The Contemplative Foundations of Classical Daoism

SUNY series in Chinese Philosophy and Culture
—————
Roger T. Ames, editor

The Contemplative Foundations
of Classical Daoism

Harold D. Roth

Cover art: *Butterfly Dream of Zhuangzi*
Japan, 19th century
Hanging scroll; paste resist on silk
Image and mount: 60 × 14⁹/₁₆ in. (152.4 × 36.99 cm)
Los Angeles County Museum of Art, Promised Gift of Robert T. Singer in honor of
Lynda Resnick, Lenore and Richard Wayne, and Prof. Harold D. Roth

Published by State University of New York Press, Albany

© 2021 State University of New York

For information, contact State University of New York Press, Albany, NY
www.sunypress.edu

Library of Congress Cataloging-in-Publication Data

Name: Roth, Harold D., author.
Title: The contemplative foundations of classical Daoism / Harold D. Roth, author.
Description: Albany : State University of New York Press, [2021] | Series:
   SUNY series in Chinese Philosophy and Culture | Includes bibliographical
   references and index.
Identifiers: ISBN 9781438482712 (hardcover : alk. paper) | ISBN 9781438482705
   (pbk. : alk. paper) | ISBN 9781438482729 (ebook)
Further information is available at the Library of Congress.

10 9 8 7 6 5 4 3 2 1

To My Teachers
And My Students

指窮於為薪，火傳也，不知其盡也。

Though we can merely point to what seems to be its fuel,
the fire passes on, and we do not know where it ends.

Zhuangzi　Chapter 3: "Mastery in Nurturing Vitality"
(Yang sheng zhu 養生主)

Contents

Part I
Contemplative Foundations and Textual Methods

Part II
Contemplative Foundations and Philosophical Contexts

Tables

Acknowledgments

The generation of the idea for this collection came out of a conversation I had with Roger Ames following the Daoist Studies conference at Boston University in late May, 2014. After a panel I organized on the *Zhuangzi* he suggested that I consider making a collection of the most important articles and chapters I had published on classical Daoism and its contemplative foundations.

This seemed like a daunting task at the time because all of these publications were in a very divergent collection of sources and published over a considerable length of time, at that point almost a quarter century. If it was not for the dedicated work of my former graduate student, Dr. Larson DiFiori, this definitely could not have been accomplished. Larson, much better skilled in the various computing advances of the 21st century than I, was able to scan each publication and convert those that had the older Wade-Giles romanization system to the more recent *pinyin* system. He then did important editing on the sources themselves that provided a strong foundation for what was finally entered into this volume. He also continued to be a support even down to these very last few days of editing and writing, giving me invaluable feedback on the new "Afterword" I wrote for the collection. I am deeply in his debt.

Samuel Goldstein, my current ABD student, did very important editing work in the autumn of 2020 making sure there was a consistency in the use of *pinyin* romanization and Chinese characters throughout the entire work and contributing important last minute edits that have proven extremely valuable. Roy Porat was also very helpful in his urging me to consider once again the problem of *Zhuangzi's* Inner Chapters and through his many conversations with me and challenges to my perspectives on so many related things. I wish to thank Roy and my graduate students in seminars the last two academic years on the *Huainanzi* and *Zhuangzi*, Christopher Yang, Tali Hershkovitz, Avery Morrow, Patrick Magoffin, and undergraduate Cameron McCartin for our endlessly interesting textual readings and discussions, even with the Covid shutdown.

There is nothing worse than laying yourself out completely for your best possible lecture only to discover half your students dozing, surfing the internet, yawning incessantly, etc. Not to say this has never happened here, but Brown University has provided me with an endless source of interesting, engaged, and progressive students in discussion with whom I have been able to develop and further develop the ideas contained in this volume. This has included over the decades my wonderful graduate students Aaron Stalnaker, Jung Lee, Jud Murray, Matt Duperon, Larson DiFiori, Adrien Stoloff, and Sherry Pan, as well as their more recent confreres.

It goes without saying that many of the ideas in these pages were developed in discussion with my mentors and friends Tu Weiming, Fritz Mote, Charles Lachman, Greg Schopen, Wayne Schlepp, Raymond Zhu, Barney Twiss, Angus Graham, Paul Thompson, Sarah Allan, Srinivas Reddy, my "partner in crime" for over three decades, Anne Heyrman-Hart, and my incredible *Huainanzi* "teammates" Andy Meyer, Sarah Queen, John S. Major, Jud Murray and Mike Puett. And a special thanks to my friend Louis Komjathy, with whom I shared many an intense conversation about classical Daoism and about Contemplative Studies, and to my "contemplative sister," Judith Simmer-Brown who has been a great source of wisdom and guidance. I would also like to thank the entire SUNY Press editing, production, and marketing teams including Chris Ahn, Laura Tendler, Anne Valentine, and especially Diane Ganeles for their professional work on this book. I reserve a special thanks for Press Co-Director James Peltz for his guidance and patience on this project and for Anne Holmes for her wonderfully thorough Index.

Finally, without my wonderful sons Zach and Gus, now young men of whom I am very proud, and the support of my life partner for over three decades, Elisabeth Baldwin Taylor, I would not have had the luxury of being able to think through many of the issues I have raised, researched, and written about in the current volume. Together, my family has enabled me to discover and—in the words of *Zhuangzi* 4—"sing my native note." I will forever be in their debt.

Permissions

The author gratefully acknowledges permission to reprint the following material:

"Psychology and Self-Cultivation in Early Taoistic Thought." *Harvard Journal of Asiatic Studies* 51, no. 2 (December 1991): 599–650. Reprinted with permission.

"Who Compiled the *Chuang Tzu?*" In *Chinese Texts and Philosophical Contexts: Essays Dedicated to Angus C. Graham*, edited by Henry Rosemont Jr., 79–128. LaSalle, IL: Open Court Press, 1991. Reprinted with permission.

"Redaction Criticism and the Early History of Taoism." *Early China* 19 (1994) 1–46. Copyright © Cambridge University Press. Reprinted with permission.

"Evidence for Stages of Meditation in Early Taoism." *Bulletin of the School of Oriental and African Studies* 60, no. 2 (June 1997): 295–314. Copyright © Cambridge University Press. Reprinted with permission.

"The Yellow Emperor's Guru: A Narrative Analysis from *Chuang Tzu* 11." *Taoist Resources* 7, no. 1 (April 1997): 43–60. Copyright © Johns Hopkins University Press. Reprinted with permission.

"Daoist Inner Cultivation Thought and the Textual Structure of the *Huainanzi*." In *The Huainanzi and Textual Production in Early China*, edited by Sarah Queen and Michael Puett, 40–82. Leiden: Brill, 2014.

"*Lao Tzu* in the Context of Early Taoist Mystical Praxis." In *Essays on Religious and Philosophical Aspects of the Lao Tzu*, edited by Mark Csikszentmihalyi and P. J. Ivanhoe, 59–96. Albany: State University of New York Press, 1999. Reprinted with permission.

"Bimodal Mystical Experience in the "Qiwulun" of *Zhuangzi*." *Journal of Chinese Religions* 28 (2000): 1–20. An edited version was reprinted under the title of "Bimodal Mystical Experience in the Qiwulun Chapter of the *Zhuangzi*." In Victor Mair, ed., *Experimental Essays on Zhuangzi, Third Edition*, edited by Livia Kohn, 199–214. Dunedin, FL: Three Pines Press, 2010. Copyright © Johns Hopkins University Press. Reprinted with the permission of the *Journal of Chinese Religions* and Johns Hopkins University Press.

"Nature and Self-Cultivation in *Huainanzi's* 'Original Way.'" In *Polishing the Chinese Mirror: Essays in Honor of Henry Rosemont Jr.*, edited by Marthe Chandler and Ronnie Littlejohn, 270–92. New York: Global Scholarly Publications, 2007. Reprinted with permission.

"The Classical Daoist Concept of *Li* and Early Chinese Cosmology." In *Studies in Honor of Li Xueqin. Early China* 35–36, edited by Wen Xing, 157–84. Berkeley: The Society for the Study of Early China. 2012–2013. Copyright © Cambridge University Press. Reprinted with permission.

"Against Cognitive Imperialism." *Religion East and West* 8 (2008): 1–23. Reprinted with permission.

"Cognitive Attunement in the *Zhuangzi*." In *Having A Word with Angus Graham: At Twenty-Five Years into His Immortality*, edited by Roger Ames and Carine Defoort, 49–78. Albany: State University of New York Press, 2018. Reprinted with permission.

"An Appraisal of Angus Graham's Textual Scholarship on the *Zhuangzi*." In *A Companion to Angus C. Graham's Chuang Tzu*, edited by Harold D. Roth, 181–220. Honolulu: University of Hawai'i Press, 2003. Permission Pending.

Introduction[1]

During the past decade and a half, the field of Contemplative Studies has slowly developed from a combination of traditional humanistic scholarship on the history and philosophy of religion, scientific research on the various forms of contemplative practice, and the direct personal experience of scholars and researchers. These three pillars of the field have a recursive relationship: the knowledge derived from each informs and reinforces the others. The field has also been developed in the crucible of college and university classrooms throughout the country and at numerous academic meetings during these last fifteen years. The theory and development of this field have been detailed in a number of publications to which I refer the reader.[2] But suffice it to say that for me, personally, my scholarship on the origins and early history of the classical Daoist tradition has developed in interaction with this emerging academic field.

The articles and book chapters selected here demonstrate a burgeoning interest in the contemplative foundations of the classical Daoist tradition that emerged over the course of my professional career—actually really over the course of my adult life. Starting with my undergraduate days as a student of Tu Wei-ming and Fritz Mote, I was drawn to the central problem of "self-cultivation" (*zixiu* 自修) that is one of the primary focuses of the classical Chinese philosophical tradition. This led me both into graduate work at McMaster University and the University of Toronto; to post-doctoral work at Tōhoku University in Sendai, Japan; and into serious and intensive personal engagement with a number of distinct traditions of contemplative practice.

In 1969 Professor Tu introduced me to a Japanese master from the Rinzai tradition, Kyōzan Jōshū Sasaki Rōshi, who had come to America in 1962 at the request of the overseas Japanese community in Los

Angeles. I eventually became involved in setting up and helping to run an annual series of seminars, held at Sasaki's affiliated Zen Centers and associated, over the years, with UCLA, Cornell, and the University of New Mexico. These lasted from 1977 until 2012. The purpose of these seminars was to bring the study of Buddhism into a monastic setting in which the usually abstract and removed academic approaches were combined with the direct experience of meditation practice. I came to see that this approach has considerable value: it takes the often-recondite study of philosophy and history and grounds it in the direct subjective experience of individuals.

Over time I gradually came to see that prior studies of the early history of Daoism were hampered in their understanding of its contemplative foundations by limits derived from a set of unreflective assumptions that restrict human cognitive possibilities to merely those that were deemed possible by our own European cultures.[3] Most pernicious of these are two: that all human beings have a genetic predisposition to a belief in gods or other supernatural beings; and that veridical human cognition is restricted to either reason or emotion—categories established by the European Enlightenment. These products of an unreflective Eurocentrism have largely contributed to a failure to recognize that early Daoist thinkers could possibly have derived their ideas about human psychology, human nature, and the nature of the cosmos through anything other than abstract rational thought or emotional responses. These cultural blinders have also contributed to the idea that contemplative experiences can never be epistemologically valid, and because of this non-veridicality, attempts to ascertain the contemplative foundations of classical Daoism are either unnecessary or, even worse, deluded.

The more I worked on Daoist origins, the more I saw that the distinctive philosophy of this tradition emerged directly from its practices of self-cultivation, practices that were essentially contemplative in nature. The evidence for these practices was embedded in the surviving textual and material traditions. While some scholars such as Arthur Waley[4] had briefly touched upon them, they were to a great extent being ignored in attempts to ascertain the historical origins and development of this very complex tradition. Because of this, it seemed, there was a failure to perceive how the tradition had developed in the times before it formed readily identifiable religious institutions at the end of the Eastern Han dynasty (ca. 180 CE). The essays that have been collected together in this volume attest to the ways in which the awareness of these contemplative bases of classical Daoist thought came to provide a decisive influence on my investigations of its historical and intellectual origins.

Humanistic cross-cultural scholarship and scientific studies of contemplative practices clearly show that they involve distinctive modes of mental concentration. These can include focusing attention on a particular object such as a sacred word, sound, or idea; or on the subjective experience of both body and mind, such as the breath. They can be done when one is sitting still or when one is moving. And, with consistent application over time, they frequently lead to deepened states of concentration, stillness, and insight into the nature of self-identity and of consciousness itself. A developing understanding of this humanistic and scientific research came to significantly broaden my perspectives on the contemplative foundations of classical Daoism and to see links among surviving texts that were previously difficult to detect. This then came to fundamentally alter my understanding of the origins of this tradition and to see through a number of extant beliefs about them that had precluded serious study of its contemplative foundations.

Scholarly perspectives in Early China Studies and in Daoist Studies have shifted markedly since I began my scholarly career more than three decades ago. Beliefs about the origins of the Daoist tradition were still attached to a number of major shibboleths, the most lasting of which is still rather prevalent in East Asia today, though no longer so in Europe and the United States.

This first shibboleth rests on the beliefs—now almost two millennia old—that the Daoist tradition began in the sixth century BCE with Lao Dan 老聃 and his singularly authored work the *Dao De jing* 道德經. Further, this person founded a Daoist "school" that included Zhuang Zhou 莊周, the sole author of the *Zhuangzi* 莊子 and other eponymous works created by later disciples such as Liezi 列子 and Wenzi 文子. Together they created and transmitted a Daoist school that contained a lofty mystical philosophy that accepted death as a natural transformation and maintained a cosmology of the Way and its Inner Power or Potency. However, this tradition of so-called "philosophical Daoism" or "Lao-Zhuang" 老莊 became singularly corrupted by its contact with superstitious peasant beliefs in longevity and immortality and polytheistic deities to form the organized Daoist religion that emerged in the second century CE and that persists to this day. This position was typified in a number of articles by Herlee Glessner Creel collected in his famous book *"What is Taoism?"*[5] But as A. C. Graham once succinctly put it, "No doubt one may think of this (Daoist) church like others as debasing the pure doctrine of its founder, but the Christian churches never departed quite as far from the gospel as this."[6]

While European Sinologists including Marcel Granet, Henri Maspero, Max Kaltenmark, Anna Seidel, Kristofer Schipper, and Isabelle Robinet[7] had all pointed to the long-standing basis of Daoism in both the folk and classical traditions of Chinese religion, it wasn't until the seminal publications of Nathan Sivin and Michel Strickmann in the late 1970s that opinions of scholars in the English-speaking world started to change to focus more on the complex and varied traditions and institutions of the Daoist religion, from its origins to the present day.[8] However, in successfully challenging the shibboleth of a school of lofty mystical Daoist philosophy contrasted with a superstitious organized Daoist religion, Strickmann, in particular, established a new shibboleth in the field, and one that has stood well into the current century: that there is absolutely no "Daoism" before the millenarian movements of the later second century of the Common Era.

Unfortunately, this shibboleth does not pass the test of historical accuracy any more than the first one does. And I'm not sure that Strickmann believed it either—at least not to the same extent as do his many influential disciples who now dominate the field of Daoist Studies. I met Strickmann only once in my life: at the "Universities of Southern California China Workshop" organized in the spring of 1988 by Robert Buswell and held at the University of Southern California. On that day, an important one in my early academic career, I presented a talk that is very closely related to the first chapter of the current collection. As one will see by reading it, the argument that day was sufficiently hesitant (referring to the traditions I was identifying as "Daoistic" rather than "Daoist"): but the intent was clear. Given his somewhat fearsome reputation, I fully expected the renowned acerbic professor to launch into a serious critique of my position. Instead, to my great surprise, he had nothing but praise. Driving with Buswell and Strickmann to dinner after the workshop, I asked him directly why he hadn't been more critical of my talk, given his public stance on this topic. He replied that he had really only asserted that there was no Daoism before the end of the Han in order to correct the extreme bias of the field of Daoist Studies in favor of "Lao-Zhuang," the supposed foundational school of Daoism to the detriment of the organized Daoist religion that followed.

Another set of factors that these fields were beginning to take into account was the information coming from the first great discovery of excavated manuscripts, at Mawangdui 馬王堆 in 1973. There an important cache of texts was discovered that included works that were known—most famously, as the two untitled manuscripts of what would shortly thereafter be called the "*Dao De jing*" (or *De Dao jing* 德道經, given the order of its two main sections[9])—and others that were previously unknown—most significantly, the so called "Four Canons of the Yellow Thearch" or *Huangdi si jing* 黃帝四經 and a group of seven medical texts.[10] When I started publishing, we were just beginning our fascination with trying to figure out the implications for the study of the *Laozi* 老子 traditions and to see if the Huang-Lao texts were some kind of fusion between "Daoism" and "Legalism." This, of course, presumed that there were distinct "schools of thought" among the historically renowned "Hundred Schools" that could really be identified by these labels. As the new millennium dawned, even this hallowed notion of pre-Han schools of thought came under increasing scrutiny.

Sarah Queen, and Michael Nylan and Mark Csikszentmihalyi wrote two very influential articles questioning the existence of pre-Han "schools of thought."[11] In these, they argued that Sima Tan, the scholar who first coined the term "Daoism" or the "Daoist School" (*Daojia* 道家), along with the other five "schools" (e.g., Confucian, Mohist, Nominalist, Naturalist, Legalist), wasn't accurately describing extant and real intellectual traditions, as has been believed for two millennia; he was organizing extant texts into bibliographic categories. While their arguments provided a welcome challenge to the anachronistic model that there were pre-Han "schools of thought," they also unintentionally reinforced the Strickmannian view that there was no "Daoism" before the end of the Han.

It is precisely these four shibboleths that have impeded our understanding of the contemplative nature and historical contours of classical Daoism:

- that there was an original "school" of philosophical Daoism called "Lao-Zhuang"

- that there was a great contrast between this "philosophical school" and the later so-called "religious Daoism" that was supposed to be descended from it;

- that there is no such thing at all as "Daoism" before the late Han millenarian rebellions;

- and that there were absolutely no "schools" of thought or even coherent and identifiable lineages in the classical Chinese philosophical and religious traditions of the pre-Han and early Han periods.

The quarter century of research contained in this volume presents significant challenges to all of them.

The contemplative foundations of classical Daoism are grounded in a distinctive form of practice that I came to define as "inner cultivation" after a work that had been glossed over by many scholars, "Neiye" 內業 or "Inward Training" (ca. 330 BCE), one of seventy-six texts in a major collection from the state of Qi 齊 on the Shandong peninsula, the *Guanzi* 管子 (compiled between 340 and 150 BCE). The surviving evidence for these practices can be found in this work, in the *Laozi* and *Zhuangzi*, and in a number of other classical texts of mixed traditions, including the *Lüshi chunqiu* 呂士春秋 (239 BCE) and the *Huainanzi* 淮南子 (139 BCE). The distinctive ideas of inner cultivation begin and end with the Way or Dao 道 as the ultimate source of the cosmos and Potency (*De* 德) as its manifestation in terms of concrete phenomena and experience; Non-Action (*wuwei* 無為) as the definitive movement of the Way, and Formlessness (*wuxing* 無形) as its spatial mode are both essential as well. There is also a common self-cultivation vocabulary that includes such results as stillness and silence (*jimo* 寂漠), tranquility (*jing* 靜), emptiness (*xu* 虛), and a variety of "apophatic," or self-negating, techniques and qualities of mind that lead to a direct apprehension of the Way. These contemplative practices that were transmitted in classical Daoism involve, first and foremost, the apophatic emptying of the normal contents of the conscious mind through concentrating on the breath and various objects of internal visualization. Specific techniques for moving meditation were also known as well, although they are most often found in the context of health and longevity practices, such as we find in the famous painting of the various positions of what archaeologists called the "Guiding and Pulling Diagram" (*Daoyin tu* 導引圖) that was found at Mawangdui. The classical Daoist Inner Cultivation tradition referred to its practices as *yangshen* 養神 or *yangxing* 養性 ("nourishing the inner spirit or innate nature"). While this tradition of practice shared concepts and some techniques with these health and longevity practices (often referred to as *yangsheng* 養生 or *yang xing* 養

形—"nourishing vitality or nourishing the body"), they practiced them much more assiduously, and they were careful to differentiate themselves from others they thought of as health freaks, as made clear in *Zhuangzi* 15, "Keyi" 刻意 ("Ingrained Opinions"), and *Huainanzi* 7, "Jingshen" 精神 ("The Quintessential Spirit").[12]

In the early stages of my research, represented in the first two chapters of this collection, I was more hesitant in how I referred to these contemplative practices, referring to them by the more general category of "self cultivation practices" in "early Daoistic thought." As my work developed, I came to see that without understanding these contemplative foundations, it was significantly more difficult to see the connections among the various surviving textual and epigraphic sources that attest to a classical Daoist tradition. Further, the very fact that coherent contemplative practices were identifiable from text to text had to imply the existence of certain social organizations, lineages of teachers and students who taught and studied the practices and kept them alive across the generations until more organized and readily identifiable religious institutions formed at the end of the Han dynasty.

Gradually in my thinking, a heuristic framework emerged that helped to make sense of the distinctive set of technical terms I was finding in these extant texts. As detailed in the second and third chapters of this collection, three distinctive categories of these technical terms were repeatedly present and could be linked to three authorial voices that a number of scholars, including Guan Feng, A. C. Graham, and Liu Xiaogan, found in the *Zhuangzi*. More than just labels that pertained to the *Zhuangzi* alone, these distinctive categories of terms were signs of overlapping chronological "phases" in the development of a classical Daoist tradition. The "Individualist" phase contains specific technical terms of a cosmology of the Way and of inner cultivation theory. Principal sources for this were the "Neiye" (Inward Training) text from the *Guanzi* collection and the "Inner Chapters" of the *Zhuangzi*. The "Primitivist" phase has the terminology of cosmology and inner cultivation of the Individualist phase, but added to this a political philosophy of creating simple agrarian communities governed by a sage who was, in essence, an inner cultivation adept. Examples of this are the *Laozi* and a section of the *Zhuangzi*, chapters 8–11. The "Syncretist" phase also has the same cosmology of the Way and inner cultivation practices as the first two phases but contains, instead, a syncretic political philosophy that advocated using the best ideas of other early intellectual lineages and subsuming them within a framework of inner cultivation cosmology and practice. The "Four Canons of the Yellow Thearch" and the *Huai-nanzi* are among the texts that contain the distinctive ideas of this phase.

One of the great challenges in identifying the contours of a classical Daoist tradition is that so little concrete evidence has survived. We are, to all intents and purposes, working with a vast jigsaw puzzle in space and time for which only a few fragmentary pieces survive. Making sense of how these fit together and how they imply other pieces requires not only a fidelity to the evidence, but also a sense of imagination and the exercise of reason. Texts do not exist in a vacuum, and they do not magically compose and transmit themselves. Human beings compose and transmit them, and they imply at least a minimal social organization. There were no bookstores at which one could buy a text and then study its contents. Circulation of written manuscripts was much more limited than many imagine. Especially in the Warring States period, before lineage masters were gathered at local courts to debate one another and advise local rulers (starting with Jixia 稷下 in the state of Qi around 340 BCE), you had to receive a text within a concrete lineage of teachers and students. And when you did that, you also received a direct transmission of the methods and techniques on which these ideas were founded: ritual practices for "Confucians"; techniques of bureaucratic organization for "Legalists'; techniques of argumentation for "Sophists"; methods of defensive warfare and reason for the "Mohists." As we shall see, these labels are not only bibliographic categories created by Han dynasty historians. These categories would have no meaning if they were not based on actual coherent lineages of teachers and students who formed lines of transmission of these texts and ideas over the generations. For classical Daoism, these lineages transmitted the practices of Inner Cultivation and the ideas on cosmology, psychology, and politics that were derived from them. These lineages—decentralized and with minimal social organization—formed the institutions that constituted classical or original Daoism. It was not until they became much more organized and became involved with large-scale political movements that these institutions finally garnered the attention of the official historians of the central government in the millenarian rebellions of the Way of Great Peace and the Celestial Masters in the latter half of the second century CE.[13]

Part I: Contemplative Foundations and Textual Methods

The first part of this collection is devoted to the careful textual analysis of the major extant sources of classical Daoism to derive evidence for both its contemplative foundations and its historical and social contexts.

Chapter 1, "Psychology and Self-Cultivation in Early Daoistic Thought," argues that the traditional belief that the origins of Daoism are found exclusively in the *Laozi* and *Zhuangzi* is misplaced. That there is a much broader range of works that complement these foundational texts, and when we take them all into account, a much broader and deeper understanding of this tradition begins to emerge. These include the four "Techniques of the Mind" (Xin shu 心術) texts from the *Guanzi* compendium, the four "YellowThearch" texts found at Mawangdui ("*Huangdi si jing*" [ca. 275 BCE]), and the *Huainanzi*. When we take these texts and their key ideas about human nature and psychology and contemplative practice into account, we start to see links among them that give us a more accurate understanding of what I then called "Daoistic Thought," but which I now feel comfortable in calling "original" or "classical Daoism," within the larger parameters of the Daoist tradition. In particular, the textual evidence provided here shows that from the very beginning, the tradition conceived of self-cultivation in terms of working and transforming energies of mind and body that later were central to organized Daoism: *qi* 氣 ("vital breath/energy"), *jing* 精 ("vital essence"), *shen* 神 ("numen" or "spirit"), and *jingshen* 精神 ("numinous essence" or "quintessential spirit"). Moreover, when we understand the contemplative practices of self-cultivation that are directly mentioned or implied in these texts, and understand the key role that these contemplative practices play in the creation of the distinctive philosophy of these works that distinguish them from other early traditions of thought and practice, we come to see that there is a much greater continuity in the entire Daoist tradition, from the classical period through the rise of the organized Daoist religion to the present day than had previously been assumed.

Chapter 2, "Who Compiled the *Zhuangzi*?," begins by examining how closely the definitions of the "Daoist School," which I think is more accurately thought of as a loosely organized lineage of teachers and students who followed a set of shared practices of "inner cultivation," fit the evidence found in the texts of this early tradition identified in chapter 1. This chapter goes on to delineate the basic ideas of an early lineage that shared in these practices in terms of three important categories of thought: cosmology, psychology, and politics; and, further, sees evidence for all of them in the distinctive sections of the *Zhuangzi* that have been identified by Graham, Guan Feng, and Liu Xiaogan: original Zhuangzi writings (chapters 1–7); the "Primitivist" or "Anarchist" sections (chapters 8–11 [first part]); and the Syncretist or "Huang-Lao" sections (parts of chapters 12–14, all of 15 and 33). Relying heavily on an analysis of the key ideas in this last authorial voice in the text, this chapter demonstrates its clear parallels with *Guanzi's* "Xinshu, shang" 心術上 (Techniques of the Mind, I) with the *Huainanzi*, and with Sima Tan's definition of a "Daoist school." The chapter finishes with an argument that the *Zhuangzi*, which transmitted the thought and practice of an original teacher, Zhuang Zhou, and his followers from the late fourth century BCE through the early Han, was likely compiled at the court of Liu An, the second king of Huainan 淮南 and the sponsor and editor of the *Huainanzi* compendium.

In chapter 3, "Redaction Criticism and the Early History of Daoism," I begin to use the methodologies of textual criticism found in Biblical Studies: in particular, form criticism, composition criticism, and redaction criticism. These involve the analysis of the ideas in a text as they are influenced by the literary form of the text (e.g., rhymed verse; argumentative essay, didactic narrative) and by the composition techniques by which the text was put together and subsequently augmented. Form criticism conducts an analysis of the standard genres or forms in which oral (or early written) tradition is cast. Redaction criticism attempts to identify the theological or ideological viewpoints of the people who assembled the various literary forms into texts and to understand the historical conditions in which they may have been created. Composition criticism examines the literary techniques of the early redactors of a tradition, and how they arranged and assembled their inherited material to create unified works. The true pioneer in applying these methods in a deliberate and self-conscious way to early Chinese works was Michael LaFargue.[14] In this chapter I apply these methods in a highly focused fashion to determine the relationship between two essays that I identified in chapters 1 and 2 as being part of the Daoist works in the *Guanzi*, "Neiye" ("Inward Training"), and "Xinshu xia" 心術下 (Techniques of the Mind II). While previous theories have ranged from their being damaged versions of the same text to the notes of two different students from the lectures of their master, a careful line-by-line textual analysis and redaction criticism of these two works yields a different conclusion, one that is extremely important in establishing the contours of classical Daoism. There is a key relationship between these two texts that testifies to an important development in any attempt to reconstruct something of the social and historical conditions in which original Daoism developed, the moment when a text from what I call the "Individualist" phase becomes applied to the complex political theories of the "Syncretist" phase. In this chapter I focus further on the three interlocking categories of technical terms that I have found in the texts of this early Daoist tradition: "cosmology," "inner cultivation," and "political thought," and provide further details of essential ideas in each category. After a detailed analysis of these two works, I conclude that "Xinshu xia" is a deliberate redacting and reorganizing of the textual material from the Individualist "Neiye" to support a program of sage rulership. This regimen is based on a cosmology of the Way and contemplative inner cultivation practices that include the emptying out of the normal contents of consciousness in a systematic fashion through a kind of breath attention training leading to the state of complete emptiness in which the adept is able to become one with the Way. An additional conclusion I came to in this chapter is that the Syncretic Daoism of the last third and early second century BCE is a direct descendant of the earlier Individualist Daoism of the "Inner Chapters" of the *Zhuangzi* and *Guanzi*'s "Neiye."

In chapter 4, "Evidence for Stages of Meditation in Early Daoism," I continue with more detailed textual, philosophical, and contemplative testimony to the existence of a distinctive tradition of early Daoism that we are justified to call "original Daoism." It becomes clear from the distinctive rhetorical structures for stages of meditation that I present from a variety of classical Daoist works that a common contemplative practice of inner cultivation had to have been both widespread and foundational to the tradition of original Daoism. The presence of this unique rhetorical structure was surprisingly found in a variety of texts that span almost two centuries in time. This rhetorical structure consists of:

- a preamble with a varied series of "apophatic" prefatory exercises through which the usual contents of consciousness—thoughts, feelings, and desires—are removed;

- a sorites-style argument in which the stages of meditation are presented in a consecutive fashion;

- a denouement that discusses the noetic and practical benefits of having attained these stages.

What this rhetorical structure indicates is that original Daoism was grounded in a practice of breath meditation whose goal was to produce a profound transformation in adepts in which the individual self is ultimately transcended in a unitive mystical experience of merging with the Way. After this, when adepts return to engaging the dualistic world again, their consciousness is radically transformed so that they spontaneously "take no action yet leave nothing undone." This provides further evidence for the conclusions that original Daoism was not a philosophical school but rather consisted of one or more related master-disciple lineages that centered on the contemplative practice of inner cultivation. This practice formed the distinctive "technique" (*shu* 術) around which these lineages formed and from which they eventually took their self-identity.

In chapter 5, "The Yellow Emperor's Guru: A Narrative Analysis from *Zhuangzi* 莊子 11" I return to the *Zhuangzi* to apply a fourth type of literary criticism from Biblical Studies, "narrative criticism," to one story in this rich narrative-filled collection. Narrative criticism is focused on the critical analysis of stories and their didactic intent. It examines which characters represent the voice of their author, which represent opposing viewpoints, and identifies the viewpoint that the author is espousing and its audience, the group at whom the narrative is aimed. While not a primary concern of narrative criticism, the development of hypotheses concerning the historical context in which the narrative was written is also part of the information that can be derived from its analysis. In this chapter, I apply narrative criticism to analyze the meaning and significance of one passage from the *Zhuangzi*, the story of the dialogue between the Yellow Emperor and his "guru" Guang Chengzi 廣成子 "Master Broadly Complete") from chapter 11, "To Preserve and Circumscribe" (*Zai you* 在宥). The central meaning of this narrative is very relevant to the early history of the Daoist tradition. Herein the Yellow Emperor symbolizes the coordination of the realm of human beings with the greater patterns of Heaven and Earth, as he does in other pre-Han philosophical and medical literature, and Guang Chengzi symbolizes the contemplative inner cultivation techniques that were characteristic of classical Daoism. The latter's teaching of these techniques—in the literary form of the same genre of rhymed verse we find in Individualist sources such as "Inward Training" and the *Laozi*—herein symbolizes the synthesis of Daoist contemplative methods and a Syncretist political philosophy of setting up the human polity—as microcosm—in parallel to the greater patterns of Heaven and Earth—as macrocosm. This, in many ways, typifies the synthesis of viewpoints contained in the "Huang-Lao" teachings that formed the final phase of the original Daoist tradition as found in the Mawangdui Yellow Emperor texts, some of the later chapters of the *Zhuangzi*, the *Huainanzi*, and most definitely in the purview of Sima Tan 司馬談 when he established the parameters of what he was calling "Daoism." The apex of this passage is the apotheosis of Guang Chengzi into a near-immortal who has "cultivated my own person for 1,200 years so that my form has never deteriorated." This provides additional evidence that the goals of longevity and immortality were as much a part of original Daoism as they became in later institutionalized Daoism.

In chapter 6, "An Appraisal of Angus Graham's Textual Scholarship on the *Zhuangzi* 莊子," I present an overview of the unique version that Graham created in his translation of this foundational work of the classical Daoist tradition. I examine his reasons for creating it and his method of doing so. Graham realized that each chapter of the text was a compilation of various literary styles and that they didn't always fit together perfectly well. His translation breaks up the chapters he translates into sections and he avoids the translation of different sections as if they were a continuous text. He also only translates those passages whose meaning he understands, which leads him to omit about 20% of the entire text. Furthermore, after translating in full the Inner Chapters as a distinctive block of related text, he then divides the remainder of the work into topical sections. In addition to examining his textual methodology, I present original research on some of these sections. I propose an earlier date than his 205 BCE for the "Primitivist" chapters: circa 243–37 BCE, and argue that there was an early version of the textual materials that became the 52 chapter original recension of the *Zhuangzi* present in the Qin court where this author wrote these chapters. I further argue that the chapters that Graham attributes to the followers of the individualist philosopher Yang Zhu 楊朱 were likely compiled by the Primitivist author to use in his defense of his "Daoist" interpretation of the concept of human nature (*xing* 性). I then present data that the authors of the "Syncretist" sections of the *Zhuangzi* shared a common vocabulary of inner cultivation practice and its results with the authors of four chapters of the *Spring and Autumn Annals of Mister Lü* (*Lüshi chun qiu* 呂氏春秋) that was created at the Qin court during this time period. Additionally I link this shared perspective with that of the authors of the Han dynasty Daoist compendium the *Huainanzi* 淮南子 and speculate that this group could have brought what I later call the "proto-*Zhuangzi*" to Liu An's 劉安 court at Huainan. Finally, I conclude that chapter 16 of the *Zhuangzi*, "Menders of Nature" (Shan xing 繕

性), is the likely product of a disciple of the "Primitivist" author who transmitted his writings with his copy of the *Zhuangzi* textual materials after the fall of Prime Minister Lü Buwei in 237 BCE and the fall of his intellectual enterprise in the Qin court.

In chapter 7, "Daoist Inner Cultivation Thought and the Textual Structure of the *Huainanzi*, I apply the hypotheses I have reached in the earlier chapters of this collection to a detailed analysis of the intellectual filiation of this important early Han philosophical work that was finally translated in 2010 by a team that included John Major, Sarah Queen, Andy Meyer, and me. [15] As a group, we often discussed this problem: was this text properly categorized as "eclectic" (*zajia* 雜家)—the category to which it was assigned in the bibliographical monograph of the *History of the Former Han Dynasty*; was it "Daoist?"; or is it an intellectual work with so varied a content that it cannot be classified into any other category than its own? One thing on which we all agreed was that the *Huainanzi* was composed and redacted according to a specific structure. The first eight of its twenty-one chapters contains a set of ideas that are foundational to the work; these constitute the "root" of the text; the remaining chapters constitute its "branches." In the further analysis I undertook in this chapter, the first two *Huainanzi* chapters provide the foundation of the entire work. And, further, each chapter of the text begins with a "Root Passage" that contains its core ideas. This forms a multilayered compositional structure that is used to reinforce the contemplative Inner Cultivation foundations of this intentionally syncretic work. This emphasis on the core contemplative practices and derivative insights of what we have identified as "original Daoism" proves that, far from being a text without affiliation, the *Huainanzi* is a rich and complex doubling down on the fundamental teachings of the final or syncretic phase of the classical Daoist tradition. In many ways, it represents its most sophisticated expression and constitutes what can be thought of as a "last-ditch attempt" to convince Han Emperor Wu that these ideas should be the ones through which the empire should be governed.

Part II: Contemplative Foundations and Philosophical Contexts

In the second part of this collection I take the foundational understanding of the contemplative basis of classical Daoism derived from the textual and historical analyses in Part I and apply it to specific texts and ideas from this tradition.

In chapter 8, "*Laozi* in the Context of Early Daoist Mystical Praxis," I analyze the evidence for mystical practices and concomitant philosophical insights contained in this foundational Daoist text. What I argue is that the *Laozi* is a complex work that contains both advice on how to govern effectively as well as concrete references to contemplative practices that involved breath cultivation, practices that share methods and metaphors with many other early sources of Daoist inner cultivation such as "Inward Training" and the *Zhuangzi*. All exhibit a complementary relationship between an apophatic introvertive meditation practice and the extrovertive application of these introvertive experiences that leads to the spontaneous ability to, in the famous phrase of this work, "take no action yet leave nothing undone" (*wuwei er wu bu wei* 無為而無不為). This basic pattern of what I called in chapter 6 complementary states and traits of Daoist apophatic inner cultivation practice can also be seen in many of the other early sources of this original Daoist tradition. This contributes to the substantial textual evidence for a common set of mystical practices that show that the *Laozi* is an important part of this tradition, but not its sole foundation.

In chapter 9, "Bimodal Mystical Experience in the "Qi wu lun" of *Zhuangzi*," I extend these arguments about the complementary introvertive and extrovertive—or "bimodal"—mystical experiences that characterize inner cultivation practices to what is arguably the most important chapter in this thirty-three-chapter collection. Contra mysticism theorist Walter Stace, I argue for the primacy of both these dimensions of mystical experience in traditions throughout the world using the analysis of this original Daoist text as the basis. Contra Lee Yearley's argument that the *Zhuangzi* avers an exclusively "intrawordly" mysticism, I maintain that both aspects are present in abundance in the text. While the "Qi wu lun" is often regarded as containing the essence of what scholars have alternately deemed "skepticism," "relativism," or "perspectivism" in the *Zhuangzi*, what I argue in this chapter is that it advocates using apophatic inner cultivation practices to attain a literally "enlightened" or "Dao-centered" mode of cognition ("great knowledge") in which all the many and varied phenomena of our experiences and our world are seen from the same perspective: one that, in the literal translation of the title, "sees all things as equal." In both this chapter and its predecessors, I have used methodologies derived from the comparative, cross-cultural study of mysticism to analyze key ideas in my original Daoist sources.

In chapter 10, "Nature and Self-Cultivation in *Huainanzi*'s 淮南子 "Yuan dao" 原道 (Originating in the Way)", I provide a close section-by-section reading of the foundational "Root Chapter" of this important work, which I regard as the ultimate and most sophisticated expression of syncretic Daoist thought. What this analysis demonstrates is that, for the author of this chapter, the world contains a normative natural order that is infused by a single divine force or power, the Way. Further, this order itself is holy and consists of natural patterns (*li* 理), innate natures (*xing* 性), natural propensities (*qing* 情), and numerical sequences (*shu* 數) that continually interact with one another in a seamless cosmic web. Human beings, while connected to this order by our innate natures, tend to fall away from it and must relearn to establish it through the "techniques of the mind," the various methods of contemplative inner cultivation practice through which we can set aside the desires, preferences, and dualistic knowledge that cause this falling away. Rulers who are able to do this achieve complete success because they are governing in accord with the normative patterns and forces that infuse the cosmos. Thus we find in this chapter an evocative and succinct expression of the key ideas of original syncretic Daoist political thought that combine inner cultivation with political philosophy such as we see in such sources as *Guanzi*'s "Techniques of the Mind," the Syncretist *Zhuangzi*, and the *Huangdi si jing* from Mawangdui.

In chapter 11, "The Classical Daoist Concept of *Li* 理 (Pattern) and Early Chinese Cosmology," I provide a sustained analysis of the origins of this absolutely central concept to the original Daoist tradition. A sophisticated understanding of this idea is commonly thought to have been the almost exclusive purview of the Neo-Confucian tradition in its theories of a cosmology of *li* and *qi*. But a careful analysis of the classical Chinese sources of these ideas demonstrates that our original Daoist texts contain a particularly sophisticated theory and development of these key concepts. While this analysis shows the presence of *li* as an important idea in several of the "Techniques of the Mind" chapters of the *Guanzi* and several chapters in the *Zhuangzi*, it is the *Huainanzi* that places a singular emphasis on this concept: ". . . we wrote these (prior) twenty chapters so that the Patterns of Heaven and Earth would be thoroughly examined," states the final summary chapter of this syncretic Daoist work, likely written by the sponsor and compiler of the entire text, Liu An 劉安, the second king of Huainan (?180–122 BCE). In accord with the root-metaphor for *li* contained in the original uses in classical China of this concept—the invisible guidelines along which jade naturally fractures—the inherent patterns of the greater cosmos contain *li* that are the guidelines that underlie all of human and cosmic experience. When human beings adapt and comply with them, they succeed; when they ignore or depart from them, they fail. Because of their practice of Daoist inner cultivation techniques, the perfected adepts in this tradition act spontaneously and harmoniously because they are totally in accord with these underlying patterns. Thus *li* can be seen as a classical Daoist explanation for why such spontaneous and harmonious action by adepts and sages is possible. Because these adepts are grounded in the direct experience of the all-pervading Way, the ultimate sources for all these patterns, their actions will always be harmonious no matter what the situation.

In chapter 12, in the process of discussing my late mentor Angus C. Graham's (1919–1991) ideas on mysticism, I present a sustained analysis of the central experiences in the entire text of the *Zhuangzi* through the lens of the Contemplative Studies perspective. This perspective, which combines third-person, second-person, first-person, and no-person perspectives, is derived from the work of Francisco Varela, William James, and Kitaro Nishida. This "contemplative phenomenology" contains aspects of both cognitive sciences and humanistic philosophy. With this perspective, I argue for what I think is the central concept that holds together the entire diverse parts of the *Zhuangzi*: "cognitive attunement." It is through the apophatic inner cultivation practices, which we have seen pervade the tradition of teachers and students that constituted "original Daoism," that adepts are able to "embody the Way." This state of experience leads to a transformed "flowing cognition" in which one sees all things as equal and is able to respond in the moment, spontaneously, and in a completely attuned harmony to whatever situation arises. Thus one is completely able to "treat oneself as other": to have no more preference for *your* particular way of doing things than for anyone else's, and thereby "throw things open to the lucid light of Nature." This contrasts with the all too prevalent "fixed cognition" in which we rigidly apply predetermined categories of true and false and self and other to the situations in which we find ourselves, like the monkeys in the famous narrative from the "Qi wu lun." In the words of chapter 22 ("Knowledge Wanders North"), "The Sage neither misses the occasion when it is present, nor clings to it when it is past. He responds to it by attuning himself." This is the key extrovertive metaphor of the original Daoist tradition, a complement to such introvertive metaphors as "cleaning out the lodging place of the numinous mind" from "Inward Training" and "sweeping clean your Profound Mirror" from the *Laozi*.

Chapter 13, "Against Cognitive Imperialism," is perhaps the most theoretical work in this collection. It contains the initial rationalization of establishing the new field of "Contemplative Studies" as a way to combat the narrow strictures into which the humanistic field of Religious Studies and the scientific field of Cognitive Science have been confined because of a narrow ethnocentricism that derives primarily from an Abrahamic worldview supplemented by a European hubris about the superiority of its own basic worldview. In this chapter I lay out an argument that is largely drawn from my prior work on the contemplative foundations of classical Daoism, with a particular reliance on my analysis of the *Zhuangzi*. It concludes with the call to expand the horizons of our conceptions of human psychology and human potential to embrace the vision that was originally derived from the contemplative insights of the sages who authored the texts of classical Daoism. I also argue that such an expansion in humanistic scholarship be reflected in research in the various Brain Sciences as well.

In an Afterword, I apply what I call the "contemplative hermeneutic" to the more recent controversy on whether or not a historically attested single author, Zhuang Zhou wrote the Inner Chapters of the *Zhuangzi* and present a new textual analysis of the parallel passages between chapter 23 of this work and the Inner Chapters of the same. This represents a direct application of the various hypotheses, data that support them, and arguments I have made throughout the prior chapters of the book to this very vexing problem.

The essays that form this collection, written over a quarter century, are aimed at countering the four shibboleths of Early China Studies and Daoist Studies that have previously prevented the field from identifying, in a historically plausible, contemplatively grounded, and textually justified fashion, some of the basic contours of classical Daoism. It remains for others to discover the details through which the practices, texts, and traditions of teachers and students from this formative classical period connected with the later and more clearly organized religious institutions of the late Han and post-Han periods. Indeed, some of this work has already been done in publications by such scholars as Livia Kohn, Fabrizio Pregadio, Mark Csíkzsentmihalyi, Ronnie Littlejohn, Steven Eskildsen, and Louis Komjathy, to name a few.[16] It is my hope that such research will be able to continue and develop even closer associations between the classical and the later periods of development in the very complex Daoist tradition, based on some of the foundations of the work contained in the present volume.

Part I

Textual Methods

Chapter 1

Psychology and Self-Cultivation in Early Daoistic Thought

One genuinely unexplored area of early Chinese thought is that of psychology. What are the basic elements that constitute the human mind? How do they interact and function together to express innate human tendencies and shape human experience? And how can they be transformed so that human beings can reach the limits of their inherent natures? While most certainly we cannot expect the ancient Chinese to have conceived of psychology in the same ways that we do, there is no doubt that as human beings they wrestled with many of the same problems that we confront today in trying to understand human consciousness and human potential.

In his 1980 book *Xianqin xinli sixiang yanjiu* 先秦心理思想研究, Yan Guocai 燕國材 differentiates between "psychology" (*xinli xue* 心理學), which is a century-old science developed in the West without parallels in ancient China, and "psychological thought" (*xinli sixiang* 心理思想), a broader category of theories about the mind, which does not necessarily contain the same Western assumptions and is definitely represented in pre-Qin thought.[1] While I agree with Yan about the need to distinguish between a definition of psychology based exclusively on Western models and a more broadly-based category, which could be called "psychological thought," I do not think that the mere use of the

I wish to express my gratitude to Angus Graham and Robin Yates for their careful reading and searching criticisms of earlier versions of this manuscript. I wish also to thank Margaret Taylor for her most helpful editorial suggestions.

21

term "psychology" must carry with it any particular set of assumptions about the nature of the mind from the wide range of Western schools of psychology simply because the term was coined in the West. Indeed, if one did wish to outline the basic ideas of "Western psychology," one would be hard-pressed to find a consensus on just what they might be. Should Western psychology be characterized by the theories of Sigmund Freud or the theories of B. F. Skinner? Instead of distinguishing between "psychology" and "psychological thought," as Yan does, should we not make a distinction between psychotherapy and psychology? In that case, I would agree that there is little evidence of anything resembling Western psychotherapy in ancient China, but I would argue that we can certainly find "psychology" there.

Here I use "psychology" as a generic term referring to any theories of the nature and activity of the human mind, independent of any specific model—either Western or Eastern.[2] While I agree with Yan that ancient Chinese ideas on psychology include such aspects as knowledge, emotion, intentionality, and human nature,[3] I would expand his list to include the entire range of experiences of self-transcendence that usually fall outside the purview of Western psychology and are considered under the general heading of "religious" or "mystical" experience.

This approach implies that ancient Chinese philosophers did conceive of an inner psychic life. Some modern scholars may wish to extend the arguments of Herbert Fingarette about the absence of such "subjective" notions in Confucius to all early Chinese thinkers, but such arguments cannot stand against the overwhelming evidence in the sources examined in the present study.[4] In these sources, an inner dimension is not merely present in human beings but is the basis for the complete realization of our inherent potential. Those scholars who question the presence of psychological theories in ancient China reveal more about their own philosophical presuppositions than about any early Chinese thinker. As I understand it, this is precisely Benjamin Schwartz's critique of Fingarette, and I wholeheartedly agree with it.[5]

Questions of human psychology were first raised in China during the fourth century BCE and, not surprisingly, were associated with the philosophical debates about human nature. Such questions are mentioned in the surviving writings of Yang Zhu preserved in the Lüshi chunqiu 呂氏春秋 and the Zhuangzi 莊子,[6] and are seen as well in the Confucian works of Mencius and Xunzi and the foundational Daoist texts, the Laozi 老子 and the Zhuangzi. Questions of the nature and functioning of the human mind do not figure prominently in any of these works save the last, or "Syncretist," stratum of the *Zhuangzi*, of early Han date.[7] But each of these texts takes for granted certain common ideas about human psychology, which may have been discussed more directly in other works that are now lost or have not received the same degree of attention from traditional and modern scholars.

One of the most ancient assumptions about human psychology in China is that the various aspects of human psychological experience are associated with, or even based upon, certain physiological substrates or conditions. Interestingly enough, this assumption is initially discussed in some of the most important passages on self-cultivation in early Chinese thought. Mencius alludes to this in 2A2, where he links the continual practice of acting ethically with the "flood-like vital energy" (*haoran zhi qi* 浩然之氣). The Inner Chapters of the Zhuangzi touch upon this in the relationship between emptiness (*xu* 虛) and the vital energy in chapter 4.[8] The *Laozi* as well touches upon this assumption in its passing mention of concentrating the vital energy (*zhuan qi* 專氣) in chapter 10. Yet despite these scattered references, none of the major Warring States philosophical texts explores the physiological basis of human psychology. This is particularly surprising of the Daoist texts, because in them the process of self-cultivation does seem to involve such mental disciplines as "the fasting of the mind" (*xin zhai* 心齋)[9] and "sitting and forgetting" (*zuo wang* 坐忘).[10] It is also surprising in light of later developments in Daoism.

Despite this apparent absence in the early Daoist tradition, the physiological basis of human psychology does play a major role in the theory and practice of the *nei dan* 內丹, or "physiological alchemy," which emerged somewhat later when Daoism became institutionalized and took on many of the characteristics we usually ascribe to a religion. The linking of psychological experience to physiological conditions—in this case to the generation and/or manipulation of the vital energy (*qi* 氣), the vital essence (*jing* 精), and the numen (*shen* 神)—contains a significant theoretical assumption.[11] If psychological experiences—especially the exalted and desirable ones traditionally attained through meditation—are based upon physiological conditions, then it is possible to attain these states through exclusively physiological means such as dietary control, the consumption of certain physical substances, and even carefully regulated physical exercise. This makes possible a whole range of *nei dan* practices, which seem to have preceded the Daoist religion but which became fully developed therein.[12]

One problem that has perplexed those scholars who have investigated the possible links between the Daoist religion and the texts it often claims as foundational, the *Laozi* and the *Zhuangzi*, is just when and from what sources did these practices of physiological alchemy enter the tradition? Some, such as Henri Maspero, have found evidence of them in these early philosophical sources.[13] Others, such as H. G. Creel and Fung Yu-lan, see them as part of a supposed corruption of Daoist philosophy caused by its intermingling with various superstitious popular elements during the Han dynasty.[14] Others-especially Japanese and Chinese scholars (such as Fukui Fumimasu, Sakai Tadao, Yamada Toshiaki, Zhou Shaoxian, and members of the Daoist Association of China)—contended that they were introduced by the shadowy group of *fang shi* 方士 (Esoteric Masters) who most certainly were involved in various alchemical techniques long before institutionalized Daoism arose.[15]

It is not my purpose here to assess the validity of each of these approaches. What I would like to point out is that all these interpretations share a common assumption that is misdirected and dooms their efforts to failure: that the *Laozi* and the *Zhuangzi* (and for some, the *Liezi*) define the parameters of early Daoist philosophy. This assumption also largely informs the scholarly attempts to interpret the Huang-Lao 黄老 texts discovered at Mawangdui 馬王堆. To refer to these as sources of "Yellow Emperor Daoism" presupposes that there already existed another, and more basic, form of Daoism—that which has come to be called "Lao-Zhuang 老莊." This assumption has also led to rather fruitless debates on whether Daoist philosophy is primarily mystical or primarily political and to such distinctions as the one Creel makes between "contemplative" and "purposive" Daoism.[16]

In fact, the earliest textual and historical sources offer little or no evidence of any lineage of early Daoist philosophy that can be labeled as "Lao-Zhuang." With one possible exception, the term does not even appear until the third century CE.[17] What we find instead, especially in the *Shi ji* 史記, is evidence of Daoism being equated with the teachings of Huang-Lao (that is, the Yellow Emperor and Laozi), teachings that embraced both mystical and political concerns in a philosophy advocating a minimalistic and naturalistic government overseen by a ruler who has experienced the ground of the cosmos—the Dao—through techniques of self-cultivation.[18] Let us look for a moment at what Sima Tan, who coined the term "Daoism" (*Daojia* 道家), has to say about this teaching:

The Daoist school enables man's numinous essence to be concentrated and unified, to move in unison with the formless, and to provide adequately for the myriad things. As for its methods, it follows the general tendency of the Naturalists (Yinyang jia 陰陽家), picks out the best of the Confucians and Mohists, and adopts the essentials of the Terminologists (Ming jia 名家) and Legalists. It shifts with the times and changes in response to things; and in establishing customs and in practical applications it is nowhere unsuitable. The general drift of its teaching is simple and easy to hold onto; much is achieved with little effort.[19]

Sima Tan, who supposedly studied with a Huang-Lao master, elaborates on this favorable assessment:[20]

The Daoist school takes no action but also says that nothing is left undone. Its substance is easy to practice, but its words are difficult to understand. Its methods take emptiness and non-being as the root, and adaptation (yin 因) and compliance (xun 循) as its practice. It has no set limits, no constant forms, and so is able to penetrate to the genuine basis of things . . . It blends with the Great Dao, obscure and mysterious, and after illuminating the whole world it reverts to the nameless.[21]

In light of these definitions, it is clear that Daoism in the *Shi ji* was not defined as "Lao-Zhuang." Rather, it was much closer to the philosophy found in a much overlooked text, the early Han compendium, the *Huainanzi* 淮南子, recognized by some as the principal surviving document of Huang-Lao thought.[22]

It is further my contention that the "Lao-Zhuang" of the Wei 魏 and Jin 晉 Neo-Daoists—with its emphasis on the mystical and cosmological aspects of these texts at the expense of the political and psychological—has strongly influenced traditional and modern understandings of philosophical Daoism, causing scholars to ignore other aspects of early Daoist thought and other relevant texts. In other words, what I am suggesting here is that Daoist philosophy is more accurately categorized as "Huang-Lao" than "Lao-Zhuang."[23]

From the above description by the Han historians, a picture of Daoism emerges that differs from the mystical cosmology of "Lao-Zhuang." What we find instead is a system of thought that blends a cosmology based on the Dao as ultimate ground of the cosmos with both psychological techniques of self-cultivation leading to immediate experience of the Dao and a political philosophy that elaborates the *Laozi*'s principle of *wuwei* 無為 ("effortless action"). Psychological techniques of self-cultivation are centered on such concepts as emptiness *(xu)*, moving in unison with the formless *(dong he wu xing* 動合無形), and reverting to the nameless *(fufan wuming* 復反無名), familiar to us from the *Laozi* and the Inner Chapters of the *Zhuangzi*. They also include a new element not found in either source, namely enabling man's numinous essence to be concentrated and unified *(shi ren jingshen zhuan yi* 使人精神專一). The political philosophy is based upon *wuwei* but is expanded to include such related ideas as shifting with the times *(yu shi qian yi* 與時遷移), spontaneous response *(ying* 應), suitability *(yi* 宜), adaptation *(yin* 因), and compliance *(xun* 循), which are not found in the *Laozi* or the Inner Chapters of the *Zhuangzi*. It also demonstrates a thoroughgoing syncretism, signs of which begin to emerge in the later strata of the *Zhuangzi*, and which attains its fullest expression in the *Huainanzi*. It is this Huang-Lao teaching that Sima Tan and Sima Qian call "Daoism."

While of course we run the risk of falling under the influence of what may be a retrospective view of early Daoism contained in the *Shi ji*, it is a viewpoint much closer in time to the origins of Daoism than that of the Neo-Daoists. Let us take as a working hypothesis the definitions of Daoist philosophy provided by the Han historians, and label "Daoist" those teachings that meet their criteria of a cosmology, psychology, and polity based on the Dao, and "Daoistic" those teachings that at least meet the most important of them, that is, those that accept the Dao as the ultimate ground of the cosmos.

By these definitions, the *Laozi* and the Inner Chapters of the *Zhuangzi*, while of course still important, are not the sole basis of philosophical Daoism. Other equally important texts contain very early theories discussing the physiological basis of human psychology and focusing on self-cultivation. I include in this list works not traditionally classified as "Daoist"—certain parts of the "Legalist" *Guanzi*, and the "Eclectic" *Huainanzi*—as well as works that have been considered at least tangentially "Daoist"—the Syncretist essays of the *Zhuangzi* and the four short Mawangdui texts tentatively identified as the lost *Huangdi si jing* 黃帝四

經.[24] In this study I focus on the "non-Daoist" works because their critical role in the early history of Daoism has gone largely unappreciated. Elsewhere I have explored their relationship to the Syncretist material, and other scholars have begun analysis of their relationship to the "Yellow Emperor" texts.[25] By thus broadening our list of sources for early Daoist philosophy, it should become increasingly possible to see more clearly the very definite links this early tradition has with the Daoist religion. Certainly the addition of this psychophysiological element to our picture of early Daoist philosophy provides a bridge to an analogous and very important element in later Daoism, the *nei dan.*

This chapter examines the theories of the physiological basis of psychology and self-cultivation discussed in three texts from the *Guanzi* and in the *Huainanzi.* These theories seem to be presupposed by, and alluded to, in several places in the *Laozi* and the *Zhuangzi* (including those mentioned above) and are crucial to any understanding of the origins and development of Daoism. In fact, these texts mark the progressive development of the psychophysiological component of early Daoist thought identified by the Han historians, and demonstrate its relationship to the political component.

The *Guanzi* Texts

The *Guanzi* is an extensive and diverse collection of texts currently in seventy-six *juan* 卷, most of which deal with various aspects of government and political thought. Its traditional ascription to Guan Zhong 管仲, a famous seventh-century BCE prime minister in the state of Qi 齊, is no longer taken literally; rather it is now generally accepted that much of the material was written in Qi and that the *Guanzi* includes an early basic text produced at the Jixia Academy 稷下, which was established there at the end of the fourth century BCE.[26] The extant recension was assembled by Liu Xiang in about 25 BCE and clearly contains material written well into the second century BCE.

The *Guanzi* was originally classified as "Daoist" in the *Han shu* 漢書 bibliography, but from the Sui onward it has been included in the Legalist section of dynastic bibliographies, although some scholars have pointed out that its basic orientation disagrees with Legalism.[27] This early classification of the *Guanzi* as Daoist is interesting because the Jixia Academy is regarded by Sima Qian as the home of Huang-Lao thought and because Allyn Rickett notes many parallels between the *Guanzi* chapters included in his new translation and the *Huainanzi*.[28] This evidence suggests the possibility that both are part of a Huang-Lao lineage and certainly warrants further analysis, which, unfortunately, cannot be attempted here. While Rickett believes that these parallels indicate that some of the extant *Guanzi* could have actually been written by Liu An's retainers, the three texts we are about to examine clearly represent an earlier phase of theories of self-cultivation and government than those in the *Huainanzi* and cannot have been written at Huainan 淮南.

The texts in question, "Xin shu shang, xia" (Techniques of the Mind, Parts I and II 心術上, 下) and "Neiye" (Inward Training 內業), have been the subject of considerable debate as to their origins and dating.[29] Liu Jie and Guo Moruo, and most scholars currently working in the People's Republic of China, take them to be the products of the Huang-Lao philosophers Song Xing 宋鈃 and Yin Wen 尹文, who were active at the Jixia Academy.[30] Machida Saburo sees them as late Qin or early Han products of Daoist thinkers, even though they contain some Confucian and Legalist concepts.[31] Rickett originally considered them to be Daoist works written in Qi at various times between the early fourth and late second centuries. Now he believes that they are from Chu 楚 and could have entered the *Guanzi* via Liu An's court at Huainan.[32] Graham prefers not to classify the earliest of the three, "Neiye," which he believes predates the split between Confucianism and Daoism.[33]

By the definition established above, I consider these texts to be, at the very least, Daoistic works whose authorship cannot be definitely established. On the basis of their style and philosophical content, it is clear that they were written at different points in time and, though related, represent different stages in the development of theories of self-cultivation. Therefore, they cannot be attributed to Song Xing and Yin Wen. "Neiye," written in rhymed verse, seems to be the oldest of the three, and there are no compelling reasons not to attribute it to someone at Jixia, as most scholars do. "Xinshu shang" contains two distinct sections. The first third is a basic text, and the remainder is a line-by-line commentary on it, which seems to have been written later, probably at the beginning of the Han.

With "Xinshu xia," we face a new problem. Close examination reveals that about 65 percent of "Xinshu xia" consists of passages that are virtually identical to about one-third of "Neiye" but are arranged in a completely different order. Did "Xinshu xia" take them from "Neiye" or vice versa? Or are they both different redactions of the same text? Rickett maintains that "Xinshu xia" is an early Han work based on *Neiye*.[34] Guo Moruo sees the two texts as notes taken independently by two students at the lectures of their master.[35] My own conclusion is that "Xinshu xia" represents a deliberate abridgment and rearrangement of "Neiye" designed to complement the ideas in "Xinshu shang," perhaps by the person who wrote the explanatory section of that text. My reasons for this are detailed below.

"Neiye" ("Inward Training")

Graham regards "Neiye" as "possibly the oldest 'mystical' text in China.'"[36] It is a collection of rhymed verses on the nature of the cosmos, the nature and activity of the human mind, and the practice of several related methods of mental and physical self-discipline aimed at physical health, longevity, and self-transcendence. Because it mentions the same "flood-like vital energy" (*haoran zhi qi*) as does Mencius and shows no awareness of the Naturalist concepts of Yin and Yang and the Five Phases, scholars have given it a relatively early date. I tend to agree with a late fourth-century BCE date for the text for another reason, namely, that it contains very little advice to the ruler and does not set its prescriptions on self-cultivation in the context of governing effectively. This political element does play a major role in "Xinshu shang" and, to a lesser extent, in "Xinshu xia," and given what we understand about Daoist philosophy and Huang-Lao thought from the various sources mentioned above, I see this placement of techniques of self-discipline in a political context as indicative of a more developed stage in the tradition. In short, "Neiye" is a manual on the theory and practice of meditation that contains the earliest references to breath control and the earliest discussion of the physiological basis of self-cultivation in the Chinese tradition.

The first section of "Neiye" concentrates on the cosmological principles that form the foundation for its theories and practices of self-cultivation. It presents the Dao as the ineffable ground of the cosmos with ideas we have come to identify as Daoistic:[37]

> The "Dao" is what the mouth cannot speak of, the eyes cannot look at, and the ears cannot listen to. It is that by which we cultivate the mind and align the physical form.[38] It is what

a person loses and thereby dies, what a person gains and is thereby born. When undertakings lose it, they fail; when they gain it, they succeed.

The Dao
Never has a root or a trunk, Leaves or flowers.
The myriad things are born by means of it
And by means of it develop.
We name it "the Dao." (16.2a2)[39]

In addition to the Dao, there is another important cosmic principle, which is closely associated with life and is on an almost equal footing, the *Jing*, or "vital essence":

For all things when the vital essence
Coalesces there is life.
Below it generates the five grains,
Above it becomes the constellated stars.
When it flows between Heaven and Earth
We call it daemonic and numinous.
When it is stored within the chest of a man
We call him a sage.
Therefore this vital energy is
Bright!—as if ascending to Heaven.
Dark!—as if entering an abyss.
Vast!—as if present within the ocean.
Lofty!—as if located on a mountain peak.[40]
Therefore this vital energy
Cannot be stopped by force
But can be secured by the Power (*De* 德).
Cannot be summoned by sound
But can be welcomed by the awareness (*yi* 意).[41]
Diligently hold onto it and do not lose it. This is called
    "developing the Power."
When the Power develops and wisdom emerges
The myriad things will to the last one be grasped.[42] (16.1a5)

The vital essence is thus that mysterious and elusive aspect of the Dao that is responsible for the generation of life and for maintaining the vitality of living organisms. That it is clearly a concentrated form of the vital energy pervading the cosmos is implicit here and explicit somewhat later in the text, when we find the following definition: "The vital essence is the essence of the vital energy" (16.2a9). It is closely linked with the Power (*De*), which in Daoistic thought represents the potency that arises in an organism from the concrete manifestation of the Dao within it and yet cannot be secured by any kind of intentional effort.

The text then discusses how the mind is naturally filled with the vital essence and naturally tends to generate and develop it. Yet the mind inevitably loses this essence because of emotions, desires, and selfishness. But if the mind can discard such disturbances, it will follow its natural tendency toward equanimity and harmony (16.1a11).

Next, the Dao is described as that ineffable and constantly moving force responsible for the vital essence filling the mind. This essence comes and goes with the Dao and is just as mysterious. Yet if we abandon the attempt to hold onto it and just still the mind (*xin jing* 心靜) and guide the vital energy (*qi li* 氣理) through breath control, this Dao can be secured (16.1b10). With this groundwork in place, the text then discusses the theory and practice of self-cultivation and the benefits obtained therefrom. These practices are based on stabilizing the mind:

> If one can align the mind and make it still,
> Only then will it be stable.
> When inwardly the mind is stable,
> The eyes and ears will perceive clearly,
> And the four limbs will be firm.
> One can thereby make a lodging place for the vital
>   essence.
> The vital essence is the essence of the vital energy.
> When the vital energy follows the Dao, there is vitality.
> With vitality, one can think,
> With thought, there is knowledge.
> But when you have knowledge, you come to a stop.
> In general, when the mind has excessive knowledge,
> It loses its vitality. (16.2a9)

This passage establishes an important link between mental stability and the vital essence. The state of tranquility creates the conditions for lodging or accumulating the vital essence within the mind and is thus intimately associated with this essence. This is further developed in the following:

> In general a person's vitality
> Depends on his peace of mind.
> When one is anxious, one loses the guiding thread.
> When one is angry, one loses the tip of this thread.
> When one is anxious or sad, pleased or angry,
> The Dao has no place to settle.
> Love and desire: still them!
> Folly and disturbance: correct them![43]
> Do not push it! Do not pull it!
> And its blessings will naturally settle in.
> And that Dao will naturally come to you,
> To rely on and take counsel with.
> If one is still, it will be obtained.
> If one is agitated, it will be lost.
> This mysterious vital energy within the mind,
> One moment it arrives, the next it departs.
> So fine, nothing can be contained within it,
> So vast, nothing can be outside it.
> The reason we lose it
> Is because of the harm caused by agitation.
> When the mind can adhere to stillness,
> The Dao will be naturally stabilized. (16.5a4)

Here once again we see the Dao (and the vital essence) conceived of as constantly moving into and out of the human mind. But if this Dao is the ultimate ground of the cosmos, how can it ever separate from any one part of it? Rather than taking these descriptions literally, I interpret them as metaphorical references to one's experience of the Dao. That is, for example, when the mind is still, it seems as if the Dao is present, and when the mind is agitated, it seems as if the Dao has departed. Also, the Dao is so intimately associated with the vital essence (herein called "mysterious vital energy" (ling qi 靈氣) that in this and other passages (e.g., 16.1a6 and 16.1b7), identical metaphors are used to describe them. The mental tranquility needed to stabilize the Dao is attained by casting aside all emotions, desires, and deliberate attempts to force it under one's control. With the Dao grounded in one's mind, the vital essence is also lodged therein, and health and well-being develop:

> When the vital essence is present, there is a natural vitality.
> And one's exterior is calm and healthy.
> Stored within, we take it to be the wellspring.
> Flood-like (*haoran*), it harmonizes and equalizes.
> And we take it to be the source of the vital energy. When
>   the source is not dried up,
> The four limbs are firm.
> When the wellspring is not drained,
> (The vital energy) freely circulates through the nine apertures
> One can then exhaust Heaven and Earth
> And spread over the four seas. (16.3a8)

The vital essence is thus seen as the source of the vital energy within the organism, and its free circulation is associated metaphorically with a higher level of comprehension of the entire cosmos. This association is further developed when the text speaks of stability and stillness leading to the ability to "carry the great circle (of Heaven) . . . tread over the great square (of Earth) . . . contemplate the ultimately transparent (*da qing* 大清) . . . and see through to the ultimately luminous (*da ming* 大明)." This is known as "daily renewing one's Power" (16.3b2). We here encounter metaphors for metaphysical knowledge, which this text often associates with the *shen*, the numinous power present within the mind:

> By concentrating your vital energy as if numinous,
> The myriad things will all be contained within you.
> Can you concentrate? Can you unify?
> Can you know good and bad fortune
> Without resorting to divination?
> Can you stop? Can you halt?
> Can you not seek it without
> But attain it within?[44]
> If you think and think, and think further about this
> But still cannot penetrate it,
> The daemonic and numinous (*gui shen* 鬼神) in you will
>   penetrate it.

It is not due to the inherent power of the daemonic and
    numinous,
But rather to the utmost development of your vital essence.
    (16.4a2)

This passage is important for establishing a link between the
numinous state within, which is viewed as a concentrated form of vital
energy, and the vital essence, which somehow confers on the numinous
the ability to foreknow. This type of metaphysical knowledge is a defining
characteristic of the numinous state and differentiates it from the vital
essence, which is responsible for this knowledge but does not of itself
know. This link is further discussed in the following:

The numen naturally resides within.[45]
One moment it goes, the next it comes,
And no one is able to conceive of it.
To lose it inevitably implies chaos;
To attain it inevitably implies order.
Diligently clean out its lodging place [the mind],
And the vital essence will naturally come to you.[46]
Still your attempts to imagine and conceive of it.
Relax your efforts to reflect on and control it.
Be reverent and diligent,
And the vital essence will naturally become stable.[47] (16.2b9)

The attainment of the numinous metaphysical knowledge is thus
associated with the stabilizing of the vital essence through the stilling
of thought and the cessation of all efforts to control this essence. This
process is metaphorically described as "cleaning out the lodging place
of the numinous," that is, the mind. This is associated with the advice,
mentioned earlier, about relinquishing desires and emotions in order
to attain stillness and mental stability. Such advice is found in other
traditions of meditation and is especially clear in Buddhism. "Neiye"
goes even further in linking this advice to what can only be a form of
breath-control meditation. Elaborating on how one might "daily renew
one's Power" and "attain it within," the text says:

In general [to practice] this Way
One must coil, one must contract,

> One must uncoil, one must expand,
> And one must be firm and regular [in this practice].
> Hold fast to this excellent [practice];
> Do not let go of it.
> Chase away the excessive [in sense perception].
> Abandon the trivial [in thought].[48]
> And when you understand the ultimate levels
> You will return to the Way and its Power. (16.3b6)

The regularized practice of coiling and uncoiling, of contracting and expanding, is clearly a method of controlled breathing, with coiling/ contracting referring to exhalation and uncoiling/expanding to inhalation.[49] Regular breathing, however, is not, in and of itself, a goal. It is a method of meditation for calming the mind and reaching the Dao inherent within. To my knowledge, this passage contains the earliest reference to the practice of breath-control meditation in the Chinese tradition. Another passage links this practice with the vital essence:

> In general in the life of human beings
> Heaven brings forth the vital essence,
> Earth brings forth the body.
> Unite these two to make a whole person.
> When they are in harmony, there is vitality;
> When they are not in harmony, there is no vitality.
> If we scrutinize too closely the Way of harmony [between
>   the two],
> Its truth is not seen,[50]
> Its evidence is not categorized.
> But if one evens out and aligns [the breathing] within the chest,
> The vital essence will flow freely within the mind.[51]
> This confers longevity. (16.4a11)

The practice of regularized and controlled breathing is thus the foundation of mental tranquility and hence of physical well-being, metaphysical knowledge, and the lodging of both the vital essence and the Way and its Power. Significantly, this practice is here also associated with the attainment of longevity. This indicates that, "Lao-Zhuang" to the contrary, there was an interest in extending the term of life at the very origins of Daoistic thought.

In addition to breath control, "Neiye" recommends one other concrete method for lodging the vital essence. The method, called "the way of eating," involves avoiding the extremes of overeating and starvation and keeping to a mean so that the vital energy can flow freely and harmony can be achieved. Eventually this method enables one to enlarge the mind, expand the vital energy, and sit calmly and motionlessly in order to "guard the One" (*shou yi* 守一) and discard all mental clutter (16.4b7). This is probably the earliest reference to this meditation technique of "guarding the One," which later became so important in Daoist and Buddhist practice.[52] Hence the practice of moderate eating complements the practice of controlled breathing. Both lead to the emotionless, desireless experience of mental tranquility associated with the vital essence and with the Way and its Power.

Thus, "Inward Training" is very much a manual for the theory and practice of self-cultivation. The physiological basis for the psychological states of calmness and stability is to be found in the unencumbered circulation of the vital energy and in the accumulation of the vital essence, that mysterious aspect of the Dao ultimately responsible for the birth and vitality of all living organisms. This accumulation of the vital essence is further accompanied by the attainment of the metaphysical knowledge of the future and of all things within Heaven and Earth that is linked to the numen and to the experience of the ground of the cosmos, the still and silent Dao. "Neiye" makes little attempt to recommend this "inward training" to the ruler. Occasionally it refers to such Confucian ideas as humaneness and "rightness" (16.2b7), and ritual and music (16.4b6), but it subordinates them to the superior methods that develop stillness and stability. Hence "Neiye" must be considered an important source of Daoistic thought that had a significant influence on the early history of this tradition, an influence that leads through the two parts of "Techniques of the Mind" to the theories of self-cultivation in the *Huainanzi*.

"XINSHU SHANG" (THE TECHNIQUES OF THE MIND, PART I)

"Xinshu shang" is very different from "Neiye." It is less than half as long as "Neiye" and for the most part is not written in rhymed verse. It is divided into a basic text, which constitutes about one-third of the overall work, and a line-by-line explanation of it. Furthermore, although it adopts the general guidelines for self-cultivation found in "Neiye," it places them in the context of advice to the ruler on how to govern effectively. This advice is placed in the cosmological framework of the Way and its Power and so meets our minimum criteria for Daoistic thought. And it centers on a number of specific ideas from the *Laozi* and on others that are listed by Sima Tan and Sima Qian in their discussions of Daoist philosophy.

The prescriptions for government by the sage are principally based on the concept of *wuwei*, which is extended to several closely related ideas such as spontaneous response (*ying*), adaptation (*yin*), compliance with natural guidelines (*xun li* 循理), and the principle of assigning tasks suitable (*yi*) to the individual. These concepts are developed in the *Huainanzi* and included in the descriptions of Daoism in the *Shi ji* as well. The prescriptions on how to attain the state of mind needed for practicing these principles center on achieving stillness (*jing*) and emptiness (*xu*); on relinquishing wisdom, desires, and preferences; and, finally, on cleaning out the mind in order to lodge the numen and develop the vital essence.

The text begins by drawing an interesting macrocosmic microcosmic parallel between the ruler, who governs his officials through non-action, and the mind, which governs the flow of the vital energy through the senses:

> The location of the mind in the body is analogous to the position of the ruler. The supervision [of the circulation of vital energy] by the nine apertures is analogous to the responsibilities of the officials. When the mind rests in its Way, the nine apertures will comply with natural guidelines.
> When lusts and desires fill the mind to overflowing, the eyes do not see colors and the ears do not hear sounds. When the superior departs from his Way, the inferiors will make mistakes in their affairs.[53] Therefore we say "the techniques of the mind are to take no action and yet to control the apertures." (13.1a5)[54]

This passage sets the themes that dominate the remainder of the text. The ruler should take no action contrary to the Dao, and his officials will adhere to their own responsibilities, just as the mind takes no action and the nine apertures follow their inherent guidelines. A further aspect to this parallel is that in order to accomplish this non-action, the ruler must literally empty his own mind so that it will function naturally in controlling his senses, thus allowing him to avoid interfering with the duties of his officials. Hence the internal mental discipline of non-action permits the external practice of non-action as a principle of government. The former is also referred to as the "techniques of the mind," which is also the title of the text.

However, before the ruler can put these practices into effect, there must be certain basic principles of social organization. For these, the text recommends some familiar Confucian and Legalist concepts, which are placed in a Daoistic framework:

> That which is empty and formless, we call the Dao.[55] That which transforms and nurtures the myriad things, we call the Power. That which is involved in the interactions between ruler and minister, father and son, and among all human beings, we call rightness. That which determines the various levels of status, courtesy, and familiarity in relationships, we call ritual.[56] That which selects things both great and small for execution and extermination, for prohibition and punishment, according to a single standard (Dao), we call laws. (13.1b2)[57]

The explanatory section of the text discusses these seemingly non-Daoistic ideas in terms of what, in my opinion, are two of the predominating concepts of early Han Daoism, suitability (yi) and conforming to natural guidelines (xun li):

> "Rightness" means that each rests in what is suitable to it. "Ritual" is that which follows the genuine feelings of human beings by going along with the natural guidelines of what is right for them, and then creating limitations and embellishments. Therefore ritual means "to have natural guidelines." Natural guidelines clarify distinctions in order to explain the meaning of rightness. Therefore, ritual is derived from rightness; rightness is derived from natural guidelines; and natural guidelines are derived from what is suitable.[58]
>
> Law is that by which uniformity is produced so that people will have no other alternative than to do what is so. Thus execution and extermination, and prohibition and punishment, are used to unify them. Therefore human affairs are supervised by law, law is derived from authority, and authority is derived from the Way. (13.3a8)

This explanatory passage clearly demonstrates the incorporation of Confucian and Legalist concepts into a framework fully consistent with the Daoist philosophy described in the *Shi ji* and the Huang-Lao thought expressed in the *Huainanzi*. The principle of suitability is particularly important in the latter text, as has been discussed thoroughly by Roger Ames.[59] The *Huainanzi*, however, elaborates on this principle by incorporating it into the Naturalist philosophy of Yin and Yang and the Five Phases of vital energy, and is thus more sophisticated than "Xinshu shang." Nonetheless, the presence of these ideas in "Xinshu shang" enables us to situate it firmly within the syncretic Daoist tradition of the early Han. This position is further confirmed by its prescriptions on how the ruler acts in conformity with the principle of non-action:

> Therefore the superior person is not enticed by likes nor oppressed by dislikes. Calm and tranquil, he takes no action, and he discards wisdom and precedent. His responses (*ying*) are not pre-arranged. His movements are not deliberately chosen. Mistakes are caused by direct intervention. The fault here is that one alters things instead of adapting to them (*yin*).
>
> Therefore, as for the ruler who is grounded in the Dao: at rest, he seems to have no knowledge; when responding to things he seems to fit together with them. This is the Way of stillness and adaptation. (13.2a3)

The ruler must therefore develop the facility to respond spontaneously to all situations, to avoid the temptation of intervening directly in them, and simply to follow along with them as they evolve. This is developed in the explanatory section as involving the relinquishment of self-interest so that one can simply respond when stimulated (*gan er hou ying* 感而後應) and follow along with natural guidelines (13.4a6). His response is so perfectly natural and spontaneous that it resembles the shadow's imaging of a shape, and the echo's responding to a sound. To do this, the ruler must be grounded in complete emptiness (13.4a14), and to be so grounded he must follow methods of self-cultivation fully consonant with those of "Neiye":

> The Dao is not far off, but it is hard to reach its limit. It rests together with man, but it is hard to grasp. Empty out your desires, and the numen will enter its abode. If the abode

is not thoroughly swept clean, the numen will not remain there.[60] (13.1a10)

The explanatory section, in elaborating on these ideas, shows the influence of "Neiye":

> The Dao lies with Heaven and Earth. So vast there is nothing beyond it; so small there is nothing within it. Therefore the text says, "it is not far off, but it is hard to reach its limit."
> Rest in it and there will be no gap between the Dao and man. Only the Sage is able to rest in the Dao. Therefore the text says, "it rests together with man but is hard to grasp."[61]
> That which the Sage directs is his vital essence.[62] Relinquish desire, and the mind will be expansive. When it is expansive, it will be still. When it is still, the vital essence is present. When the vital essence is present, one experiences complete solitude (du 獨). In complete solitude there is clarity (ming 明). With clarity comes the numen. The numen is the most honored. Thus when the abode is not cleaned out, the honored one will not dwell in it. Therefore the text says, "if it is not thoroughly swept clean the numen will not reside there." (13.2b5)

Just as in "Neiye," here there is a close relationship between the experience of the Dao achieved by "cleaning out the lodging place," that is, by emptying the mind of desire and knowledge—and the stillness associated with the vital essence. The presence of this essence is linked to the experience of complete solitude, which is an important technical term in the Zhuangzi. I understand it as a metaphor for the unitive consciousness attained in many of the world's great mystical traditions.[63] After solitude comes clarity, a term in "Neiye" that I take to refer to the light that develops in states of meditative trance and the clarity of mind it imparts when one emerges from such states. Finally, this clarity is associated with the numen, the source of metaphysical knowledge that transcends selfhood and rationality. Here we are but one step removed from the Huainanzi's concept of the numen as the locus of the Dao within all human beings.

In only one other instance does "Xinshu shang" discuss self-cultivation (13.1b6), and it adds little to the above. It recommends "cleaning out the dwelling" and adds to this the prescriptions to "open its doors" (the senses), "relinquish selfishness" (*chu si* 出私), and "stop talking." This confers numinous clarity (*shen ming* 神明). Unlike in "Neiye," this advice is placed firmly within the context of how the sage is to rule and how he is to develop the ability to be responsive, impartial, and unconfused. Finally, one other passage (13.3a3) discusses the vital essence and links it to the Power, the lodging place of the Dao within phenomena that generate life.

Hence the physiological basis of self-cultivation is not a major topic in "Xinshu shang." There can be no question, however, that what is discussed is clearly based on "Neiye." And, most importantly, when self-cultivation is discussed, it is placed within a political context fully consonant with the syncretic nature of Daoist thought in the late Warring States and early Han. Perhaps because "Xinshu shang" scarcely touches on self-cultivation, the author of its explanatory section found it necessary to borrow about one-third of "Neiye" to form the basis for the second part of "Xinshu."

"XINSHU XIA" (TECHNIQUES OF THE MIND, PART II)

As mentioned above, about 65 percent of "Xinshu xia" is virtually identical with the middle part of "Inward Training" (16.2b–4b), but the material is presented in a completely different order. More precisely, this middle part can be divided into several sections. The order of these sections is totally different in "Xinshu xia."

The first difference one notices between the two texts is that "Xinshu xia" lacks the passages from "Neiye" that describe the Dao as the ultimate ground of the cosmos. If indeed "Xinshu xia" was created to complement "Xinshu shang," this is to be expected, because such passages are already included in "Xinshu shang."[64]

The second striking difference is that whereas "Neiye" contains virtually no application of self-cultivation to the problems of governing, such an application is one of the primary concerns of "Xinshu xia." Passages on the use of self-cultivation for governing constitute the 35 percent of "Xinshu xia" that has no parallel in "Neiye." These passages seem to serve the purpose of linking the sections on self-cultivation and setting them in a political context.

An excellent example of this occurs toward the beginning of "Xinshu xia." It is located after a section on how to develop "inward Power" by aligning the flow of vital energy within the organism:

Therefore, only after the awareness and vital energy are stabilized will the body be aligned.[65] The vital energy is what fills
the body. The alignment of the vital energy is the standard
pattern of its movement.[66] When what fills the body does
not move according to a standard, the heart will not attain
it [the Power].[67] When the movement of the vital energy is
not aligned [in the ruler], then the people will not submit.

Therefore the sage is like Heaven: selflessly he covers;
he is like Earth: selflessly he supports. Selfishness is what
disrupts the world of human beings.

In all cases, things already come bearing names (*ming*
名). The sage adapts and uses these, and so the world of
human beings is well governed. If actualities (*shi* 實) are not
injured [by their names], then the world of human beings is
not disrupted and will be well-governed. (13.4b9)

This passage seems designed to bring out the political benefits of
developing "inward Power." It also mentions several concepts that pertain
to the behavior of the sage-ruler in "Xinshu shang"—being selfless or
impartial, being adaptable, and making use of names and actualities (not
previously discussed but found at 13.3b9). "Xinshu xia" then returns to its
"Neiye" parallels and brings together two verses on mental concentration
that are separated in "Neiye" (16.4a6 and 4a2). The second of these, the
passage on concentrating and unifying the vital essence translated above,
talks of developing the numinous ability to foreknow that is associated
with the utmost level of the vital essence (13.5a2).

"Xinshu xia" continues with another section from a different location
in "Neiye" (16.2b2) but alters the opening line to comment on the vital
essence. "Neiye" reads: "What unifies things and is able to transform, call
it "the numen" (*yi wu neng hua wei zhi shen* 一物能化謂之神). "Xinshu
xia" instead reads: "What unifies the vital energy and is able to change,
is called the vital essence" (*yi qi neng bian yue jing* 一氣能變曰精).

The next line is virtually identical in the two sources: "What unifies affairs and is able to alter in unity with affairs is called knowledge."
However, "Xinshu xia" inserts the following connective, which is absent
from "Neiye":

Compiling and selecting are the means of classifying affairs.[68]
The utmost level [of the vital essence] and (the ability] to
change are the means of responding (*ying*) to things. Compile

and select, and there will be no disorder. Develop the utmost vital essence and be able to change, and there will be no annoyances. (13.5a8)

Once again "Xinshu xia" provides a comment, which brings out the political implications of the theories of self-cultivation that are taken from "Neiye." Furthermore, there are several other passages in which "Xinshu xia" connects verses that are separated in "Neiye," thus enabling the second of these verses to comment on the first.[69] This seems to me to be a deliberate effort to rationalize the text of "Neiye" and to place it in a political context. The politicization of self-cultivation and the absence of cosmology in "Xinshu xia" suggest that "Xinshu xia" has deliberately abridged and reorganized material on self-cultivation from "Neiye," probably to complement "Xinshu shang," which generally ignores the topic of self-cultivation but contains cosmology.

Therefore, while "Xinshu xia" does not add to our understanding of the physiological basis of psychology and self-cultivation in early Daoistic thought, it does show evidence of a conscious attempt to incorporate these theories into a political context, an attempt that links it to the Daoism of the *Laozi* and of the early Han historians. When it is considered together with "Xinshu shang," we have a text that contains the three basic elements of Daoism as defined in the *Shi ji*: cosmology, psychology, and political thought.

By contrast, "Neiye" is almost exclusively concerned with cosmology and psychology. It is therefore "Daoistic," according to our definition, but not yet "Daoist." Its influence on both parts of the "Daoist" "Xinshu" is undeniable. By incorporating the psychology and cosmology of "Neiye" into a political context, the "Xinshu" texts mark a significant turning point in early Daoist history, the point where "Daoistic" becomes "Daoist." All three *Guanzi* texts are part of a philosophical lineage that is related to both the *Laozi* and the "Syncretist" chapters of the *Zhuangzi* and leads directly to the *Huainanzi*. Future studies will no doubt demonstrate that the "Yellow Emperor" texts from Mawangdui are part of the same lineage. It is this lineage that the early Han historians call "Daoism."

The *Huainanzi*

The themes thus far discussed in the three *Guanzi* texts are continued and greatly developed in the *Huainanzi*. The physiological basis of psychological experience is a constant concern in this text as part of its discussions of the theory and practice of self-cultivation. As in the two "Xinshu" texts, self-cultivation is presented in the context of enabling the ruler to govern effectively in accord with *Laozi*'s principle of *wuwei* and the related concepts of spontaneous response (*ying*), suitability (*yi*), adaptability (*yin*), and compliance with natural guidelines (*xun li*), all of which are found as well in the *Shi ji* description of the Daoist school of philosophy.

The *Huainanzi* has another characteristic of the Daoists mentioned in the *Shi ji* but seen only sporadically in the *Guanzi* texts; namely, it utilizes ideas from other pre-Han schools of thought. This is undoubtedly the principal reason why the *Huainanzi* has been traditionally overlooked as a major source of Daoist philosophy and why since the *Han shu* bibliography it has been classified as Eclectic (*zajia* 雜家).[70] Because of this classification, it is only relatively recently that scholars have begun to appreciate its unifying aspects: that despite the presence of Confucian, Legalist, and other strands of thought, the dominant outlook in both cosmology and political theory remains Daoist. In light of the frequent (fifty-seven) quotations from the *Laozi* and the overall orientation toward minimalistic and naturalistic government by a Daoistically perfected ruler, it appears that the *Huainanzi* authors considered themselves the inheritors of the teachings and spirit of the *Laozi*. They ranged far and wide in pre-Han thought in their effort to adapt this teaching to the times and to provide the Daoist ruler with a compendium of knowledge about the nature of the cosmos and the human beings inhabiting it.

After the *Laozi*, the next most pervasive influence on the *Huainanzi* is the Yin-yang/Five Phases philosophy, which was supposedly systematized by Zou Yan, and which Joseph Needham calls "Naturalism."[71] In the *Huainanzi*, this philosophy appears for the first time in Chinese intellectual history as an all-encompassing paradigm for phenomenal change. As such, it is relevant to the complete spectrum of human endeavors.[72]

The *Huainanzi* is a work of twenty essays on a wide variety of topics from cosmology and astronomy to warfare and government. A twenty-first essay, most likely written by Liu An, the sponsor and editor of the text, provides a summary of the other essays and a rationale for their inclusion and arrangement. In addition to Liu An, history records the names of eight of the other authors. These came from a larger group of scholars and *fang shi*, whom Liu had assembled and supported at his court in Huainan beginning in about 150 BCE. Liu An presented the text to his nephew, Han Emperor Wu, in 139 BCE, seventeen years before Liu met his end (perhaps by his own hand) when Wudi sent a contingent of troops to Huainan to quell Liu An's incipient rebellion.[73]

The *Huainanzi* is one of three known philosophical works written at Huainan: the "Inner Book," as opposed to an "Outer Book" of thirty-three chapters lost since the Han, and a "Central Book" of eight chapters devoted to the techniques of inner alchemy, which is extant today only as fragments assembled into reconstituted redactions by a number of late Qing scholars.[74] The presence of *fang shi* at Liu An's court, along with the Huang-Lao philosophers who wrote the *Huainanzi*, is the first clearly documented historical evidence for interaction between the two groups most influential in the later rise of the Daoist religion. Needless to say, it is also possible that these two groups were in contact long before this time.

The physiological basis of psychology and self-cultivation is discussed throughout the *Huainanzi*, but it is given particular attention in the seventh essay, "Jingshen" 精神 (The Numinous Essence). Internal evidence suggests that the authors of the *Huainanzi* were aware of the three *Guanzi* texts analyzed above. In the twenty-first essay, "Yao lüe" 要略 (Summary of the Essentials), a "book of Guan Zhong" is mentioned. This indicates that at least one recension of the *Guanzi* had taken shape by the middle of the second century BCE, and that a copy was present at Huainan. Rickett affirms this likelihood as well.[75]

There are four specific references to the "techniques of the mind" ("Xinshu") in the *Huainanzi*, and they occur in the context of discussions on the benefits to the ruler of possessing a cultivated mind. The first essay, "Yuan Dao" 原道 (Getting to the Source of the Way),[76] explains that Xu Yu refused to accept Yao's offer to govern because he believed it was first necessary to clarify what was within himself:[77]

> The essentials of ruling the empire:
> Do not lie in other things,
> They lie in the self.
> They do not lie in other men,
> But in one's own person.[78]
> Once one finds one's person, one will find all the myriad
>   things therein.
> Once one thoroughly understands the essay on the tech-
>   niques of the mind, the desires, likes, and dislikes all
>   become extraneous.[79] (1.15a1)

This theme is continued in the fourteenth essay, "Quanyan" 詮言 (Inquiring Words):

> Zhan He[80] said: "I have never heard of a case in which one's person was put in order and the state was chaotic . . ." When one gets to the source of the Decree of Heaven, orders the techniques of the mind, makes likes and dislikes conform to natural guidelines, and acts in accordance with one's true conditions and nature, then the way of order (*zhi dao* 治道) is comprehended. When one gets to the source of the Decree of Heaven, then one is not deluded by bad or good fortune. When one orders the techniques of the mind, then one is not led astray by pleasure and anger.[81] When one makes likes and dislikes conform to natural guidelines, then one does not desire what is useless. When one acts in accordance with one's true conditions and nature, then desires do not exceed their appropriate limits. If one is not deluded by bad or good fortune, then in activity and in stillness one will conform to natural guidelines. If one is not led astray by pleasure and anger, then rewards and punishments will not affect one. If one does not desire what is useless, then one does not interfere with one's nature by desire.[82] If desires do not exceed their limits then one understands what is sufficient to nourish one's nature. Of these four principles of action, do not seek them from outside and do not borrow them from others; return to the self and they will be attained.[83] (14.2a2)

Two other references to the techniques of the mind occur in similar contexts in chapters 7 (7.11al) and 21 (21.4b2). Quite clearly, for the authors of the *Huainanzi*, the techniques of controlling the mind consist in relinquishing desires and making emotions conform to guidelines emerging from one's inherent nature. In fact, this concept of human nature is one of the *Huainanzi*'s principal elaborations on the theories from the *Guanzi* texts. The other major development in the *Huainanzi* pertains more directly to the physiological basis of human experience and involves the term *jingshen*. These are both discussed below.

Human Nature

A series of interlocking ideas form the basis for theories of psychology and self-cultivation in the *Huainanzi*, and the most basic of these is the concept of human nature (*xing* 性). This is one of the central concerns of the *Huainanzi*, and despite the variety of topics in the half-dozen essays in which this concept is discussed in detail, there is a fairly consistent understanding in all of them.[84] To the authors of the *Huainanzi*, as to earlier thinkers, this term referred not only to the basic abilities with which human beings are born, but also, as Graham points out, to the spontaneous tendencies of a living organism throughout its lifetime.[85] This concept, so important in the Yangist and Confucian writings of the later Warring States period, is totally absent from the *Laozi* and most of the *Zhuangzi*.[86] Yet it is one of the most critical ideas in the *Huainanzi*.

The development of this predominantly non-Daoist concept by the authors of the *Huainanzi* is undoubtedly related to the interest in human psychology in late-Qin and early Han Daoist circles that is attested to by the three *Guanzi* texts analyzed above. However, despite this interest, the *Guanzi* texts virtually ignore the concept of human nature. Because the *Huainanzi* does not ignore human nature, it represents a further level of development in this Daoist lineage of thought.

In the *Huainanzi*, the concept of human nature is intimately connected with two of its main themes—government and self-cultivation—as the following passage, which sounds like a Daoist version of the *Daxue* ("Great Learning"), shows:

> Those who are able to be in possession of the empire certainly do not neglect their states. Those who are able to be in possession of their states certainly do not lose their families. Those who are able to regulate their families certainly do not neglect their persons. Those who are able to cultivate their persons certainly do not forget their minds. Those who are able to reach the source of their minds certainly do not impair their natures. Those who are able to keep their natures whole certainly have no doubts about the Dao.
>
> Therefore Guang Chengzi said:[87] "Diligently protect what is within you; fully prevent it from being externalized. Excessive knowledge is harmful. Do not look! Do not listen! Embrace the numen by being still and the body will be naturally aligned. There has never been anyone who was able to know the other without first grasping it in himself." (14.2b7)

Thus for the ruler, the basis of effective government is found in self-cultivation, which itself involves keeping one's inherent nature unimpaired and whole. Precisely why this is important stems from the basic characteristics of one's nature:

> Clarity and serenity constitute the nature of human beings. (18.1a4)

> The nature of water is clear but soil muddies it.[88] The nature of human beings is calm and still, but lusts and desires disrupt it . . . (2.10a8)

> Human nature has no aberration. But when it is immersed in customs for a long time, it is replaced; and when it is replaced, man forgets his foundation and identifies with what seems to be his nature. Therefore the sun and moon desire radiance, but floating clouds cover them. Great rivers desire clarity, but sand and stones muddy them. Human nature desires equanimity (*ping* 平), but lusts and desires interfere with it. Only the sage can abandon external things and return to himself. (11.4a9)

Thus human nature is the serene and pure essence of one's being; it is impaired by the passions and replaced by the various customs that are external to it. It is further conceived of as a dynamic essence that is extremely beneficial when actualized in one's daily life:

> To act in accord with one's nature is called the Way. To grasp one's heavenly nature is called the Power. When this nature is lost, only then is benevolence esteemed. When this Way is lost only then is rightness esteemed . . . Therefore when benevolence and rightness are established, the Way and the Power are exiled. (11.1a4)

> If someone who has become lost sailing and does not know East from West sees the Pole Star, then he realizes his position. Our nature is the Pole Star of human beings. If one has the means to see it oneself, then one will not mistake the true condition of other things.[89] But if one lacks the means to see it oneself, then in every move one will be deluded. If one follows desire and thus loses one's nature, then one's movements will never be properly aligned. If one regulates the self in this way, there will be danger; if one governs

the state in this way, there will be chaos; if one directs the army in this way, there will be defeat. Therefore if one does not hear the Way, one is unable to return to one's inherent nature. (11.4a11)

Therefore, the inherently serene and pure nature within human beings not only can, but must, be used as a basis for action in the phenomenal world. It serves as an inner guide in all of one's interactions. For governing the state it is particularly important because it enables one to see the "true condition of other things" (*wu zhi qing* 物之情). The ninth and eleventh essays build on this idea to develop the governing technique of suitability, in which the ruler assigns tasks that are appropriate to the nature and talents of the individual. Only the ruler grounded in his own inherent nature is able to see clearly into the true nature of others. The self-cultivation of the ruler that enables this clarity of mind is discussed in the following:

> Therefore in the perfect man's way of ordering, the mind dwells together with the numen, and the physical form and nature are harmonized. In stillness, he embodies the Power; in movement, he flows freely with natural guidelines (*tong li* 通理). He follows his spontaneous nature (*ziran zhi xing* 自然 之性) and goes along with inevitable transformations. Being clear, he takes no action (*wu wei*), and the empire is naturally harmonized. Being tranquil, he has no desires, and the people are naturally innocent (*zi pu* 自樸). (8.4b5)

This passage links the experience of stillness with the embodiment of the Power, which, as previously stated (11.1a4), means to realize one's inherent nature. It also establishes that this nature is the basis for spontaneous action that fully accords with *li*, the natural guidelines or patterns present in any situation. This concept of *li* refers to those invisible and fundamental guidelines, or patterns, inherent in the cosmos that establish the boundaries for the development of phenomena and for their interaction with one another. It is another important idea in the *Huainanzi*. As chapter 21 states: "This book and its essays are the means by which we learn to flow freely with the various natural guidelines" (21/1a4–5). It is through their inherent nature that human beings are directly connected to these cosmic patterns. When human beings can ground their actions in this nature and thereby act spontaneously, they always act in accord with these patterns and hence in harmony with the cosmos. What we have here is a theory that provides a basis for the notions of non-action and spontaneity established in the *Laozi* and the "Inner Chapters" of *Zhuangzi*. It explains just why these concepts are valid and how they work. The effects on human experience of being grounded in one's nature are dealt with in detail in passages such as these:

> Stillness and quietude, and placidity and tranquility, are the means by which we nourish our nature. Harmony and serenity, and emptiness and nothingness, are the means by which we nourish the Power. When the external does not becloud the internal, then human nature will attain what is suitable to it. When one is tranquil, unmoving, and harmonious, then the Power secures its position.[90] To nourish the nature and thereby rule in the world, and to embrace the Power and thereby last out one's years, may be called embodying the Way.[91] If you can act in this manner, the blood will flow without obstruction and the five orbs will not have excessive vital energy. Bad and good fortune will not confound you, and praise and blame cannot soil you. (2.11b8)

The sage relies on his mind: the multitude rely on their desires. The superior person manifests aligned vital energy; the inferior person manifests aberrant vital energy.[92] That which inwardly goes along with one's nature and outwardly accords with what is right, and which in its movements complies with natural guidelines and is not bound up in external things, this is the aligned vital energy. That which is stimulated by fragrances and tastes, excited by sound and color, evoked by pleasure and anger, and which if you are not careful leads to trouble, this is the aberrant vital energy. Aberrant and aligned vital energy injure one another; desire and nature interfere with one another. Both cannot be established together. When one flourishes, the other falls away. Therefore, the sage relinquishes desire and preserves his nature.[93] (14. 7a10)

These selections establish a definite relationship between human nature and the vital energy that is the basis of human physiology. In the first, by nourishing one's nature through stillness and tranquility, one establishes a proper flow of vital energy throughout one's being. In the second, by spontaneously going along with this inner nature, one generates true vital energy and acts in a proper and suitable fashion. Thus the mechanism by which the spontaneous action that emerges from one's inner nature and operates in harmony with the natural guidelines inherent in any given situation is conceived of as correctly aligned vital energy (*zheng qi* 正氣). These ideas are clearly related to those passages in the three *Guanzi* texts that discuss the benefits to one's health and well-being gained by stilling the mind, circulating the vital energy, and accumulating the vital essence. In the *Huainanzi*, these ideas are tied together by the concept of a pure and tranquil inner nature, which spontaneously connects human beings to the natural guidelines governing the movements and interactions of all phenomena in the cosmos.

Another idea that is frequently repeated and echoes the *Guanzi* texts is that desires and emotions are harmful and interfere with the realization of the inner nature. For example:

> Joy and anger are aberrations of the Way. Anxiety and grief are lapses of the Power. Likes and dislikes are excesses of the mind. Lusts and desires are the fetters of human nature. When a person is extremely angry, the Yin is damaged. When a person is extremely happy, the Yang collapses. Weak vital energy causes dumbness. Shock and fright bring about madness. When anxiety and grief abound, rage builds up. When preferences and annoyances abound, misfortunes follow one another.
>
> Therefore when the mind does not grieve or rejoice, this is the perfection of the Power. When it is absorbed (*tong* 通) and does not alter, this is the perfection of stillness.[94] When lusts and desires do not fill it up, this is the perfection of emptiness. When there is nothing liked or disliked, this is the perfection of equanimity. When it is not confused by external things, this is the perfection of purity.[95] Those who are able to practice these five will be absorbed in the numinous light (*shen ming*). Those who are absorbed in the numinous light are those who actualize what is within them. (1.12b6)

In the practice of self-cultivation, when one attempts to develop stillness in order to become grounded in one's pure nature, both emotions and desires are harmful. However, unlike the *Guanzi*, which advocates the complete elimination of both emotions and desires, the *Huainanzi* differentiates between the two. Whereas desires are not inherent in human nature and actually impair it, the emotions are harmful only when they are unnatural or excessive. Another essay speaks of emotions as being spontaneous:

Moreover joy and anger, and sadness and happiness, arise spontaneously when stimulated. Therefore the outburst of sobbing from the mouth and the outpouring of tears from the eyes are both things that build up on the inside and take shape on the outside. By way of illustration it is like water flowing downwards and smoke burning upwards . . . (11.5a6)

Now three years of mourning force a person to do what he cannot naturally do, and so he is using what is false to support what is genuine. But three months of mourning cut off grief and stifle one's nature. The Confucians and Mohists have not sought the beginnings and ends of man's true feelings but instead endeavor to practice restrictions that are mutually contradictory. (11.6a8)

To the extent that emotions represent a spontaneous response to a given situation, they are part of one's nature. This passage makes clear that only when emotions are forced to be unnatural—by the unsuitable mourning rituals of the Confucians and Mohists, for example—do they actually go against human nature. Desires, by contrast, are always to be abjured. They never derive from one's inherently pure nature and are not conducive to stillness. In an interesting way, this attitude echoes the first chapter of the "Doctrine of the Mean," which speaks of both the mental equilibrium experienced before the arising of the emotions and the harmony experienced after they attain the appropriate degree of fulfillment. Both are aspects of following one's inner nature, and they are paralleled by the concepts of inward stillness and the proper outward expression of emotion found in the *Huainanzi*.

The concept of human nature in the *Huainanzi* is thus a significant element in its theories of psychology and self-cultivation. The authors of the *Huainanzi* also explain in detail how mental tranquility, emotions, desires, and preferences develop and function according to the concepts of the vital energy, the vital essence, and the numen. This is discussed in the following section.

The Physiological Basis of Human Experience

Two of the central concepts in the *Huainanzi*'s presentation of the physiological basis of human experience are familiar to us already from the three *Guanzi* texts: the vital essence and the numen. To these the *Huainanzi* adds several concepts not seen in the *Guanzi*: the numinous essence (*jing shen*)—the purified, or essential, vital energy of the numen—and the five orbs of vital energy (*wu zang* 五臟), often translated as the "five organs," or "five viscera."[96] The *Huainanzi*'s use of these new ideas often parallels that of the earliest Chinese medical texts, the *Huangdi nei jing su wen*黃帝內經素問 and *Huangdi nei jing ling shu* 黃帝內經靈樞, which may have been taking shape when the *Huainanzi* was being written.

THE VITAL ESSENCE

The concept of the vital essence is similar in the *Huainanzi* and the three *Guanzi* texts, but it receives less emphasis in the *Huainanzi*. In most psychological contexts, it has been replaced by the concept of the "numinous essence" (*jingshen*). In the *Huainanzi*, the vital essence is also a concentrated or essential form of the vital energy, and it is found outside the human organism as well as within it, as described in the following passage. (Note that the numinous essence, by contrast, is never naturally found outside of human beings.)

> The combined vital essences of Heaven and Earth become the Yin and the Yang. The concentrated vital essences of the Yin and the Yang become the four seasons. The dispersed vital essences of the four seasons become the myriad things . . . (3.1a8)

Elsewhere the vital essence appears to be the medium through which sound travels and is recognized (16.1b5), the medium through which a ruler's intention to attack a city is sensed by animals living in it (20.8b3), and the medium through which the aura of the self-cultivated ruler is sensed by his subjects, and which is more effective in governing them than punishments and executions (9.2b3). The operant principle in these usages seems to be the Naturalist concept of *gan ying* 感應, often translated as "resonance," by which a thing, when stimulated, spontaneously responds according to the natural guidelines of the particular phases of vital energy engendered in itself and active in the situation. The vital energy is the medium through which this mechanism functions.

When the vital essence occurs within the human organism, it is invariably associated with the numen and its activities:

> Therefore the mind is the ruler of the physical form and
>   the numen is the treasure of the mind.
> When the physical form toils without rest, it will collapse.
> When the vital essence is used incessantly, it will be exhausted.
> Hence the sage values and exalts it,
> And does not permit it to rush out. (7.4b5)

> When the vital essence flows into the eyes, then vision is
> clear. When it resides in the ears, then hearing is acute. When
> it rests in the mouth, then speech is appropriate. When it is
> collected in the mind, then thinking comprehends. Therefore
> block these four gateways. Then throughout one's entire life
> there will be no suffering and the hundred joints will not be
> sickly, die, be born, be empty, or be full. We call this a "true
> person."[97] (8.8a1)

The vital essence is responsible for various kinds of acute perception and clear cognition, but can be overused and thereby exhausted.
Its relationship to cognition is what links it to the numen, which in the
Huainanzi is ultimately responsible for cognition. Perhaps in keeping with
the usages above, it serves as a medium for the transfer of information
between outside and inside, but the text does not clearly state this.
The vital essence is gradually used up by perception and cognition and
is conceived of as flowing out of the body during these activities. It is
preserved by "blocking the gateways," which I assume refers to the less
strenuous forms of sensory deprivation associated with sitting in silence
while being engaged in breath-control meditation. During the periods of
meditation, sensory stimuli are reduced to a minimum, thus preventing
the egress of the vital essence. In contexts such as these throughout
the *Huainanzi*, the more common term found is *jingshen*, the numinous
essence, and there is reason to believe that in these passages *jing* also
means *jingshen*, as explained below.

THE NUMEN

The *shen*, or numen, is the dominant idea in the psychological theories
of the *Huainanzi*, where it receives a fuller treatment than in any other
text known up to that time. In the *Huainanzi*, *shen* is something ultimately unfathomable, and the authors were probably aware of the basic

definition in the *Xici zhuan* 繫辭傳 of the *Yi jing* 易經, that the numen is beyond the reach of Yin and Yang (*Yinyang bu ce zhi wei shen* 陰陽不測之謂神), which are the two most fundamental aspects of the Dao (*yi yin yi yang zhi wei Dao* 一陰一陽之謂道).[98] Just as in the *Guanzi* texts, the numen is repeatedly associated with metaphysical knowledge, especially knowledge of the future, and this kind and means of knowledge are often referred to by the term *shen ming*, "numinous light," the closest English equivalent for which might be "intuition." It is this numen that must be guarded and preserved, for it is both involved in all forms of mystical experience and the foundation of normal daily cognition. Therefore, the self-cultivation advocated by the authors of the *Huainanzi* is referred to as *yang shen* 養神, "nourishing the numen." This technique basically involves the same prescriptions as those in the *Guanzi* texts, namely attaining the psychological states of calm and stillness by relinquishing thoughts, emotions, and desires—the same practices referred to above as *yang xing* 養性, "nourishing the nature."[99] In fact, these are linked together in the following passages:

> The highest man puts his person in order by nourishing the
>   numen. The next highest nourishes the physical form.
> When the numen is clear,
> The attention (*zhi* 志) is in equilibrium,
> And the hundred joints are all in repose,
> This is the foundation for nourishing the nature. (20.8b11)

> Therefore one who does not hear about the Way will have no means to return to his nature. The sage-kings of old were able to attain it within themselves. Consequently, their decrees were effective, their prohibitions worked, their fame was passed on to later generations, and their Power spread throughout the four seas. Therefore, whenever one is about to undertake a task, one must first put one's awareness in equilibrium and clarify the numen. When the numen is clear and awareness is in equilibrium, things can be properly aligned [with natural guidelines]. (11.4b4)

In this and other passages, nourishing or returning to one's nature involves purifying the numen. Furthermore, just as one's inherent nature can be impaired by thoughts, desires, and emotions, so too can the numen:

> When the numen is injured by pleasure and anger, thought and worry, it becomes exhausted, but the physical form remains. (2.2b10)

> The nature of water is clear, but soil muddies it.[100] The nature of man is calm and still, but lusts and desires disrupt it . . . When the numen is clear, lusts and desires cannot disrupt it. (2.10a8, 10b5)

To the authors of the *Huainanzi*, the numen is the locus of the inherent tranquility of human nature. When cultivated or preserved, it can serve as the "pole star" that guides human cognition and actions to accord spontaneously with natural guidelines. The *Huainanzi* details how this happens by indicating the critical role the numen plays in the process of cognition:

> That which is still from man's birth is his heavenly nature. Movement only after it is stimulated causes this nature to be impaired. When external things arrive and the numen responds, this is the activity of perception. When perception comes in contact with external things, preferences arise from that. When preferences are formed, perception is enticed by externals, one cannot return to the self, and the natural guidelines (*tianli* 天理) are destroyed. Therefore those who penetrate the Dao do not use the human to replace the natural. They outwardly transform together with things and inwardly do not lose their true state. (1.5a6)

So it is the response of the numen, the inherently tranquil aspect of human nature, to external things that brings about the process of perception, which, if not beclouded by preferences, occurs according to natural guidelines. The numen does not itself perceive, because it resides outside the energetic systems of the human organism. Its role is rather different:

> Now why is it that people can see clearly and hear acutely; that the weight of the body can be supported, and that the hundred joints can be bent and stretched; that one's discrim-

ination can determine white from black and discern ugliness from beauty; and that perception can differentiate similarities and differences and distinguish this from that? Because the vital energy infuses these activities and the numen directs them. (1.17a1)

So the basic human experiences of perception and cognition are guided or coordinated by the numen, as another line also states: "The physical form is the abode of life; the vital energy is what uses life; and the numen is what organizes life" (1.16b6).

The role of the numen in cognition is elaborated on in the following passage:

If someone's attention is lodged in something and his numen is consequently tied up in it, then even if he stumbles over tree roots or bumps into tree limbs when taking a walk, he remains unaware of what has happened.[101] If you wave to him, he cannot see you; if you call to him, he cannot hear you. It is not that his eyes and ears have left him.[102] Why, then, can he not respond? It is because his numen has lost its hold. Therefore, when it is lodged in the small, it forgets the great; when it is lodged in the inside, it forgets the outside; when it is lodged in the upper, it forgets the lower; when it is lodged in the left, it forgets the right. When there is nowhere it does not infuse, there is nothing in which it does not lodge. Therefore those who value emptiness take the tip of an autumn hair as their mansion. (1.17a3)

In this passage, the numen has "lost its hold"—presumably its ability to organize and coordinate the cognition of the whole environment in which the person is operating—when the attention becomes occupied with any one element of this environment to the exclusion of the others. This also happens when emotions and desire cloud the mind. Thus emptying the mind and restoring balance or equilibrium to one's attention help to clarify the numen. The numen is thus closely related to awareness but is not the specific awareness of any one thing. Rather, it is more the element, or principle, of pure consciousness that runs through all awareness, as the following passage indicates:

> The numen is the fount of knowledge. When the numen is clear, knowledge is illumined.[103] Knowledge is the storehouse of the mind. When knowledge is impartial, the mind is composed. Men never mirror themselves in surging floodwaters; they mirror themselves in still water, because it is tranquil . . .[104] When the mirror is bright, dust cannot sully it. When the numen is clear, desire cannot disrupt it. (2.10a11, 10b5–6)

The mirror-like clarity of the numen is the basis of illumined knowledge and full cognition. Other passages state that it is "easy to make murky but difficult to make clear" (2.12a12) and that wine is one of the things that makes it murky (13.19a9). So the numen is the element of consciousness at the basis of all normal awareness; it is also an agent, or force, responsible for coordinating the various systems of vital energy in the human organism. These systems, in turn, are the physiological basis of human cognition and knowledge. But if this numen is intrinsically pure—and ultimately outside the energetic configurations of the human being—then how can it coordinate them? An answer can be found in some material from the one essay in the *Huainanzi* that contains a highly specific analysis of the physiological basis of human experience: *jing shen*.

To the authors of the *Huainanzi*, the transcendent numen accomplishes its various activities through the medium of its vital essence, which is called *jing shen*, "numen-as-vital essence," or "numinous essence." In his classic work on Chinese medical theory, Manfred Porkert explains what happens to the concept of *shen* when combined with the word *jing*:

> From the basic definition of *shen* in the *Xi ci*, "Something the polarity of which cannot be determined . . ." it is always inferred that *shen* by itself is not only inexhaustible but also unfathomable and undefinable. In spite of this to speak of the manifestation of *shen* is to imply what elsewhere is explicitly stated: the simultaneous presence of a structive complement to *shen*, either structive capacity (*ling* 靈) or structive potential (*jing* 精), in combination with which *shen* may concretely manifest itself.[105]

The numinous essence is thus the concrete manifestation of the numen. The concept of numinous essence walks the fine line between mind and body. The numen is sentient; the vital essence is not. So what is the numinous essence? For the authors of the *Huainanzi*, it is simply the actual stuff that constitutes the numen, its physiological basis. It is what enables the numen to interact with all the energetic systems of the human organism. The numinous essence might be thought of as the interface between the sentient and insentient, or the psychological and the physical. It is a blend of both aspects and thus appropriate for a worldview that did not strongly value such boundaries. Let us examine the mechanism by which the human organism functions, as presented in the *Jing shen* essay.

THE NUMINOUS ESSENCE

The numinous essence, which is received from Heaven, is ultimately responsible for coordinating the flow of vital energy through the five orbs. The *Jingshen* essay discusses the development and birth of the human being, at which time the five orbs begin to function. The flow of the vital energy within each orb governs the activity of a specific sense organ. The pulmonary orb governs the eyes, the renal controls the nose, and so on (gallic mouth; hepatic-ears; spleen-tongue). The orbs interact with one another in a complementary manner, and each has its conduits and connections through which flow the two aspects of the vital energy: the material aspect (*xue* 血, often translated as "blood") and the ethereal (*qi*). The coordination of all five orbs is accomplished by the mind (7.2a5). After discussing the parallels between the heavenly macrocosm and the human microcosm, the text presents a model of the healthy functioning of the entire organism:

> For this reason, when the material and ethereal forms of vital energy[106] can be concentrated in the five orbs and do not rush outward, then the chest and the abdomen will be full and lusts and desires will be removed. When the chest and abdomen are full and lusts and desires are removed, then the ears and eyes are clear and hearing and vision are acute. When the eyes and ears are clear and hearing and vision are acute, then we call it clarity (*ming*).
>
> When the five orbs can be coordinated within the mind and their flow is not reversed, then mental fluctuations are conquered and the flow of vital energy is not misaligned.[107] When mental fluctuations are conquered and the flow of vital energy is not misaligned, then the numinous essence is abundant and the vital energy is not dispersed. When

the numinous essence is abundant and the vital energy is not dispersed, then the organism functions according to natural guidelines. When the organism functions according to natural guidelines, then the mind is unperturbed. When it is unperturbed, it is absorbed (*tong*). When it is absorbed, it is numinous. When it is numinous, there is nothing that vision does not see,[108] nothing that listening does not hear, and nothing that action does not accomplish. For this reason, worries and misfortunes cannot enter and the aberrant vital energy cannot intrude. (7.2b1)

The five orbs are coordinated in the mind. The numen, located in the mind, coordinates the activities of the five orbs through the medium of the numinous essence. Therefore, in the passage quoted above (8.8a1), the vital essence, which circulates to the senses and results in perceptual acuity, must be the vital essence of the numen, in other words, the numinous essence.

The text then details the disruption of the harmonious functioning of the human organism, which occurs through overstimulation of the senses. This causes the five orbs to oscillate and the numinous essence to rush out through the nine apertures. One will then have no way to know good or bad fortune in advance (7.2b10). But when the preferences and desires that cause this externalization of vital energy and numinous essence are removed, one becomes still and serene, the numinous essence is preserved, and one can "contemplate the antecedents of the past and observe the aftermath of the future" (7.3a4). Herein is the basis of the metaphysical knowledge that is associated with the numen throughout this work and in the *Guanzi* texts as well. This knowledge transcends space and time, just as the numen is the pure core of consciousness that transcends its differentiations. In another essay, the experience of transcendence is linked to man's inherent nature:

For this reason those who have gotten through to the Dao return to clarity and stillness. Those who have thoroughly seen through all things end in Non-action. To use calmness to nourish one's nature, to use serenity to stabilize one's numen, is to enter the Gateway of Heaven. That which is called Heaven is pure, simple, whole, and luminous. It has never had any impurities. (1.7b6)

Thus, by nourishing one's nature and stabilizing one's numen, one becomes unified with Heaven and ultimately with the Dao. This is only one of many passages in the *Huainanzi* that links the numen with both metaphysical knowledge and the mystical experience of self-transcendence. The *Huainanzi* does not often talk directly of techniques to accomplish these mystical experiences, other than recommending the attainment of stillness and the stabilization of the numen, but in several passages it does suggest a form of breath-control meditation:

> Now Wang Qiao and Chi Songzi[109] puffed out and sucked in, exhaled the old and inhaled the new. They left their bodies behind, cast aside knowledge, embraced simplicity, and returned to the genuine. And so they roamed in the profound subtleties of the universe and had free access to the cloudy sky above. If you now wish to study their Way but do not understand their methods of nourishing the vital energy and stabilizing the numen, and simply imitate their exhaling and inhaling, sometimes bending, sometimes stretching, then clearly you will not be able to ride the clouds and ascend into the distance. (11.8b11)

This passage criticizes those who simply imitate without really understanding these two techniques of famous Immortals. It is similar to the criticism of those who practice Daoist gymnastics in the *Jing shen* essay (7.6a10), and who nourish the body but not the nature and the numen. Thus specific methods of breath-control meditation were known to the authors of the *Huainanzi* and were undoubtedly included in their "Daoist arts." It is worth noting here too that such techniques were associated not just with longevity, but with immortality. This could indicate a relationship between these techniques and the *fang shi*, the esoteric masters who were present at Liu An's court and who were pursuing immortality at this time.

Conclusions

The theories in the *Huainanzi* concerning the physiological basis of psychology and self-cultivation are derived, at least in part, from analogous theories in the three texts of the *Guanzi*. There are most certainly some differences between these two sources. To begin with, the concept of the vital essence from the earliest of the *Guanzi* texts, "Neiye," is much less important in the *Huainanzi*, where it is largely supplanted in psychological contexts by the numinous essence. Correspondingly, the concept of the numen is much more fully elaborated in the *Huainanzi*, as is the entire "phase energetic" basis of human experience. Furthermore, the detail with which the *Huainanzi* discusses the concept of human nature, as well as the entirety of human physiology, was unprecedented in the non-technical literature before that time. Nonetheless, the general orientation of the *Guanzi* texts to the theory and practice of self-cultivation is continued in the *Huainanzi*.

The three texts from the *Guanzi* and the *Huainanzi* clearly demonstrate that theories of the physiological basis of human experience were present both in China from at least the fourth century BCE and in the tradition of philosophical Daoism from its inception. And at least from the time of the *Laozi*, they were placed alongside Daoist methods of government. It is simply not accurate to define Daoist philosophy exclusively in terms of "Lao-Zhuang" and to argue over whether it is mystical or political. We have for too long been misled by the weight of tradition.

Rather, the evidence of the sources discussed above shows that Daoist philosophy—the "Huang-Lao" of the Han historians, not the "Lao-Zhuang" of the Wei and Jin literati—embraced both self-cultivation and politics into one coherent system based upon a cosmology of the Dao. And further, early Daoist theories of self-cultivation were grounded in the physiology of human experience. These theories do not represent some alien element injected into Daoism during a supposed corruption in the Han. They were there from the outset. Thus, in addition to the cosmological and the political, there is a psychological, or psychophysiological, element that can be seen in philosophical Daoism when we move beyond the boundaries of "Lao-Zhuang." This psychophysiological element clearly continues into the Daoist religion in the form of the various techniques of self-cultivation based upon the numen, the vital essence, and the vital energy. Other research has already pointed to close philosophical parallels between the sources discussed in this study and the Syncretist *Zhuangzi*, and has begun to link these works with the "Yellow Emperor" texts from Mawangdui. Their possible relationship to the early physical cultivation literature from Mawangdui and to the *Huangdi neijing* must also be explored. Such future research holds the promise of clarifying our understanding of early Daoist history and of finally demonstrating the continuity in the Daoist tradition.

Chapter 2

Who Compiled the *Zhuangzi* 莊子?

Introduction

It has long been recognized that the *Zhuangzi* is not a homogeneous text. As early as the seventh century, scholars were expressing doubts about the integrity of the work,[1] and four centuries later, the famous poet and scholar Su Dongpo 蘇東坡 (1036–1101) concluded that chapters 28–31 could not have been written by the historical Zhuang Zhou 莊周, the man to whom the entire text had traditionally been ascribed.[2] In fact, the Southern Song scholar Luo Miandao 羅勉道 (fl. ca. 1260) actually established a new, twenty-six-chapter edition of the *Zhuangzi* in which he followed Su's conclusions by connecting chapters 27 and 32, and relegating chapters 28–31, and two more Luo himself doubted, 15 and 16, to a scrap bin at the end of his volumes, where they remained without commentary.[3] However, despite these doubts about certain chapters, many scholars have continued until quite recently to attempt to present the ideas in the text as if they contain a unified position.[4]

It is largely because of the research of Angus Graham, building on the earlier work of Guan Feng 關鋒, that we are now able to identify six basic strata and groups of authors of the three major sections of the extant thirty-three-chapter recension of the *Zhuangzi*, which consists of the *neipian* 內篇 ("Inner" Chapters: 1–7), the *waipian* 外篇 ("Outer" Chapters: 8–22), and the *zapian* 雜篇 ("Mixed" Chapters: 23–33).[5]

1. Chapters 1–7: The writings of the man the Han 漢 historians call Zhuang Zhou, a contemporary of King Hui of

Liang 梁惠王 (370–319 BCE) and King Xuan of Qi 齊宣王 (319–301 BCE). This section contains all the major themes for which the *Zhuangzi* has been renowned—the "free and easy wandering" of the sage grounded in the Dao, the relativity of all human experience, equanimity toward life and death, and so on. In addition, Graham has recovered fragments that he believes were originally included in this section from the "Mixed" Chapters to which they may have been displaced when the text underwent a major revision at the hands of the commentator Guo Xiang 郭象 (ca. 300 CE).

2. Chapters 8–11: Essays by an individual who was strongly influenced by the *Laozi*. Guan Feng omits the last section of the chapter.

3. Chapters 12–16, 33: Guan sees most of 12–14 (minus certain rather vaguely defined sections), and 15 and 16, which are individual integral essays, as written by early Han followers of the philosophers Song Xing 宋鈃 and Yin Wen 尹文, who were in attendance at the famous Jixia Academy 稷下 founded by King Xuan of Qi, and who are included in the group of "Huang-Lao" 黃老 philosophers there.[6] He agrees with Tan Jiefu 譚戒甫 that chapter 33 (minus the final section on Hui Shi), the famous last essay in the book that presents a criticism and syncretic vision of six schools of thought, was written by Liu An 劉安, the King of Huainan (?180–122 BCE.). Graham includes the following sections of these chapters as the writings of a group of early Han eclectic Daoists he refers to as the "Syncretists": 12/1–18, 13/1–45, 60–64, 14/1–5; also 11/66–74, and all of 15 and 33. He does not include 16, which he maintains is unlike any other section in the book.[7] The conclusions of both men point to one of the principal difficulties with chapters 12–14, that they include many sections that seem unrelated to the "Syncretist" outlook. I have more to say about them below.

4. Chapters 17–22: Material that often imitates the themes and style of the "Inner" Chapters, which both scholars

conclude represents the writings of later followers of Zhuangzi. Guan includes chapter 23 in this group.

5. Chapters 23–27, 32: A heterogeneous collection of fragments that probably originated in the other strata of the book. Graham finds some material here that belongs in the "Inner" Chapters.

6. Chapters 28–31: These are the chapters that initially caused scholars to doubt the homogeneity of the entire work. They represent a collection of materials from the "Individualist" School of Yang Zhu 楊朱, which Graham dates to about 200 BCE. Guan does not include 30 in this group, and maintains that it is the work of a philosopher named Zhuang Xing 莊幸 that was erroneously added because of the similarity in name with Zhuangzi.[8]

The text of the *Zhuangzi* therefore must have been written and transmitted over about two centuries until it was compiled at some point during the first century of the Han. Because of the predominance of the traditional view of at least majority authorship by *Zhuangzi* and the tendency to place him at the head of early Daoist philosophy along with the mysterious figure of Lao Dan 老丹, the reputed author of the *Laozi*, the value of this text as a document for unraveling what I would like to call the "hidden history" of early Daoist thought is just beginning to be appreciated. In this context, the question of just who might have compiled the text, and when it might have been done, gains added significance.

In recently completed research, I have discovered what I believe is a significant textual and philosophical relationship between three essays in the supposedly "Legalist" *Guanzi* 管子, a work associated with the state of Qi 齊, whose composition, transmission, and compilation span roughly the same time period as the *Zhuangzi*, and the supposedly "Eclectic" *Huainanzi* 淮南子, an early Han Daoist compendium of thought written under the sponsorship and direction of the above-mentioned Liu An and completed in 139 BCE.[9] The earliest of the *Guanzi* essays, "Neiye" 內業 ("Inward Training"), is a contemporary of the "Inner" Chapters of *Zhuangzi*, and presents the physiological basis of human psychology and self-cultivation grounded in a cosmology of the Dao. This text is unarguably the basis of the more sophisticated theories later developed

in the *Huainanzi*, particularly in its seventh essay titled "Jingshen" 精
神 ("The Numinous Essence"). The next two essays from the *Guanzi*,
"Xinshu shang," "Xinshu xia" 心術上, 心術下 ("The Techniques of the
Mind," parts I and II), place these theories in the context of very Dao-
ist-sounding advice to the ruler on how to govern effectively in keeping
with the *Laozi*'s 老子 principal prescription of *wuwei* 無為 ("Non-action").
These essays, probably completed early in the Han, also contain very
strong textual and philosophical parallels with the *Huainanzi*, and form
a major part of its intellectual inheritance.

I have argued that these four works are part of the same lineage
of thought, and that they very closely fit the description of the "Daoist
School" (*Daojia* 道家) given by Sima Tan 司馬談 (d. 110 BCE) in his
important preface to the *Shiji* 史記. It is this school that is alternately
referred to by the Han historians as "Huang-Lao."[10] The existence of
this school before the Han, and its associations with the Jixia Academy
in Qi, are attested to in the *Shiji*, even if the attribution of texts to its
philosophers and its relationship to Legalism are rather problematic.[11]
Nonetheless, it is this lineage of thought that first receives the label of
"Daoism," not the mystical philosophy of "Lao-Zhuang," 老莊 which is
virtually unknown as a distinct philosophical lineage in the Han. In
fact, the linking of the mystical aspects of *Laozi* and *Zhuangzi* into the
category "Lao-Zhuang," which has so dominated the traditional understanding of the early history of Daoist thought, seems instead to have
been inaugurated by the Wei 魏 and Jin 晉 *Xuanxue* 玄學 ("Profound
Learning") literati.[12]

The fact that theories of the physiological basis of psychology and
self-cultivation are an integral part of the Huang-Lao tradition and hence of
early Daoist philosophy, and the fact that analogous theories are found later
in what scholars have called "Religious Daoism," indicates the possibility
of a more tangible relationship between the two than can be discovered
if one defines philosophical Daoism exclusively as Lao-Zhuang.[13]

It is in the context of these theories on the nature of philosophical
Daoism that the question of who compiled the *Zhuangzi* is significant. If
we are ultimately able to place this compiler in a philosophical lineage,
then we shall learn more about this lineage and be able to derive a more
complete picture of early Daoism and its links to later forms.

There are several theories about who compiled the *Zhuangzi* that
will form the starting point for our inquiry. Guan Feng maintains that
the text was compiled by the scholars who assembled at the court of Liu

An for a period of roughly three decades beginning in about 150 BCE.[14] He provides no justification for this conclusion, but one might infer that because he believes that the final chapter was written by Liu An, the text could not have been completed until then. Graham argues that the Syncretists were the compilers and gives evidence that at least three of the three-word phrases that became titles in the "Inner" Chapters can be found in the Syncretist parts of the text.[15] He also, I think, conclusively demonstrates that, contrary to Guan's opinions, the author of the last chapter shares the technical vocabulary of these other chapters and can be readily placed in the same lineage of thought, although stylistic differences indicate that it is likely that he did not write these others.[16] Therefore, our search for the compiler of the *Zhuangzi* resolves itself into the question of determining the identity of these Syncretists. We also ask the related but distinct question of whether the author of any of the Syncretist chapters can be justifiably identified as the compiler, or if instead we must look elsewhere within a Syncretist tradition.

Guan Feng's theory on the tradition of these chapters is that with the exception of chapter 33, they were written by the followers of Song Xing and Yin Wen, who are identified with Huang-Lao, though in the *Shiji*, Graham does not further specify just who these "eclectic Daoists" might have been, although at one point he does distinguish their outlook from the "equally eclectic" *Huainanzi*.[17] An additional theory is provided by Benjamin Schwartz, who maintains that the Syncretists are actually members of the Huang-Lao school of Daoist thought.[18]

In the following study, I attempt to situate the Syncretist chapters in the lineage of Daoist philosophy of which the three *Guanzi* essays and the *Huainanzi* form an integral part, a lineage that I believe can be labeled "Huang-Lao." I do this by analyzing the main elements of the philosophy of these chapters and comparing them with the thought of the *Guanzi* and *Huainanzi* material. I end with a consideration of the question of whether the author of any of these chapters might also have been the compiler of the entire work, and speculate on a possible date for this compilation.

The Lineage of the Syncretists

In the Syncretist chapter 33 "Tianxia" 天下 ("Below in the Empire"), the author contrasts the comprehensive philosophy, which he calls the *Daoshu* 道術 ("Methods or Tradition of the Way"), with the more limited *fangshu* 方術 ("Methods or Tradition of a Formula") represented by six groups of philosophers who only understood one aspect of this comprehensive Way. He includes in this group both Lao Dan and Zhuang Zhou, each of whom he admires for the profundity of their attainments in self-cultivation, but who were unable to derive much practical value from them. His own way is a blending of the best aspects of these and other early systems of thought, especially the Confucians and Legalists (most clearly explained in chapter 13), into a comprehensive system based in a cosmology of the Dao that is referred to as the *Tiandi zhi Dao* 天地之道, the Way of Heaven and Earth (HYC, 15/7–8; 33/84). This idea of a comprehensive Dao that embraces cosmology, psychology, and political thought is not exclusive to the Syncretist. It is found in two of the three *Guanzi* essays mentioned above, as well as in the *Huainanzi* and in Sima Tan's description of the Daoist school, and is often given the same label.

The concept of *Daoshu* is found in six places in the *Huainanzi*, and here it appears to be given a more specific meaning than it is by the Syncretists as those methods of self-cultivation conducive to creating the tranquility of mind needed to govern effectively.[19] For example, we read that the Sage "inwardly cultivates the techniques of the Way and outwardly does not adorn himself with Benevolence and Rightness" (2/7b), and that he does not use these techniques to seek after fame but rather to cultivate his own person (*xiushen* 修身) so that he is able to follow the Way of Heaven (*Tian Dao* 天道 14/4b). Elsewhere we find the scholar Tian Pian 田駢 (a Huang-Lao teacher at Jixia criticized in *Zhuangzi* 33) teaching the King of Qi 齊王 about the techniques of the Way and urging him to broaden his focus from the concerns of the state to the appreciation of the cosmological context in which his state exists, thus enabling him "to govern through not governing" (12/2b). It is this latter use of the idea of *Daoshu* that approaches the Syncretist meaning of the term.

If the scope of the *Daoshu* in the *Huainanzi* is somewhat more restricted than for the Syncretist, this is most certainly not the case in Sima Tan's description of Daoism. In fact, Tan's description is so close to the spirit of the Syncretists' *Daoshu* that one might justifiably suspect a Syncretist influence on his very choice of the term *Daojia* as a label for this system of thought. Tan says that methods (*shu* 術) of the Daoist school:

> . . . follow the general tendency of the Naturalists (*Yinyang jia*陰陽家), pick out the best of the Confucians and Mohists, and adopt the essentials of the Terminologists (*Ming jia* 名家) and Legalists . . .

SIMA TAN'S ESSAY

Sima Tan's discussion of the six schools of thought presented in a colophon to the *Shiji* is important for a number of reasons. First, it parallels the Syncretists' examination of pre-Han thought in chapter 33 in that it examines the world of philosophy in the Han from a perspective based in a vision of the kind of comprehensive syncretic Daoism that informs these chapters in the *Zhuangzi* and that finds some limited value in other schools of thought.[20] Second, it is one of the few sources whose date we can approximate with certainty, because we know that Tan died in 110 BCE. Finally, because Tan studied with a Huang-Lao teacher and clearly embraced the Daoist position as his own, we can conclude that his syncretic perspective and his description of the Daoist school are accurate reflections of the Huang-Lao tradition's self-understanding.[21] Let us examine what the tradition that first receives the name of Daoism looks like to Sima Tan:

> The Daoist school enables man's Numinous Essence (*jingshen* 精神) to be concentrated and unified, enables him to move in unison with the Formless (*wuxing* 無形), and to provide adequately for the myriad things. As for its methods, it follows the general tendency of the Naturalists, picks out the best of the Confucians and Mohists, and adopts the essentials of the Terminologists and Legalists. It shifts with the times, changes in response to things, and in establishing customs and in practical applications it is nowhere unsuitable. The general drift of its teachings is simple and easy to hold onto; there is much achievement for little effort.[22]

In addition to the syncretism noted above, Tan touches on theories of government and psychology in this paragraph. Daoists provide adequately for all things (*danzu wanwu* 膽足萬物), and exhibit a flexibility in governing that enables them to respond to the transformations of things (*ying wu bianhua* 應物變化) and establish suitable customs and practical measures. This kind of flexibility is the main theme of chapter 11 of the *Huainanzi*, "Qi su" 齊俗 ("Placing Customs on a Par"), which applies *Zhuangzi's* vision of the relativity of human experience from the perspective of the Dao in chapter 2 ("Qi wu lun" 齊物論) to questions of social organization.[23] In addition, Tan suggests techniques of self-cultivation that enable humans (in particular, the ruler) to preserve the essential energy (*jing* 精) of the Numen, which in the psychological theory of the *Guanzi* essays and the *Huainanzi* is the core of human consciousness, simultaneously the ground of the self and the source of metaphysical knowledge. These unexplained methods of self-cultivation (which are detailed in our earlier sources) also enable one's movements to harmonize with the Formless.

Tan proceeds to criticize the then prevalent Confucian theories of an active ruler for doing too much, and explains that it is better for him to rely on methods that relinquish strength, desire, and intellectual brilliance. The reason for this, he says, is that:

> When the Numen is overused it becomes depleted; when the body is overworked it becomes worn out. For the body and Numen to be restlessly active and to then wish to live as long as Heaven and Earth, is something that's never been heard of.[24]

A further description of Daoism is provided in a later passage:

> The Daoist school takes no action (*wuwei* 無為), but it also says that nothing is left undone. Its substance is easy to practice, but its words are difficult to understand. Its methods (*shu*) take Emptiness (*xu* 虛) and Non-being (*wu* 無) as the root, and Adaptation (*yin* 因) and Compliance (*xun li* 循理) as its practice. It has no set limits, no constant forms, and so is able to explore the genuine basis of things (*neng jiu wu zhi qing* 能究物之情) . . . It blends with the Great Dao, obscure and mysterious (*hun-hun ming-ming* 混混冥冥), and after illuminating the whole world it reverts to the Nameless (*fan wuming* 反無名).[25]

In this description we continue to see the blend of cosmological, psychological, and political elements established above. The basis for this philosophy is *Laozi's* concept of Non-action, which involves the twofold practice of emptying the mind until one experiences Non-being, and then returning to the world and acting effortlessly through Adaptation and Compliance. This dual practice of stillness and action is characteristic of Huang-Lao philosophy. It is present in both the *Guanzi* essays and the *Huainanzi*; and I would argue that it is also present in the Syncretist *Zhuangzi*, where it is given the now famous name of *nei sheng wai wang* 內聖外王 ("inwardly a sage, outwardly a king").

This, then, is Daoism, as seen by the man who coined the term. Sima Tan's discussion contains a number of important technical terms and phrases that are found in the sources of Daoist thought I have already analyzed, and which I hope to show are contained in the Syncretist writings as well. In addition, it shows Huang-Lao to be a comprehensive system of thought that advocates a flexible government that draws its measures from the best of the other schools, which bases them in an understanding of universal principles, and which is headed by a Sage-ruler who has achieved the deepest levels of tranquility through techniques of self-cultivation.

THREE DAOISTIC ESSAYS IN THE *GUANZI*

The three Daoistic essays in the *Guanzi* are important early sources for the philosophical lineage that I believe can be called Huang-Lao, and they present the outlines of a system of thought that is most fully developed in the *Huainanzi*. Their dates and authorship have been intensely debated, and the opinions generated have a direct relationship to the question of authorship of the Syncretist chapters of the *Zhuangzi*. The prevailing opinion to this day in China is the one established forty years ago by Guo Moruo 郭沫若, that they are the products of Song Xing and Yin Wen, two of the Jixia Academy Huang-Lao scholars.[26] Because of the strong textual and philosophical parallels he sees between these texts and all but chapter 33 of the Syncretist *Zhuangzi*, Guan Feng concludes that they must have been written by the later followers of these men.[27]

This theory holds true if all three *Guanzi* texts were written at roughly the same time. However, a close reading of them shows that based on style and philosophical content, this cannot have been the case. "Neiye" (Inward Training) is written in rhymed verse, and because it mentions the same *haoran zhi qi* 浩然之氣 "Floodlike Vital Energy" (16/3a9) as does *Mencius* (2A2), and shows no awareness of the Naturalist concepts of Yin 陰 and Yang 陽 and the Five Phases (*wuxing* 五行), I agree with other scholars that it is clearly the earliest of the three, and can be dated to around 300 BCE.[28] "Xinshu shang" (Techniques of the Mind, I) contains two distinct sections, the first third being a basic text, and the remainder a line-by-line commentary on it that, for reasons I present below, I believe was written in the early Han, contemporary or slightly later than the Syncretist *Zhuangzi*. About two-thirds of the remaining essay, "Xinshu xia," consists of passages that constitute about one-third of "Neiye," which are rearranged and rationalized in what I have concluded was a deliberate attempt to create a companion essay to "Xinshu shang," which elaborates on the application of the self-cultivation techniques of "Neiye" to the enlightened government of the Daoist ruler.[29] These reasons underscore what Graham also concludes is the very dubious attribution of these essays by Guo Moruo.[30]

Despite the fact that they cannot be products of Song Xing and Yin Wen, their influence on the *Huainanzi*, and the numerous conceptual parallels they share with Sima Tan's descriptions, indicate their importance in the lineage of Huang-Lao philosophy. "Neiye," which Graham feels is ". . . possibly the oldest 'mystical' text in China,"[31] presents theories on the nature and activities of the human mind and on the practice of several related methods of mental and physical self-discipline aimed at health, longevity, and self-transcendence, which are grounded in a cosmology of the Dao that shows striking parallels with the *Laozi*. For example we read:

> The "Dao" is what the mouth cannot speak of, the eyes cannot look at, and the ears cannot listen to. It is that by which we cultivate the mind (*xiu xin* 修心) and adjust the body. It is what a person loses and thereby dies, what a person gains and is thereby born. When undertakings lose it they fail; when they gain it they succeed.

> The Dao
> Never has a root or trunk,
> Leaves or flowers.
> The myriad things are born by means of it
> And by means of it develop.
> We name it "the Dao." (16/2a2–4)

One of the main features that distinguishes this text from the *Laozi* is its emphasis on the importance of the *jing* ("Vital Essence"), which is conceived of as the mysterious aspect of the Dao that is responsible for the generation of life and the maintenance of vitality. It is defined as a concentrated form of *qi* 氣 ("Vital Energy"), and is closely linked with the concept of *de* 德, the potency that arises in an organism from the manifestation of the Dao within it.

The text speaks of the importance of settling the Dao within one's mind and generating and lodging the Vital Essence. This is accomplished by guiding the Vital Energy through a practice of regular breathing (16/1b10–2a4, and 3b6–7), so that the mind becomes tranquil (*jing* 靜) and stable (*ding* 定) (16/2a9–b1). It points out repeatedly that emotions, desires, and knowledge interfere with this process and can actually be detrimental to one's physical and psychological well-being (16/5a4–5a9; 2a9–b1). But if they can be cast aside through these practices, then one can attain a level of experience associated with metaphysical knowledge and eventually self-transcendence:

> By concentrating your Vital Energy like a Numen
> The myriad things will all be contained within you. Can
>   you concentrate? Can you unify?
> Can you know good and bad fortune
> Without resorting to divination? Can you stop? Can you
>   halt?
> Can you not seek it outwardly
> But attain it inwardly?[32]
> If you think, and think, and think further about this
> But still cannot penetrate it,
> The daemonic and numinous (*gui shen* 鬼神) in you will
>   penetrate it.
> It is not due to the inherent power of the daemonic and
>   numinous,
> But rather to the utmost development of your Vital
>   Essence. (16/4a2–5)

Therefore, one concentrates the Vital Energy through controlled breathing. Or rather, because the concept of *qi* includes the breath, this really refers to breath-concentration. By concentrating the *qi* in this manner, one attains the metaphysical knowledge of the future that is associated with the Numen. Throughout this text and others related to it, the Numen is seen as the source of this kind of metaphysical knowledge. It is also worthy of note that the Numen itself is conceived of as a concentrated form of *qi*, or in other words, it is made of the Vital Essence, the most concentrated form of *qi*. Although the concepts of Numen and Vital Essence remain distinct in this text, the principal difference is that the Numen is associated with sentience while the Vital Essence is not; they later blend together in the *Huainanzi* into the concept of Numinous Essence (*jingshen*), the manifestation of the Numen within the systems of Vital Energy that constitute a human being.[33] The important point here is that this text maintains that the psychological states of calmness and tranquility that allow one to stabilize the Numen are based on the physiological substrates associated with the Vital Essence, a concentrated form of the Vital Energy that pervades the cosmos. When, through controlled breathing, one chases away perception, thought, and emotions, one can return to the Way and the Power (*fan Dao De* 反道德) (16/3b7). Elsewhere these practices are said to lead to longevity (16/4a11–b2) and to the ability to "embrace unity" (*shou yi* 守一), a concept that becomes important in later religious Daoist techniques of meditation.[34]

The above passage contains significant textual and philosophical parallels with two other sources in addition to the *Huainanzi*. The concept of concentrating and unifying (*zhuan yi* 摶一) the Vital Energy here is virtually identical to Sima Tan's "concentrating and unifying the Numinous Essence" (*zhuan yi* 專一). And lines 3–8 in this passage from "Neiye" are repeated almost verbatim in one of the "Mixed" Chapters of the *Zhuangzi* (23/34–5), in which Laozi is explaining the meaning of the method of protecting one's vitality (*wei sheng zhi jing* 衛生之精). Even if "Neiye" and *Zhuangzi* draw from a common source, the point remains that the compiler of the latter was aware of such techniques. It is not surprising therefore that related concepts should appear in the Syncretist material, as we see below.

The most significant difference between "Neiye" and "Xinshu shang" is that whereas little or no attempt is made in the former to recommend these practices of self-cultivation to rulers as ways to enable them to govern more effectively, the latter is devoted to precisely that. The theories of government are placed in the context of a cosmology of the Dao that parallels the *Laozi*, and they center on an elaboration of the concept of *wuwei* that is found therein. The elaboration involves a number of closely related ideas that are found in Sima Tan's description of the Daoists, such as *ying* 應 ("spontaneous response"), *yin* 因 ("adaptation"), *xun li* ("compliance with Patterns"), and the principle of assigning tasks that are suitable to the individual (*yi* 宜). The prescriptions for self-cultivation in order to attain the state of mind needed to practice these principles center on *jing* 靜 ("stillness") and *xu* ("emptiness"), relinquishing wisdom, desires, and preferences, and finally on cleaning out the mind in order to lodge the Numen and develop the Vital Essence. These close conceptual and textual parallels with both Sima Tan and the *Huainanzi* that are found most frequently in the explanatory section of this work make Rickett's conclusion of an early Han date even more probable.[35]

Because two-thirds of the text of "Xinshu xia" are a restatement of the theories and techniques of self-cultivation found in "Neiye," it provides little new information. Yet it does contain a linking passage that nicely sums up the unique blend of cosmology, psychology, and politics, which I believe is a hallmark of this lineage of thought. After a passage taken from "Neiye" that discusses aligning the flow of Vital Energy in the body (*zheng xing* 正形) by not allowing external things to disrupt the senses, and not allowing the senses to disrupt the mind, a practice called developing "inward power," the text reads:

> Therefore, only after the awareness and Vital Energy are stabilized will the body be aligned.[36] The Vital Energy is what fills the body. The alignment [of the Vital Energy] is the standard pattern of its movement. When what fills the body does not move according to a standard, the heart will not attain it [the power]. When the movement [of the Vital Energy] is not aligned [in the ruler], then the people will not submit. Therefore the Sage is like Heaven: selflessly (*wusi* 無私) he covers; he is like Earth: selflessly he supports. Selfishness is what disrupts the world. (13/4b9–12)

THE *HUAINANZI*

The *Huainanzi* is unique among our sources: its date is relatively certain: 139 BCE; we know who wrote it: Liu An and the eight retainers listed in Gao You's 高誘 preface (ca. 212 CE); and it is a well-organized and coherent set of twenty essays, each with a specific topic, followed by a final essay (*Yao lüe* 要略) that summarizes each of the others and explains the rationale for their inclusion and order of presentation in the text. In short, it is a compendium of knowledge about the nature of the cosmos and the human beings who live within it that was intended to give the enlightened ruler all that he needed to govern effectively. Continuing along the general outlines laid out in the *Laozi* and the three *Guanzi* essays, it embraces the interrelated themes of cosmology, psychology, and politics, and presents the most sophisticated and thoroughly syncretic discussion of them that is found in the entire tradition. Sima Tan's discussion of the Daoist school so closely parallels the basic philosophical stance and terminology of the *Huainanzi* that it could serve as a summary of the entire work. It would not be at all surprising if he had the *Huainanzi* in mind when he wrote this essay. I fully agree with K. C. Hsiao that it is the principal representative of Huang-Lao philosophy in the Han.[37]

The themes that are present in the three *Guanzi* essays are elaborated in the *Huainanzi*, and there is solid textual as well as philosophical evidence that its authors were aware of the earlier material.[38] The physiological basis of psychology and self-cultivation found in "Neiye" is explained in great detail in this work, particularly in its seventh essay, "Jingshen" ("The Numinous Essence"). As in the two parts of "Xinshu," it is presented in the context of enabling the ruler to govern effectively in accord with *Laozi*'s principle of Non-action and with the related concepts of Spontaneous Response, Suitability, Adaptation, and Compliance with Natural Patterns, which are the hallmarks of Daoism for Sima Tan as well. Another of these hallmarks for Tan that is present in the *Huainanzi* is the utilization of certain aspects of the philosophy of other pre-Han schools of thought in a syncretic perspective that remains grounded in a cosmology that is thoroughly Daoist. It is undoubtedly this frequent use of material from other lineages of thought that resulted in the bibliographical classification of the Huainanzi as "Eclectic" (*zajia* 雜家). It is not that this syncretic perspective is new; it is fully consonant with that of the *Xinshu* essays and, I believe, with the Syncretist *Zhuangzi*. It is just that this syncretism is so thoroughly absorbed by the authors that it appears almost natural. Roger Ames's excellent analysis of the ninth essay, "Zhu shu" 主術 ("The Art of Rulership"), shows how completely Legalist and Confucian concepts are absorbed into a Daoist perspective on government.[39]

The *Huainanzi* does not merely continue the established themes of the Daoist syncretic tradition, it innovates within that tradition as well. Three innovations are worthy of note. First is the incorporation of the Naturalist cosmology of Yin and Yang and the Five Phases of *qi*, which is present in many of the essays.[40] Second is the development of the understanding of the nature and activities of the Numen, and of the mind in general, explained in terms of Naturalist philosophy.[41] Finally is the development of a Daoist theory of human nature, which the *Huainanzi* authors probably took over from the Primitivist *Zhuangzi*, but which they present in a much more comprehensive fashion as the foundation of their theories of psychology, self-cultivation, and government.[42]

Despite this syncretism, it is clear that the two primary influences on the text of the *Huainanzi* are the *Laozi* and the *Zhuangzi*. Even though the *Huainanzi* advocates a philosophy of government whose syncretic use of certain aspects of Confucianism (in their own place, of course) would have offended the authors of the *Laozi*, the general outlines on cosmology and government are the same: Dao and *wuwei*. The differences in complexity and sophistication between the two texts, which could, following Schwartz, be characterized as "primitivist" versus "syncretist," are due to the vastly different social and political conditions at the times each was written. Certainly the *Huainanzi* authors regarded the *Laozi* as canonical. It is quoted ten times more often than any other work, and an entire essay, "Dao ying" 道應 (The Responses of the Dao), is devoted to illustrating philosophical points from *Laozi*.[43] The text of the *Zhuangzi* is, most significantly, treated in a considerably different way. Although ideas, or sentences, or sometimes whole paragraphs from the *Zhuangzi* are found in the *Huainanzi*, by one count, five times more frequently than is material from the *Laozi*, only once in the entire work is the text actually quoted.[44] And quite often the *Zhuangzi* material is presented in a different context, or interpreted differently.[45] This suggests a much less hallowed status for the *Zhuangzi*: it is beloved, but it is not canonical. And, as we shall see, its text may not have even been fixed at this time.

THE THOUGHT OF THE SYNCRETISTS IN CONTEXT

The philosophy found in what Graham defines as the Syncretist chapters of the *Zhuangzi* (11/66–74; 12/1–18; 13/1–45; 14/1–6; 15; 33) shares striking parallels in terminology and in general outlook with the three *Guanzi* essays and the *Huainanzi*, and shows similarities as well with Sima Tan's description of Daoism. The Syncretist philosophy exhibits the three interlocking elements that form the basis of the thought detailed in these other sources: cosmology, psychology, and politics. I analyze these parallels by first presenting a table of the shared terminology and then proceed to a discussion of the main features of the Syncretists' philosophy in which I identify similar material in these other sources.

TECHNICAL TERMINOLOGY

In table 2.1, I compare the technical terms of the Syncretists with those found in "Xinshu shang" and *Huainanzi*. I have chosen to focus primarily on "Xinshu shang" because among the three *Guanzi* essays it presents the most complete expression of the three aspects of Daoist thought I have identified.

While there is a remarkable consistency in terminology among the three sources, there is a marked difference in frequency of occurrence (see table 2.1). This is due in part to the varying lengths of the sources: the *Huainanzi* is easily fifteen times longer than the Syncretist *Zhuangzi*, which in turn is about twice as long as "Xinshu shang." This must also be due in part to the terminology that was current at the time when each was written.

The most common terms to all are The Way of Heaven, Non-action, Stillness, and Emptiness, which is separated in the table because it is used in both cosmological (emptiness of the Dao or the Way of Heaven) and psychological (emptiness of the mind) contexts in each of the sources. Interestingly, all four terms are found in the *Laozi*, which is a strong indication of its influence. However, the syncretism that places Confucian and Legalist ideas under a Daoist umbrella, which all three sources exhibit, is certainly not found there. In addition to the syncretism in methods of government, the remaining political concepts are all found in Sima Tan, a fact that gives a strong indication that all the sources are part of the same lineage of thought.

The frequency of use of the terms must be related to the stage of development of the tradition. Based on this table, the *Huainanzi* must be closest in time to Sima Tan, and, of course, we know it is. "Xinshu shang" would be next, followed by the Syncretist *Zhuangzi*. The single occurrence of *ying* 應 in *Zhuangzi* 15 could indicate that it is the latest of these chapters, possibly a contemporary of "Xinshu shang." This impression is reinforced by the context: the phrase *gan ying* 感應 is found in both of the other sources and thought to be a key term in Naturalist philosophy. Also, chapter 15 contains more of these terms than any other chapter, although this may not be entirely fair because chapter 33 is largely devoted to discussing the philosophies of others. However, it is significant that chapter 15 contains almost all of the psychological terms. This is a strong indication of its links to the *Guanzi* essays and the *Huainanzi*, and to its relatively late date.

Table 2.1. The Technical Terminology of the Syncretists

Terms	"Xinshu shang"	Zhuangzi	Huainanzi
1. COSMOLOGY			
Way of Heaven Tian zhi dao 天之道	13/3a2, 3b6	11/72(3), 73; 13/1b	10/1a; 12/5b; 14/14b; 15/2a; 20/2b 20 times, especially chs. 3, 9, 15
Way of Heaven and Earth Tiandi zhi dao 天地之道		15/7–8; 33/84	3/12a; 7/2a; 20/6a
Non-action* Wuwei 無為	13/1b12; 2a3, 12; 4a1, 8	18 times, especially 13/5–10, 17–24	41 times, especially chs. 1, 9, 14
Formless* Wuxing 無形	13/1b2; 3a5; 3b2	33/62; also 6/29 and 11 times in rest	31 times, especially chs. 9, 14
2. PSYCHOLOGY			
Stillness Jing 靜	13/19; 2a3; 2b4, 7, 8; 3b6	17 times, esp. 13/1–17; 15/10–17; 33/49, 50, 57	33 times, especially chs. 1, 9, 14, 15
Cast off Wisdom and Precedent Qu zhi yu gu 去智與故	13/2a3; 4a8; 2b11 (no precedent)	15/11; 13/36 is similar	1/5a, 9a; 6/7b; 7/10a (verbs different; object same)
Cast off Desires* Qu yu 去欲	13/2b9–10; 3b7	12/5 (have no desires); 15/14 (implied)	2/4b; 14/2a, 7b, 10a; and throughout ch. 7
Techniques of the Mind Xin shu 心術	Title; 2a12	13/26	1/15a; 7/11a; 14/2a; 21/4b
Vital Essence Jing 精	13/2b7; 3a4	12/17; 15/20–21; 33/3, 54	23 times, especially chs. 2, 7, 8
Numinous* Essence Jingshen 精神		13/4, 26; 15/18–19	Title of ch. 7; 34 times especially chs. 1, 7

continued on next page

Table 2.1. Continued

Terms	"Xinshu shang"	Zhuangzi	Huainanzi
Human Nature Xing 性		Only in Primitivist	90 times, especially chs. 1, 2, 7, 11
Longevity* Shou 壽	Neiye, 16/4b7	13/7; 15/7	4/5a, 7a; 7/3a, 11a; 10/3b
3. POLITICS			
Nourishing the Myriads* Yu wanwu 育萬物	13/1b2	13/22; 15/19; 33/5, 7	5/17a; 9/7a; 10/4b; 12/16a, 22a; 15/3a
Spontaneous Response* Ying 應	13/2a4, 6; 3b3, 9, 11; 4a9; 5a1, 2, 3	15/11	40 times, especially in chs. 1, 15
Adaptation* Yin 因	13/2a3; 3a8; 3b10; 4a1, 9; 5a1	11/67, 71; 13/33 (yin-jen)	1/10b; 9/1a, 7a; 14/8a; 15/8a, b; 20/3b, 4a; 21/2a
Compliance* Xun 循	13/1a5	12/9; 15/11	1/7b; 7/4b; 9/1a, 3a; 10/7b; 11/6b; 14/2a, 3b, 4b; 19/3a
Suitability* Yi 宜	13/3a8, 3b3	13/34	17 times, especially chs. 11, 13
Syncretism, especially Legalism, Confucianism*	13/1b5; 3a8-b1	13/27–41; 15/7; 33/2–6	In many chs., especially 9, 11, 13, 19
4. OTHER			
Emptiness* Xu 虛	13/1a10, 1b2; 2b10; 2b12; 3b6; 4a5, 8, 11; 5a1, 3	13/1–17; 15/8, 13, 15	49 times, especially chs. 1, 2, 7

*Terms that are also attributed to the *Daojia* in Sima Tan's Essay on the Six Traditions

THE WAY OF HEAVEN; THE WAY OF HEAVEN AND EARTH

Both Guan Feng and Graham note that one of the unique characteristics of the Syncretist philosophy is the importance given to the Way of Heaven or the Way of Heaven and Earth.[46] It almost seems that in these phrases, and in the hierarchical list of governing measures in 13/32–41, as Graham says, the Way has assumed a secondary position.[47] In chapter 15, after the author criticizes the limited points of view of five groups of men who seem to include the Primitivists ("the hermits of mountains and valleys" who have "finicky notions"), the Confucians ("the stay-at-home scholars" who expound "Goodwill and Duty"), the Legalists ("The annexers of lands" who are "interested only in governing"), Zhuangzi himself ("The untroubled idler" who is "interested only in Doing Nothing"), and the Esoteric Masters (*fang shi* 方士) ("Grandfather Peng's ripe old agers" who practice the "guide-and-pull" exercises *Daoyin* 導引 to stimulate the flow of Vital Energy), the author continues:

> As for being lofty without having finicky notions, improving oneself without bothering about Goodwill and Duty, governing without caring about deeds and reputations, living untroubled not by riverside or seaside, living to a ripe old age without "guide-and-pull," and forgetting them all and possessing them all, being serene and unconfined and having all these glories as the consequence, this is the Way of Heaven and Earth, the Power which is in the sage.[48] (15/7–8)

Here the Way of Heaven and Earth seems to refer to the syncretic philosophy of the author, which takes the best from these limited points of view and blends them in the Power of the sage. The other use of this phrase at 33/84 is consonant with this interpretation.

In the *Huainanzi*, the Way of Heaven and Earth pertains more to cosmology. It is the basis for determining the calendar (3/12a), and it is responsible for the macro-microscopic parallels between universe and human beings and for their numinous aspects (7/2a–b). These two interpretations are not necessarily incompatible. One could maintain that the sagely Way is parallel to the cosmic Way. This is in fact the pattern in the Syncretist discussion of the Way of Heaven.

The Syncretist fragment at the end of chapter 11 (66–74) makes the distinction between the Way of Heaven and the Way of Man:

. . . To be exalted by Doing Nothing (*wuwei*) is the Way of Heaven, to be tied by doing something is the Way of Man. The sovereign's is the Way of Heaven, the minister's is the Way of Man. That the Ways of Heaven and of Man are far apart is not to be overlooked.[49] (11/72–4)

Here *wu-wei* has both a cosmological aspect as the Way of Heaven, and a human aspect as it is manifested in the sovereign. These two aspects are continued in chapter 12:

The Master said:

"The Way is the shelterer and sustainer of the myriad things. Vast, vast is its greatness. The gentleman has no choice but to scrape out everything in his heart for it.

"It is the doer of it by Doing Nothing that we call 'Heaven,' the teller of it by Doing Nothing that we call 'Power. . . .' "[50] (12/6–8)

Heaven clearly accomplishes its tasks (for example, of completing the myriad things through its circuitings—13/1) by *wuwei*. The sage who practices this form of selfless and effortless action is following the Way of Heaven. In a sense, he is the microcosm to the macrocosm of Heaven.

This passage also points out an important distinction that sometimes gets overlooked in these chapters. Despite the importance of Heaven, it has not actually replaced the Dao as ground of the cosmos. The two other passages, which Graham refers to as the "rhapsodies on the Way," affirm that the Dao still has this position (12/12–13; 13/60–62). I would argue that the significance of the Way of Heaven or the Way of Heaven and Earth is in its emphasis on the practical manifestation of the vast and profound Dao within the universe. Rather than a fundamental shift in cosmology, we have a shift in focus that seems perfectly in keeping with the overall practicality of the Syncretists.

This understanding of the Way of Heaven as the manifestation of the Dao within the cosmos is paralleled in both "Xinshu shang" and the *Huainanzi*. In the explanatory section of the former, we read:

The Way of Heaven is empty and formless. Empty, then it does not wear out. Formless, then there is nothing that it bumps against. Because there is nothing that it bumps against, it flows everywhere through the myriad things and does not change. The Power is the lodging of the Way . . . Non-action (*wuwei*) we call the "Power." Therefore there is no gap between the Way and the Power. (13/3a2–7)

In this passage, the Way of Heaven, although we cannot identify it as an object, is manifested throughout the phenomenal world. While we cannot objectify it, it can be "lodged," or experienced. The *Huainanzi*, as well, talks of this intangible, yet palpable Way:

The Vital Energy of Heaven is called *hun* 魂 the Vital Energy of Earth is called *po* 魄. If you return them to the Profound Chamber (*xuanfang* 玄方), then each will rest in its abode. If you protect them and don't let them slip away, then above you will circulate freely with Vast Unity (*Taiyi* 太一). The Vital Essence of Vast Unity circulates freely in the Way of Heaven. The Way of Heaven is profound and silent. It is without contents, without guidelines. You cannot reach the limits of the Way of Heaven. It is deep and cannot be fathomed. Ascending, it transforms along with human beings, and knowledge cannot grasp it. (9/1b6–8)

This passage speaks of the mystical experience of merging with the Dao, here conceived of as *Tai yi*. Yet even this most profound of experiences has a physiological basis, a Vital Essence, and it is this that flows freely within the Way of Heaven. Thus once again while this Way is mysterious and cannot be objectified, it can be experienced. The text proceeds to discuss the ideal reign of Shen Nong, a sage-ruler who was able to experience this profound Way and the benefits his subjects derived from it.

The *Huainanzi* puts more emphasis on the intangible qualities of the Way of Heaven than do the other two texts. Yet despite this it retains their emphasis on the experiential possibilities. The source for this concept of the Way of Heaven, the *Laozi*, does this as well:

Without venturing outside
One can know the whole world
Without looking out a window
One can see the Way of Heaven.

The farther one goes
The less one knows.
Therefore the sage knows without doing
Sees without naming
Completes without acting. (chapter 47)

NEI SHENG WAI WANG 內聖外王: THE HARMONY OF THE PSYCHOLOGICAL AND THE POLITICAL

Another of the central elements in the philosophy of the Syncretist *Zhuangzi* that is recognized by Guan, Graham, and others is the concept of being "inwardly a sage, outwardly a king" (*nei sheng wai wang*), which is found in chapter 33 (33/14). Elsewhere in the "Way of Heaven" chapter it is referred to as "in stillness a sage, in motion a king" (*jing er sheng, dong er wang* 靜而聖, 動而王) (13/10). It is paralleled in "Xinshu shang" by the concept of the "Way of stillness and adaptation" (*jing yin zhi Dao* 靜因之道) (13/2a3–7), and throughout the *Huainanzi* in the idea that in order to govern effectively, the ruler must cultivate the limits of his innate nature. This harmony between the psychological and the political is one of the hallmarks of this lineage of thought, even though it may not always be conceived of in precisely the same terms.

A classic statement of this position begins the "Heaven and Earth" chapter of *Zhuangzi*:

> The ruler finds his source in the Power and is full-formed by Heaven . . . We say then that in profoundest antiquity ruling the empire was Doing Nothing; it was simply a matter of the Power which is from Heaven . . .
>
> Hence it is said of those who of old were pastors of the empire that they desired nothing (*wu yu* 無慾), yet the empire had enough; they did nothing, but the myriad things were transformed; they were still from the depths (*yuan jing* 淵靜), but the Hundred clans were settled.[51] (12/2–6)

This passage maintains that the balance between inner cultivation and outer manifestation in the ruler is crucial to the flourishing of the empire. By being "still from the depths" and "desiring nothing," the ruler is able to be grounded in the Power and completed by Heaven. Through manifesting this profound inner experience through selfless and effortless action, he is able to govern effectively. In so doing, he models himself after Heaven. These ideas are reiterated in 13/17–21, which also maintains the distinction seen in 11/72–74 between the role of the ruler and that of his ministers. The ruler is the one who must be self-cultivated according to these guidelines.

The action of the sage-king in the phenomenal world is spoken of in similar terms in the passage from "Xinshu xia" examined above, in which the ruler is said to be like Heaven in that he selflessly covers, and like Earth in that he selflessly supports (13/4b11–12). It is paralleled in the opening section of "Xinshu shang" and its commentary (13/1a5–8, 2a7–11) in which the analogy is made between the non-acting position of the mind within the body, which through its emptiness of desires enables the senses to perceive accurately, and the empty and non-acting position of the ruler in the empire. "When the one above departs from his way," the passage concludes, "the ones below lose their activities."

The emphasis on the harmony between the inner realization of the ruler and his outward activity is found throughout the *Huainanzi*. For example:

> Therefore the sage inwardly cultivates the root (*xiu qi ben* 修其本) and outwardly does not adorn himself with the branches. He preserves his Numinous Essence and puts an end to wisdom and precedent (*zhi yu gu* 智與故) . . . Therefore calmly (*moran* 漠然) he takes no action and there is nothing that is not done (*wuwei er wu bu wei*). Tranquilly he does not govern, and there is nothing that is ungoverned. (1/8b12–9a2)

Stillness

The discussion of the "inner sageliness" of the ruler in the Syncretist *Zhuangzi* centers on the development of stillness (*jing*), which is viewed as the common basis of both cosmos and psyche. In the long essay that begins the Way of Heaven chapter, we read:

> Emptiness and stillness, calm and indifference (*tian yan* 恬惔), quiescence (*ji mo* 寂漠), Doing Nothing, are the even level of heaven and earth, the utmost reach of the Way and the Power; therefore emperor, king or sage finds rest in them. At rest he empties, emptying he is filled, and what fills him

sorts itself out. Emptying he is still, in stillness he is moved, and when he moves he succeeds. In stillness he does nothing; and if he does nothing, those charged with affairs are put to the test. If he does nothing he is serene; and in whoever is serene, cares and misfortunes cannot settle, his years will be long.[52] (13/4–7)

This passage again shows the balance between the inward realization of stillness attained through emptying the mind and the outward manifestation of Non-action. It is quoted in the "Finicky Notions" essay, where stillness, calm, and indifference (tian yan) are associated with concepts that find parallels in the three Guanzi essays:

If he [the sage] is even and unstrained, calm and indifferent,
Cares and misfortunes cannot enter,
The deviant energies (xieqi 邪氣) cannot make inroads.
Therefore his Power is intact and his daemon (shen) is
    unimpaired.[53] (15/8–10)

The association of states of stillness and tranquility with the Vital Energy and Essence and the Numen are found throughout the Guanzi essays and the Huainanzi. For example, in "Xinshu shang":

That which the sage directs is his Vital Essence. Relinquish desire and the mind will be expansive. When it is expansive it will be still. When it is still the Vital Essence is present. When the Vital Essence is present one experiences solitude (du 獨). In solitude there is clarity (ming 明). With clarity comes the Numen. The Numen is the most honored. Thus when the abode is not cleaned out, the honored one will not dwell therein. (13/2b5–10)

In the Huainanzi, in the context of removing lusts and desires through controlled breathing, which leads to the proper flow of Vital Energy within the entire organism, we read:

When the Numinous Essence is abundant and the flow of Vital Energy is not dispersed then the organism functions according to Pattern (li 理). When the organism functions according to

Pattern [the mind] is even. When it is even [the Numinous Essence] flows freely. When [the Numinous Essence] flows freely [the mind] is numinous. When it is numinous there is nothing that vision does not see, nothing that listening does not hear, and nothing that action does not accomplish. For this reason cares and misfortunes cannot enter and the deviant vital energy cannot make inroads. (7/2b5–9)

There are certainly differences in the ways of conceiving of this process of achieving the stillness of mind necessary to govern effectively in the three passages. But it is important to note that in each, this level of tranquility is given a physiological basis (Vital Energy or Essence, or Numinous Essence), and is associated with the Numen. In all our sources, the emptying of the mind of knowledge, desires, and emotions is referred to as either lodging or nourishing the Numen. Other examples are found in "Neiye" (16/2b9–12, 5a4), *Zhuangzi* (15/14–16), and *Huainanzi* (i.e., 7/4b2–7, 20/8b11–9a1). The *Zhuangzi* and second *Huainanzi* passages both refer to these methods as *yang shen* 養神.

Stillness and Motion

The harmony between inner realization and outer manifestation characterized as *nei sheng wai wang* is directly related to stillness and motion in all of our sources. Not only do they all identify stillness with Yin and motion with Yang (*Zhuangzi* 13/14, 15/10; "Xinshu shang" 13/2b3–4; *Huainanzi* 7/4b4–5), but they also conceive of the spontaneous response of the sage grounded in stillness in terms of the Naturalist idea of *gan ying* (*Zhuangzi* 15/11; "Xinshu shang" 13/4a5; *Huainanzi*, i.e., 7/5b1–2), and agree that he "casts off wisdom (or knowledge) and precedent" (see above chart). An important statement of these ideas is found in the "Finicky Notions" chapter of *Zhuangzi*:

Hence it is said that the sage
In his life proceeds with Heaven
In his death transforms with other things In stillness shares
    the Power in the Yin
In motion shares the surge of the Yang.
He will not to gain advantage make the first move
Will not to avoid trouble take the first step

> Only when stirred will he respond,
> Only when pressed will he move,
> Only when it is inevitable will he rise up.
> Rejecting knowledge and precedent
> He takes his course from Heaven's pattern (*xun Tian zhi li* 循天之理).[54] (15/10–12)

These ideas are paralleled in "Xinshu shang":

> . . . Therefore the Superior Person is not enticed by likes, not pressed by dislikes. Calm and tranquil (*tian yu* 恬愉), he takes no action (*wuwei*), and casts off wisdom and precedent (*qu zhi yugu* 去智與故). His responses (*ying*) are not something prearranged. His movements are not something (deliberately) chosen . . . (13/2a2–3)

> [*Commentary*] . . . When a person is pressed by dislikes then he loses what he likes. If he is enticed by likes then he forgets what he likes. This is not the Way. Therefore the text says "He is not enticed by likes, not pressed by dislikes." When one is not pressed by dislikes then dislikes do not lose their Pattern (*li*), and desires do not exceed what is genuinely needed. Therefore the text says "The Superior Person, calm and tranquil, takes no action and casts off wisdom and precedent." Thus it says that he is empty (*xu* 虚) and pure (*su* 素).

> "His responses are not something prearranged. His movements are not something (deliberately) chosen." This says that he adapts (*yin* 因). Adaptation means that he abandons the self and takes other things as his models. Only when stirred will he respond (*gan er hou ying*). It is not something prearranged. To move according to Pattern is not something [deliberately] chosen . . . (13/4a7–10)

In the *Huainanzi*, we find similar descriptions:

> Therefore the Sage adapts to the times (*yin shi* 因是) and is thereby secure in his position. He matches his contemporaries

and enjoys what he does. Sadness and joy are deviations from the Power. Pleasure and anger go beyond the Way. Likes and dislikes are the scorchings of the mind. Therefore it is said:

In his life proceeds with Heaven,
In his death transforms with other things. In stillness he
    closes up with the Yin,
In motion he opens up with the Yang.
His Numinous Essence is placidly (*tanran* 澹然) limitless
It is not dispersed amidst phenomena
And the entire world naturally submits. (7/4b2–5)

. . . The Perfect Person . . . His form is like withered wood. His mind is like dead ashes. He forgets his Five Orbs (*wu zang* 五臟—the systems of vital energy in the organism), and loses his physical body.

He knows without studying.
He sees without looking.
He completes without acting.
He regulates without disputing
When stirred he responds
When pressed he moves . . . (7/5a12–b2)

All three texts exhibit close textual and conceptual parallels in describing the activity of sages. They emphasize that these sages must attain stillness through relinquishing desires and preferences, and the *Huainanzi* even uses the famous simile of withered wood and dead ashes from the "Inner" Chapters of the *Zhuangzi* (2/2). They also maintain that when sages are grounded in stillness, they will respond in a purely spontaneous fashion in accord with the natural guidelines of Heaven's patterns. This spontaneity is the basis of the ideas of Non-action, Adaptation, and Compliance, which are also mentioned by Sima Tan. The *Huainanzi*, as the most developed text among the three, provides the most sophisticated analysis of the physiological basis of the experience of stillness, conceiving of it as the preservation of the Numinous Essence, the most rarified form of the Vital Energy that actually constitutes the Numen. This represents an elaboration of similar ideas in the other sources that have been discussed above.

These passages again demonstrate the conceptual similarity among our sources, and show that the Syncretist *Zhuangzi* is part of the same tradition as the other texts.

THE POLITICAL PHILOSOPHY OF THE SYNCRETISTS

The Syncretists' theories of government are concentrated in the long essay at the head of "The Way of Heaven" (13/1–45), in which the author expounds the Ways of Heaven, the Emperor, and the Sage. In addition to the principles of Non-action, Adaptation, Spontaneous Response, and Compliance, discussed above, this philosophy contains three other significant aspects: nourishing the myriad things, deriving measures from the natural guidelines that constitute the Patterns of Heaven, and the use of ideas drawn from the political philosophy of the Confucians and Legalists within a Daoistic framework. All three aspects are included in Sima Tan's description of the Daoists.[55]

Nourishing the Myriad Things

The idea of the sage's nourishing of the myriad things (*yu wanwu* 育 萬物) is found in several locations in the Syncretist *Zhuangzi*, and is implied in the idea of being Pastor to the Empire (*chu Tianxia* 畜天下) found at 12/5 and 13/17. It essentially means the sage-ruler, though the profundity of his self-cultivation, which connects him with the ground of Heaven and Earth, and through the appropriateness of his selfless actions, which manifest this ground, is able to not only provide sufficiently for his people, but to also aid in assuring that the processes of Heaven and Earth function harmoniously. As "Below in the Empire" says:

> Did not the men of old provide for everything? They were peers of the daemonic-and-illumined (*shen ming* 神明) and equals of heaven and earth, they fostered the myriad things and harmonised the empire, their bounty extended over the Hundred Clans.[56] (33/6–8)

Nourishing the myriad things is discussed once in the basic text of "Xinshu shang" as a characteristic of the Power (13/1b2), and the explanatory section makes it clear that the Power develops in the sage from the lodging of the Dao (13/3a2–8, quoted above in the section on the Way of Heaven). Hence the sage who is able to develop the Power will also possess this nurturing ability.

As the latest text among our sources, the *Huainanzi* develops this idea the furthest. It speaks in general terms of the ruler's ability to nourish. For example:

> The Way of the Ruler is round: it revolves without any starting points. He transforms and nourishes as if numinous. He is empty and vacant, he adapts (*yin*) and complies (*xun*), and he always lays back and does not anticipate. (9/9a10–11)

It also discusses specific measures that embody this, such as "making use of the masses" (*yong zhong* 用眾) so that each will be able to develop his own inner nature, and "benefitting the people" (*li min* 利民). These ideas are fully discussed by Roger Ames in his excellent analysis of the "Art of Rulership" essay.[57]

Comprehending the Patterns of Heaven

The idea of complying with heaven's patterns (*Tian li* 天理) occurs only once in the Syncretist *Zhuangzi* in the "Finicky Notions" chapter quoted above (15/10–12). Here it refers to the guidelines that direct the spontaneous responses of the sage who cultivates stillness. However, it is clearly implied in the Syncretist notions that the hierarchical structure of government and society must be based on parallel structures in Heaven and Earth:

> The ruler comes first, the minister follows; the father comes first, the son follows . . . the senior comes first, the junior follows . . . Being exalted or lowly, first or last, belongs to the progressions of heaven and earth; therefore the sage takes his model from them. Being exalted if of heaven, lowly if of earth, are the stations of the daemonic-and illumined; spring and summer first, autumn and winter last, is the sequence of the four seasons . . . Heaven and earth are supremely daemonic yet have sequences of the exalted and the lowly, the first and the last, how much more the Way of Man! If you expound a Way without their sequences, it is not their Way. If you

> expound a Way which is not their Way, from what will you
> derive a Way?[58] (13/27–32)

This passage provides a clear example that the Way of Heaven and
Earth advocated by the Syncretists has cosmological, social, and political
dimensions. It is a way that embraces Confucian and Legalist concepts
of social order and government, as is demonstrated in the continuation
of this passage, which is quoted in the next section.

These dimensions are also discussed in the commentarial section
of "Xinshu shang":

> "Rightness" (yi 義) means that each rests in what is suitable
> (yi 宜) to it. "Ritual" is that which accords with the genuine
> feelings of human beings by going along with the Patterns
> of what is Right for them, and then creating limitations and
> embellishments. Therefore "Ritual" means to have Patterns.
> Patterns are what clarify distinctions and thereby convey the
> meaning of Rightness. Therefore Ritual is derived Rightness;
> Rightness is derived from Patterns; and Patterns accord with
> the suitable.
>
> Law is that by which uniformity is produced so people
> will have no other choice to do what is so. Thus execution
> and extermination, prohibition and punishment, are used to
> unify them [the people]. Therefore human affairs are super-
> vised by Law; Law is derived from authority (quan 權), and
> authority from the Way. (13/3a8–b1)

This passage emphasizes that the key Confucian ideas of Rightness
and Ritual are grounded in the notion of Pattern. These natural Patterns,
which guide the spontaneous expression of human emotions, are the basis
for the Rituals that are the social forms through which these emotions
can be manifested. Rightness means what is suitable in a given situation,
and this is determined by the Patterns inherent in that situation, especially the particular social relationship involved. Rightness determines
the appropriate Ritual; both are based on Pattern. The Patterns here
are the natural guidelines through which human nature is expressed
and the hierarchical guidelines of society that mold its expression. The
cosmological dimension of these Patterns is only implicit here. This is,
however, not the case in the next paragraph, in which the cosmological
basis of Law and authority is directly proclaimed.

The value of understanding and complying with Heaven's Patterns is well understood by the authors of the *Huainanzi*. In fact, it is their rationale for writing the book. In the twenty-first essay, "Yao lüe" 要略 (Summary of the Essentials), we read:

> Therefore we wrote this book of twenty chapters so that the Patterns of Heaven and Earth would be explored, the affairs of the human world would be encountered, and the Way of Emperors and Kings (*Diwang zhi Dao* 帝王之道) would be fully at one's disposal. (21/5b1–2)

The concern to comprehend the Patterns of the cosmos clearly led to the writing of such essays as #3, "Tian wen" 天文 ("The Patterns of Heaven"), #4, "Di xing" 地形 ("The Forms of Earth"), and #5, "Shice" 時則 ("The Seasonal Ordinances"). The idea of complying with Patterns is seen in this last essay in the idea that only certain types of human activities are appropriate to a given season, and the specific idea of *xun li* occurs in several locations, for example, 117b, 9/1a, 13a, and 14/4b. Finally, the idea that Pattern is the basis of Ritual and Rightness, found in "Xinshu shang," occurs as well in the *Huainanzi*:

> "Rightness" is what complies with Patterns and practices what is suitable. "Ritual" is what embodies genuine [emotions] and controls their expression. "Rightness" is to be suitable. "Ritual" is to embody. (11/6b11–7a1)

Political Syncretism

The classic expression of the political syncretism of the Syncretist *Zhuangzi* is found in the hierarchy of governing principles that constitute the "Great Way" in chapter 13. This passage exhibits the blending of Confucian and Legalist ideas in a Daoist context that is a hallmark of these chapters:

> Therefore the men of old who made clear the Great Way
> first made Heaven clear
> and the Way and the Power were next:
> and when the Way and the Power were clear, Goodwill
>   and Duty were next:
> and when Goodwill and Duty were clear, portions and
>   responsibilities were next:

and when portions and responsibilities were clear, title and
performance were next:

and when title and performance were clear, putting the
suitable man in charge was next:

and when putting the suitable man in charge was clear,
inquiry and inspection were next:

and when inquiry and inspection were clear, judging right
and wrong were next:

and when judging right and wrong was clear, reward and
punishment were next.[59] (13/32–36)

"Xinshu shang" only briefly deals with Confucian and Legalist
social and governmental principles in the passage quoted in the previous
section. It is a commentary on a passage in the basic text that provides
a definition of terms and an indication of their relative value, which,
while not as specific as the list in the *Zhuangzi*, is consonant with it:

That which is empty and formless we call the Dao. That which
transforms and nourishes the myriad things we call the Power.
That which is involved in the interactions between ruler and
minister, father and son, and among all human beings, we call
Rightness. That which determines the various levels of status,
courtesy, and familiarity in relationships we call Ritual. That
which selects things both great and small for execution and
extermination, for prohibition and punishment, according to
a single standard (Dao), we call Law.[60] (13/1b2–5)

The political philosophy of the *Huainanzi* exhibits all the major elements
that we have been discussing in the other sources, but presents them in
a much more sophisticated synthesis than is found in the shorter and
earlier works. Because of this, there are no single passages that encap-
sulate the *Huainanzi*'s political thought that can be quoted. Instead, I
provide a summary of the ninth essay, the "Art of Rulership," in which
this philosophy attains its fullest expression. For a more comprehensive
treatment, I refer the reader to Ames's excellent study of this essay, on
which the following summary is based.[61]

The political thought of the *Huainanzi* centers first and foremost on
the person of the sage-ruler, who cultivates himself in solitude and who
embodies the principle of Non-action. This ruler governs without concern
for his own benefit, and must establish an administrative hierarchy based

on clear differences between the responsibilities of ruler and officials, which are found in the Legalist notion of *shi* 勢 ("political advantage"). However, unlike in Legalist thought, the relationship between ruler and officials is governed by what Ames calls "a reciprocity, a harmony in which each position responds to the other."[62] Furthermore, *shi* is not used as an instrument of the ruler's own power and self-maintenance, but as a "device for maintaining a desirable political organization conducive to universal personal realization."[63]

This selfless ruler follows a program of policies aimed at "utilizing the people" (*yong zhong*) adapted from Confucianism and Mohism) in such a way that each is able to find work that is suitable to his own individual talents and abilities, and to thereby become more spontaneous and harmonious with his own inherent nature. An essential element of governmental policy is *fa*, "Law," strongly altered from its Legalist service in reinforcing the power of the ruler to a notion of universal law applicable to the ruler himself.

There is also in this political philosophy what Ames calls "a sustained effort to subordinate the interests of the ruler to the welfare of the people."[64] This is embodied in the adaptation of the Confucian concept of "benefiting the people" (*li min*) found throughout the text. The contributions of Confucian thought in this essay can also be seen in the presence of ideas such as "benevolence" (*ren* 仁) (e.g., 9/2b3–4, 22a12), "uprightness" (*zhi* 直) (e.g., 9/17b8), "sincerity" (*cheng* 誠) (e.g., 9/23a6), and "trustworthiness" (*xin* 信) (e.g., 9/23a4).

Finally the essay calls on the ruler to comprehend and act in compliance with the Patterns of the cosmos in order for his policies to be fully effective. This emphasizes once again that the structure of society and government must reflect the structure of the cosmos that contains it.

The political philosophy of the *Huainanzi* thus exhibits not a mere synthesis of the earlier social and political ideas of other schools, but rather a thorough integration of them within a framework that remains fundamentally Daoist, that is, one that maintains a cosmology of the Dao and shows a concern for psychology and self-cultivation. It is fully in accord with the earlier sources, but is much more detailed.

CONCLUDING REMARKS

The clear terminological and conceptual parallels between the Syncretist *Zhuangzi* and the four other sources studied above provide convincing evidence that they are not isolated texts, but are rather part of the same lineage of thought. The fact that there are also individual differences among them points to the fact that each had its own author, and each was written at a different point in time under unique circumstances. The early Han was a period when the Daoist political perspective was being seriously considered at the Imperial Court, and the challenge to the Daoists of the time was to create a system of government complex and specific enough to be practical, yet faithful to the founding vision of the *Laozi*, written with a much simpler social and political unit in mind. These texts are, I believe, all the results of this effort. Because of the striking similarities between the philosophy in all these sources and Sima Tan's description of Daoism, I must conclude that they are all part of the philosophical lineage that the Han historians call Huang-Lao. I must therefore also agree with Schwartz that the Syncretist chapters of the *Zhuangzi* are an integral part of this lineage of thought.

Now that we have located the Syncretist chapters in a philosophical tradition, we must return to the question of who within this tradition might have compiled them.

Did a Syncretist Author Compile the *Zhuangzi*?

By situating the Syncretist chapters of the *Zhuangzi* within the Huang-Lao tradition, we have taken a major step toward identifying the compiler of the entire text. The question remains, was it one of the authors of these documents, or was it someone else in this tradition?

The two opinions already mentioned on the compilation are those of Guan Feng and Graham. Guan states that the text was compiled by the retainers of Liu An, the second king of Huainan, the sponsor, editor, and partial author of the *Huainanzi*. He provides little evidence, however, to support his statement. Graham suspects that one of the Syncretist authors compiled the text and placed "Below in the Empire" at the end ". . . to show the irresponsible genius of Zhuangzi in proper perspective."[65] Additional evidence, he believes, is found in the presence of three phrases that became titles in the "Inner" Chapters in the Syncretist writings. However, now that we have placed the philosophy of the Syncretist *Zhuangzi* within the same lineage of thought as the *Huainanzi*, and we know that the authors were not isolated individuals, how does this change the analysis of this problem?

Although it is true that phrases from the titles of three of the "Inner" Chapters ("Qi wu" 齊物, "Da zong" 大宗, and "Di wang" 帝王) occur in the Syncretist *Zhuangzi*, phrases from six of the "Inner" Chapters are also found in the *Huainanzi* (see table 2.2).

Using the same reasoning, one could conclude that the even more frequent occurrence of "Inner" Chapter titles in the *Huainanzi* is an indication that the text was compiled by the authors of this later work. However, this is far from the only piece of evidence that points us in the direction of Huainan. Looking to others than the Syncretists helps to resolve the thorny problem of what I call "textual shuffling" in these chapters.

"Textual Shuffling" in the Syncretist *Zhuangzi*

One of the principal contributions of Graham's new translation of the *Zhuangzi* lies in his identification of several unique points of view in the book. This is especially valuable because there are some chapters (especially 11–14) in which more than one viewpoint is represented. Armed with this knowledge, we no longer have to try to rationalize the diverse sections of any of these chapters into one point of view. For example, in chapter 11, "Keep It in Place and in Bounds" (*zai you* 在宥), Graham has identified at least three viewpoints: Primitivist (1–28, 57–66), Immortalist (28–57), and Syncretist (66–74). However, as is often the case, increased knowledge raises new questions. The relevant

Table 2.2. *Zhuangzi* "Inner Chapter Titles" as Phrases in the *Huainanzi*

Phrase	*Huainanzi* Location
1. "Xiao yao" 逍遙	1/15; 19/8b; 21/6a
2. Qi wu 齊物	Occurs as *Qi-su*, title of chap. 11
3. "Yang sheng" 養生	7/10b; 20/8b–9a; 21/5a
4. "Ren jian" 人間	Title of chap. 18; 2/3b; 2/4a; 9/13b
5. "De chong fu" 德充符	No occurrences
6. "Da zong" 大宗	1/11a; 2/9a, 9b
7. "Di wang" 帝王	10/6a; 18/17a; 19/2b; 21/2b, 5b

one here is that if one of the Syncretist authors compiled the *Zhuangzi*, why are diverse viewpoints present in chapters 11–14?

A possible answer to this question lies in the fact that the extant recension of the Zhuangzi in thirty-three chapters established by the "Profound Learning" scholar Guo Xiang (ca. 300 CE) is not the original recension of the text. The Bibliographical Monograph to the *Hanshu* written by Ban Gu 班固 (ca. 80 CE) lists a fifty-two-chapter version, and most scholars agree that Ban Gu's work was largely based on the lost *Qi lüe* 七略 of Liu Xiang 劉向 (ca. 10 BCE). In addition, several of the third-century commentaries included in Lu Deming's 陸德明 *Jingdian shiwen* 經典詩文 were based on this fifty-two-chapter text: those of a certain "Mr. Meng" 孟氏, and the much more frequently cited one of Sima Biao 司馬彪.[66] Therefore, it is likely that this fifty-two-chapter version represents the original recension of the text.

Several scholars, including Ma Xulun 馬敘倫 and Graham, suggest that when Guo Xiang revised the text, he took the sections he thought were valuable from the nineteen discarded chapters and placed them into the thirty-three chapters he retained.[67] Despite compiling the most complete collection of the lost *Zhuangzi* fragments, neither Ma nor Wang Shumin 王樹民 could discover Guo's rationale, nor any way of determining which fragments from the discarded material he had placed into the extant text.[68] However, Lu Deming's collection of earlier commentaries does give us one possible method. Whenever Lu Deming does not cite one of these early commentaries written before Guo Xiang for a particular section of text, and that section contains a different viewpoint from that of a prior section or the remainder of the chapter, we may suspect that that particular section was placed there by Guo Xiang and originated in the chapters he discarded. This method is not perfect: there is evidence that Lu sometimes omitted comments from earlier scholars, especially Sima Biao.[69] Also, it assumes that Lu did not bother to look in other chapters within the fifty-two to find comments for these shuffled fragments. But it has been used before (for example, by Graham in identifying the Syncretist fragment at 11/66–74) and can give us a rough idea at least of which sections may have been shuffled into the extant text by Guo Xiang. Knowing this, we can better determine if Guo Xiang is responsible for the divergent ideas in chapters 12–14.

In table 2.3, I have analyzed the text of the most heterogeneous of the Syncretist chapters, "Heaven and Earth" (#12), into its fifteen sections, and have provided the category into which Graham placed each of these sections. I have also indicated whether or not there are any comments from pre-Guo Xiang scholars for these sections included in Lu Deming's work, and have included brief comments on the topic of the section.

Table 2.3 shows that, despite a considerable degree of apparent heterogeneity in chapter 12, at the very least some of it must have been present in the version of this chapter included in the original fifty-two-chapter recension, and that we cannot blame it all on Guo Xiang. This evidence represents a strong argument that the author of one of the Syncretist chapters could not have also compiled the entire book, for what could his rationale have been for including so much non-related material? It suggests instead that the compiler must have had a somewhat more liberal

Table 2.3. "Textual Shuffling" in *Zhuangzi* 12

Section	Graham Category	Early Commentary	Comments
1–6	Syncretist	No	The Way of the ruler
6–12	Syncretist	Yes	"Rhapsody on the Way"
12–18	Syncretist	No	"Rhapsody on the Way"
18–20	Untranslated	Yes	Yellow Emperor
20–26	Untranslated	No	Yao and Xu You
26–33	Immortality	Yes	Yao and the border guard
33–37	Utopia	No	Yao's rule
37–41	Rationalizing the Way	No	Great Beginning; Graham: broken-off mutilated Autumn Floods dialogue
41–45	Confucius and Laozi	Yes	Daoist self-cultivation
45–52	Untranslated	No	Government of Sage
52–69	Stray Ideas	Yes	Methods of Mr. Hundun
69–77	Untranslated	No	Government of Sage
77–83	Utopia	Yes	When Supreme Power reigns
83–95	Primitivist-related	Yes	Criticism of hypocrisy
95–102	Primitivist	No	Five ways to lose one's nature; Graham: moved to Primitivist 8/26

viewpoint, one that would have been willing to include, for example, stories about the Yellow Emperor (18–20) and Immortality (26–33) in a chapter whose overriding theme, it seems to me, is the government of the sage-king. However, we need not necessarily look outside the tradition of the Syncretists for the compiler. A later member of this tradition could easily have done this, someone who might have been rather more sympathetic to the Yellow Emperor and Immortality than an early Han Syncretist author. Given the presence of Esoteric Masters (*fang shi*) at the court of Liu An, men whom we know from the *Shiji* honored both that legendary ruler and that ultimate goal, I would suggest that we look to Huainan to find our compiler. There is considerable evidence that if we did this, we would be looking in the right direction.

THE *ZHUANGZI* AT HUAINAN

A significant part of the argument for placing the compiler of the *Zhuangzi* at the court of Liu An has already been presented. The Syncretist chapters are part of the same philosophical lineage as the *Huainanzi*. There are about three hundred locations in the latter text that contain ideas, phrases, or entire paragraphs borrowed from the former, only one of which is attributed to *Zhuangzi*. The ideological heterogeneity of chapters 11–14 indicates that an author of the Syncretist chapters is unlikely to have been the compiler. There are additional pieces of information that bolster the case.

To begin with, there can be no doubt that a version of the material contained in the extant *Zhuangzi* was at the court of Liu An and was influential in the writing of the *Huainanzi*. In addition to the many borrowings we can identify, Wang Shumin has located eleven passages from the lost *Zhuangzi* material that are presently in the *Huainanzi*, and he suspects there are many more.[70] The influence of the *Zhuangzi* can be seen as well in the titles and topics of two of the essays in the *Huainanzi* chapter 11 "Qi su" 齊俗, in which the author applies the idea from the "Qi wu lun" of the relativity of human experience to the subject of human customs, and chapter 18 "Ren jian" 人間.

However, the viewpoint of the authors of the *Huainanzi* is clearly different from that of the Inner Chapters of *Zhuangzi*. They have the Syncretists' concern for government, which Zhuangzi would have disdained. And when *Zhuangzi* material is used, it is often in a context that is alien to the man who wrote the "Inner" Chapters. For example, see the Naturalist cosmogonic explanation of the famous infinite regress in the "Qi wu lun" (2/49–52) at *Huainanzi* 2/1a, which is intended to demonstrate the futility of precisely the kind of reasoning used by the *Huainanzi* author. This suggests a strong influence from the *Zhuangzi*, but not yet any clearly identifiable viewpoint associated with the text, most certainly not one determined primarily from the "Inner" Chapters. This suggests to me a text in transition.

The name of Liu An is attached to two essays on the *Zhuangzi* that were included in the original fifty-two-chapter recension of the text. They are no longer extant, but a few lines from each of them have been preserved in the commentary on the *Wen xuan* 文選 written by Li Shan 李善 (d. 689), where they are accompanied by a comment from Sima Biao, thus indicating they were included in his edition of the text.[71] These fragments are as follows:

From the "Explanatory Colophon to the *Zhuangzi*" (*Zhuangzi hou jie*):

Geng Shizi 庚市子 was a sage, a man without desires. There were men who were quarreling over valuables. Geng Shizi divided some jade among them and they stopped quarreling.

This is attached to a line from the text that is now lost.

From the "Summary of the Essentials of *Zhuangzi*" ("*Zhuangzi lüeyao*"):

The gentlemen of river and ocean, the hermits of mountain and valley (*shangu zhi ren* 山谷之人) make light of the Empire, treat the myriad things as trifles, and traverse in solitude.

The two essays represented by these fragments must have been included in the three-chapter explanatory section (*jie shuo* 解說) of Sima Biao's edition.[72] They must have been included among the materials that "came from Huainan," which, in the colophon to the fragmentary Kozanji manuscript edition of the *Zhuangzi*, Guo Xiang says he discarded.[73] They not only indicate an active interest in the *Zhuangzi* by Liu An, but they also indicate that the text of the *Zhuangzi* must not have been fixed until it left Huainan. This is the only reason I can see for the inclusion of two of Liu An's essays in the original recension.

For all these reasons, I think it likely that the text of the *Zhuangzi* was compiled at the court of Liu An. However, I do not think it is possible to identify the actual compiler. Guan Feng maintains the opinion that "Below in the Empire" is actually the second of the lost *Zhuangzi* essays of Liu An, the "*Zhuangzi lüeyao*" 莊子略要 (The Summary Essentials of *Zhuangzi*). Indeed, it does bear a striking resemblance to the title of the final essay of the *Huainanzi*, "Yao lüe" 要略 (A Summary of the Essentials), which is likely to have been written by Liu. This seems to be the principal reason to identify him as the author. However, there are a number of reasons why this is unlikely.

To begin with, the "Yao lüe" essay of the *Huainanzi* is a summary of each of the chapters of the text with a rationale for their inclusion and their order. This is certainly not the case for chapter 33 of *Zhuangzi*. Second, it contains a discussion of the philosophy of Mozi 墨子 (21/7a), which is rather different from that found in "Below in the Empire." It is included in a section that explains the social and political conditions that led to the creation of certain philosophical texts and schools of thought, and does not criticize them from any superior standpoint. Third, the *Huainanzi* is written in regular parallel prose with rhymed verse interspersed; *Zhuangzi* 33 is not. Finally, there is a distinct possibility that the fragment from Liu An's *Zhuangzi lüeyao* quoted above can be linked to the opening section of *Zhuangzi* 15, "Finicky Notions," in which the author criticizes the "hermits of mountain and valley" (*shangu zhi shi* 山谷之士) (15/1). Liu An speaks of these hermits in the above fragment using virtually the same phrase. This fragment could have been part of a summary of this chapter, similar to the summaries of the Huainanzi essays in "Yao lüe." For these reasons, it is highly unlikely that Liu An is the author of "Below in the Empire." His "Explanatory Colophon" was probably a brief running commentary on the text appended to the end of it, as many early commentaries were, and his "Lüe yao" was probably a summary of the text similar to the final essay of the *Huainanzi*. It is a shame that Guo Xiang did not think these essays were worthy of transmission. Nonetheless, their presence in the initial version of the *Zhuangzi* provides further evidence for locating the compilation of the text at the court of Liu An.

The Date of Compilation of the *Zhuangzi*

Now that we have placed the compiling of the *Zhuangzi* at the court of Liu An, we have narrowed the possible date for this to between about 150 and 122 BCE, the years when Liu and his retainers were active. Is it possible to be even more precise? There are a few bits of evidence that could be construed to indicate that the text was compiled during the latter half of this period.

Wu Zeyu 吳則虞 mentions that in the "Outer" Chapters, all the occurrences of the character *heng* 恆 have been changed to *chang* 常.[74] This was a taboo that began during the reign of Wendi 漢文帝 (180–57 BCE) and would hold for the next two reign periods of Jingdi 漢景帝 (157–40) and Wudi 漢武帝 (140–87): The only two occurrences of *heng* in the "Outer" Chapters are in locations for which there is no Sima Biao commentary recorded by Lu Deming (12/25 and 13/58). Hence they could be part of fragments inserted there by Guo Xiang.

There are occasional comments in some of the chapters that look like interpolations that could have been inserted by a Huang-Lao compiler. For example, Graham has noted two comments critical of the notion of "abandoning affairs" at the beginning of the "Fathoming Nature" chapter "Da sheng" 達生 (19/4, 5) that come from a position of advocacy of involvement in the world that could be syncretist.[75] He also mentions four glosses in the Primitivist chapters that introduce an aphorism, three of which are taken from *Laozi* (e.g., 11/28) PT.[76] This pattern of illustrating a saying from *Laozi* with a story or a brief argument is found throughout the *Huainanzi*, especially in essay #12. Finally, there is a peculiar gloss at 33/9–10 that explains the utility of the Four Classics (*Shi* 詩, *Shu* 書, *Liji* 禮記, *Yue* 樂) and adds two others (*Yi* 易 and *Chunqiu* 春秋). There was a revival of the study of the Six Classics under Han Wudi, and in the year 136 BCE, academic posts in the government bureaucracy were established for scholars who specialized in each of them.[77]

Finally, there is a brief comment about the Yellow Emperor's ascent to Heaven in the "Inner" Chapters (6/33) that scholars have concluded is a late interpolation.[78] Yu Yingshi 余英時 maintains that this legend was originated by *fang shi* during the reign of Wudi in their quest for political legitimacy. There were certainly *fang shi* at the court of Liu An who could have inserted this idea into a text that was being compiled there.

There is one final piece to the puzzle: the frequent unattributed borrowings from the *Zhuangzi* by the authors of the *Huainanzi*, and the totally random nature of these borrowings, suggests that they were not only thoroughly familiar with the *Zhuangzi* materials, but that the text may have still been in flux while the *Huainanzi* was being written. This is also suggested by the fact that the Liu An essays were included in the original fifty-two-chapter recension.

Based upon this admittedly circumstantial evidence, I would like to suggest the possibility that the *Zhuangzi* was compiled at the court of Liu An after the *Huainanzi* was written, after the Six Classics were formally acknowledged with posts in the bureaucracy, and after the *fang shi* began advocating their legend of the Yellow Emperor's ascent. This would approximate the date of compilation of the *Zhuangzi* to about 130 BCE.

Final Conclusions

I believe that the evidence presented in this study demonstrates that the authors of the Syncretist chapters of the *Zhuangzi* were not isolated individuals, but were part of the lineage of thought that is called in the *Shiji* both the Daoist school and Huang-Lao. The Syncretist philosophy contains the three aspects that are characteristic of this philosophical lineage: a cosmology based on the Dao; a psychology whose theories are given a physiological basis in such concepts as the Vital Energy, Vital Essence, and the Numen, which provides the theoretical basis for techniques of self-cultivation directed to the sage ruler; and finally a political theory that begins with the Non-action of the self-cultivated ruler and that adopts elements from the political thought of other pre-Han schools, and that is based on an understanding of the Patterns of the cosmos of which human society is an integral part.

To be sure, there are certain differences in emphasis among the sources we have been considering that clearly indicate that none is from the same author or group of authors. But the striking conceptual and terminological parallels provide clear evidence that what we have here are different authors within the same philosophical lineage.

These conclusions enable us to begin to clarify the nature of Daoist philosophy and to begin to see it independent of the restrictions that have traditionally been imposed on our understanding of it by the category of "Lao-Zhuang." When we do so, we can begin to see, particularly in the element I have labeled "psychology," the possibilities of connections with parallel elements in the later Daoist religion. This would suggest that, despite the fact that the origins of this religion remain obscure, it does not represent the radical break with philosophical Daoism that many have suggested.

Our search for the compiler of the *Zhuangzi* has enabled us to place its final chapters in a philosophical lineage, and also to trace its compilation to the court of Liu An, the King of Huainan. For the reasons presented above, I believe that the text of the *Zhuangzi* was not fixed until after the completion of the *Huainanzi*. Further evidence, admittedly scanty, has enabled the approximation of the date of compilation to 130 BCE. So while we have not actually identified the actual compiler of the *Zhuangzi*, we have been able to place him in a philosophical lineage, locate him in a specific place, and approximate when he completed his project. That may be as close to identifying him as it is possible to get.

Chapter 3

Redaction Criticism and the
Early History of Daoism

Introduction

Much of my previous textual research has involved the use of a type of textual criticism that employs systematic processes in order to determine the content of a hypothetical archetype that is ancestral to all the extant versions of an original text.[1] But in light of some important research in New Testament studies that deals with the literary aspects of textual criticism, I would to like to attempt a case study employing a different type of textual criticism that has potentially considerable benefits for the study of early Chinese thought. The literary aspect of textual criticism I discuss in this chapter involves the analysis of the ideas in a text as influenced by its literary forms, by its linguistic style and patterns, by the composition techniques and redaction strategies through which a text was originally created and subsequently augmented,

This chapter is a revised version of a paper read at the 1994 Meeting of the Association for Asian Studies on a panel entitled, "Textual Criticism and Cultural History." I wish to thank the panel organizer, Susan Cherniack and the other panel members, William Boltz, Benjamin Elman, and John Henderson, for their insightful comments on the first version of this article. In addition I wish to thank the anonymous re viewers, the journal editor, Sarah Queen, and John Major for their detailed criticisms of the second version of this article. All their thoughtful comments have, in one way or another, found their way into this final version and have helped me sharpen my arguments and clarify my abstruse prose.

and through the structure and content of its narratives and embedded myths. It is my opinion that examining these literary aspects of early Chinese texts can provide valuable testimony to help ascertain the actual historical conditions in which these texts were written and so provide evidence for the origins and evolution of the various pre-Han intellectual lineages.

The literary aspect of textual criticism I wish to deal with derives from the research of twentieth-century scholars of the New Testament on the related methodologies they call "form criticism" and "redaction criticism."[2] In beginning to adapt these methods to the study of early Chinese philosophical texts, I am following the lead of two scholars who, it seems to me, implicitly follow them: William Boltz and Victor Mair (on the *Laozi* 老子), and one scholar who explicitly follows them, Michael LaFargue, also on the *Laozi*.[3] Form criticism and redaction criticism are, in essence, an attempt to bring consistent methodological rigor to the logic of deriving historical evidence from the literary form, composition methods, and redaction strategies found in early Christian texts, specifically the Synoptic Gospels. The former represents "an analysis of the standard genres or 'forms' (stories, songs, sayings, and so on) in which oral tradition is cast and an attempt to interpret each unit of oral tradition in the context of some concrete life setting in which it was originally used."[4] The latter is "an analysis of the techniques and intentions of those who wove the material into longer compositions."[5] Particularly relevant for the present study is redaction criticism, because of its concern with the interaction between inherited tradition and later interpretive viewpoint in the effort to understand "why the items from the tradition were modified and connected as they were," and because of its concern to identify ideological viewpoints expressed in and through the composition of a given text.[6]

In this chapter, I would like to demonstrate the methods and results of redaction criticism in the context of studying a particularly difficult textual problem that has important implications for our understanding of the early history of Daoism. This problem is the often-debated relationship between two essays in the *Guanzi* 管子, "Neiye" 內業 ("Inward Training") and "Xinshu xia" 心術下 ("Techniques of the Mind" II). By applying the methodology of redaction criticism, I hope to demonstrate that the latter is a deliberate rearrangement and restatement of the former, not vice versa, as some have argued.[7]

Some Hypotheses on the Early History of Daoism

There is a larger context in which the results of this particular demonstration of redaction criticism are relevant, namely the attempt to delineate the foundations of what might be called "original Daoism." As with the attempt to reach an understanding of any of the Chinese traditions of this antiquity, the paucity of surviving textual and historical evidence and the continuing possibility of new archaeological discoveries reduce one to the development of plausible hypotheses rather than definitive conclusions. Therefore, what I suggest in this chapter are hypotheses and not conclusions. Nevertheless, I think strong arguments about the nature of early Daoism can be made, and redaction criticism can play a significant role in providing the justification for some of these arguments. Further, while I am fully aware of the difficulties inherent in the use of the term "Daoism," as pointed out in a seminal article by Nathan Sivin,[8] I am still of the opinion that a carefully circumscribed use of this term is better than no use at all. In the following section, I endeavor to present my hypotheses on early "Daoism" in such a way as to avoid at least some of the pitfalls of imprecision that Sivin outlines.

In previous research I have argued that there is no original school of Daoism called "Lao-Zhuang" 老莊 (probably a third-century AD literati creation) and that the textual origins of Daoism are not even to be found *exclusively* in these two works.[9] My argument here is based on looking back at Warring States and early Han textual sources from the perspective of Sima Tan 司馬談, the man who coined the term we translate as "Daoism," *Daojia* 道家.[10] There is no historical evidence for such a "Lao-Zhuang school" of thought in this period, if by "school" one means a well-organized group of masters and disciples with a well-defined textual canon and self-identity. Daoism, as defined by Sima Tan, is much closer to the kind of syncretic philosophy found in the *Huainanzi* 淮南子 than to either the *Laozi* 老子 or the *Zhuangzi* 莊子, the presumed foundational texts of this "school."[11] In "Who Compiled the *Zhuangzi*?," I argued that the thought found in those chapters of *Zhuangzi* that A. C. Graham labeled as "Syncretist" bears such close similarities with the "Daoism" of Sima Tan and the *Huainanzi* that they can be considered part of the same tradition. This implied that the category of Syncretic Daoism that Graham found in the *Zhuangzi* could be extended to other texts, as Guan Feng 關鋒 and others have asserted.[12] Indeed, both Guan and Liu Xiaogan 劉笑敢 link the syncretic Daoism of the *Zhuangzi* with philosophers from the Huang-Lao 黃老 tradition, which the *Shiji* 史記 traces back to the Jixia 稷下 Academy in Qi 齊 (originated ca. 310 BCE), and which it shows was one of the dominant ideologies of the Western Han imperial court during the first six decades of its rule.[13]

One of the essential characteristics of the Han syncretic Daoism found in the above sources is the presence of a well-developed vocabulary of what I initially called "psychology and self-cultivation," but which I now prefer to call "inner cultivation" after the text that I think contains the earliest surviving expression of it, the *Guanzi* essay titled "Neiye" 內業 ("Inward Training"). This philosophy is characterized by theories of how to make the mind tranquil through a systematic practice of guided breathing, a tranquility that leads to profound states of self-transformation. In my study "Psychology and Self-Cultivation in Early Daoistic Thought" I presented the textual evidence that the psychological thought of the *Huainanzi* derives directly from a series of three often overlooked essays in the *Guanzi*: "Neiye," "Xinshu shang" 心術上 (Techniques of the Mind, I), and "Xinshu xia" 心術下 (Techniques of the Mind, II).[14] This textual evidence of influence implies that all these sources are in some way linked together, and it is one of the principal challenges facing scholars of the early history of Daoism to determine precisely how. That is one of the concerns of the present study.

In addition to showing philosophical links between the syncretic Daoism of the *Zhuangzi* and other early Huang-Lao sources, Guan Feng and Graham demonstrate the parallels between the sections of *Zhuangzi* Graham attributes to a "Primitivist" author (chapters 8–10 and the first half of 11) and the *Laozi*. This is another important link because it suggests that both textual sources are closely related to one another. Both sets of philosophical links demonstrate that the strata of the *Zhuangzi* are not isolated phenomena and suggest that they may be related to broader textual traditions.

The methodology used by Guan Feng, Graham, and Liu Xiaogan to identify the various strata of the *Zhuangzi* represents a type of literary criticism in which shared technical terms, parallel or identical phrases, and common grammatical structures are the criteria for the inclusion of material in their distinct categories of authorial voices or ideologies. As we have seen, all three scholars develop arguments about the relationships between these strata and other early Daoist sources, and a careful reading of their works shows that they do so by simply extending this methodology. In my work on the inner cultivation theories in the *Guanzi* essays and the *Huainanzi*, I used the very same method to identify influence. In other words, I assumed that the repeated occurrence of certain group-ings of technical terms in a number of different texts had a significance for identifying important philosophical relationships among these texts. Working from a grouping of the technical terms used to characterize Daoism by Sima Tan, I further developed a series of three general cat-egories for these terms that represent three interlocking philosophical concerns: cosmology, inner cultivation, and political thought.[15] These characteristic groupings of technical terms form what might be called a "semantic pattern" that can be used as a guide to delineate commonali-ties and differences among the possible early textual sources of Daoism.

The category of cosmology includes such familiar technical terms as Dao and De, non-action (*wuwei* 無為), formlessness (*wuxing* 無形), and the Way of Heaven (*tian zhi Dao* 天之道). Under the second category I include such ideas as tranquility (*jing* 靜), emptiness (*xu* 虛), desirelessness (*wuyu* 無欲), selflessness (*wusi* 無私), circulating the vital breath (*xing qi* 行氣), and the vital essence (*jing* 精). The final category of political philosophy is the one in which the most variety can be seen among the early Daoist textual sources, and it is dominated by the technical terminology of the early Han Syncretists. It includes such concepts as non-action (*wuwei* 無為), spontaneous response (*ying* 應), adaptation (*yin* 因), compliance (*xun* 循), suitability (*yi* 宜), and, for certain texts, the use of Legalist and Confucian political and social thought. While many of these terms occur at times in other contemporaneous philosophical texts, their consistent use together to form a distinctive vocabulary that occurs in the context of the above three principal concerns is, I think, extremely significant.

Pulling together the insights of Guan Feng, Graham, and Liu Xiaogan on the stratification of the *Zhuangzi* and the relationships of these strata to other early Daoist texts, and utilizing the method of identifying "semantic patterns," I would like to suggest the existence of three "aspects" or, perhaps, "phases" of early Daoism, that are attested to by a number of extant texts, including—but by no means limited to—*Laozi* and *Zhuangzi*.

The first, or "Individualist," aspect is essentially apolitical and is concerned exclusively with individual transformation through inner cultivation placed in the context of a cosmology of the Dao. It is rep-resented by "Neiye" and the seven "Inner Chapters" of *Zhuangzi*. The second, or "Primitivist," aspect adds a political dimension to the first, one that advocates the return to a more simple and basic form of social organization found in the agrarian utopias of the legendary past. It is represented by the *Laozi* and the Primitivist chapters 8–11 of the *Zhuangzi*. The third and final aspect, the Syncretist, shares the cosmology and inner cultivation theory of the former two, but takes a different direction with its political thought. It advocates, instead, the establishment of a more complex, hierarchically organized central government that accords with the models provided by the patterns of Heaven and Earth. It also exhibits a syncretic use of ideas from Confucian, Mohist, and Legalist sources within a Daoist cosmological and political framework. It is represented in a number of texts including, at least, *Jingfa* 經法 and *Daoyuan* 道原 from the "Huang-Lao Boshu" 黃老帛書, *Guanzi*'s "Xinshu shang," the Syncretist chapters 12–15 and 33 of the *Zhuangzi*, and the *Huainanzi*.[16] It also matches closely the description of "Daoism" given by Sima Tan. The only chronology I would like to suggest is that the first aspect is likely to have been the earliest. This will be another of the questions upon which the present study can shed some light.

To this point in my analysis, these three aspects are essentially textual phenomena. While the relevant texts were undoubtedly produced by persons who were part of distinct master-disciple lineages, we cannot yet link these texts with any degree of certainty to the few specific Daoist lineages to which the historical record attests.[17] The considerable evidence of the semantic patterns found in these sources seems to preclude the possibility that these three aspects of early Daoism are entirely unrelated. Whether they represent distinct phases in a continuous tradition or three closely related, but distinct, lineages is not, at this point, completely certain. This is one question that I hope the present redaction criticism can help to clarify. What *is* certain, however, is that all three have one very important characteristic in common.

As even a casual perusal of the semantic criteria presented above will show, all three aspects are linked together by a shared vocabulary and concern for the method of practice I have called "inner cultivation." This practice involves the progressive emptying out of the ordinary contents of consciousness—thoughts, feelings, desires—through an inner contemplative process involving guided and regularized breathing. It produces states of deep tranquility with a profound noetic content, states not normally attainable without deliberate effort, which have a powerful transformative quality for the adept.[18] It also yields the practical gains of mental acuity and dispassionate objectivity that would have been attractive goals to rulers as well as adepts.

Furthermore, it is not merely a common concern for inner cultivation that ties together all the above textual sources. If it were only this, then we should also have to include a number of other texts that show an awareness of guided breathing and some of the vocabulary of inner cultivation, such as *Mengzi* 孟子, *Xunzi* 荀子, and the Yangist essays in the *Lüshi chunqiu* 呂氏春秋, to say nothing of the physical hygiene texts in the important medical corpus from Mawangdui.[19] The other component that the textual sources of Daoism contain that is not found in these other works is the characteristic cosmology of Dao and De 德, the Way and its inner power. Indeed, I would contend that it is precisely the practice of inner cultivation—carried to a degree not evidenced in these non-Daoist textual sources—that produces the profound noetic experiences from which this characteristic cosmology of the Dao derives.[20]

Just as the presence of such a cosmology allows us to differentiate a Yangist source from a Daoist one, so too does it enable us to distinguish the mundane practitioner of inner cultivation for health and hygiene from the adept who follows it to its ultimate levels. Such distinctions are old and authentic and emerge from important early textual sources, such as the related criticisms, found in both the *Zhuangzi* and the *Huainanzi*, of those who nourish the body (*yang xing* 養形) through the gymnastic and respiratory exercises of "guiding and pulling" the vital breath (*dao yin* 導引).[21] These are contrasted with the superior methods characterized as "nourishing the numen" (*yang shen* 養神) or "nourishing one's innate nature" (*yang xing* 養性).

Therefore, the semantic elements common to all three aspects I have delineated are the characteristic cosmology and the philosophy of inner cultivation. These elements strongly suggest a well-developed tradition of practice. For this reason, I would contend that the three aspects are more than a textual phenomenon. They are products of one or more master-disciple lineages that followed the theory and practice of inner cultivation to the attainment of the profound experiences of self-transformation that gave rise to their characteristic cosmology. It is to these master-disciple lineages and to the distinctive cosmology and philosophy of inner cultivation they produced that we can give the name "Daoism."

To be sure, I do not mean to suggest by this usage that throughout the Warring States period there was a self-conscious "school" of philosophy that called itself "Daoism." Rather, what I am trying to suggest is that there were a number of related master-disciple lineages who shared common practices of inner cultivation and a sufficiently common philosophical outlook that they can be grouped together under the rubric term "Daoism," which can then be divided into the Individualist, Primitivist, and Syncretist aspects based on the semantic criteria derived from their surviving textual testimony. The situation changed in the late Warring States/early Han, when the Syncretists do seem to have attempted to define themselves as a distinct tradition, perhaps what could even be called a "school." Evidence for this includes the creation of the legend of Lao Dan 老丹 as the author of the *Dao De jing*, as brilliantly clarified by Graham, and the Syncretist self-identification as the sole practitioners of the comprehensive *Dao shu* 道術 (Techniques of the Way) in *Zhuangzi* 33.[22]

It is to this Syncretist tradition, of course, that Sima Tan first gave the name of "*Daojia*," and we would not go amiss, I think, in seeing it as the first true "school" of Daoism. Precisely what we call the earlier and less clearly organized lineages is partly a semantic question. In earlier work I suggested they be designated as "Daoistic," but this is giving Sima Tan perhaps too decisive a role in our analysis and underplaying the commonalities of cosmology and inner cultivation found in all three aspects.[23] It also suggests that we might be able to determine when this "proto-Daoism" became "Daoism." While I am confident this process did come about, I am not certain that we will ever be able to identify precisely when it happened.

What we call this "proto-Daoism" is also partly a historical question. For while we have identified three aspects of early Daoism and suggested their association with master-disciple lineages, we have not provided decisive evidence for their suggested chronology nor for whether they are phases of one continuous tradition or distinct, but related, traditions. This is where the text-critical methods developed in New Testament studies can possibly be of assistance.

Using form and redaction criticism, Mair and LaFargue argue that the *Laozi* probably originated in a community of practitioners of inner cultivation and that it was transmitted orally in discrete, easily memorized units or forms until these were written down at some point in the third century BCE.[24] These insights are valuable, for they begin to provide a more clearly defined context for these works, albeit a somewhat speculative one. I think it is also the case that "Neiye" was produced in such a practicing community of masters and disciples. I also agree with LaFargue in his contention that these two texts are not purely speculative philosophy but are filled with concepts derived directly from self-cultivation experience.[25] Inner cultivation, as practiced by the "Neiye" teachers, leads directly to the cosmology of the Dao that is a hallmark of what I think we can call early Daoism. As I argued above, it is not the casual practice of inner cultivation for health and hygiene that is the basis of this distinctive cosmology, but rather a sustained effort over many years. Daoist inner cultivation is thus, I maintain, a technical art, in certain respects analogous to astronomy and medicine, whose mastery demanded years of training and practice.[26] It is hard to imagine, given these demands and the models provided by the later and more institutionalized mystical traditions found in China and elsewhere, that a mastery of these techniques could have been accomplished outside closely knit communities of masters and disciples.

The Primitivist and Syncretist aspects of early Daoism represent, in my view, deliberate attempts to apply these techniques of Daoist inner cultivation to the problems of government. It is possible that each developed within a distinct community of Daoist inner cultivation practitioners toward the end of the fourth or early in the third century BCE that might have directly descended from the "Neiye" lineage. It is my hope that the following redaction criticism of "Xinshu xia" can contribute to the clarification of this possible relationship.

Four Daoist Essays in the *Guanzi*

There are four related essays in the *Guanzi*, a complicated collection now containing seventy-six *pian* 篇 (chapters) arranged in twenty-four *juan* 卷 (books) that originated in Qi 齊 circa 300 BCE and to which material may have been added until 26 BCE, when Liu Xiang 劉向 established the extant recension.[27] These four essays focus on Daoist inner cultivation practices and their application to the problems of government. Guo Moruo's 郭沫若 very influential theory attributing these essays to a school of Jixia Huang-Lao thinkers that included Song Xing 宋鈃 and Yin Wen 尹文 has been discredited by Graham,[28] but, because of the semantic criteria outlined above, their linkage to some Daoist lineage is, in my opinion, beyond question. All four texts exhibit the irregular rhyme patterns thought to be characteristic of Chu dialect, but because there is so little overlap in these patterns among the four, Allyn Rickett concludes each had a different author.[29] I focus principally on the two of them that are the most closely related, "Neiye" and "Xinshu xia." I discuss "Xinshu shang" ("Techniques of the Mind" I) because it shares its title with the latter, and leave untouched the least relevant essay for the present study, "The Purified Mind" (*Baixin* 白心).

"Neiye" is almost exclusively written in rhymed verse, with the rhymes occurring most often at the end of every second four-character line.[30] While in extant editions there are only two or three general divisions in the text, it is possible to identify a greater number of distinct units based on semantic, syntactic, and phonological criteria. I have arranged the text into twenty-two separate stanzas and find my divisions closest to those of the Gustav Haloun/Jeffrey Riegel arrangement.[31] Other arrangements have been suggested.[32] Each of these units of rhymed verse can stand independently, and, on the model of form criticism, could represent discrete forms of oral transmission that were assembled by the composer of the original written text.[33]

"Xinshu shang" is a very different type of work than "Neiye." It is composed of two distinct parts: the first third is a series of discrete statements, many in rhymed verse; the final two-thirds is a prose commentary elucidating the first part. Whereas "Neiye" is almost exclusively devoted to the practice and philosophy of inner cultivation, "Xinshu shang" focuses on the application of inner cultivation to the problems of government. Its principal argument is that inner cultivation is the sine qua non of *wuwei* 無為 government, giving the ruler the "inner power" (*de*) to realize the ineffable Way, the mental acuity to perceive the relationship between names and actualities, the ability to judge things with an objective impartiality and to respond spontaneously to any event that arises.[34] Not only does this text promote the inner cultivation program of "Neiye," but its specific use of the "Neiye's" distinctive metaphor for this program, "cleaning out the abode of the numen," is concrete evidence of its debt to "Neiye" and, in my opinion, the group of practitioners who transmitted it.[35] I have elsewhere concluded that "Xinshu shang" shares the intellectual concerns and technical vocabulary of the late Warring States and early Han Syncretic Daoism that in the latter period was called "Huang-Lao."[36]

"Xinshu xia" is an unusual text in that roughly 65 percent of it is made up of passages borrowed from the middle section of "Neiye," which deals primarily with inner cultivation, but it omits those verses surrounding this middle section that deal primarily with descriptions of the ineffable forces of the Dao and the "vital essence" (*jing* 精).

These borrowed passages from "Neiye" are presented in an order quite different from that of their source text, and they often contain variant readings. The 35 percent of original material in "Xinshu xia" that is almost exclusively in prose presents a philosophical position quite similar to that of "Xinshu shang." As we shall see, it often serves to comment on "Neiye" verses, to link passages that are separated in "Neiye," or to reframe the topic of a verse extracted from "Neiye."

Two explanations have been put forward to explain the differences between the "Neiye" material in these two sources. On the one hand, Guo Moruo argues that "Neiye" and "Xinshu xia" represent distinct texts based on the notes of two different students taken at the lectures of their Jixia teacher, with the latter representing the more faithful version that was damaged in transmission, losing its beginning and ending sections and having its order disrupted by the shuffling of bamboo strips.[37] On the other hand, Rickett contends that "Xinshu xia" is a distinct text that brings out the political implications of "Neiye," but it is based on an entirely different version of the text than our extant one, a version with many variants readings that, during its early transmission, lost its beginning and ending sections.[38] What I hope to demonstrate is a third alternative: that "Xinshu xia" is an original prose essay in which the author *deliberately* extracted and rearranged the verses from "Neiye" for the purpose of advocating the techniques and philosophy of inner cultivation as part of the arcana of rulership. It thus complements "Xinshu shang," and it is no accident that the two are placed together in the Guanzi and labeled as parts of one distinct essay.[39]

Linguistic Data for Comparative Dating

There is a consensus among recent scholars that "Neiye" is considerably earlier than either of the "Xinshu" texts, and I also concur. Before presenting the redaction criticism that, I think, demonstrates this conclusively, I would like to summarize the grammatical evidence that also argues for this conclusion.

The research of Bernhard Karlgren on the patterns of grammatical "auxiliaries" in the Lu and Zuozhuan 左轉 dialects and in the literary language of the third century BCE can sometimes provide a valuable test for comparative dating. Here I list only those of Karlgren's auxiliaries that are represented in our three Guanzi texts, and to these I add several others not mentioned by him but that are found therein.[40]

I. "Neiye" only uses *ru* 如 (ten times) but never *ruo* 若; for "like, as," except in two locations, which I believe, for other reasons, to be interpolations.[41] Both "Xinshu" essays only use ruo.[42] This "Neiye" usage is, for Karlgren, characteristic of the *Zuozhuan* dialect.

II. "Neiye" always uses the postverbal preposition *yu* 於 (twenty-six times), but never uses *hu* 乎. The "Xinshu" texts use both equally, except where "Neiye" material is being borrowed, wherein it almost always uses <u>yu</u>. Once again, "Neiye" follows the *Zuozhuan*.[43]

III. "Neiye" always clearly distinguishes among its negatives, frequently using the negative imperative *wu*[4] 勿 + verb (indicating the implicit object pronoun *zhi* 之, translated as "do not VERB it"), and clearly distinguishing it from *wu*[2] 無 and *bu* 不.[44] The "Xinshu" texts never use wu[4]. Otherwise "Xinshu shang" distinguishes among the negative imperative *wu*[2] 毋, *wu*[2] 無, and *bu*. "Xinshu xia" three times uses the negative imperative *wu*[2] 毋 for the three clearly distinguished negatives of "Neiye," thus indicating a possible blurring of distinctions among these negatives, which is thought to be a Han characteristic.[45]

IV. The "Xinshu" texts both use the pre-nominal preposition *yu* 與 "together with"; "Neiye" never uses it.[46]

V. The commentarial sections in "Xinshu shang" and "Xinshu xia" quite frequently use the nominalizing particle *zhe* 者 (forty-three and eighteen times, respectively). In the latter, *zhe* is often inserted into a phrase borrowed from "Neiye" in order to clarify the author's understanding of "Neiye." *Zhe* is virtually absent from both the first part of "Xinshu shang" (two occurrences) and from "Neiye" (four occurrences).[47] This is understandable because these commentarial sections of "Xinshu shang" and "xia" are both attempts to interpret earlier verse materials.

A number of these linguistic features indicate an earlier date for "Neiye." Its exclusive use of *ru* 如, the postverbal preposition *yu* 於, and the negative imperative with implicit object *wu*[4] 勿 probably mark it as a fourth-century BCE work, along with the *Zuozhuan* and *Mencius*.

This is reinforced by the evidence of its distinctive literary structure as a composition of parallel rhymed verses that was probably assembled from a number of independent original "forms" that lent themselves to easy memorization and verbal transmission, much in the manner of the *Laozi*. Further, "Neiye" does not contain the kind of sustained argumentation found in third century BCE philosophical essays and it shows only a very loose principle of organization between its verses. Its absence of any discussion of yin-yang theory and virtual absence of any political concerns further reinforce the impression of its antiquity.[48]

The largely verse form of the first part of "Xinshu shang" probably indicates that it is older than the rest of "Xinshu." The equal use of the postverbal prepositions *yu* 於 and *hu* 乎 throughout "Xinshu" fits Karlgren's characteristics of the third-century BCE literary language, but the exclusive use of *ruo* 若 does not. The distinctive use of the prenominal *yu* 與 throughout both parts of "Xinshu" indicates a common literary style, but the predominant use of the nominalizing particle *zhe* in the "Xinshu shang" commentarial sections and in "Xinshu xia" indicates a close relationship among these two and probably indicates they are later than the verse section of "Xinshu shang." The evidence for the blurring of distinctions among negatives in "Xinshu xia" could possibly push its date into the early Han, although the examples are too few for a definitive conclusion.

This linguistic evidence clearly indicates that the first explanation for the parallels between "Neiye" and "Xinshu xia," which both represent the notes of two students from the teachings of their master, is not supported. I adduce further evidence against this explanation below.

The Structure of "Xinshu xia"

As mentioned above, it is my contention that "Xinshu xia" is a coherent essay whose author deliberately rearranged and edited the material he borrowed from "Neiye" in order to support his arguments. I demonstrate this with tables 3.1 and 3.2 (pp. 120–121). Table 3.1 contains my division of "Neiye" into twenty-two distinct units of verse with a suggested topic for each unit. I also indicate the location of each unit in the *Sibu congkan* 四部叢刊 edition of the *Guanzi* and the parallel "Xinshu xia" section. Table 3.2 contains my division of "Xinshu xia" into seven sections, each of which contains a varying number of distinct semantic units. Here I provide a tentative suggestive topic for each unit, along

Table 3.1. The Structure and Topics of Neiye; "Xinshu xia" Parallels

NY: Sections and Topics		Location	XS2 Parallel
I.	Jing (Vital Essence)/De (Inner Power)	16.1a5	
II.	Jing and the Mind	1a11	
III.	Ineffable Dao and De	1b2	
IV.	Dao and Inner Cultivation	1b10	
V.	Dao: Ineffable and Creative	2a2	
VI.	Inner Cultivation and Jing	2a6	XS2 V.E, VII.C
VII.	The One	2b1	XS2 IV.A,C; V.A
VIII.	Benefits of Inner Cultivation	2b3	XS2 V.C
IX.	Inner Cultivation and De	2b6	XS2 I. A,B
X.	Inner Cultivation: Grasping the Shen (Numen)	2b8	XS2 I.C
XI.	Inner Cultivation: Attaining the Shen	2b9	
XII.	Inner Cultivation: Dao and the Tranquil Mind	3a2	XS2 V.B; VII.C,E
XIII.	Health Benefits of Jing	3a8	XS2 VII.D
XIV.	Inner Cultivation and Mystical Experience	3b1	XS2 VI.A
XV.	Guided Breathing, Dao, and De	3b6	
XVI.	Benefits of Inner Cultivation	3b8	XS2 VI.B,D
XVII.	Concentrate qi (Vital Breath)	4a2	XS2 III.A–C
XVIII.	Avoid Excesses	4a8	
XIX.	Inner Cultivation and Vitality	4a11	
XX.	Vitality, Emotions, Confucian Virtues	4b5	XS2 VII.A
XXI.	The Way of Eating; The One	4b7	
XXII.	Inner Cultivation, Vitality, Emotions	5a4	

NB: Roman numerals in all tables refer to the comparative critical versions of both texts found in the Appendix to this chapter (pp. 141–48).

Table 3.2. The Structure and Topics of "Xinshu xia"; "Neiye" Parallels

XS2: Sections and Topic	NY Parallels
Inner Cultivation and Inner Power	
Inner Cultivation and *De*	NYIX, 1–6(7)
The *Shen* (Numen)	NY IX, 7; X, 1–3(6)
*Inner Cultivation: Attaining *De*	NY X, 4–6
Inner Cultivation: Benefit to the Sage	
*Guided Breathing: The People Submit	NONE
*The Sage Is Selfless	NONE
Sage Regulates Names: World Is Ordered	NONE
Inner Cultivation: Concentrate Qi	
Concentrate Awareness/Unify Mind	NY XVII, 13–14
Inner Concentration/Numinous Insight	NY XVII, 3–6(14)
Numinous Insight and *Jing*	NY XVII, 7–12(14)
Inner Cultivation: The One: Benefits to the Ruler	
Unifying: *Jing* and Wisdom	NY VII, 1–2(9)
Benefits for Ruler	NONE
The Ruler Who Can Unify	NY VII, 5–6(9)
The Inner Cultivation of the Sage Ruler	
The Sage Regulates Things	NY VII, 7–8(9)
The Sage: Calm Mind, Calm State	NY XII, 10–13(22)
The Sage: Calm Mind, Ordered World	NY VIII, 1–4(7)
‡Way of the Sage: Helps People, Not Self	NONE
Way of the Sage: Spontaneous Response	NY VI, 7–8
Inner Cultivation: Personal and Political Benefits	
Tranquility/Mystical Experience	NY XIV, 1, 3–12(16)
Perfected Mind: Personal/Political Benefits	NY XVI, 1–13(19)
Loving and Hating the People	NONE
Loving/Hating: Rewards/Punishments	NY XVI, 14–15(19)
Inner Cultivation and Vitality	
Vitality/Emotions/Confucian Virtues	NY XX, 1–5, 7–8,10–11(12)
Benefits of Calmness	NONE
Vitality and Thought	NY XII, 14–19(22); VI, 18–19
*Vitality and Vital Breath	NY XIII, 3, 6–11
*Sage Reaches Heaven/Earth	NY XII, 4–6(22)

*Therefore (*shi gu* 是故).
†Thus it says (*gu yue* 故曰).
‡Thus (*gu* 故).

with the number of the unit of verse and specific lines (and total number of lines in the verse) from "Neiye."[49] For the full texts of "Xinshu xia" and its "Neiye" parallels, see the Appendix.

Table 3.1 shows the way in which "Neiye" is composed of distinct stanzas, some of which, such as I and II and III–V, seem to be clustered around a common theme. Others, such as III, VI, and VIII, simply begin new themes that have no apparent relationship to their predecessors. On the other hand, table 3.2 shows a more apparent logical relationship both within and between the sections of "Xinshu xia." The first four sections alternate between discussing the personally transformative effects of inner cultivation and the benefits of such transformations for the ruler. The next three sections blend these complementary concerns by focusing on the Way of the sage ruler.

A comparison of the two tables shows that stanzas of "Neiye" ranging from VI to XX have been borrowed, in all amounting to eleven of the twenty-two stanzas. This could indicate that the text of "Neiye" used by the "Xinshu xia" author was damaged, as suggested in Rickett's theory of the latter's origins. However, closer examination indicates that some of the topics of the "Neiye" stanzas omitted in "Xinshu xia" are included in "Xinshu shang." For example, "Neiye" III–V deals with the Way as an ineffable cosmic force, yet several passages in "Xinshu shang" discuss the same topic in similar terms: 13.1a10 and 2b5; 1b2 and 3a2; 1b6 and 3b1. Further, the important verse in "Neiye" on cleaning the abode of the numen in stanza XII, which is also not included in "Xinshu xia," is paralleled by the "Xinshu shang" passages at 13.1a11 and 2b8. This looks very much as if the author of "Xinshu xia" was not only aware of "Xinshu shang," but was intentionally avoiding redundancy in the text he was creating to complement it.

Furthermore, because "Neiye" is composed of formerly independent units of verse, it contains some thematic repetition that would need not to be repeated by the "Xinshu xia" author.

For example, "Neiye" XX, included in "Xinshu xia" and dealing with how vitality is built by the relinquishing of emotions, covers essentially the same themes as "Neiye" XVIII, XIX, and XXII, which are not in "Xinshu xia." So the omission of "Neiye" material is not necessarily due to a damaged version of "Neiye," as Rickett would have it. It is more likely to indicate editorial decisions made by the "Xinshu xia" author.

Guo Moruo has suggested that the different sequence of the "Neiye" material in "Xinshu xia" is due to the shuffling of bamboo strips in the latter. Rickett has suggested that "Xinshu xia" is based on a damaged copy of "Neiye" that was arranged differently, but does not accept Guo's shuffling theory to explain the different sequence of "Neiye"'s stanzas in "Xinshu xia." So if we examine this sequence more closely in table 3.2, we see the following: IX, X, XVII, VII, XII, VIII, VI, XIV, XVI, XX, XII, XIII, XII. It would be a very strange shuffle that would *naturally* result in such a sequence. On the other hand, if we accept the alternative explanation, that this rearrangement was the result of editorial activity by the "Xinshu xia" author, then we have no need to assume a damaged copy of "Neiye" in the first place. Even if we accept the accidental shuffling theory, how are we to explain the fact that different lines from the same "Neiye" stanza show up in non-contiguous sections of "Xinshu xia"[50] For example, "Neiye" VI is found at both "Xinshu xia" V.E (where lines 8 and 9 are borrowed) and VII.A (where lines 20 and 21 are borrowed), and "Neiye" XII is found at both "Xinshu xia" V.B (which borrows lines 10–13), VII.C (which borrows lines 14–20), and VII.E (which borrows lines 4–6).[51] The bamboo strips of "Neiye" would have had to have been not only shuffled, but also cut up into small segments like the tiles of a scrabble game to explain how they would have naturally fallen into the sequence in which they are now found in "Xinshu xia." Clearly, then, the omission of "Neiye" passages in "Xinshu xia" and the new sequence in which those included are found are not the result of a damaged or altered original, but the result of editorial activity. So if the "Neiye" version that formed the basis for "Xinshu xia" was not damaged, what of the theory that it was a markedly different edition?

Redaction Strategies and the Ideology of "Xinshu xia"

REDACTION STRATEGIES IN THE BORROWED MATERIAL

The theory that the "Xinshu xia" author used a different edition of "Neiye" than the one now found in the *Guanzi* is based as much on the rearrangement and omission of sections of the borrowed material as it is on another "Xinshu xia" feature: its versions of "Neiye" passages have a considerable number of variant readings when compared with the received text of "Neiye," and sometimes lines occur in a different order, even within the same verses of these two texts. To explain these differences, I have identified a number of what I call "redaction strategies" on the part of the "Xinshu xia" author.[52] They fall into two general categories based upon the two distinct types of material in "Xinshu xia": strategies in the borrowed material and strategies in the original material. As will be seen, many of the strategies are not mutually exclusive.

IDEOLOGICAL EMENDATIONS

An important principle of redaction criticism is to attempt to locate evidence of the arrangement and editing of earlier sources to conform to a new ideological position. While by no means does every variant between the two texts indicate ideological emendation, a significant number of them do. Here are some examples:[53]

- "Neiye": *wanwu* 萬物, "the myriad things"; "Xinshu xia": *Tianxia* 天下, "All-under-Heaven, the world": I.B.3. *Tianxia* is also used four times in the original material in "Xinshu xia": 11.B.4, 11.C.3,4, VI.C.2. This original material in "Xinshu xia": was, I contend, part of the redacting and reframing of lines and passages taken from "Neiye" done to suit a new viewpoint.

- "Neiye": *zhong de* 中得, "grasping it within your center"; "Xinshu xia": *nei de* 內德, "Inner Power": I.C.3.

- "Neiye": *jen* 人, "human beings"; "Xinshu xia": *min* 民, "the people": V.C.3, VII.A.l. *Min* is also used three times in the original material in "Xinshu xia": 11.A.5,V.D.l.V.D.4.

- "Neiye": *junzi* 君子, "exemplary person"; "Xinshu xia": *shengren* 聖人, "sage": V.A.1. *Sheng(ren)* is also used four times in the original material in "Xinshu xia": 11.B.l, 11.C.2, V.E.l, VILE.I.

- Neiye": *cong wu qian* 從物遷, "shifts according to things"; "Xinshu xia": *ying wu* 應物, "spontaneously responds to things": V.E.6. *Ying* also occurs once in the original material, at IV.B.2.

If taken individually, these emendations reveal little; they could have come from a variety of non-"Daoist" sources. If taken together, as I think they must be, these ideological emendations form a pattern: they are changes in the direction of the more "political" position that is characteristic of the late Warring States and early Han syncretic Daoism found in the "Syncretist" *Zhuangzi*, "Xinshu shang," and the other sources of this phase that I mentioned in the "Introduction." The concept of the "myriad things" refers to all phenomena in the world; "all-under-Heaven" refers only to the human polity and is a particular concern of this form of Daoism. The second emendation, to "Inner Power," conforms to what I think is an increasing sense of tradition that developed in this lineage after the writing of the *Laozi* during the latter half of the third century BCE. "Inner Power" is, of course, one of the central tenets of this text. I have identified the concept of "spontaneous response" (*ying*) as a critical technical term in this syncretic Daoism.[54] The exemplar of the sage is also one of its central focuses, as seen, for example, in the "Tianxia" 天下 chapter of *Zhuangzi*'s famous phrase, "inner sageliness, outer kingliness" (*nei sheng, wai wang* 內聖外王).[55]

RHETORICAL EMENDATION

Another type of emendation quite common in the borrowed material is changing the "Neiye" readings in order to suit the context of making an argument consistent in "Xinshu xia." There are five examples of this, including:

Table 3.3. Rhetorical Emendation in "Xinshu, xia"

"Xinshu xia" 心術下 13.5b9	"Neiye" 內業 16.3b1
VI.	XIV.
A.1 人能正靜者: If a man can be regular (in breathing) and be tranquil:	1. 人能正靜: If a man can be regular (in breathing) and be tranquil:
	2. 皮膚裕寬, His flesh will be relaxed,
	3. 耳目聰明, His ears and eyes will perceive clearly,
2. 筋<朋>「韌」而骨強。[56] His muscles will be elastic and his bones strong.	4. 筋信(伸)而骨強。 His muscles will be supple and his bones strong
3. 能戴大圜者, If he is able to hold up the Great Circle [of Heaven],	5. 乃能戴大圜 He will then be able to hold up the Great Circle [of Heaven]

continued on next page

4. 體乎大方。 He will embody the Great Square [of Earth].	6. 而履大方 And tread firmly over the Great Square [of Earth].
5. 鏡大清者, If he mirrors the Great Clarity,	7. 鑒於大清, He will reflect the Great Clarity
6. 視乎大明。 He will gaze into the Great Luminosity.	8. 視於大明 And will gaze into the Great Luminosity
7. 正靜不失, Be regular and tranquil and do not lose it,	9. 敬慎無忒 Reverently be aware and do not waver,
8. 日新其德, And you will daily renew your Inner Power,	10. 日新其德, And you will daily renew your Inner Power,
9. 昭知天下, Intuitively understand all-under-Heaven	11. 遍知天下 Thoroughly understand all-under-Heaven
10. 通於四極。 And penetrate the Four Directions.	12. 窮於四極 And exhaust the Four Directions.
	13. 敬發其充 To reverently bring forth what fills you:
	14. 是謂內得。 This is called "grasping it within."
	15. 然而不反 If you do this but fail to return,
	16. 此生之忒 This will cause a wavering of your vitality.

This table demonstrates a number of significant rhetorical emendations:

VI.A.1 and 7: The stated topic of this section in "Xinshu xia" is regularizing the circulation of the vital breath in the body and making the mind tranquil (*ren neng zheng jing zhe* 人能正靜者); this topic corresponds with the topic of the borrowed material from "Neiye" XIV. Both versions parallel each other rather well until we find a significant emendation: where "Neiye" reads "Reverently be aware without being excessive" (*jing shen wu* 敬慎無忒; line 9), "Xinshu xia" reads "be regular and tranquil and do not lose it" (*zheng jing bu shi* 正靜不失; line

7). This emendation restates the topic of the section. By doing this, the author eliminates the vagueness of "Neiye" (i.e., "reverently be aware" of what?) and affirms that the final three verses of this section refer to the practice of regularizing the breathing and making the mind tranquil.

Other examples of this type of emendation are found at IV.A.1 (in which the emendation from "Neiye" *shen* 神 to "Xinshu xia" Jing 精 continues the topic of III.C.5, and the emendation from "Neiye" *hua* 化 to "Xinshu xia" *bian* 變 conforms to the reading in the next line); VI.B.1 and 11 (which is exactly the same pattern as VI.A.1 and 7); VII.D.2 and 4; and VII.E.4. In addition, the textual variants at VI.A.9 and 10 in "Xinshu xia" (*zhaozhi tianxia, tongyu siji* 昭知天下, 通於四極) are identical to the "Xinshu xia" readings at I.B.3–4, and are likely, as well, to be emendations for rhetorical consistency.

TRANSPOSITION

The transposition of the borrowed material in "Xinshu xia" takes two basic forms. There are several instances of the transposition of lines of verse within a section of the borrowed material. A good example occurs in "Xinshu xia" III, which generally parallels "Neiye" XVII. In the former, the two lines that open the "Neiye" section are omitted ("By concentrating your vital breath as if numinous, the myriad things will all be contained within you."). In their place is an emended version of the last three lines in the "Neiye" section (lines XVII, 16–18), which have been transposed to the beginning of the "Xinshu" section in order to announce its new topic.

Table 3.4. Transposition in "Xinshu, xia"

"Xinshu xia" 心術下 13.5a2	"Neiye" 內業 16.4a2
III.	XVII.
A.l. 專於意, 一於心 Concentrate your awareness, unify your mind;	1. <博>「搏」氣如神, By concentrating your vital breath as if numinous,
2. 耳目端, 知遠之<證>「近」。 Then your ears and eyes will perceive acutely and you will know the far-off to be near.	2. 萬物備存。 The myriad things will all be contained within you.

continued on next page

B.1. 能專乎, 能一乎。 Can you concentrate? Can you unify?	3. 能專, 能一乎。 Can you concentrate? Can you unify?
2. 能毋卜筮 Can you not resort to divination	4. 能無卜筮 Can you not resort to divination
3. 而知凶吉乎。 Yet know bad and good fortune?	5. 而知<吉凶>「凶吉」乎。 Yet know bad and good fortune?
4. 能止乎, 能已乎。 Can you stop? Can you cease?	6. 能止乎, 能已乎。 Can you stop? Can you cease?
5. 能毋問於人 Can you not ask it from others,	7. 能勿求諸人 Can you not seek it in others,
6. 而自得之於己乎。 Yet grasp it within yourself	8. 而得之己乎。 Yet attain it within?
C.1. 故曰: Therefore it says:	
2. 思之思之不得, If you reflect and reflect on it and do not grasp it,	9. 思之思之又重思之, You reflect on it, reflect on it, and again reflect on it,
	10. 思之而不通; You reflect on it and still do not penetrate it;
3. 鬼神教之。 The daemonic and numinous will instruct you.	11. 鬼神將通之。 The daemonic and numinous will penetrate it.
4. 非鬼神之力也, This is not due to the power of the daemonic and numinous,	12. 非鬼神之力也。 This is not due to the power of the daemonic and numinous,
5. 「其」精氣之極也。 But rather to the utmost refinement of its vital breath.	13. 精氣之極也。 But rather to the utmost refinement of your essential vital breath.
	14. 四體既正, When the four limbs are squared,
	15. 血氣既靜, And the blood and vital breath are tranquil,
	16. 一意摶心。 Unify your awareness; concentrate your mind,

	17. 耳目不淫。 Then your ears and eyes will not be overstimulated.
	18. 雖遠若近。 Then even the far-off will seem to be near.

This example of transposition also includes several small, but significant rhetorical emendations. Note that the "Xinshu" variants in III.A.I are consistent with the order of argumentation in III.B.1 (that is, "concentrate . . . unify," not vice versa, as in "Neiye" XVII.16):

"Xinshu xia," 心術下 13.5a2	"Neiye" 內業 16.4a6
III	XVII
A.1. 專於意, 一於心 Concentrate your awareness, unify your mind;	14. 一意<搏>「摶」心。 Unify your awareness; concentrate your mind,
2. 耳目端, Then your ears and eyes will perceive acutely	15. 耳目不淫。 Then your ears and eyes will not be overstimulated.
3. 知遠之<證>「近」。 And you will know the far-off to be near.	16. 雖遠若近。 Then even the far-off will seem to be near.
B.1. 能專乎, 能一乎。 Can you concentrate? Can you unify?	

In addition, the variants "Neiye" 17 *bu yin* 不淫: "Xinshu xia" A.2 *duan* 端 and "Neiye" 18 *sui yuan ruojin* 雖遠若近: "Xinshu xia" A.3 *zhi yuan zhi jin* 知遠之<證>「近」。 appear to be rhetorical emendations by the "Xinshu xia" author to make his argument even stronger. To have acute perception seems a more desirable goal than simply to have perception that is not overstimulated. To "know that the far-off is near" seems a more precise statement of the noetic content that results from inner cultivation than "Neiye's" vaguer "even the far-off will seem to be near."

Even more common than the transposition of individual lines of verse between our two texts is the transposition of entire sections of "Neiye" to suit the different context of a new argument in "Xinshu xia." This can be seen in a general fashion in the two tables. A good example of this redaction strategy is found in "Xinshu xia" V (see Appendix), which constructs a consistent argument from the last three lines of "Neiye" VII, the last four lines of "Neiye" XII, the first four lines of "Neiye" VIII, and the last two lines of "Neiye" VI. Several other redaction strategies can be seen in "Xinshu xia" V. In the borrowed material from "Neiye," there is ideological emendation at V.A.1 ("Neiye" *junzi* 君子: "Xinshu xia" *shengren* 聖人) and semantic recontextualization at V.B. In the original material, there is expository commentary at V.D and framing at V.E. I discuss these last three strategies below.

SEMANTIC RECONTEXTUALIZATION

Semantic recontextualization refers to the change in meaning that occurs when the transposition of borrowed material from "Neiye" places it in a new context that is significantly different from its original context. It is one of the most common redaction strategies in "Xinshu xia" because there is such a great deal of transposition in it. A prime example of this is "Xinshu" V.B., which is borrowed from "Neiye" XII.

Table 3.5.1. Semantic Recontextualization in "Xinshu, xia" Part 1

"Xinshu xia" 心術下 13.5a12	"Neiye" 內業16.2b3
V	VII
A.1. 聖人裁物， The Sage regulates things,	7. 君子使物 The exemplary person directs things,
2. 不為物使。 He is not directed by them.	8. 不為物使。 He is not directed by them.
	9. 得一之理 He grasps the patternings of the One.
	XII. 16.3a2
	1. 道滿天下。 The Way fills all-under-Heaven.
	2. 普在民所 It is everywhere that people are
	3. 民不能知。 But people are unable to understand this.

	4. 一言之解； The explanation of this single word:
	5. 上察於天， It reaches up to Heaven above,
	6. 下極於地。 It stretches down to Earth below;
	7. 蟠滿九州。 It fills up the Nine Continents, encircling them.
	8. 何為解之？ What is this explanation of it?
	9. 在於心安。 It resides in the mind's being calm.
B.1. 心安是國安； When his mind is calm, the state is calm.	10. 我心治，官乃治。 When my mind is controlled, my senses are thereby controlled.
2. 心治是國治也。 When his mind is controlled, the state is controlled.	11. 我心安，官乃安。 When my mind is calm, my senses are thereby calmed.
3. 治也者，心也； What controls them is his mind.	12. 治之者心也。 What controls them is my mind,
4. 安也者，心也。 What calms them is his mind.	13. 安之者心也。。。 What calms them is my mind . . .

The transposition of an ideologically emended version of the last few lines from "Neiye" VII to this new position in which they introduce the topic of "Xinshu xia" V is part of the semantic recontextualization of "Neiye" XII, lines 10–13. Whereas in "Neiye," the context is purely one of individual cultivation, in "Xinshu" the context is the sage's cultivation and how it relates to the good order in his state. This recontextualization is further developed by the ideological emendation of "Neiye"'s *guan* 官 (senses) to "Xinshu"'s *guo* 國 (state). The cumulative effect of these emendations strikingly transforms the meaning of the borrowed material from "Neiye" and provides a succinct statement of the Syncretist position of the value of inner cultivation for rulership:

Table 3.5.2. Semantic Recontextualization in "Xinshu, xia" Part 2

"Xinshu xia" 心術下13.5a12	"Neiye" 內業16.3a4
V	XII
B.1. 心安是國安; When his mind is calm, the state is calm.	10. 我心治, 官乃治。 When my mind is controlled, my senses are thereby controlled.
2. 心治是國治也。 When his mind is controlled, the state is controlled.	11. 我心安, 官乃安。 When my mind is calm, my senses are thereby calmed.
3. 治也者, 心也; What controls them is his mind.	12. 治之者心也。 What controls them is my mind,
4. 安也者, 心也。 What calms them is his mind.	13. 安之者心也。。。 What calms them is my mind . . .

Other examples of semantic recontextualization are found at the following locations in "Xinshu xia": IV.A.1–2; V.E; VI.D; VII.E; and VII.C, which, because it is made up of two transposed passages from "Neiye," involves a double semantic recontextualization.

OMISSION

Examples of the deliberate omission of lines from the borrowed stanzas of "Neiye" abound in "Xinshu xia." See, for example, above, where V.A uses only two lines of the nine lines of "Neiye" VII, and V.B uses only four of the twenty-two lines of "Neiye" XII. Another example is VI.A (see Appendix), which uses ten of the sixteen lines of "Neiye" XIV, omitting only lines 2–3 and 13–16. Given the substantial evidence of deliberate editorial emendation of the borrowed material, we can no longer entertain the theory that such omissions are the result of a defective source-edition.

ADDITION

As mentioned in the section on the linguistic evidence for dating these "Xinshu" texts, "Xinshu xia" contains eighteen instances of the use of the nominalizing particle *zhe* 者, many of which are in the borrowed material. Examples are found at I.A.1,3; 11.A.3,4; and VI.A.1,3,5. Most of these additions of *zhe* are used to delineate nominal clauses and thereby show the "Xinshu xia" author's understanding of the grammatical and logical relationships in the relevant sentences. They are clearly additions because they do not occur in parallel passages in "Neiye."

Another example of addition is the insertion of the connective conjunctions *shi gu* (therefore) and *gu yue* (thus it says) between verses of the borrowed material to indicate conclusion and quotation, respectively. We also find *gu* 故 introducing a linking and explanatory passage of the original material at V.D. The locations of these conjunctions in "Xinshu xia" are shown in table 3.2 on page 121.

REDACTION STRATEGIES IN THE ORIGINAL MATERIAL

From our examination of the ideological emendations and the other redaction strategies in the borrowed material of "Xinshu xia," we are beginning to develop a picture of the ideology of its author, who seems to share some of the concerns and vocabulary of the authors of "Xinshu shang" and the Syncretist *Zhuangzi*. This general impression is strongly reinforced by the original prose material in "Xinshu xia," which constitutes roughly 35 percent of the entire text. This original material not only gives us a fuller understanding of the ideology of the author, but it also provides us with three new categories of redaction strategies: 1. linking; 2. expository commentary; and 3. framing. I give one example of each and also analyze its ideological content. These categories are not exclusive, and often one passage exhibits more than one strategy.

LINKING

Linking passages provide politically oriented connectives between both contiguous and non-contiguous parts of the borrowed material and between the borrowed and original material. I select an example of the latter because it leads into the next category, expository commentary.

The "Xinshu xia" opening passage I.A–C largely parallels "Neiye" passages IX and X and deals with the practice and personal benefits of inner cultivation. It discusses how regularizing the flow of the vital breath within body and mind leads to developing Inner Power and numinous insight into the most profound workings of the world, both human and non-human. It ends with the following passage, which is borrowed from "Neiye":

Table 3.6. Linking Passages in "Xinshu, xia"

"Xinshu xia" 心術下 13.4b8	"Neiye" 內業 16.2b9
I.G.1. 是故<曰> Therefore,	X
2. 無以物亂官 Do not disrupt your senses with external things,	4. 不以物亂官, To not disrupt your senses with external things,

continued on next page

3. 毋以官亂心。 Do not disrupt your mind with your	5. 不以官亂心。 To not disrupt your mind with your senses.
4. 此之謂內德。 This is called "Inner Power."	6. 是謂中得。 This is called "grasping it within your center."

This is followed by the second section of "Xinshu xia," which begins with a passage (II.A) that links this personal cultivation with the expository commentary in II.B and C:

"Xinshu xia" 13.4b9

II.A.1. 是故

Therefore,

2. 意氣定然后<反>「身」正。
When the awareness and vital breath are stable, only then will one's person become regular.

氣者, 身之充也。
The vital breath is what fills the body

行者, 正之義。
Its circulation is what "being regular" refers to.

5. 充不義則心不得。
When what fills the body does not circulate well, then the mind will not attain it (Inner Power).

6. 行不正則心不得。
When your circulation (of vital breath) is not regular, the people will not submit.

This linking passage brings out the political significance of the inner cultivation of the sage ruler: when he has developed the Inner Power spoken of in the opening section of "Xinshu xia," the people will simply submit to his rule. This theme is continued in the next two passages from this section that are presented immediately below. Other linking passages occur at V.D; VI.C; and VII.B.

EXPOSITORY COMMENTARY

The expository commentary elaborates the political implications of the apolitical material borrowed from "Neiye." It is particularly valuable as a source for the ideology of the "Xinshu xia" author. Perhaps the main focus of "Xinshu xia" is the sage ruler, who uses inner cultivation techniques to develop Inner Power, a well-ordered mind, numinous insight, and the ability to apprehend intuitively all things within heaven and earth, particularly those that pertain to effective governing. The practical applications of this profound transformation are frequently provided in the original material in "Xinshu xia." For example:

"Xinshu xia" 13/4b11

II.B.1. 是故, 聖人

Therefore, the Sage:

2. 若天然, 無私覆也。
Like heaven, he selflessly covers;

3. 若地燃, 無私戴也。
Like earth, he selflessly supports

4. 私者亂天下者也。
Selfishness: it is what makes all-under-heaven disordered.

The image of the sage covering and supporting his people as heaven and earth do for the myriad things is found in several pre-Han philosophical texts. It is one of the important images in Syncretic Daoist sources, including *Daoyuan* from the *Huang-Lao Boshu* 黃老帛書 (line 2) and the "Yuan Dao" chapter of *Huainanzi* (1.2b5). In Syncretic Daoism, this image symbolizes the important tenet of "nourishing the myriad things," which I have discussed elsewhere.[57] Selflessness is also advocated in "Xinshu shang" (13.1b8 and 3b8). The expository commentary from "Xinshu xia" continues:

"Xinshu xia" 13/4b12:

II.C.1. 凡物戴名而來

Whenever things come bearing names,

2. 聖人因而<財>「戴」之
The Sage adapts to them and regulates them

3. 而天下治。
And all-under-heaven is well-ordered.

實不傷, 「名」不亂於天下
When actualities are not damaged and names are not disordered in all-under-heaven,

5. 而天下治。
Then all-under-heaven is well-ordered.

The establishment and regulation of names and actualities are often taken to be the equivalent of the regulation of performance (*xing* 形) and title (*ming* 名) within a bureaucracy, and its development is attributed to the "Legalist" administrative philosopher Shen Buhai 申不害.[58] It is an important aspect of the sage ruler's political activity throughout the Jing *fa* of the *Huang-Lao Boshu*, in the Syncretist Zhuangzi, and in "Xinshu shang."[59]

FRAMING

Framing passages surround brief selections from "Neiye" and provide them with a new context. Section V.E. provides an excellent example.

Table 3.7. Framing in "Xinshu, xia"

"Xinshu xia" 心術下 13.5b7	"Neiye" 內業16.2a6
V.	VI.1. 天主正; For Heaven, the most important thing is to be regular.
E.1. 聖人之道: The Way of the Sage:	2. 地主平 For Earth, the most important thing is to be tranquil.
2. 若存若亡。 It is as if it exists and does not.	3. 人主<安>「靜」。 For man, the most important thing is to be tranquil.
3. 援而用之, Take hold of it and make use of it.	4. 春秋冬夏, 天之時也。 Spring, autumn, winter, and summer, are the seasons of Heaven.

4. 歿世不亡。 To the end of your days do not lose it.	5. 山陵川谷, 地之<枝>「材」。 Mountains, hills, rivers, and valleys, are the resources of Earth.
	6. 喜怒取予, 人之謀也。 Pleasure and anger, taking and giving, are the devices of man.
	7. 是故, 聖人: Therefore, the sage:
5. 與時變而不化; And you will alter with the seasons but not be transformed,	8. 與時變而不化, Alters with the seasons, but doesn't transform,
6. 應物而不移; Spontaneously responds to things but not be moved.	9. 從物「遷」而不移。 Shifts according to things, but doesn't change places.
7. 日用而不化。 Make use of it daily and you will not be transformed.	

The redaction strategy of framing here changes the context. In "Neiye," the first six lines present Heaven-Earth-Man parallels. The last three lines tack on a conclusion that seems to have, at best, a weak logical relationship to the preceding material. These latter lines discuss the sage's ability to respond to things in a general fashion. The context in "Xinshu xia" is the Way of the sage and refers to something much more specific, namely, the entire program for government by rulers made numinous by methods of inner cultivation that is the subject of both parts of "Xinshu." Notice that the tone of "Xinshu xia" V.E. is hortatory rather than simply expressive, as if a ruler were being encouraged to take up such a program. Notice, too, the ideological emendation in "Xinshu xia" V.E.6, which changes "Neiye"'s "shift according to things" 從物「遷」 to "spontaneously respond to things" *ying wu er bu yi* 應物而不移. As discussed previously, spontaneous response is one of the key benefits conferred upon the ruler who practices inner cultivation, according to Syncretic Daoist ideology. It is also found in a "Xinshu xia" linking passage at IV.B.2.

Other commentarial, linking, and framing passages in "Xinshu xia" provide further information about the author's political ideology: IV.B: the wisdom of prioritizing endeavors and the inner cultivation that develops spontaneous responsiveness; V.D, which recommends nonpunitive restrictions and criticizes profit-taking officials; and VI.C, which discusses how a good circulation of vital breath in the ruler can cause love between him and his subjects. All fit well with the ideology of Syncretist Daoism I have discussed elsewhere.[60]

Therefore, the ideological emendations in the borrowed material in "Xinshu xia" and the ideology found in the original material place its author squarely in the tradition of late Warring States and early Han Syncretic Daoism and make it a companion text to "Xinshu shang." In addition, the ideological emendations in the borrowed material found in "Xinshu xia" indicate that the edition from which it borrowed its "Neiye" material was significantly closer in its readings to our extant "Neiye" than was previously thought. However, because not all of the textual variants can be explained as ideological emendations, the possibility that a different edition of "Neiye" was used cannot be entirely ruled out. But it most certainly was not a totally distinct version missing its beginning and ending sections.

Implications

The evidence I have presented on the structure and redaction strategies of "Xinshu xia" shows that it was a carefully constructed essay on the political benefits of inner cultivation that deliberately restructured and emended its borrowed material from "Neiye." It also demonstrates, along with the linguistic analysis, that Neiye" was the earlier of the two essays. This has a number of implications for our understanding of the early history of Daoism, especially when combined with the form-critical work on the *Laozi* done by Mair and LaFargue.

The deliberate use of this foundational text of inner cultivation in the context of the Syncretic Daoist program for sage rulership seems to support the theory that what came to be called "Daoism" in the former Han dynasty began as an apolitical self-cultivation movement and only later developed a political dimension. "Xinshu xia" itself provides one piece of concrete evidence of such a project being deliberately undertaken. When considered together with the textual evidence of the influence of "Neiye" and the two "Xinshu" essays on the *Huainanzi* that I analyzed in "Psychology and Self-Cultivation in Early Daoistic Thought," (chapter X in this collection), it would lend considerable support to the theory that the Syncretist Daoism of the late third and early second centuries BCE was a direct descendant of the earlier Individualist Daoism.

Furthermore, the very fact that "Neiye," a fourth-century BCE text, was edited and recontextualized in so dramatic a fashion, perhaps a century and a half after it was first written down, suggests not only that its brand of Individualist Daoism might be a direct ancestor of Syncretic Daoism, but also that there might have been a significant continuity in Daoist inner cultivation practices between these two aspects. This could suggest that both are not simply aspects, but actually "phases" of a continuous tradition. It could even imply lineal descent through a series of masters and disciples.

Of course this is not an inevitable conclusion from the results of this redaction criticism. One could argue that the activities of the "Xinshu xia" author only bear witness to events that occurred at the time of its composition. In such a reading, this author could have simply adapted the text of "Neiye" to his own ideological agenda without feeling part of the same tradition or being in any way related by lineage to the people who wrote it. This is certainly possible, but there are several factors that would seem to argue against it.

First, "Neiye" is not just a text of inner cultivation; it is a text of *Daoist* inner cultivation. The "Xinshu xia" author did not choose to adapt any of the physical cultivation manuals that Harper, for one, presumes to have existed in the late Warring States period; he adapted one with a cosmology that he shared.[61] This would seem to indicate that he did not select "Neiye" at random, but was able to identify its common cosmology as an important ancestor, if not an integral part, of his own tradition.

However, being part of the same tradition does not necessarily equate with being part of the same lineage of practitioners. The support for this latter hypothesis must be more specific than the surviving evidence can bear. What I offer is only conjectural argumentation along the following lines derived, in part, from the form and redaction criticism of the *Laozi* and the brilliant, but unpublished, research of David Keegan on the *Huangdi nei jing* 黃帝內經 and its relationship to early Han medical lineages.[62]

I have already argued that the "Neiye" was produced by a lineage that specialized in the practice and theory of techniques of inner cultivation used to attain profound experiences of self-transformation. This suggests that Daoist inner cultivation is, indeed, a technical art like that of the physician, to be gained only after many years of practice, the learning of which requires participation in such a lineage. In a fascinating picture of medical apprenticeship in the early Han, Keegan describes how one physician, Cang Gong 倉公 (fl. ca. 200–150 BCE), came to study under a famous physician and how he received from him, in a formal ceremony, copies of the texts his teacher felt were critical to his practice of medicine.[63] For the next three years, Cang learned the correct interpretation of these texts and their practical application from his teacher. These texts were clearly not, Keegan concludes, "for general distribution or for self-help."[64]

I would like to suggest the possibility that "Neiye" was a similar kind of text, one whose possession was only for an initiate into Daoist inner cultivation practices. Given the extreme degree of editorial liberties he took with this text, the "Xinshu xia" author seems to have been extremely familiar with it and to have felt that he thoroughly understood it. This familiarity bespeaks a practical, not just an intellectual, understanding. Also, the hortatory nature of the text suggests such a practical understanding. If the author is, indeed, attempting to persuade rulers of the value of this new application of inner cultivation techniques to governing, he must have been certain that he could teach them if the ruler decided to learn them from him. All of these factors argue, at the very least, for membership in a common tradition, if not for a lineal connection between the Individualist author of "Neiye" and the Syncretist author of "Xinshu xia."

Whether or not we accept this membership in one tradition, there can be little doubt that the Daoist inner cultivation techniques of "Neiye" were directly incorporated into the early Han syncretic Daoism that Sima Tan described. These conclusions therefore question the assumption that the *Laozi* was really the foundational text of Daoism, although it seems to have been accorded that status after the deliberate lineage-building activities of the early Han mentioned above. Because it combines a Primitivist political agenda with its well-known cosmology of the Way and inner cultivation practices quite similar to those of "Neiye," and because of this new evidence for the chronological priority of pure inner cultivation practices, it would seem that the *Laozi* is a later development. While of course the *Laozi* was extremely influential on Han Daoist Syncretism, as its frequent quotations in the *Huainanzi* certainly attest, it is clear that "Neiye" was an older and, arguably, an equally important influence. It is also clear that inner cultivation theory did not come into Daoist Syncretism from the *Laozi*, but directly from "Neiye" instead. What we have then in "Neiye" is not just the oldest "mystical text in China," as Graham would have it,[65] but quite possibly the oldest extant text of Daoism.

Of course further work on this hypothesis will have to be done, work that would provide a detailed redaction criticism of the "Neiye" itself. In addition, it will be necessary to examine more carefully what I referred to as the "deliberate lineage-building" activities of the early Han Syncretic Daoists and to see how they might be linked to the evidence provided by the Han histories. The overall effect will, I hope, be a clarification of the early history of Daoism that would better enable us to see its links to the institutionalized Daoist religion of the later Han and beyond. Most assuredly such research will benefit considerably from the kind of text-critical methodologies I have presented herein, which I offer in the hope that others will also see their value.

Appendix: The Text of "Xinshu xia" with "Neiye" Parallels

The following critical texts of "Xinshu xia" and "Neiye" are based upon the *Sibu congkan* edition of the *Guanzi*, the location in which is provided at the beginning of each verse of the text. I have also made emendations occasionally based upon Riegel, "The Four 'Tzu Ssu' Chapters of the *Li Chi*," 151–79, and upon my own research, principally based upon Xu Weiyu 許維遹, Wen Yiduo 聞一多, and Guo Moruo, *Guanzi jijiao*. I list only the emendations from this work that I accept and their rationales. I do not list the emendations from this work that I do not accept, many of which use variants in one of these texts to emend the other. I have been very conservative about emending the texts for such reasons because each is an independent text, not simply a unique edition of the same text, and emending one based upon the other only conflates the two and obscures the distinctive characteristics of each.

The base-edition or lemma for *Guanzi jijiao* is the *Sibu congkan* edition. The authors also collated it with the four other oldest extant editions, those of Liu Ji 劉績 (ca. 1500), Zhu Dongguang 朱東光 (1579), Zhao Yongxian 趙用賢 (1582), and an "old edition" in the personal collection of Guo Moruo. For further information on these editions, see Rickett, *Guanzi: Political, Economic, and Philosophical Essays from Early*

China, 31–40. In addition, Guo Moruo et al. include the emendations of many nineteenth- and twentieth-century textual critics whose names I include whenever I cite their emendation.

The following symbols are used in the critical texts:

<A> delete character A
「B」 insert character B
A (B) read character A as B

I have divided the two texts into sections based upon considerations of meaning, rhyme, and meter. Whenever a particular topic or line of reasoning is completed and a new one begins, I have started a new section, one that does not violate the rhyme scheme when the text in question is in verse. Connective conjunctions such as *shi gu*, *gu*, and *gu yue* often signal such a change of topic and hence the beginning of a new section or subsection. I have further divided the texts into numbered lines, each representing a minimum syntactic unit of a complete sentence or a complete clause within a sentence containing, at least, a subject and a verb. In addition, I have also given connective conjunctions their own separate lines, in part to emphasize their occurrence because of their significance for understanding the structure of argumentation in the texts and in part to maintain the parallelisms that are so frequent in both texts.

As indicated above, "Neiye" is written in parallel rhymed verse, with the rhymes occurring most often at the end of every second four-character line. The sections of "Xinshu xia" that are borrowed from "Neiye" often retain the rhyme, even when there are variant readings between the two. Most of the original material in "Xinshu xia" is in parallel prose, and the way I have chosen to present it should enable the reader to see the parallelisms.

"Xinshu xia"	"Neiye"
I. 13.4b5	IX. 16.2b6
A.1. 形不正者	1. 形不正
2. 德不來。	2. 德不來。
3. 中不精者	3. 中不靜
4. 心不治。	4. 心不治。
5. 正形飾德	5. 正形攝德
6. 萬物畢得。	6. <天仁地義則>[66]
	7. 淫然而自<至>「來」。[67]

B1. 翼然而自來,
  2. 神莫知其極。
  3. 昭知天下,
  4. 通於四極。

C.1. 是故〈曰〉[69]
  2. 無以物亂官
  3. 毋以官亂心。
  4. 此之謂内德。

X. 16.2b8

  1. 神明之極
  2. 照乎知萬物。
  3. 中義守不忒。[68]

  4. 不以物亂官,
  5. 不以官亂心。
  6. 是謂中得。

II. 13.4b9

A.1. 是故
  2. 意氣定然後后〈反〉「身」正。[70]
  3. 氣者, 身之充也。
  4. 行者, 正之義也。
  5. 充不美, 則心不得。
  6. 行不正, 則民不服。

B.1. 是故, 聖人
  2. 若天然, 無私覆也。
  3. 若地然, 無私載也。
  4. 私者, 亂天下者也。

C.1. 凡物載名而來
  2. 聖人因而〈財〉「裁」之[71]
  3. 而天下治。
  4. 實不傷「名」不亂於天下[72]
  5. 而天下治

III. 13.5a2

A.1. 專於意, 一於心
  2. 耳目端,
  3. 知遠之〈證〉「近」。[73]

B.1. 能專乎, 能一乎。
  2. 能毋卜筮
  3. 而知凶吉乎?
  4. 能止乎, 能已乎。
  5. 能毋問於人
  6. 而自得之於己乎。

C.1. 故曰
  2. 思之, 思之不得,
  3. 鬼神教之。

XVII. 16.4a2

  1. 〈摶〉「摶」氣如神,[74]
  2. 萬物備存。

  3. 能摶, 能一乎。
  4. 能無卜筮
  5. 而知〈吉凶〉「凶吉」乎。[75]
  6. 能止乎, 能已乎。
  7. 能勿求諸人
  8. 而得之己乎。

  9. 思之思之又重思之。
  10. 思之而不通,
  11. 鬼神將通之,

4. 非鬼神之力也,　　　　　　　12. 非鬼神之力也。
5. 其精氣之極也。　　　　　　　13. 精氣之極也。
　　　　　　　　　　　　　　　14. 一意〈搏〉「摶」心。
　　　　　　　　　　　　　　　15. 耳目不淫。
　　　　　　　　　　　　　　　16. 雖遠若近。

IV. 13.5a7	VII. 16.2b1

A.1. 一氣能變曰精。　　　　　　　1. 一物能化, 謂之神。
　2. 一事能變曰智。　　　　　　　2. 一事能變, 謂之智。
　　　　　　　　　　　　　　　3. 化不易氣, 變不易智;
　　　　　　　　　　　　　　　4. 唯執一之君子能為此乎。

B.1.〈慕〉「募」選者, 所以等事。
　2. 極變者, 所以應物也。
　3.〈慕〉「募」選而不亂。[76]
　4. 極變而不煩。

C.1. 執一之君子,　　　　　　　　5. 執一不失,
　2. 執一而不失;　　　　　　　　6. 能君萬物。
　3. 能君萬物。
　4. 日月之與同光,
　5. 天地之與同理。

V. 13.5a12	VII. 16.2b3

A.1 聖人裁物,　　　　　　　　　7. 君子使物,
　2. 不為物使　　　　　　　　　8. 不為物使
　　　　　　　　　　　　　　　9. 得一之理。

B.1 心安是國安;　　　　　　　XII. 16.3a2
　2. 心治是國治也。　　　　　　　1. 道滿天下。
　3. 治也者, 心也。　　　　　　　2. 普在民所,
　4. 安也者, 心也。　　　　　　　3. 民不能知。
　　　　　　　　　　　　　　　4. 一言之解;
　　　　　　　　　　　　　　　5. 上察於天,
　　　　　　　　　　　　　　　6. 下極於地。
　　　　　　　　　　　　　　　7. 蟠滿九州。
　　　　　　　　　　　　　　　8. 何謂解之?
　　　　　　　　　　　　　　　9. 在於心安。
　　　　　　　　　　　　　　　10. 我心治, 官乃治。
　　　　　　　　　　　　　　　11. 我心安, 官乃安。
　　　　　　　　　　　　　　　12. 治之者心也。
　　　　　　　　　　　　　　　13. 安之者心也。。。

VIII. 16.2b4

C.1. 治心在中:	1. 治心在於中;
2. 治言出於口,	2. 治言出於口,
3. 治事加於民。	3. 治事加於人,
	4. 然則天下治矣。
	5. 一言得而天下服;
	6. 一言定而天下聽。
	7. ⟨公⟩「此」之謂也。 [77]

D.1. 故功作而民從,
  2. 則百姓治矣。
  3. 所以操者, 非刑也。
  4. 所以危者非怒也。
  5. 民人操, 百姓治,
  6. 道其本治也。
  7. 至⟨不⟩「丕」至無;[78]
  8. 非⟨所人⟩「人」而(能)亂「司。」[79]
  9. 凡在有司執制者之利非道也。

V. 13.5b7   VI. 16.2a6

E.1. 聖人之道:	1. 天主正;
2. 若存若亡。	2. 地主平;
3. 援而用之,	3. 人主⟨安⟩靜。[80]
4. 歿世不亡。	4. 春秋冬夏, 天之時也。
5. 與時變而不化;	5. 山陵川谷, 地之⟨枝⟩「材」。[81]
6. 應物而不移;	6. 喜怒取予, 人之謀也。
7. 日用之而不化。	7. 是故, 聖人:
	8. 與時變而不化,
	9. 從物「遷」而不移。[82]

VI. 13.5b9   XIV. 16.3b1

A.1. 人能正靜者:	1. 人能正靜:
2. 筋肕⟨朋⟩「韌」而骨強。[83]	2. 皮膚裕寬,
3. 能戴大圓者, 體乎大方。	3. 耳目聰明,
4. 鏡大清者,	4. 筋信(伸)而骨強。[84]
5. 視乎大明。	5. 乃能戴大圓
6. 正靜不失,	6. 而履大方,
7. 日新其德。	7. 鑒於大清,
8. 昭知天下,	8. 視於大明。
9. 通於四極。	9. 敬慎無忒;
	10. 日新其德。

11. 遍知天下,
12. 窮於四極。
13. 敬發其充,
14. 是謂內得。
15. 然而不反;
16. 此生之忒。

XV. 16.3b6

1. 凡道:
2. 必寬必舒,
3. 必堅必固。
4. 守善勿舍,
5. 逐淫澤薄。
6. 既知其極,
7. 反於道德。

VI. 13.5b12	XVI. 16.3b8

B.1 〈金〉「全」心在中, [85]　　　　1. 全心在中,
2. 不可匿。　　　　　　　　　　　2. 不可蔽匿。
3. 外見於形容,　　　　　　　　　3. 〈和〉「知」於形容, [86]
4. 可知於顏色。　　　　　　　　　4. 見於膚色。
5. 善氣迎人,　　　　　　　　　　5. 善氣迎人,
6. 親如弟兄。　　　　　　　　　　6. 親於弟兄。
7. 惡氣迎人,　　　　　　　　　　7. 惡氣迎人,
8. 害於戈兵。　　　　　　　　　　8. 害於戎兵。
9. 不言之言,　　　　　　　　　　9. 不言之聲,
10. 聞於雷鼓。　　　　　　　　　10. 疾於雷鼓。
11. 〈金〉「全」心之形:　　　　　11. 心氣之形,
12. 明於日月,　　　　　　　　　12. 明於日月,
13. 察於父母。　　　　　　　　　13. 察於父母。

C.1. 昔者, 明王之愛天下。
2. 故天下可附。
3. 暴王之惡天下。
4. 故天下可離。

D.1. 〈貨〉「賞」之不足以為愛, [87]　　14. 賞不足勸善。
2. 刑之不足以為惡。　　　　　　　15. 刑不足懲〈過〉「惡」。[88]
3. 〈貨〉「賞」者, 愛之末也。
4. 刑者惡之末。

　　　　　　　　　　　　　　　　16. 氣意 得
　　　　　　　　　　　　　　　　17. 而天下服。
　　　　　　　　　　　　　　　　18. 心意定
　　　　　　　　　　　　　　　　19. 而天下聽。

VII. 13.6a6	XX. 16.3b5
A.1. 凡民之生也,	1. 凡人之生也,
2. 必以正〈乎〉「平」。[89]	2. 必以平正。
3. 所以失之	3. 所以失之
4. 以喜樂哀怒。	4. 必以喜怒憂〈患〉「樂」。[90]
5. 節怒莫若樂;	5. 是故
6. 節樂莫若禮;	6. 止怒莫若詩;
7. 守禮莫若敬。	7. 去憂莫若樂;
	8. 節樂莫若禮;
8. 外敬而內靜者,	9. 守禮莫若敬;
9. 必反其性。	10. 守敬莫若靜。
	11. 內靜外敬,
	12. 能反其性。
	13. 性將大定。

	XII. 16.3a5
B.1. 豈無利事哉?	
2. 我無利心。	
3. 豈無安處哉。	
4. 我無安心。	
C.1. 心之中又有心。	14. 心之中又有心〈馬〉「焉」。[91]
	15. 彼心之心,
2. 意以先言。	16. 〈音〉「意」以先〈言〉「音」。[92]
3. 意然後刑(形);	17. 音然后形,
4. 刑(形)然後思;	18. 形然后〈言〉「名」;[93]
5. 思然後知。	19. 〈言〉「名」然后使(事)。
	20. 使(事)然后治。
	21. 不治必亂;
	22. 亂乃死。

	VI. 16.2a11
	15. 精也者, 氣之精也。
	16. 氣道乃生,
	17. 生乃思,
	18. 思乃知,
	19. 知乃止矣。
6. 凡心之刑(形),	20. 凡心之形
7. 過知失〈王〉「生」。[94]	21. 過知失生。

VII. 13.6b1	XIII. 16.3a8
D.	1. 精存自生,
1. 是故	2. 其外安榮,
2. 內聚以為原。	3. 內藏以為泉原。
	4. 浩然和平,
	5. 以為氣淵。
3. 泉之不竭,	6. 淵之不涸,
4. 表裡遂通。	7. 四體乃固。
5. 泉之不涸,	8. 泉之不竭,
6. 四支堅固。	9. 九竅遂〈通〉「達」。 [96]
7. 能令用之,	10. 乃能窮天地,
8. 被〈服〉「及」四〈固〉「圉」。 [95]	11. 被四海。。。

	XII. 16. 3a2
E.1. 是故聖人:	1. 道滿天下。
2. 一言解之:	2. 普在民所,
3. 上察於天,	3. 民不能知。
4. 下察於地。	4. 一言之解;
	5. 上察於天,
	6. 下極於地。
	7. 蟠滿九州。
	8. 何謂解之?
	9. 在於心安。。。

Chapter 4

Evidence for Stages of
Meditation in Early Daoism

Introduction

The role of some form of breathing meditation in most of the world's great mystical traditions has long been known, but few have seen much evidence for this in early Daoism. By "early Daoism," I mean the formative stages of the tradition, from its mysterious origins to the completion of the *Huainanzi* 淮南子 (139 BCE). Perhaps scholars have seen so little evidence of meditative practice in early Daoism because they have tended to focus almost exclusively on its famous foundational works, *Laozi* 老子 and *Zhuangzi* 莊子, and have, furthermore, tended to treat them as works of abstract philosophy. In my research, I have been particularly interested in the experiential basis of the philosophy found in the *Laozi* and the *Zhuangzi* and in a variety of other related texts that have hitherto been generally overlooked as sources for early Daoism. In order to clarify the context for the present investigation of meditative stages, I would like to present briefly the most relevant hypotheses from this research:[1]

1. There is no original school of Daoism called "Lao-Zhuang." Such a pairing is probably a third-century AD literati creation. Indeed, the textual origins of Daoism are not even to be found exclusively in these two texts.

2. In the formative period of Daoism we can identify, from extant textual sources, three "aspects" or, perhaps, "phases."

The first, or "Individualist," aspect is essentially apolitical and is concerned exclusively with individual transformation in the context of a cosmology of the Dao. It is represented by the *Guanzi* 管子 essay titled "Neiye" 內業 (Inward Training) and the seven "inner chapters" of *Zhuangzi*. The second, or "Primitivist," aspect adds a political dimension to the first, one that advocates the return to a more simple and basic form of social organization found in the agrarian utopias of the legendary past. It is represented by the *Laozi* and chapters 8–11 and 16 of the *Zhuangzi*. The third and final aspect, the "Syncretist," shares the cosmology and self-transformation theory of the former two, but advocates, instead, the establishment of a more complex, hierarchically organized central government that accords with the models provided by the patterns of Heaven and Earth. It is represented by all of the following texts:

From the Mawangdui *Huang-Lao boshu* 黃老帛書 (*Silk Manuscripts of Huang Lao*):
    "Jing fa" 經法 (Normative Standards)
    "Shiliu Jing" 十六經 (Sixteen Canons)
    "Dao Yuan" 道原 (The Source that is the Way)
From the *Guanzi*:
    "Xinshu, shang," and "Xinshu, xia" 心術上, 下 (Techniques of the Mind, I and II)
From the *Zhuangzi*: parts of the following chapters:
    12. "Tian di" 天地 (Heaven and Earth)
    13. "Tian Dao" 天道 (The Way of Heaven)
    14. "Tian yun" 天運 (The Circuits of Heaven)
From the *Zhuangzi*: all of the following chapters:
    15. "Keyi" 刻意 (Ingrained Opinions)
    33. "Tianxia" 天下 (Below in the Empire)
The *Huainanzi*.
    By the Han dynasty, this Syncretist aspect was called "Huang-Lao," 黃老 and formed the first true "school" of Daoism. The only chronology I have suggested is that the first aspect is likely to have been the earliest.

3. All three of these aspects share two very important characteristics. First, they contain a common vocabulary

and concern for a method of practice I have called "inner cultivation." This essentially apophatic practice involves the progressive emptying out of the usual contents of consciousness—thoughts, feelings, desires—through an inner contemplative process that is based on a form of guided and regularized breathing. This practice produces states of deep tranquility with a profound noetic content, states that have a powerful transformative quality. It also yields the practical gains of mental acuity and dispassionate objectivity that would have been attractive goals to rulers as well as adepts. Second, these texts all contain the characteristic cosmology of Dao and De 德 that we have come to identify as essential to whatever we define as Daoism. Indeed, I would argue that it is precisely the practice of inner cultivation, carried to its ultimate conclusion, that produces the profound noetic experiences from which this characteristic cosmology derives.

4. Daoism in this formative period was not a philosophical school but rather consisted of one or more related master-disciple lineages that centered on the practice of inner cultivation. This practice formed the distinctive "technique" (shu 術) around which these lineages formed and from which they eventually took their self-identity.[2] Indeed, this central focus on technique rather than philosophy may very well be true not just for the Daoists but for all the other pre-Qin schools, as Professor Fukui Fumimasa has recently observed.[3] The philosophical texts produced by these Daoist lineages were based in this practice, and the cosmology and self-transformation theories they contain were derived directly from it. Thus, although there is little, if any, concrete information about the social structure of these lineages that has hitherto been derived from extant sources, one might speculate that they may have more closely resembled small communities of religious practitioners than philosophical schools in the early Greek model.

I should like to begin this investigation with the following question. If it is indeed true that early Daoism is grounded in a practice of guided breathing meditation, then we should expect that its textual sources also contained evidence of stages of meditation, such as we find in many of the other great meditative traditions, from Eastern Orthodox Christianity to Samkhya Yoga and the Indian and Tibetan traditions of Buddhism. These traditions all contain very detailed descriptions of stages of increasing profundity leading to whatever they conceived of as the ultimate level of mystical experience or gnosis. Furthermore, recent neurophysiological studies in the West have attempted to identify and compare these stages of meditation and tie them to specific levels of psychological experience.[4] The question is: can we find any evidence of comparable stages in early Daoist meditation?

If we were to limit ourselves to only those texts that have hitherto been presumed to be the sole extant sources of early Daoism, the *Laozi* and the *Zhuangzi* (especially the "Inner Chapters"), while there is some concrete evidence for meditative practice in them, there is virtually no evidence for meditative stages.[5] The only exception to this is the wonderful narrative of how the Self-reliant Woman (*Nüyu* 女偊) trained the talented Bu-liang Yi 卜梁倚.[6] Although this passage shows stages that ultimately end in the foundational introvertive mystical experience of union with the Dao, the connection to guided breathing practice can only be inferred.

However, if we look beyond the *Laozi* and the "Inner Chapters" of *Zhuangzi* to other texts, it is possible to find some important testimony that is relevant to our question. In a search through relevant early Daoist sources, I have located seven passages that provide clearer evidence for the existence of stages of meditation in texts that span the entire formative period of early Daoism. These passages demonstrate a consistency in technical terminology and rhetorical structure that is both striking and suggestive. I now proceed to present and analyze these passages.

A Common Rhetorical Structure in Early Daoist Passages on Meditative Stages

What first called my attention to some of these passages was a similar method of reasoning in them. As I analyzed them further, I noticed that they exhibited a common rhetorical structure. It can be divided into three component parts.

1. A preamble in which the practices that prepare the adept for the later stages are discussed. These practices are apophatic: they all involve a removal of the usual contents of consciousness: perception, thought, desires, and feelings. This is common to all systems of meditation practice in religious traditions throughout the world.

2. A sorites-style argument in which the stages of meditation are presented in a consecutive fashion. A sorites argument is one that presents a series of propositions in which the predicate of each is the subject of the next. Thus it follows the form "A then B, B then C, C then D . . ."[7]

3. A denouement that discusses the noetic and practical benefits of having attained these stages.

Of the seven passages to be examined in this chapter, only one does not contain the first part and one does not contain the third part of this rhetorical structure.

Passage 1: *Xing qi yu pei ming* 行氣玉佩銘 (The twelve-sided jade knob inscription)

This inscription was found on a twelve-sided jade knob that may have served as the knob of a staff, or as a kind of pendant. Guo Moruo 郭沫若 finds it similar to the style of characters in an inscription from the state of Han that was found in a village near Luoyang and dated to approximately 380 BCE.[8] However, Joseph Needham finds that its rhetorical structure and technical terminology are very close to the earliest inscription on the Five Phase theory found on a jade sword hilt from the state of Qi 齊 that is dated to about 400 BCE.[9] He further suggests that the jade knob might be even earlier. In any case, both agree that this is the earliest extant evidence for the practice of guided breathing in China.

The inscription[10]

行氣: 深則蓄; 蓄則伸; 伸則下; 下則定; 定則固; 固則萌; 萌則長; 長則退; 退則天。天機舂在上; 地機舂在下。 順則生; 逆則死。

To circulate the Vital Breath:
Breathe deeply, then it will collect.

When it is collected, it will expand.
When it expands, it will descend.
When it descends, it will become stable.
When it is stable, it will be regular.
When it is regular, it will sprout.
When it sprouts, it will grow.
When it grows, it will recede.
When it recedes, it will become heavenly.
The dynamism of Heaven is revealed in the ascending;
The dynamism of Earth is revealed in the descending.
Follow this and you will live; oppose it and you will die.

The inscription follows the rhetorical structure of a sorites argument and a denouement. It assumes development from a stage of mental agitation to one of regular and patterned breathing. This is accomplished by first taking a deep breath and then intentionally cycling through a series of exhalation and inhalation sequences until the breathing becomes stable and regular. To do so enables one to reach an inherent, natural pattern of breathing in which one need not exert the will any further. Experiencing this, one then directly apprehends the dynamisms of Heaven and Earth (*Tian ji* 天機, *di ji* 地機) through the ascending and descending of the breath.

That an inherent, natural pattern of breathing is reached by this practice is implied by the use of the character *Tian* 天 (heaven, nature) as the last predicate in the sorites. It is further implied in the sentence that concludes the denouement on the benefits of this practice. The use of the contrasting verbs *shun* 順 (to follow, accord with) and *ni* 逆 (to oppose, resist) implies an object that is either followed or opposed. In the later *Huang-Lao boshu*, these contrasting verbs are extremely important technical terms, and their explicit object is the *li* 理, the various fundamental patterns or natural guidelines that pervade human beings and the cosmos that the sage must clearly penetrate, and in parallel to which he must set up the institutions of his government.[11] These contrasting terms are also found in the Yin-Yang 陰陽 texts from Yinqueshan 銀雀 山, where their use is virtually the same as in the *Huang-Lao boshu*.[12] Indeed, it is likely that these Yin-Yang texts, or others like them, were the basis for the preoccupation with the cosmological justification of human rule in the Huang-Lao works from Mawangdui.[13] Passage 2 below is from these Mawangdui Huang-Lao texts, and it demonstrates this specific usage of *ni* and *shun* with *li* as their stated object. While the jade knob inscription is rather early for an explicit discussion of the concept of *li*, the use of these contrasting verbs suggests an implicit understanding that the breathing practice brings one into compliance with, and reveals, an underlying pattern.

The term "dynamism of Heaven" is also found in the context of breath meditation in a passage in *Zhuangzi* 6, "Da zong shi" 大宗師.[14]

古之真人:
其寢不夢
其覺不憂
其食不甘
其息深深。
真人之息以踵; 眾人之息以喉。屈服者: 其嗌言若哇。其耆欲
　　深者,
其天機淺。

The Genuine of Antiquity:
Their sleep was without dreams,
Their waking was without cares,
Their eating was without sweetness,
Their breathing was deeply deep.
The breathing of the Genuine is from their heels. The breathing of the multitude is from their throats. The submissive talk in gulps as though retching. In those whose desires are deep, the dynamism of Heaven is shallow.

The exact meaning of "the dynamism of Heaven" (*Tian ji*) is unclear. The *Zhuangzi* sees it as the opposite of being filled with desires, and so it appears to represent an achievement in apophatic cultivation. It is also associated with the profound breathing of the Genuine, the adepts who cultivate themselves according to Daoist practices. If we gloss this passage with our jade knob inscription, the dynamism of Heaven could refer to a particularly deep pattern of breathing associated with inhalation, where the diaphragm feels as if it is ascending. The meaning of this term is difficult to pin down; it appears to be the kind of cryptic metaphor that Donald Harper finds in the breath cultivation literature from Mawangdui and that occurs in later Daoist religious literature.[15] Such metaphors would have been well understood by the community of practitioners who engaged in these techniques, but without further information about such a community and its beliefs, all we can do is make an educated guess at its meaning. In any case, the use of this term in the context of breath cultivation in *Zhuangzi* is indicative of a possible connection between this text and our jade knob inscription.

Before leaving this inscription, it is important to note that, as the first source that contains the characteristic sorites reasoning in dealing with stages of meditation, it serves as the prototype for the rest. However, it does not contain the explicit phenomenology of meditation stages that we find in the following six passages, but only presents stages in the actual breathing practice.

Passage 2: *Huang-Lao boshu*, *"Jing fa"* 黃老帛書 6: *"Lun"* 論 (*sorting*)

The so-called *"Huang-Lao boshu"* are the four silk manuscripts discovered at Mawangdui in 1973 that precede, on the same scroll, one of the two manuscripts of the *Laozi* found among the cache of texts in tomb number three. These texts, of course, started the "Huang-Lao craze" in scholarship that has gone a long way toward reshaping our understanding of early Daoism. Without wishing to enter into the various debates that have arisen around these texts over issues such as ascertaining their dates, elucidating their relationships to one another, determining whether or not they are the long-lost *Huangdi Sijing* 黃帝 四經 (Four Canons of the Yellow Emperor), and so on, I would briefly present my current thinking about these works in order to contextualize the passage I have selected from them.

In previous studies I have linked these texts with the Syncretic aspect of early Daoism found in such sources as the "Xinshu" essays from *Guanzi*, chapters 12–15, 33 of *Zhuangzi*, *Huainanzi*, and Sima Tan's 司馬 談 foundational description of the "Daoist School" (*Daojia* 道家).[16] While the *Huang-Lao boshu* are much more explicit than these other sources on the various mechanisms of government and do exhibit some differences in technical terminology, I believe that their sharing of the same basic orientation and many technical terms is sufficient to class them with this group. Their differences may indicate their earlier date or perhaps the existence of regional lineages in this Syncretic Daoist tradition.

Of paramount importance in their vision of an ideal society is that it should be ruled by a sage-king who has developed a gnostic wisdom enabling him to see through the complex and constantly changing continuum of daily affairs to the underlying patterns that underpin and direct them. Seeing these patterns clearly, he can then establish his state in parallel to them, being always careful not to do anything that is contrary to them. In order to develop this rare and numinous clarity, the sage must cultivate what we would today call a higher level of consciousness by the assiduous application of the apophatic techniques of inner cultivation. The *sorites* structures in these passages will be italicized.

理之所在謂之(道)。物有不合於道者, 謂之失理。失理之所在, 謂之逆。逆順各自命也, 則存亡興壞可知(也)。存亡之知)生惠(慧), (慧)生正, (正)生靜。靜則平, 平則寧, 寧則素, 素則精, 精則神。至神之極, (見)知不惑。帝王者, 執此道也。是以守天地之極, 與天俱見, 盡□┌于四極之中, 執六枋(柄)以令天下, 番三名以為萬事□┌, 察逆順以觀于霸王危亡之理, 知虛實動靜之所為, 達於名實(相)應, 盡知請(情)偽而不惑, 然後帝王之道成。[17]

That wherein natural guidelines are located, we call it [the Way]. When there are things that have not united with the Way, we call them things that have lost their natural guidelines. That wherein the loss of natural guidelines is located, we call deviation. Because deviation and compliance cause one another, then preservation and loss, flourishing and destruction can be understood.

[*The knowledge of preservation and loss*] *generates wisdom.*[18]
Wisdom generates alignment.
Alignment generates tranquility.
When one is tranquil, one becomes equanimous.
When one is equanimous, one becomes serene.
When one is serene, one becomes unadorned.
When one is unadorned, one becomes purified.
When one is purified, one becomes numinous.

When one becomes perfectly numinous, then (seeing) and knowing are never deluded. Emperors and kings took hold of this Way. Therefore, they maintained the limits of Heaven and Earth, saw (and knew) together with Heaven. They exhausted [missing graph] . . . within the four directions; took hold of the Six Handles in order to make decrees to all under Heaven; inspected the three names in order to make the myriad endeavors . . . [missing graph]; discerned deviation and compliance in order to observe the patterns of the destruction of hegemons and kings; understood what makes things empty or full, active or tranquil; comprehended the mutual resonance between name and reality; exhaustively understood the true and the false without delusion. Only then did the Way of emperors and kings become completed.

Passage 2 is an important source for understanding the nature of Huang-Lao epistemology. It presents the results of this practice of inner cultivation in a series of psychological stages of increasing profundity that lead to the attainment of a numinous level of awareness in which "seeing and knowing are never deluded" (*jian zhi bu gan* 見知不惑). Notice again the characteristic sorites reasoning and the presence of a clear preamble and a clear denouement.

In the preamble, knowledge of the preservation and loss of inherent patterns within the cosmos and within the individual person lead to an enlightened wisdom about how to follow them. This yields a condition in which both body and the flow of vital breath are aligned (*zheng* 正), presumably according to these inherent patterns, and next, to mental tranquility (*jing* 靜). This calmness is followed by equanimity (*ping* 平), serenity (*ning* 寧), and a condition of purity (*su* 素) that is elsewhere, in *Laozi* 19, defined as being selfless (*shao si* 少私). These are followed by a state of refined mental concentration (*jing* 精) and finally a numinous awareness (*shen* 神). The denouement speaks of the benefits to the ruler of this practice: it gives him the ability to see and understand unerringly the deeper patterns that underlie heaven and earth and to have a profound insight into all the various techniques that make for a successful and harmonious government.

Passage 3: *Lüshi chunqiu* 呂氏春秋 3.4: "*Lun ren* 論人" (Sorting out others)
The *Lüshi chunqiu* was completed in 239 BCE by scholar-retainers who had been gathered together at the Qin court by Prime Minister Lü Buwei 呂不韋. It is a difficult book to assess because it consists of essays written by followers of a number of different schools of practice that included the Confucians, Mohists, Yin-Yang Naturalists, Logicians, Legalists, Agriculturalists, Yangists, Daoists, and others.[19] It is therefore easy to see why from Han times on it has received the bibliographical classification of "eclectic" (*zajia* 雜家). Modern scholars have attempted to identify one or another of these ideological viewpoints as the dominant

position in the entire text, but they invariably rely on one or several chapters of the total of 26 in order to establish their positions.[20]

Tian Fengtai 田鳳台 has demonstrated that each of the 147 original essays in the 26 chapters exhibits a consistent structure of discourse.[21] This suggests that a structure was preestablished by the editors, and then teachers from each school were asked to write essays on given topics that conformed to this structure. Andrew S. Meyer has identified certain chapters (nos. 3, 5, 17, and 25) as having been written by members of the Huang-Lao lineage of early Daoism, and, in general, I concur with his assessment.[22] They exhibit the same basic philosophical orientation as the other Syncretist texts I have identified; namely, they are based in a cosmology of the Dao; they show clear evidence of inner cultivation theories directed primarily at the ruler; and they advocate that the thus-enlightened sovereign rule by modeling his government after the greater patterns of Heaven and Earth.

The first of the two passages selected from the *Lüshi chunqiu* comes from the first of its Syncretist chapters, no. 3, the "Third month of spring." This essay, "Sorting out others," discusses how the ruler who practices inner cultivation techniques is able to sort out the relative strengths and weaknesses of his ministers because of the clear and objective functioning of his own consciousness.[23]

主道約, 君守近。太上:反諸己。。。 何謂反諸己也。適耳目,
節嗜欲, 釋智謀, 去巧故而游意乎無窮之次(註: ＝舍)。事心乎
自然之塗(途)(註: ＝道)。若此則無以害其天矣。無以害其天
則精, 知精則知神, 知神, 之謂得一。凡彼萬形得一後成。故知
一則應物變化闊大深不可測也。德行昭美比於日月不可息也。
豪士時之遠方來賓不可塞也。意氣宣通無所束縛不可收。。。
故知知一則歸於樸。。。。

The Way of the ruler is concise. The lords hold it close to them. Its highest principle is to return to the self . . .

What do I mean by "returning to the self"? Relax the ears and eyes, limit lusts and desires, let go of wisdom and scheming, cast off cleverness and precedent, let your awareness roam in the Limitless, and set your mind on the Path of Spontaneity.

If you do this then there will be nothing that injures the heavenly in you.

When there is nothing that injures the Heavenly in you then you will be concentrated.

When you know how to be concentrated then you will know the numinous.

When you know the numinous, this we call attaining the One.

All the myriad forms attain the One and thereby develop.

Therefore if you know the One you will respond to the alterations and transformation of the myriad things. You will be vastly grand and profoundly deep so that you cannot be fathomed. Your power and actions will be brilliant and beautiful; like the sun and the moon, you cannot be exhausted. Great scholars will quickly arrive and guests from afar will come in an endless line. Your awareness and vital breath will be expansive and penetrating and nothing can bind or restrain them . . . Therefore if you know how to know the One then you will return to the Unhewn . . .

This passage begins with preparations we recognize from other early Daoist sources that include relaxing perception, restricting desires, and relinquishing various sorts of biased intellection.[24] This leads to a condition in which "nothing harms the heavenly" or natural in you, a phrase that seems to echo the jade knob inscription's use of the same term. Here I take the "heavenly" to refer not just to the natural and spontaneous side of one's nature that Daoists cultivate, but, because of the parallel to the jade inscription and the following discussion of stages of meditation, also to the naturally calm and patterned breathing that will arise from following this mental discipline that produces tranquility.

From here, the passage provides a brief list of successive stages of meditation in the characteristic sorites rhetorical structure. *Jing*, which I usually translate as the "vital essence," is a concentrated or refined form of *qi* 氣, the "vital breath or energy."[25] In the Inner Cultivation tradition, it is associated with the most refined states of consciousness, those of complete tranquility. I have argued that the *jing* should be considered a "physiological substrate" of such psychological experiences of tranquility.[26] Here it indicates simultaneously the refined *qi* that develops from the practice of naturally patterned breathing and the tranquil state of mental concentration that develops from this practice. This is followed by the experience of the *shen*, the numinous, a core level of consciousness that is without will or desire and that is the source of unbiased thinking, clear intuition, and the mystical experience of merging with the Dao.[27] Indeed, herein, the numinous stage is followed by the stage called "attaining the One," which I take to indicate precisely this experience of unitive consciousness.

The denouement to this passages states that after this ultimate stage of meditation is attained, the consciousness of the ruler is profoundly transformed. Among other results, he is able to spontaneously respond to things, be impenetrably profound and unattached, and be able to return to the "unhewn," one of the *Laozi*'s images for the desireless spontaneity of the Dao within the perfected sage.

Passage 4: *Lüshi chunqiu* 25.3: "You du" 有度. (Having limits)

Passage 5: *Zhuangzi* 23: "Gengsang Chu" 庚桑楚

I consider these two passages together because they are two different versions of the same passage, with very few variations between them. The *Lüshi chunqiu* could possibly be quoting the *Zhuangzi* passage, but not vice versa, because the Zhuangzi contains several sentences after it begins the quotation that are not in the *Lüshi chunqiu*. It is also possible that both are quoting from yet a third text. While each passage occurs in a generally different context (*Lüshi chunqiu*: short anonymous essay; Zhuangzi: long narrative attributed to Laozi 老子), they share a common polemical criticism of the Confucian virtues. Both argue not that these virtues are worthless, but that they can only be attained by the superior Daoist inner cultivation practices.

Chapter 25 in the *Lüshi chunqiu*, the "Si shi lun" 似順論 (Essay on Appearing to Comply), is devoted to demonstrating how Daoist inner cultivation practice gives the ruler the ability to overcome the inherent imperfections of the common, ego-based self and thereby be able to ascertain those governmental measures that truly comply with the greater patterns of Heaven and Earth. It is easy to be misled, the author argues, if one relies on the ego alone to govern. Echoing the passage from *Lüshi chunqiu* 3 quoted above, this essay speaks of the superiority of "holding onto the One" (*zhi yi* 執一), which I take to mean experiencing a complete unity with the Dao and then carrying this over into one's daily affairs. To do so enables one to realize the "essentials of our nature and destiny" (*xing ming zhi qing* 性命之情).

LSCQ 25.3: "You du" (Having limits)[28]

。。。唯通乎性命之情, 而仁義之術自行矣。

先王不能盡知, 執一而萬物治。使人不能執一者, 物〈感〉「惑」之也。故曰, 通〈意〉「志」之悖, 解心之繆, 去德之累, 通道之塞。貴、富、顯、嚴、名、利六者, 悖〈意〉「志」者也。容、動、色、理、氣、意六者, 繆心者也。惡、欲、喜、怒、哀、樂六者, 累德者也。智、能、去、就、取、舍六者, 塞道者也。此四六者不蕩乎胸中則正。正則靜, 靜則清明, 清明則虛, 虛則無為而無不為也。

. . . If one can only see through to the essentials of our nature and destiny, then the techniques of humanity and rightness will proceed on their own.

The Former Kings were unable to exhaust knowledge; they held onto the One and the myriad things were ordered. If humans are not able to hold onto the One, things will delude them. Therefore it is said,

"Break through the perturbations of the will,
Release the fetters of the mind,
Cast off the constraints to Inner Power,
Break through the blockages of the Way.

Nobility, wealth, fame, authority, reputation, and profit: these six are what perturb the will. Demeanor, action, sex, patterns, vital breath and imagination: these six are what bind up the mind. Hatred, desire, pleasure, anger, grief and joy: these six are what constrain Inner Power. Wisdom, talent, departing, approaching, accepting and rejecting: these are what block the Way.

When these four sets of six do not disturb what is within your chest,
then one becomes aligned.
When one is aligned, one becomes tranquil.
When one is tranquil, one becomes clear and lucid.
When one is clear and lucid then one becomes empty.
When one is empty, then one takes no action and yet nothing is
left undone."

Chapter 23 of the Zhuangzi, "Gengsang Chu," contains an extended narrative of a quest for Daoist inner cultivation practices that carries the seeker, Nanrong Chu 南榮趎, from master Geng to Geng's own master, Laozi. This narrative contains several inner cultivation sayings, including what appears to be an extended verse quotation from *Guanzi*'s "Inward training" essay ("Neiye") that is recited by Laozi (HYC 62/23/34).[29] The entire narrative shows an awareness of both the *Laozi* (in its pairing of Dao and De [e.g., 23/32] and its use of the image of the pure mind of the child [23/35]) and the "Inner Chapters" of *Zhuangzi* (e.g., in its use of the meditative images of "body like withered wood . . . mind like dead ashes" (23/41)). It also show an important conceptual link with the *Lüshi chunqiu* 25 passage in speaking of the benefits of Daoist inner cultivation in terms of returning to the "essentials of our nature" (*qing xing* 情性 [23/29]). While "Gengsang Chu" does not directly discuss government, in light of its use of material from both the *Laozi* and the earlier sections of the *Zhuangzi*, I think it likely to have been written by a Syncretist Daoist author who was intentionally imitating the style of the "Inner Chapters."

"Gengsang Chu"[30]

。。。故曰：至禮有不人。至義不物。至知不謀。至仁無親。
至信辟金。徹志之勃(悖)。解心之謬(繆)。去德之累，達道之
塞。貴、富、顯、嚴、名、利，勃志也。容、動、色、理、
氣、意六者，繆心也。惡、欲、喜、怒、哀、樂六者，累德也。
去、就、取、與、知、能六者，塞道也。此四六者不盪(蕩)胸
中則正。正則靜，靜則明，明則虛，虛則無為而無不為也。。。

. . . Therefore it is said, "perfect courtesy does not objectify others, perfect rightness does not objectify things, perfect knowledge does not scheme, perfect humaneness has no kin, perfect trustworthiness disdains gold.

Penetrate the perturbations of the will,
Release the fetters of the mind,
Cast off the constraints to Inner Power,
Pass through the blockages of the Way.

Nobility, wealth, fame, authority, reputation and profit: these six are what perturb the will. Demeanor, action, sex, patterns, vital breath and imagination: these six are what bind up the mind. Hatred, desire, pleasure, anger, grief and joy: these six are what constrain Inner Power. Wisdom, talent, departing, approaching, accepting, and rejecting: these are what block the Way.

When these four sets of six do not disturb what is within your chest,
then one becomes aligned.
When one is aligned, one becomes tranquil.
When one is tranquil, one becomes lucid.
When one is lucid, then one becomes empty.
When one is empty, then one takes no action and yet nothing is
    left undone. . . ."

The preparatory practices in both passages involve eliminating various kinds of psychological disturbances that interfere with the harmonious functioning of the sage's consciousness. Conceived of in four groups of six items each, they can be summarized as 1. things that perturb the will, causing it to seek after external things (wealth, fame, profit) and to ignore the internal; 2. things that bind up the mind, causing it to move uncontrollably from one thing to the next; 3. the emotions and desires, which tie down one's natural and spontaneous responses; and 4. the various aspects of analytical thought that operate on a dualistic level and hence block one's realization of the Dao. When these disturbances do not disrupt the natural breathing in one's chest, then one begins to attain the higher stages of meditative experience.

These passages present a series of meditative stages in the characteristic sorites rhetorical structure as follows: *zheng* 正: the simultaneous alignment of the body and vital breath; *jing* 靜: the tranquility that it produces; (*qing*) *ming* 清明: the clarity and luminosity associated with deep meditative experience in many traditions throughout the world; *xu* 虛: complete emptiness, wherein consciousness is totally devoid of content. It is in this profound introvertive experience that the adept directly apprehends the One, the Dao.[31]

The Denouement presents the practical benefits of this process of inner cultivation by using one of the most characteristic phrases of the *Laozi*: *wuwei er wu buwei* 無為而無不為. Thus, holding onto this experience of the One amid the vicissitudes of daily life enables one to take no intentional action and yet accomplish whatever task one undertakes.

Passage 6: *Guanzi* 管子 13: "Xinshu shang" 心術上 (Techniques of the mind, I)

The *Guanzi* is a complicated collection of essays mostly devoted to political and economic thought that contains seventy-six essays in twenty-two chapters (*juan* 卷). It originated in the state of Qi toward the end of the fourth century BCE and was added to over a period of perhaps two centuries. "Xinshu shang" is one of four related essays in this collection that discusses Daoist inner cultivation practice and its benefits for rulership. It is particularly closely related to "Neiye," which is devoted exclusively to this practice and its cosmic context and eschews any explicit discussion of its political applications. "Xinshu shang" takes the inner cultivation theories from "Neiye" and applies them to government, arguing that they give the sage ruler the mental clarity, spontaneous responsiveness, and "inner power" (*De*) to practice the *wuwei* 無為 art of rulership. This distinctive application of inner cultivation to government coupled with its presentation of a cosmology based on Dao and De and its deliberate use of Confucian, Mohist, and Legalist ideas within this Daoist framework identifies "Xinshu shang" as one of the most important sources for Syncretist Daoism.[32] "Xinshu shang" consists of two related parts: a series of terse statements, often in verse, and a line-by-line explanation of these statements, mostly in prose. In our sixth passage, the verse statement presents an image taken from "Neiye" in which the inner cultivation practice of emptying the mind and attaining numinous awareness is conceived of as a process of sweeping clean the abode of the numen (*shen* 神).[33] The explanation presents the stages of meditative experience that derive from this process of emptying:

Guanzi 管子 13: "Xinshu shang"
Statement[34]

道不遠而難極也。與人並處而難得也。虛其欲, 神將入舍。
掃除不絜, 神<乃>「不」留處[35]

The Way is not far off yet it is difficult to reach its limit.
It dwells together with man but is difficult to grasp.
Empty out your desires and the numen will enter its abode.
If the abode is not purified, the numen will not reside there.

Explanation

道在天地之間也。其大無外, 其小無內。故曰 "不遠而難極
也。"<虛>「並處」之與人也無間。[36]唯聖人得虛道。故曰 "
並處而難得。"<世>「聖」人之所職者精也。[37]去欲則<宣>
「正」, [38]<宣>「正」則靜矣。靜則精, 精則獨<立>矣。[39]獨
則明, 明則神矣。神者至貴也。故館不辟除, 則貴人不舍。故
曰 "不潔則神不處。"

The Way lies within Heaven and Earth. So vast, there is
nothing outside it; so minute, there is nothing within it.
Therefore the text says, "It is not far off yet it is difficult to
reach its limit." It dwells together with man, without any gap.
Only the sage is able to attain the empty Way. Therefore
the text says, "It dwells together with man but is difficult to
grasp."

That which the Sage directs is his [inner] concentration.
Cast off desires and your body and breathing will become aligned.
When you are aligned, you will become tranquil.
When you are tranquil, you will become concentrated.
When you are concentrated, you will become detached.
When you are detached, you will become lucid.
When you are lucid, you will become numinous.

The numinous is the most honored. Thus when the lodging
place is not cleaned out, the honored one will not dwell in it.

Therefore the text says ". . . if it is not thoroughly purified the numen will not reside there."

The preparatory stages are spoken of briefly as "purifying the abode of the numen" in the statement and "directing one's inner concentration" by "relinquishing desire" in the explanation. The text next proceeds, using the characteristic *sorites* reasoning, through a series of familiar stages: *zheng*: alignment of the body and vital breath; *jing* 靜: tranquility; *jing* 精: a refined state of mental concentration; *ming*: lucidity; and, finally, the attainment of numinous awareness, *shen*. The only new variant in this sequence is the stage referred to as "solitude" (*du* 獨), which occurs between *jing* 精 and *ming*. This term is found elsewhere in similar contexts in early Daoist literature and seems to refer to a particularly deep form of inner concentration in which duality has completely dissolved.[40]

There is no denouement presenting the benefits of inner cultivation here because the author is herein commenting on a statement that does not address these benefits. Furthermore, because the entire essay contains many references to these benefits, there is apparently no need to present them here.[41]

Passage 7: *Huainanzi* 淮南子 7: "Jingshen" 精神 (The Quintessential Spirit)

The Huainanzi is a work of twenty-one essays on a wide variety of topics that was intended as a compendium of knowledge for the Daoist ruler. Completed in 139 BCE by the retainers of Liu An, the second king of Huainan, it represents the final flowering of Huang-Lao thought before it was eclipsed by Confucianism under the Han Emperor Wu. It can be seen as a final attempt on the part of Liu An 劉安 and his Huang-Lao philosophers to dissuade the emperor from his developing conviction that Confucian doctrines were best for ruling the unified empire.

The "Jingshen" essay contains the most complete presentation of inner cultivation theory found in China to this point, and it fully discusses both its physical and its self-transformative benefits. It is therefore not surprising that the apophatic preparatory practices that we have seen in the preambles of our other passages are so fully set forth in our selection from this essay.[42] Even a cursory glance at them, however, will show that, while more explicit than our previous passages, they contain many familiar ideas. The basic process involves intentionally stabilizing the breathing, eliminating desires, harmonizing perception, and conquering perturbations of the will and attention so that the mind is focused, the numinous essence is abundant, and the vital breath is retained:

> 夫<面>「血」氣能專於五藏而不外越則胸腹充而嗜欲省矣。
> 胸腹充而嗜欲省則耳目清聽視達矣。耳目清聽視達謂之明。
> 五藏能屬於心而無乖則勃志勝而行不僻矣。勃志勝而行<之>
> 不僻則精神盛而氣不散矣。精神盛而氣不散則理, 理則均, 均
> 則通, 通則神, 神則以視無不見<也>, 以聽無不聞也, 以為無不
> 成也。是故憂患不能入<也>, 而邪氣不能襲。

Now if the blood and vital breath are concentrated within the Five Orbs and do not flow out:

> Then the chest and belly are replete
> And lusts and desires are eliminated.
> When the chest and belly are replete
> And lusts and desires are eliminated
> Then the ears and eyes are clear
> And hearing and vision are acute.
> When the ears and eyes are clear
> And hearing and vision are acute,
> We call this "lucidity."

When the Five Orbs (and their associated emotions) can be assimilated by the mind and their functioning is without error:

Then perturbations of the will will be conquered
And the circulation (of the vital breath) will not be awry.
When perturbations of the will are done away with
And the circulation (of the vital breath) is not awry,
Then the numinous essence is abundant
And the vital breath is not dissipated.

When the numinous essence is abundant and the vital breath is not dissipated,
Then one is breathing according to natural guidelines.

When one breathes according to natural guidelines,
One attains equanimity.
When one attains equanimity one becomes fully absorbed.
When one becomes fully absorbed
One becomes spirit-like.
When one is spirit-like then:
> *With vision there is nothing unseen,*
> *With hearing there is nothing unheard,*
> *And with actions there is nothing incomplete.*

For this reason
Anxiety and worry cannot enter
And aberrant vital breath cannot seep in.

In the *sorites* section of this passage, the author states that these conditions give rise to patterned and regular breathing *li* 理, which I regard as analogous to the alignment of the vital breath in our exemplary passages 2 and 4–6 and to attaining the "heavenly" or natural flow of breathing in passage 3 and the jade knob inscription. This is followed by the experience of balance (*jun* 均), which seems virtually identical to the equanimity (*ping* 平) of passage 2. Next, one becomes fully absorbed (*tong* 通), which I take to mean that there are no psychological obstructions to one's awareness, which now penetrates to the deepest levels of consciousness.[43] Finally, one reaches the familiar numinous awareness, the level of pure and spontaneous consciousness that the Inner Cultivation tradition often sees at the core of one's being. The denouement speaks of the benefits of this introvertive practice in terms similar to those we have seen before. They, in fact, parallel the *"wuwei"* rhetoric seen in the *Laozi* and in passages 4 and 5 above.

Analysis

Table 4.1 summarizes the testimony of these passages on the existence of stages of meditation in early Daoism.[44] It shows how all six passages (not including the jade tablet) follow the same rhetorical structure, with almost no deviation from it.

Table 4.1. Comparative Table of Early Daoist Meditation Stages

	黃老帛書經 法6:論	呂氏春秋 3.4:論人	呂氏春秋 25.3:有度	莊子 23 庚桑楚	管子 13:2b 心術上	淮南子 7: 精神
Preamble: preparatory stages	(存亡之知)生惠(慧)生正	適耳節目嗜欲釋智謀去巧故	通志解心去德通道塞	徹志解心去德達道塞	除館:去欲職精	血氣胸腹嗜欲勃志行精氣盛散 / 專氣充腹省欲勝志不行神氣不
Sorites: consecutive stages of meditation	正	無害其天	正	正	正	理
	靜		靜	靜	靜	
	平				均	
	寧					
	素	精				
	精		清明	明	精	通
					獨	
	神	神	虛	虛	神	神
		得一			得虛道	
Denouement: benefits	至神之(見)極,知不惑。…	應物變化淵深不可測…歸於樸。	無為而無不為也。	無為而為也。	得虛道	視無不見,聽無不聞,為無不成

	Huang-Lao boshu "Jingfa" Ch. 6 "Assessing"	*Lüshi chunqiu* Ch. 3.4 "Assessing Others"	*Lüshi chunqiu* Ch. 25.3 "Having Limits"	*Zhuangzi* Ch. 23 "Gengsang Chu"	*Guanzi* Ch. 13.2b "Techniques of the Heart-mind I"	*Huainanzi* Ch. 7 "Numinous Essence"
Preamble Preparatory Stages	[Knowledge of preservation and loss] generates wisdom. Wisdom generates alignment.	Harmonize ears and eyes; limit lusts and desires; let go of wisdom and scheming; cast off cleverness and precedent ...	Break through perturbations of the will; release the fetters of the heart-mind; cast off constraints to inner power; break through blockages of the Way	Penetrate perturbations of the will; release the fetters of the heart-mind; cast off the constraints to inner power; pass through blockages of the Way.	Clean out the lodging place; cast off desires; direct inner concentration.	Concentrate blood and breath; fill the chest and belly; eliminate lusts and desires; purify seeing and hearing; conquer perturbation of the will ...
Sortes Consecutive Stages of Meditation	Aligned	Nothing injures the celestial	Aligned	Aligned	Aligned	Patterned
	Tranquil		Tranquil	Tranquil		
	Equanimous				Balanced	
	Serene					
	Unadorned					
	Concentrated	Concentrated			Concentrated	Absorbed
					Solitary	
			Clear and lucid	Lucid	Lucid	
	Numinous	Numinous			Numinous	Numinous
		Attain the One	Empty	Empty	Attain the empty Way	
Denouement Benefits	Perfectly numinous; then seeing and knowing are never deluded ...	Respond to alterations and transformations of things; be grand and deep; be unfathomable ... return to the unhewn	Take no action and yet nothing is left undone	Take no action and yet nothing is left undone		Seeing: nothing is unseen; hearing: nothing is unheard; acting: nothing is unaccomplished

While there is certainly some variation among the specific phrases of the preamble, all, except the *Huang-Lao boshu* passage, advocate a number of related types of apophatic processes in which the consciousness of the adept is emptied of its normal contents, which include lusts and desires, various kinds of intellectual activity, and various other egotistical cognitions within the untransformed individual. It seems likely that these processes occur during the practice of breath meditation, which, according to our sources, seems to result in the practitioner experiencing a deep and natural breathing in which the flow of the vital breath is perfectly regular and aligned. The *Huainanzi* passage provides the most direct evidence of this in its presentation of the initial stages of apophasis in which the "blood and vital breath are concentrated within the Five Orbs and the chest and belly are replete with vital breath."

The apophatic processes found in these passages generally fit well with other early textual sources of Daoism. "Neiye" also talks of calming the mind through regular breathing and through the elimination of desire, perception, and intellection and offers a general characterization of these processes in the metaphor of "sweeping clean the abode of the numen."[45] In the *Zhuangzi* we find two metaphors for apophasis, the "fasting of the mind" and "sitting and forgetting." The latter metaphor is even associated with specific phrases that are quite similar to those in our sources, for example:

堕肢體。黜聰明。離形，去知，同於大通。

I drop off limbs and body, expel eyesight and hearing, cast off knowledge, and merge with the Universal Thoroughfare.[46]

While there are variations in the different lists of meditative stages, both in terms of detail and of individual technical terms, there is a remarkable similarity among them. This is especially true given that they are separated in time by about a century and a half (or more, if we consider the jade knob), and that they come from a wide variety of textual sources. Particularly striking is the consistent order in which the common terms occur. For example, *zheng* and *jing* 靜 invariably occur in the same order: alignment of body and breath precedes tranquility; and *jing* 精 and *shen* also always occur in the same order: refined mental concentration always precedes numinous awareness. This order has ample precedent in the Inner Cultivation tradition. For example, we find that alignment precedes tranquility in four passages in "Neiye" and that mental concentration preceding numinous awareness is implicit there as well.[47]

In the *Huang-Lao boshu* and *Huainanzi* passages, the numinous inner awareness of the *shen* is the ultimate attainment. In the *Lüshi chunqiu*, *Zhuangzi*, and *Guanzi* passages, there is the further level of attainment: the One, emptiness, or the empty Way. Elsewhere I have argued that phrases such as these refer to one of two major aspects of mystical experience in early Daoism, the "introvertive" union in which the individual totally merges with the Way.[48] This then leads to a second mystical experience when the adept returns from the introvertive union to the world of multiplicity and simultaneously perceives both unity and diversity in experiencing the world through a self-less ego. This "extrovertive" mystical experience is at the basis of Zhuang Zhou's 莊 周 being able to "see all things as equal" in chapter 2 of the *Zhuangzi* and of the ability to "do nothing and yet leave nothing undone" in the *Laozi*. Such extrovertive mysticism is also the basis of the benefits of apophatic practice presented in the denouement in our passages.

There is also a striking consistency in the benefits of inner cultivation among our sources. All maintain that such practice gives one the ability to perceive what others cannot, to respond spontaneously in a way that most people cannot respond and to act effortlessly and selflessly and yet accomplish anything one undertakes. These undoubtedly would have been attractive qualities of mind for both practitioners and the various rulers of late Warring States and early Han China to whom most of the texts that contain these passages seem to have been addressed.

IMPLICATIONS

The passages analyzed in the present study demonstrate a distinct similarity in rhetorical structure and technical terminology. The most reasonable explanation for this is that these passages are, in some fashion, related to one another. Yet they come from diverse textual sources that few have seen as related. I have taken the similarities in these passages to be indicative of their having derived from a common basic practice of breath meditation whose goal is to produce a profound transformation in the practitioner in which the individual ego is gradually calmed, clarified, and then ultimately transcended in a unitive mystical experience, after which it is returned to the phenomenal world and reconstituted from a more universal perspective. I see these passages as having been written by practitioners of this discipline who developed a relatively consistent way of conceiving of and contextualizing these experiences.

When taken together, these passages provide compelling evidence for the presence of stages of meditation in early Daoism. They also provide a fuller context for the few references to meditative praxis found in the *Laozi* and the "Inner Chapters" of *Zhuangzi*. While it must remain beyond the present discussion, these meditative stages, while certainly much less detailed here than in other cultures in which meditation is practiced, show striking parallels with those enumerated in the yogic traditions of Central and South Asia and the meditative traditions of the Christian West.[49] This could imply that there are certain fundamental commonalities in psychological experiences of transformation that are found cross-culturally and throughout human history.

Chapter 5

The Yellow Emperor's Guru

A Narrative Analysis From *Zhuangzi* 莊子 11

Introduction

Of all the philosophical and religious works in the Chinese tradition, perhaps none contains as many varied and interesting literary forms as the *Zhuangzi*. Within its thirty-three chapters we find aphorisms, dialogues, poetry, instructions, explanatory and polemical essays, and narratives of various kinds, all filled with a panoply of characters both mythological and historical. As such, it provides an extremely fertile source for literary criticism and one that has remained virtually untapped.

Literary and historical criticism of religious works has been pioneered in the twentieth century by New Testament scholars working on the Synoptic Gospels. Their methods can be summarized under the heading of what one scholar—Stephen D. Moore—calls the "four criticisms": form, redaction, composition, and narrative.[1] Form criticism conducts an analysis of the standard genres or forms in which oral (or early written) tradition is cast and attempts to interpret each in terms of the "life setting" (*Sitz im Leben*) in which it was produced.[2] Redaction criticism attempts to identify the theological or ideological viewpoints of the people who assembled the various literary forms into the texts as we now have them and to understand their own sociohistorical conditions.[3] Composition criticism examines the literary techniques of the early redactors of a tradition, how they arranged and assembled their inherited material to create unified works.[4] It is a holistic variant of redaction criticism in which the entire text is the context for interpreting any part of it.[5]

175

Indeed, these three methodologies are not unknown in sinology—even if they are not explicitly identified by these labels. Most relevant here is the research of Guan Feng 關鋒, Angus Graham, and, more recently, Liu Xiaogan 劉笑敢 on the various ideological viewpoints found among the thirty-three chapters of the *Zhuangzi*.[6] Even if they do not all agree on the details, they are at various times implicitly utilizing all of the traditional forms of literary and historical criticism found in New Testament studies.

Narrative criticism differs from these other three methods in that it came into New Testament studies during the past two decades from outside the field—from the more general and theoretical area of literary criticism.[7] Narrative criticism further differs in that its principal concern is not to identify inherent ideology or to relate the text to its sociohistorical conditions. Its main task is the critical analysis of narrative: what is the story (plot, characters, setting) and how is it communicated—that is, what is its form or "rhetoric?" For narrative critics, ideology is inseparable from story: form is content; content is form. They are also interested in identifying the "point of view" of the narrator and locating the "narratee" or implicit reader to whom the narrative is being addressed. In general, literary criticism looks askance at the possibility or necessity of deriving the original meaning intended by the author of a text and speak of it as the "intentional fallacy." At its most extreme, literary criticism locates meaning in the responses of each reader to the text; so the text becomes not the original written or oral work but the multiplicity of individual reactions to the text by those who read it.

Despite its general lack of interest in authors' ideology and historical circumstances, narrative criticism—at least in its less extreme forms—has much to offer the other three criticisms. Stephen Moore suggests that its analytical methods can help to identify the ideology of the authors of narratives and of those who compiled them into larger works, even if this is not a central concern for literary critics per se.[8] Indeed, that is my interest in pursuing narrative criticism here. I would like to apply some of the most relevant techniques of narrative criticism to analyze the meaning and significance of one passage from the *Zhuangzi*, the story of the dialogue between the Yellow Emperor and his "guru" Guang Chengzi 廣成子 ("Master Broadly Complete") from chapter 11, "To Preserve and Circumscribe" ("Zai you" 在宥).[9] I seek to locate the key ideas expressed in the narrative, identify how they are communicated, and attempt to place them in a larger historical context. Because I am attempting to use narrative criticism in the service of redaction criticism to answer questions about the historical and philosophical context of the narrative, I depart from its more narrowly circumscribed purpose. I have therefore deemed this project a "narrative analysis" rather than a "narrative criticism."

A Narrative Analysis of *Zhuangzi* 11/28–44

SUMMARY OF THE STORY

After ruling for nineteen years, an apparently dissatisfied Yellow Emperor goes to have an audience with the sage Guang Chengzi atop Vacant Merged Mountain. There, he asks about the essentials *jing* 精 of the utmost Way so he can use them to assist in nurturing the people.

Guang Chengzi rebukes him, saying how dare he ask about the substance of the very things of the cosmos that he has destroyed. Ever since he has been ruling, the basic patterns of the cosmos have been out of harmony.

The Yellow Emperor then gives up the empire and builds a special hut with mats of white reeds, where he stays in seclusion for three months. He then returns to have a more formal audience with Guang Chengzi, who now faces south like an emperor. He asks a new question: "How can I cultivate myself (*zhi shen* 治身 so that I can attain long life?" Guang Chengzi then provides detailed instructions on the utmost Way.

These instructions entail an internally focused meditation in which one casts aside sense perception and knowledge, does not belabor the body or agitate the vital essence, attains tranquility and stability, and can thereby keep the spirit firmly within the body. This confers longevity: indeed, Guang Chengzi claims to have lived for 1,200 years. It also facilitates an ascent to the source of yin and yang and a complete merging with Heaven and Earth. If one can cultivate himself like this, he advises, then all living things will flourish by themselves.

The Yellow Emperor is struck with awe. The master goes on to teach him about the implications of merging with the utmost Way that is unending and unfathomable. When you merge with what is immortal, in essence, you become immortal. This was done by the great emperors of the past and will be done again by the great kings to come (and you could be one of them, your majesty!).

The Rhetorical Structure of the Story

THE PLOT AND SETTING

The overall rhetorical structure of the story is in the form of a dialogue in which the Yellow Emperor requests information from a specialist teacher or from a trusted minister. This structure is known in a number of other important sources from both the naturalist technical literature and the philosophical literature. In the former, we find it, for example, in the Yin-Yang 陰陽 military text recently excavated from Yinqueshan 銀雀山 titled "Didian 地典."[10] We also find this dialogue structure in the "Ten Questions" (Shiwen 十問) medical text unearthed at Mawangdui 馬王堆.[11] It is also the predominant literary device in the two Huangdi nei jing 黃帝內經 texts. In the philosophical literature, it occurs in four of the sections of the "Sixteen Canons" (Shiliu jing 十六經) text included among the Huang-Lao works excavated at Mawangdui, often called the Huang-Lao boshu 黃老帛書 (The Silk Manuscripts of the Yellow Emperor and Laozi 老子).[12] The significance of this overall rhetorical structure is not to be overlooked; we return to it below.

In this group of texts, there are two dialogues that are most relevant to our passage from Zhuangzi 11, because in both the Yellow Emperor is taught techniques of inner or spiritual cultivation. These are the fourth instruction in the "Ten Questions" physical hygiene text from Mawangdui and the third section (titled "The Five Regulators" [Wuzheng 五正]) of the "Sixteen Canons" text in the Huang-Lao boshu.[13] Of further interest is that, in the former, the teacher of the Yellow Emperor is a certain Rong Chengzi 容成子, a name quite similar to Guang Chengzi; in the latter, the teacher is a certain Yan Dan 闊聃, a name quite similar to Lao Dan 老聃, the reputed identity of Laozi.

In addition to this overall structure, the narrative has an internal structure that can be divided into three sections: 1. an introduction in two parts, each containing the narrative setting of audiences between the Yellow Emperor and Guang Chengzi; 2. the instructions on inner cultivation; 3. a denouement in which the type of immortality being taught is clearly specified. Among all the other Yellow Emperor passages in the texts mentioned above, narratives are found much more in the philosophical literature than in the technical literature. And virtually none, I would argue, provides as complete or as complex a narrative structure as our passage from *Zhuangzi* 11 (with the possible exception of its parallel narrative in the *Huang-Lao boshu* "Five Regulators" text).

While the names of the characters are different, the narrative immediately following our Yellow Emperor passage in *Zhuangzi* 11 has the same rhetorical structure. It is a dialogue between two characters named Cloud General (Yun Jiang 雲將), who represents a perplexed ruler, and Vast Obscurity (Hong Meng 鴻蒙), who represents a teacher adept at spiritual cultivation. Furthermore, it also contains the same tripartite internal structure of introduction-instruction-denouement. Looking at this from a composition-critical standpoint, I think these two passages were placed together because the compiler or redactor of our extant *Zhuangzi* also recognized their parallels. While there is no time to analyze this second passage in detail, because its rhetorical structure is so close to our *Zhuangzi* 11 passage, it can be used as a gloss.

THE CHARACTERS AND THEIR SYMBOLISM

Of the two characters in our narrative, the Yellow Emperor is the much better known. Indeed, several recent studies have explored the various symbolic associations of this important mythological figure, and they are so numerous that one might be concerned that he might be suffering from a bad case of multiple personalities.[14] Nonetheless, certain definite characteristics do appear.

The Yellow Emperor is a primal ancestor of the Chinese people and, depending on the text, either the first or one of the first of the five emperors. He is seen as the inventor of certain basic cultural institutions and the conqueror of various barbarians and enemies. He is also depicted as a god of the center and of the earth, an "axial deity." Beyond this, his image often depends on the filiation of the particular text in which he appears. Confucian texts emphasize his wisdom at ruling and his ability to pick and utilize able ministers. Daoist texts emphasize his associations with the various "esoteric arts."

It is in this latter context that his dialogues in the naturalist technical literature are relevant to his image in our narrative. In these sources, the Yellow Emperor learns from the experts about the various technical arts such as warfare, physical hygiene, and medicine—as we have already seen—and other arts, such as yin-yang and five phase cosmology, astronomy, calendrics, immortality—if we can extrapolate from his name being found in the titles of long-lost works in these sections of the *Hanshu* "Bibliography." The rhetorical device of the Yellow Emperor as the paradigmatic student of techniques (and the one student who can't be flunked!) is certainly important in this literature and plays a major role in the symbolic context for the audience in our *Zhuangzi* narrative. However, what is never addressed in this technical literature (perhaps because it was already understood) is the even more basic question of why the Yellow Emperor wants to know all of this in the first place. A clear and resounding answer to this question is found in the *Huang-Lao boshu* texts from Mawangdui.

Here, for example in the "Sixteen Canons," the Yellow Emperor is putting this kind of technical knowledge to work in the service of his sage rulership, his humane nurturing of the people. In the first section, "Establishing the Mandate," we find a powerful image of his method of rulership:

> In ancient times, the natural disposition of the Yellow Ancestor began from his love of reliability. At first he fashioned himself into an exemplary image with four faces to assist his unified mind. Reaching out from the center to all four directions, he aligned with what was in front of him, what was behind him, what was to his left, and what was to his right. Then, walking through these positions, he completed his alignments and, for this reason, was able to become the ancestor of all under Heaven.[15]

This provides a symbolic explanation of the image of the Yellow Emperor as an exemplary ruler who fully aligns the human polity (of which he is the primary representative) with the forces and patterns of Heaven and Earth, thus manifesting the triad of "*tian-di-ren* 天地人." Why? Because, in his own words, "I am in awe of Heaven, love the Earth, and cherish the people."[16] We see further evidence of this activity in this section and in the next one, "Observation" (*guan* 觀), where the Yellow Emperor governs in accord with the overarching patterns of Heaven and Earth, particularly yin and yang. Thus he establishes the calendar in order to "match the movements of the sun and moon" and at the appropriate time regulates the people's work in order not to oppose the seasons of Heaven.[17] Here his most important techniques come from his knowledge of yin and yang, their associations and their seasonal alternations. In

Robin Yates's meticulous study of the Yin-Yang texts from Yinqueshan, we see in great detail all the myriad categorizations of phenomena and the seasonal prohibitions that Sima Tan 司馬談 undoubtedly had in mind when he said, "the techniques of the Naturalists magnify the importance of omens and proliferate prohibitions and taboos, causing people to feel constrained and to fear many things."[18] Regulating what the people should do on every day of every month of every season is the way to ensure that human beings act in harmony with the greater forces of Heaven and Earth. The answer to the question of why the Yellow Emperor wants to know all these things he is taught in Naturalist technical literature could very well be that he wants to know them in order to better govern and nurture the people as he does in the "Sixteen Canons."

The Yellow Emperor appears in nineteen passages in the *Zhuangzi*, only two of which are in the "Inner Chapters." In most of these he appears in his well-defined role as one of the five foundational emperors and is often simply mentioned in a passing reference. He is only really criticized twice, in the Primitivist polemic that immediately precedes our narrative from chapter 11 and in what I think is a Primitivist criticism of the decline of inner power caused by civilization in chapter 16, "Menders of Nature" (*Shan xing* 繕性).[19] There are three narratives that could be relevant to the image of the Yellow Emperor in our passage.

In *Zhuangzi* 24, "Ghostless Xu" (Xu Wugui 徐無鬼), the Yellow Emperor goes to look for the "Great Clod" on Mt. Shady, gets lost, and meets a sagely boy tending horses.[20] Impressed with the boy's spiritual depth, he asks him how to take care of all under Heaven. After first declining to answer, the boy gives him a simple instruction: it is no different from tending horses. Simply get rid of whatever would harm them. The Yellow Emperor kowtows and calls the boy "Heavenly Master" (*tianshi* 天師) (an interesting phrase because of its parallels to later Daoism, though probably without that kind of meaning here). This story follows the same overall rhetorical structure as our passage, but the instructions to the Yellow Emperor are extremely simple and seem to advocate non-action rather than a regimen of inner cultivation. Although this passage has a similar rhetorical structure to our narrative from *Zhuangzi* 11, the content is too different to help with our analysis.

In chapter 22, "Knowledge Wanders North" ("Zhi bei you" 知北游), the character Knowledge has a lengthy discussion with the Yellow Emperor, who lectures him on the superiority of non-action and quotes three chapters from *Laozi*: 56, 18, and 48.[21] This could indicate that the narrative was written after the development of a self-conscious tradition in which the Yellow Emperor and Laozi became symbolic spokesmen.

In chapter 14, "The Circuits of Heaven" ("Tian yun" 天運), there is an extremely important narrative in which the Yellow Emperor sets forth a very interesting musical performance of a piece called the "Pond of Totality."[22] What this seems to represent is a ritual reenactment of all the most important patterns, forces, and phenomena in Heaven and Earth. It is most instructive to see the Yellow Emperor here in the role of maestro, the conductor of the grand cosmic communion between Heaven, Earth, and Humankind. This fits well with his image in the "Sixteen Canons" text from the Mawangdui *Huang-Lao boshu*.

There is considerably less information to associate with Guang Chengzi. In fact, what little there is seems to stem from our *Zhuangzi* passage. *Huainanzi* 淮南子 14, "Inquiring Words" ("Quan yan" 詮言), quotes several lines from the instructions section of our narrative in a slightly different order, but adds nothing to our knowledge of the identity of this teacher.[23] Later Daoist sources, starting with Ge Hong's 葛洪 *Shen Xian zhuan* 神仙傳, classify him as an immortal, and some say that Guang Chengzi is simply another name for Laozi.[24] This theory is also stated by the early Tang Daoist commentator Cheng Xuanying 成玄應.[25] But because these sources are late, they can only tell us about how Guang Chengzi came to be thought of in the Daoist tradition.

As mentioned above, the fourth instruction in the "Ten Questions" physical hygiene text from Mawangdui contains a dialogue between the Yellow Emperor and a certain Rong Cheng 容成 in which the latter gives instructions in a form of breath meditation that, however, differ substantially from the instructions in *Zhuangzi* 11.[26] While it also talks about the vital essence and spirit, this text is both more specific and more abstruse than the latter. While giving instructions in breathing, it contains a number of cryptic metaphors that bespeak an esoteric teaching needing the firsthand explanations of a teacher. Rong Cheng is associated with physical cultivation techniques, especially sexual practices in later sources.[27] He also appears in lists of cultural founders in the *Lüshi chunqiu* 呂氏春秋 and *Huainanzi* as the inventor of calendrics.[28] Finally, some later Daoist sources identify him with Guang Chengzi.[29] While the parallel in the overall rhetorical structure of these two sources is suggestive, given the differences in their instructions and the differences in their names, we cannot identify these two teachers with one another. Thus, whatever we are to learn about Guang Chengzi must come directly from our *Zhuangzi* narrative.

The Ideology and Rhetoric of the Narrative

It is now time to examine how these various elements of the story and its form come together in the narrative to express the ideology and point of view of its author. At first glance, the tripartite structure, introduction-instructions-denouement, makes it appear that the main focus is on the instructions themselves. Let us examine this further.

In the first audience in the introduction, the Yellow Emperor comes to Guang Chengzi requesting a secret teaching that would enable him to govern by "putting yin and yang to service in order to perfect the growth of everything" and thereby nurture the people.[30] Guang Chengzi rebuffs him with a very pointed criticism. He says that the Yellow Emperor has not just made ruins of everything, but that he has also failed specifically in the mission we have seen him symbolically charged with in other sources: to coordinate the human world with the greater patterns of Heaven and Earth. It has rained before clouds fanned, leaves have fallen off trees while they were still green, and the sun and moon have grown increasingly dim.

In the parallel narrative that immediately follows, this problem is made more specific. The Yellow Emperor–like figure, Cloud General, is already aware of the fact that the world has become disordered: "the vital energy (qi 氣) of Heaven is inharmonious and the vital energy of Earth is in disarray. The six vital energies are discordant, and the four seasons are not regular."[31] Later in the narrative, his teacher, Vast Obscurity, refers to this situation in phrases reminiscent of the "Normative Standards" text in the *Huang-Lao boshu* collection from Mawangdui:[32]

Whatever disorders the warp of Heaven
And goes against (ni 逆) the true basis of things
Dark Heaven will not bring to completion.
It will disperse herds of beasts
And birds will sing at night
Disasters will strike grasses and trees
And calamities will affect reptiles and insects.[33]

Clearly, then, this problematic situation in both narratives works off the image of the Yellow Emperor as the coordinator of human beings with the greater patterns of Heaven and Earth, the political with the cosmological that would have been understood by the audience of the narrative. Because he has failed so miserably in this mission, the

Yellow Emperor is dismissed by a distrusting Guang Chengzi: "you of the shallow fawner's heart, why should you deserve to be told about the utmost Way?"[34]

The Yellow Emperor next does a most interesting thing: he relinquishes the throne, builds a special hut, furnishes it with nothing but mats of white straw (perhaps symbolizing purity), and lives there in retirement for three months. This retreat period is three years in the parallel story in the "Five Regulators" section of the "Sixteen Canons" from the *Huang-Lao boshu* and Cloud General also disappears for three years before his second audience with Vast Obscurity. These would have been well-known periods of retirement to the audience for this narrative: three months was the mourning period for Mohists, and three years was the period for Confucians, and Liezi 列子 retired for three years after Huzi's 壺子 demonstration of his superiority over the shaman in *Zhuangzi* 7.[35]

This looks very much like a ritual act of purification on the part of the Yellow Emperor that causes a major shift in his personality. When he returns for the second audience, he treats Guang Chengzi with the utmost respect. Indeed, the teacher has now symbolically assumed the role of emperor and faces south, while his student bows and kowtows before him. The student then asks to be taught about how to regulate or cultivate himself (*zhi shen*) in order to attain long life. He receives this instruction, which is presented mostly in tetrasyllabic verse. This literary form is also found in the "Inward Training" essay from *Guanzi* that I maintain is the origin of an Inner Cultivation tradition of breath-meditation that was the primary technique in the early "Daoist" lineages and suggests that this instruction may have originated in an oral tradition within such a lineage and later been incorporated into this story.[36] Indeed, the instruction of Guang Chengzi bears striking similarities with "Inward Training": both talk about righting the body and attaining tranquility, reducing or eliminating perception and knowledge, preserving the vital essence, attaining longevity, and, most importantly, guarding the spirit or numen within.[37] These apophatic techniques, and others like them, are widely attested in other extant texts from this general time period, such as other treatises in the *Guanzi*, the *Lüshi chunqiu*, the *Huainanzi*, and, as we shall see below, even in the *Zhuangzi*.[38] *Laozi*, too, contains evidence of this kind of apophatic practice.[39] Moreover, similar advice is given to Cloud General in the parallel narrative in chapter 11. In our narrative, however, Guang Chengzi puts a unique twist on the results of this form of spiritual cultivation, which I think is a significant invention of the author and not part of the original verse instruction:

我為女遂於大明之上。至彼至陽之原也。
為女入於窈冥之門，至彼至陰之原也。
天地有官，
陰陽有藏，
慎守女身，
物將自壯。
我守其一，
以處其和。
故我修身千二百歲矣。吾形未常衰。

I will take you to a place above the Greatly Luminous
Reaching that which is the source of the Ultimate Yang.
I will take you through the Dark and Mysterious Gateway
Reaching that which is the source of the Ultimate Yin.
Heaven and Earth have their own offices;
Yin and Yang have their own treasuries.
Attentively guard your own person
And things will flourish by themselves.
I guard their unity within me
So that I may settle where they harmonize.
Thus have I cultivated my own person for 1200 years so that
my form has never deteriorated.[40]

The apex of Guang Chengzi's teaching resides here. In wonderfully evocative language, he explains that the ultimate goal of his practice is to merge completely with the unifying power in the cosmos, the Way, which is the ultimate source of Yin and Yang and of Heaven and Earth. This is the answer to the problem of how to once again set the world aright, cultivate yourself, and attain this profound union. When you can dwell in this unity, all things will flourish by themselves. This is very much a "Laoist" *wuwei* 無為 conclusion, and it is echoed in the parallel Cloud General passage, when Vast Obscurity teaches about "mind nourishing" (*xin yang* 心養):

汝徒處無為
而物自化。
墮爾形體，
吐爾聰明。
倫與物忘，
大同乎涬溟。

> Just settle yourself in non-action and things will transform
> by themselves.
> Drop off your bodily form.
> Spit out your intellect.
> Forget your relationships with things.
> And you may merge in the totality of the boundless.[41]

Because Guang Chengzi can do this, he has lived for 1,200 years. The point is that through becoming one with what is eternal, one becomes eternal too.

So that no one misses this understanding of longevity and immortality, the author provides an elaboration in the denouement to our narrative, where Guang Chengzi states:

> The things that belong to that are inexhaustible, but all men
> think they have an end. The things that belong to that are
> immeasurable, but people all think they have a limit. Those
> who attain my Way are like the emperors of the past and the
> kings to come. Those who lose my Way begin in the light
> of day and afterwards end up as earth . . .[42]

He then leaves his pupil and becomes one with the Way.

The Point of View of the Author

Literary critics distinguish between the point of view of the narrator and the author, but in this case, it seems to me that they are the same: the advocacy of the spiritual self-cultivation of the ruler as the essential element and most important technique of rulership. It is through this that the Yellow Emperor can assist in maintaining the delicate harmony and balance of the universal triad of Heaven, Earth, and Humankind. If he can become totally one with the Way, all the myriad things will develop and interact on their own in perfect harmony presumably because the forces of Heaven and Earth and yin and yang can take care of things by themselves. It is not a rejection of the existence of these overriding patterns and forces, but rather a recognition that they can function well when left alone, as long as the ruler is spiritually perfected. It seems to be aimed at those who maintain that successful government is based upon the detailed intentional coordination of the political and the cosmological, a description that sounds very much like the Yin-Yang Naturalist thinkers we encountered in the many texts from Yinqueshan. This kind of manipulation will not work if the ruler is not spiritually perfected.[43] With this understanding of the story, rhetoric, and ideology of this narrative, we can now attempt to place it in a larger literary and intellectual context.

The Literary and Philosophical Context of the Narrative

There are several issues to be dealt with in order to determine the narrative context of our passage and to help complete our study of its meaning and implications. The first is the relatively straightforward issue of its location within the text of the *Zhuangzi*; this is a composition-critical question. The second is its role in the context of the *Zhuangzi*: why was it included in the text?

THE NARRATIVE'S LOCATION IN THE *ZHUANGZI*

According to A. C. Graham, the first part of chapter 11 (lines 1–28) is a Primitivist essay, a polemic written by the same author as chapters 8–11.[44] Our Yellow Emperor narrative runs from lines 28–44, and the Cloud General narrative that parallels it runs from lines 44–57. The remainder looks very much like a pastiche of fragments with no overriding theme. Lines 57–61 are part of a Primitivist argument that Graham tacks onto lines 83–95 from chapter 12.[45] He classifies the fragment in lines 61–63, a paragraph deploring "treating things as things," as a "stray idea" on the theme of self-alienation.[46] Lines 63–66 contain a brief "Great Man" story, and the remainder of the chapter, lines 66–74, is a Syncretist fragment discussing the importance of hierarchy in the government of the sage similar to the "Way of Heaven" (*Tian Dao* 天道) chapter's discussion of hierarchy in 13/27–41.[47]

Whenever one sees this kind of hodgepodge in the *Zhuangzi* that contains no apparent theme and no rationale for inclusion, one is naturally led to suspect the mysterious hand of the third century redactor Guo Xiang 郭象, who reduced the original 52 chapter recension to our received text of 33. One way to detect his editorial work is to look for both a shift of viewpoint and the absence of early commentaries predating Guo for any section of text.[48] These features suggest that the segment in question was not in this position in the original recension seen by these early commentators and very well could have been placed there by Guo when he broke up the other nineteen chapters.

Indeed, there are no extant commentaries earlier than Guo for the last quarter of chapter 11, lines 57–74. Given this and their varying viewpoints, they appear not to have been part of the original chapter. However, there are early commentaries for our two narratives, indicating that both were part of the chapter 11 from the outset. But why, because their viewpoints seem to share so little with the Primitivist polemic in the first part of the chapter?

The answer, I think, is twofold. First, the Primitivist polemic ends with a criticism of sage-emperors, beginning with the Yellow Emperor. Because our narrative contains the Yellow Emperor, the Han dynasty compiler may have included it here. The Cloud General narrative was added because its rhetorical structure is so close to that of our narrative. That is the simple reason.

The more complex reason is that there may not be that great a difference in the ideology of these two narratives and the Primitivist polemic in chapter 11. After all, both of our narratives end with a Laoist "non-action" perspective, and this they most certainly share with the first part of the chapter. The absence of inner cultivation theories in the various Primitivist polemics in the *Zhuangzi* need not indicate they were unimportant to their author, only that they were not relevant to the arguments he was making in them. Moreover, while a fuller analysis would be tangential to the current discussion, there do seem to be inner cultivation images in chapter 11, for example, the sage who "sits as still as a corpse, looks as majestic as a dragon, and from the silence of the abyss speaks with a voice of thunder."[49] Thus, it appears not only possible, but even likely, that Guang Chengzi may have been thought of as a Laoist teacher—if not by the author of our narrative, then certainly by the *Zhuangzi* compilers. This proves quite an interesting theory. If true, in light of our interpretation of the point of view of these narratives at the end of chapter 11, it could indicate that *Zhuangzi* compilers thought that the origins of their syncretic Huang-Lao lineage were to be found in a combination of Yin-Yang and Primitivism or "Laoist" theories of cosmology, self-cultivation, and government.

THE NARRATIVE'S PURPOSE IN THE *ZHUANGZI*

Turning to the role our narrative has in the context of the remainder of the *Zhuangzi*, we have already explored, in our discussion of him as a character in our story, the eighteen other passages in which the Yellow Emperor appears. The closest parallels to it are the Cloud General-Vast Obscurity narrative from chapter 11 and the Yellow Emperor's dialogue with the boy in 24. Both have essentially a "Laoist" or "Primitivist" message: cultivate yourself and do not intervene too much. However, the image of the Yellow Emperor as the conductor of the grand ritual symphony called the "Pond of Totality" is much more a Syncretist image, very much in keeping, for example, with the image of this sage ruler in the *Huang-Lao boshu*. Graham has identified both Primitivist and Syncretist ideologies in the text and further asserted that the latter were its compilers. I have theorized further that these Syncretists were part of the Huang-Lao lineage of the early Han that descended from the authors of the Mawangdui Huang-Lao texts and that dominated the court of Liu An 劉安, second king of Huainan 淮南, where I concluded the *Zhuangzi* was compiled circa 130 BCE. Given our understanding of the ideology of our narrative and these hypotheses about early Daoist lineages, I propose that our narrative was included in the *Zhuangzi* because its Syncretist compilers thought it symbolized something extremely important in their own tradition: the initial merging of the Naturalist cosmological and political thought with Daoist techniques of spiritual cultivation.

Robin Yates has insightfully identified two significant differences between the Yin-Yang texts from Yinqueshan and the four distinct works in the *Huang-Lao boshu* from Mawangdui. First, while the Yinqueshan and the Mawangui texts both share a belief in the fundamental importance of complying with the various patterns and cycles of Heaven and Earth, the latter texts do this in a much more general fashion. They simply do not contain the thoroughgoing details of the former—either in classifying phenomena or in daily prohibitions. Second, there seems to be no interest in Daoist spiritual cultivation in the Yin-Yang sources. Indeed, this kind of inner cultivation is absolutely essential in order to give the ruler the "penetrating insight" through which "seeing and knowing are never deluded."[50] Elsewhere I have shown how the essay titled "Assessing" ("Lun" 論) in the "Normative Standards" presents the ruler's self-cultivation in terms of a series of consecutive stages of breath-meditation that conforms to a rhetorical structure found in a number of other principal sources for the early Daoist practice of spiritual cultivation.[51] The important point to be made here is that the Mawangdui Huang-Lao philosophical texts (at least most of them) look very much like a melding of Yin-Yang philosophy with Daoist cosmology and techniques of meditation. As such, they are closely related to our narrative. Perhaps the principal difference is that they pay more attention to the yin-yang side of things, to human compliance with the patterns of the cosmos. As such, they appear to represent a further development of the initial combination of Huang and Lao that we find in our narrative.

It is therefore not surprising that the one source outside the *Zhuangzi* with the closest parallel to our narrative in terms of rhetorical structure and content is the "Five Regulators" section in the "Sixteen Classics" from Mawangdui. Here we find the Yellow Emperor asking advice on government from a certain Yan Dan, who urges him to look within:

> If your majesty does not yet know your own person, then submerge yourself fully within your source and thereby seek the inner model. Once you attain the inner model then you will know by yourself how to humble your own person [i.e., control your egotistical desires].[52]

Yan Dan elaborates: the true test of one's self-cultivation is not to fight when one feels compelled to by egotistical desires and emotions, but rather to learn how to control them. The Yellow Emperor next retires to live in seclusion atop Extensive Hope Mountain and spends three years seeking within through a practice of quiet reclining (*tian wo* 恬臥).[53] He then dispassionately goes out to defeat his archenemy, Chi You, who has violated the patterns of Heaven. This narrative further reinforces the viewpoint that the spiritual cultivation of the ruler is an essential technique of government

A still further development of this combination of Huang and Lao can be seen in the one chapter of the *Zhuangzi* that contains the strongest parallels with the instructions of Guang Chengzi from our narrative, chapter 15, "Finicky Notions" ("Ke yi" 刻意). This is an integral essay on how to "nourish the spirit" (*yang shen* 養神) whose author takes pains to differentiate clearly this practice from that of "nourishing the body" (*yang xing* 養形), which is followed by the physical hygiene practitioners of breath control and the "guiding and pulling" gymnastic exercises who take Pengzi 鵬子 as their founder. I consider this to be one of the last additions to the *Zhuangzi* for a number of reasons. First, its technical language and logic of argumentation are extremely close to the "Spiritual Essence" ("Jing shen" 精神) essay of the *Huainanzi*. Second, it shares many phrases with other important early sources of Daoist inner cultivation theory, including the "Inward Training" and "Techniques of the Mind I" essays from the Guanzi and the "Inquiring Words" essay from the *Huainanzi*.[54] Third, it quotes several sentences from the Syncretist chapter 13 of the *Zhuangzi*.[55] And finally, it contains two sentences used by Sima Tan in his presentation of the ideas of the Daoist lineage.[56]

In this essay, we see an advocacy of an apophatic practice quite similar to that of Guang Chengzi: limiting perception and relinquishing emotions, desires, and wisdom in order to become empty and tranquil and thereby preserve the vital essence and guard the spirit. However, there are some subtle but important differences. First, the "Finicky Notions" author makes no claims to attaining immortality, however one wants to conceive of it. Quoting an unnamed source, he says:

> That the sage is born is because Heaven moves;
> That the sage dies is because things transform.
> Tranquil, he shares the power of the Yin;
> Acting, he shares the surging of the Yang.

Second, this essay mentions some specific benefits for the sage ruler who practices this nurturing of the spirit, and it sees this practice as an integral part of its comprehensive philosophy for rulership, which it calls "The Way of Heaven and Earth." For example:

> [The Sage] responds only after he is stirred.
> Acts only after he is pressed.
> Rises up only when it is unavoidable.
> He casts off knowledge and precedent
> And complies with the patterns of Heaven (*Tian li* 天理).
> Therefore he has no disasters from Heaven
> And no attachments to its things.
> He is not blamed by people
> Nor attacked by ghosts . . .

In making the first point clear, the author of "Finicky Notions" is distinguishing his position from that of the seekers of immortality who may have followed similar cultivation practices, at least in pre-Han times. In making the second point, the author of "Finicky Notions" shows a further integration of inner cultivation practice into the Huang-Lao philosophy of rulership. Our narrative from *Zhuangzi* 11 advocates this Way but does not have much to say about the benefits for rulership for the sage who practices it (except for merging with the cosmos). In "Finicky Notions," we see the sage ruler able to respond spontaneously to whatever arises and simply follow along with the greater patterns of Heaven, thereby avoiding all the various calamities that can befall a ruler.

The final piece of evidence I wish to present in support of this theory that our narrative of the Yellow Emperor and Guang Chengzi symbolizes regarding the origins of Huang-Lao thought is the passage from the "Inquiring Words" essay (#14 "Quanyan" 詮言) of the *Huainanzi* that quotes part of the latter's instructions. After arguing that the foundation of establishing order in a state is ultimately grounded in the ruler's cultivation of the emptiness and tranquility wherein the Way abides, the passage continues in a fashion reminiscent of the rhetoric of the Confucian "Great Learning" (*Daxue* 大學):

> Those who are able to be in possession of the empire
> Certainly do not neglect their states.
> Those who are able to be in possession of their states
> Certainly do not lose their families.
> Those who are able to regulate their families
> Certainly do not neglect their persons.
> Those who are able to cultivate their persons
> Certainly do not forget their minds.
> Those who are able to reach the source of their minds
> Certainly do not impair their natures.
> Those who are able to keep their natures whole
> Certainly have no doubts about the Way.

> Therefore Guang Chengzi said:
> Diligently guard what is within you;
> Fully prevent it from being externalized.
> Excessive knowledge is harmful.
> Do not look! Do not listen!

Embrace the numen by being still
And the body will be naturally aligned.

There has never been anyone who was able to understand other things without first attaining it in within himself. Thus the *Yijing* 易經 says: "Tie it up in a bag. No blame. No praise."[57] (14/2b4–11)

The point of this argument is its advocacy of the spiritual self-cultivation of the ruler as the essential tenet of rulership. It is most instructive that Guang Chengzi is used as the spokesman for this method of inner cultivation. It indicates that, for the *Huainanzi* circle and its audience, he was the foundational teacher of this method and its integration into a larger philosophy of government.

I have previously suggested that the literary circle at the court of Liu An was responsible for compiling the 52-chapter recension of the *Zhuangzi*.[58] This means that the people who wrote the *Huainanzi* also compiled the *Zhuangzi*. I think it is no accident that the only two references to Guang Chengzi in the received literature are in these two texts. The author of the *Huainanzi* 14 passage quoted above seems to have drawn his summary of the instructions of Guang Chengzi from our Yellow Emperor narrative in *Zhuangzi* 11. The fact that he uses these instructions in the context of an argument that advocates what is perhaps the essential tenet of Han Dynasty Huang-Lao thought—the need for Daoistic spiritual cultivation of the ruler—is a strong indication that the *Huainanzi* authors saw our *Zhuangzi* narrative as symbolizing the initial merging of the teachings of Huang and Lao that were the foundations of their tradition. It is for this reason, I think, that this narrative was included in the *Zhuangzi*.

Conclusions: The Significance of the Narrative for the Early History of Daoism

In our analysis of this narrative of the Yellow Emperor and Guang Chengzi, we have seen how its various elements combine to communicate the point of view of its author. It is a clarion call for the Daoistic spiritual cultivation of the human ruler who attempts to coordinate the cosmological with the political. Prior to meeting his "guru," the Yellow

Emperor had failed in his rulership because his lack of self-realization had caused him to create a society that was fundamentally out of harmony with the greater patterns of Heaven and Earth. Only after he is able to cultivate himself and merge completely with the Way can he follow a governmental course of Non-action that enables the cosmos to evolve as it should according to these greater patterns and forces, especially yin and yang. In this narrative, the Yellow Emperor symbolizes the attempt to coordinate the cosmological and political by means of enacting ordinances based on Naturalist theories of yin and yang. Guang Chengzi symbolizes the Laoist philosophy of spiritual cultivation coupled with *wuwei* government and an implicit cosmology of the Way. Thus each character symbolizes one of the two most essential elements of Huang-Lao thought.

Of course Huang-Lao thought, as we know it, in the silk manuscripts from Mawangdui, in the Syncretist sections of the *Zhuangzi*, various essays in the *Guanzi*, the *Huainanzi*, and Sima Tan's discussion of the six lineages cannot be simply reduced to these two factors. It contains a much broader intellectual range and includes ideas borrowed from the Confucians, Mohists, Terminologists, and Legalists. However, it is arguably the case that in Sima Tan's assessment, these borrowed ideas were secondary; Daoistic spiritual cultivation and a political philosophy of coordinating the human polity with the greater patterns of the cosmos were the primary elements of the distinctive Daoist philosophy. So why could our narrative not be intended to represent the inception of Huang-Lao thought rather than its mature development?

A further consequence of seeing Guang Chengzi as a Laoist symbol in our narrative is that it associates it with the Laoist ideology in the Primitivist polemic from the first part of the chapter and hence with the Primitivist essays in chapters 8 through 10 as well. Not only does this suggest a rationale for our narrative's inclusion in this chapter, but it also indicates that there may very well have been a significant element of spiritual cultivation implicit in the Primitivist position. The fact that Guang Chengzi claims great longevity and immortality further suggests a close relationship between early seekers of these goals and early Daoistic inner cultivation theories. It is of further interest that the Syncretist author of the "Finicky Notions" essay found it necessary to differentiate his teachings on spiritual self-cultivation from those of the longevity seekers who simply "nurture the body." Symbolic fragments such as these suggest that there might have been a closer relationship between early Daoistic lineages and the various physical cultivation experts, as Donald Harper has been arguing.

In conclusion, by analyzing this one narrative from the *Zhuangzi*, I hope I have indicated something of the possible information that lies buried within its text for what I like to call the "hidden history" of Early Daoism. I hope further that this narrative analysis has indicated just a little of the potential that such a textual methodology has for studies of the historical, social, and philosophical contexts of early Chinese thought in general, and Daoism in particular. Narrative criticism, along with its complementary methodologies of form, redaction, and composition criticism, represents important tools of "textual archaeology" that, when combined with the fruits of physical archaeology, contain the promise of bringing us closer to deciphering the original meaning and significance of the ideas of those who walked the earth so long ago in a culture so different from own.

Appendix: Guang Chengzi's Instructions on Inner Cultivation:

至道之精，
窈窈冥冥。
至道之極，
昏昏默默。
無視無聽，
抱神以靜，
形將自正。
必靜<心>[必]清，
無勞女形，
無搖女精，
乃可以長生。
目無所見，
耳無所聞，
心無所知：
女神將守形，
形乃長生。
慎女內，
閉女外，

多知為敗。
我為女遂於大明之上。
至彼至陽之原也。
為女入於窈冥之門,
至彼至陰之原也。
天地有官,
陰陽有藏。
慎守女身,
物將自壯。
我守其一,
以處其和。

The quintessence of the Perfect Way
Is obscure, obscure, and deep, deep.
The zenith of the Perfect Way
Is dark, dark, silent, silent
Do not look; do not listen
Embrace the spirit using stillness
Then the body will become aligned on its own.
You must be still; you must be pure
Do not toil your body
Do you disturb your vital essence
And you will thereby attain long life.
When the eyes have nothing to see
When the ears have nothing to hear
When the mind has nothing to know:
Your spirit will be preserved within your body
And your body will attain long life.
Be attentive to what lies within you
Prevent it from becoming externalized
Excessive knowledge will destroy you.
I will take you to a place above the Greatly Luminous
Reaching that which is the source of the Ultimate Yang.
I will take you through the Dark and Mysterious Gateway
Reaching that which is the source of the Ultimate Yin.
Heaven and Earth have their own offices;
Yin and Yang have their own treasuries.
Attentively guard your own person

And things will flourish by themselves.
I guard their unity within me
So that I may settle where they harmonize.
Thus have I cultivated my own person for 1200 years so that
my form has never deteriorated.

Chapter 6

Revisiting Angus C. Graham's Scholarship on the *Zhuangzi* 莊子

Angus Graham's philosophical insights into the *Zhuangzi* were founded upon his methodical criticism and analysis of the text. In what follows I will attempt to analyze and assess Graham's scholarship on the text of the *Zhuangzi* by trying to understand the perspective from which he approached the text, the perspective that led to his many important and controversial insights. I will also attempt to expand upon his achievements by offering answers to a number of questions that Graham's research raised, but did not answer, including that of how the various intellectual voices that he identified came to be incorporated into the text.

Introduction

When Angus Graham's almost complete translation of the *Zhuangzi* was published in 1981 it represented a radical break with all complete English translations extant at that time.[1] Rather than translate the entire chapter as a whole as his predecessors James Legge, Herbert Giles, and Burton Watson had done, with the implicit assumption that it was the creation of one person (as per the *Analects* of Confucius or the *Way and its Power* of Laozi), Graham treated the text as a collection of distinct (and mostly Daoist) philosophical positions, which he carefully identified and contextualized. This was part of a deliberate strategy on his part to confront

---

This chapter has been edited from its original source to better fit the current volume.

the realities of the text as he saw them and we cannot appreciate his singular contributions to our understanding of what is arguably the most significant work of foundational Daoism without grasping how he saw the problems of the text and what to do about them.

Basing himself on the work of a number of contemporary East Asian scholars—the most important of whom was Guan Feng 關峰[2]— and upon his own research on the text, Graham implicitly applied the principles of form, redaction, and composition criticism that he learned during his undergraduate studies in Theology at Oxford.[3] He saw that the *Zhuangzi* was far from the homogenous product of a single author but was rather a heterogeneous product that embraced at least five distinct philosophical positions that could be identified as Daoist or related to Daoism. These were:

- The historical Zhuangzi of the "Inner Chapters;"

- The "school of Chuang Tzu": his followers;

- The Primitivist, a "pugnacious" thinker philosophically related to the *Laozi* 老子;

- The Yangists: followers of the "hedonist" philosopher Yang Zhu 楊朱;

- The Syncretists: early Han eclectic Daoists distinct from the Huainan 淮南 circle.

He further concluded that most of the original scrolls of the text were neither separate essays nor chapters in what we would call a "book" but were instead compilations of various literary forms including narratives, prose, aphorisms, songs, and poetry that were initially put together in the early Han 漢 by someone from the final "Syncretist" stratum. He recognized that the extant recension of Guo Xiang 郭象 (fl. ca. 300 CE) in thirty-three chapters was not the original recension of the text in 52 chapters listed in the "Bibliographical Monograph" of *The History of the Former Han Dynasty* (*Hanshu Yiwenzhi* 漢書藝文 志) and that its many textual corruptions and dislocations resulted at least in part from Guo's editing as he attempted to fit fragments of the chapters he excised into those he retained. He also asserted that the text contained a series of philosophically subtle and significant technical terms that had to be clearly elucidated by understanding their intellectual context before they could be accurately translated.

For Graham the principal failing of all previous complete translations—including that of Watson, which he admired for its outstanding literary qualities—was a failure to come to grips with these outstanding textual, linguistic, and philosophical problems. He reserved praise solely for the work of Arthur Waley who, in *Three Ways of Thought in Ancient China*, had attempted to translate only those passages whose problems he felt he was able to resolve rather than translate continuously through them to create an English prose style Graham labeled as the "Rambling Mode." In "Two Notes on the Translation of Taoist Classics," Graham defines this translation style as that "which drifts inconsequentially between sense and nonsense with an air of perfect confidence."[4] It results from the translator's attempt to render the entire text as if it were constituted of unified and integral chapters while ignoring the various literary forms, shifting philosophical positions, and corrupt passages that in reality constitute it. "What seems to be the rambling style of the great Taoist," Graham writes, "is in the first place an evasive tactic of the scholar who has lost the thread, who is trudging from sentence to sentence with his dictionaries and commentaries and hoping for the best.[5]"

In order to avoid this problem, Graham made the following decisions:

1. to offer (in the spirit of Waley) integral translations of only those "blocks of text" that are homogeneous. These are: the inner chapters; the Primitivist essays that constitute chapters 8–10 and the first part of 11; the Yangist chapters 28–31; the complete Syncretist essays in 15 and 33; chapter 16 (which Graham failed to link with any known philosophy); and any complete episode extracted from miscellaneous chapters.

2. to provide a clear intellectual context for each of these,

3. to differentiate between the various literary forms in the translation. This involved distinguishing between verse, songs, aphorisms, propositions, provisional formulations, and comments and treating only "true essays," such as those of the Primitivist, as consecutive paragraphed prose.

4. while striving to retain the order of material in the extant recension, to rearrange and patch in those fragments from the textually heterogeneous Mixed Chapters (23–27) that could plausibly be relocated into the Inner Chapters.

5. to translate only those philosophically significant passages from the Outer (chapters 8–22) and Mixed Chapters (chapters 23–33) that can be classed as "school of Chuang Tzu" material and to group them by theme such as those that present, for example, tales of Zhuangzi and meetings between Confucius and Lao Dan 老丹.

By following these guidelines Graham attempted to provide a translation that was intellectually nuanced and linguistically precise, that never fell into the "Rambling Mode," yet did justice to Zhuangzi as both philosopher and poet. The foundation for these guidelines and for the translation that was shaped by them was Graham's research on the various aspects of the text of the *Zhuangzi* and it is to this that I shall now turn.

Rearrangement of the Text

Perhaps the most original and controversial aspect of Graham's scholarship on the *Zhuangzi* is his reconstruction and rearrangement of the text. The reconstruction involves putting passages back together that he felt were originally whole but had been fragmented due to textual corruption and to the drastic editorial work of the fourth century commentator Guo Xiang. The rearrangement involves his establishment of thematically based reconstituted redactions of whole passages from the Outer and Mixed chapters that were distributed randomly throughout these sections of the work. I will analyze each of these in turn.

There are seven significant textual reconstructions accomplished by Graham in his translation of the *Zhuangzi* and these are detailed and justified in the textual notes:

1. chapter 2, p. 49: adding the poem, "Heaven turns circles . . ." from 14/1–4.[6]

2. chapter 3, pp. 62–63: adding "Hence as the ground which the foot treads . . . we do not know how to put our questions to it" from 24/105–11, 32/50–52, 24/103–5.[7]

3. chapter 5, p. 79: adding a bracketed commentary misplaced in 6/17–19 but relevant here

4. chapter 5, pp. 79–82: a major reconstruction involving rearrangement of 5/41–52 and the insertion of fragments from the end of chapters 24 and 23.

5. chapter 6/1–20, p. 85: a major reconstruction involving

   - relocation of 6/11–14 to after 6/89 (p. 91): ". . . when the sage goes to war"

   - relocation of 6/17–19 to chapter 5 as in item 3 above

   - relocation of 6/22–24, the little episode of the fish on dry land, to after 6/73

   - insertion of fragments from 24/97 and 96 on the True Man after poem at 6/17

6. chapter 17/1–53, pp. 144–49:a reconstruction of the "autumn floods" dialogue involving:

   - relocating 17/24–28 as a separate "great man" fragment on p. 150

   - insertion of 22/16–21 ("Heaven and earth have supreme beauty . . .") on p. 148–49

7. chapter 8, p. 202: insertion of a fragment at line 26 from 12/96–102: "Century old wood is broken to make a vessel . . . a leopard in its cage has got somewhere too."

In all the above cases, Graham makes cogent arguments based upon both meaning and upon grammar. He moves fragments from contexts in which their meaning seems out of place to those in which their meaning fits. He then justifies the move by detailing similarities in specific unique phrases, particle usage, and technical terminology between the relocated fragment and its new context. For example, in the first relocation he reconstructs what he believes to be the original ending to the Ziqi 子

綦 narrative by adding the introductory poem from chapter 14, "The Cycles of Heaven (Tianyun 天運)." He justifies this by an argument from meaning: "The poem carries on Ziqi's question about who it is that causes things to begin and end, with the same metaphor of a wind blowing through everything." He then follows up with an argument from grammar and terminology:

> As in the first two episodes of ch. 2, the ending of things is described in terms of 'stopping of themselves' (14/2 自止 similar to 2/9 自己) and being 'sealed up' (14/2 緘, variant 咸 in Sima Biao's text; similar to 2/9 咸 2/12 緘); we also find the metaphor of the trigger which starts things off (機 14/2 cf. 2/11).

He also provides corroborating evidence in the form of a Tang dynasty Buddhist source citing the poem as an example of the distinctive thought of the Inner Chapters He argues further that the poem must have been excised from chapter 2 by Guo Xiang because it duplicated the opening of chapter 14, which needed to be retained because the chapter title was taken from it.

In general, Graham makes a reasonable case in favor of each recon-struction. A minor problem with all of them is that they are difficult to locate in the translation, even by using the finding list on pages 36–39 of *Chuang Tzu: the Inner Chapters*, and the reconstructions make comparisons between Graham's translation of these passages and all oth-ers virtually impossible. Graham ameliorated this in the first paperback edition of 1986 by providing alist of each *Zhuangzi* chapter and where it is found in his translation. This has been included in all subsequent reprints. My major hesitation in accepting all of them is that it is not clear how many of these textual dislocations could have taken place. Graham only provides such an explanation for the reconstruction of the end of the Ziqi narrative and it is a plausible one. The second, third, and fourth reconstructions could be explained if we assume that damaged versions of chapters 3 and 5 were transmitted along with their missing passages, which found their way into the ends of chapters 23, 24, and 32. If so however, was this the case in the original 52-chapter recension or in the expurgated Guo Xiang recension? Also how did 6/17–19 get displaced to this location in chapter 6 from chapter 5? The reconstruc-tion in chapter 6 implies that several larger fragments were displaced from later to earlier in the chapter. Perhaps all could be explained if we assume that a series of bamboo strips simply became detached from their proper positions in the redaction of the original 52-chapter recension that Guo Xiang possessed and that he simply tacked them onto the ends of chapters 23, 24, 32, and 12 (in the seventh reconstruction) or found new places for them in chapters 5 and 6 (or in chapter 22, for the dislocated fragment from chapter 17). While this is certainly not impossible by any means, it does seem rather implausible. If true, we should all have less confidence that the text we now have of the thirty-three chapters that survived Guo Xiang's excision is an accurate reflection of those chapters in the original recension.

Graham's thematically based textual rearrangements derive from his identification of the different philosophical positions in the text and upon topics within those positions. These rearrangements remind me of the scholarly practice of creating reconstituted redactions of lost works. Originating during Qing 清 dynasty with scholars like Ma Guohan 馬國翰 and Tao Fangqi 陶方琦, these redactions collected passages from the indirect testimony to lost works.[8] A superb modern example of this genre is Wang Shumin's 王樹民 collection of lost fragments for the *Zhuangzi*.[9] Of course the major difference is that Graham assembled passages from within one extant textual collection while these other scholars worked from a great variety of sources of indirect testimony; yet both were reestablishing lost works of distinct philosophical viewpoints.

The first of these rearrangements is the group of sixteen passages Graham assembles from chapters 23–27 and 32 that he considers directly related to the Inner Chapters by virtue of the fact that they contain themes and the highly specific technical terminology of logical debate that would "hardly have outlasted" the lifetime of Zhuangzi. In addition to this principal rationale for their inclusion, Graham concluded that the chapters from which they were taken "include strings of miscellaneous pieces, some no more than fragments, which may come from any or all of the authors in the Chapter" (p. 100). He implies that the passages he includes in this section came from Zhuangzi without explicitly stating so. Other scholars, such as Liu Xiaogan 劉笑敢, have taken the similarities in meaning and wording between these passages and those of the Inner Chapters to indicate that the chapters in which they are found are the product of later disciples attempting to emulate their master.[10]

In fact both these theories could be right. If we analyze, for example, chapter 23, "Gengsang Chu" 庚桑楚, we see that it is made up of two distinct parts. The first is a long continuous narrative involving a quest for the Dao undertaken by a character named Nanrong Chu 南榮 趎 who first studies with Gengsang and later with his teacher Lao Dan. While it is arguable where this narrative ends, I see it continuing to line 42. The second part of chapter 23 is a collection of eleven different fragments with no discernable link to one another except for their being distillations of general Daoist wisdom. These fragments could have been added to an original narrative by the Syncretist compilers in the second century BCE or to an original short chapter (recall that Zhuangzi 15 has twenty-two lines and 16 has twenty-one) by Guo Xiang from material he wanted to save from chapters he was deleting. Without subjecting these chapters to a detailed composition criticism we cannot settle the issue.

Graham also provides a small collection of passages from the Syncretist position taken from chapters 11–14 and divides them into two sections, "Syncretist Fragments" (pp. 268–70) and "Three Rhapsodies on the Way" (pp. 271–73). These chapters are often taken together as representing a coherent viewpoint, although Graham sees them as miscellaneous collections containing some Syncretist material. Again I would argue that without a detailed composition criticism we cannot reach conclusions about which position is correct. I presented a partial composition criticism of chapter 12 in the second chapter of the present volume, arguing that the presence of Syncretist and non-Syncretist material therein was not the result of tampering on the part of Guo Xiang but was part of the original version of this chapter. However, I did not take it farther to see if I could find a rationale for the inclusion of each of the fifteen passages that make up the chapter.[11] I did conclude that this chapter was assembled by a later Syncretist than the author of its overtly "Syncretist" passages and that this person was a member of the Huainan circle of Liu An 劉安.

By far the most extensive collection of thematically rearranged passages is contained in Graham's "'School of Chuang Tzu' selection" (pp. 116–94). Drawn principally from chapters 16–22 but including passages from chapters 11–14, 23–26, and 32, they are organized into ten topical headings such as "stories about Chuang Tzu," "dialogues of Confucius and Lao Tan," "the advantages of spontaneity," and so on, and they constitute Graham's most significant reorganization of the text. This section results directly from his decision to translate only those passages that are clearly understandable, have a definite viewpoint, and are intellectually interesting, and from his conclusion that there was no organized school of Zhuangzi surviving his death but rather a tradition of "thinking and writing in the manner of Chuang Tzu" that led to these writings. There are a number of problems however with this methodology.

To begin with, removing these many passages from their contexts within specific chapters makes it impossible to perform a composition criticism of how each of the chapters was assembled using Graham's translation alone. This in turn makes it impossible to derive any shred of historical evidence about who might have written the material in these chapters and who might have assembled them into these units. Furthermore without this kind of information we have little idea of how the Inner Chapters might have been transmitted after the death of their author. Indeed, I would argue that it makes more sense to see at least some of these chapters—particularly 17–22—as the products of the followers of Zhuangzi who were attempting to continue writing in his style and practicing the meditative inner cultivation techniques he advocates in the Inner Chapters. Certainly this is the position of many Chinese scholars, including Liu Xiaogan, and of the doctoral thesis of Brian Hoffert.[12] Graham's decision to rearrange this material also fails to give any evidence for why the various philosophical positions that he accurately identifies actually became assembled into a text and in many ways leaves us with more questions than it answers. Of course, when he did this research, Graham was not primarily concerned with such historical issues; he was concerned with providing a clear and coherent translation, first and foremost. Nonetheless, I would argue that their resolution will only augment the insights into the philosophical positions in the text that he identifies. In addition, this radical rearrangement of the material in these chapters makes comparison with other translations impossible, except for the very short chapter 16 which he translates as a whole.

Redaction Criticism

Graham's expertise in both philosophy and philology come together again in his influential study, "How Much of Chuang Tzu did Chuang Tzu Write?" This work, which implicitly adheres to the principles of redaction criticism, was the first in the West to differentiate the distinct philosophical positions in the text and provide a detailed rationale for so doing. He begins with the question that many have taken for granted:

can we provide evidence that the Inner Chapters were written by one person? In the most thorough analysis in this article Graham proceeds to identify four general categories of linguistic tests through which he compares the Inner Chapters with the Outer and Mixed Chapters:

1. idioms: for example, those concerning life and death, perfection, and distinctive turns of phrase such as "How do I know?" *wu hu zhi* 惡乎知 and "it is caused by Heaven// man" *wei ren/tian shi* 爲人//天使

2. grammar: for example, "never yet" *wei shi* 未始 and "only now" *nai jin* 乃今.

3. philosophical terms: for example, "that which fashions and transforms" *zao hua zhe* 造化者 and "lodging place" *yu* 寓.

4. persons and themes: for example, the madman of Chu as a spokesman for the author of the Inner Chapters and the absence of any textual parallels to the *Laozi* in the "inner chapters."

Acknowledging that these tests are heterogeneous, of unequal value, and in need of refinement, Graham nonetheless maintains that they indicate a sufficient consistency in philosophical outlook, technical terminology, and literary style so that we need not seriously question that they were written by a single hand. He also uses these tests to identify fragments in the Mixed Chapters that can be used to reconstruct damaged passages in the Inner Chapters and he demonstrates this with a detailed reconstruction of the introductory essay to chapter 3.

Working independently of Graham but using similar kinds of linguistic tests—some more detailed, some less—Liu Xiaogan reached a similar conclusion on Zhuangzi's authorship of the Inner Chapters and further argued that they are a "mid-Warring States" creation whose contents were written mostly by Zhuangzi but compiled by his disciples.[13] One of the strengths of the latter's much more lengthy work—and a weakness of Graham's—is that Liu briefly summarizes and then criticizes the work of some other Chinese scholars who did not think that the Inner Chapters were all the creation of the hand of Zhuangzi. While Graham indirectly disproves them, it would have been fascinating if he had directly taken on, for example, the theory of Wang Shumin that the extant Inner Chapters were the creation of Guo Xiang's revised arrangement and that the true thought of Zhuangzi can be found scattered throughout the collection.[14]

Graham uses similar but more limited linguistic tests to identify the distinctive thought and style of three other unique philosophical positions in the Outer and Mixed sections of the text. First, we have the "Primitivist" (chapters 8–11/line 28), whom he identifies with some confidence as a single author who takes the view that civilization and its attendant devices and values have destroyed the essentially pure nature of human beings. Thus man's innate tendency to perceive things clearly and to realize the Power (*De* 德) that emerges from the spontaneous attainment of the Way is blocked, and disorder and chaos reign. Graham concludes that this individual was an exponent of Laozi's ideal of a minimalist government and only incidently interested in Zhuangzi, who lived at a particular moment during the Qin-Han interregnum very close to 205 B.C.

While recognizing that the only four chapters with thematic titles outside the Inner Chapters are a group (chapters 28–31) that share a number of important similarities with the Primitivist material (e.g. figure of Robber Zhi 盜蹠, vitriolic criticism of Confucians and Mohists, fondness for a primitive agrarian Utopia, criticism of the damaging influences of culture, the equal harmfulness of moralist and criminal), Graham sides with Guan Feng in concluding that they are attributable to the later followers of the philosopher Yang Zhu. He finds that they contain a number of the key phrases and ideas that other sources attribute to his distinctive philosophy, including: "keeping one's nature intact" (*quan xing* 全性), "protecting one's genuineness" (*bao zhen* 保眞), not risking life and health for the sake of material possessions. Although he sees a similar, but more pronounced, nonmystical side to these chapters and the Primitivists, he attributes the similarities between these two groups of chapters as their being products of the same general time period.

Liu Xiaogan treats the commonalities between these two groups of chapters not as an indication of temporal proximity but as an indication of a common philosophy. Basing himself on the presence of several similar phrases and narratives between these groups, he links them together under the title of the "Anarchist school," which he takes from passages with a similar point of view in the much later *Baopuzi* 抱樸子.[15] This is one of Liu's weaker arguments. He totally fails to examine whether or not these two groups of chapters share the same underlying philosophy and does not seriously examine Guan Feng's assertion that the second group is Yangist. He also concludes that the second group, despite its close ties with first group, "are not products of the legitimate branch of Chuang Tzu's later followers" but were influenced by Zhuangzi and his school.[16] Yet he fails to tell us why he reached this conclusion. Indeed, the relationship between these two groups is essential to understanding why the latter group—the most anomalous chapters in the entire work—were even included. (I will return below to a more detailed consideration of these two closely related groups of chapters).

Graham applies linguistic criteria to identify the final philosophical position in the text, which he calls "the Syncretists." This group advocated a comprehensive Daoist social and political philosophy they called "the Way of Heaven and Earth" governed by an enlightened sage-king who embodies the spontaneous workings of the Way commended in the "inner chapters." He includes whole chapters 15 and 33 in this group but only adds the opening sections of chapters 12–14 and various other fragments. By contrast Guan Feng and Liu Xiaogan see these chapters as solid blocks advocating a similar point of view, one whose central philosophy is similar to that identified by Graham. Guan sees them as the products of the school of Song Xing 宋鈃 and Yin Wen 尹文, identified as Huang-Lao 黃老 philosophers in the *Records of the Grand Historian* (*Shiji* 史記;) Liu thinks they represent the ideas of Huang-Lao Daoists.[17] Their differences with Graham point to a methodological contrast to which I will return.

One of the main criteria Graham uses for his conclusion that only the introductory sections of chapters 12–14 were written by the Syncretists is the absence of post-verbal use of the particle *hu* 乎 common in the rest of the *Zhuangzi*. However this may not be as significant as he suggests. I have checked for the use of post-verbal *hu* 乎 and post-verbal *yu* 於 (the preposition it is often seen as synonymous with in these usages) in two clearly datable works of this general time period, the *Lüshi chun qiu* 呂氏春秋 (ca. 240 B.C.) and *Huainanzi* 淮南子 (139 B.C.). In both works post-verbal *hu* and *yu* seem to be used interchangably, even with the same verb. The ratio of their use seems to shift between these two works. In the former, *hu* is used after verbs about 27% of the time (*yu* follows verbs about 73%) and in the latter it is used about 10% of the time (with *yu* occurring about 90%).[18] This could suggest that the distinctions between their useages were becoming blurred by the time of the *Lüshi chun qiu* as *yu* was gradually eclipsing *hu* in these post-verbal positions. Whatever the case, I would conclude that the absence of post-verbal *hu* is not a reliable indicator of anything more than perhaps the style of a particular Syncretist writer, if that. Using it to determine authentically Syncretist passages, as Graham did, may eliminate some that are.

One final point to note is that Graham says little more in this article about the "school of Chuang Tzu" material. He does not feature it as a subject of any of his linguistic tests beyond the tests for authorship of the Inner Chapters because it seems he has already concluded that its linguistic contrasts with them indicate a later group of followers of "Chuang Tzu's own branch of Taoism." By contrast Liu sees these chapters and Graham's "rag-bag" chapters as the creations of the "Transmitter School" of Zhuangzi's followers.[19] As to this latter group, Liu presents phrases or terms from each of these Mixed Chapters that are similar to or identical with phrases or terms in the "inner chapters." While these may be true, they cannot be used to establish that the entire chapter shares the same philosophical position. Graham's work clearly demonstrates that these chapters do contain material related to the Inner Chapters as well as material related to all other philosophical positions found in the Chapter. Now that he has put forth his arguments only a detailed redaction and composition criticism of them will establish their provenance.

The Problem of Zhuangzi's Syncretists

One of the distinctive characteristics of Graham's identification of the philosophical positions in the text in contrast to the scholarship of others such as Guan and Liu is that he makes little attempt to link these positions with other contemporary intellectual lineages and in the questions of how the text came to be constituted with so many differing intellectual positions. What he does say about its textual history is simple and straightforward:

1. Zhuangzi wrote the seven inner chapters and related passages in the late fourth century B.C.;

2. later followers who wrote in his style created chapters 17–22;

3. a single Primitivist author influenced by the Laozi wrote chapters 8–11/28 in about 205 B.C.;

4. the Yangist miscellany is roughly contemporaneous with the Primitivist writings;

5. the Syncretists who wrote parts of chapters 12–14 and all of 15 and 33 also compiled the entire text sometime in the early Han.

In an article in the *festschrift* for Graham included at chapter 2 in the present volume, I argued that it was possible to link the group he identified as the Syncretists with a series of other works under the rubric of "Huang-Lao" or syncretic Daoism.[20] Working with three categories of technical terms, "cosmology, psychology/self-cultivation, and political thought," I found distinct commonalities between the *Zhuangzi*'s Syncretists and the authors of three of the "Techniques of the Mind" essays in the *Guanzi* 管子, the *Huainanzi*, and in Sima Tan's 司馬談 definition of the Daoist lineage. I concluded that these commonalities indicated all belonged to the same lineage of practice and thought and that this constituted the sole surviving Daoist lineage in the early Han. In his reflections on this piece Graham largely agreed with these conclusions although he took exception to my identification of this lineage as "Huang-Lao" and to my argument that members of the Huainan circle actually compiled the *Zhuangzi*.[21] Graham's comments suggest agreement with linking the Syncretists from the *Zhuangzi* with these other syncretic Daoist works as the lineage that first defined "Daoism." I think it is possible to extend these links even farther.

Andrew Meyer has argued that there are four chapters in the *Lüshi chun qiu*—3, 5, 17, and 25—that are largely made up of essays written by members of this Syncretic Daoist tradition.[22] Since, as Wang Shumin and Liu have argued, there are a significant number of common passages between the *Zhuangzi* and this work, it is important to examine its possible relationship to the *Zhuangzi* and possible role in its transmission. Using the terms identified by Graham and myself as characteristic of Syncretic Daoism I have constructed the following table based on a preliminary investigation:

Table 6.1. Syncretic Daoist Technical Terms in the *Lüshi chun qiu*

Categories and Terms	Chapters 3, 5, 17, 25	Remainder of Text
	COSMOLOGY	
天之道 The Way of Heaven	Chapter 3 (3x); Chapter 25 (1x)	Chapter 7 (1x); Chapter 20 (1x)
天地之道 The Way of Heaven and Earth	none	none
無爲 Non-action	Chapter 3 (2x); Chapter 17 (3x) Chapter 25 (3x)	Chapter 12 (1x) in Postface Chapter 13 (1x)
無形 Formlessness	Chapter 17 (1x)	Chapter 18 (2x)
理 Natural patterns	Chapter 3 (3x); Chapter 5 (5x) Chapter 17 (12x); Chapter 25 (4x)	43 x
	PSYCHOLOGY	
靜 Mental tranquillity	Chapter 3 (2x); Chapter 5 (5x) Chapter 17 (13x); Chapter 25 (4x)	none
虛 Mental emptiness	Chapter 17 (3x); Chapter 25 (3x)	none
去智與故 Eschew wisdom and precedent	Chapter 3.4 去巧故 Chapter 17.5 去想去意 Chapter 17.3 棄智	none

continued on next page

Table 6.1. Continued

Categories and Terms	Chapters 3, 5, 17, 25	Remainder of Text
去欲 Eschew desire	Chapter 17.5 去愛惡之心	none
心術 Techniques of the mind	none	none
精「氣「Vital essence	Chapter 3 (9x)	9x
精神 Quintessential spirit	Chapter 3 (2x)	Chapter 8 (1x)
性 Innate nature	Chapter 3 (3x); Chapter 5 (2x) Chapter 17 (10x); Chapter 25 (3x)	48x (including 15x in Chapter 1)
壽 Longevity: desire for/ techniques of	Chapter 3 (2x); Chapter 5 (2x); Chapter 17 (1x); Chapter 25 (1x)	Chapter 1 (3x); Chapter 2 (1x); Chapter 4 (1x)
神明 Spirit-like clarity	none	none
	POLITICAL THOUGHT	
因 Adaptation	Chapter 17 (4x)	none
應 Responsiveness	Chapter 3 (3x); Chapter 17 (7x) Chapter 25 (3x)	59x

Categories and Terms	Chapters 3, 5, 17, 25	Remainder of Text
循 Compliance	Chapter 25 (2x) 理 Chapter 3 (2x) 順性 Chapter 17 (1x) 順天	Chapter 12 (1x) in Postface
宜 Suitability	Chapter 17 (1x)	none
育萬物 Nurturing the myriads things	none	Chapter 21 (1x)
畜下 Tend the people	Chapter 17 (1x) 畜人	Chapter 2 (1x); Chapter 8 (1x)
王天下 Rule the state	none	Chapter 2 (2x); Chapters 6, 17, and 17 (1x each)
(五)帝(三)王 The Five Thearchs and /Three Kings	Chapter 17 (1x)	
	ADDITIONAL	
黃帝 The Yellow Thearch (favorable)	Chapters 3 and 5 (1x each)	15x

NB: In the table "x" stands for "times."

This table shows that there are a significant amount of shared technical terms between the Syncretic tradition of the *Zhuangzi*, the "Techniques of the Mind" texts in the *Guanzi*, the later *Huainanzi*, and now these four chapters of the *Lüshi chun qiu*. Of particular importance are the psychological terms from the Inner Cultivation tradition that advocates a meditation practice that involves the removal of thoughts, desires, and prior intellectual committments of all kinds, in an attempt to create a condition of tranquillity and emptiness needed to act selflessly and successfully in the world as characterized by phrases such as *wuwei er wu buwei* 無爲而無不爲 (take no action yet nothing is left undone). Such terms as *jing* 靜 and *xu* 虛 (tranquillity and emptiness) and phrases such as *qu qiaogu* 去巧故 casting off cleverness and precedent—or casting off thoughts and ideas//wisdom// and the mind of love and hate) are definitely part of the technical vocabulary of those who followed this practice.[23] It is clearly commended to the ruler in essays from these four chapters such as 17.2, 17.8, and 25.3. A further similarity with Zhuangzi's Syncretists is that inner cultivation is first and foremost to be practiced by the ruler, who maintains a similar hierchical structure to that found in, for example, *Zhuangzi* 13:[24]

凡君也者, 處平靜、任德化以聽其要, 若此則形性彌 (贏) 〔嬴〕, 而耳目愈精; 百官慎職, 而莫敢愉 (綎) 〔綖〕; 人事其事, 以充其名。名實相保, 之謂知道。

As a general principle, a lord should dwell in tranquillity and quiescence and depend on the transforming influence of his Power in order to hear what is essential. In this way his bodily frame and inborn nature will gather an ever-greater harvest and his ears and eyes will have ever more energy. The hundred officials will all be careful in their duties, and none will dare be lax or remiss. It is by doing his job a man satisfies the meaning of his title.

　　When title and reality match,
　　This is called "knowing the Dao." (*Lüshi Chun qiu* 17.4, "Not Personally")[25]

These chapters also show a degree of use of other philosophical concepts such as the matching of name and reality here taken from the Legalists that is another hallmark of the Syncretic Daoist tradition. Other important Syncretist ideas such as "adaptation" (*yin* 因) and "compliance with natural patterns" (*xun li* 循理), and "spontaneous responsiveness (*ying* 應) are also found here. To be sure, such terms as "formlessness" (*wuxing* 無形), "The Way of Heaven and Earth" (*tiandi zhi Dao* 天地之道), "nurturing the myriad things" (*yu wanwu* 育萬物) and several others do not have the same importance in these *Lüshi chun qiu* writings as in other Syncretist works. Nonetheless, there is enough evidence in these tables to support further research on the theory that Syncretic Daoists wrote these chapters and that they were part of a larger intellectual tradition that not only included the Syncretists who wrote the material Graham identified in the *Zhuangzi* but also led directly to them.

The Problem of Zhuangzi's Primitivist

There is considerable evidence from the Primitivist and Yangist sections of the *Zhuangzi* of certain intriguing parallels with the *Lüshi chun qiu* that warrant further examination and that could present a challenge to Graham's conclusions that these two sections were written at a moment during the Qin-Han interregnum. Indeed, Liu Xiaogan lists a total of twenty-six parallel passages between the two texts, eleven of which come from chapter 28, "Yielding the Throne."[26] He uses them as evidence that the entire *Zhuangzi* was already extant and served as the source for the *Lüshi chun qiu* parallels, yet his logic is flawed. He assumes without question and without establishing criteria for directionality of borrowing that the *Zhuangzi* is always the source. He never considers the possibility that both texts were drawing on common oral or written sources or that the *Lüshi chun qiu* might have been the source for the *Zhuangzi*. Indeed, Graham concludes that the only parallel with the Primitivist chapters (10/10 and LSCQ 11.4) is from a common source.[27] Furthermore, the only parallel with the Syncretist chapters is a narrative at *Zhuangzi* 12/33–37 and *Lüshi chun qiu* 20.2 in which the latter's version is almost twice as long, thus making it more likely that it was the source and not vice versa.[28] Nonetheless, the fact that *Lüshi chun qiu* 9.5 shows an awareness of the Cook Ding 庖丁 narrative (which itself is much too specific to the *Zhuangzi* to have come from a common source) and the fact that *Lüshi chun qiu* 14.8 contains almost verbatim the narrative about Zhuangzi and the mountain tree that begins chapter 20, indicates that some version of the *Zhuangzi* text was present at the court of Lü Buwei

呂不韋 and that it probably contained material from Zhuangzi and his immediate disciples. If an early recension of the *Zhuangzi* were present at the Qin 秦 court circa 240 B.C. and if it contained writings of Zhuangzi and his disciples, then what of the other three sections of the text that Graham has identified and how might that affect his dating of them?

After dispensing with the possibility that *Lüshi chun qiu* 11.4 took its version of the Robber Zhi narrative from *Zhuangzi* 10, Graham provides two pieces of evidence to support his concusion that the Primitivist wrote during the Qin-Han interregnum. The first is the following phrase from the Primitivist chapter 10, "Rifling Trunks (Qu qie 胠篋):"[29]

然而田成子一旦殺齊君而盜其國 . . . 十二世有其國。

> However Tian Chengzi 田成子 in one morning murdered the lord of Qi and stole his state . . . and (his family) possessed the state of Qi for twelve generations.

The Tian family ruled Qi until it fell to Qin in 221 B.C. Thus, Graham reasons, the Primitivist author must have written these words after the Qin unification. However since no tense for the verb *you* 有 is indicated, another possible reading is that "(his family) has possessed the state of Qi for twelve generations." Qian Mu 錢穆 lists twelve formal changes of rulership in Qi, where the Tian family effectively governed the state, beginning with Tian Qi's 田乞 murder of the Yan family heir on the death of Duke Jing 景公 in 489 B.C. and continuing until the last Qi ruler, Wang Jian 王建, who ruled from 264 B.C. until the Qin conquest.[30] Thus the Primitivist could have been writing at any point after 264 B.C., when the last Tian family member ascended the throne of Qi.

Additional evidence Graham provides for the interregnum date are several Primitivist references to a present age of death and destruction amidst which Confucians and Mohists "start putting on airs and flipping back their sleeves among the fettered and manacled." He argues that this must be a reference to the revival of philosophical schools during the period following the death of the First Emperor but there is another intriguing possibility that takes us to the decade during which the *Lüshi chun qiu* was written and compiled. According to historical sources, at the same period Lü Buwei was inviting scholars to come to the Qin court to write a philosophical blueprint for governing the empire to be, he was undertaking several campaigns against rival states. Between

249 and 243 B.C. he directed three successful campaigns against the states of Zhao 趙, Han 韓, and Wei 衛 and effectively destroyed them as independent entities.[31] It is possible that the turmoil the Primitivist writes about is what he has seen in one of these three states, ironically victimized by armies directed by the man who at the same time was opening his court to scholars of all intellectual persuasions, including of course the Confucians, Mohists, and the Yangists who the Primitivist also detests. Indeed, the courts of Zhao and Wei entertained numerous scholars of various schools before this time and some of the retainers who went to Qin could have easily come from one or both of these intellectual centers.

Furthermore there is intriguing textual evidence that places Graham's Primitivist at the court of Lü Bu-wei during this period. The one phrase that Graham demonstrates is the most characteristic of the Primitivist's writing—"the essentials of our nature and destiny" (*xingming zhi qing* 性命之情)—is found excusively in only one other Warring States philosophical work: the *Lüshi chun qiu*.[32] This distinctive phrase occurs nine times in the *Zhuangzi*, all of which are in the Primitivist chapters or related passages.[33] In the *Lüshi chun qiu* there are twelve uses in six passages and they are distributed in an interesting fashion across the entire work:

> 1.3: twice in same passage (p. 3/lines 12,13);
> 13.5: twice in same passage (67/5);
> 16.2: once (92/5);
> 17.4: once (103/6);
> 17.5: thrice in same passage (104/3,4);
> 25.3: thrice in same passage (162/9,17).[34]

It is important to note that the essay 1.3, "Giving Weight to the Self" (Zhong ji 重己) is one of the five essays in the *Lüshi chun qiu* that Graham follows Feng Yulan 馮玉蘭 in identifying as Yangist. And that essays 17.4 "Not Personally" (Wugong 勿躬), 17.5 "Knowing the Measure" (Zhi du 知度), and 25.3 "Having the Measure" (You du 有度) are in the group that I have earlier linked with Syncretic Daoism. These form an interesting pattern that we need to contextualize.

A distinctive theory of the inborn nature of human beings is completely absent from Daoist works written prior to 240 B.C. This includes *Guanzi's* "Inward Training" ("Neiye" 內業), *Zhuangzi's* Inner Chapters and most of the "school of Chuang Tzu" material identified by Graham, and the *Laozi*.[35] The first enunciation of such a theory is in the Primitivist chapters of the *Zhuangzi* and I have argued that it emerged from dialogue with the Yangists rather than the Confucians because it shares a similar—but not identical—vision of human nature. For the Yangists, the single most important of the spontaneous tendencies of human nature is longevity.[36] They argued that human beings tend to live long if they keep themselves from being disturbed by the "external things" of this world such as fame and profit. The second important aspect of human nature is the desire of the five sense faculties (eye, ear, nose, tongue, skin) for sense-objects. It is the senses' desire for their objects that in a fundamental way helps to maintain the health and the development of the organism, thus enabling it to realize its inherent tendency for longevity. However the senses themselves need to be regulated and limited to only the "suitable" amount of stimulation. Over-stimulation causes the senses to be impaired and eventually damaged. Thus there is a suitable amount of stimulation that is conducive to the health and development of the human organism and that suitable amount must be determined by Sages; the senses on their own do not have the ability to do this. Self-cultivation for the Yangists therefore consists of nourishing one's inherent nature by strictly limiting sense stimulation to the appropriate degree needed to maintain health and vitality. One of their principal practices was to prevent the loss of one's finite supply of "essential vital energy"(*jing* 精), which is lost due to over-stimulation of the senses. The Yangists shared an understanding of how the human organism functioned with the thinkers of the Inner Cultivation tradition and with early Chinese medical philosophers and practitioners who envisioned a body-mind complex made up of various systems of *qi* 氣 (vital energy).

The Primitivist understanding of "the essentials of our nature and destiny" seems to be an expansion of the Yangist position from within the Yangist model of human nature. Just like the Yangists, in their theory of human nature the Primitivists chose to focus on the senses. They argue that it is not merely the desire of our senses for sense-objects that constitutes our inborn nature, but, rather, their spontaneous tendency to perceive clearly and accurately that does. Furthermore, contra the other traditions that focus on human nature, the Primitivist argues that this spontaneous tendency can only be realized if the senses are unimpaired by either the Yangist rational attempt to limit their stimulation or the Confucian attempt to circumscribe them by the moral dictates of humanity and rightness or by cultural standards of beauty and taste. Thus, the Primitivist theory of human nature is based on a sense perception model just as is the Yangist and both differ distinctly from Confucian virtue models that entail the conquering of the senses because they easily lead to self indulgence.

An excellent contrast between Yangist and Primitivist theories can be seen in the following two passages:

Lüshi chun qiu 2.3, "The Essential Desires" (Qingyu 情欲)

天生人而使有貪有欲。欲有情, 情有節。聖人修節以止欲, 故不過行其情也。故耳之欲五聲, 目之欲五色, 口之欲五味, 情也。此三者, 貴賤愚智賢不肖欲之若一, 雖神農、黃帝, 其與桀、紂同。聖人之所以異者, 得其情也

Heaven generates human beings and causes them to have lusts and desires. Desires have essential aspects. These essential aspects have limits. The Sage cultivates these limits in order to regulate his desires. Thus they do not exceed what is essential to them. Therefore the ear's desire for the Five Tones, eye's desires for the Five Colors, the mouth's desire for the Five Flavors: these are the essentials. The noble and base, the foolish and the wise are not alike, but in desiring these they are as one. Even Shen Nong 神農 and the Yellow Emperor are the same as (the tyrants) Jie 桀 and Zhou 紂 when it comes to these. The reason that the sage is different is because he attains the essentials . . .[37]

Zhuangzi 8, "Webbed Toes" (Pianmu 駢拇)

且夫屬其性乎仁義者, 雖通如曾史, 非吾所謂臧也; 屬其性於五味, 雖通如俞兒, 非吾所謂臧也; 屬其性乎五聲, 雖通如師曠, 非吾所謂聰也; 屬其性乎五色, 雖通如離朱, 非吾所謂明也。吾所謂臧, 非仁義之謂也, 臧於其德而已矣; 吾所謂臧者, 非所謂仁義之謂也, 任其性命之情而已矣; 吾所謂聰者, 非謂其聞彼也, 自聞而已矣; 吾所謂明者, 非謂其見彼也, 自見而已矣。

Moreover whomever keeps his nature subordinate to Humanity and Rightness, though as intelligent as Zeng 曾 and Shi 史, is not what I would call a fine man; and whomever keeps his nature subordinate to the Five Tastes, though as intelligent as Yu Er 俞兒, is not what I would call a fine man either. Whomever keeps his nature subordinate to the Five Tones, though as intelligent as Music-Master Kuang 師曠, does not have what I would call good hearing; and whomever keeps his nature subordinate to the Five Colors, though as intelligent as Li Zhu 離朱, does not have what I would call good eyesight. When I call someone a fine man, it is not Humanity and Rightness that I am talking about, but simply the fineness in his Power; nor when I call someone a fine man is it the Five Tastes I am talking about, but simply a trust in the essentials of our nature and destiny. When I say someone has good hearing, I mean not that he hears something, but simply that he hears with his own ears; and when I say someone has good eyesight, I mean not that he sees something, but simply that he sees with his own eyes.[38]

The point being made here is further clarified in *Zhuangzi* 16, "Menders of Nature:" "If someone else lays down the direction for you, you blinker your own Power."[39] The Power is what develops from the spontaneous manifestation of our inborn nature to perceive things clearly. To do so spontaneously and harmoniously and completely without self-consciousness is what constitutes our innate nature. Perhaps borrowing images from *Laozi*, the Primitivist argues in chapter 9, "Horses Hooves (*Mati* 馬蹄):" "In the Simple (*su* 素) and Unhewn (*pu* 撲) the nature of the people is found."[40] The Confucians with their pre-established categories of morality and the Yangists with their rational determination of stimulation into such categories as Five Tones, and so forth, introduce a strong element of self-consciousness into the human psyche and destroy our innate ability to function spontaneously and harmoniously. And so the Primitivist laments in "Horses Hooves:"

> 夫赫胥氏之時, 民居不知所為, 行不知所之 . . . 及至聖人, 屈折
> 禮樂 . . . , 縣跂仁義 . . . 而民乃始踶跂好知, 爭歸於利 . . . 此
> 亦聖人之過也。

In the time of the House of Hexu 赫胥氏 (when Power was at its utmost), the people when at home were unaware of what they were doing, when travelling did not know where they were going. . . . Then came the sages, bowing and crouching to Rites and Music . . . groping in the air for Humanity and Rightness . . . and for the first time the people were on tiptoes in their eagerness for knowledge. Their competition became centered on profit. . . . This too is the error of the sages.[41]

If we return to examine the six passages in which the dozen occurences of the phrase, "the essentials of our nature and destiny" are found in the *Lüshi chun qiu*, an interesting pattern emerges. The initial use is in Chapter 1 and this is the only occurrence of this phrase in the first twelve chapters of the work (the "Almanacs"), the only ones that conform completely to Lü Buwei's original plan. The Postface to this first major division is dated August 11, 239 B.C., but then Lü's political difficulties grew as he became increasingly compromised by his involvement in the so-called "Lao Ai 嫪毐 Affair." He was removed from the office of Prime Minister in 237 B.C. and committed suicide two years later when the future First Emperor exiled him to Shu 蜀 (Sichuan). During this difficult period Lü must have had to increasingly concentrate on political affairs instead of his book, which seems to have been hastily finalized and could not follow his original plan for it.[42] Thus the initial use of our phrase is Yangist; both it and the theory of inborn human nature that includes it, seems to have been topics for debate and discussion in Lü's intellectual circle. The five remaining uses of the phrase "the essentials of our nature and destiny" seem to either extend it or challenge it. Let us examine all these uses in their contexts:

> 1.3, "Giving Weight to the Self" argues that our individual life is our most precious possession that must be attentively guarded by the reasoned and moderate fulfillment of the senses and that whomever injures it "does not fathom the "essentials of our nature and destiny." As we have seen, these essentials are the desire of the senses for sense objects and the need to rationally regulate them.[43]
>
> 13.5, "Carefully Listening" (Jinting 謹聽) argues that Yao 堯 found Shun 舜 worthy and Shun found Yu 禹 worthy because "They listened with their own ears" and thus relied upon "the essentials of nature and destiny." Thus this phrase must refer to the senses' tendency to perceive clearly and accurately.[44]

In 16.2, "Observing the Age" (Guan shi 觀世), Liezi 列子 refuses the gift of grain from Prince Yang of Zheng 鄭子陽 even though he is starving because the prince was only offering it based on someone else's recommendation and did not directly know of Liezi's abilities on his own: "Would he also kill me based on someone elses' recommendation?" he reasons. Later Prince Yang was killed in a rebellion and Liezi, not being associated with him, survived. Because he declined after seeing how things might change, he "was well-versed in the essentials of our nature and destiny" states the author. Here it seems to entail using our inborn tendency to perceive and know things clearly rather than to rely on others as a basis for making decisions and is thus a similar use to that of 13.5.[45]

17.4, "Not Personally, (Wugong 勿躬)" argues that sage-kings, by nourishing their spirit and cultivating their Power, govern effectively because their inner cultivation prevents them from interfering with the work of their officials and meddling in the lives of the people. Thus "good rulers take care to preserve the essentials of nature and destiny," which here seems to refer to the inherent tendency for their spirits to be united with the Grand Unity (Taiyi 太一) a synonym for the Dao, and to thereby attain the Power. This implies that it is a natural human tendency for the mind to be tranquil and unbiased because at our deepest levels humans are grounded in the Dao.[46]

In 17.5, "Knowing the Measure (Zhi du 知度)," the essentials of according with the Dao are to be found in knowing the essentials of nature and destiny to which the superior ruler submits by relinquishing love and hatred and using emptiness and nonaction as his foundation for governing others. This use seems consistent with the prior one.[47]

25.3, "Having the Measure (You du 有度)," quotes the teaching of Jizi 季子 that all those who are able to penetrate (tong 通) "essentials of our nature and destiny" are able to govern effectively because they have controlled their selfish impulses and become impartial and selfless. Confucian and Mohist dicta of humaneness and morality are alien to nature: only by penetrating the essentials of nature and destiny will people become spontaneously humane and moral. Realizing these essentials involves holding fast to the One by an apophatic practice of emptying the mind. Again here the spontaneous tendency to become tranquil and realize our innate union with the Dao is meant by this phrase.[48]

It looks like the understanding of our phrase in the Syncretic Daoist essays in chapters 17 ("Not Personally" and "Knowing the Measure") and 25 ("Having the Measure"), directly contradicts that in the Yangist "Giving Weight to the Self." In the latter, the individual self is the focus of cultivation; it is the self that rationally regulates the natural desires of the senses for sense objects. In the former three essays the focus of self cultivation is on the ontological basis to human nature in the Dao that can only be attained when these selfish concerns can be set aside. Indeed, their position is similar to what emerged in the *Huainanzi* a century later but which the Syncretist authors in the *Zhuangzi* were completely silent about.[49] Indeed, the concept of human nature is totally absent from their writings.

The uses of our phrase in the essays chapters 13, "Carefully Listening," and 16, "Observing the Age," seem to be working within the same model we find in the Yangist understanding of human nature in "Giving Weight to the Self" and the three other early Yangist essays, 1.2, "Making Life the Foundation" (Ben sheng 本生), 2.2, "Valuing Life" (Gui sheng 貴生), and 2.3, "The Essential Desires" (Qingyu). In these instances the model is that of sense perception. For the Yangists it is the desire of the senses for sense objects that is the inborn tendency of human nature and in these two other passages it is the tendency of the senses to perceive clearly that is this basis. In fact the understanding of human nature in 13.5 and 16.2 seems strikingly close to that in *Zhuangzi's* Primitivist in its assumption that this inborn nature consists of the spontaneous tendency of the senses to perceive clearly and accurately and that this must be the basis of an enlightened awareness.[50]

Given this theoretical similarity with the Primitivist and given the earlier argument that the Primitivist developed his theory of human nature by extending a Yangist model, I think it likely that the Primitivist developed his own unique theory in response to the four early Yangist essays of the *Lüshi chun qiu*. There are two possible scenarios for how this happened:

- He read the text at some later point in time (as Graham would have it);

- He was present at the court of Lü Buwei and either participated in the disputations that led to the writing of the text or read the text perhaps when the initial twelve chapters were completed in 239 B.C.

As for the former scenario, we have already noted the problems with Graham's justification for his late date of authorship. Furthermore, given the vagaries of textual transmission, especially during the latter half of the third century B.C., it is much more likely that the Primitivist formed his ideas in dialogue with the Yangists at the court of Lü Buwei than that he came across them in written form forty years later in some other place. Moreover, if the Primitivist had read the entire *Lüshi chun qiu* text he would have seen that the Syncretic Daoist authors of 17 and 25 had already given a Daoist response to the Yangist misunderstanding of "the essentials of our nature and destiny." And if he had read the entire text and then disagreed with the authors of 17 and 25, he would have been prompted to include a criticism of them in his attack. Yet this is not the case.

Therefore, I think it likely that the Primitivist wrote his essays in direct response to the early Yangist essays of the *Lüshi chun qiu* and before others authored the Syncretic Daoist challenges to the Yangist theory of human nature now found in chapters 17 and 25. This places him in Qin after Lü Buwei's last military campaign in 243 B.C., the devastation from which he seems to have witnessed, and before Lü was removed from office in 237. Furthermore, given what Graham describes as his "pugnacious attitude" in these writings, it would seem that he became disaffected with the entire enterprise and with its director. Indeed, if we look carefully at his representation of Robber Zhi in "Rifling Trunks," one can almost see Lü Buwei: "The man who steals a buckle is put to death; the man who steals a state becomes a lord, and at the gates of a lord you'll see the humane and righteous."[51]

For a number of reasons I think that the Primitivist was also a follower of the *Zhuangzi* of the "Inner Chapters. First, his essays were included in the book; I think with further study we will find that all of the thirty-three chapters had some relationship to the first seven. Second, while social criticism predominates in these chapters, they are not totally without mystical concerns. For example, the exemplary person when forced to rule does so through nonaction (*wuwei* 無為) and

". . . sitting still as a corpse he will look majestic as a dragon; from the silence of the abyss he will speak with a voice of thunder . . . He will move with the numinous and proceed with the Heavenly, will be relaxed and nonacting. . . ."[52] Third, as Graham notes in "How Much of Chuang Tzu . . ." the phrase *zai you* 在宥 ("to locate and circumscribe [one's nature]") found in Zhuangzi 11 is also present in the Inner Chapters[53] Finally, the Primitivist shares the same essential concern of the Inner Chapters: the most important thing one can engage in in this life is the cultivation of the numinous and spontaneous qualities of one's being and the concomitant development of Inner Power and manifestation of the Way. The Primitivist embeds these qualities in human nature and argues that to first realize them and then fulfill them constitute "the essentials of our nature and destiny."

Therefore, I conclude that these Primitivist chapters were written during the debates that presumably occurred at the Qin court of Lü Buwei before and during the writing of the *Lüshi chun qiu* by a lineal descendant of the historical Zhuang Zhou 莊周 who is also likely to have brought the extant writings of his teacher and his tradition to the court. This person responded particularly to the Yangists and from them adapted a number of unique concepts into early Daoist thought including the notion of inborn nature. However, due to the excessively combative and polemical nature of his writings, the Primitivist chapters were not included in the *Lüshi chun qiu*, if, indeed, they were ever even submitted for inclusion.

The Problem of Zhuangzi's Yangists

This then brings us to a reconsideration of the four Yangist chapters and why they are included in the *Zhuangzi*. Graham identifies them as Yangist because they contain many of the technical terms that independent sources say characterized their philosophy, terms such as "honoring life" (*guisheng* 貴生), "giving weight to life" (*zhongsheng* 重生), and "keeping life (or nature) intact" (*quansheng/xing* 全生/性). To be sure these terms also abound in the five Yangist essays in the *Lüshi chun qiu*. However if these Zhuangzi chapters really are Yangist, as Graham would have it, then how did they find their way into the *Zhuangzi*? If they are not Yangist, as Liu Xiaogan would have it, then why do they contain so many Yangist ideas? Part of the explanation may be found in the eleven shared narratives between Zhuangzi 28 and the *Lüshi chun qiu*:

Table 6.2. Shared Narratives in *Zhuangzi* 28 and the *Lüshi chun qiu*

Narrative in *Zhuangzi* 28	HYZZ Loc.+ Graham trans	Location in *Lüshi chun qiu*	Knoblock/Riegel
1. Yao 堯 and Xu You 許由	28/1–3; ACG 224	2.2	80
4. Shun 舜 and farmer	28/8–9; ACG 225	19.1 longer	475
5. King Danfu 大王亶父	28/9–15; ACG 225	21.4	557–58
6. Prince Sou flees	28/15–18; ACG 226	2.2	81
7. Master Hua 子華子	28/18–23; ACG 226	21.4	558
8. Lu Jun 魯君 and Yan He 顏闔	28/23–31; ACG226–27	2.2 slightly fuller	81–82
9. Master Lie 子列子	28/31–35; ACG 227	16.2 has conclusion	380–81
14. Master Zhan 瞻子	28/56–59; ACG229–30	21.4 omits conclusion honoring Mou of Wei	558–59
15. Confucius trapped	28/59–68; ACG230–31	14.6	325–26
16. Shun and Wuze 無擇	28/68–70; ACG 231	19.1 longer; has key variants and conclusion	475–78
17. Tang 湯 and Jie 桀	28/70–78; ACG 231–32		
18. Bo Yi 伯夷 and Shu Qi 叔齊	28/78–87; ACG 232–33	12.4 longer; many variants; approving	266–68

To begin with, six of the eleven shared narratives are found in Yangist essays of the *Lüshi chun qiu*. All of these are fairly close textually with only a handful of variants among them. Four of the remaining five vary rather more extensively from their *Zhuangzi* counterparts and three of those have different conclusions. While Graham thinks that the *Lüshi chun qiu* was the source and Liu would have it the other way round, I find it difficult to determine a clear direction of borrowing between them. I would hypothesize that both texts draw on a common source, perhaps a Yangist collection of tales for use in disputation that could be used for different ends, depending upon one's ideological persuasion. Graham argues that the *Zhuangzi* collection of these passages is Yangist but perhaps there is another explanation.

The last three narratives in "Yielding the Throne" are different from the rest, as Graham has noted. To him they they are examples of the wasting of life that the Yangists so detested but if we look to their *Lüshi chun qiu* parallels we see that they were put to different uses. *Lüshi chun qiu* 19.1, "Departing from the Conventional" (Li su 離俗) argues for an extreme Confucian position that we can track back to *Mencius* 6A10, that if one keeps life at the expense of what is Right one is not an ethical person. Here these men who killed themselves rather than dishonor their sense of "Reason and Rightness" (yi li 義理) are honored; the *Zhuangzi* parallel omits this conclusion. In *Lüshi chun qiu* 12.4, "Sincerity and Purity" (Cheng lian 誠廉), the story of Bo Yi and Shu Qi, who starved themselves to death rather than serve a corrupt (Confucian) Zhou conquest, looks every bit a Mohist attack against the Yangists in its conclusion that it is more important to keep intact one's principles of benefit for all, rather than selfish gain even at the cost of one's life. Of course "Yielding the Throne" excoriates these men for their "lofty punctiliousness and harsh code of conduct."

Now while these narratives could have been collected by the Yangists, their use by Confucian and Mohist extremists in the *Lüshi chun qiu* suggests that such views were being argued in the Lü Buwei circle. The Primitivist is particularly harsh in his denunciation of both these groups and if, indeed, he was present there he could have also been interested in collecting these passages for use in arguing for a different vision.

One possibility not envisioned by Graham and Liu is that *Zhuangzi* 28, rather than being a Yangist compilation or the writings of a disciple of Zhuangzi, is a collection of narratives for use in disputation against the Yangists, Confucians, and Mohists—but drawn from them—that was created by the Primitivist.[54] Indeed, this could have been inspired by the idea of practicing "saying from a lodging-place (Yuyan 寓言)," which is advocated in a brief essay in chapter 27 Graham links to the Inner Chapters.[55] On this theory then, the Primitivist would be the author of Zhuangzi 29 and 31.[56] This would explain the commonality of the figure of Robber Zhi to both chapters 29 and 10, and many other shared technical terms and metaphors such as their interest in inborn nature, their strong anti-Confucianism, their promoting of a primitive agrarian Utopia, the touches that Graham recognizes as "mystical" in "Robber Zhi" such as the advice: "Return and seek what is from Heaven in you . . . Take your course from Heaven's pattern. . . . and . . . In accord with the Way walk your meandering path."[57] It would also explain some of the Taoist sounding phrases in chapter 31, "The Old Fisherman, (Yufu 漁父)" such as "Carefully guard the Genuine in you" and "The Genuine is the means by which we draw upon Heaven, it is spontaneous and irreplaceable" and ". . . it is from the Way that the myriad things take their course."[58] And it would also explain the six examples of shared narratives between the Primitivist essays and these "Yangist" chapters enumerated by Liu Xiaogan.[59]

If these four "Yangist" chapters were actually created by the Primitivist, they would have entered the Zhuangzi along with his essays now found in chapters 8–11 and would have been included because the Primitivist was himself a follower of Zhuangzi and was the person who brought what existed of the Zhuangzi text to Lü Buwei's court. However if the Primitivist left the court in a huff, how then did his text get transmitted from there? Perhaps the anwer is to be found in the resolution of another problem: the classification of chapter 16, "Menders of Nature."

The Problem of Chuang Tzu 16, "Menders of Nature" (Shanxing 繕性)

The classification of Chapter 16 "Menders of Nature" has been problematic. Liu Xiaogan links it to the "Huang-Lao" chapters of the text but Graham finds it unlike anything else in the entire work and refuses to classify it.[60] In my opinion this chapter is very close to the Primitivist material.

There are two principal reasons why Graham fails to link "Menders of Nature" to the Primitivist writings, although he does see some strong parallels. The first is that this chapter contains a series of Confucian definitions derived from Daoist concepts. These are found in the thirty-seven graphs found at 16/3–4.[61] The second is that chapter 16 does not have any of the expressions characteristic of the Primitivist's very distinctive style.

However, scholars since the Song dynasty have questioned the authenticity of the Confucian definitions in these two lines. Recently they include Qian Mu, Guan Feng, and Chen Guying 陳鼓應.[62] Since, as Graham has pointed out, there are a number of other places in the text that appear to be glosses inserted by a compiler (see for example four quotations from the *Laozi* he feels were inserted into the Primitivist essays), there is every reason to believe that these sentences were written by a Syncretist editor who was contending that Daoists and Confucians weren't that different after all. This will be clearer if we examine the disputed passage (which contains 37 graphs whose translation I have italicized) in context:

古之治道者, 以恬養知; 生而无以知為也, 謂之以知養恬。知與恬交相養, 而和理出其性。夫德, 和也; 道, 理也。德无不容, 仁也; 道无不理, 義也; 義明而物親, 忠也; 中純實而反乎情, 樂也; 信行容體而順乎文, 禮也。禮樂徧行, 則天下亂矣。彼正而蒙己德, 德則不冒, 冒則物必失其性也。

The men of old who cultivated the Way used calm to nurture knowing. They knew how to live but did not use knowing to do anything; one may say that they used knowing to nurture calm. When knowing and calm nurture each other harmony and pattern issue from our nature. The Power is the harmony, the Way is the Pattern. *The Power harmonizing everything is Humaneness; the Way patterning everything is Rightness; when Rightness is clarified and we feel close to other things, this is Loyalty; . . . when something pure and real from within you gets expressed, there is Music; when trustworthy conduct has a harmonious embodiment that conforms to elegant patterns, there are Rites.* When Rites or Music are universally practiced, the world falls into disorder. If something else lays down the

> direction for you, you blinker your own power. As for the Power, it will not venture blindly; and things that do venture blindly are sure to lose their own natures."[63]

The most striking thing about this passage is the contrast between the problematic sentences and the two that immediately follow them. How can the author be advocating Rites and Music and other Confucian virtues in one breath and then criticizing them in the next? Criticism of the deleterious effects of culture, which would include such virtues, is the norm in this essay rather than the anomaly. Furthermore there are no absolutely no places in the entire essay in which Confucian values are advocated. If we take these thirty-seven graphs as an editor's gloss and remove them, then the essay can be definitively linked with the Primitivist chapters.

In addition to sharing the Primitivist interest in the Way and its Inner Power as we see in the above passage, the author of "Menders of Nature" shares the following themes with the Primitivist:

1. Both advocate and defend the life of the hermit.

2. Both criticize cultural institutions for meddling with inborn nature:

   a. Confucian practices and ideas

   b. "wisdom"

   c. cultural norms of taste, beauty, etc.

3. Both harken back to primitive Utopias and use very similar descriptions.

4. Both detail the decline from this and see it as a loss of Power, which they concur in defining as the ability to act and live spontaneously in accord with the Way;

5. Both are unique in the text for their being pivotally concerned with inborn nature and "nature and destiny."[64]

However there are a few differences. First, as Graham points out, the author of "Menders of Nature" does not use any of the distinctive expressions of the Primitivist author. Second, he is more positive about the possibility that certain kinds of knowledge (properly harmonized with quiescence; not used to do anything) can be beneficial. Third, he criticizes the Confucians and Yangists, as does the Primitivist, but not the Mohists, perhaps indicating he wrote at a slightly later time when they were no longer a viable intellectual rival. Finally he talks positively about Pattern (*li* 理), an idea much further developed by the Syncretic lineages of early Daoism and, by the way, a particular concern of the authors of the *Lüshi chun qiu*.

For all these reasons I conclude that the author of "Menders of Nature" was a different person than the author of the Primitivist essays, but because of their shared perspective and opinions, this author was likely a disciple who wrote at a slightly later time. Like the Primitivist, he is a believer in the type of minimalistic government found in *Laozi* and he uses technical terms from the latter, most importantly Dao, *De*, the Unhewn (*pu* 樸), and spontaneity (*ziran* 自然). On the theory that his teacher, the Primitivist author, left the Qin court a bitter man, he could very well have left his student in charge of his writings and of a copy of the extant *Zhuangzi* text. This author of "Menders of Nature" might have found a home with the Syncretist Daoist authors of *Lüshi chun qiu* 17 and 25 and it was this group that continued to transmit the *Zhuangzi* text, now expanded by the addition of the Primitivist essays in chapters 8–11 and his disciple's essay in chapter 16. On this theory, later members of this Syncretist tradition added the remainder of the *Zhuangzi* text and transmitted all this material into the Han where it eventually ended up in Liu An's court in Huainan.[65] This theory, while admittedly tentative and in need of further corroboration, has the benefit of explaining how the different strata of the text that Graham accurately identified all came to be part of it.

Conclusion

Angus Graham's groundbreaking research on the different authorial voices in the *Zhuangzi* stopped short of answering a number of key questions about the history of the text, the most important of which is how the diverse positions he correctly identified came to be considered part of the text. I have tried to answer some of these questions by focussing on the relationship of the Syncretist, Primitivist, and Yangist sections to material in the *Lüshi chun qiu*. Based upon the evidence and arguments

evinced above, I would present the following theory of the early textual
history of the *Zhuangzi*:

By the time Lü Buwei announced the establishment of an intellectual center at the Qin court in about 250 B.C., the text consisted of
the material now found in the Inner Chapters and most—if not all—of
the "school of Chuang Tzu" material now found in chapters 17–22. In
addition much of the material in chapters 23–27 and 32 could also have
been written by this time. Future composition criticism of these conflated
chapters will hopefully establish all the different viewpoints contained
within them and how they were compiled.

This early recension was brought to the Qin court by a follower
of the historical Zhuangzi who later penned the chapters Graham calls
"Primitivist." He wrote them in response to Yangist ideas now found in
the *Lüshi chun qiu* but left the court in disgust over the prevalence of
Yangist, Confucian, and Mohist ideas there and over his contempt for Lü
Buwei himself, whom he may have satirized through the figure of Robber
Zhi.Before leaving, the Primitivist compiled the collection of narratives
in "Yielding the Throne" and tried his hand at using some of them in
"Robber Zhi" and "The Old Fisherman." After he left, his writings were
added to the text, perhaps by his disciple, who penned "Menders of
Nature." As the Lü Buwei circle collapsed after 235 B.C., this disciple
may have left Qin with the Syncretic Daoist group that authored many
of the essays in *Lüshi chun qiu* 3, 5, 17, and 25. I have elsewhere argued
that this group was the first to attempt to self-consciously build something that could be called a Daoist "school" and that they transmitted
Daoist practices and texts into the Han dynasty.[66] At some point this
group added their own ideas to the text of the *Zhuangzi* and decades
later brought it to the court of Liu An at Huainan (a theory Graham
took to be "an attractive conjecture"). Thus the original recension of
the *Zhuangzi* was finally established.

Of course much of this is hypothetical and awaits further research.
It is difficult to say how much the textual interference of Guo Xiang
has altered the materials on which we may base our final conclusions.
But there is no doubt that we would be much farther from a resolution
of the many questions that have surrounded the text of the *Zhuangzi* for
over a millenium without the innovative scholarship of Angus Graham.

Daoist Inner Cultivation Thought and the Textual Structure of the *Huainanzi* 淮南子

Introduction

The issue of the intellectual filiation of the *Huainanzi* is one that has vexed scholars for generations. Is it an "Eclectic" work (*zajia* 雜家), as it was categorized in the *Bibliographical Monograph of the History of the Former Han*? Is it a "Daoist" work, as others have categorized it? Is it a work that self-consciously eschews any and all intellectual affiliation, claiming for itself a uniqueness that makes it *the* essential philosophical blueprint for ruling the Han empire? Our *Huainanzi* translation team has gone over all these arguments time and again and agreed to disagree.[1] In this chapter, I present an argument for the *Huainanzi* being a work of the Inner Cultivation tradition that received the label "Daoist" from Sima Tan 司馬談 in his famous and influential discourse, "On Six Lineages of Thought" in chapter 130 of the *Historical Records*. When one analyzes the carefully organized series of nesting Root-Branch structures in the text, it becomes clear that while the authors did incorporate a great variety of ideas from earlier intellectual traditions into the unique synthesis they created in the *Huainanzi*, the ideas and practices of the Daoist Inner Cultivation tradition constitute the normative foundation into which all these other ideas are integrated. I begin by presenting an overview of previous research on this tradition of practice and philosophy,

---

I would like to dedicate this chapter to the memory of Arun Stewart, Brown class of 2011: "Alas! Heaven has bereft me." *Lunyu* XI.9.

then proceed to discuss how the carefully crafted Root-Branch structures in the book demonstrate how the ideas from this tradition provide the normative foundation of the entire book. Then I conclude with how this textual analysis impacts theories of the intellectual affiliation of the *Huainanzi*.

The Inner Cultivation Tradition

Those of us who have studied the surviving textual sources from the late Warring States and early Han are confronted with an array of separate texts. Given the limited production and circulation of written works in this period, it simply isn't logical to conclude they are all produced independently of one another.[2] Indeed, some of them cite or borrow material from others, such as *Mencius* citing the *Analects*, the "outer chapters" of the *Zhuangzi* 莊子 and the *Huainanzi* citing the *Laozi* 老子, and so on; so we know that at least some later authors were aware of earlier written works. But even if the *Mencius* never cited the *Analects* by title or Confucius by name, we would understand the two works were intellectually related because they share a common set of philosophical concerns, most important of which are benevolence (*ren* 仁), propriety (*li* 礼), knowledge (*zhi* 知), rightness (*yi* 義), and filiality (*xiao* 孝). These philosophical concerns, furthermore, are positively valued in these two works and in a third major work of this early intellectual tradition, the *Xunzi* 荀子. These concepts form a unique field of discourse and techniques that can be used to differentiate distinctive intellectual lineages in pre-Han China. The very existence and survival of works like the *Analects*, the *Mencius*, and the *Xunzi* implies that there must have been some sort of social organization to create, copy, and transmit them.[3] Relying on the evidence of a teacher-student social relationship that we find in many sources starting with the *Analects*, we can postulate that this is the basis for the social organization that created, preserved, and transmitted the texts of the distinctive philosophical lineages in pre-Han China.

Indeed, Mark Lewis posits the existence of such groups that were outside the "ambit of the state" that

> . . . were formed by master-disciple traditions that relied on writing both to transmit doctrine or information and to establish group loyalties. . . . Internal evidence of shifting usage and doctrinal contradictions shows that several of these

works evolved over long periods of time. The masters were invented and certified as wise men in this progressive rewriting by disciples, while disciples in turn received authority from the prestige they generated for their master . . .[4]

In addition, Fukui Fumimasu has insightfully observed that these intellectual lineages were not only organized around texts and ideas: they were grounded in distinctive practices or techniques.[5] We read in the historical record that the thinkers who considered themselves the inheritors of the tradition of Confucius and that of Mozi 墨子 had a distinctive set of core practices that centered on ritual performance for the former and logical argumentation and defensive warfare for the latter. These core practices and concomitant ideas, as well as a body of teachers and narrative stories—a kind of lore—formed the basis for an emerging sense of a distinctive lineal identity.

It is these distinctive practices that formed the basis for the famous identification of the distinctive *jia* 家, often translated—I think mis-leadingly—as "schools," but better rendered as intellectual "lineages" or "traditions" of the pre-Han period by Sima Tan. In writing his "Analysis of the Six Intellectual Traditions," he focused on the particular techniques that each one practiced: ritual for the Confucians, economy in state expenditures for the Mohists, rectification of state hierarchies for the Legalists, and intellectual syncretism and apophatic self-cultivation for the Daoists.[6] While the precise nature of Sima's project is the subject of a lively recent debate, even if we concede that Sima Tan retrospectively labeled philosophical traditions according to his own intellectual inter-ests, it is beyond doubt that he drew his comments about the "Daoist tradition" from the unique constellations of ideas that I have identified as "Inner Cultivation."[7]

The extant texts of this tradition include works often regarded as foundational to "Daoism," such as the *Laozi* and *Zhuangzi*, as well as a set of others that have been often overlooked, such as the four so-called "Techniques of the Mind" ("Xinshu") works within the *Guanzi* 管子, the *Lüshi chunqiu* 呂氏春秋, some excavated works such as the "Silk Manuscripts of Huang-Lao (*Huang-Lao boshu* 黃老帛書), and others.[8] A conceptual analysis of these works shows that the ideas they advocated can be organized into three general categories: Cosmology, Self-Cultivation, and Political Thought.[9] These ideas in many ways begin and end with a common understanding of the Way (*Dao* 道) as the ultimate source of the cosmos, Potency (*De* 德) as its manifestation in terms of concrete phenomena and experience, Nonaction; (*wuwei* 無為) as its definitive movement, and Formlessness (*wuxing* 無形) as its characteristic mode. There is also a common self-cultivation vocabulary that includes stillness and silence (*ji mo* 寂 漠), tranquility (*jing* 靜), emptiness (*xu* 虛), and a variety of apophatic, self-negating techniques and qualities of mind that lead to a direct apprehension of the Way. Let us explore these in more detail.

Inner Cultivation Practices

Simply put, the basic practice of inner cultivation is to unify or focus attention on one thing, often the inhalation and exhalation of the breath for a sustained period of time. Through this, one comes to gradually empty out the thoughts, perceptions, and emotions that normally occupy the mind and develop an awareness of the presence of the Way that resides at the ground of human consciousness. We can analyze these apophatic or "self-negating" practices into a number of basic categories.

POSTURE AND BREATHING: "SITTING AND FORGETTING"

To begin with, inner cultivation involves proper posture: an aligned sitting position for body and limbs is frequently recommended. For example, we see frequent references to this in "Inward Training," and we also find the famous narrative in *Zhuangzi* about "sitting and forgetting" (*zuo wang* 坐忘).[10] Often accompanying advice on posture is recommendation for breath cultivation. Cultivating the breath or vital energy (*qi* 氣) is a foundational practice in all the major sources of inner cultivation. It is often spoken of as concentrating or refining the breath (*zhuan qi* 專氣), as in this *locus classicus* from *Laozi* 10. Focusing on one's breathing is in essence a concentration of the attention.

In addition to proper posture and concentration of breath and attention, these Inner Cultivation texts also present a wide variety of techniques that have the effect of emptying out the normal contents of consciousness and hence approaching the Dao by apophatic means. Principal among these is the very frequent admonition in "Inward Training" to restrict or eliminate desires (*jing yu* 靜 欲, *jie yu* 節欲) (e.g., verses XXV and XXVI)[11] that occurs in similar form in the *Laozi* as "to minimize or be without desires" (*gua yu* 寡 欲, *wu yu* 無 欲) (chapters 1, 19, 37, 57). The *Zhuangzi*, the *Guanzi* ("Techniques of the Mind" 1), and the *Lüshi chunqiu* also contain similar and identical phrases.[12] Other related apophatic techniques include restricting or eliminating emotions, a staple of "Inward Training" (see verses III, VII, XX, XXI) as in verse XXV: *"When you are anxious or sad, pleased or angry, the Way has no place to settle within you."* Restricting or eliminating thought and knowledge is also commended in Inner Cultivation texts; so, too, is restricting or in some cases completely eliminating sense-perception.

Taken together, these passages recommend an apophatic regimen that develops concentration by focusing on the breathing and stripping away the common cognitive activities of daily life, something that must, of practical necessity, be done when not engaged in these activities, hence while sitting unmoved in one position. There is a wide variety of metaphorical descriptions of these apophatic regimens. These include the idea that following the Way involves "daily relinquishing" (*risun* 日損) in *Laozi* 48, *Zhuangzi*'s famous phrases of the "fasting of the mind" (*xin zhai* 心齋) in chapter 4, and "sitting and forgetting" (*zuo wang* 坐忘) in chapter 6. Both *Zhuangzi* 23 and *Lüshi chunqiu* 25.3 talk of "casting off the fetters of the mind" (*jie xin mou* 解心繆 or 謬). Another common phrase with a few close variations is "to discard/reject/relinquish wisdom/knowledge/cleverness and precedent/scheming" (*qu/qu/qi/shi* 除/去/棄/釋 *zhi/zhi/qiao* 智/知/巧 *gu/gu/mou* 故/固/謀).[13] Finally, who can forget the beautifully evocative parallel metaphors for these apophatic mental processes as "diligently cleaning out abode of the vital essence" (*jingqu jing she* 敬除精舍) "sweeping clean the abode of the spirit" (*saoqu shen she* 掃除神舍) in "Techniques of the Mind" 1 and "Washing clean the Profound Mirror" (*di qu xuanjian* 滌去玄鑑) from *Laozi* 10, a metaphor echoed in *Zhuangzi* 5:

> 人莫鑑於流水而鑑於止水 . . . 鑑明則塵垢不止, 止則不明也 . . .

> *None of us finds our mirror in flowing water, we find it in still water. . . . If your mirror is clear, dust will not settle. If dust settles then your mirror is not clear.*[14]

RESULTANT STATES: TEMPORARY EXPERIENCES
OF A TRANSFORMATIVE NATURE

The direct results of following these apophatic psychological practices is remarkably similar across many early texts of the Inner Cultivation tradition, thus indicating a consistency of actual methods and some sharing of ideas and texts. It is useful to borrow an important contrast from cognitive psychologists and talk about these results in terms of "states," which pertain to the inner experience of individual practitioners and tend to be transient, and in terms of "traits," which pertain to more stable character qualities developed in interactions in the phenomenal world.[15]

Probably the two most common resultant states of Inner Cultivation practices are "tranquility" (jing 靜), the mental and physical experience of complete calm and stillness, and "emptiness" (xu 虛), the mental condition of having no thoughts, feelings, and perceptions, yet still being intensely aware. States of tranquility and emptiness are both closely associated with a direct experience of the Way, perhaps the ultimate result of apophatic Inner Cultivation practices. There are a number of striking metaphors for this experience of unification of individual consciousness with the Way; three use the concept of merging to express it. Chapter 56 of Laozi contains advice on apophatic practice (e.g., "block the openings and shut the doors [of the senses]") and identifies the ultimate result as "Profound Merging" (xuantong 玄同). Zhuangzi 6 parallels with Laozi 56; therein Yanhui 顏回 teaches Confucius about the apophatic practice of "sitting and forgetting"; the ultimate result of which is "merging with the Great Pervader" (tong yu datong 同於大通).[16] Chapter 2 of Zhuangzi also engages this metaphor for the Way, stating that the Way "pervades and unifies" (Dao tong wei yi 道通為一) phenomena as different from one another as a stalk from a pillar, a leper from the beauty Xishi.[17] It is important to also note that these profound states of experience of the Way are quite often linked with preserving the spirit internally or becoming spirit-like (shen/rushen 神/如神) in "Inward Training" (see, for example, verses IX, XII, XIII), "Techniques of the Mind," the Lüshi chunqiu 3.4, and the Huang Lao boshu ("Jing fa" 經法 6). They are further associated with a highly refined and concentrated form of vital energy called the Vital Essence (jing 精) in "Inward Training" verses V, XIX, and these latter three sources.[18]

RESULTANT TRAITS: ONGOING COGNITIVE ALTERATIONS

As the direct result of the experience of these various dimensions of union with the Way—which, if we understand them correctly, are internal experiences attained in isolation from all interactions with the phenomenal world—adepts develop a series of what are best thought of as traits, more or less continuing alterations in one's cognitive and performative abilities that were highly prized by rulers and literati subjects alike for obvious reasons.

Perhaps the most famous of these is the idea that one can take no deliberate and willful action from the standpoint of one's separate and individual self, and yet nothing is left undone (*wuwei er wu buwei* 無 為而無不為). This works because adepts have so completely embodied the Way that their actions are perfectly harmonious expressions of the Way itself in any given situation. One of the most famous phrases in the *Laozi*, we find this in many of the other early sources of "inner cultivation," including the Outer and Miscellaneous chapters of the *Zhuangzi* and three inner cultivation essays in *Lüshi chunqiu*.[19]

These traits of immediate and uncontrived responsiveness describe well one of the ideas for which the *Laozi* is famous: spontaneity (*ziran* 自 然). A quality of both the Way and the cultivated sage in chapters 17, 23, 25, and 51, it refers to their natural, instantaneous and non-reflective responses to the phenomenal world. In a fundamental fashion, this almost magical ability to spontaneously accomplish all without seeming to exert any deliberate action is frequently associated with a great deal of Potency (*de* 德), an idea often associated with charisma. Potency is a kind of aura of spontaneous efficacy that develops in a person and is visible for all to see through repeated experiences of tranquility, emptiness, and merging with the Way. We find it all the early sources of inner cultivation theory, often in conjunction with apophatic techniques.

Additional cognitive improvements are also found in inner cultivation sources. These include perceptual acuity and cognitive accuracy (e.g., notice the phrase "mirror things with great purity" (*jian yu daqing* 鑑於 大清), which utilizes the metaphor of the mirror found in *Laozi* 10 and *Zhuangzi* 4); mental stability; impartiality; and the ability to "roll with the punches" that is so valued in the *Zhuangzi* notion of "*yinshi* 因是." Graham translates this in a very literal fashion: "the that's it which goes by circumstance." The concept is really that of flowing cognition, totally changing and transforming according to the situation, and it is exemplified in many of the narratives of the *Zhuangzi*: the "free and easy wandering" of chapter 1; the monkey keeper handing out nuts in chapter 2; Cook Ding in chapter 3; Cripple Shu in chapter 4, Wang Tai in chapter 5, Master Lai in chapter 6, Huzi 壺子 in chapter 7. There are many other examples in the rest of the text. All these individuals respond without egotism, without selfishness, without insisting on any one fixed point of view: that is how they survive and flourish. This kind of indifference to fortune or misfortune and creative spontaneous responsiveness to all situations is characteristic of people "in whom Potency is at its utmost."[20]

The basic contours of inner cultivation can be described as follows. Apophatic practices of sitting still and concentrating on one's breathing lead to gradual reductions in desires, emotions, thoughts, and perceptions. States of experience result from these reductions that make one feel tranquil, calm, still, and serene; these are states in which one's consciousness is empty of its usual contents and in which one feels unified with the Way. These states lead to a series of beneficial cognitive changes and the development of new traits such as acute perception, accurate cognition, selflessness, and impartiality; the ability to spontaneously be in harmony with one's surroundings no matter what the situation; and the ability to be flexible and adjust to whatever changes may come one's way. Table 7.1 summarizes these practices and results.

Despite the lack of precise identities among the specific terms assembled and discussed here, there is a remarkable consistency in their basic interrelationships and relatively focused range of meanings.[21] This, I would argue, indicates the presence of a distinctive intellectual tradition that transmitted both ideas *and* apophatic practices. But it is a tradition that was dynamic in its ability to change as the historical circumstances demanded. Thus developed several later Inner Cultivation works that centered on the political application of these apophatic techniques

One of the primary areas of change in the Inner Cultivation tradition is the application of its practices to the fundamental concern of the late Warring States Chinese thinkers: rulership. The *Laozi* (e.g., chapters 37, 46) begins to address how some of the traits derived from inner cultivation practice are beneficial for rulership. For one, they give sage rulers a distinct lack of attachment to themselves and their own desires that leads to making better decisions in governing (e.g., chapters 22, 49). Later texts such as "Techniques of the Mind" 2 and *Zhuangzi* 13 and 33 demonstrate thinking aimed at applying the techniques, states, and traits of inner cultivation to governing. They developed catchphrases for these applications: for example, "the Way of tranquility and adaptation (*jing yin zhi Dao* 靜因之道) in the former, "tranquil and sagely, active and kingly" (*jing er sheng, dong er wang* 靜而聖, 動而王) and "internally a sage, externally a king" (*nei sheng wai wang* 內聖外王) in the latter.[22] This trend continued into the *Huainanzi*, which embellished this unlikely mix of apophatic inner cultivation practices and results and political thought into a sophisticated new synthesis.

Table 7.1. A Summary of Inner Cultivation Ideas

Cultivation Practices	Posture:	Apophatic Techniques:
	Aligning the body; zheng xing 正形, zheng siti 正四體 keeping it still: xing an er bu yi 形安而不移	Restricting desires, gua yu 寡欲, jie yu 節欲, wu yu 無欲,
		Restricting thoughts, chu congming 出聰明, qu zhi 屈知, qi zhi 棄知, qu zhi 去知
	Breathing	Restricting perceptions: sai qi dui bi qi men 塞其兌閉其門;
	Concentrate zhuan qi 專氣,	yi qi er mu 遺其耳目; duo zhiti li xing 墮支體離形,
	Order qi li 氣理,	chu congming 出聰明,
	Guide qi dao 氣導,	
		Apophatic Metaphors:
	Attention	Mind fasting xin zhai 心齋,
	Focus on the One shou yi 守一,	Sitting + Forgetting zuo wang 坐忘,
	Focus on ctr. shou zhong 守中	Casting off mental fetters jie xin mou 解心繆,
		Sweeping clean numinous lodge saochu shenshe 掃除神舍
		Cleaning off the Profound Mirror diqu xuanjian 縧去玄鑑
		The Way of Stillness + Adapting jing yin zhi dao 靜因之道

continued on next page

Table 7.1. Continued

Resultant States	Tranquility *jìng* 靜 Emptiness *xu* 虛 Calmness *an* 安 Equanimity *qi* 齊 Repose *níng* 寧 Stillness *jì* 寂 Silence *mo* 漠 Serenity *tián* 恬	Detachment *dan* 淡 Refined/concentrated *jīng* 精 Spirit-like *shen* 神 Hold fast to the One *zhi yi* 執一 Attaining Empty Way *de xu Dao* 得虛道 Halting the Way *zhi Dao* 止道 Guarding/Returning to the Ancestor *shoulfan zong* 守/反宗
Resultant Traits	Nonaction *wuwei* 無為 All done *wu buwei* 無不為 Potency *de* 德 Resonance *gan ying* 感應 Spontaneity *ziran* 自然 Perceptual acuity *jian yu daqing* 鑑於大清 Instant + accurate knowledge: *jian zhi bu huo* 見知不惑	Suppleness *ruo* 弱 Pliancy *rou* 柔 Mental stability *ding xin* 定心, *zhi xin* 治心 Selflessness *wusi* 無私 Impartiality *gong* 公 Simplicity *su* 素 Wholeness *pu* 樸 Mastery of Mental Techniques *xinshu* 心術 Flowing cognition *yinshi* 因是 Following the Way of stillness and adaptation *jìng yin zhi dao* 靜因之道

So with this understanding of the inner cultivation practices, results, and insights, I argue that these are the basis for the *Huainanzi*'s syncretic approach to living in and governing the world.

Inner Cultivation in the *Huainanzi*

The *Huainanzi*, taken as a whole, is filled with the technical vocabulary of inner cultivation. One need merely tabulate the preponderance of the cosmological idea of the Way (329 of a total of 606 occurrences of 道 in the text) in comparison with, for example, the Confucian idea of benevolence (*ren* 仁) (145 occurrences; but many are critical, such as "When benevolence and rightness were established, the Way and Potency were cast aside").[23] One could come up with equally impressive totals for many of the other terms of the Inner Cultivation tradition in the *Huainanzi* (see table 7.2 on page 210). There are many interesting patterns to note in this table, especially the ways in which the presence of Daoist technical terms (Dao, De, *wuwei*, etc.) tend to cluster in the chapters that are most clearly devoted to the concerns we have identified as belonging to the Inner Cultivation tradition, such as chapters 1–2, 7, 11, 12, and 14. If we look further, we can see surprising clusters of Daoist ideas in unexpected chapters, such as 6, 8, 9, 13, and 15. While this is interesting, it is important to realize that it is not the mere presence of these ideas, but their absolutely pivotal role in the entire text that argues that they are foundational to the brilliant syncretism of the *Huainanzi*.

The Root-Branch Structure of the Text

In our recently published translation, we have asserted that the *Huainanzi* relies on the metaphor of roots and branches to structure the first twenty chapters of the book.[24] The twenty-first and final chapter, "A Overview of the Essentials" ("Yao lüe" 要略), is an summary of the rest of the book. As Sarah Queen has pointed out, this summary, likely to have been written at the very end of the writing project and also likely to have been written by its sponsor, Liu An 劉安, the second king of Huainan淮南, can give us helpful insights into the structure and composition of the text. Reflecting back on the text as a whole, the author of this final essay states:

Table 7.2. Distribution and Frequency of Key Inner Cultivation Terms in the *Huainanzi*

HNZ chap	Dao 道 Way	Cosmic Dao	De¹ 德 Potency	Dao De 道德 Way+Potency	Wu Wei 無為 Non-action	Jing 精 Essence	Shen 神 Spirit	Qing⁴ 清 Clear	Wu Xing 無形 Formless	Jing² 靜 tranquil	Xu³ 虛 Emptiness	Tian 恬 Serenity
1	33	29	20	0	6	6	31	5	12	7	8(2)	6
2	36	29	23	2	2	8	33	11	1	8	11	4
3	9	7	20	0	0	7	11	9(9)	0	1	10(10)	1
4	2	1	1	0	0	0	8	9(9)	0	0	2(2)	0
5	4	1	13	0	0	0	5	0	0	5(1)	1	0
6	23	12	10	3	0	6	8	2	2	0	2(1)	0
7	14	11	8	1	2	23	33	9	5	7	7(1)	2
8	22	16	20	4	1	8	12	3	1	5	2 (1)	0
9	50	19	16	0	7	9	14	6	0	10(3)	7(1)	1
10	28	6	21	3	0	7	2	3(2)	1	0	4(4)	0
11	30	19	15	5	0	0	7	7(3)	2	0	11(3)	0
12	53	33	12	0	10	6	9	4	0	4(3)	1	0
13	53	24	16	5	0	2	16	3(2)	0	0	4(2)	0
14	61	39	16	3	12	0	8	0	4	0	7(2)	4
15	33	25	17	0	1	4	11	3(2)	9	13(5)	17(11)	0
16	12	4	8	2	4	2	8	4(4)	3	0	3(3)	2
17	13	3	4	2	0	3	4	3(1)	3	2	1(1)	1
18	31	7	14	0	2	0	4	1	1	2(1)	0	1
19	17	3	5	0	4	5	8	2(1)	0	1	1(1)	0
20	48	22	15	2	0	9	19	9(4)	2	3(2)	3(3)	1
21	34	19	17	6	0	10	7	5	1	8(3)	3	1
N=	606	329	271	38	51	115(5)	260	98(37)	47	80(20)	105(49)	25

1. *De* does not include seven astronomical uses in the pairing *xing-de* ("recision and accretion").
2. *Jing* non-technical uses in parentheses, i.e., the phrase dong/jing "movement and stillness"; read N=80–20=60.
3. *Xu*: non-technical uses in parentheses, i.e., *xuyan* "falsehoods"; read N=105–49=56.
4. *Qing*: technical uses in the sense of cosmic or cognitive clarity; non-technical uses in parentheses mostly *qingzhuo* "clear and muddy"; read N=98–37=61.

21.1

夫作為書論者，所以紀綱道德，經緯人事，上考之天，下揆之
地，中通諸理。雖未能抽引玄妙之中 (才)〔哉〕，繁然足以觀終
始矣。揔要舉凡，而語不剖判純樸，靡散大宗，則為人之惛惛
然弗能知也；故多為之辭，博為之說，又恐人之離本就末也。
故言道而不言事，則無以與世浮沉；言事而不言道，則無以與
化游息．故著二十篇 . . .

We have created and composed these writings and discourses
as a means to
    knot the net of the Way and its Potency,
    and weave the web of humankind and its affairs.
    Above investigating them in Heaven,
    below examining them on Earth,
    and in the middle comprehending them through Patterns
      (*li* 理).

Although these writings are not yet able to fully draw out the
core of the Profound Mystery, they are abundantly sufficient
to observe its ends and beginnings. If we [only] summarized
the essentials or provided an overview and our words did not
discriminate the Pure, Uncarved Block and differentiate the
Great Ancestor, then it would cause people in their confusion
to fail to understand them. Thus,

    numerous are the words we have composed,
    and extensive are the illustrations we have provided,

yet we still fear that people will depart from the root and
follow the branches.

    Thus,
    if we speak of the Way but do not speak of affairs, there
    would be no
    means to shift with the times.
    if we speak of affairs but do not speak of the Way,
    there would be no means to move with (the processes of)
    transformation.
Therefore we composed the following twenty essays . . .[25]

Thus we can see that the authors of the *Huainanzi* regarded the Way as the root and normative foundation of the cosmos and human affairs as the branches. They took it as their most important task to "discriminate the Pure, Uncarved Block and differentiate the Great Ancestor," namely to attempt to describe the origins of the entire cosmos and to identify how its foundational Way is manifested within the phenomenal world, particularly within the daily experience of human beings. They also set about to "in the middle comprehend The Way and its Potency through the Patterns (*li* 理) through which they operate in the phenomenal world." This very understanding operates within the Root-Branch metaphorical structure. The author of this final essay further states that while sages can know the branches simply by attaining the root, most people, including scholars and implicitly Emperor Wu, to whom this book was presented by its compiler and his uncle, Liu An, in 139 BCE, must rely on the detailed explanations of the book in order to understand how the root of the Way is manifested throughout the world.

Given these concerns, it became apparent to us that although the *Huainanzi* does not traditionally contain any internal divisions (like, for example, the *Zhuangzi*, with its "inner-outer-mixed" structure), it does contain a basic division of its chapters into those that contain the philosophical foundations for the others and those that are derivative of them, in other words, "Root Section" and "Branch Section." Indeed, we are not the first to suggest a similar division: Charles LeBlanc, for example, has suggested that the first eight chapters constitute the "Basic Principles" (chapters 1–8) of the entire work and that the second half is concerned with "Applications and Illustrations" (chapters 9–20).[26] In an essay in this volume, Martin Kern supports these conclusions by demonstrating that the titles of the first twenty chapters of the text rhyme, and that the first rhyme sequence ends with the title of chapter 8. The title of chapter 9 begins a new rhyme sequence.[27]

In our analysis, the first eight chapters provide the basic philosophy of the whole text, and the remaining chapters contain a variety of detailed illustrations of how these basic philosophical principles work in the phenomenal world. In the "Root Section," we find all the basic cosmology, cosmogony, epistemology, self-cultivation theory, and theories on history, sagehood, and politics that the authors regard as foundational; in the "branch chapters," we find illustration of these foundations presented in a variety of literary styles, such as "overviews" (*lüe* 略), "discourses" *lun* 論,

sayings (*yan* 言), and persuasions (*shui* 說).This is completely consistent with the grand plan of the work presented in chapter 21, which involves attaining a comprehensive balance between the cosmology of the Way and its Potency and the variety of its manifestations in the human world.

Within this "Root Section" of the *Huainanzi*, the first two essays provide the cosmological, cosmogonic, and self-cultivation foundations for the all chapters of the "Root Section," and, by extension, for the entire book; in effect, they are the "Root Chapters" of the whole work. As Andy Meyer has argued, "every level of the compositional structure of the *Huainanzi* stands in a 'root' relationship to what comes after it. The further one gets toward the beginning of the text, the more fundamental the realm one encounters."[28] It is no accident that these essays, "Originating in the Way" ("Yuan Dao" 原道) and "Activating the Genuine" ("Chu zhen" 俶真), each borrows heavily from the *Laozi* and the *Zhuangzi*, respectively. In order to understand the pivotal role played by inner cultivation theory and practice within brilliant philosophical synthesis of the *Huainanzi*, one must comprehend the philosophy in these two chapters first and foremost.

Cosmology and Inner Cultivation in the "Root Chapters" of the *Huainanzi*

In chapters 1 and 2 and, indeed, throughout the entire work, the Way is the power and force that "covers heaven and upholds Earth." It embraces the entire cosmos; flowing through it, it sustains and nurtures all its phenomena and enables each of them to fulfill its nature. Chapter 1 begins with a beautiful poetic rhapsody on the Way, the longest paean on this topic in all of early Chinese philosophical literature. It reads, in part:

> 夫道者, 覆天載地, 廓四方, 柝八極, 高不可際, 深不可測, 包裹
> 天地, 稟授無形。源流泉 (滂) 〔浡〕, 沖而徐盈; 混混汩汩, 濁而
> 徐清。 . . . 山以之高, 淵以之深, 獸以之走, 鳥以之飛, 日月以
> 之明, 星歷以之行, 麟以之游, 鳳以之翔。

As for the Way:
  It covers Heaven and upholds Earth.
  It extends the four directions

and divides the eight end points.
So high, it cannot be reached.
So deep, it cannot be fathomed.
It embraces and enfolds Heaven and Earth
It endows and bestows the Formless.
Flowing along like a wellspring, bubbling up like a font,
 it is empty but gradually becomes full.
Roiling and boiling,
 it is murky but gradually becomes clear. . . .
. . . Mountains are high because of it.
Abysses are deep because of it.
Beasts can run because of it.
Birds can fly because of it.
The sun and moon are bright because of it.
The stars and timekeepers move because of it.
Unicorns wander freely because of it.
Phoenixes soar because of it.[29]

This understanding of the role of the Way in the cosmos expands upon—but is entirely in keeping with—all the earlier sources of inner cultivation theory.

According to these two "Root Chapters" in the *Huainanzi*, the universe is structured by the various innate natures (*xing* 性) of things that determine their course of development and their actions and the great patterns (*li* 理) that govern the characteristic ways that things act and interact with one another. These natures and patterns are thoroughly infused with the empty Way, which mysteriously guides their spontaneous processes of development and of daily activity. This entire complex world functions completely spontaneously and harmoniously and needs nothing additional from human beings.

It is because of this normative order that sages can accomplish everything without exerting their individual will to control things. In other words, they practice "Non-Action," (*wuwei* 無爲), which is effective because of the existence of this normative natural order. Sages cultivate themselves through the "Techniques of the Mind" (*xin shu* 心術) in order to fully realize the basis of this order within.[30] By realizing the Way at the basis of their intrinsic nature, sages can simultaneously realize the intrinsic natures of all phenomena. Thus *Huainanzi* 1 reads:

是故聖人內修其本, 而不外飾其末, 保其精神, 偃其智故, 漠然
無為而無不為也, 澹然無治 (也) 而無不治也。所謂無為者, 不
先物為也; 所謂〔無〕不為者, 因物之所為〔也〕。所謂無治
者, 不易自然也; 所謂無不治者, 因物之相然也.

> Therefore sages internally cultivate the root [of the Way
> within them]and do not externally adorn themselves with
> its branches.
> They protect their Quintessential Spirit (*jingshen* 精神) and
> dispense with wisdom and precedent (*zhi yu gu* 智與故).
> In stillness they take No Action (*wuwei* 無為) yet nothing is
> left undone (*moran wuwei er wu buwei* 漠然無為而無不為).
> In tranquility they do not govern but nothing is left
> ungoverned.
> What we call "taking No Action" is to not anticipate the
> activity of things.
> What we call "nothing left undone" means to adapt to what
> things have [already] done.
> What we call "to not govern" means to not change how
> things are naturally so.
> What we call "nothing left ungoverned" means to adapt to how
> things are mutually so.[31] (*yin wu zhi xiangran* 因物之相然)

While the *Huainanzi* authors are clearly grounding theses ideas upon
earlier inner cultivation cosmology, they expand upon it in asserting that
everything within Heaven and Earth is both natural and supernatural,
secular and sacred. ("The world is a spirit-like vessel *shenqi*" *gu tianxia
shenqi* 故天下神器.[32]) Therefore, the natures and patterns that underlie
and guide all these phenomena that are ultimately direct expressions of
the Way and that enable it to be manifest in the phenomenal world
attain a normative prominence that is mostly unfamiliar to the Abrahamic
traditions of the West. That is, these patterns, sequences, propensities,
and natures are themselves holy or divine.[33] They are the basis through
which all the multitudinous phenomena in the world adhere and function in harmony and as such serve as the models and standards for the
communities of human beings who are an integral part of this order.
While we found the beginnings of a similar understanding of the *li* in
the later "Techniques of the Mind" and *Zhuangzi* essays, the *Huainanzi*

authors build upon these to present a more fully articulated version of this position and an emphasis on the holy nature of these underlying Patterns. Human beings can either ignore this normative natural order and fail in their endeavors or they can follow it and succeed.

According to chapter 2 of the *Huainanzi*, human beings, despite having attained a harmonious society in keeping with these principles in the ancient past, tend to fall away from this normative natural order and lose their spontaneous functioning in accord with it. This is a major theme of the "Primitivist" chapters 8–11 of the *Zhuangzi*.[34] Humans must learn to get back in touch with this natural and spontaneous side within themselves; it is that part of us that is directly connected to the normative patterns through which the Way subtly guides the spontaneous self-generation of all things. Inner cultivation practices are the primary ways in which human beings can realize the deepest aspects of our intrinsic nature, that part of our being that is directly in touch with the Way and, through it, with the inherent patterns and structures of the universe.

As for the political realm, in order to govern effectively, rulers must follow the apophatic inner cultivation techniques that put them directly in touch with the Way. As the text clearly states:

天下之要, 不 (任)〔在〕於彼而在於我, 不在於人而在於 (我) 身, 身得則萬物備矣。徹於心術之論, 則嗜欲好憎外 (失)〔矣〕。

The essentials of the world:

> Do not lie in the Other
> But instead lie within the Self.
> Do not lie within other people
> But instead lie within your own person.

When you fully realize it [the Way] in your own person then the myriad things will all be arrayed before you. When you thoroughly penetrate the teachings of the Techniques of the Mind then you will be able to put lusts and desires, likes and dislikes outside yourself.[35]

Through these inner cultivation practices, these "Techniques of the Mind," sage rulers are able to develop the valuable cognitive trait of being able to discern these natures, propensities, and patterns of all phenomena and then not interfere with how the myriad things follow them. This seems to be an expansion of the *Huang Lao boshu* idea that, for the Cultivated, "seeing and knowing are never deluded" (*jian zhi bu huo* 見知不惑).[36] These inner cultivation practices are conceived of in almost the exact same terms as they are in the earlier sources of this tradition. As we have seen, this entails the systematic elimination of desires, emotions, thoughts, and sense perceptions that usually flood the conscious mind. Through this, one may break through to the set of profound experiences of contact with the Way that the *Huainanzi* authors embellish through passages such as these:

故心不憂樂, 德之至也; 通而不變, 靜之至也; 嗜欲不載, 虛之至也; 無所好憎, 平之至也; 不與物 (散) 〔殽〕, 粹之至也。能此五者, 則通於神器。通於神器者, 得其內者也. 是故以中制外, 百事不廢 . . .

Thus, when the mind is not worried or happy, it achieves the perfection of
>   Potency.
When the mind is inalterably expansive, it achieves the perfection of
>   tranquility.
When lusts and desires do not burden the mind, it achieves the perfection of
>   emptiness.
When the mind is without likes and dislikes, it achieves the perfection of
>   equanimity.
When the mind is not tangled up in things, it achieves the perfection of
>   purity.
If the mind is able to achieve these five qualities, then it will break through
>   to spirit-like illumination (*shenming* 神明).
To break through to spirit-like illumination is to realize what is
>   intrinsic.
Therefore, if you use the internal to govern the external,
>   then your various endeavors will not fail.[37]

The *Huainanzi* authors innovate upon earlier Inner Cultivation foundations by proffering a theory of human nature that avers that several important "states" that result from apophatic practice are actually inherent in the basic natures of all human beings. They are there to be discovered through practice. Perhaps the most important of these is tranquility. In *Huainanzi* 2 "Activating the Genuine" we read:

水之性真清而土汩之, 人性安靜而嗜欲亂之。夫人之所受於天者, 耳目之於聲色也, 口鼻之於 (芳) 臭 〔味〕也, 肌膚之於寒燠, 其情一也, 或通於神明, 或不免於癡狂者, 何也? 其所為制者異也。是故神者智之淵也, (淵) 〔神〕清則智明矣; 智者、心之府也, 智公則心平矣。人莫鑑於 (流沫) 〔流潦〕, 而鑑於止水者, 以其靜也; 莫窺形於生鐵, 而窺 〔形〕於明鏡者, 以 (覩) 其易也。夫唯易且靜, 〔故能〕形物之性 〔情〕也. 由此觀之, 用也 〔者〕必假之於弗用 〔者〕也, 是故虛室生白, 吉祥止也。夫鑑明者塵垢弗能薶, 神清者嗜欲弗能亂。

The nature of water is clear, yet soil sullies it.
The nature of human beings is to be tranquil, yet desires
　　disorder it.
What human beings receive from Heaven are [the tendencies]
　　　for ears and eyes [to perceive] colors and sounds,
　　　for mouth and nose [to perceive] fragrances and tastes,
　　　for flesh and skin for [to perceive] cold and heat.
The basic tendencies are the same in everyone, but some
　　penetrate to spiritlike
　　　illumination,
　　　and some cannot avoid derangement and madness.
　　　　Why is this?
　　　That by which they [these tendencies] are controlled
　　　　is different.
Thus,
　　the spirit is the source of consciousness; if the spirit is
　　　clear, then consciousness
　　　　is illumined.
　　Consciousness is the storehouse of the mind; if conscious-
　　　ness is impartial, the
　　　　mind will be balanced.
　　No one can mirror himself in flowing water, but [he can
　　　observe] his reflection

in standing water because it is still.
No one can view his form in raw iron, but [he can] view
his form in a clear
mirror because it is even.
Only what is even and still can thus give form to the
nature and basic tendencies
of things. Viewed from this perspective, usefulness
depends on what is not used.
Thus when the empty room is pristine and clear, good
fortune will abide there.[38]
If the mirror is bright, dust and dirt cannot obscure it.
If the spirit is clear, lusts and desires cannot disorder
it.[39]

Thus apophatic inner cultivation restores the mind to its natural state of tranquility. Through this experience, one can develop the various traits we have seen in the earlier tradition such as impartiality, perceptual acuity and cognitive accuracy (mirroring).

In *Huainanzi* 2, the very evolution of human cultural history is conceived of in terms derived from the Inner Cultivation tradition. For these authors, human cultural history is an inevitable devolution from an idyllic utopian condition in which all people can spontaneously manifest their deepest natures and live in harmony into an age of disorder and chaos in which only the most motivated and gifted of human beings can return to their foundation. This devolution is both natural and inexorable. It occurs on parallel levels in both the social macrocosm throughout history and the individual human microcosm as we develop from infancy to adulthood.

It is inevitable that an individual human being will fall away from the grounding in the Way that they experience as infants as they mature into an individuated person endowed with subject-object consciousness. It is also inevitable that human society will become increasingly more complex and technologically sophisticated over time. The assertion of the *Huainanzi* is that, paradoxically, although both of these processes are inevitable, they entail perils and vulnerabilities that will prove self-destructive if ignored. Given the intrinsic defects of the human condition, the key to human flourishing is a "return to the Way" through the apophatic inner cultivation practices described above. People who can do this "Activate the Genuine" and are sometimes called by that name, "the Genuine" (*zhen ren* 真人), as well as the Perfected (*zhi ren* 至人), or Sages (*sheng ren* 聖人). They are also said to have a great deal of Potency (*de* 德).

This cultural and individual human devolution itself is paralleled by the very evolution of the cosmos detailed in the cosmogonic passages at the beginning of chapter 2 (echoed in the briefer versions that begin chapters 3, 7, and 14) from a primordial nameless unity to the multifaceted phenomenal world in which human beings are embedded. This tri-leveled devolution is itself an expression of the same Root-Branch processes that structure the text as a whole. Just as the cosmos has differentiated into the complex world of things and affairs, human beings evolve from the un-self-conscious purity of the infant to the multidimensional complexity of adulthood and human society that evolves from primitive idyllic utopia to sophisticated civilization. At these latter stages of complexity, there is a natural tendency to fall away from the inherent harmony of the social world and individual consciousness, and human beings must counteract this by taking measures to preserve the supremacy of the originating root—the Way—in both individual and society.

In sum, then, these are the foundational ideas of the *Huainanzi*; they are thoroughly grounded in the earlier Inner Cultivation tradition. It is my contention that despite the variety of ideas from earlier intellectual traditions that abound throughout the text, the philosophy of these first two chapters provides the basis, the foundation, the "root" for all twenty chapters of the *Huainanzi*.

Inner Cultivation in the "Root Passages" of Each Chapter

The influence of inner cultivation ideas throughout the *Huainanzi* can be seen in a further analysis of the Root-Branch structure *within* each chapter. The following table demonstrates that most of the *Huainanzi* chapters begin with a foundational or "Root Passage" that a) is completely consistent with the normative Daoist inner cultivation philosophy of the first two "Root Chapters" of the text, and b) provides the foundation for the central arguments in the remainder of the chapter. The following table examines this phenomenon:

Table 7.3. Inner Cultivation Ideas in the "Root Passages"

HNZ Chapter and Main Theme	"Root Passage"
1. Cosmology of Way; inner cultivation	1. Rhapsody on the Way
2. Potency, inner cultivation; perfection; historical devolution	2. Cosmogony from *Zhuangzi* 2
3. Astrology/astronomy	3. Cosmogony of *Taishi* 太始 and yin yang
4. Geography	4. About geography
5. Seasonal ordinances	5. About seasonal ordinances
6. Five Phase resonance	6. Narrative of Resonance
7. Psychological/spiritual cultivation	7. Cosmogony of spirit/mind/body
8. History as devolution	8. The Historical Utopia of *Taiqing* + Way
9. Rulership techniques	9. Ruler's techniques: *wuwei*; *wuyan* 無言; *qingjing* 清靜
10. Moral psychology of human exemplars	10. Way/Feelings of Sages who embody it
11. Ritual and customs	11. Following nature = following the Way
12. How Dao manifests in the world	12. Knowing the Way
13. The fluidity of sage rulership	13. A Utopia of Potency when sages ruled
14. Sayings and comments on sage rulership	14. Cosmogony of Taiyi
15. Military techniques	15. Military in antiquity to pacify and protect
16. Collections of sayings for disputation	16. Hun/Po-Souls' Dialogue on the Way
17. Collections of sayings for disputation	17. According with Heaven and Earth
18. Inner cultivation needed to live among others	18. The Wise follow nature and accord with the Way
19. Diligent work needed for cultivation	19. *Wuwei* isn't really not working hard
20. The qualities of sage rulership	20. Sages achieve spirit-illumination

As table 7.3 shows, when we carefully examine the "Root Passages" at the beginning of each *Huainanzi* chapter, we find that they contain ideas from the two "Root Chapters" of the entire text, chapters 1 and 2. The only possible exceptions to this are the technical chapters 4 "Terrestrial Forms" ("Dixing" 地形) and 5 "Seasonal Rules" ("Shize" 時則), which form a set with chapter 3 "Celestial Patterns" ("Tianwen" 天文), although one could argue that because they are a set, the cosmogonic root passage for chapter 3 plays this role for chapters 4 and 5. Let's examine these data more closely.

To begin with, all of the cosmogonic "Root Passages" (in chapters 2, 3, 7, and 14) are consistent with the cosmology of the Way in enunciated in chapters 1 and 2. For example, the "Root Passage" of chapter 7 draws the following inner cultivation conclusion:

是故聖人法天順情, 不拘於俗, 不誘於人, 以天為父, 以地為母, 陰陽為綱, 四時為紀。天靜以清, 地定以寧, 萬物失之者死, 法之者生。夫靜漠者, 神明之宅也; 虛無者, 道之所居也。是故或求之於外者, 失之於內; 有守之於內者, (失)〔得〕之於外。譬猶本與末也, 從本引之, 千枝萬葉莫得不隨也。

For this reason, the sages:
    Model themselves on Heaven,
    Accord with what is genuine.
    Are not confined by custom,
    Nor seduced by other men.
    They take Heaven as father,
    Earth as mother,
    Yin and Yang as warp,
    The four seasons as weft.
    Through the tranquility of Heaven they become pure,
    Through the stability of Earth they become calmed.
Among the myriad things
    Those who lose this perish,
    Those who follow this live.
    Tranquility and stillness are the dwellings of spirit-like
      illumination,
    And emptiness and nothingness are where the Way resides.
For this reason,
    those who seek for it externally, lose it internally,
    and those who preserve it internally attain it externally as well.

It is like the roots and branches of trees: none of the thousands of limbs and tens of thousands of leaves does not derive from the roots.[40]

Chapter 14's "Root Passage" is also consistent with inner cultivation theory:

稽古太初, 人生於无, 形於有, 有形而制於物。能反其所生, 若未有形, 謂之真人。真人者, 未始分於太一者也。

In antiquity, at the Grand Beginning (*Tai chu* 太初) human beings came to life in "Non-being" and acquired a physical form in "Being." Having a physical form, [human beings] came under the control of things. But those who can return to that from which they were born, as if they had not yet acquired a physical form, are called "The Genuine." The Genuine are those who have not yet begun to differentiate from the Grand One.[41]

Note here the concept of "The Genuine" (*zhen ren*), which is developed most extensively in HNZ 2 but also appears in chapters 6, 7, and 8.

While not obviously indebted to inner cultivation theory on first reading, the narrative "Root Passage" that begins chapter 6 concludes with a statement that is totally consistent with its ideas:

夫全性保真, 不虧其身, 遭急迫難, 精通于天。若乃未始出其宗者, 何為而不成!

Now if you keep intact your nature and guard your authenticity,
　　And do not do damage to your person,
　　[When you] meet with emergencies or are oppressed by
　　　　difficulties,
　　Your Essence will penetrate [upward] to Heaven;

You will be like one who has not yet begun to emerge from his Ancestor—how can you not succeed?[42]

Despite the extensive discussion of the moral psychology of sagehood in Chapter 10, the authors take care to argue that ethical values often associated with the Confucian tradition are subordinated to the more fundamental concepts of the Daoist inner cultivation philosophy from the two "Root Chapters." We see this in its "Root Passage":

道至高無上, 至深無下, 平乎準, 直乎繩, 員乎規, 方乎矩, (句) 〔包〕裹宇宙而無表裏, 洞同覆載而無所礙。是故體道者, 不哀 不樂, (不怒不喜) 〔不喜不怒〕, 其坐無慮, 其寢無夢, 物來而名, 事來而應。

> The Way at its highest has nothing above it;
> at its lowest it has nothing below it.
> It is more even than a carpenter's level,
> straighter than a marking-cord,
> rounder than a compass,
> and more square than a carpenter's square.

> It embraces the cosmos and is without outside or inside. Cavernous and undifferentiated, it covers and supports with nothing to hinder it.

> Therefore those who embody the Way
>   are not sorrowful or joyful;
>   They are not happy or angry.
>   They sit without disturbing thoughts
>   And they sleep without dreams.[43]
>   Things come and they name them.
>   Affairs arise, and they respond to them.[44]

The more one examines them, the more one discovers that most of the "Root Passages" in the *Huainanzi* contain cosmological and inner cultivation ideas drawn from—or closely related to—the foundational concepts in chapters 1 and 2. As we have already seen, the "Root Passages" in chapters 3, 7, 10, and 14 unmistakably present various aspects of the cosmic Way. In addition, the "Root Passages" in chapters 8, 13, and 15 (this last one discusses the ideal military in antiquity) present antiquarian Utopian societies in keeping with the vision of them and their tendency to devolution outlined in chapter 2. Look, for example, at the beginning of the "Root Passage" of chapter 8, which depends for its meaning on the technical vocabulary of inner cultivation:

太清之治也, 和順以寂 (漢) 〔漠〕, 質真而素樸, 閑靜而不躁, 推移而无故, 在內而合乎道, 出外而調于義, 發動而成于文, 行快而便于物, 其言略而循理, 其行悅而順情, 其心愉而不偽, 其事素而不飾 . . .

The reign of Grand Purity (*Tai qing* 太清)
Was harmonious and compliant (*he xun* 和順) and thus silent
    and indifferent (*ji mo* 寂漠);
Substantial and true (*zhi zhen* 質真) and thus plain and simple
    (*su pu* 素僕).
Contained and tranquil (*jing* 靜), it was not intemperate;
Exerting and shifting, it [followed] no precedents.
Inwardly it accorded with the Way,
Outwardly it conformed to Rightness.
When stirred into motion, it formed [normative] patterns
    (*xunli* 循理);
When moving at full speed, it was well matched to things.
Its words were concise and in step with reason,
Its actions were simple (*su* 素) and in compliance with
    circumstances.
Its heart was harmonious and not feigned,
Its [conduct of] affairs was simple and not ostentatious.[45]

Less obviously linked to chapters 1 and 2, but nonetheless still connected, are the "Root Passages" in the following chapters:

Chapter 11, "Integrating Customs" ("Qi su" 齊俗), contains a discussion of the fluidity and efficacy of customs and rites. Simply put, in this "Root Passage," following one's nature is said to be following the Way:

率性而行謂 之道; 得其天性謂之德.

"Following one's nature and putting it into practice is called the Way; attaining one's Heaven (-born) nature is called Potency."[46]

Chapter 12, "The Responses of the Way" ("Dao ying" 道 應), is made of narratives that illustrate various sayings from Laozi; the "Root Passage" is a dialogue between two characters called Grand Purity (*Tai qing*) and Nonaction (*wuwei* 無為) on the theme of "knowing the Way" (*zhi dao* 知道).[47]

Chapter 15, "An Overview of the Military" ("Bing lue" 兵 略), the "Root Passage" discusses the use of the military in an antiquity when the military was only used to "pacify the chaos of the world and eliminate harm to the myriad people." 古之用兵 . . . 平天下之亂, 而除萬民之害 也.[48] We later read in this chapter that the military is an outgrowth of the natural response of great sages such as the Yellow Thearch and Yao 堯 and Shun 舜 to greedy and cruel rulers who have lost the Way and that it may only be used against a state or ruler who is "without the Way." The military and its commander only succeed to the extent that they accord fully with the Way:

兵失道而弱, 得道而強; 將失道而拙, 得道而工; 國得道而存,
失道而亡。

The military is
weak if it loses the Way;
strong if it obtains it.
　　The commander is
inept if he loses the Way;
skillful if he obtains the Way.
　　The state
that obtains the Way survives;
that loses the Way perishes.[49]

In Chapter 16, "A Mountain of Persuasions" ("Shui shan" 說山), a chapter containing a collection of short narratives to be used in disputation, the "Root Passage" is a humorous dialogue between the *hun* 魂 and *po* 魄 souls on the nature of the Way, Nonaction, and Formlessness.[50] Its style and tone are similar to many dialogues in the *Zhuangzi*.

Chapter 17, "A Forest of Persuasions" ("Shui lin" 說林), begins with a narrative about the importance of roaming by adapting to the greater patterns of Heaven and Earth (*yin tiandi yi you* 因天地以游).[51]

Chapter 18, "Among Others" ("Ren jian" 人間), opens with a "Root Passage" that states that the Wise follow their inherently tranquil and serene innate natures and accord with the Way. "They hold to the One in order to respond to the many" (zhi yi ying wan 執一應萬). This passage elaborates:

居智所為, 行智所之, 事智所秉, 動智所由, 謂之道

What the wise are at rest, where the wise go in motion, what the wise wield in affairs, that from which the wise act: this is known as "the Way."[52]

Chapter 19, "Cultivating Effort" ("Xiu wu" 修務) has a "Root Passage" that debates how to understand wuwei, about whether to take a quietist or an activist interpretation of it. While it seems at first to be critical of an important Daoist virtue, what the authors are really criticizing is the interpretation that wuwei literally means "doing nothing":

若吾所謂「無為」者, 私志不得入公道, (耆)〔嗜〕 欲不得枉
正術, 循理而舉事, 因資而立〔功〕, (權)〔推〕 自然之勢, 而曲
故不得容者 . . .

What I call non-action [means]
    not allowing private ambitions to interfere with the public
      Way,
    not allowing lustful desires to distort upright techniques.
[It means] complying with the inherent patterns of things
    when initiating undertakings,
    according with the natural endowments of things when
    establishing accomplishments,
and advancing the natural propensities (i.e., spontaneous tendencies) of things so that misguided precedents are not able to dominate.[53]

This understanding of wuwei fits perfectly with the advice in the "Root Chapters" 1 and 2 to follow apophatic inner cultivation techniques so that rulers relinquish personal self-aggrandizement and become impartial and thereby accord with the greater patterns of the cosmos, thus enabling the human polity to flourish.

Chapter 20, "The Exalted Lineage" ("Taizu" 泰族), begins with a "Root Passage" containing a cosmology in which Heaven is given many of the characteristics of the Way found elsewhere in the text, including "spirit-illumination" (*shenming* 神明), and argues that sages must take it as their model. The authors elaborate:

遠之則邇, (延)〔近〕之則疎; 稽之弗得, 察之不虛; 日計无筭,
歲計有餘。

Move away from it; it nears.
Approach it; it recedes.
Search for it; it will not be obtained.
Examine into it, it is not insubstantial.
Reckon it by days; it is incalculable.
Reckon it my years; there is a surplus.[54]

These examples (from chapters 3, 6–8, 10–20) show that, with the possible exceptions of chapters 4 and 5, the "Root Passages" of each chapter of the *Huainanzi* contain ideas derived from the two "Root Chapters" 1 and 2.[55] Given the intentional Root-Branch structure in the organization of the entire text, the location of these passages at the beginning of each chapter shows that Inner Cultivation tradition ideas are given pride of place throughout the *Huainanzi*.

Furthermore, in many of the *Huainanzi* chapters, the "Root Passage" also provides the foundational ideas for the remainder of the essay. Exceptions to this rule are some of the later chapters that are written in specific literary forms and that contain no obvious line of reasoning that links its various sections together, such as 16, 17, and 19. A complete analysis of each and every example of this is well beyond the scope of the present discussion, but I would like to present two examples.

The "Root Passage" in chapter 9, "The Techniques of the Ruler" ("Zhu shu" 主術) outlines the essentials of governing through Non Action and discusses the need for the ruler to attain states of experience that can only be derived from inner cultivation practices. The whole passage is too long to quote here; this is the first half:

人主之術, 處无為之事, 而行不言之教, 清靜而不動, 一度而不
搖, 因循而任下, 責成而不勞。是故心知規而師傅諭 (導)〔道〕,
口能言而行人稱辭, 足能行而相者先導, 耳能聽而執正進諫。
是故慮无失策, (謀)〔舉〕无過事, 言為文章,〔而〕行為儀表於
天下, 進退應時, 動靜循理 . . .

The ruler's techniques [consist of]
>   Establishing non-active management
>   And carrying out wordless instructions.
>   Quiet and tranquil, he does not move;
>   By [even] one degree he does not waver;
>   Adaptive and compliant, he relies on his underlings;
>   Dutiful and accomplished, he does not labor.

Therefore,

though his mind knows the norms, his savants transmit the
>   discourses of the Way;
though his mouth can speak, his entourage proclaims his words;
though his feet can move forward, his master of ceremonies leads;
though his ears can hear, his officials offer their admonitions.[56]

Therefore,

>   his considerations are without mistaken schemes,
>   his undertakings are without erroneous content.
>   His words [are taken as] scripture and verse;
>   his conduct is [taken as] a model and gnomon for the world.
>   His advancing and withdrawing respond to the seasons;
>   his movement and rest comply with [proper] patterns (*xun li* 循理).[57]

The remainder of *Huainanzi* 9 lays out in considerable detail the philosophy of government by the enlightened Daoist ruler and is the single longest chapter in the entire book, an indication of its significance. Its theory of rulership is completely reliant on the personal development of the ruler, which is the direct result of the apophatic inner cultivation practices outlined in chapters 1 and 2 and in the earlier sources of this tradition. According to this work, the ruler must cultivate himself through apophatic inner cultivation techniques. These include reduction of thoughts, desires, emotions, and the gradual development of emptiness and tranquility. The ruler is able to accomplish this and is able to develop his Potency and perfect his Vital Essence (*zhijing* 至精), and through this to penetrate through and directly apprehend the essences of Heaven and Grand Unity (*Taiyi* 太一), another metaphor for the Way.

This connects the ruler directly to the invisible cosmic web of the correlative cosmology of *qi*, and its various types (yin and yang) and phases (*wuxing* 五行) and refinements *jing* 精 that form the very fabric of the normative natural order the *Huainanzi* authors see in the universe.

With this connection, the enlightened ruler can invisibly influence the course of events in the world and affairs among his subjects through the types of resonance (*gan ying* 感應) detailed in chapter 6, which we also saw as developing in the later works of Inner Cultivation such as "Techniques of the Mind" 2. Experiencing the most profound states of inner cultivation also enables the ruler to develop many of the traits envisioned in earlier sources such as reducing desires to a minimum, impartially designating responsibilities within the government hierarchy, having a cognition devoid of emotions, and being able to spontaneously adapt to whatever situations arise, without hesitation.

Many narrative examples are given of past rulers who attained this level of cultivation. Chapter 2 argues that as human society and culture devolved, sage rulers adapted to the times by utilizing various ideas on governing taken from earlier Confucian and Mohist traditions and other sources. For the authors of this chapter, a cosmology of the Way and a discipline of apophatic inner cultivation is now—and has always been—the root of good rule. However, it is also important to utilize the ideas and methods of these earlier intellectual traditions. Such ideas, including benevolence, rightness, ritual, music, standards, measures, rewards, punishments, and so forth, are all the product of the spontaneous devolution from high antiquity described in chapter 2. But each set of ideas and techniques became indispensable to human order in the age in which it spontaneously arose, just as cosmic phenomena like Heaven and Earth became intrinsic to cosmic order at the point in the cosmogonic process in which they emerged. Given this, in order to function as a harmonious and organic whole, each of these ideas must be correctly prioritized in the order of their historical development and thus in the order of their normative distance from the undifferentiated "root" of good order, the Way. Thus a ruler in the current age cannot rule without the techniques of lesser thinkers like Confucius, Mozi, Han Fei 韓非, and so forth, because human society has spontaneously evolved into a complex form that necessitates their employment.

Chapter 11, "Integrating Customs," while superficially about the importance of maintaining a fluid approach to enforcing customs and rituals throughout the empire, is really a treatise that proffers the clearest statement of a Daoist theory of human nature written to this point. Its "Root Passage" signals this important move right from the beginning:

> 率性而行謂之道, 得其天性謂之德。性失然後貴仁, 道失然後
> 貴義。是故仁義立而道德遷矣, 禮樂飾則純樸散矣, 是非形則

百姓 (眩) 〔眩〕 矣, 珠玉尊則天下爭矣。凡此四者, 衰世之造
也, 末世之用也。

> Following nature and putting it into practice is called "the
>   Way,"[58]
> attaining one's Heaven[-born] nature is called "Potency."
> Only after nature was lost was Humaneness honored,
> only after the Way was lost was Rightness honored.
> For this reason,
>   when Humaneness and Rightness were established, the
>   Way and Potency receded;
>   when Ritual and Music were embellished, purity and sim-
>   plicity dissipated.[59]
> Right and wrong took form and the common people were
>   dazzled;
> Pearls and jade were revered and the world set to fighting
>   [over them].

These four were the creations of a declining age, and are the
implements of a latter age.[60]

This passage asserts that the self-cultivation that is essential to
governing the state and governing oneself is grounded in developing
an awareness of one's inmost nature. Practicing Confucian norms of
Humaneness and Rightness, and so forth are inferior expressions that
live at a kind of second-order distance from realizing this. This idea is
elaborated later in the chapter:

世之明事者, 多離道德之本, 曰禮義足以治天下, 此未可與言
術也。所謂禮義者, 五帝三王之法籍風俗, 一世之迹也。譬若
芻狗土龍之始成 ...

五帝三王, 輕天下, 細萬物, 齊死生, 同變化, 抱大聖之心, 以
(鎮) 〔鏡〕 萬物之情, 上與神明為友, 下與造化為人。今欲學
其道, 不得其清明玄聖, 而守其法籍憲令, 不能為治亦明矣。

Many of those who oversee affairs in the world depart from
the source of the Way and its Potency, saying that Ritual
and Rightness suffice to order the empire. One cannot discuss
techniques with such as these. What is called "Ritual and

Rightness" is the methods, statutes, ways, and customs of the Five Thearchs and the Three Kings. They are the remnants of a [former] age. Compare them to straw dogs and earthen dragons when they are first fashioned. . . .[61]

The Five Thearchs and the Three Kings
    viewed the world as a light [affair],
    minimized the myriad things,
    put death and life on a par,
    matched change and transformation.

They embraced the great heart of a sage by mirroring the dispositions of the myriad things.

    Above they took spirit-illumination as their friend,
    below they took creation and transformation as their
      companions.

Now if one wants to study their Way, and does not attain their pure clarity and mysterious sagacity, yet maintains their methods, statutes, rules, and ordinances, it is clear that one cannot achieve order.[62]

That we need to follow a practice of self-cultivation to get in touch with our inmost natures is a natural result of the historical devolution that this chapter presumes and that is first enunciated in *Huainanzi* 2. Because of this devolution, many different customs have developed throughout all the many and varied cultures within the empire. Nonetheless, this does not imply that the people who practice these varied customs and rituals have different innate natures:

> 原人之性, 蕪濊而不得清明者, 物或堁之也。羌、氐、樊、翟, 嬰兒生皆同聲, 及其長也, 雖重象狄騠, 不能通其言, 教俗殊也。今令三月嬰兒, 生而徙國, 則不能知其故俗。由此觀之, 衣服禮俗者, 非人之性也, 所受於外也。夫竹之性浮, 殘以為牒, 束而投之水, 則沉, 失其體也。金之性沉, 託之於舟上則浮, 勢有所(枝)〔支〕也。夫素之質白, 染之以涅則黑; 縑之性黃, 染之以丹則赤。人之性無邪, 久湛於俗則易。易而忘其本, 合於若性。故日月欲明, 浮雲蓋之; 河水欲清, 沙石濊之; 人性欲平, 嗜欲害之。唯聖人能遺物而反己

If the original nature of human beings is obstructed and sullied, one cannot get at its purity and clarity—it is because things have befouled it. The children of the Qiang 羌, Dii 氐, Bo 棥, and Dee 翟 [barbarians] all produce the same sounds at birth. Once they have grown, even with both the *xiang* 象 and *diti* 狄騠 interpreters,[63] they cannot understand one another's speech; this is because their education and customs are different. Now a three-month-old child that moves to a [new] state after it is born will not recognize its old customs. Viewed on this basis, clothing and ritual customs are not [rooted in] people's nature; they are received from without.

It is the nature of bamboo to float, [but] break it into strips and tie them in a bundle and they will sink when thrown into the water—it [i.e., the bamboo] has lost its [basic] structure.

It is the nature of metal to sink, [but] place it on a boat and it will float—its positioning lends it support.

The substance of raw silk is white, [but] dye it in potash and it turns black.

The nature of fine silk is yellow, [but] dye it in cinnabar and it turns red.

The nature of human beings has no depravity; having been long immersed in customs, it changes. If it changes and one forgets the root, it is as if [the customs one has acquired] have merged with [one's] nature.

Thus

the sun and the moon are inclined to brilliance, but floating clouds cover them;

the water of the river is inclined to purity, but sand and rocks sully it.

The nature of human beings is inclined to equilibrium, but wants and desires harm it.

Only the sage can leave things aside and return to himself.[64]

The author of "Integrating Customs" thus provides a series of metaphors for the pure, unsullied, and calm innate nature of human beings. These metaphors are characteristic of what some have called the "Discovery Model" of human nature, in which a perfectly complete nature is "discovered" and then serves as a guide for all of one's activities in the world, especially ethical ones. This contrast with the "Development Model" well known through metaphors of the natural growth of plants, as in the famous passage in *Mencius* 2A:2.[65] *Huainanzi* 11 also exhibits another of the characteristics of the "Discovery Model": innate nature, when accessed, can serve as the ultimate source of direction in human affairs. The text continues:

夫乘舟而惑者，不知東西，見斗極則寤矣。夫性、亦人之斗極也。（以有）〔有以〕自見也，則不失物之情；無以自見〔也〕，則動而惑營。譬若隴西之遊，愈躁愈沉。

Someone who boards a boat and becomes confused, not knowing west from east,

will see the Dipper and the Pole Star and become oriented. [Innate] Nature is likewise a

Dipper and a Pole Star for human beings.

If one possesses that by which one can see oneself, then one will not miss the genuine disposition of things.

If one lacks that by which one can see oneself, then one will be agitated and ensnared.

It is like swimming in the Longxi; the more you thrash, the deeper you will sink.[66]

If one follows the contemplative inner cultivation practice of calming the mind to get in touch with one's innate nature, it can serve as the basis (the "Pole Star") for making all the key decisions in one's life:

是故凡將舉事, 必先平意清神[67]。意平神清, 物乃可正。 . . .

夫耳目之可以斷也, 反情性也; 聽失於誹譽, 而目淫於采色, 而欲得事正, 則難矣。夫載哀者聞歌聲而泣, 載樂者見哭者而笑。哀可樂 (者) 、笑可哀者, 載使然也, 是故貴虛。故水 (擊) 〔激〕則波興, 氣亂則智昏。 (智昏) 〔昏智〕不可以為政, 波水不可以為平。故聖王執一而勿失, 萬物之情 (既) 〔測〕矣, 四夷九州服矣。夫一者至貴, 無適於天下。聖人 (記) 〔託〕於無適, 故民命繫矣。

For this reason, whenever one is about to take up an affair, one must first stabilize one's intentions and purify one's spirit (*ping yi qing shen* 平一清神).
    When the spirit is pure and intentions are stable
    only then can things be aligned . . .
That the ears and eyes can judge (impartially) is because one returns to one's true nature (*qing xing* 情性).
    If one's hearing is lost in slander and flattery
    and one's eyes are corrupted by pattern and color,
if one then wants to rectify affairs, it will be difficult.
    One who is suffused with grief will cry upon hearing a song,
    one suffused with joy will see someone weeping and laugh.
    That grief can bring joy
    and laughter can bring grief—
being suffused makes it so. For this reason, value emptiness.
    When water is agitated waves rise,
    when the qi is disordered the intellect is confused.
    A confused intellect cannot attend to government;
    agitated water cannot be used to establish a level.

Thus the sage king holds to the One without losing it and the true conditions of the myriad things are discovered, the four barbarians and the nine regions all submit. The One is the supremely noble; it has no match in the world. The sage relies on the matchless; thus the mandate of the people attaches itself [to him].[68]

The authors of "Integrating Customs" are advocating here the apophatic inner cultivation practices of chapters 1 and 2, and the earlier Inner Cultivation tradition, as the way to bring the mental stability needed to resist strong emotions that will bias one's awareness and thus cloud judgment. This mental stability allows the adept to empty consciousness and apprehend true nature, which is ultimately based in the Way. Thus the "Root Passage" of chapter 11 serves as the foundation for the entire chapter.

Conclusions

The Root-Branch structure in the *Huainanzi* operates on a number of distinct—yet interrelated—levels to help determine the way in which its individual chapters are organized to form a coherent whole and by which the arguments within its individual chapters are constructed. As we have seen, the "Root Section" of the work is made of up of the first eight chapters. The "Root Chapters" of this "Root Section" and hence of the entire work are chapters 1 and 2, which are thoroughly infused by a philosophy that is taken from the major works of the pre-Han Inner Cultivation tradition. Within most of the twenty chapters of the text, there is a "Root Passage" that contains core ideas for the entire chapter. Despite the great variety of philosophical positions taken from a number of the "Hundred Schools" that are represented within the *Huainanzi*, the "Root Passages" in most of the chapters contain ideas that are found within, or are closely derived from, the first two "Root Chapters" of the text, chapters 1 and 2. It is in this way that the multilayered compositional structure of the text is used to assert and reinforce the normative Inner Cultivation foundations of this admittedly and deliberately syncretic work. Metaphorically speaking, we can think of these Inner Cultivation ideas as providing the veins with the leaves of the text that occur on multiple levels throughout:

Table 7.4. Nesting Root-Branch Textual Structures in the *Huainanzi*

	Roots	Branches
The "Root Section"	Chapters 1–8	Chapters 9–20
The "Root Chapters"	Chapters 1–2	Chapters 3–8
The "Root Passages"	First passage in most chapters	The rest of the chapter

This analysis of the structure and significance of the multilayered Root-Branch textual structures challenges arguments that the *Huainanzi* cleaves to no particular intellectual tradition.[69] The common technical terminology and basic understanding of apophatic inner cultivation practice and its pivotal role in cultivating individual potential and in governing society that we have discovered in the *Huainanzi* argue that it is this tradition that dominates the philosophical orientation of this text. While it would take us too far afield in this chapter to fully examine the arguments surrounding the hypothesis that the *Huainanzi* is not affiliated with "Daoism" or with any one intellectual tradition, in essence they boil down to three items:

- The text never explicitly states that it is "Daoist;"

- The text contains the ideas from many different pre-Han intellectual traditions;

- The idea that *Huainanzi* adheres to no one intellectual tradition is principally supported by this statement in the final summary chapter.

非循一跡之路, 守一隅之指, 拘繫牽連於物, 而不與世推移也

. . . . We have not followed a path made by a solitary footprint, nor adhered to instructions from a single perspective, nor allowed ourselves to be entrapped or fettered by things so that we would not advance or shift according to the age . . .[70]

Understanding the Root-Branch compositional structure of the text and the significance of its "Root Chapters," and the "Root Passages" within each chapter, makes possible the contextualization of the *Huainanzi's* use of ideas taken from the Confucians, Mohists, and other early intellectual traditions. The Way is the supreme root from which are derived all these branch ideas that are valuable, yet of lesser importance in the overall cosmic scheme. This makes possible a Dao-based syncretism that links the *Huainanzi* to a number of other texts that advocate similar intellectual positions: "Techniques of the Mind" 1 and 2 from the *Guanzi*; the *Huang-Lao boshu*; the "syncretic" chapters of the *Zhuangzi* (12–15, 33); and certain chapters in the *Lüshi chunqiu* (3, 5, 17, and 25).[71]Could adhering to this Dao-based syncretism possibly be the underlying meaning of the phrase "We have not followed the path made by a solitary footprint"? The brilliant syncretism of the *Huainanzi*, which seamlessly makes use of the best ideas on rulership from many earlier philosophical traditions yet remains thoroughly grounded in a Daoist inner cultivation cosmology, philosophy, and practice, is brilliantly epitomized as a "path with many footprints."

When an awareness of this Dao-based syncretism of the *Huainanzi* is combined with the profusion of ideas and techniques from the Inner Cultivation tradition that pervades the text and links it to other early textual sources of this tradition, it also suggests that there may have been something more to early "Daoism" than just a bibliographical category or an arbitrary invention by a Han historian. This is not to suggest that the Inner Cultivation tradition that so dominates the philosophical outlook of the *Huainanzi* called itself "Daoist:" this was a later term first affixed to it by Sima Tan. Of course that would be the reason the *Huainanzi* (and, in actuality, *all* the pre-Han Inner Cultivation texts) do not refer to themselves as "Daoist": the precise term and category hadn't yet been "invented"!

There are some who would challenge this assertion, insisting instead that the philosophy of the "inner chapters" of *Zhuangzi* is distinctly different from that of the *Laozi* and that both differ in kind from the ungrounded "eclecticism" of the *Huainanzi*.[72] To this I would counter that there is every bit as much consistency amid difference in these textual sources as we find between the *Analects* and the writings of Xunzi. In these works, which few challenge belong to one intellectual tradition, what holds them together is, as we have seen, both a consistent set of technical terms (*ren, li, zhi, yi*) and an equally consistent set of practices, mostly involving rituals and education. If we looked back on the Confucian tradition from the perspective of Xunzi, we would see that despite obvious differences, he was clearly working within the same field of discourse and techniques as were Confucius and Mencius.

Our analysis of the textual structures of the *Huainanzi* not only provides important testimony to the importance of Inner Cultivation thought in the text, but it also places it squarely within the same field of discourse and technique as the earlier Inner Cultivation textual sources we have mentioned. Taken together, these textual sources are too closely related in terms of philosophy and practices to have arisen independently or from random contact between their authors. These close textual relationships can only mean that these are the product of a distinctive social organization that we are remiss *not* to recognize as a "tradition." This becomes apparent when we stop looking for evidence of early intellectual traditions as exclusively made of ideas and not practices. In his famous work *After Virtue*, philosopher Alistair MacIntyre has this relevant comment on the nature of traditions:

> . . . a tradition is constituted by a set of practices and is a mode of understanding their importance and worth; it is the medium by which such practices are shaped and transmitted across generations . . .[73]

With this in mind, the inner cultivation practices we have discussed may have initially been associated with some contrasting ideas of governing (e.g., the "individualism" and avoidance of politics in *Guanzi*'s "Inward Training" and the sophisticated political syncretism of the *Huainanzi*), but, like the Rites for the Confucians, they are the backbone of a distinctive tradition of teachers and students that stretches over two centuries from its apocryphal origins to the time of Han Wudi 漢武帝. In his brilliant analysis of a distinctive tradition of Chinese medicine that stretches over three centuries to the present, Volker Scheid brings this point home:

> . . . a practice relies on the transmission of skills and expertise between masters and novices. As novices develop into masters themselves, they change who they are but also earn a say in defining the goods that the practice embodies and seeks to realize. To accomplish these tasks human beings need

narratives: stories about who they are, what they do, and why they do it. Traditions provide these narratives. They allow people to discover problems and methods for their solution, frame questions and possible answers, and develop institutions that facilitate cooperative action. But because people occupy changing positions vis-à-vis these narratives, traditions are also always open to change . . .[74]

In the last analysis, this understanding of tradition as a changing phenomenon grounded in practice may proffer the best explanation of the coherence of the early lineages of masters and disciples that likely formed the basis for Sima Tan's definition of Daoism. Our analysis of the Root-Branch textual structures of the *Huainanzi* only buttresses this conclusion.

Part II

Contemplative Foundations and Philosophical Contexts

Chapter 8

The *Laozi* 老子 in the
Context of Early Daoist Mystical Praxis

To know others is to be clever
To know oneself is to be clear . . .

—*Laozi* 33

Introduction

One of the few areas of agreement between sinologists and scholars of Comparative Religion is in regarding the *Laozi* as an important work of mysticism. Scholars from Wing-Tsit Chan to Benjamin Schwartz in the former group and from Walter Stace to Wayne Proudfoot in the latter group share this common understanding of the text as they make use of it in a wide variety of intellectual endeavors.[1] While this is by no means a unanimous view (see the contrary opinions of D. C. Lau and Chad Hansen), it is certainly held by a great many scholars.[2] Despite this surprising unanimity, when one examines the views of these scholars more closely, there is an equally surprising lack of a comprehensive discussion of why they regard the *Laozi* as a mystical text in the first place.

Some scholars simply use the term "mysticism" uncritically, as in Chan's accurate but overly general observation that the *Laozi* is a "com-

I wish to express my gratitude to Angus Graham and Robin Yates for their careful reading and searching criticisms of earlier versions of this manuscript. I wish also to thank Margaret Taylor for her most helpful editorial suggestions.

bination of poetry, philosophical speculation, and mystical reflection."[3] Others use passages from the *Laozi* to illustrate their general theories about mysticism. For example, Stace uses chapters 4 and 14 in his discussion of the epistemology of mystical experience to illustrate an important characteristic of the "objective referent" of mystical experience, namely that it is paradoxically spoken of as a "vacuum-plenum."[4] Proudfoot uses chapter 1 of the *Laozi* to illustrate how the supposed ineffability of mystical experience is really a characteristic of grammatical rules embedded in religious doctrine.[5] Two fuller approaches are found in the writings of Livia Kohn and Benjamin Schwartz. In her pioneering study of Daoist mysticism, Kohn correctly accepts the assumption that the mystical philosophy of the *Laozi* and *Zhuangzi* 莊子 is derived directly from the experience of practicing mystics, and she usefully defines such philosophy as ". . . the theoretical, conceptual description of the mystical worldview . . . the intellectual framework that provides an explanation and systematic interpretation of increasingly sophisticated spiritual experiences."[6] She founders, however, in a largely unsuccessful attempt to integrate several contradictory approaches in mysticism theory to forge her own definition. Furthermore, her discussion of the mysticism of the *Laozi* is simply an analysis of its philosophy with no specific attempt to demonstrate how this philosophy is mystical, according to her definitions.[7]

While hardly a thorough textual analysis, Schwartz provides a more sustained attempt to demonstrate the presence of mystical philosophy in the *Laozi*.[8] Arguing from a cross-cultural foundation that is rare among sinologists, Schwartz sees mystical philosophy in the *Laozi*'s cosmology of the paradoxically determinate and indeterminate *Dao*, the source of meaning for all human beings that can only be known through the "higher direct knowledge" of gnosis. However, in an effort to deflate arguments asserting the non-mystical nature of the *Laozi* based upon the absence of specific techniques for attaining mystical experience in the text, Schwartz downplays the importance of such techniques and emphasizes, instead, the vision of reality with which they are associated. In my opinion, he does not need to take such an approach.

What I attempt to demonstrate in this chapter is that mystical praxis is at the very heart of the *Laozi*. While, of course, it is not present in all its chapters, there is sufficient textual evidence for both mystical praxis and its resultant mystical experience in the work to provide a firm basis for any future scholars who wish to pursue the demonstration of how these two closely related aspects of mysticism are the foundations of the mystical philosophy of the text. Prior scholarship has not noted the extent of such textual evidence because the *Laozi* largely has been regarded as a work of philosophy produced by a school of philosophy. In order to counter this prevailing view, I first summarize my recent research on the historical and religious context from which the *Laozi* emerged. I next present the elements of mysticism theory that I have found most valuable in developing definitions of early Daoist mysticism. I then proceed to a study of the passages on mystical praxis and mystical experience in the *Laozi* in which I attempt to explain their meaning and significance by comparing them with parallel passages in a number of other important textual sources of early Daoist mysticism.

Historical Context

In contrast to the traditional view, I do not regard the *Laozi* and *Zhuangzi* as the sole foundational texts of Daoism. Nor do I think there was a "Lao-Zhuang" 老莊 school of Daoist thought until its retrospective establishment by the Profound Learning (*xuanxue* 玄學) literati of the third century CE. Indeed, I have grave doubts that any of Sima Tan's 司馬談 so-translated "schools of philosophy" were "schools," as we might think of them today, with a clear self-identity and a well-defined organization and curriculum, much less schools whose principal raison d'etre was philosophical speculation.[9]

Rather, my research has suggested that, particularly in the case of Daoism, the foundational texts of the tradition were produced within one or more closely related master-disciple lineages whose principal focus was learning and practicing specific techniques (*shu* 術).[10] Indeed, these techniques are so central to the tradition that from a very early period, that of the "inner chapters" of the *Zhuangzi* (ca. 300 BCE), they are referred to as the "techniques of the Way" (*Dao shu* 道術).[11] While these eventually came to include methods of political and social organization and a variety of investigations of the natural world (and their associated yinyang and Five Phase theories), the single most important technique was that of guiding and refining the flow of vital energy or vital breath (*qi* 氣) within the human organism.[12] This seems to have been accomplished in two possibly complementary ways, the first a kind of active or moving meditation whose postures resembled modern positions in taiji 太極 and qigong 氣功, and the second a kind of still, sitting meditation that involved regularized natural breathing.[13] It is this second form, which entails the apophatic practice of removing the normal contents of the mind to produce a profound tranquility with a decisively noetic character, that I have called "inner cultivation."[14]

According to this view, the texts we have come to regard as the foundations of Daoist philosophy are not filled with abstract metaphysical speculation that has no basis in nondiscursive experience, but are, rather, works written to elucidate the insight attained from inner cultivation practices and to discuss their practical benefits. This latter aspect would have been particularly critical in late Warring States China in order to persuade local kings of the value of adapting the teachings being advocated and thereby winning their favor and a position within the court from which to continue these pursuits. We have some historical certainty that such conditions did exist, for example, at such disparate courts as those of the states of Qi 齊 (ca. 320–260 BCE), Qin 秦 (ca. 241 BCE), and, later, the Han 漢 state of Huainan 淮南 (ca. 150–122 BCE). Each court produced a book containing collections of teachings from a variety of Daoist and non-Daoist lineages: the *Guanzi* 管子, the *Lüshi chunqiu* 呂氏春秋, and the *Huainanzi* 淮南子, respectively, which are all important sources for early Daoist thought.

Therefore, it is my contention that the *Laozi* can best be understood by placing it—as much as we possibly can, given the limits of the extant textual corpus—within its historical context. Perhaps the most ambitious attempt to do this until now is the work of Michael LaFargue in his innovative application of the Biblical Studies methodologies of form and redaction criticism to the *Laozi*.[15] While LaFargue's work is not without its problems, it has developed some important hypotheses about the nature of the text and its origins. One of the most important (and one that I currently share) is that the *Laozi* is the product of a group or community whose foundation was first and foremost a shared practice of "self-cultivation." According to LaFargue, it is from this practice that many of the more "mystical" passages in the text arose, sayings that I examine in this chapter.

The attempt to apply these "mystical" teachings to the problems of governing in late Warring States China constitutes an important element of the *Laozi*. The particular form of political thought it advocates helps to define one of the three principal phases of early Daoism (the "Primitivist" as opposed to the "Individualist" and the "Syncretist") I have identified in previous publications.[16] However, in this chapter I focus not on the distinctive political philosophy of the *Laozi* but rather on the evidence it contains for this community's practice of inner culti-vation and how it relates to similar evidence in the other early textual sources of Daoism. Most relevant among these sources is the essay titled "Inward Training" ("Neiye" 內業) from the *Guanzi*. I also place the *Laozi*'s evidence for inner cultivation in the context of evidence for analogous apophatic practices and results in the other early Daoist textual sources mentioned above.

Theoretical Context: Mysticism, Meditation, and the *Laozi*

Seeing the *Laozi* as the product of a lineage involved in apophatic practices of directed breathing meditation enables us to put the text directly into dialogue with similar practices in other cultures and traditions and with modern Western scholarship on the philosophical and psychological implications of such practices. In the following section, I define those elements of mysticism theory that I think are most relevant to the study of the *Laozi* and show how they are related to one another.[17]

The cross-cultural study of "mysticism" is very much a modern Western phenomenon that began with the publication of William James's *Varieties of Religious Experience* in 1902.[18] This work presents a phenom-enology of religious experiences and identifies the subset of mystical experiences as being 1. ineffable; 2. noetic; 3. transient; 4. passive; and 5. transformational.[19] Following the lead of James, scholars from Evelyn Underhill to Robert Forman have pursued the study of mysticism along the following two lines, clearly adumbrated by Peter Moore:

> The philosophical analysis of mysticism comprises two over-lapping lines of inquiry: on the one hand the identification and classification of the phenomenological characteristics of mystical experience, and on the other the investigation of the epistemological and ontological status of this experience. The first line of inquiry is generally focused on the question whether the mystical experiences reported in different cultures and religious traditions are basically of the same type or whether there are significantly different types. The second line of inquiry centres on the question whether mystical experiences are purely subjective phenomena or whether they have the

> kind of objective validity and metaphysical significance that
> mystics and others claim for them . . .[20]

In other words, the former line deals with the nature and characteristics of mystical experience and the latter deals with the various philosophical claims that are made on the basis of mystical experience. These overlapping lines of inquiry indicate that two fundamental aspects of mysticism are mystical experience and the mystical philosophy that is derived from it.

Walter Stace delineates two fundamental forms of mystical experience, "extrovertive" and "introvertive."[21] Extrovertive looks outward through the senses of the individual and sees a fundamental unity between this individual and the world. In this form there is a simultaneous perception of the one and the many, unity and multiplicity. Introvertive mystical experience looks inward and is exclusively an experience of unity, that is, an experience of unitive or what some scholars (Forman et al.) call "pure" or object-less consciousness.[22] I have found this basic differentiation to be extremely useful and see it in early Daoism in what I call the "bimodal" character of its mystical experience, a concept that I explain further below.[23]

For Stace, mystical philosophy takes its most fundamental concepts from mystical experience. First and foremost are the varying notions of "the One" in different religious traditions that are ultimately derived from the introvertive mystical experience of complete union. Brahman for Hindu mystics, God for Christian mystics, the One for Plotinus, the *Dao* 道 for the Daoists, the unconditioned for "Hinayana" Buddhists—these are all philosophical expressions of the "universal self" that is derived from this unitive experience.[24] While scholars may wish to debate whether these concepts are derivative of mystical union or cause this experience, the fact remains that there is a very intimate connection between these two aspects of mysticism.[25]

Peter Moore argues that a particularly crucial element of mysticism is the intimate connection between mystical experiences and what he calls "mystical techniques," the practices that are used to "induce" them.[26] He distinguishes between two primary techniques that represent the "immediate preconditions" for mystical experience, "meditation" and "contemplation." The former entails "the disciplined but creative application of the imagination and discursive thought to an often complex religious theme or subject-matter." The latter, a development of the former, entails the attempt "to transcend the activities of the imagination and intellect through an intuitive concentration on some simple object, image, or idea."[27] It seems to me that focusing on one's breathing in a systematic fashion would be an example of the latter. While this differentiation is instructive, because of the relatively poor state of our knowledge of the specifics of early Daoist mystical techniques—in particular, how the imagination and intellect are used in them—and because of the use of the former term in common parlance, I have used—and continue to use—"meditation" to refer broadly to both of these techniques.

Mystical techniques are further clarified in the writings of Robert Forman and Donald Rothberg. Forman, following the phenomenological tradition of James and Stace, argues that the "Pure Consciousness Event (PCE)" (defined as a wakeful though contentless [nonintentional] consciousness)—his version of the latter's introvertive mystical experience—comes about through a systematic process of "forgetting."[28] This is elaborated upon by Rothberg:

> Robert Forman . . . has proposed a model of mystical development (in many traditions) as involving the "forgetting" (Meister Eckhardt's term) of the major cognitive and affective structures of experience . . . In this process of "forgetting," there is an intentional dropping of desires, ideas, conceptual forms (including those of one's tradition), sensations, imagery, and so on. The end of this process is a contentless mystical experience in which the constructs of the tradition are transcended . . .[29]

Citing the twelve-year research project on meditative praxis in three Indo-Tibetan traditions by the psychologist Daniel Brown, Rothberg argues that the spiritual path involves, in many traditions, "a process of progressive deconstruction of the structures of experience."[30] These include, for Brown, attitudes and behavioral schemes, thinking, gross perception, self-system, and "time-space matrix."[31] This is not to argue that the spiritual path is the same in every tradition. Indeed, as Rothberg argues, "each path of deconstruction or deconditioning is itself constructed or conditioned in a certain way."[32] Nor do he and Forman argue that pure consciousness is the only goal of all mystic paths. Indeed, the entire Forman collection intentionally passes over the important extrovertive aspect of mystical experience, unfairly denigrated by Stace, and, I would argue, extremely important to the understanding of early Daoist mysticism.[33]

In a recent review essay, I argued for the presence of a "bimodal" mystical experience in early Daoism, particularly evident in the "inner chapters" of the *Zhuangzi*.[34] The first mode is an introvertive unitive consciousness in which the adept achieves complete union with the *Dao*. This corresponds, in general, with Stace's "introvertive mystical experience" and with Forman's "Pure Consciousness Event." The second is an extrovertive transformed consciousness in which the adept returns to the world and retains, amid the flow of daily life, a profound sense of the unity previously experienced in the introvertive mode. This experience entails an ability to live in the world free from the limited and biased perspective of the individual ego. This second mode corresponds, in general, to Stace's "extrovertive mystical experience," although I would regard it as a quite profound subcategory of it.[35] This bimodal character of mystical experience is, actually, quite prevalent in mystical experience across traditions, but it is often overlooked by scholars, who tend to focus on the introvertive mode exclusively.[36] While evidence for its presence is not as strong in the *Laozi* as in the *Zhuangzi*, it is, as we shall see, most certainly there.

Finally, in the philosophical analysis of mysticism there is also a great deal of attention paid to mystical language, and herein I am concerned with one particular subset of it, the unique language that evolves within mystical praxis. Brown witnessed this in his study of Tibetan monastic communities, where there was a body of teachings about the internal states attained through mystical praxis to which an adept could compare his or her experience. He goes on:

> In such traditions, where meditation practice is socially organized, a technical language for meditation experience evolved. This language was refined over generations. The technical terms do not have external referents, e.g., "house," but refer to replicable internal states which can be identified by anyone doing the same practice, e.g., "energy currents," or "seed meditations." Much like the specialized languages of math, chemistry, or physics, technical meditation language is usually intelligible only to those specialized audiences of yogis familiar with the experiences in question . . .[37]

LaFargue sees this kind of language present in the *Laozi*, and I concur.[38] I would also extend this to the other textual sources of early Daoism, including, most importantly, "Inward Training." The great challenge facing modern scholars who wish to study this specialized mystical language is to make sense of what it really meant to the people who used it. While this is not as much a problem when technical terms are primarily descriptive, as for example, in *Zhuangzi*'s famous prescription for how to just "sit and forget," the more metaphorical the language becomes (see, later in the same sentence, "I . . . merge with the universal thoroughfare"), the more challenging it is to interpret.[39] In this chapter, I attempt to explain the meaning of some of the important technical terms and phrases of mystical praxis in the *Laozi* through extensive cross-referencing to other early Daoist works and through cross-cultural comparisons to mystical techniques in other traditions. I see this attempt as a plausible reconstruction, but certainly not the only one possible.

Using the above definitions of the various aspects of mysticism, I concentrate on presenting and analyzing the textual evidence for mystical techniques and their resultant mystical experiences in the *Laozi* under the general heading of "mystical praxis." In doing this, I make extensive use of relevant passages from the other important works that I have identified in my research on the historical context of early Daoism. Because of the practical limitations of the present article, I do not make anything more than general assertions about the relationship of mystical experience to mystical philosophy in the *Laozi* and leave a more detailed study for another time.

Mystical Praxis in the *Laozi*

Mysticism and Meditation in Early Daoism

Perhaps the most direct passage on mystical praxis in the *Laozi* is chapter 10:

> Amidst the daily activity of the psyche, can you embrace the
>   One and not depart from it?
> When concentrating your vital breath until it is at its softest,
>   can you be like a child?
> Can you sweep clean your Profound Mirror so you are able
>   to have no flaws in it?
> In loving the people and governing the state, can you do it
>   without using knowledge?

When the Gates of Heaven open and close, can you become feminine?
In clarifying all within the four directions, can you do it without using knowledge?[40]

Because this passage contains the kind of technical language of meditation that Brown found in his Tibetan communities and LaFargue sees in the *Laozi*, it has caused scholars great difficulty. Lau sees "some sort of breathing exercise or perhaps even yogic practice" here, but considers it an atypical passage that could have come from a school interested in the prolongation of life, not the avoidance of untimely death that characterizes the *Laozi*.[41] Chan rejects the entire claim that breathing meditation is involved: "The concentration of *qi* (vital force, breath) is not yoga, as Waley thinks it is. Yoga aims at transcending the self and the external environment. Nothing of the sort is intended here."[42] Their failure to understand the passage has a twofold origin: failure to understand the larger context of early Daoist mystical praxis and the *Laozi* passages that contain evidence of it and failure to understand the nature of mysticism. After examining mystical praxis in the *Laozi* in the light of these two critical understandings, I return to an analysis of this passage.

A familiar place to begin discussing the greater context of early Daoist mystical praxis is with the *Zhuangzi* passage on "sitting and forgetting." Here Confucius's favorite disciple Yan Hui ironically "turns the tables" on his master by teaching him how to "sit and forget" (*zuo wang* 坐忘):

(CONFUCIUS:) What do you mean, just sit and forget?

(YAN HUI:) I let organs and members drop away, dismiss eye sight and hearing, part from the body and expel knowledge, and merge with the universal thoroughfare. This is what I mean by "just sit and forget."[43]

To let "organs and members drop away" (*duo zhi ti* 墮肢體) means to lose visceral awareness of the emotions and desires, which, for the early Daoists, have "physiological" bases in the various organs.[44] To "dismiss eyesight and hearing" (*chu cong ming* 黜聰明) means to deliberately cut off sense perception. To "part from the body and expel knowledge" (*li xing qu zhi* 離形去知) means to lose bodily awareness and remove all thoughts from consciousness. To "merge with the universal thoroughfare" (*tong yu datong* 同於大通) seems to imply that, as a result of these practices, Yan Hui has become united with the *Dao*.[45]

The *locus classicus* for these apophatic practices is the "Inward Training" essay from the *Guanzi*, which I date to the second half of the fourth century BCE. Herein such practices are metaphorically referred to as "cleaning out the abode of the numinous mind" (*shen* 神). The numinous mind refers to an elusive and profound level of awareness that comes and goes within consciousness. It has its own unique physiological substrate, its "vital essence" (*jing* 精), and its presence confers a psychological clarity and centeredness.[46] Elsewhere in the text, these apophatic practices are linked to a guided breathing meditation that involves sitting with the body erect and the limbs squared and stable and refining the vital breath (*qi*).[47] It is through the refinement of the vital breath that emotions and desires are stilled, sense perception is restricted, the attention is unified and the mind is concentrated, and experiences of increased tranquility are produced through which one gradually reaches the deepest levels wherein the Way is attained.[48] This breathing practice is spoken of metaphorically in the following passage:

> For all to practice this Way:
> You must coil, you must contract,
> You must uncoil, you must expand,
> You must be firm, you must be regular in this practice.
> Maintain this excellent practice; do not let go of it.
> Chase away excessive perception;
> Abandon trivial thoughts.
> And when you reach the ultimate limit (*ji* 極)
> You will return to the Way and its Inner Power (*De* 德).[49]

In this passage, I interpret coiling/contracting to refer to the activity of exhalation in the breathing cycle and uncoiling/expanding to refer to the activity of inhalation. It is also important to note here the occurrence of the foundational pairing of the Way and its Inner Power (Dao and De). In this fourth-century BC text, its use predates all extant recensions of the *Laozi* and suggests that "Inward Training" may very well be closely connected to it. It also demonstrates a concrete link between the apophatic breathing practice of "Inward Training" and the attainment of a profound level of experience at which one is in touch with the Way and its Inner Power.

This general type of apophatic prescription and result is also found elsewhere in the "inner" *Zhuangzi*[50] and in other textual sources for early Daoism, including the Daoist essays of the *Lüshi chunqiu*, later chapters of the *Zhuangzi*, the inner cultivation essays of the *Guanzi*, and the *Huainanzi*, as I have discussed in chapter 2 of the present volume (for a summary, see Table 2.1).[51] Therein I identified a rhetorical structure of mystical praxis in early Daoism that has the following tripartite structure:

1. Preamble in which a variety of apophatic practices are listed that prepare the adept for the later stages of meditative experience. Typically, these feature various prescriptions for removing the normal contents of the mind: sense perception, desire, the emotions, knowledge and scheming, wisdom and precedent.

2. A *Sorites*-style argument (if x then y, if y, then z . . .) in which consecutive stages of meditative experience are presented. These include alignment of the body and breathing (*zheng* 正), tranquility (*jing* 靜), equanimity (*ping* 平 or *jun* 均), being unadorned (*su* 素), being concentrated or purified (*jing* 精), being clear or lucid (*ming* 明), having a numinous awareness (*shen* 神), and, finally, attaining the One or the empty Way, (*de yi* 得一, *de xu Dao* 得虛道), or becoming completely empty (*xu* 虛). These practices in the preamble and their results in the sorites section correspond, in general, with the basic deconstructive processes and results of mystical praxis that are enumerated by Brown.[52]

3. A *Denouement* in which the practical benefits of the first two parts are enumerated. These include instantaneous accurate cognition (*jian zhi bu huo* 見知不惑), spontaneous responsiveness to things (*ying wu bianhua* 應物便化), being able to return to the Unhewn (*gui yu pu* 歸於樸), having perception in which nothing is unperceived (*shi wu bujian* 視無不見), and taking no action and yet leaving nothing undone (*wuwei er wu buwei* 無為而無不為).

Examining this rhetorical structure from the standpoint of mysticism theory, we can see that the first part corresponds with the concept of mystical techniques, the second part with that of introvertive mystical experience, and the third part with that of extrovertive mystical experience, or, at least, with a discussion of the unique mode of cognition and action associated with it. I make use of these three related categories to guide my analysis of mystical praxis in the *Laozi*.

MYSTICAL TECHNIQUES IN THE *LAOZI*

The discussion of mystical techniques in the *Laozi* should begin with the second line of chapter 10, which talks of refining the vital breath and parallels material in "Inward Training," but I postpone analysis of this line until the end of the article, when I can do a comprehensive analysis of the whole passage.

The first aspect of apophatic practice in early Daoism that is usually presented in our sources is to reduce to a minimum or entirely eliminate sense perception. We have evidence of such a practice and advice related to it in several passages in the *Laozi*. In chapter 52 we read:

> Block your openings
> Shut your doors,
> And to the end of your life you will not run dry.
> Unblock your openings,
> Increase your striving,
> And to the end of your life you will never get what you
>   seek . . .

This is echoed in chapter 56:

> Block your openings,
> Shut your doors.
> Blunt your sharpness,
> Untangle your knots.
> Blend into your brightness,
> Merge with your dust.
> This is called the "profound merging."
> Therefore,

> You can neither get close to it nor stay away from it.
> You can neither help it nor harm it.
> You can neither honor it nor debase it.
> Therefore it is honored by all under Heaven.

The openings and doors refer to the sense apertures.[53] Both passages suggest the beneficial effects of the limitation or removal of sense perception.[54] Chapter 56 moves beyond sense perception and makes a broader reference to other aspects of apophatic practice. I take "blunting sharpness" to refer to setting aside clear-cut perceptual and conceptual categories and "untangling knots" to refer to removing attachments to various aspects of the self. The next two lines speak metaphorically of merging with two contrasting qualities, darkness and light, which are perhaps symbolic of the emotional moods of the self.

Overall, this process is called "profound merging" (*xuantong* 玄同), another challenging technical metaphor used by the *Laozi* authors. The use of the term "profound," which is a characteristic of the Way in chapter 1, seems to suggest that this process leads to a merging or union with the Way itself, a foundational introvertive mystical experience that I discuss further in the next section. This interpretation is further supported by the phrase "merge with the Universal Thoroughfare" (*tong yu datong*) from the sitting and forgetting passage in *Zhuangzi*. The conclusion to *Laozi* 56 provides more evidence for such an interpretation. It suggests that "profound merging" is something that cannot be approached through dualistic categories or activities, but only through their removal. This is why it is valued by all under Heaven.

Chapter 12 also makes reference to limiting the sense desires and gives an explanation of why this is needed:

> The five colors blind one's eyes;
> The five notes deafen one's ears;
> The five flavors damage the palate;
> Galloping on horseback and hunting madden the mind;
> Hard to obtain goods hinder one's progress.
> For this reason, the sage is for the belly, not for the eye.
> Therefore he discards that and takes up this.

The activities of the senses, riding and hunting, and the pursuit of material goods all seem to reinforce attachment to the individual self and also prevent it from being centered. They must be set aside if one is to make any kind of progress in inner cultivation. In this context, being "for the belly, not for the eye" would seem to refer to restricting sense perception by focusing on the regular circulation of the breath, which is centered in the belly. This is a well-known meditative technique in many traditions.[55] According to Brown, with "sense-withdrawal," the meditator "learns to disengage from external reality and the impact of sense objects so as to bring awareness carefully to bear on the stream of consciousness."[56] As a result, an increasing inner concentration develops. Furthermore, the belly is the location of the famous lower "cinnabar field" (*dantian* 丹田), so central in later Daoist meditation as the place where the One resides, where the vital essence accumulates, and where the practitioner must focus attention in order to eliminate desires and emotions.[57] While anachronistic for our purposes, this theory could have emerged from such early breathing practices.

A further rationale for restricting sense perception comes from the theories of the Inner Cultivation tradition. As already mentioned, in these sources, the vital essence (*jing*) is associated with tranquility and with the numinous mind as their "physiological" substrate. It is also a source of health and vitality in the organism. It is therefore extremely important not to waste this vital essence. However, it is normally consumed during the everyday activities of sense perception, which are enhanced by its presence. As the *Huainanzi* says:

> When the vital essence flows into the eyes then vision is clear.
> When it resides in the ears then hearing is acute.
> When it rests in the mouth then speech is appropriate.
> When it is collected in the mind then thinking comprehends.
> Therefore if you block these four gateways
> Then one's person will suffer no calamities.
> The hundred joints will not be sickly,
> Will not die, will not be born,
> Will not be empty, will not be full.
> We call (those who can do) this "the Genuine" (*zhen ren* 真人).[58]

If one can retain the vital essence, one can also retain the inner tranquility and numinous mind with which it occurs. This is a further reason to restrict sense perception.

To this point we have seen references to the removal of sense perceptions, desires, emotions, attachment to selfish concerns, and conceptual categories in the *Laozi*. There are further references to the removal of various aspects of thought. First, we have the famous prescription in chapter 19: "Eliminate sageliness, discard knowledge, and the people will benefit a hundred fold." This is similar to such phrases as to "cast off wisdom and precedent" (*qu zhi yu gu* 去智與故), which is commonly found in inner cultivation sources.[59] This chapter ends in the three appended statements:

> Manifest the Unadorned and embrace the Unhewn.
> Reduce self-interest and lessen desires.
> Eliminate learning and have no worries.[60]

This passage restates the need to move past self-interest, desire, and learning, which, as we have seen above, is inherent to early Daoist apophatic practice. The latter connects with the famous passage in chapter 48 about losing accumulated learning in order to cultivate the Way. We also find here two technical terms, the "Unadorned" (*su*) and the "Unhewn" (*pu*), which seem to refer to states of mind that would have been well understood in the community of inner cultivation practitioners that produced the *Laozi*. Our analysis of these terms takes us into the next section on mystical praxis in the *Laozi*.

INTROVERTIVE MYSTICAL EXPERIENCE IN THE LAOZI: THE PROFOUND MERGING

In the context of mystical praxis that I have been developing, I would argue that both the Unadorned and the Unhewn refer to states of mind that arise from apophatic practice. In *Laozi* 19, the Unadorned is associated with selflessness. In the *Huang-Lao boshu* 黃老帛書, it refers to a meditative state that arises after tranquility and equanimity and precedes the refined state of inner concentration that is linked to the vital essence (see Table 4.1). In *Laozi* 19, the Unhewn is linked with having few desires. In chapter 28, the Unhewn appears as an undifferentiated state attained through being like a valley and developing constant Inner Power (*De*). In chapter 37, it is referred to as "nameless" and free from desire, and it is said that this desireless state is brought about through tranquility. As technical terms of meditation, it is difficult to know for certain what their meanings are. However, what we can say is that both arise from the cultivation of tranquility and stand in the spectrum of stages of introvertive meditation bounded by two other important technical terms in the *Laozi*, tranquility (*jing*) and emptiness (*xu*). Chapter 16 presents them both:

> Complete emptiness is the ultimate limit (*ji*).
> Maintaining tranquility is the central (practice).
> The myriad things arise side-by-side
> And by this I contemplate their return.
> Heaven makes things in great numbers.
> Each one returns to its root.
> This is called "tranquility."
> Tranquility: this means returning to the inevitable (*ming* 命).
> To return to the inevitable is a constant.
> To know this constant is to be lucid.
> Not to know this constant is to be confused.
> If you are confused you will create misfortune.
> To know this constant is to be detached.
> To be detached is to be impartial.
> To be impartial is to be kingly.
> To be kingly is to be with Heaven.
> To be with Heaven is to be with the Way.
> If you are with the Way, to the end of your days you will
> suffer no peril.[61]

The statement that "complete emptiness is the ultimate limit" fits well with the fact that emptiness appears as the penultimate meditative state in several of our early Daoist sources, as can be seen in Table 4.1. So, too, does the emphasis on maintaining tranquility, which develops directly from apophatic practice at an earlier level, just following the alignment of the body and breathing.

These two terms frame a series of meditative stages in early Daoist praxis that include the Unadorned and the Unhewn. Given its nameless, desireless, and undifferentiated characteristics (all adjectives applied also to the Way), the latter term seems to refer to the unitive consciousness attained by merging with the Way.

As for the remainder of this chapter, whereas many commentators—starting with Wang Bi—see this as referring to the production of the things of the phenomenal world, in the context of the opening lines on emptiness and tranquility, I would argue that it is a phenomenological description of how one observes the arising and passing away of the contents of consciousness during guided breathing meditation. Accordingly, the myriad thoughts, emotions, and perceptions are metaphorically spoken of as the things that Heaven makes. Just as inevitably as these things arise while one is sitting in meditation, they pass away and out of consciousness. As one deepens this practice, when all these contents disappear and no longer recur, one returns to a condition of tranquility. This proceeds through a series of stages of increasing profundity until one reaches an ultimate level at which one is utterly empty.

If one knows about this inevitable process, one will realize that the variegated contents of the stream of consciousness are transient, and one can become detached from them. This lack of attachment confers the ability to be impartial in everyday interactions, as even the opinions and preferences of the individual self are also seen to be transient. This impartiality is the human counterpart of the dispassionate objectivity of Heaven, which "treats the myriad things as straw dogs" (chapter 5) and an important aspect of the desireless Way (chapter 37). It is a quality of mind the *Laozi* authors see as critical to cultivate in the ruler, and I have more to say about it in the following section on extrovertive mystical experience. Following the apophatic practice of the *Laozi* authors will produce it.

Chapter 16 also appears to be connected to the coiling and uncoiling passage from "Inward Training" through the concepts of reaching the ultimate limit (*ji*) of apophatic practice and returning to the Way found in both. The coiling and uncoiling of breathing meditation yield a profound tranquility, which, at its ultimate level, results in complete emptiness. In complete emptiness, one returns to the Way. Moreover, as we have seen, the attainment of, first, tranquility, and then emptiness through apophatic practice is found in the *Lüshi chunqiu* 25, *Zhuangzi* 23, and *Guanzi* "Techniques of the Mind I" ("Xinshu shang" 心術上) meditation passages summarized in Table 4.1. Indeed, in the last passage, the ultimate result is "to attain the empty Way" (*de xu Dao*). Finally, in *Zhuangzi's* "fasting of the mind" passage, the attainment of emptiness through apophatic practice leads directly to merging with the Way: "It is only that the Way coalesces in emptiness. Emptiness is the fasting of the mind."[62] All these passages provide a fuller context from which to interpret *Laozi* 16.

The cultivation of this state of emptiness is highly prized by the authors of the *Laozi*. This valuation results in some of the most famous images of the text: the nothingness at the hub of the wheel, inside the clay vessel, and within the empty room in chapter 11; the empty Way that use cannot drain in chapter 4 (*chong* 沖; not *xu* 虛; this image is repeated in chapter 35, where the emptiness of the Way is implied by the recurrence of this non-draining metaphor, and in chapter 45, where the Way is implied by the emptiness and non-draining metaphor from chapter 4); the empty space between Heaven and Earth that is never exhausted in chapter 5; the spirit of the empty valley that use will never drain in chapter 6, the empty ravine and valley in chapter 28 and the expansive valley in chapter 15; and, the blank mind of the fool in chapter 20.

Furthermore, tranquility, the "central practice" and the root to which all things inevitably return from chapter 16, is repeatedly emphasized in the text. The prescription to hold fast to the center (*shou zhong* 守中) in chapter 5 seems to refer to this "central practice" (*zhong* 中) of tranquility (chapter 16). In chapter 37, we read that "if one ceases to desire by being tranquil, all under Heaven will settle of its own accord." Chapter 45 states that "if one is clear and tranquil, one can set all under Heaven aright." Chapter 61 states that the feminine overcomes the masculine through tranquility. Both emptiness and tranquility are central to the metaphorical description of the ancient skilled practitioners of the Way in chapter 15:

> The ancients who excelled at manifesting the Way:
> Were subtle and marvelous, profound and penetrating,
> So deep they could not be conceived of.
> It is only because they could not be conceived of that if I
> were forced to describe them I would say they were:
> Tentative, as if fording a stream in winter.
> Hesitant, as if in fear of being surrounded.
> Solemn, as if someone's guest.
> Melting, like thawing ice.
> Undifferentiated, like the Unhewn.
> Murky, like muddy water.
> Vast, like a valley.
> When muddy water is made tranquil, it gradually becomes clear.
> When the calm is made active, it gradually springs to life.
> Those who maintain this Way do not wish to become full.
> It is only because they do not wish to become full that they
> can wear out yet be complete.[63]

The apophatic practice of breathing meditation is the process through which the normal contents of the self become emptied out and the murky consciousness gradually becomes clear. Tranquility, the Unadorned, emptiness, the Unhewn, and the "profound merging," all discussed above, are technical terms that refer to various stages in the process of intro-vertive meditation leading to the experience of union with the Way. The attainment of the state in which all normal conscious contents are emptied out would certainly qualify as an "introvertive mystical experi-ence" for Stace and a "Pure Consciousness Event" for Forman. Yet, for the *Laozi* authors, as we begin to see in chapter 15, when completely calm, one can still return to activity. The sages who do so maintain a clear and empty mind and detachment from the self that present few clearly defined characteristics to others. Hence they can only be described metaphorically. This, then, leads us to our third and final category of mystical praxis in the Laozi.

EXTROVERTIVE MYSTICAL EXPERIENCE IN THE *LAOZI*:
HOLDING FAST TO THE ONE

This detachment from self spoken of in chapter 15 is also mentioned in chapter 7, where the sage's lack of self-interest (*wusi* 無私) parallels that of Heaven and Earth and confers longevity, and in chapter 19, where lack of self-interest is called "manifesting the Unadorned" (*xian su* 見素). It is an integral part of the *Laozi*'s unitive expression of extrovertive mystical experience that places a strong emphasis not on some unitive conscious experience, but on the mode of cognition and being in the world that it confers. An excellent place to begin examining it is chapter 48:

> Those who cultivate learning gain something every day.
> Those who cultivate the Way lose something every day.
> They lose and further lose until they arrive at the point of taking no deliberate action.
> They take no deliberate action and yet nothing is left undone . . .

This saying is a succinct summary of apophatic practice, which can be thought of as the systematic loss of thoughts, feelings, perceptions, and, eventually, the self. Deliberate action comes from the biased perspective of the individual self. When this perspective is eliminated through apophatic practice, one still acts, but from a different center. While there are no passages that explicitly identify this new center for nondeliberate action, we can identify it through the famous phrase *wuwei er wu buwei*. For not only is this a mode of acting that develops as the result of apophatic practice, but it also is the mode of acting of the Way. Chapter 37 begins with the sentence "The Way constantly takes no deliberate action and yet nothing is left undone." Thus the sage, when completely empty, acts precisely as the Way acts. This suggests that the sage has become one with the Way and provides further support for our interpretation of the "profound merging" in chapter 56.

The table of early Daoist meditative stages in Table 4.1 shows a similar pattern to *Laozi* 48. The *wuwei* phrase—or some variation of it—is the result of apophatic practice in each of the six passages summarized therein. I would argue that this table indicates the presence of the two basic modes of mystical experience, introvertive and extrovertive. The final stage of the introvertive mode is spoken of as becoming empty, but also as both "attaining the One" in *Lüshi chunqiu* "Assessing Others" and "attaining the empty Way" in *Guanzi*'s "Techniques of the Mind I." The former suggests the attainment of a unitive consciousness, in other words, Stace's introvertive mystical experience and Forman's "Pure Consciousness Event." The latter suggests that the "object" of this unitive consciousness is the Way, and seems to confirm LaFargue's theory that the concept of the Way developed as the hypostatization of "the quality of mind one is cultivating internally" in the *Laozi*.[64]

The extrovertive mode of mystical experience occurs in the table as the result of the introvertive. The variations on *wuwei* are modes of selfless experience, experience that is extremely efficacious precisely because it is selfless. It comes from the Way and not the individual self. If this is true, we would expect that there would be some evidence in the Laozi of the retaining of some sense of the empty Way experienced at the pinnacle of introvertive mystical experience when one returns to the phenomenal world. I would assert that such evidence is found in the closely related concepts of holding on to (*zhi* 執), maintaining (*bao* 保) or holding fast to (*shou* 守) the Way, and embracing (*bao* 抱) the One.[65]

There are several important prescriptions to "hold on to" or "maintain the Way" in the *Laozi*. In chapter 14, we have the saying:

> Hold on to the Way of the present
> In order to manage the things of the present.
> And to know the ancient beginning.
> This is called the thread running through the Way.[66]

Chapter 15 talks of one who "maintains the Way" being first tranquil and clear, then calm and active. In chapter 32, "holding fast to the Way" results in all things spontaneously submitting to one's rule. In chapter 52, we read of the Way as mother of all things (as in chapters 1 and 25):

> All under Heaven had a beginning
> And we take this to be the mother of all under Heaven.
> If you attain the mother, you will know the children.
> If you know the children, return to hold fast to the mother,
> And to the end of your life you will never see danger.

As in chapter 14, holding fast to the Way (the mother) enables one to know intimately all things that are generated because of it (its children) because the Way continues to be their basis, as well as one's own. Other benefits of being in touch with the Way come about because of the transformed consciousness this confers. Because of it, one is able to be selfless and desireless and to take no deliberate action and yet accomplish everything one undertakes.

Further related aspects of these benefits are explored in the other early sources of Daoist inner cultivation theory. Some examples are given in the table. According to the *Huang-Lao boshu* essay "Assessing," "seeing and knowing are never deluded." In the "Assessing Others" essay of the *Lüshi chunqiu*, after attaining the One, one can "respond to the alterations and transformations of things and return to the Unhewn." In the "Numinous Essence" essay of the *Huainanzi*, "in seeing, nothing is left unseen, in hearing nothing is left unheard, in acting, nothing is left undone." All of these are possible because after the "profound merging" with the Way at the pinnacle of introvertive mystical experience, one retains a sense of this unitive power when one returns to the world of the myriad things. Retaining this experience of unity upon this return is further presented in the "embracing the One" passages in the *Laozi*.

In chapter 22, after a description of the sage as being "bowed down then preserved" that contains further metaphors of self-yielding as opposed to self-asserting, we read:

> Therefore the Sage embraces the One and is a model for all
>   under Heaven.
> He does not show himself, and so is conspicuous.
> He does not consider himself right, and so is illustrious.
> He does not brag and so has merit.
> He does not boast and so endures . . .[67]

This means that sages can be selfless because they are able to embrace the One. Why? By retaining a sense of this unitive ground amid daily life, they have an unbiased source for their actions that is not the individual self. For *Zhuangzi*, in the "Essay on Seeing Things as Equal" ("Qi wu lun" 齊物論), this non–self-based orientation leads to a complete freedom from attachment to basic conceptual categories, as in the famous "three every morning" story in which the monkey keeper spontaneously adapts his feeding plan to that of the monkeys.[68] For *Zhuangzi*, to "see all things as equal" means to regard them from this unbiased perspective of the One. Therefore, "holding fast to the One" (and its many variants) can justifiably be seen as the central descriptive metaphor in the *Laozi* for its understanding of what, in mysticism theory, is called the extrovertive mystical experience.

LAOZI 10 AS A SUMMARY OF MYSTICAL PRAXIS

With this understanding of mystical praxis in the *Laozi*, we can now return to analyze the critical chapter 10 that discusses "embracing the One" and links it with guided breathing meditation and other aspects of inner cultivation and its application to daily life:

> Amidst the daily activity of the psyche,[69] can you embrace
>   the One and not depart from it?
> When concentrating your vital breath until it is at its softest,
>   can you be like a child?
> Can you sweep clean your Profound Mirror so you are able
>   to have no flaws in it?
> In loving the people and governing the state, can you do it
>   without using knowledge?
> When the Gates of Heaven open and close, can you become
>   feminine?

In clarifying all within the four directions, can you do it
without using knowledge?

This passage is probably the most important evidence for guided breathing
meditation in the *Laozi*, and it contains three close parallels to "Inward
Training." In the first line, "embracing the One" is seen as something
one adheres to amid everyday psychological activities. I take this to mean
talking about retaining the sense of the consciousness experienced in
introvertive mystical experience when one returns to the phenomenal
world. It is paralleled in "Inward Training" by the concepts of "holding
on to the One" (*zhi yi* 執一) amid the daily transformations of things
and the daily alterations of events, thus enabling the sage to "master
the myriad things,"[70] and of "holding fast to the One" (*shou yi* 守一) in
the following passage:

> When you broaden your mind and relax it,
> Expand your vital breath and extend it,
> And when your physical form is calm and unmoving:
> You can hold fast to the One and discard the myriad vexations.
> You will not be lured by profit,
> Nor will you be frightened by harm.
> Relaxed and unwound, yet acutely sensitive,
> In solitude you delight in your own person.
> This is called "revolving the vital breath";
> Your thoughts and deeds resemble Heaven's.[71]

This passage implies that "holding fast to the One" is accomplished
through guided breathing meditation. It confers a selflessness that prevents
being lured by profit or frightened by harm, results similar to those in
Laozi 22 for the sage who "embraces the One." "Inward Training" contains the *locus classicus* for this concept of *shou yi*, a central tenet of the
early Inner Cultivation tradition that became extremely important in the
practice of meditation in later Daoist religion. There it sometimes refers
to what I have called the extrovertive mystical experience of seeing unity
amid the multiplicity of the phenomenal world and sometimes refers to
a specific meditative technique for focusing on the One, both in sitting
in silence and in the affairs of daily life.[72]

"Concentrating the vital breath" is a second important tenet in the
Inner Cultivation tradition of early Daoism. It seems to refer to developing
a refined and subtle level of breathing in introvertive meditation. Once

again, its *locus classicus* in the extant literature is in "Inward Training":

> By concentrating your vital breath as if numinous,
> The myriad things will all be contained within you.
> Can you concentrate? Can you unify?
> Can you not resort to divination yet know bad and good
> fortune?
> Can you stop? Can you halt?
> Can you not seek it in others,
> But attain it within yourself?
> You think and think and think further about this.
> You think, yet still do not penetrate it.
> The daemonic and numinous in you will penetrate it.
> It is not due to the inherent power of the daemonic and
> numinous.
> But rather to the utmost refinement of your essential vital
> breath.
> When the four limbs are set squarely
> And the blood and vital breath are tranquil:
> Unify your awareness, concentrate your mind.
> Then your eyes and ears will not be overstimulated.
> Then even the far-off will seem close at hand.[73]

When one sits in a stable posture and practices a form of guided breathing meditation, one becomes increasingly tranquil and the breathing becomes concentrated and subtle. This leads to a well-focused mind, minimal perception of the external world, and a numinous awareness in which "the myriad things will all be contained within you." This sounds very much like the attainment of a unitive consciousness. Retaining it when one returns to interact with the phenomenal world results in the lack of self-consciousness possessed by the child in the second line of *Laozi* 10.

In the third line of this chapter, we encounter the phrase "sweep clean your Profound Mirror" (*ti chu xuanjian* 滌除玄鑒), an abstruse meditational metaphor that Lau interprets as "cleaning out the mind."[74] This phrase is extremely close in meaning to one of the most important metaphors for apophatic practice in the Inner Cultivation tradition, which is first found in "Inward Training":

> There is a numinous awareness that naturally lies within.
> One moment it goes, the next it comes,

And no one is able to conceive of it.
If you lose it you are inevitably disordered;
If you attain it you are inevitably well-ordered.
Reverently clean out its abode (the mind)
And its vital essence will come on its own.
Still your attempts to imagine and conceive of it.
Relax your efforts to reflect on and control it.
Be serious and reverent and its vital essence will naturally
  settle.
Grasp it and don't let go,
Then the eyes and ears will not be overstimulated,
And the mind will have no other focus.
When a properly aligned mind lies within your center,
The myriad things will be seen in their proper context.[75]

To "reverently clean out the abode" of the numinous awareness shares the syntax and key verb (*chu* 除) of *Laozi* 10's "sweep clean your Profound Mirror." The metaphor is repeated in the related *Guanzi* essay "Techniques of the Mind I," where emptying the mind of desires is synonymous with "sweeping clean" (*saochu* 掃除) the abode of the numinous awareness.[76] The "Inward Training" verse seems to imply that the cleaning process involves setting aside the attempt to conceive of or control the numinous awareness. Then the mind will be ordered and concentrated on an inner meditation that allows the "myriad things to be seen in their proper context," a rather vague phrase that perhaps parallels the "myriad things will all be contained within you" from the previous passage.

The presence of all three parallels between *Laozi* 10 and "Inward Training" provides further evidence that the two works are closely related. I would hypothesize that the lineages of practitioners that produced each work shared a common apophatic meditative practice but, because of perhaps regional traditions and the particular experiences of individual teachers, developed somewhat different metaphors for conceiving of their practice and its results.

Conclusion

When taken together, these passages provide important testimony to the presence of mystical praxis in the *Laozi*. They further indicate that the *Laozi* is not an isolated product but was part of a greater tradition of lineages that shared a common meditative practice as their basis. Furthermore, this practice, as much as we can tell from the surviving textual evidence, is similar to apophatic meditative practice in many other cultural and religious traditions. This practice also yields both introvertive and extrovertive mystical experiences that seem to be similar to those in other traditions; I have made no attempt here to claim that these experiences are identical. What I have claimed is that these experiences are the likely basis of the distinctive cosmology and political theory of sage rulership for which the *Laozi* is renowned.

Chapter 9

Bimodal Mystical Experience in the "Qi wu lun" 齊物論 Chapter of the *Zhuangzi* 莊子

During the past fifteen years, scholars of Western philosophy have analyzed the text of the *Zhuangzi* in a number of books, including two excellent collections of essays, Victor Mair's *Experimental Essays on the Chuang Tzu* and Paul Kjellberg and P. J. Ivanhoe's *Essays on Skepticism, Relativism, and Ethics in the Zhuangzi*.[1] One of the most significant issues raised therein is that of epistemology: is the author, Zhuangzi, a "skeptic" in denying that human cognition in its various aspects can give any reliable knowledge of "truth"; or is he a "relativist" in admitting that the truths derived from cognition are relative to the standpoint of the person asserting them and hence not objectively true.[2] With certain exceptions that I indicate below, most of the authors either deny, neglect,

This chapter was originally published in *Journal of Chinese Religions* 28 (2000), 31–50. I wish to thank the editors for their kind permission to reprint. I am much indebted to Professor Scott Cook of Grinnell College for organizing the Association for Asian Studies panel for which I initially wrote this manuscript. He also included a version of it in his excellent collection, *Hiding the World in the World: Uneven Discourses on the Zhuangzi* (Albany: State University of New York Press, 2003), 15–32. There is yet another version included in the expanded edition of *Experimental Essays on Zhuangzi*, ed. Victor Mair (Dunedin, FL: Three Pines Press, 2010), 195–211. I also wish to thank my former colleague Professor Sumner B. Twiss of Brown University (now at Florida State University) and my graduate students Aaron Stalnaker (now at Indiana University) and Jung Lee (now at Northeastern University) for their valuable criticisms of an earlier version of this manuscript.

307

or, at best, only point to the mystical dimension of the text. I hope to demonstrate that this mystical dimension is critical to the understanding of Zhuangzi's epistemology.

In recent research on the historical and textual origins of several related lineages of the Daoist tradition of the fourth to second centuries BCE, I argued that these lineages are experientially based in mystical praxis.[3] That is, they share a common basic practice of breathing meditation. This practice led its adepts to profound mystical experiences that provided insights into the nature of the world and of a fundamental moving power that infused it and everything within it that they called the Dao. This is not to say that only members of these lineages practiced breathing meditation, but only to say that it was these adherents who took this practice to its furthest limits. Textual evidence for this breathing practice survives in the Duodecagonal Jade Tablet Inscription, the *Laozi* 老子, several essays in the *Guanzi* 管子 ("Neiye" 內業 and "Xinshu shang" 心術上 and "Xinshu xia" 心術下), the Mawangdui 馬王堆 "Huang-Lao" 黃老 texts, the *Lüshi chunqiu* 呂氏春秋, and the *Huainanzi* 淮南子. Related practices are also found in the *fang shu* 方術 texts from Mawangdui and Zhangjiashan 張家 山, but these finds cannot be classified as "Daoist" because they show no evidence of the distinctive cosmology of the other sources and because they seem to be part of their own distinctive medical tradition.[4]

In my research I have referred to this Daoist breathing practice as "inner cultivation." It involves following or guiding the breath while one is in a stable sitting position. As one does this, the normal contents of consciousness gradually empty out, and one comes to experience a tranquility that, as one's practice develops, becomes quite profound. Eventually one comes to fully empty out the contents of consciousness until a condition of unity is achieved, which is spoken of with a number of related phrases, such as "attaining the One" and "attaining the empty Way." After this experience, one returns and lives again in the dualistic world in a profoundly transformed fashion, often characterized by an un-self-conscious ability to spontaneously respond to whatever situation one is facing. This new mode of being in the world is frequently char-acterized by the famous phrase from *Laozi*: "doing nothing, yet leaving nothing undone" (*wuwei er wu buwei* 無為而無不為). I argue that there is concrete evidence that the author of the "Inner Chapters" of the *Zhuangzi* was aware of—and likely followed—such an inner cultivation practice.

These two complementary results of the practice of inner cultiva-tion show a noteworthy similarity with the two fundamental categories of mystical experience that Walter Stace has seen in religious traditions throughout the world: introvertive and extrovertive. He defines the former as a "unitary" or "pure" consciousness that is non-temporal and non-spatial and is experienced when the individual self loses its individuality in the One, and the latter as "the unifying vision—all things are One" coupled with "the more concrete apprehension of the One as an inner subjectivity, or life, in all things."[5] For him, this unity is directly perceived within the experience and will later be variously interpreted depending on the "cultural environment and the prior beliefs of the mystic."[6]

I have argued that Stace's phenomenological model of what I have called "bimodal" mystical experience can be fruitfully applied to the case of early Chinese mysticism, though it needs certain modifications.[7] Stace strongly values the introvertive over the extrovertive, a bias caused by his almost exclusive reliance on Indo-European textual sources for his theories and by his limited reading of these sources.[8] While this is a doubtful contention even among these sources, it is certainly not true of early Chinese mystical writings, especially the *Zhuangzi*. Indeed, Lee Yearley argues that with Zhuangzi, we have neither the Christian "mysticism of union," in which a union occurs between an "unchanging Real and the changing but still real particular individual"; nor do we have the Indian (Hindu-Buddhist) "mysticism of unity," in which the mystic attains unity by uncovering an inherent identity with a monistic principle that is the sole reality of the universe.[9] Rather, Zhuangzi espouses what Yearley calls an "intraworldly mysticism," in which ". . . one neither obtains union with some higher being nor unification with the single reality. Rather, one goes through a discipline and has experiences that allow one to view the world in a new way."[10]

While embracing Yearley's insights into what he calls "intraworldly mysticism," I see them as a corrective, rather than a replacement for, Stace's phenomenological model. That is, what I hope to demonstrate in this chapter is that what he calls "intraworldly mysticism" is not an entirely new mode of mystical experience, but rather a uniquely "Zhuangzian" form of Stace's extrovertive mode. As such, it is integrally related to the introvertive mode, although I would most certainly concur with Yearley that the unity attained fits into neither of his two categories of Indo-European mystical experience. For Zhuangzi, the Stacian "objective referent" of this introvertive mystical experience—the Way—is not a static metaphysical absolute (and Chad Hansen is most certainly correct in arguing that such a concept is not present in the *Zhuangzi*[11]), but rather a continuously moving unitive force that can be merged with when consciousness is completely emptied by inner cultivation practice, and can then serve as a constant guiding power throughout the many activities and circumstances of daily life.

Mystical Praxis in the Inner Chapters of the *Zhuangzi*

Before analyzing the evidence for bimodal mystical experience in the "Qi wu lun" of the *Zhuangzi*, I would like to briefly touch base with the evidence for inner cultivation practice in the "Inner Chapters" as a whole (of course I am assuming here a common authorial viewpoint in these seven initial chapters of the text). There are four passages that attest to this, two of which I only summarize, two of which I analyze:

1. The "fasting of the mind" dialogue in which Confucius teaches Yan Hui 顏回. Here Hui is told that he must completely empty out his consciousness to find the Way, and then he will be able to act spontaneously in the world and thereby "fly by being wingless" and "know by being ignorant" (4/24–27).[12]

2. The brief mention of how the Genuine breathe from their heels while the Common breathe from their throats, a passage that also implies that such breathing manifests a profound "mechanism of Heaven" (*Tian ji* 天機) (6/6–7). I have written elsewhere how the latter key technical term demonstrates an awareness of the breathing practice outlined in the oldest epigraphic source for inner cultivation, the Duodecagonal Jade Tablet Inscription.[13]

The third passage is the famous dialogue in which Yan Hui ironically "turns the tables" on his master by teaching *him* how to "sit and forget" (*zuo wang* 坐 忘)

(CONFUCIUS:) "What do you mean, just sit and forget?"

(YAN HUI:) "I let organs and members drop away, dismiss eyesight and hearing, part from the body and expel knowledge, and

> merge with the Great Pervader. This is what I mean by 'just sit and forget.'" (6/92–3; Graham CT: Inner Chapters, 92)[14]

To let "organs and members drop away" (*duo zhi ti* 墮支體) means to lose visceral awareness of the emotions and desires, which, for the early Daoists, have "physiological" bases in the various organs.[15] To "dismiss eyesight and hearing" (*chu cong ming* 出聰明) means to deliberately cut off sense perception. To "part from the body and expel knowledge" (*lixing chüzhi* 離形屈知) means to lose bodily awareness and remove all thoughts from consciousness. These are all familiar as apophatic aspects of the breathing meditation found in other sources of inner cultivation theory. To "merge with the Great Pervader" (*tong yu datong* 同於大通) seems to imply that, as a result of these practices, Yan Hui has become united with the Dao. Notice here the anti-metaphysical tendency of this final phrase: it implies the reality of the Way without establishing it as any kind of abstract metaphysical absolute.

There is another passage in chapter six that I think provides clear and incontrovertible evidence of the presence of a Stacian-type introvertive mystical experience: the dialogue between the "Self-Reliant Woman" (*nüyu* 女偊), who has "the Way of a sage but not the stuff of a sage," and her disciple, Buliang Yi 卜梁倚, who has the reverse qualities. While here we do not find concrete evidence of inner cultivation practice, we see its results in a series of stages: 1. After three days, he could put the human world (*tianxia* 天下) outside himself; 2. After seven days, he could put things outside himself; 3. After nine days, he could put life outside himself. And once he could do this, he could "break through to the Brightness of Dawn, see the Unique, be without past and present, and then enter into the unliving and undying. That which kills the living does not die, that which gives birth to the living does not live . . ." (6/39–43; Graham CT: Inner Chapters, 87).

In early Daoism, there is only one power that is beyond living and dying in the cosmos, one power that generates life and brings about death: the Way. In this passage, Buliang Yi has gradually stripped away all the contents of consciousness until he has reached an experience of totally merging with the Way. This certainly qualifies as the penultimate introvertive mystical experience. Its presence here indicates the author's awareness of such an experience; in the "Qi wu lun," we see further references to this experience and how it relates to the extrovertive mode that is spoken of much more frequently.

Skepticism in the "Qi wu lun"

Most of the essays that discuss the related issues of skepticism, relativism, and perspectivism in the *Zhuangzi* center almost exclusively on the "Qi wu lun." In general, most authors agree that all three are present but disagree about the extent to which they dominate the philosophical discourse and the degree of thoroughness with which they are applied. Hansen argues for a perspectival relativism in the text. In the "Qi wu lun," we find that all the doctrines of the Confucians and Mohists that each school thinks are true have a truth only relative to the perspective and viewpoint of each of the schools themselves:

> What is it is also other; what is other is also it. There they say "that's it," "that's not" from one point of view. Here we say "that's it," "that's not" from another point of view. Are there really it and other? Or really no it and other? . . . (2/29–31; Graham CT: Inner Chapters, 53)

"The strategy," Hansen argues, "is to show that all discrimination, evaluation, classification, and so forth, are relative to some changeable context of judgment."[16] This relativity of judgment implies that the knowledge it yields is likewise only relatively true and that there is, for Zhuangzi, no standpoint from which anything can be known to be objectively true. According to Hansen, this skepticism most certainly extends to the "mystical monist's" claim for a metaphysical, absolute One beyond the world of distinctions. He sees the parodying of Huishi's statement that "heaven and earth are born together with me and the myriad things and I are one" (2/52–53) to be a critique of precisely this position.

Lisa Raphals argues that the "Qi wu lun" demonstrates the use of skeptical methods but not the presence of skeptical doctrines.[17] That is because it emphasizes the distinction between small knowledge (*xiaozhi* 小知) and great knowledge (*dazhi* 大知). She equates the former with ordinary knowing, "with *shifei*, the language and practice of moral judgment," and the latter with illumination (*ming* 明), *Dao*, and *jue* 覺 "awakening."[18] The presence of the latter notion shows that the author was *not* an adherent to skeptical doctrines because he asserts the existence of a greater form of knowledge, something a true skeptic would never do.

A true skeptic would say that we cannot know whether or not there are greater or lesser forms of knowing because we cannot know for certain whether knowing really knows anything real. Raphals recognizes three possible ways to interpret this essay that include a skeptical reading (Zhuangzi seeks great knowing but questions whether it is possible) and a mystical reading, that "unitive mystical experience is the source of the knowing Zhuangzi refers to as "great," which she says could be compatible with a skeptical reading but which she declines to pursue.[19] It is compatible with a skeptical reading only if that skepticism is applied to the knowing of mundane life. This is an important insight, and I pursue it in line with Raphals's unexplored mystical reading of the "Qi wu lun."

Thus Raphals differs from Hansen on the issue of the thoroughness of Zhuangzi's skepticism: Hansen argues that it is applied to all forms of knowing; Raphals argues that there is a kind of knowing that is exempted from the skeptical critique, "illumination." I argue that this represents a distinctive mode of knowing that arises in the sage after the penultimate introvertive mystical experience of merging with the Dao and that it represents Zhuangzi's understanding of the kind of cognition that occurs within what Yearley calls "intraworldly mysticism," which I prefer to regard as a type of extrovertive mystical experience.

In his first of two articles on the philosophy of the *Zhuangzi*, P. J. Ivanhoe also examines the question of whether Zhuangzi was a skeptic, and in the process throws considerable light on this distinctive mode of knowing advocated in the text.[20] He provides a valuable definition of four kinds of skepticism and examines whether or not each can be found in the *Zhuangzi*[21] He concludes that:

i.   Zhuangzi was not a sense skeptic because the two dream passages in "Qi wu lun" imply that there is knowledge but that the problem is that we don't usually know how to reach it;

ii. that Zhuangzi was not an ethical skeptic because his skill passages present paradigms of persons who embody the Way;

iii. that Zhuangzi was an epistemological skeptic about intellectual knowledge but not about intuitive knowledge (he doubted, in Ryle's distinction, "knowing that," but not "knowing how"); and

iv. that Zhuangzi was a language skeptic who mistrusted proposals about what is right and wrong (not that there are right and wrong actions) and who doubted the abil-

ity of words to express the Dao. Ivanhoe maintains that
Zhuangzi used proposals that he constantly negated to
therapeutically undermine our confidence in proposals
that are the products of our scheming minds.[22]

Ivanhoe argues further that Zhuangzi uses a kind of perspectivism aimed at
dismantling intellectual traditions and leading to a process of unlearning
so that one can get back in tune with the Dao (Ivanhoe 1993, 645).[23]
This is greatly aided by the processes of "sitting and forgetting" and
"fasting of the heart and mind" by which we forget "the narrow and
parochial views which society has inflicted upon us."[24] Thus Ivanhoe
concurs in general with Raphals's argument that Zhuangzi excludes an
important mode of knowing from his skeptical probing. For him it is
the intuitive knowledge of the Dao; for her it is the great knowledge of
illumination. In my analysis, these are simply two aspects of the same
cognitive mode that arises within the extrovertive mystical experience.

Two Distinctive Modes of Consciousness in the "Qi wu lun"

Angus Graham made an important breakthrough in translating and
understanding the "Qi wu lun" when he identified a number of key technical terms also found in the Mohist Canons.[25] Most important for this
analysis are the contrasting demonstratives *shi* 是 and *fei* 非, which he
renders as "that's it" and "that's not" and for the Mohists were judgments
rendered about the truth or falseness of propositions about knowledge
and the contrasting pronouns *shi* 是 and *bi* 彼, which he renders as "It"
and "Other." Both pairs are used in the text to represent the conflicting
intellectual positions of the various philosophers:

> . . . And so we have the "that's it," "that's not" of Confu-
> cians and Mohists, by which what is it for one of them for
> the other is not, what is not for one of them for the other
> is . . . (2/26; Graham, CT: Inner Chapters, 52)

In a more general sense, *shi* and *fei* also stand for basic positions
or standpoints that individuals take in the world and for the conceptual
categories and intellectual commitments that are associated with them,
as Hansen accurately understands.[26] In this light, Zhuangzi differentiates

between two modes of adherence to such viewpoints that are symbolized in the text as *weishi* 為是 (the "that's it" which deems, or the contrived "that's it") and *yinshi* 因是 (the "that's it" which goes by circumstance, or the adaptive "that's it").[27]

In the former mode, one rigidly applies a preestablished way of looking at the world to every situation in which one finds oneself; in the latter mode, one lets the unique circumstances of the situation determine one's understanding and approach to it. The former involves a rigid attachment to oneself and one's intellectual commitments; the latter involves a complete freedom from such an attachment, a freedom to act spontaneously as the situation demands. From the psychological perspective, each represents a distinct mode of consciousness containing its own distinctive mode of knowing. The quintessential contrast between these two modes is found in the famous "three every morning" passage:

> A monkey keeper handing out nuts said, "Three every morning and four every evening." The monkeys were all in a rage. All right," he said, "four every morning and three every evening." The monkeys were all delighted. Without anything being missed out either in name or in substance, their pleasure and anger were put to use; his too was the "that's it" which goes by circumstance. This is why the sage smoothes things out with his "that's it, that's not," and stays at the point of rest on the potter's wheel of Heaven . . . (2/38–40; Graham CT: Inner Chapters, 54)

The monkeys are attached to one fixed way of seeing the underlying reality of the seven nuts; the keeper is not. They symbolize the *weishi* mode, a mode also characteristic not only of the Confucians and Mohists, but also of Zhaowen 昭文 the zither virtuoso, music-master Kuang 曠, and Zhuangzi's old friend Huishi 惠施 (2/43–44; Graham CT: Inner Chapters, 54). "All illumined an It that they preferred without the Other being illumined" . . . and "so the end of it all was the darkness of chop logic" (2/45; Graham CT: Inner Chapters, 55). Each developed his own unique viewpoint on the world and came to prefer It and only It and thereby left no room to adapt any Other. They were therefore fixated in this position and, like the monkeys, could never set it aside to see another way. "Therefore the glitter of glib implausibilities is despised by the sage. The "that's it" which deems he does not use, but finds for things lodging places in the usual. It is this that is meant by "using Illumination" (*yi ming* 以明) (2/47; Graham CT: Inner Chapters, 55).

By contrast, the monkey keeper is able to shift his conceptual categories—his way of conceiving of the same underlying reality—to harmonize with that of the monkeys because he is not attached to any one particular way of seeing this reality. His is the *yinshi* mode of consciousness that adapts spontaneously to the situation, an "illumined" consciousness that exhibits an intuitive knowledge that knows *how* to act without even knowing *that* it is acting. That is, the sage acts without self-consciousness and without being governed by any directing principle. His consciousness knows spontaneously how to respond because it is not confined to any one particular perspective.

Zhuangzi seems to be operating from this mode of consciousness throughout the "Qi wu lun." The language skepticism and therapeutic use of perspectivism that Ivanhoe has noted are possible because the author is unconfined by any one way of looking at things. For example, in the Gaptooth and Wang Ni 王倪 dialogue, Zhuangzi says, "how do I know that what I call knowing is not ignorance? How do I know that what I call ignorance is not knowing?" (2/66; Graham CT: Inner Chapters, 58). Or, in the Lady Li 麗姬 story, "How do I know that to take pleasure in life is not a delusion? How do I know that we who hate death are not lost children who have forgotten the way home?" (2/78–9; Graham CT: Inner Chapters, 59). Self-negating propositions and challenges to the culturally accepted ways of looking at the world abound in this chapter. They are examples of an illumined cognition that becomes possible when attachment to a rigid and fixed worldview is abandoned.

Furthermore, Zhuangzi makes it clear that abandoning a fixed viewpoint is concomitant with abandoning attachment to the self. For example, he seems to quote and largely approve of the saying "Without an Other, there is no Self; without Self, no choosing one thing rather than another" (2/14–15; Graham CT: Inner Chapters, 51). That is, if you lose the distinction between self and other, then you lose the self and, with it, any bias toward choosing one thing rather than another. There is also another relevant argument: ". . . No thing is not 'other'; no thing is not 'it.' If you treat yourself too as 'other,' they do not appear. If you know of yourself, you know them" (2/27; Graham CT: Inner Chapters, 52). It and Other do not appear because "treating yourself as other" (*zibi* 自彼) involves abandoning attachment to your self. That is, it involves having the same attachment to your self that you have to anything else.

This lack of self-attachment is an essential characteristic of the free and spontaneously functioning consciousness that Zhuangzi is advocating.

Zhuangzi has several related metaphors for the unique type of cognition of this *yinshi* consciousness, which stays "at the point of rest on the potter's wheel of Heaven (2/40)": using illumination (2/23, 2/29, 2/47; Graham CT: Inner Chapters, 52, 53, 55); opening things up to the light of Heaven (*zhao zhi yu tian* 照之于天) (2/29; Graham CT: Inner Chapters, 52); and, as Raphals has already pointed out, "great knowing" and "greatly awakened" knowing. All these imply a fundamental shift in perspective away from attachment to one's individual viewpoint and toward freedom from such attachment that involves going along with the responses that emerge spontaneously from the Heavenly within one. So far we find that this *yinshi* mode of consciousness fits well with Yearley's "intraworldly mysticism," Raphals's understanding of "great knowledge," and Ivanhoe's intuitive "knowing how." What I would like to argue here is that for Zhuangzi, this *yinshi* consciousness with its characteristic mode of knowing is not the sole result of mystical praxis: there is another equally important experience on which it rests.

Introvertive Mystical Experience in the "Qi wu lun"

There is a series of passages in the "Qi wu lun" that talk about the *yinshi* mode of consciousness coming to an end. Perhaps the most important one is the following:

> If being so is inherent in a thing, if being allowable is inherent in a thing, then from no perspective would it be not so, from no perspective would it be not allowable. Therefore when a "that's it" which deems picks out a stalk from a pillar, a hag from beautiful Hsi Shih, things however peculiar and incongruous, the Way pervades and unifies them. As they divide they develop, as they develop they dissolve. All things whether developing or dissolving revert to being pervaded and unified.
>
> Only those who penetrate this know how to pervade and unify things. The "that's it" which deems they do not use, but find lodging-places in daily life. It is in daily life that they make use of this perspective. It is in making use of this perspective that they pervade things. It is in pervading things

that they attain it. And when they attain it they are almost there. The "that's it" which goes by circumstance comes to an end. It ends and when it does, that of which we do not know what is so of it, we call the Way. (2/33–37)[28]

This is an extremely rich passage that must be carefully analyzed. Zhuangzi begins the passage with a reiteration of what some scholars have called his relativism or perspectivism. There are no perspectives, no viewpoints from which a thing is always so, is always true. The normal mode of *weishi* consciousness clearly differentiates things such as a stalk and a pillar, a hag and a beauty, and simultaneously makes preferences based on these perceptual distinctions. However, it is only the Way that can pervade these things and unify them. That is, it is the one and only perspective from which all things are seen just as they are, without bias, without preference, the only perspective from which "all things are seen to be equal," of equal value and worth (or lack thereof, as in the title of this chapter). It is just this kind of seeing that is the essential defining characteristic of the "great" or "awakened" knowing of the *yinshi* mode of consciousness that is developed by those rare people who can penetrate through (*da* 達) the common *weishi* mode. In this passage Zhuangzi clearly states that such people possess the exact same ability that the Way has to "pervade and unify" (*tong weiyi* 通為一) all things.

Using this ability, these sages find temporary lodging places, that is, viewpoints to which they are completely unattached, within the common experience of everyday living. The passage then reiterates that in using this Way-like perspective, the sages pervade things just as the Way pervades them. And in pervading things like this, these sages attain the Way itself. It is at this point that their distinctive everyday mode of *yinshi* consciousness come to an end and they have the experience of merging with the Way itself. This is symbolized by the phrase "that of which we do not know what is so of it, we call the Way." Knowing what is so of something implies a separation between the self that knows and the object that is known. But the Way can never be known as an object; it can only be "known" when the distinction between self and other, subject and object, dissolves in the introvertive mystical experience of uniting or merging with the Way. Thus the extrovertive mystical experience of "pervading and unifying things" must depend on the introvertive mystical experience of merging with the Way. Or, rather, there is a recursive relationship between the two modes of this bimodal mystical experience. In other words, once one loses the self temporarily by merging with the Way and then returns to the everyday dualistic world, one is no longer attached to oneself, and then the *yinshi* consciousness arises.

This, then, is the way in which this bimodal mystical experience operates in the "Qi wu lun" to generate the distinctive cognition that makes use of the skeptical methods that Hansen and Raphals identify and the distinctive form of linguistic skepticism that Ivanhoe identifies. These can be practiced because sages are not attached to their individual selves because they have already gone through the experience of total self-forgetting or total self-emptying in which they merge with the Way. But after this introvertive experience, they return to the world of everyday living, while at the same time retaining their prior condition of contact with the Way, the "Great Pervader" and unifier of all things. This condition of simultaneously seeing unity within multiplicity (or, to paraphrase Stace, of apprehending the One as an inner subjectivity in all things) is one of the significant characteristics of the extrovertive mystical experience. We might best describe it as a "Dao-centered" mode of being in contrast with the "ego-centered" mode of being that most of us are enmeshed in and that Zhuangzi symbolizes as the "that's it which deems."

There are other passages that speak of the intimate relationship between the introvertive and extrovertive modes of mystical experience in *Zhuangzi*. For example,

> What is It is also Other; what is Other is also It. There they say "that's it," "that's not" from one point of view. Here we say "that's it," "that's not" from another point of view. Are there really It and Other? Or really no It and Other? Where neither It nor Other finds its opposite is called the axis of the Way. When once the axis is found at the center of the circle there is no limit to responding with either, on the one hand no limit to what is it, on the other no limit to what is not. Therefore I say: "The best means is Illumination." (Graham CT: Inner Chapters, 53; 2/29–31)

In other words, after the experience of merging with the Way, one has discovered the "axis at the center of the circle" within, and so when one carries this experience back into everyday life and naturally maintains a connection to the Way, one can always respond spontaneously and harmoniously to whatever the situation demands, to whatever set of It/ Other or "that's it"/"that's not" categories are found in the limited *weishi* viewpoints of those with whom one is interacting. This is the particular skill or knack of the monkey keeper, and, in another passage, a similar circular metaphor, "staying at the point of rest on the potter's wheel of Heaven," is also used to characterize it (2/40; Graham CT: Inner Chapters, 54). The Way is the very center within the sage from which the "great" or "awakened" knowing of the *yinshi* mode of consciousness operates. The metaphor of a center implies impartiality: the center is equally distant from—or close to—any point on the circle. Therefore, there is no bias; no thing is only It and not Other.

It is from this "Way-centered" perspective that Zhuangzi rejects all forms of propositions that attempt to establish true knowledge from a limited perspective. For example, we find his rejection of a series of intentionally paradoxical propositions, including Huishi's famous "heaven and earth were born together with me and the myriad things and I are one," which looks, at first, to be a concise statement of an extrovertive mystical experience. Zhuangzi says:

> Now that we are one, can I still say something? Already having called us one, did I succeed in not saying something? One and the saying make two, two and one make three. Proceeding from there, even an expert calculator cannot get to the end of it, much less a plain man. Therefore if we take the step from nothing to something we arrive at three. How much worse if we take the step from something to something! Take no step at all, and the "that's it" which goes by circumstance will come to an end. (2/52–55; Graham CT: Inner Chapters, 56)

Zhuangzi rejects Huishi's saying because it is made from a dualistic, *weishi* standpoint. That is, when one is truly united with the myriad things, one cannot say anything because in this experience of unity there is no self from which such a statement can be made. Only after one is separated, in his words, after one has "taken the step from nothing to something," can one even make such a statement. But what is the point of making such a statement? It cannot give one true knowledge of the condition of unity because one is already functioning in a dualistic consciousness when such a statement is made. The only way of "knowing" such a unity is to experience it in a non-dual fashion. It can never be adequately described by propositional knowing, which simultaneously reifies the self that asserts the truth of the propositions ("Without Other there is no Self. Without self, no choice between alternatives . . ."). Propositional knowing is, in Ryle's words, a "knowing that." Non-dual knowing, on the other hand, is a "knowing how." Knowing *that* is the knowing of the *weishi* mode of consciousness. Knowing *how* is the knowing of the *yinshi* mode of consciousness and, as we shall see, is linked with the many skill passages in the text that are particularly collected in chapter 19, "Fathoming Life" ("Da sheng" 達 生). Notice, too, that here again, in the last sentence, Zhuangzi mentions the unity that comes about after the *yinshi* mode comes to an end. This unity is spoken of in one final passage that I would like to analyze:

> The men of old, their knowledge had arrived at something: at what had it arrived? There were some who thought that there had not yet begun to be things—the utmost, the exhaustive, there is no more to add. The next thought there were things but there had not yet begun to be borders. The next thought there were borders to them but there had not yet begun to be "that's it," "that's not." The lighting up of "that's it," "that's not" is the reason why the Way is flawed. The reason why the Way is flawed is the reason why love becomes complete. It anything really complete or flawed? Or is nothing really complete or flawed? . . .

Lisa Raphals sees these as stages in the history of knowledge but also acknowledges the possibility of a mystical reading in which these stages represent the return from an undifferentiated mystical experience to the perceptual and linguistic distinctions of the phenomenal world, and I concur with the latter interpretation.[29] When one is merged with the Way in the introvertive mystical experience, there are neither things nor a self that perceives them. When one emerges, one returns to a perceiving self and a perceived world of things, and such a return is inevitable. Establishing borders among things, I think, implies identifying them with words and ideas, and at this point one is living in the *yinshi* mode of consciousness. It is only when one begins to use these labels to establish propositional knowledge about these things and its concomitant preferences that one gets into trouble because one simultaneously reifies the self that knows and the objects known, giving both an ultimate truth that Zhuangzi thinks they do not have. One here ventures into the *weishi* mode of consciousness of the dream that Zhuangzi satirizes with such phrases as "Yet fools think they are awake, so confident that they know what they are, princes, herdsmen, incorrigible" (2/83; Graham CT: Inner Chapters, 60). It is in this mode that we are prevented from penetrating through to the Way that pervades and unifies. It is this mode that is the dream from which we must awaken and understand that the mode in which most of us function every day is really the "ultimate dream." How are we to accomplish this awakening? I would argue that it is by following the apophatic practice of breathing meditation that is mentioned elsewhere in the Inner Chapters and that, I think, formed the distinctive technique around which Zhuangzi and his community of early Daoists formed.

Great Knowledge

So what, then, for Zhuangzi, constitutes "great knowledge" or "awakened knowledge?" Great knowledge consists of knowing *how* dualistic cognition—in other words, knowing *that*—and all forms of propositional knowledge that arise from it are true only relative to the standpoint and the circumstances of the knower. This type of cognition entails directly experiencing how to take all things as equal by pervading and unifying them, just as the Way does. As I see it, "all things" refers not to just external phenomena but also to all aspects of one's own experience, including the very self we take to be our foundation. This is what Zhuangzi means when he says that one must treat oneself as other (*zibi*). This does not imply the total negation of dualistic cognition, but the relativizing or perspectivizing of it. This is what is meant by "finding lodging-places in daily living." Dualistic cognition and propositional knowledge may be useful in certain specific circumstances, but when the circumstances change, as they inevitably do, one must abandon them and allow oneself to respond to the new situation without their determining influence. This yields an awareness that is able to focus completely on what is taking place in the present moment.

So when Zhuangzi dreams he is a butterfly in the famous story, he is totally experiencing being a butterfly, and he has none of the conceptual categories of Zhuangzi the man. Then when he wakes up, he is again the man who remembers the sensation of being a butterfly. His question about his own identity arises from his total lack of attachment to any one way of looking at things, even to the standpoint of his own self. This is a perfect demonstration of the total fluidity of conceptual categories that is one of the essential defining characteristics of the *yinshi* mode of consciousness.

This distinct quality of psychological freedom and concomitant total concentration is at the heart of all the many skill passages throughout the text that Yearley, Ivanhoe, and others quite rightly point to as paradigmatic examples of the results of "intraworldly mysticism" and "intuitive knowing." These passages contain stories of masters of the *yinshi* consciousness, the "that's it" that goes by circumstance, who can totally concentrate on whatever task they are involved in, be it carving an ox, catching a cicada, plunging over the Spinebridge Falls,[30] carving a bellstand, or even serving in government—albeit reluctantly. Note that the last two "fast" in order to still their minds to prepare them for the tasks confronting them.[31]

Indeed, I would like to suggest that the cultivation of such a mode of consciousness—of a "Dao-centered" mode of being—was one of the central focuses within the community of Zhuangzi and his later disciples. Evidence of it can be seen scattered throughout the entire thirty-three-chapter work. The depiction of this mode of consciousness in the text of the *Zhuangzi* constitutes a major contribution to the cross-cultural study of extrovertive mystical experience that sets this mode squarely on a par with the introvertive, thereby helping to counteract the Stacian bias and clearly indicating the bimodal character of mystical experience in early China.

Chapter 10

Nature and Self-Cultivation in
Huainanzi's 淮南子 "Yuan Dao" 原道
(Originating in the Way)

Introduction

"Originating in the Way" ("Yuan Dao" 原 道) is an essay containing a beautiful poetic rhapsody on the cosmology of the Way (*Dao* 道) and its Inner Power (*De* 德) in the tradition of the *Laozi* 老子, certainly one of the canonical sources for this particular essay and for the book as a whole. In it we see a detailed examination of how these cosmic foundations are manifested within the world and a detailed description of how sages are able to use their unique penetrating vision of these foundations, attained through self-cultivation, to bring peace and harmony to the realm. Coming at the beginning of the entire twenty-one-essay book and written at a time when its compiler Liu An 劉安 was trying to dissuade his nephew, Emperor Wu 武帝, against the arguments of his Confucian (*Ru* 儒) advisors, this essay serves a number of purposes.

First, it is a summary of the activist Daoist argument for government by a ruler enlightened by Daoist inner cultivation practices and by their overarching cosmology of an intimately interrelated universe interfused by the unifying power of the Way and governed by discoverable patterns and sequences and predictable natures that tend toward harmony when not interfered with by the desires of the human ego.[1] Second, it contains an implicit appeal to rulers—Emperor Wu of the Han in particular—to adapt this Daoist position as the official ideology of government and,

325

understandably, a number of implicit critiques of the Confucian tradition and its contemporary practitioners. Third, as lead essay of the collection, it sets out general themes that are pursued in more details in the remainder of the work. Its importance for understanding the entire book and for looking back upon the earlier Daoist tradition and seeing it in a clearer light cannot be overemphasized.

In the great religious traditions of the West, we have come to be familiar with the notion of a transcendent source for moral and political authority, a divine lawgiver who set up the universe and its phenomena and the laws that govern them and who stands apart from his creation.[2] The natural world is that creation, and both this world and human beings who are made in God's image to dominate and control it have little divinity inherent within them. The divine is to be sought in another, transcendent realm, a sacred region that is, for the most part, denied to the living.

By contrast, one of the distinctive hallmarks of early Daoist cosmology is a complete fusion of the two realms that we can roughly describe as the transcendent and the immanent, the noumenal and the phenomenal, the sacred and the secular, the supernatural and the natural. They depict a universe totally infused with inherent divinity, a divinity that is contained in the everyday activities of the phenomena that constitute it as well as in the phenomena themselves. It is a universe of precision and order, whose activities are governed by natural guidelines and propensities, and whose phenomena are governed by their inherent natures so that they act in predictable ways. Human beings are an integral part of this universe and as a result are subject to its laws. Moreover, all this is thoroughly interfused by a force that guides the spontaneous activity of all things according to their inherent natural laws. This force is, of course, the Way, a unitive power that transcends any single phenomenon yet is paradoxically immanent within all of them. The Way guides the self-generation of all phenomena and remains at the basis of them throughout their existence.

Because the natural world to the early Daoists is thus both natural and supernatural, secular and sacred, the natures and patterns that constitute it attain a normative prominence that is mostly unfamiliar to us in the West. That is, these patterns, sequences, propensities, and natures are themselves divine. They are the basis through which all the multitudinous phenomena in the world adhere and function in harmony and as such are to serve as the models and standards for the communities of human beings who are an integral part of this order. Thus Nature is holy in and of itself—to be respected, adhered to, even worshiped. According to the early Daoists, human beings can either ignore this normative natural order and fail in their endeavors, or they can follow it and succeed.[3] This is the choice the authors of "Original Way" present to their intended audience of regal readers. Inner cultivation is the primary way in which human beings can both, on a macrocosmic level, follow this divine natural order and, on a microcosmic level, fully realize its elements within them. I would like to summarize this important essay in order to demonstrate how it elaborates upon the basic position I have just outlined.

"Original Way" can be divided into a number of distinct sections, each of which contains a particular argument; one problem is of course that most of us who have worked on it divide the text differently. Thus D. C. Lau sees thirty-three paragraphs in his critical edition (Lau and Chen 1992), but organizes them into twenty-two sections in the translation he did with Roger Ames (Lau and Ames 1998).[4] Kusuyama Haruki has twenty-one sections (1979), while Zhang Shuangdi 張雙棣 sees eleven (1997).[5] I have also organized the text into eleven sections in which I have identified a principal theme and a consistent line of argumentation, although my eleven concur with Chang's in only about a third of the cases. The Lau, the Lau-Ames, and the Kusuyama divisions also seldom converge completely.

On the Nature of the Way (1/1/3–24)[6]

This section discusses how the Way interfuses the entire phenomenal world and how the mythical organizer deities Fu Xi 伏羲 and Nü Wa 女媧 "grasped the handles of the Way," in other words, made use of it to bring order to the entire world. It contains some of the most beautiful and evocative poetic verses on the Way in all of early Daoist literature. For example:

As for the Way:
It covers the Heavens and upholds the Earth.
It extends the four directions
And divides the eight endpoints.
So high, it cannot be reached.
So deep, it cannot be fathomed.

It embraces and enfolds the Heavens and the Earth
It endows and bestows the Formless.
Flowing along like a wellspring, bubbling up like a fount,
It is empty but gradually becomes full.
Roiling and boiling
It is murky but gradually becomes clear.

Therefore, pile it up: it fills all within the Heavens and the
  Earth.
Stretch it out: it encompasses all within the Four Seas.
Extend it limitlessly: nothing marks dusk and dawn.
Roll it out: it expands to the Six Coordinates.
Roll it up: it doesn't make a handful.
It is constrained but able to extend.
It is dark but able to brighten.
It is weak but able to strengthen.
It is pliant but able to become firm.
It stretches out the Four warp-threads and binds yin and
  yang.
It suspends the cosmic rafters and displays the Three
  Luminaries.
It is saturating and soaking,
Subtle and minute.

Mountains are high because of it.
Abysses are deep because of it.
Beasts can run because of it.
Birds can fly because of it.
The sun and moon are bright because of it.
The stars and time keepers move because of it.
Unicorns wander freely because of it.
Phoenixes soar because of it. (1/1/3–8)

Thus the Way is the ultimate cause for the existence of the entire universe
and all the myriads of things within it. Yet paradoxically it cannot be
fully perceived nor conceived of by human beings. It has the qualities of
a highly refined energy that enables all things to spontaneously realize
the dynamism that emerges from their inherent natures, yet unlike an
energy it can never be exhausted.

Cosmic Rulership: The Ability of Great Rulers to Merge the Spiritual and Political Orders (1/1/26–2/11)

The sage-kings Feng Yi 馮夷 and Da Bing 大丙 are the first exemplars of enlightened Daoist government. They ruled the cosmos by "grasping the handles of the Way" and governed by following the natural tendencies in the phenomenal world:

> Thus if you take the heavens as your canopy
> Then nothing will be uncovered.
> If you take the earth as your carriage,
> Then nothing will not be supported
> If you take the four seasons as your mounts
> Then nothing will not be employed.
> If you take the yin and the yang as your charioteers
> Then nothing will not be complete.
>
> Therefore, why is it that they hastened forth but did not
>   wobble,
> Went far but did not weary
> Their four limbs did not weaken,
> Their perceptual acuity did not diminish
> And they could comprehend the shapes and outlines of the
>   eight outlying regions and the nine fields of the heavens?
> Because they grasped the handles of the Way and roamed
>   in the land of the inexhaustible.
> Therefore, the affairs of the world cannot be controlled.
> You must draw them out by following their natural direction.
> The alterations of the myriad things cannot be fathomed.
> You must grasp their essential tendencies and guide them
>   to their homes. (1/2/9–12)

The main point here is that human beings cannot succeed by going against the fundamental principles of the natural world. They must discover them and then not interfere with how the myriad things follow these principles in order to govern effectively and enable the human world to flourish. In other words, the human ruler must, like these sage-kings, have the wisdom to discern and to then adhere to the greater patterns of the heavens and the earth.

The Inherent Spontaneity of
the Natural World (1/2/13–3/13)

Natural phenomena (water mirror, echo, shadow, etc.) act spontaneously and respond harmoniously to whatever situation they are in all without any kind of intentional effort. In effect, they constitute a normative natural order. To penetrate the Way is to understand this and to learn how to not go against this natural order by gradually coming to realize its workings within your own being. Later sections argue that the only way to do this is through a process of inner cultivation.

> Now when a water mirror comes in contact with shapes, it is not because of wisdom and precedent that it is able to flawlessly reflect the square, round crooked and straight.
>
> Therefore, the echo does not respond at random and the shadow does not independently arise. They mimic sounds and forms and naturally do so without intent.
>
> That which is tranquil from our birth is our heavenly nature. Responding only after being stimulated, our nature is harmed. When things arise and the spirit responds, this is the activity of perception. When perception comes into contact with things, preferences arise. When preferences take shape and perception is enticed by external things, it cannot return to the self and the heavenly patterns are destroyed.
>
> Thus those who penetrate through to the Way do not use the human to alter the heavenly. Externally they transform together with things but internally they do not lose their true responsiveness. (1/2/13–16)

This passage argues that human beings fall away from this normative natural order and lose their spontaneous functioning as part of a kind of natural development of perception. The senses' desire for sense objects generates preferences and enticements, and people become so obsessed with them that they lose touch with their innate nature and natural spontaneity. Humans must learn to get back in touch with this natural and spontaneous side within themselves; it is that part of us that is directly connected to the normative patterns through which the Way subtly guides the spontaneous self-generation of all things. To realize this is to "follow the Great Way" (1/3/1), to not have a "crafty mind" and to know yourself completely, thus implying that the Way resides within the deepest layers of human beings.

Contrasting the Heavenly (Natural) and the Human (1/3/15–4/10)

The qualities, tendencies, and properties of the things of the natural world emerge from their innate natures (*xing* 性) and their natural (*ziran* 自然) propensities.

> Plants like duckweeds take root in water.
> Plants like trees take root on land.
> Birds beat their wings in the air in order to fly.
> Wild beasts stomp on solid ground in order to run.
> Serpents and dragons live in the water.
> Tigers and leopards live in caves.
> All this is the nature of the heavens and the earth.
>
> When two pieces of wood are rubbed together they make fire.
> When metal and fire are close together the metal becomes molten.
> Round things always spin.
> Hollow things excel at floating.
> This is their natural propensity. (1/3/15–17)

This section also discusses how human beings at the periphery of civilization adapt to their environment, that is, to the assemblage of innate natures and natural propensities in the various phenomena that constitute it. Here we see the important Syncretic Daoist principle of *yin* 因 (going along with, adapting to these natures and propensities of things). We also see the principle of suitability (*yi* 宜): each thing is intimately connected to its environment: there is a kind of inherent resonance between innate nature and natural environment that must be accorded with:[7]

> Tree-dwellers nest in the woods;
> Water dwellers live in caves.
> Wild beasts have beds of straw;
> Human beings have houses.

> Hilly places are suitable for oxen and horses.
> For travel by boat it's good to have a lot of water.
> The Xiongnu 匈奴 produce grass mats,
> The Gan 干 and Yue 越 make clothes of kudzu.
>
> Each produces what it urgently needs in order to adapt to the aridity or dampness. Each accords with where it lives in order to defend against the cold and the heat. All things attain what is suitable to them, things accord with their niches. From this viewpoint the myriad things definitely accord with what is natural to them, so why should the sage interfere with this? (1/3/21–22)

All these things are part of a normative natural order that humans are part of but fall away from, and this order gets further obscured by the development of such Confucian virtues as "wisdom and precedent." Humans must practice inner cultivation in order to return to their inherent connection to this natural order:

> Therefore, those who penetrate the Way return to clarity and tranquility. Those who look deeply into things end up not competing with them. If you use calmness to nourish your nature, and use quietude to stabilize your spirit, then you will enter the Heavenly Gateway.
>
> What we call "Heavenly"
> Is to be pure and untainted, unadorned and plain.
> And to never begin to be tainted with impurities.
> What we call "human"
> Is to be biased because of wisdom and precedent.
> Devious and deceptive,
> To look back to past ages and resort to convention.
> Thus that the ox treads on cloven hooves and grows horns
> And that the horse has a mane and square hooves
> Is what is Heavenly (i.e., natural).
> Yet to put a bit in a horse's mouth
> And to put a ring through an ox's nose,
> Is what is human.
> Those who comply with the Heavenly roam with the Way.
> Those who follow the human resort to convention.

Now you can't talk to a fish in a well about great things because it is confined by its narrow space. You can't talk to a summer bug about the cold because it is restricted to its season. You can't talk to petty scholars about the Utmost Way because they are confined by conventions and constrained by teachings.

> Thus sages do not allow the human to interfere with the
>   Heavenly
> And do not let desire confuse their genuine responsiveness.
>   (1/4/3–9)

The concept of the Heavenly (*tian* 天) is here used as a general term for this normative natural order. Randall Peerenboom finds a similar use in the *Huang-Lao boshu* 黃老帛書, and argues that "nature" provides a more accurate translation.[8]

Self-Cultivation and Non-Striving (1/4/10–5/8)

Sages cultivate themselves so that they do not strive to act contrary to Nature (*wuwei* 無為) and do not interfere (*wushi* 無事) with its normative patterns and principles. So Shun did not speak but transformed his environment in a numinous fashion because of his high degree of inner cultivation: In order to do this:

> Sages internally cultivate the root (of the Way within them)
> And do not externally adorn themselves with its branches.
> They protect their quintessential spirit (*jingshen* 精神) and
>   dispense with wisdom and precedent.
> Unperturbed, they do not strive to act yet there is nothing
>   left undone.
> Detached, they do not strive to govern but nothing is left
>   ungoverned. (1/4/22–23)

Sages do not assert their own wills and force things to conform to them but rather accomplish their ends by complying with and blending with other things:

> Thus those who attain the Way
> Their wills are weak but their deeds are strong.

Their minds are empty but their responses correspond (*dang*
當). (1/4/28)
Therefore, the pliant and weak are the supports of life
And the hard and strong are the disciples of death. (1/5/6–8;
Laozi chapter 76)

The message here is clear: there is a normative and harmonious order
in nature. Sages cultivate themselves and become empty and tranquil so
that they can accord with this natural order. Once they are able to attain
this harmony, they can act without effort and govern without striving
because they do not allow any self-interested actions to interfere with
the spontaneous evolution and transformations of this normative order.

Self-Cultivation and Timely Action (1/5/8–23)

It is important that sages do not act in advance of the correct moment.
If they act in advance of it, then disaster will result. When they detect
that moment, they act spontaneously in response to it.

Why? Because those who act in advance have a hard time
acting with wisdom,
But those who follow after have an easy time acting efficaciously.

What we call "following after" does not mean being stagnant
without breaking out of it or being congealed and not flowing.
It is, rather, to value being able to accord with the (Heavenly)
sequences (*shu* 數) and act at the right moment. (1/5/15–16)

These Heavenly sequences are the precisely measured movements of the sun, moon, stars, planets, and constellations
that govern the heavens and are the basis of determining
time. Following means to act in accord with them and act
in a timely fashion but in order to do this, sages practice
inner cultivation:

Therefore sages guard the Pure Way and embrace the limits
of the feminine principle. They adapt to things and comply
with them, they respond to alterations spontaneously, they
constantly follow and do not precede.

Because of their tranquility they are pliant and weak,
Because of their stability they are relaxed and calm.
They defeat the great and grind down the hard, and none is
able to compete with them. (1/5/22–23)

The notion of timely action pervades much of early Chinese thought and certainly undergirds the hermeneutical basis of the various commentaries to the *Yijing* 易經 (Book of Changes). In this section of "Original Way," the emphasis on following after rather than acting in advance is also based in this notion, but I think it is further related to the more general idea of the non-assertiveness of the human will over the normative natural order contained in such concepts as *wuwei* and *wushi* (non-interference). For humans to act in advance of the right moment is a selfish and almost "unholy" act that will inevitably result in failure. This is stated more dramatically in earlier *Huang-Lao* works such as the "Four Measures" (Sidu 四度) section of the "Normative Standards" (Jing fa 經法) section in the *Huang-Lao boshu*. For example:

When activity and tranquility do not correspond to the right
moment
We call this deviance.
When generating and killing do not correspond (to the
Heavenly patterns *Tian li* 天理)
We call this cruelty. . . .
With deviance, you lose the Heavenly (correspondences *Tian
dang* 天當).
With cruelty, you lose (the goodwill) of human beings. . . .
When you lose the Heavenly (correspondences) there will
be famine.
When you lose (the goodwill of) human beings there will
be enmity. . . .
When activity and tranquility align with (the patterns of)
the Heavens and the Earth
We call this "civility" (*wen* 文).
When punishments and prohibitions correspond to the right
season,
We call this martiality (*wu* 武).[9]

This notion of Heavenly correspondences (*Tian dang*) is central to the *Huang-Lao boshu*. It refers to the matching of human endeavors to the greater patterns of the cosmos. These patterns are the *li* 理, the natural guidelines that direct the spontaneous interactions of all things. They form a vast matrix in space and time in which human beings are embedded and which guide the spontaneous responses of things that arise from their innate natures (*xing*) as they interact with one another. As a result of these hidden guidelines, the universe is precise and ordered. Human beings have these natures and guidelines within themselves but often do not realize it and fail to act in harmony with these greater forces. If they govern a state, then disaster results. The authors of "Original Way" shared in this vision but added to it an additional element derived from inner cultivation practice. Sages follow apophatic methods of emptying the mind of all desires, thoughts, and emotions that constitute the factors that interfere with human realization of these innate forces. Removing these enables them to experience these forces working within them as microcosms and in the greater world as macrocosm. Thus when these *Huainanzi* authors state above that ". . . those who attain the Way . . . Their minds are empty but their responses correspond (*dang* 當)," they do so as part of a tradition at least a century old that placed a great deal of emphasis on realizing the right thing to do at exactly the right moment by uncovering the normative natural order inherent in that situation.

The Normative Metaphor of Water (1/5/25–6/7)

The authors of "Original Way" often used the metaphor of water to express the most important aspects of this normative order:

> Of all things under the Heavens none is more pliant than water.
> Nonetheless it is so great that its limits cannot be reached. . . .
> Therefore,
> It is neither partial nor impartial,
> It overflows and surges through
> And vastly merges with the heavens and the earth.
> Without favoring the left or the right,
> It coils and swirls and twists round and round,
> And it ends and begins with the myriad things.
> This is what we call "Perfected Inner Power." (1/6/6–7)

. . . Now the reason that water is able to achieve its Perfected Inner Power within all under the heavens is that it is gentle and soaking, moist and slippery.

Thus, in the words of Lao Dan:
The most pliant things in the world
Ride roughshod over the most rigid.
This is because they emerge from what has no existence
And enter into what has no spaces.
I thereby understand the benefits of acting without striving
    (*wu-wei*). (1/6/9; *Laozi* 43)

The importance of the water metaphor in the Daoist tradition has recently been recognized by Sarah Allan and received a new impetus with the discovery of the "Vast Unity Generates Water" (*Taiyi sheng shui* 太一生水) text at Guodian 郭店 (see Allan 1998; Allan and Williams 2000).[10] In both this text and in "Original Way," water moves and acts as the Way does. It is also something from which we can learn about how the Way works in the world and also a normative model for how the sages act. When they encounter difficulties, they do not meet them with force but rather with a mental attitude based upon the model of the persistent weakness of water. This is a quality of mind to be cultivated and is related to the notions of weakness, pliancy, non-striving, and non-assertiveness. It is through this normative model of water that we can, as the *Laozi* says, understand the benefits of acting without asserting the human will over and against the patterns of Nature.

Cultivating The One (1/6/11–7/2)

The Formless (*wuxing* 無形) and the One are metaphors for the Way. They are certainly described in very similar terms to the Way:

What we call the Formless is a designation for the One.
What we call the One is matchlessly united with all under
    the heavens.
When standing by itself it is lofty,
When dwelling by itself, it is amorphous.

It permeates the Nine Heavens above,
And threads through the Nine Regions below. . . .

Therefore, you may look for it but you will never see its form;
You may listen for it but you will never hear its sound;
You may touch it but you will never feel its contours.
It is a formlessness from which forms are generated;
It is a soundlessness from which the Five Tones call out.
It is a tastelessness from which the Five Flavors take shape.
It is a colorlessness from which the Five Colors develop.
  (1/6/16–20) . . .

As for the Way: when the One is established then the myriad things all are born (1/6/24).

Therefore, the Formless and the One are both mysterious and omnipresent. They provide the basis from which all sense objects continuously emerge and the foundation from which phenomenal things are continuously born. The implication seems to be that this aspect of the Way serves as a kind of baseline from which all values emerge. Because it is also at the basis of all human beings, sages are able merge with the One through inner cultivation practice and apply it to daily life:

Therefore, clarity and tranquility are the perfection of Inner
  Power
And the pliant and weak are the essentials of the Way.
Emptiness and nothingness, calmness and serenity are the
  ancestors of the myriad things.
To quickly respond when stimulated; to boldly return to the
  Foundation,
This is to be merged with the Formless. (1/6/15–16)

Therefore, when the Perfected govern:
They conceal their mental acuity,
They extinguish their literary brilliance.
Relying on the Way, they set aside wisdom and act impartially
  toward the people.

They are restrictive in what they guard (the One)
And they reduce what they seek after.
They cast off enticements and longings,
Discard lusts and desires.
And reject thoughts and deliberations. . . .

Therefore, sages make use of the One Measure to comply
 with the tracks of things.
They do not alter its suitability
They do not change its constancy.
They follow it as their level;
They take hold of it as their plumb line.
And they intimately accord with its correspondences (*dang*).
 (1/6/29–7/1)

Through a process of "inner cultivation," sages are able to become calm and tranquil and penetrate through to a direct inner apprehension of the Formless One within their own beings. This subsequently gives them the clarity and serenity and freedom from egotistical desires that enable them to govern impartially by constantly referring back to this "One Measure" as their guiding power.

The benefits of this include freedom from attachment, spontaneous responsiveness in any situation, impartiality, and the ability to recognize and comply with the greater patterns and propensities of the heavens and the earth. Cultivating the One is thus what puts sages directly in tune with the normative natural order.

Inner Cultivation and its Personal Benefits (1/7/4–8/9)

While previous sections have argued that inner cultivation enables sages to penetrate the Way and make use of its Inner Power, they have not detailed how this process works. This is addressed here:

Thus when the mind is neither worried nor joyful you attain
 the perfection of Inner Power.
When it is unified and does not alter you attain the perfection
 of tranquility.

> When lusts and desires are not borne by the mind you attain
> the perfection of emptiness.
> When the mind is without likes and dislikes you attain the
> perfection of equanimity.
> When the mind is not mixed up with things you attain the
> perfection of purity.
> If you are able to attain these five qualities then you will
> break through to Spirit-like Clarity (*shenming* 神明).
> If you break through to Spirit-like Clarity then you will realize
> your deepest interiority. (1/7/4–8)[11]

Therefore, it is through the systematic elimination of the emotions, distractions, desires, preferences, thoughts, deliberations, and attachments to sense-objects that usually flood the conscious mind that one may break through to the level of "Spirit-like Clarity" and realize what lies at the basis of one's own inner being. We know from the previous section that what lies deep within one's innermost core of one's being is the One Way. This subsequently confers benefits throughout one's life:

> When treading through dangers and traversing defiles
> You will never forget your Profound Support.
> If you are able to preserve this here,
> Then your Inner Power will not diminish.
> The myriad things commingle in profusion,
> And you can revolve and transform together with them.
> And thereby listen to all under the heavens.
> It is like galloping with the wind at your back.
> This is called "perfect Inner Power."
> If you attain perfect Inner Power then you will be truly
> joyous. . . . (1/7/15–16)

On true joy:

> What I call "joy" how could it refer to the so-called joy of
> residing in the Lofty Terrace . . . or to galloping on a level
> highway; or to hunting the auspicious turquoise kingfisher.
> What I call "joy" refers to realizing your own deepest interiority. (1/7/20)

Therefore if you have the resources to realize your own deepest interiority, then beneath lofty forests and within the bowels of the deepest caves you will have what it takes to respond appropriately to your situation. But if you do not have the resources to realize your own deepest interiority, then although you take all under the heavens as your own family and the myriad people as your servants and concubines, you will not have what it takes to nurture life. (1/7/23–6)

This section ends with a further discussion of what joy is not. It is not the extremely transient pleasures of the senses that give enjoyment when they are present but pass away quickly leaving sadness. Why is this?

Because you do not use what lies within you to bring joy to what lies outside but rather use what is outside you to bring joy to what lies within. (1/8/3)

Therefore, if you do not realize the center that lies within you then you will take your commands only from the outside and use them to falsely adorn yourself . . . (1/8/4–5)

Thus when they hear good words and sound advice, even
   fools know to accept it.
When they are told of perfect Inner Power and lofty actions,
   even the unworthy know to yearn for it.
Yet while those who accept it are many, those who make
   use of it are few.
While those who yearn for it are many, those who practice
   it are few.
Why is this so? Because they do not know how to return to
   their innate natures. (1/8/6–8)

Inner Cultivation and the Benefits it
Confers on the Ruler (1/8/10–9/13)

This section presents an elaborate argument about the benefits of inner cultivation practice for rulership:

Therefore if you do not realize (what lies deep) within your own mind (*bu de yu xin* 不得於心) and still want to control the vital energies of all under the heavens, this is like having no ears yet wanting to tune bells and drums and like having no eyes and wanting to enjoy pattern and ornament. You will, most certainly, not be up to the task.

It also unequivocally states the holiness or divinity of the normative natural order:

Thus, all under the heavens is a spirit-like vessel (*tianxia shenqi* 天下神器): you cannot impose your personal will on it; those who do so will be defeated; those who try to hold onto it will lose it. Now that Xu You 許由 devalued all under the heavens and would not trade places with Yao was because he had the intention of leaving behind all under the heavens. Why was this so? Because he thought that you should act on all under the heavens by adapting to it (and not trying to impose your own will upon it).

The essentials of all under the heavens
Do not lie in the Other
But instead lie within the Self.
Do not lie within other people
But instead lie within your own being (*shen* 身).
When you realize what rests within your own being then the
    myriad things will all be arrayed before you.

When you thoroughly comprehend the discussions of the Techniques of the Mind then you will be able to put lusts and desires, likes and dislikes outside yourself. (1/8/14–17)

This passage argues that there is a normative natural order implicit within the world, and this is why the world is called a "spirit-like vessel." As we have seen, it is made up of the various innate natures of things that determine their course of development and their actions and the great patterns inherent in the cosmos that govern the characteristic ways that things interact with one another. These natures and patterns are thoroughly infused with the empty Way, which mysteriously guides their spontaneous processes of development and of daily activity. This entire complex world functions completely spontaneously and harmoniously and needs nothing additional from human beings. All sages need to do is to recognize these natures and patterns and adapt to them. It is because of this normative order that sages can accomplish everything without exerting their individual will to control things. In other words, *wuwei* functions because of the existence of this normative natural order. Sages cultivate themselves through the "Techniques of the Mind" in order to fully realize the basis of this order within.[12] By realizing the Way at the basis of their own deepest interiority, sages can simultaneously realize the basis of the interiority of all phenomena. Hence the saying "the myriad things will all be arrayed before you." The section continues:

> Now to possess all under the heavens, why must it consist of grasping power, holding onto authority, wielding the handles of life and death and using them to put one's own titles and edicts into effect? What I call possessing all under the heavens is certainly not this. It is realizing your own deepest interiority and that's all. Once I am able to realize it then all under the heavens will also be able to realize me. When all under the heavens and myself are mutually realized, then we will always mutually possess each other. And so how could we fail to fill in any space between us? . . .
>
> What I call "to realize your own deepest interiority" means to fulfill your own being. If you fulfill your own being then you will become united with the Way. (1/8/21–25)

Thus when you realize your own deepest interiority, you unite with the Way that interfuses the phenomenal world. As you do this, you return to your innate nature and attain your natural propensity to act spontaneously and harmoniously. All things have this propensity, and it is also called the "Heavenly Dynamism" (*Tianji* 天機). Sages experience both enticements and privations, but neither can cause their minds to be displaced in their focus on their true natures because of their realization of this "dynamism":

> Because inwardly they have the means to penetrate the Heavenly Dynamism they do not allow honor or debasement, poverty or wealth to make them weary and lose their focus on Inner Power. . . .

> Therefore when the realization of the Way is secured and does not depend on the vagaries of the myriad things, momentary transformations do not determine my ability to spontaneously realize it. What I am calling "realization" means realizing the true responses of my nature and destiny and resting securely in the calmness that it produces . . . (1/9/3–8)

In early Chinese thought, what happens to people over the course of their lives is seen as a combination of two factors over which we have little or no control: the inherent nature and talents we are born with (*xing* 性) and all the various life circumstances that are beyond our control (*ming* 命). The *Zhuangzi* 莊子 follower whom Graham deemed "the Primitivist" was the first Daoist to derive a foundational idea from these terms and use it as the basis of his unique philosophy.[13] For him, the "true responses of my nature and destiny" (*xing ming zhi qing* 性明 之情) meant the spontaneous and harmonious reactions that arise from that deepest part of our beings in response to the various circumstances in which we find ourselves throughout the course of our lives. These are often obscured by the psychological effects of culture that produce a self-consciousness that prevents us from uncovering this instinctive connectivity with the rest of the world. The authors of "Original Way" seem to be using this phrase with the same meaning. It seems to be an elaboration of their idea of the "Heavenly Dynamism."

There is a further poetic extolling the praises of those who realize the Way (*de Dao zhe* 得道者) in this section. It echoes descriptions in the *Laozi* and *Zhuangzi* and ends with the following summation:

> Therefore, they are not content with prosperity
> Nor do they suffer with privation.
> They do not take honor as security
> Nor do they take debasement as danger.
> Their bodies, spirits, vital energy, and attention
> Each dwell in appropriate activities
> And they thereby follow the workings of the heavens and
> the earth. (1/9/11–13)

These "workings of the heavens and the earth" are the normative natural order that sages discover and rely on.

Techniques of the Mind:
Underlying Principles of Inner Cultivation (1/9/15–10/10)

This final section discusses the basis of inner cultivation as depending on preserving the inherent balance between the functioning of the four basic aspects of human beings: physical body (*xing* 形), vital energy or breath (*qi* 氣), spirit (*shen* 神), and will or attention (*zhi* 志). These aspects and the relationships among them can be seen as part of the normative natural order that exists in human beings and that, if their balance is not interfered with, will enable humans to function spontaneously and harmoniously.

> Now the physical form is the abode of the life force,
> The vital energy is what infuses the life force,
> And the spirit is what regulates the life force.
> If one of these loses its position then the other two are harmed.
>
> Therefore, sages ensure that each rests in its suitable position,
> preserves its specific functions, and that they do not interfere
> with each other. (1/9/15–16)

The body has the usual variety of life activities it performs, all of which are infused with vital energy or breath; sense perception is among the most important of these. All these activities must be directed by the spirit if the proper balance of four aspects is to be maintained. Clogging up consciousness with the lusts and desires that arise from the senses causes the spirit to lose its focus, and sometimes when this happens, even madness results. The antidote for this is inner cultivation practice, which cleanses the mind by a process of emptying and thus gradually restores the inherent balance between these activities:

> Thus for those in whom the spirit is the ruler,
> The body will follow and will benefit from this.
> For those in whom the body is the governor
> The spirit will follow and will be harmed by this.
> People who are covetous and filled with desires
> Are blinded by political power and profit
> And are enticed by their lust for fame and station. (1/10/3–4)

So if you let your body and its sense desires and desires of the ego govern your spirit, then you will every day squander your spiritual essence until it will disappear. However, there is another way:

> Now the vital essence, spirit, vital energy, and attention:
> If you are tranquil and infused by them then you will daily
>   get stronger.
> If you are agitated and squander them then you will daily
>   grow older.
> Therefore sages will nourish their spirits,
> Harmonize and soften their vital breath
> Level out their bodies
> And sink and float, plunge and soar through life along with
>   the Way.
> In calmness they relax into it
> When pressed they employ it.
> Their relaxing into it is like their taking off clothes;
> Their use of it is like the (automatic) shooting of a crossbow.
> If you can be like this then among all the transformations
>   of the myriad things there will be none that you will not
>   welcome
> And among all the alterations of the hundreds of endeavors
>   there will be none that you will not spontaneously respond
>   to. (1/10/8–10)

Thus by practicing inner cultivation that calms mind and body and yields a deep state of tranquility, sages enable the four basic aspects of their beings to function spontaneously and harmoniously in accord with their inherent natural guidelines. This then allows them to fall into the "Heavenly Dynamism," the normative natural order of which they are an integral part and thus act completely in accord with the Way.

Conclusion

Thus the attitude toward nature and self-cultivation found in the "Original Way" chapter of the Huainanzi can be summarized as follows:

1. There is a normative natural order in the Heavens and the Earth that is established—and interfused—by a single divine force called the Way.

2. This order consists of natural patterns, innate natures, spontaneous propensities, and numerical sequences, all of which govern the behavior of everything in the world, including human beings. It is also called the "Heavenly Dynamism."

3. This normative natural order is divine or holy.

4. Human beings, while connected to this order by their innate natures, tend to fall away from it in their activities, and they must learn how to reestablish their connection to it.

5. Humans can accomplish this through "Techniques of the Mind"—in other words, inner cultivation practice— through which they can set aside lusts and desires, likes and dislikes, and wisdom and precedent, all of which have separated them from their innate natures and wasted their inherent potential for true happiness.

6. Rulers who are able to do this achieve complete success and happiness because they govern in accord with the normative patterns and forces that infuse the Heavens and the Earth.

Afterward

The *Huainanzi*'s approach to self-cultivation in the context of a normative natural order has remained influential within the various traditions of the Daoist religion, although the details and the depth of this influence have varied over the course of the two millennia or so since its creation. Indeed, Michael Saso asserts that the *Huainanzi* is one of the principal works upon which the modern Daoist training manual whose use he observed in Taiwan, "Origins of Religious Daoism" (*Daojiao yuanliu* 道教原流), is based, and thus expresses many of "the fundamental ideals of religious Taoism."[14] Indeed, the strong likelihood that there was a copy of this text included in the Northern Sung recension of the Daoist Canon of 1016 and the distinct possibility of its inclusion in Tang recension of circa 740 indicates that the *Huainanzi* was considered an important part of the philosophical foundations of the tradition from its earliest times.[15] Given its central role in the *Huainanzi*, the theories of nature and self-cultivation in "Original Way" are at the very heart of these philosophical foundations of the entire Daoist tradition.

To a great extent, the masterful work of Henry Rosemont Jr. has dealt with the natural tendencies of human beings and the political organizations that can best be developed to harness and direct them. Hence his work in traditional Chinese thought has cleaved to the Confucian tradition, which, over the course of two millennia, has directly dealt with these problems in normative and innovative ways. However, such questions are not the sole purview of the Confucians; Daoist thinkers have grappled with them as well, although their contributions have long been overlooked because they are not contained in those works that Chinese literati have favored, the *Laozi* and the "Inner Chapters" of the *Zhuangzi*. In the *Huainanzi*, we find a novel approach to these problems that grounds human nature in a normative natural order and recommends that government be organized in light of this foundational insight. The authors of "Original Way" thus find a source of human nature that inherently links human beings with something greater than their own individual natures, the normative natural order in which all people are embedded. In so doing, they provide a Daoist theory of human nature that offers an explicit cosmological dimension that is arguably only implicit in the classical Confucian sources that Professor Rosemont has so deftly analyzed.

Chapter 11

The Classical Daoist Concept of
Li 理 (Pattern) and Early Chinese Cosmology

Introduction: *Li*, Jade, and Cosmology

In her pioneering application of Lakoff and Johnson's "Metaphor Theory" to classical Chinese thought, Sarah Allan identifies the root-structures of some of the most significant ideas therein. She demonstrates that profound and lasting ideas sometimes derive from very commonplace observations human beings make about the world in which we find ourselves embedded.[1] Allan argues that these long-lasting concepts of the Chinese worldview derive directly from fundamental or "root-metaphors" that are themselves derived directly from these natural observations and experiences. Allan argues that the most powerful of these root-metaphors are those based on human observations of how water operates within the cosmos and of the natural growth and life cycle of plants. We can see them operative in many of the descriptive passages of how the Way works within the world from the classical Daoist tradition and in how the Confucian tradition developed its ideas of "self-cultivation" from its sprout-like tendencies into effulgent moral virtues.

Because Allan did not set out to write a completely comprehensive analysis of all the major ideas of classical Chinese philosophy, there are some concepts she did not include. In the following analysis, I would like to concentrate on one important idea that she did not study, an idea that has its origins in fairly specific and concrete observations of the natural world, an idea that was supposed to have been developed as a key cosmological term within the Song "Neo-Confucian" tradition: the concept of *li*, often translated as "principle," but in early sources best thought of as "Inherent Pattern" or "Natural Guidelines."[2] In what follows I argue that this idea, far from being a Song dynasty philosophical invention, was really developed as a central concept of a "normative natural order" within the texts of the classical Daoist tradition. I also demonstrate how this major cosmological concept is itself grounded in a root-metaphor that ultimately must have been derived by the guild of workers in the precious and highly valued mineral of jade.

Jade as Symbol and Metaphor

While jade objects are found in many places in the world, perhaps in no other civilization has jade been as prized as in China. For more than seven thousand years, the Chinese have regarded jade as the most precious of all materials and have seen in it many important symbolic qualities. In the early Confucian tradition, jade represented both an object of great value as well as highly prized virtuous qualities that the tradition espoused. For example, in the surviving sayings of the extremely influential Confucian philosopher Mencius (391–308 B.C.E.), we find jade used as the symbol of the enduring strength of sageliness:

集大成也者、金聲而玉振之也。金聲也者、始條理也; 玉振之也者、終條理也。始條理者、智之事也; 終條理者、聖之事也。[3]

(5B1) . . . The perfect ensemble begins with the sound of the bronze bell and ends with the sound of jade chimes, the bronze bell anticipating the harmony at the beginning of the concert and the jade chimes bringing harmony to a conclusion at its close. The harmony at the opening is the work of wisdom; the harmony at the close is the work of sageliness . . .[4]

In the later traditions of the organized Daoist religion, the ageless surface texture of jade came to be associated with immortality and transcendence. Perhaps the most significant example of this association is the Jade Emperor (*Yuhuang* 玉皇), who rules over a celestial pantheon including numerous immortals and nature gods. While gaining popularity in Chinese religion from the tenth century forward, graphic depictions may date back to as early as the sixth century.[5]

While such understandings of jade are well known and well documented, they treat jade as a symbol. While we could cite many more such well-known examples, I would like to show a different aspect of jade, a certain specific quality of jade that serves as a root-metaphor for an absolutely pivotal concept in the Chinese ideas of how the universe functions: the notion of inherent patterns or *li*. So we find that in its single oldest extant definition, *li* is actually derived from one of the most important characteristics of jade, the presence of regular veins or striations in the untreated mineral that cause it to split or fracture along predictable lines when cut. These veins or striations were called *li* "patterns." The oldest Chinese etymological dictionary, the *Shuowen jiezi* 說文解字 (ca. 100 C.E.), contains the following definition:[6]

理, 治 玉 也。

Patterns, are what form regular structures in jade.

The later commentator Duan Yucai 段玉裁 (1735–1815) provides a further explanation:

理 為 剖 析 也。玉 雖 至 堅, 而 治 之 得 其 鰓 理, 以 成 器 不 難, 謂 之 理。

"*Li*" is to fracture (along regular lines). Although jade is extremely hard, because its structures occur along regular inner patterns, making utensils with it is not difficult. This is how we define "*li*."

So the *li* are patterns inherent to a block of uncut jade that permit it to be split or cut along regular lines. Think of them as veins along which the material will fracture in a predictable way. It is this very concrete observation of how jade naturally reacts when it is actually worked by artisans that formed the root-metaphor of what was to become a central concept to Chinese cosmology.

In what follows, I trace the path of how this idea of Pattern developed in the early Chinese philosophical traditions from its specific meaning as an essential characteristic of jade into this cosmological cornerstone.

Classical Non-Daoist Sources on *Li*

The character *li* is completely absent from the collection of sayings of Confucius (?551–489 B.C.E.), the *Analects* (*Lun yu* 論語). However, about a century later, we find it does occur in three passages from the sayings of his follower Mencius, who is famous for the contention that human nature is basically good because, among other reasons, it has the tendency to prefer order and justice. In the most famous, *li* means "order":

> 心之所同然者何也？謂理也、義也。聖人先得我心之所同然耳。故理義之悅我心，猶芻豢之悅我口。 [7]

> (6A7) . . . And what is it that all minds have in common? I call it Order (*li*) and Rightness (*yi* 義). Sages were the first to discover what our minds have in common. Order and Rightness please our minds like the flesh of animals pleases our palates . . .[8]

For this extremely influential Confucian thinker, a sense of order and of right and wrong is innate to the human mind. This appears to represent a sense of psychological or perhaps social order but does not have an obvious derivation from the root-metaphor of the natural fracture lines in jade.

Li means order in another passage:

> 貉稽曰:「稽大不理於口。」[9]

> (7B19) (A disciple named) Mo Ji said, "I am largely undisciplined (i.e., disordered) in what I say."

Li, defined as psychological or social order, is a very common usage throughout the early Confucian tradition. More than a century after Mencius, amid a very different theory of human nature, we read in the essay that "Human Nature Is Bad" by Xunzi 荀子 (298–238 B.C.E.):

> 人之性惡, 其善者偽也。今人之性, 生而有好利焉, 順是, 故爭奪生而辭讓亡焉; 生而有疾惡焉, 順是, 故殘賊生而忠信亡焉; 生而有耳目之欲, 有好聲色焉, 順是, 故淫亂生而禮義文理亡焉。

然則從人之性, 順人之情, 必出於爭奪, 合於犯 (分)〔文〕亂理而
歸於暴。故必將有師法之化、禮義之道, 然後出於辭讓、合於
文理而歸於治。用此觀之, 然則人之性惡明矣, 其善者偽也。[10]

Human nature is bad: whatever goodness there is derives from
conscious effort. If we examine human nature we see that from
birth human beings are fond of benefiting themselves. Because
they obey this urge, conflict and greed develop and courtesy and
modesty disappear. From birth human beings have envy and
hatred. Because they obey this tendency, violence and thievery
develop and conscientiousness and trustworthiness disappear.
From birth they have the desires of the senses and so they
are fond of sounds and colors. Because they obey these urges,
therefore licentiousness and chaos flourish and the cultured
Order (*li*) created by Ritual and Rightness disappear. From
this we understand that when human nature obeys human
instincts, conflict and theft will inevitably emerge and unite to
destroy culture and disrupt Order. Therefore, inevitably there
will develop the transformational efforts of the old masters
who follow the Way of Ritual and Rightness; only then will
courtesy and modesty emerge to unite society with a cultured
order and return people to being under control. Because of this
it is clear that human nature is evil and whatever goodness
there is derives from conscious effort.

This notion of a cultured social order created by the practices of obedience
to accepted ritual forms and canons of justice is repeated throughout this
work. For Xunzi, these practices represent the thin socializing line that
separates human beings from beasts. The understanding of *li* as socializing
order is a hallmark of this "realistic" subtradition in early Confucianism,
opposed to the "idealistic" tradition of Mencius. As such, we see similar
passages in those essays included in two collections of the writings of
a variety of early intellectual traditions, such as the *Guanzi* 管子 (ca.
333–139 B.C.E.) and *Lüshi chunqiu* 呂氏春秋 (239 B.C.E.) that seem to
reflect the Xunzian position.

In the former we see a link to the principle of the rectification of
names; that is, having specific names refer to specific realities creates a
kind of structured social discourse and hence order. Several early traditions assert the absolute necessity of this structured order of matching

names and titles to realities and performance: Confucians, Nominalists, and Legalists. This passage could be influenced by any or all of them:

Guanzi 18, *pian* 篇 55:

(脩)〔循〕名而督實，按實而定名。名實相生，反相為情。名實當則治，不當則亂。名生於實，實生於德，德生於理，理生於智，智生於當。[11]

Complying with names, we inspect realities; in contact with realities we establish names. Thus names and realities give birth to each other, they are based on being mutually responsive. When names and realities match then there is order; when they do not match there is chaos. Names are born from realities, realities are born from potency, potency is born from structure; structure is born from wisdom; wisdom is born from matching.

In the *Lüshi chunqiu*, we see many similar usages but also some new ones that start to take the notion of *li* more directly into the realm of self-cultivation, an important term of art in early Chinese thought that refers to practices that aim at realizing your potential as a human being. First we read:

湯問於伊尹曰：「欲取天下若何？」伊尹對曰：「欲取天下，天下不可取。可取，身將先取。」凡事之本，必先治身，嗇其大寶。用其新，棄其陳，腠理遂通。精氣日新，邪氣盡去，(及)〔終〕其天年。此之謂真人。[12]

Tang 湯 interrogated Yi Yin 伊尹: "Desiring to gain control of the empire, how shall I proceed?" Yi Yin replied, "Though you may desire to gain control of the world, the empire cannot be taken. Before it can, you must first gain control of your own person." The foundation for all undertakings rests in the necessity of first regulating your own person and being sparing with "your great treasure" (i.e., your allotment of primal vital energy or *qi* 氣). Use the fresh (vital energy) and expel the stale so that the circulation (of the *qi* 氣) in your fascia veins (*li*) remains free-flowing.[13] Then your essential vital energy will be renewed daily and the stale vital energy will be fully expelled so that you will attain your natural life span. Those who can do this we call "The Genuine."[14]

So here *li* refers to the inner veins or meridians through which the *qi* or vital energy courses through the outer fascia, the connective tissue within the body. The use of *li* here implies an organized system of energy veins. This passage seems to come from a self-cultivation tradition that worked with limiting the expenditures of vital energy so as to attain longevity, ideas associated with the teaching of the thinker Yang Zhu 楊朱, a contemporary of Mencius. In this next passage, the meaning of *li* expands:

夫樂 (之) 有適, 心 (非)〔亦〕有適。人之情, 欲壽而惡夭, 欲安而惡危, 欲榮而惡辱, 欲逸而惡勞。四欲得, 四惡除, 則心適矣。四欲之得也, 在於勝理 。勝 理以治身則生全 (以)〔矣〕, 生全則壽長矣。勝理以治國則法立 〔矣〕, 法立則天下服矣。故適心之務在於勝 理 。[15]

. . . Just as pleasure leads to contentment, the mind can be made content. It is human instinct that we desire longevity and loathe dying young, that we desire security and we loathe danger, that we desire glory and loathe disgrace, that we desire ease and loathe toil. If these four wishes are attained and these four aversions are eliminated then the mind will be content. The attainment of these four desires lies in mastering the patterns (*li*) (of vital energy flow within your body). If you master these patterns and thereby regulate your person then your vitality will stay whole. If your vitality stays whole then you will attain longevity. If you master these patterns (in yourself) and thereby regulate the state, then a legal system can be established; if you master a legal system then the world will submit (to your rule). Therefore the task of finding contentment for the mind rests in mastering the system (of vital energy flow within your body).[16]

This text continues the line of argumentation found in the prior passage, but here *li*'s meaning expands to encompass the structure of the entire system of veins or meridians through which vital energy flows in the body. To master this system is a key practice for the Yangists who wish to do whatever they can to preserve their vitality and attain longevity. Here the meaning of *li* is as an inherent overall structure or pattern for the flow of *qi* in the body. Yangists advocate mastering the sensory input that feeds this ordered system so that human beings can fulfill their potential to live a long life.

It would take us too far afield to analyze in detail each and every textual source that mentions *li* in the classical period. To make a quick summary, the term *li* occurs only once in the *Zhou yi* 周易, the basic text of the *Yi jing* 易經, and it is rare in Legalist works such the *Shangjun shu* 商君書 (four occurrences), the *Shenzi* 申子 (one occurrence), and the *Hanfeizi* (five passages). When it does occur in these texts, it often means "order," "structure," or "system" and, on occasion, "pattern." What is strikingly absent from these usages is a cosmological context: it is rare to find the *li* referring to anything more than these prosaic uses. This is not at all the case for the evolving tradition of Inner Cultivation that has come down to us under the name of "Daoism."

Inner Cultivation and Classical Daoism

The designation "Daoism" was first applied circa 110 B.C.E. by the great historian Sima Tan 司馬談 to the tradition of masters and disciples who practiced a form of contemplation I have referred to as "inner cultivation," after the oldest surviving work of this tradition, "Inward Training ("Neiye" 內業), written down in about 325 B.C.E.[17] It is one of seventy-six texts included in the massive *Guanzi* collection that is devoted mainly to political and economic thought and that was compiled over a century and a half mostly in the state of Qi 齊 on the Shandong peninsula, one of two major regional origins of this tradition. This Inner Cultivation tradition produced a number of works, including several I survey in this chapter, the "Techniques of the Mind" texts ("Xinshu shang" 心術上, "Xinshu xia" 心術下) from the *Guanzi*, the *Zhuangzi* 莊子, and the *Laozi* 老子. Until very recently, these latter two texts were regarded as the sole foundational works of Daoism and were believed to represent its "philosophical" early core, in contradistinction to the institutional religion of the same name that formed following the collapse of the two millenarian rebellions it inspired circa 185 C.E. However, recent research has demonstrated that the textual origins of this tradition are much broader than these two works and that when this wider range of early sources are brought into consideration, the apparently great gulf between "philosophical" and "religious" Daoism is seen to be a product of "literati selection" rather than based in historical realities.[18]

Rather than accept the extreme bifurcation of the Daoist tradition into various categories that deny the fundamental continuity between the early Inner Cultivation texts and the later institutionalized tradition that begins with the millenarian rebellions in the second century C.E., I have argued that even though they did not deem themselves "Daoists," the teacher-student lineages of the Inner Cultivation tradition can be regarded as the foundation of the developments from the late Han and on.[19] Louis Komjathy has proposed that we designate this period as "classical Daoism," and I see no reason to deny this apt categorization.[20]

The teachers in this early Inner Cultivation tradition taught contemplative techniques that involved the gradual emptying out of the normal contents of conscious experience through practices in which the attention was trained to concentrate on one thing and the body was kept still and unmoving. The major object of focus was the inhalation and exhalation of the vital breath, which was conceived of as a practice that concentrated and refined it. As you progressed in this inner contemplative path, your desires were reduced, your thoughts came less frequently, your perceptions of the outside world dimmed, and an awareness of an inner light developed. Metaphors for these practices abound in this literature; for example: "sweeping clean the lodging place of the spirit" (*saochu shenshe* 掃除神舍), "cleaning your Profound Mirror" (*dichu xuanjian* 滌除玄鑑), "the fasting of the mind" (*xin zhai* 心齋), and "sitting and forgetting" (*zuo wang* 坐忘).[21] A number of important states of experience resulted from these practices: tranquility (*jing* 靜), calmness (*an* 安), stillness (*ji* 寂), repose (*ning* 寧), equanimity (*qi* 齊 or *ping* 平), and emptiness (*xu* 虛).[22] Attaining these states would eventually lead one to be able to directly experience, or merge with, the foundational power or force that resided at the base of all phenomena, both worldly and unworldly, the Way or Dao. This power was conceived of as being transcendent of any specific phenomenon in the world but also simultaneously immanent within them as the natural force that impelled them to develop and to act in the world. Attaining the Way or "merging with the Great Pervader" (*tong yu datong* 同於大通) is not, however, an end in itself.[23] When you return to living in the world of dualities, you are completely transformed and develop a whole series of beneficial cognitive and physical traits. These include a mental and physical suppleness and pliancy, perceptual acuity and instant understanding of situations, impartiality and selflessness, a charisma that draws people to you, and an almost magical ability to accomplish tasks without exerting your will, conceived of in the famous phrase "to take no action and leave nothing undone or unaccomplished" (*wuwei er wu buwei* 無為而無不為).[24] This produces what the *Zhuangzi* calls "flowing cognition" (*yinshi* 因是), which entails the ability to respond spontaneously (*ziran* 自然) and totally efficaciously (*gan ying* 感應) to whatever situation you find yourself involved in.[25]

As members of this Inner Cultivation tradition, these early practitioners of the "Techniques of the Way" (*Dao shu* 道術) found themselves teaching not just in their preferred mountain hermitages but also in the intellectual centers of various states. There they were not only required to debate followers of other early intellectual traditions as well as occasionally give advice to ministers of state and even the royal families, but they likely were also challenged to explain precisely why it was that the contemplative practices they advocated were able to produce such efficacious cognitive capacities to spontaneously and harmoniously respond to any and all situations. It wasn't enough to explain that this was possible because these practices yielded a direct experience of the Dao or Way; why was it that the Way, which seemed to defy ready intellectual characterization of any kind (viz. *Laozi* 1: "The Way that can be spoken of is not the Constant Way . . ."), was able to create the condition for this kind of successful action? This is precisely where our special term of study today, *li*, enters into the picture. Let's take a step back and examine how this term evolved in this early Daoist Inner Cultivation tradition to play this exceedingly important cosmological role.

Li in the Classical Works of Daoism

As mentioned above, the *Laozi* and *Zhuangzi*, particularly its first seven "inner chapters," have for almost two millennia been considered the foundations of the Daoist tradition, although this traditional shibboleth is gradually collapsing amid the weight of the textual evidence, both received and recently excavated, of a much broader and deeper early tradition. Nonetheless, these two texts are still relatively early, so we turn to them to being our quest for evidence of the "cosmicization" of *li*.

Laozi (ca. 275 B.C.E.)

Li does not occur in the text; it *is* found in the Heshang Gong 河上公 commentary to three chapters, 59, 65, and 74. In 65 it occurs in the phrase *shun li* 順理 often found in Syncretic Daoist works. In commenting on the line

> 玄德深矣, 遠矣: 與物反矣, 乃至於大順。[26]

> (People of) Profound Potency are deep and far reaching: they return together with things and thereby achieve grand compliance.

The commentary states:

> 玄德之人, 與萬物反異, 故能至大順。順者, 天理也。[27]

> People of Profound Potency return to the world of phenomena and thus are able to achieve grand compliance. That to which they comply are the Heavenly Patterns (*li*).

However, because the dating of that commentary is rather vexed (ranging from circa 140 B.C.E. to 250 C.E.), let us turn to the other presumed foundational text, *Zhuangzi*.

Zhuangzi (ca. 300–140 B.C.E.)

In this relatively long work of three main strata (Inner, Outer, and Mixed sections) there are a total of thirty-seven occurrences of the term *li*; only one of them is in the oldest stratum, but it is a significant occurrence, in the "The Master of Nurturing Vitality" chapter that contains the famous narrative in which Cook Ding gives his secrets for his great skill at carving oxen. Responding to Lord Wenhui's 文惠君 query about the source of his marvelous skill, the Cook says:

> 臣之所好者道也, 進乎技矣。始臣之解牛之時, 所見噝非牛者。
> 三年之後, 未嘗見全牛也。方今之時, 臣以神遇而不以目視, 官

知止而神欲行。依乎天理, 批大郤, 導大窾, 因其固然。... 今
臣之刀十九年矣, 所解數千牛矣, 而刀刃若新發於硎。[28]

What your humble servant is fond of is the Way: I have dis-
tanced myself from all thoughts of "skill." When I first began
to butcher oxen I saw nothing but oxen wherever I looked.
After three years I stopped seeing the ox as a whole. These
days your humble servant is guided by the intuitive spirit in me
and I don't even (deliberately) use my eyes to see; my senses
know where to stop and then loose the intuitive drive from
within me. I rely completely on the Patterns of Heaven (*Tian
li* 天理), I cleave along the main seams, I am guided by the
great cavities, I go along with what is inherently so. . . . That's
why after nineteen years the edge of my cleaver is as fresh as
though it were just sharpened on the grindstone.

In this passage, the *li* are the invisible natural patterns through which
the Cook is able to intuitively link up with the oxen in order to spontaneously move his cleaver through the interstices of the oxen without
even resorting to deliberately using his senses. Such narratives of intuitive skill are important for their exemplars of people who have attained
the way. We find this idea continued in one of the last chapters of this
Zhuangzi collection, which, like the *Guanzi*, contains material compiled
over a century and a half. This chapter probably dates from the early
or middle second century B.C.E. after China had been unified under
the Han 漢 Empire:

故曰: 夫恬惔寂漠虛無無為, 此天地之平而道德之質也。故
曰: 聖人休 (休) 焉, 〔休〕則 平易矣, 平易恬惔, 則憂患不能入,
邪氣不能襲, 故其德全而神不虧。故曰: 聖人之生也天行, 其
死也物化; 靜而與陰同德, 動而與陽同波; 不為福先, 不為禍始;
感而後應, 迫而後動, 不得已而後起。去知與故, 循天之理。故
無天災, 無物累, 無人非, 無鬼責。其生若浮, 其死若休。不思
慮, 不豫謀。光矣而不耀, 信矣而不期。其寢不夢, 其覺無憂。
其神純粹, 其魂不罷。虛無恬惔, 乃合天德。[29]

Therefore it is said "Calm imperturbability, still silence, empty
nothingness, and Non action are the balanced qualities of
Heaven and Earth and the substance of the Way and its
Potency."

Therefore it is said, "Sages find their rest in them; when at rest they are balanced and at ease. When they are balanced and at ease and are calmly imperturbable then anxieties and cares cannot enter and the deviant vital energies cannot infuse them. Therefore their Potency is complete and their spirits are not diminished."

Therefore it is said that "Sages in their lives proceed with Heaven and in their death transform with all things. At rest, they have the same Potency as the Yin; in movement they surge together with the Yang. They do not prioritize good fortune; they do not deprecate misfortune. When stimulated they spontaneously respond; when pushed they spontaneously move; only when it is inevitable will they arise. They cast off wisdom and precedent and comply with the Patterns of Heaven . . .

This passage provides further details of the cognitive capacities of Sages, another exemplar of the Daoist Inner Cultivation tradition. Following these contemplative practices, they are calm and imperturbable and able to completely avoid disturbing emotions and anxieties and hence able to spontaneously and harmoniously respond to any and all situations. Avoiding preconceived notions of any and all kinds, they are able to accomplish this efficacious spontaneity because they "comply with the Patterns of Heaven (*Tian li*)." These are the invisible natural patterns that guide the spontaneous movement of all living things. Hence the idea of *li* is expanding from one of order and structures within individual things to the notion of the patterns and order that are found writ large in the universe.

Guanzi "Neiye" (ca. 330 B.C.E.)[30]

As we have seen, the *Guanzi* is a collection that includes the writings of many different intellectual traditions compiled over a great temporal range. Although it uses our term *li* more than one hundred times, and many of its uses are of the more prosaic kind, there are a number of significant occurrences that give further evidence of the development of this idea within the Daoist Inner Cultivation tradition. In the short collection of rhymed verses of early Daoist wisdom poetry that is arguably the oldest work on breath meditation in the entire East Asian cultural tradition, the development of tranquility is linked to a regular and patterned breathing (*li*), not one that is forced or irregular. This an essential practice through which one may experience the Way:

凡道無所, 善心安(愛) [處]。心靜氣理, 道乃可止。彼道不遠,
民得以產; 彼道不離, 民因以(知) [和]。³¹

VERSE V

1 The Way has no fixed position;
2 It abides within the excellent mind.
3 When the mind is tranquil and the vital breath is regular (*li*),
4 The Way can thereby be halted.
5 That Way is not distant from us;
6 When people attain it they are sustained
7 That Way is not separated from us;
8 When people accord with it they are harmonious.³²

The following passage picks up the thread of vital breath and vital energy circulation through a systematic pattern (*li*) of pathways that we saw in *Lüshi chunqiu* 5/4.2 that came from the Yangist tradition. The main difference is that here these practices of *qi* circulation are used not just to attain the proper stimulation of the senses, but instead are used to directly experience the Way. This link is further developed in the last verse in "Inward Training":

靈 氣在心, 一來一逝, 其細無內, 其大無外。所以失之, 以躁
為害。心能執靜, 道將自定。得道之人, 理丞而 (屯) 〔毛〕 泄,
匈中無敗。節欲之道, 萬物不害。³³

VERSE XXVI

1 That mysterious vital energy within the mind,
2 One moment it arrives, the next it departs.
3 So fine, there is nothing within it;
4 So vast, there is nothing outside it.
5 The reason we lose it
6 Is because of the harm caused by mental agitation.

7 When the mind can hold on to tranquility,
8 The Way will become naturally stabilized.
9 For people who have attained the Way:
10 It (the mysterious vital energy) permeates the veins of the fascia and saturates the hair.[34]
11 Within their chest, they remain unvanquished.
12 Follow this Way of restricting sense-desires
13 And the myriad things will not cause you harm.[35]

Here these patterns of *qi* circulation are seen to extend into the hair and skin of the Daoist adept, thus providing both psychological *and* physical transformations. While *li* is thus used in this very specific sense, it also finds a much broader perspective as well:

一物能化謂之神，一事能變謂之智。化不易氣，變不易智，惟執一之君子能為此乎！執一不失，能君萬物。君子使物，不為物使，得一之 理 。[36]

VERSE IX

1 Those who can transform things while unifying with them we call spirit-like;
2 Those who can alter events while unifying with them we call wise.
3 Only Exemplary Persons who hold fast to the One are able to be like this.
4 Hold fast to the One and do not lose it
5 And you will be able to be an exemplar to the myriad things.
6 Exemplary Persons act upon things
7 And are not acted upon by things
8 Because they grasp the Patterns of the One (*yi zhi li* 一之理).[37]

Here the notion of *li* once again refers to these comprehensive patterns or natural guidelines whose realization enables inner cultivation adepts to be masters of their own fate. These patterns are seen here to be linked to—and, in all likelihood, derived from—the Way (i.e., the One); holding fast to the Way enables one to be unified with things in that you are sharing with them common patterns of interaction that derive directly from the Way. These patterns of the Way may in this text be thought of to parallel the systematic pathways of vital energy circulation in the individual human organism in a striking homology quite common to this tradition, the parallel between the universal macrocosm and the human microcosm. In this next passage in a later text, whose ideas represent an application of inner cultivation thought of "Inward Training" to the problem of governing the human polity, the "body politic" is seen to parallel the "political body":

Guanzi "Xinshu shang" (ca. 275–250 B.C.E.)[38]

心之在體, 君之位也; 九竅之有職, 官之分也。心處其道, 九竅循理; 嗜欲充 (益) 〔盈〕, 目不見色, 耳不聞聲。故曰: 上離其道, 下失其事。.[39] 〔故曰:心術者, 無為而制竅者也。〕

VERSE I[40]

The position of the mind in the body
[Is analogous to] the position of the ruler [in the state].
The functioning of the nine apertures (the sense organs open
    to the "outside" world)
[Is analogous to] the responsibilities of the officials.
When the mind keeps to its Way,
The nine apertures will comply with their inherent patterns (li).
When lusts and desires fill the mind to overflowing,
The eyes do not see colors, the ears do not hear sounds.
When the one above departs from the Way,[41]
The ones below will lose sight of their tasks.
Therefore we say, "the techniques of the mind are to take
    no action (wuwei 無為) and yet control the apertures."[42]

This means that the sense organs will function properly and spontaneously if they are not interfered with by the mind. This occurs because each has an inherent pattern of activity that derives from its individual characteristics and its relation to the whole body. By implication, the various officials of a government will also function properly if they are not interfered with by the ruler. This is the concept of "Wuwei government" through which the ruler establishes a strict set of expected performance guidelines for all his ministers and then simply lets them function according to them without his direct interference. So here the *li* refer to a set of patterns or natural guidelines through which the sense organs spontaneously function. These patterns are also relevant to the emotions, which contain inherent energies that must be expended to the proper degree and no more or less. A commentary section states:

人迫於惡, 則失其所好; 怵於好, 則忘其所惡。非道也。故曰:
「不怵乎好, 不迫乎惡。」惡不失其理, 欲不過其情, 故曰: 「
君子。」「恬愉無為, 去智與故」, 言虛素也。「其應非所設
也, 其動非所取也」, 此言因也。因也者, 舍己而以物為法者
也。感而后應, 非所設也; 緣理而動, 非所取也.⁴³

Most people are so burdened by their dislikes that they lose sight of what they like. They are so enticed by what they like that they forget what they dislike. This is not the Way. Therefore, [the text] says:
    "They (Exemplary persons) are not enticed by likes
    Nor oppressed by dislikes."
Their dislikes do not lose sight of their inherent patterns (*li*). Their desires do not exceed what is essential to them. Therefore [the text] says:
    "Exemplary persons, calm and tranquil, take no action
    And discard wisdom and precedent."
Therefore this says that they are empty and unadorned.
    "Their responses are not contrived,
    Their movements are not chosen."
This says that they are adaptable. To be adaptable is to relinquish the self and take other things as standards. To respond only when stimulated is not something you contrive to do. To move according to inherent patterns (*li*) is not something you [deliberately] choose to do.

So these Patterns serve to guide the spontaneous and efficacious activities of those who practice Non-Action. That is, because of their cultivation of a profound experiential contact with the Way, they spontaneously move according to the inherent Patterns in which they and those with whom they are interacting are embedded. The "Techniques of the Mind" also sees Patterns as pertaining not just to human beings but to all things in the cosmos:

VERSE VII

物固有形, 形固有名, 名當, 謂之聖人。故必知不言〔之言〕, 無為之事, 然後知道之紀。殊形異埶, 不與萬物異理, 故可以為天下〔始〕。[44]

Things inherently have forms; forms inherently have names.
Persons who match names [and forms], call them Sages.
Therefore, one must know the unspoken word and the non-acting deed.
Only then will one know how the Way sorts things out.
Though they have distinct forms and different conditions,[45]
[Sages] do not have different inherent patterns (**li**) than all other living things.
Therefore, they can become sources for the entire world.

Although sages behave differently than the multitude, because they are human, they share the same inherent guidelines that ultimately emerge from the Way. The main difference is that sages have cultivated themselves through apophatic inner cultivation practice and so have no selfish biases that would prevent them from spontaneously complying with their inherent guidelines; the multitude cannot do this.

Li in the *Huainanzi* 淮南子

Huainanzi continues with the cosmological development of the term *li* and adds a number of important dimensions that were to continue deep into the later Daoist tradition. Among its ninety-two occurrences of the term, there are of course examples of the most prosaic uses we have already discussed. But there are a very significant number—too many to detail—of cosmologically significant usages, beginning with the summary of the overall purpose of the entire work, a compendium of all the world's knowledge deemed necessary in order to govern the world in accord with the basic principles of the Daoist Inner Cultivation tradition. The summary twenty-first essay, in ending its recitation of the rationale for each of its twenty previous chapters, writes:

故著書二十篇, 則 天地之理究矣, 人間之事接矣, 帝王之道備
矣。 46

Therefore we wrote these writings in twenty chapters so that
The Patterns of Heaven and Earth would be thoroughly
    examined,
The affairs of human relationships would be comprehensively
    engaged,
And the Way of [the Five] Emperors and [Three] Kings would
    be fully described.47

For the authors of the *Huainanzi*, who present very detailed explanations
of how all human experiences and cosmic events arise and pass away,
the *li* represent the identifiable and constant guidelines these experiences
and events follow throughout the courses of their development and their
interactions with one another. Within the psychology of human beings,
there are important Patterns of perception and of the emotional life that
emerge from our distinctly human nature:

人生而靜, 天之性也。 感而後動, 性之害也。 物至而神應, 知
之動也。 知與物接, 而好憎生焉。 好憎成形, 而知誘於外, 不
能反己, 而天理滅矣。 故達於道者, 不以人易天, 外與物化, 而
內不失其情。 48

That which is tranquil from our birth is our heavenly nature.
Stirring only after being stimulated, our nature is harmed.
When things arise and the spirit responds, this is the activity of perception. When perception comes into contact with
things, preferences arise. When preferences take shape and
perception is enticed by external things, our nature cannot
return to the self, and the Heavenly Patterns are destroyed.
    Thus those who break through to the Way do not use
the human to change the Heavenly. Externally they transform
together with things, but internally they do not lose their
genuine responses.49

So the *li* here are natural and spontaneous patterns through which we
perceive the objects in our environment. However, there is a natural
tendency for most people who have not practiced an apophatic discipline
to be so enmeshed in their own selfish perspectives that they naturally

develop biases and preferences that distort how they see the world. Only those who have followed inner cultivation practices are able to stay grounded in these natural and spontaneous patterns of clear and accurate perception and genuine responsiveness.

原天命, 治心術, 理好憎, 適情性, 則治道通矣。原天命則不惑
禍福, 治心術則不 (忘) 〔妄〕喜怒, 理好憎則不貪無用, 適情性
則欲不過節。不惑禍福則動靜循理, 不妄喜怒則賞罰不阿, 不
貪噲用則不以欲 (用) 害性, 欲不過節則養性知足。凡此四者,
弗求於外, 弗假於人, 反己而得 矣。⁵⁰

> Trace to the source Heaven's decree,
> Cultivate the techniques of the mind,
> Regulate (li) likes and dislikes,
> Follow your disposition and nature,
> And the Way of cultivating oneself will come through.
> If you trace to the source Heaven's decree, you will not be
> deluded by bad or good fortune.
> If you cultivate the Techniques of The Mind (Xinshu), you
> will not be unrestrained in your happiness and anger.
> If you regulate your likes and dislikes, you will not covet
> what is useless.
> If you follow your disposition and nature, your desires will
> not exceed the appropriate limits.
> If you are not deluded by bad or good fortune, your movement
> and stillness will comply with inherent Patterns
> If you are not unrestrained in your happiness and anger, your
> rewards and punishments will not be partial.
> If you do not covet what is useless, you will not allow your
> desires to harm your nature.
> If your desires do not exceed the appropriate limits, you will
> nurture your nature and know contentment.
>
> As a general rule, these four things cannot be sought after in
> what is outside the self nor can you bestow them on others.
> You can obtain them only by returning to the self.⁵¹

Here we see two distinct but related meanings of li. In the verbal use, to regulate likes and dislikes, what is really meant here is not just simply restricting or cutting off the emotions but making them comply with their own inherent natural guidelines. As we see in chapter 11:

且喜怒 哀樂, 有感而自然者也。故哭之發於口, 涕之出於目, 此皆憤於中而形於外者也。譬若水之下流, 煙之上尋也, 夫有 (熟)〔孰〕推之者! 故強哭者雖病不哀, 強親者雖笑不和。情發 於中而聲應於外, 故蓋負羈之壺 (餐)〔飧〕, 愈於晉獻公之垂 棘; 趙宣孟之束脯, 賢於智伯之大鍾。故禮豐不足以效愛, 而 誠心可以懷遠。[52]

Further, pleasure, anger, grief, and joy arise spontaneously from a stimulus. Thus,

> A cry issues from the mouth.
> Tears flow from the eyes—
> All burst forth from within
> And take form externally.
> It is like
>> Water flowing downward
>> Or smoke rising upward.
> What compels them? Thus,
>> Though one who forces oneself to cry feels pain, he does not grieve;
>> Though one who forces intimacy will laugh, there is no harmony.
> Feelings come forth from within and sounds respond externally.[53]

So emotions have their own inherent patterns of expression; the *Huainanzi* authors condemn Confucian ritual practices for falsely extending emotions and not serving as proper outlets for the natural energies that all emotions entail:

夫 三年之喪, 是強人所不及也, 而以偽輔情也。三月之服, 是 絕哀而迫切之性也。夫儒、墨不原人情之終始, 而務以行相反 之制, 五縗之服。[54]

The three-year mourning period (of the Confucians) forces a person to what he cannot reach; thus he supplements his feelings with pretense.

The three-month observance breaks off grief, coercing and hacking at nature.

The Confucians and the Mohists do not [find the] origin [of their doctrines] in the beginnings and ends of human feelings and are committed to practicing mutually opposed systems [for] the five grades of ritual observance.[55]

In the other use of *li* in the passage from chapter 14, having one's movements and rests comply with inherent Patterns means one goes along with the inherent invisible structures in all situations. The idea of "complying with Patterns" is found repeatedly throughout the *Huainanzi* as an important quality of sages. We read later in chapter 14 that

聖人無思慮, 無設儲, 來者弗迎, 去者弗將。人雖東西南北, 獨立中央 . . . . . . 故不為 (善)〔好〕, 不 避醜, 遵天之道; 不為始, 不專己, 循天之理。[56]

The sage has no conscious deliberations;
he has no fixed ideas.
He neither welcomes what arrives
nor sends off what departs.

Though others occupy positions north, south, east, and west,
he alone is established at the center. . . .

Thus,

he does not encourage what he likes,
nor does he avoid what he dislikes;
he simply follows Heaven's Way.
He does not initiate,
nor does he personally assume authority;
he simply complies with Heaven's Patterns.[57]

That fact that the origins of these Patterns is Heaven emphasizes that they are not the direct products of the human will; they come from the power that lies beyond the influence of human beings. A. C. Graham persuasively argues that Heaven in early China (in addition to symbolizing the contrasting half of the universe to Earth) is that power or force responsible for all that happens to us that is beyond our control. Thus it is often said to be the source of our human nature (*xing* 性) and all the events that we find ourselves in that we do not influence, that is, *ming* 命 or "fate." Thus the implication that these Patterns are derived from Heaven emphasizes their universal applicability and their complete naturalness. But the *Huainanzi* authors also see a range of Patterns as emerging from an even more fundamental source, the Way or Dao:

故體道者逸而不窮, 任數者勞而無功。夫峭法刻誅者, 非霸王之
業也; 箠策繁用者, 非致遠之 (術)〔御〕也。離朱之明, 察箴末於
百步之外,〔而〕不能見淵中之魚。師曠之聰, 合八風之調, 而不
能聽 十里之外。故任一人之能, 不足以治三畝之宅也。 (脩)
〔循〕道理之數, 因天地之自然, 則六合不足均也。 58

Therefore those who embody the Way are relaxed and never exhausted.

Those who rely on [inferior] methods work hard but achieve little.

To resort to harsh laws and arbitrary punishments is not the practice of hegemons and kings.

To repeatedly use sharp whips is not the method of those who travel far.

Li Zhu's 離朱 vision was so acute that he could pick out the tip of a needle beyond a hundred paces, but he could not see the fish in the deep.

Music Master Kuang's 曠 hearing was so accurate that he could harmonize the tones of the Eight Winds, yet he could not hear anything beyond three miles.

Thus to rely on the talents of one person is insufficient to govern a holding of three *mu* 畝 (a half acre).

But if you comply with the numerous Patterns of the Way (*Dao li*) and follow the spontaneity of Heaven and Earth, then none within the Six Coordinates will be able to be your equal. 59

In this passage, complying with the Patterns of the Way provides a foundation that gives you a mystical ability that even the paragons of human abilities cannot normally attain. In the following passage, the same phrase is used to indicate the superiority of this compliance with the greater Patterns of the Way when compared with men who are widely presumed to be the most learned and wise paragons of human knowledge and sage rulership:

> 湯、武, 聖主也, 而不能與越人乘 (幹)〔軡〕舟而浮於江湖; 伊 尹, 賢相也, 而不能與胡人騎驍〔馬〕而服駒駼; 孔、墨博通, 而不能與山居者入榛薄、〔出〕險阻也。由此觀之, 則人知之 於物也, 淺矣。而欲以偏照海內, 存萬方, 不因 道〔理〕之數, 而專己之能, 則其窮不 (達)〔遠〕矣。故智不足以治天下也。[60]

> [King] Tang 湯 [of Shang 商] and [King] Wu 武 [of Zhou 周] were sage rulers but could not equal the people of Yue 越 in managing small craft and staying afloat through rivers and lakes.

> Yi Yin was a worthy prime minister but he could not equal the Hu 胡 people in mounting fine steeds or taming wild northern horses.

> Confucius and Mozi 墨子 were erudite but could not equal the mountain-dwelling people in navigating dense undergrowth or traversing dangerous passes.

> From this perspective human knowledge, in relation to things, is shallow. Desiring to illuminate all within the seas and preserve the ten thousand places, if the ruler does not follow the numerous Patterns of the Way but relies on his own ability instead, then he will not reach his goal. Thus wisdom is not sufficient to rule the world.[61]

In chapter 11, we read that the Patterns of the Way do not rely on human knowledge: they are objective and impartial and immune to the petty and constantly shifting judgments of human beings:

> 天下是非無所定, 世各是其所是而非其所非, 所謂是與〔所謂〕 非各異, 皆自是而非人。由此觀之, 事有合於己者, 而未始有是

也; 有忤於心者, 而未始有非也。故 求是者, 非求道理也, 求
合於己者也; 去非者, 非批邪施〔也〕, 去忤於心者也。忤於我,
未必不合於人也; 合於我, 未必不非於俗也。至是之是無非,
(之非至非) 〔至非之非〕無是, 此真是非也。[62]

In the world, "right" and "wrong" have no immutable basis.
Each age affirms what it [deems] right and rejects what it
[deems] wrong. What each calls right and wrong is different,
[yet] each [deems] itself right and others wrong.

Seen from this [basis], there are facts that accord with one's
   self, yet they are not originally "right."
There are those that are repellent to one's heart, yet are not
   originally "wrong."
Thus,
those who seek what is "right" do not seek the Patterns of
   the Way; they seek what accords with their selves.
Those who reject what is "wrong" do not criticize what is
   crooked, they discard what is repellent to their hearts.
   What is repellent to me is not necessarily not in accord
      with others.
   What accords with me is not necessarily not rejected by
      custom.
   The "right" of the utmost right has no wrong,
   The "wrong" of the utmost wrong has no right.
This is genuine "right" and "wrong." . . .[63]

Among the most important of the Patterns of the Way is the pattern of
"taking no action yet leaving nothing undone." What does this entail?
It means experiencing a flowing mode of cognition based on your direct
apprehension of the Way so that, in the following passage, you act
completely spontaneously and totally un-self-consciously and beneficially
toward others and are completely devoid of any attempt to take credit
for your deeds:

有智而無為, 與無智者同道; 有能而無事, 與無能者同德。其智
也, 告之者至, 然後覺其動也;〔其能也〕, 使之者至, 然 後覺其為
也。有智若無智, 有能若無能, 道理為正也。故功蓋天下, 不施
其美; 澤及後世, 不有其名; 道理通而人為滅也。[64]

> To have knowledge but to take no action is at one with the
> Way of no-knowledge;
> To have ability but not intervene, is at one with the Potency
> of no-ability.
> This knowledge is such that, only when someone comes to
> report it do you become aware that you have [already] acted;
> This ability is such that, only after someone comes to employ
> you do we become aware that you have already done it.
> > When having knowledge resembles no-knowledge,
> > When having ability resembles no-ability,
> The Patterns of the Way are rectified.
> Thus,
> > When your merit spreads over the world but does not
> > evoke praise,
> > And when your beneficence extends to future ages, but
> > does not earn fame,
> The Patterns of the Way will pervade [the world], and human
> artifice will be destroyed.[65]

Thus, for the *Huainanzi* authors, the Patterns of Way, of Heaven, of Earth, and of human beings constitute essential elements of a normative natural order.[66] This universal order is elsewhere in chapter 1 described as a "spiritlike vessel" (*shenqi* 神器).[67] It is made up of the various innate natures (*xing*) of things that determine their course of development and their actions and of those great patterns inherent in the cosmos that govern the characteristic ways in which things interact with one another that I have been discussing.[68] These natures and patterns are thoroughly infused with the empty Way, which mysteriously guides their spontaneous processes of development and their daily activities. This entire complex world functions completely spontaneously and harmoniously and needs nothing additional from human beings. All sages need to do is recognize these natures and patterns and adapt to them. It is because of this normative order that sages can accomplish everything without exerting their individual will to control things. In other words, they practice "non-action," which is effective because of the existence of this normative natural order. Sages cultivate themselves through the "Techniques of the Mind" in order to fully realize the basis of this order within. By realizing the Way at the basis of their innate nature, sages can simultaneously realize the intrinsic natures of all phenomena and gain a mystical insight into the world that even the paragons of wisdom and talent cannot attain.

Conclusions

The root-metaphor of the natural fracturing of jade along guidelines inherent within it is deeply buried within the cosmological uses of *li* in the classical Daoist Inner Cultivation tradition. Jade patterning is an excellent metaphor for the basic inherent patterns of the cosmos to which we must adapt and comply: both are not only structured; they also represent *natural* tendencies, unlike the more prosaic uses of *li* in classical non-Daoist works. Just as jade fractures along its patterned veins, so too do the patterns of the cosmos provide the natural guidelines and pathways along which realized human beings flow. Sages according with them can act spontaneously, but their actions will not be random and chaotic, nor will they be selfish and biased. This concept of *li* achieves prominence in the later texts of classical Daoism because it provides the basis to explain *how* the earlier Daoist concept of spontaneity is able to operate. It provides the underlying normative basis for efficacious and harmonious activity in the cosmos. Because sages and adepts are grounded in and infused by an all-pervading Way that manifests its power through universal patterns, their actions will always be harmonious and efficacious.

Chapter 12

Cognitive Attunement
in the *Zhuangzi* 莊子

I suspect that some states that we call mystical are as natural as
the relief of sorrow by tears and are suppressed by certain cultures,
much as grown men may be forbidden to weep.

—A. C. Graham, "Mysticism and the
Problem of Private Access"[1]

I first met Angus Graham on a bright day in the late autumn of 1981. I
was an unemployed PhD student working on a series of radio programs
for *Ideas*, a popular show produced by the Canadian Broadcasting Corporation.[2] I had persuaded the CBC to send me to England to interview
some of the great Sinologists of the day, and Graham, of course, was
one of them.

I had been a huge fan since my last year at university, when his
initial translation of the second chapter in the *Zhuangzi*, the "Qi wu
lun" 齊物論 (Essay on seeing things as equal), published in the History
of Religions 1968 Bellagio Conference issue, had helped me crack the
Zhuangzi's coded secrets (or so I thought). After entering his office at
SOAS, I picked my way carefully through the narrow pathway from
door to desk, dodging wobbly stacks of book and piles of offprints and
photocopied articles. Having been advised by Sarah Allan, whom I had
interviewed the previous day, that the good professor was fond of cognac
and cigars, I placed them before him on his desk and then proceeded to
ready my battery-operated cassette recorder and handheld mic.

377

Almost three hours later, we were sitting in the near dark. The cognac bottle was entirely emptied; the cigars were gone, and a deep smoky haze filled the room. Professor Graham was holding forth on the topic of how Zhuangzi would have driven an automobile. I can still hear the twinkle in his voice as he went on about Zhuangzi: "He would go here . . . and there . . . but never arrive *anywhere*." Signaling the end of the interview, Graham stood up and said, "Let's go to dinner. You *do* have an expense account, don't you?" I saw the look of great anticipation disappear from this face as I shook my head back and forth. "Oh, very well," he said resignedly, "let's get some pasta!"

One of the topics on which he expounded that late fall afternoon was his idea that the insights from the "Qi wu lun" about the relativity of things from the perspective of the Way, or the person who had embodied the Way, bore certain distinct resemblances to the twentieth-century discovery of the Heisenberg principle of indeterminacy in physics. In Graham's mind, the insights of a Chinese philosopher from two and a half millennia ago could be relevant to modern philosophers as well as scientists because of certain basic elements of human experience and of the natural world that transcend culture and time.

Graham's wide-ranging curiosity and fascination with both scientific and humanistic knowledge enriched his own scholarship and broadened Chinese textual analysis. I have no doubt that he would have been a supporter of the new academic field of Contemplative Studies,[3] which is devoted to the study of human contemplative experience across cultures and through history, drawing on both scientific and humanistic perspectives. Contemplative experience was most definitely a subject that Angus Graham and I discussed numerous times. He even wrote an essay on the subject, published in the posthumous collection edited by David Hall, *Reason within Unreason*.[4] In this essay, Graham wrote of his inherent fascination with mystical experience yet expressed skepticism about the epistemological validity of something so subjective: "The great obstacle to the man of reason in coming to terms with mysticism is its appeal to the authority of an experience outside the public domain, and least accessible perhaps to the analytic cast of mind."[5]

He then proceeded to describe some of his own experiments with what he ended up calling "The Common Felicity," a deliberately cultivated, momentary, and direct cognitive apprehension of the fleeting moments of beauty in one's environment. While not claiming them as precisely "mystical," Graham saw in their spontaneity and profundity that "human capacity for awareness [is] raised to its highest pitch."[6]

Using the language of Reason, Graham was trying to identify the existence of a commonly accessible and immensely significant mode of experience that is, in itself, not inherently rational. I would like to call this experience "cognitive attunement"[7] and discuss a more recent and scientifically informed way of presenting it, via the lens of Contemplative Studies. I begin by elucidating a model for "contemplative phenomenology," a set of philosophical and scientific ideas that provide the intellectual foundation for this emerging field. Then I apply this model to demonstrate that cognitive attunement is the central theme around which the entire *Zhuangzi* collection is organized.

Contemplative Phenomenology

Contemplative Studies examines the philosophy, psychology, and cognitive activity of contemplative experience. It focuses on the many ways human beings have found to concentrate, broaden, and deepen conscious awareness as the gateway to cultivating more meaningful, ethically responsible, and personally fulfilling lives. Scholarship in this emerging field attempts to identify the varieties of contemplative experiences, find meaningful scientific and philosophical explanations for them, cultivate first-person knowledge of them, and critically assess their nature and significance.[8]

As we define it, "contemplation" includes the focusing of the attention in a sustained fashion leading to deepened states of concentration, tranquility, insight, and "contextualizing" orientations. Such experiences occur on a spectrum from the rather common experiences of absorption in an activity such as reading a book or playing a sport to the profound and transformative experiences that are deliberately cultivated within religious traditions.[9] When intentionally cultivated, contemplative experiences can become the basis for a clear and spontaneous cognition that is able to attend effortlessly to whatever presents itself. Such experiences can also serve as the basis for the development of various "other-regarding" ethical orientations, such as empathy and compassion, love and loving kindness. Results of this type have become the basis for serious scientific research in areas such as effortless attention, flowing cognition, mindfulness, and compassion.[10]

Contemplative Studies derives its orientation to experience from the work of the late cognitive neuroscientist Francisco Varela, one of the founders of the Mind and Life Institute. He was influenced by both phenomenology and the cognitive sciences. Varela makes a crucial distinction between first-person and third-person events and experiences:

> By first-person events we mean the lived experience associated with cognitive and mental events. Sometimes terms such as "phenomenal consciousness" and even "qualia" are also used, but it is natural to speak of "conscious experience" or simply "experience." These terms imply here that the process being studied (vision, pain, memory, imagination, etc.) appears as relevant and manifest for a "self" or "subject" that can provide an account; they have a subjective side.
>
> In contrast, third-person descriptions concern the descriptive experience associated with the study of other natural phenomena. Although there are always human agents in science who provide and produce descriptions, the contents of such descriptions . . . are not clearly or immediately linked to the human agents who come up with them . . . Such "objective" descriptions do have a subjective-social dimension, but this dimension is hidden within the social practices of science. The ostensive, direct reference is to the "objective," the "outside," the content of current science that we have today concerning various natural phenomena such as physics and biology.[11]

Contemplative Studies as a field embraces the recommendations of Varela and the philosopher Evan Thompson that serious scientific and philosophical study of contemplation must take into account first-person subjective experience.[12]

A second significant distinction that arises from this fertile interface between cognitive science and phenomenology is the interlinked concepts of second-person experience and intersubjectivity. This elaboration of the "I-You" hypothesis asserts that human beings are fundamentally and biologically social animals—something not at all foreign, of course, to Mencian Confucianism. And that, as Evan Thompson argues, "Individual human consciousness is formed in the dynamic interrelation of self and other, and is therefore inherently intersubjective."[13] Danish philosopher Dan Zahavi adds: "The phenomenologists never conceive of intersubjectivity as an objectively existing structure in the world which can be described and analyzed from a third-person perspective. On the contrary, intersubjectivity is a relationship between subjects which must be analyzed from a first-person and second-person perspective."[14]

In other words, intersubjectivity is not merely an abstract intellectual concept: it can only be known and understood by doing; by astute observations of lived interactions with others. Furthermore, Thompson concludes that intersubjectivity inherently involves empathy: "The concrete encounter of self and other fundamentally involves empathy, understood as a unique and irreducible kind of intentionality."[15] Cognitive scientists and neuroscientists have been very interested in developing measures of empathy and compassion and studying ways to entrain it. Their work in the past few decades has been copious.[16]

Therefore, from these perspectives, third-person experience entails an activity of consciousness that objectifies an apparently external world of things and facts as well as an internal world of ideas and feelings. This third-person objectification of an internal world of experience is significant in the construction of the idea of a fixed or permanent self-identity; it is also the root of self-consciousness. Second-person experience involves intersubjective communication that at its best is spontaneous and un-self-conscious and is grounded in empathy inherent in the I-You relationship. First-person experience is the basis of subjectivity; the experience of what we commonly perceive as the internal contents of our consciousness or minds. Consistent with this model, I would like to add a fourth dimension of consciousness: what I call "no-person experience."

"No-person experience" is immediate experience in the present moment that is non-intentional and non-self-referential. It occurs within the experiencing subject, within first-person experience on a moment-to-moment basis. I have derived this concept from a number of extant sources, both Western and Eastern. The first is William James's notion of "pure experience" as expressed in the following passage: "The instant field of the present is always experienced in its 'pure' state, plain, unqualified actuality, a simple that, as yet undifferentiated as to thing and thought."[17] Yoko Arisaka goes on to say: "According to James, 'pure experience' is not a subjective experience, but a 'simple that,' an immediate *thisness* of experience which can be taken as subjective or objective states."[18] When one reflects on the activity of knowing, experience splits into two terms, one of which becomes the knowing subject and the other the known object. Thus, for James, prior to the retrospective experience that divides into subject and object, pure experience is itself a unity that is neither subject nor object.[19]

Influenced by James and his understanding of Zen metaphysics, Nishida Kitarō also put forth his own concept of "pure experience." For him, in contrast to James, while pure experience is both prereflective and immediate, it transcends both subject and object in such a way that it does not contain any specific individual content: "The difference between 'my' flow and 'your' flow is not a fundamental fact, but is the result of the different ways in which the same pure experience is abstracted."[20] Thus, in pure experience, one cannot make absolute distinctions between oneself and another. So for Nishida, individuality emerges from a continuum of undifferentiated experience: "It is not that experience exists because there is an individual; but that an individual exists because there is experience."[21] In my analysis, the difference here is that James, as an empiricist, does not question the given nature of the external world, while Nishida, influenced by the Yogacara-based idealism that lingers in Zen metaphysics, does. For James, pure experience has content; it's noetic. For Nishida, pure experience is devoid of any specific content, as is true for the Yogacara concept of *citta matra* (mind-ground).[22]

Recent research in the brain sciences supports James's understanding of pure experience.[23] This research has identified two types of cognition that recognize environmental data spontaneously and without intentionality. First, Aaron Seitz and Takeo Watanabe have pioneered research on what they call Task-Irrelevant Perceptual Learning (TIPL). Second, Arthur Reber has researched a major mode of cognition, "tacit knowledge," that was initially suggested by philosophers Gilbert Ryle and Michael Polanyi. What is Task-Irrelevant Perceptual Learning? In their abstract, the authors state: "The basic phenomenon is that stimulus features that are irrelevant to a subject's task (i.e., convey no useful information to that task) can be learned due to their consistent presentation during task-performance."[24]

TIPL does not stand in opposition to theories of attention, but operates instead in concert with attention. Where attentional learning is best to enhance (or suppress) processing of stimuli of known task relevance, TIPL serves to enhance perception of stimuli that are originally inadequately processed by the brain. In this phenomenon, low-level sub-(attentional) threshold cues are perceived without the subjects deliberately attending to them. If these cues are raised to the attentional threshold, they are not noticed or learned because of the greater strength of the cues to which the subject is paying attention. Thus, TIPL is a form of passive cognition in which information is processed while deliberately attending to a different, much stronger, stimulus. As Seitz writes, "Task-irrelevant perceptual learning is distinguished from other forms of perceptual learning in that it is not dependent on attention being directed toward, nor having awareness of, the stimulus array during the period of learning. Stimulus arrays that are unnoticed, and even subliminally presented, can be learned through task-irrelevant perceptual learning when presented in conjunction with appropriate reinforcing events.[25]

"Tacit knowledge" is literally "knowledge that cannot be put into words."[26] This broad definition covers four general types: knowledge or know-how that

1. Often cannot be made explicit or codified (e.g., language learning);

2. May be made explicit or codified, but we don't understand how to achieve it or how to explain it (e.g., problem solving);

3. We exercise without being aware that we are exercising it, such as in automatic habits or routines that we carry out, often very skillfully, but with a minimum of conscious attention (e.g., driving, catching a baseball);

4. We exercise without being able to explain how we do it (e.g., walking, running).

Tacit knowledge is often contrasted with propositional knowledge, which is derived from logical analysis that separates itself from what it is analyzing. It is a "knowing how" that involves embodied understanding often put into action, whereas propositional knowledge is a "knowing that." The contrast between tacit and propositional knowledge parallels the contrast between first-person and third-person experience.

The research on TIPL points to perception and cognition that occur without being actively pursued within the context of a self or of self-identity. It is non-intentional and hence spontaneous. I postulate that something like this is going on in "no-person experience" and also in James's concept of "pure experience." A perceptual world is cognized on a moment-to-moment basis before we bring that cognition to full awareness. The research on tacit knowledge points to cognition and action that occur spontaneously and non-intentionally that leads to the automatization of a whole range of tasks we perform on a daily basis, from brushing our teeth to driving a car. It is impossible to pay attention to every single item of perceptual data that arises in performing these tasks. When we are first learning them, we inevitably have to be much more intentional about taking in these data. But after they become automatic, we sometimes perform them without much intentionality or self-consciousness at all.

Psychologists have been researching a related area of experience that they refer to as "effortless attention." To quote Brian Bruya:

> Under normal circumstances, the expectation is that expenditure of effort increases with the level of demands until effort reaches a maximum point at which no increase is possible . . . Sometimes, however, when the level of demand reaches a point at which one is fully engaged, one is given over to the activity so thoroughly that action and attention seem effortless.[27]

Mihalyi Csíkszentmihályi's extensive research focuses on the broader phenomenon of effortless, autotelic (self-reinforcing) experience across a wide range of human activities spanning all cultures and times. Ranging from sports to games of chance to deep listening and intimate conversations, he identifies a common and rewarding experience achieved in all of them he calls "flow," or "optimal experience." "Flow states" are characterized by an often non-intentional focusing of the attention, an awareness centered in the present moment, a complete absorption of body and mind in the activity at hand that is infinitely self rewarding. Psychological research on effortless attention and flow states ranges from self-reporting measures to designing environments and methods that induce such states deliberately, as can be seen in the range of scientific and philosophical articles that Bruya has collected. In most instances, meditation and yoga techniques are not used in this research.

Finally, the neuroscientific study of meditation has made an important distinction between "states" of experience and "traits" induced by these states.[28] "State" refers to the altered sensory and cognitive awareness that can arise during meditation practice. "Trait" refers to the lasting changes in these dimensions that persist in the meditator irrespective of being actively engaged in meditation. Regular meditation practice can produce relatively short-term states as well as long-term changes in traits. According to Rael Cahn and John Polich:

> State changes from the meditative and religious traditions are reported to include a deep sense of calm peacefulness, a cessation or slowing of the mind's internal dialogue, and experiences of perceptual clarity and conscious awareness merging completely with the object of meditation, regardless of whether a mantra, image, or the whole of phenomenal experience is the focal point . . . Trait changes from long-term meditation include a deepened sense of calmness, increased sense of comfort, heightened awareness of the sensory field, and a shift in the relationship to thoughts, feelings, and experience of self.[29]

Neuroscientific research has identified two basic categories of meditative practices: "concentrative" and "receptive."[30] Concentrative meditation techniques involve a top-down focusing of the attention on a specific mental or sensory activity: a repeated sound, an imagined image, or specific body sensations such as the breath. Repeated practice over time can lead to one-pointed modes of attention. Receptive meditation is a more effortless, involuntary, and inclusive form of practice in which one learns to allow any thoughts, feelings, and sensation to arise while remaining an unattached observer without judgment or analysis. It taps into spontaneous, pre-attentive intuitive mechanisms and can lead to forms of "choiceless awareness" free of thoughts.[31] The results of these practices include a shift from what James Austin calls a self-referential "egocentric" cognitive orientation to an other-referential "allocentric" orientation. In addition to improved attentional focus, these results include increased bodily awareness, improved emotional regulation through decreased reactivity, and "detachment from identification from a static sense of self."[32]

Neuroscientific research often focuses on studying meditative states by examining brain activity during meditation. Third-person measuring devices such as the EEG (electroencephalogram) fMRI (functional magnetic resonance imaging) and MEG (magnetic encephalography) are used. Research on meditative traits focuses on the long-term implications of meditative practice by comparing the brains of experienced and novice meditators to non-meditating controls or asking these groups to react to various stimuli during and after meditation. In addition, Varela and Thompson have pioneered the field of "neurophenomenology," which pursues research that combines these third-person measures with simultaneous first-person reports.[33]

To summarize: the contemplative phenomenology outlined above identifies four modes of experience: third-person, second-person, first-person, and no-person experience. "No-person experience" is non-intentional, non-self-conscious, and immediate. It resembles James's notion of "pure experience" in that it is pre-reflective, yet is unlike Nishida's notion in that it is noetic and provides specific content. Cognitive scientific research on "task-irrelevant perceptual learning" and "tacit understanding" supports these models of consciousness in demonstrating that perception and cognition can occur that is momentary, spontaneous, non-intentional, and non-propositional. Psychological research on "effortless attention" and on "flow" explore states of non-intentional cognition, and spontaneous and concentrated action arise that could be viewed as similar to "non-person experience" and to a range of experiences of "tacit knowledge." Finally, neuroscientific research on meditation differentiates between states (temporary experiences of concentration) and traits (longer-lasting alterations in cognitive functioning). It identifies two modes of contemplative practice: concentrative and receptive, intentional attention focusing leading to a narrower, one-pointed awareness and an opening of the field of attention to embrace thoughts, feelings, and perceptions without judgment leading to a choiceless awareness. These practices result in a shift from egocentric modes of information processing to allocentric ones and lead to increased detachment from a static sense of self-identity.

These philosophical and scientific perspectives lead to what I would like to call a condition of "cognitive attunement" that enables one to live free of attachment to rigid, egocentric third-person objectifications of self and other; free from excessive self-consciousness; able to act effortlessly, without intentionality, in a mode of no-person orientations to first-person, second-person, and third-person experience.

Cognitive Attunement in the Zhuangzi

I approach the Zhuangzi presupposing a number of hypotheses about the text and composition that Angus Graham presented and that my own work elaborated upon:[34]

- That this is a collection written by a number of distinct authorial voices compiled over perhaps a century and a half;

- That the text contains a pre-Han core, much of which represents the ideas of (but not necessarily the writings of) an initial author or authors and several later generations of disciples;[35]

- That the work was compiled into a fifty-two-chapter original recension at the court of Liu An 劉安, the second king of Huainan 淮南, and sponsor and contributor to the work that bears his name, the *Huainanzi* 淮南子;[36]

- That the apparent disparate authorial voices in the text, for the most part, shared not only a very specific intellectual lineage of master and disciple, but also a common set of contemplative practices and goals;

- That identifying the nature and results of said practices is essential for understanding the organizing principles of the text and constitutes an important missing piece of the jigsaw puzzle that is the pre-Han classical Daoist tradition.

I would like to propose and then argue the following hypotheses:

1. "Cognitive Attunement"[37] is the central theme and main goal advocated in most of the *Zhuangzi*, including the sections Graham identifies—and to which I concur—as being representative of the historical Zhuang Zhou 莊周 (chapters 1–7); the sections created by the people whom I have argued are his lineal descendants: the "Primitivists" (chapters 8–11.5, 16), the "Syncretists" (chapters 12–15, 33), and the authors of the "School of Zhuangzi" materials (chapters 17–22 and parts of chapters 24–27).

2. Cognitive Attunement is a trait change that involves a transformation of cognitive processing away from a self-conscious reliance on third-person doctrines, dogmas, and self-analyses to an increasing reliance on the phenomenology of the "no-person" perspective. It also includes the development of effortless attention and flow-like optimal experience.

3. Cognitive Attunement is a trait change that results from the apophatic contemplative practices discussed in the text.

Let's examine the evidence in the text for these hypotheses. The goal of a free and fluid consciousness that derives from a fundamentally different mode of cognition can be found throughout the text; motifs and exemplars abound in all sections. To begin with, we have the famous "free and easy wandering" of the first chapter that, I would contend, epitomizes a freedom from being confined to the narrow set of third-person conceptual analyses of oneself and the world that confine our vision and creativity, like the cicada, the turtle dove, and the quail, who cannot conceive of the possibility of—nor imagine the perspective of—the giant Peng 鵬 bird.[38] This freedom that comes from being unconfined to one third-person way of looking at things enables the imagination that permits the stranger who recommended the hand salve to the king of Wu to be enfeoffed, Zhuangzi to see the value in his friend Huizi's 惠子 gourds, and Xu You 許由 to refuse the Empire offered to him that all others would value. Zhuangzi herein links this freedom of the spirit to being selfless:

The utmost (zhi ren 至人) are selfless (wuji 無己),
The daemonic (shen ren 神人) take no credit for their deeds,
The sagely (shengren 聖人) are nameless (wuming 無名).[39]

I would aver here that being selfless means these exemplars are exceptional human beings (ren 人) who are completely free of attachment to a fixed self-identity, which, from the standpoint of a contemplative phenomenology, is a third-person construction abstracted out of the continuous flow of experience. They are able to allow it to continuously arise and to pass away and thus have no interest in gaining credit or fame. To be selfless here implies that they are un-self-conscious in their actions in the world.

The characteristic of selflessness associated with this altered cognition is found scattered throughout the text. For example, in chapter 7, we find the exemplar of the Nameless Man, who gives this advice: "let your heart roam with the flavourless, blend your energies with the featureless, in the spontaneity of your accord with other things leave no room for selfishness . . ."[40] In chapter 11, we find the teaching that Great Persons (da ren 大人):

> In describing and sorting out shapes and bodies remain joined with them in ultimate sameness. In ultimate sameness they have no self, and without a self, from where would they get to have anything? The man who perceives something is the "gentleman" you were yesterday; the man who perceives nothing is the friend of heaven and earth.[41]

This is dense but worth unpacking. If we take "having no self" to mean "being without self-consciousness," then we can see that these cognitive exemplars do differentiate things and persons as objects in their environment. Yet they do not divide the world up into rigid ideas of self and other. People who perceive others in opposition to a self (the "gentleman" of yesterday) are contrasted with people who do not do this and who are therefore friends of all things. This contrast is also found in chapter 12, wherein Lao Dan 老丹 instructs Confucius that ". . . to forget things and to forget heaven is called forgetting the self. The person who forgets himself may be said to have entered heaven."[42] From the viewpoint of contemplative phenomenology, to "forget things and forget the self" means to not objectify them from the third-person perspective. This lack of self-consciousness allows one to not become attached to one's constantly changing self-identity. We see here and repeatedly throughout this text, despite the different authorial voices contained within it, that this liberated way of cognizing the world and oneself is referred to be being "heavenly." It is frequently contrasted with the human.

In chapter 4, after Confucius teaches Yanhui 顏回 about the contemplative practice he calls "the fasting of the mind" (*xin zhai* 心齋), he makes this contrast: "What has man for agent is easily falsified; what has Heaven for agent is hard to falsify. You have heard of using wings to fly. You have not yet heard of flying by being wingless; you have heard of using the wits to know, you have not yet heard of using ignorance to know."[43]

If you act from the usual human perspective you usually act falsely; acting from the heavenly perspective means you usually act in truth. This genuine action is metaphorically equated with flying wingless and using ignorance to know. These are not just meaningless paradoxes, they point to the uniquely transformed cognition that is advocated throughout the text: cognition that knows completely without self-consciousness. In terms of contemplative phenomenology, it's acting in the world from the no-person perspective.

This contrasting of human and heavenly perspectives is found in many other passages throughout the various authorial voices in the text. In chapter 6, we find the "True Men of Old," who clearly grasped "what is Heaven's doing and what is man's." In contrast to common people who breathe from their throats, these sages breathed "from their heels," had few desires and cravings, and in them "the dynamism of the Heavens" (*Tian ji* 天機) was deep. They

> . . . did not know how to be pleased that they were alive, did not know how to hate death . . . were pleased with the gift they received, but forgot it as they gave it back. It is this that is called "not allowing the thinking of the heart to damage the Way, not using what is of man to do the work of Heaven" . . . when unified they were of Heaven's party; when divided were of man's. Someone in whom neither Heaven nor human is victor over the other, this is what is meant by the True Person.[44]

This contrast is brought out further in the final passage of the previous chapter in which Zhuangzi schools his Logician friend Hui-shi in the "essentials of being human." For Zhuangzi, these consist in the very problematic dividing up of the external world into arbitrary categories of "that's it" (*shi* 是) and "that's not" (*fei* 非), which come about from the attachment to third-person judgments of value based on a fixed self-identity. These cause ordinary humans to "inwardly wound themselves by likes and dislikes." By contrast, true sages "constantly go by the spontaneous and do not add anything to the process of life."

> [These sages] buy at the market of Heaven . . . (which means) to be fed by Heaven. Having received their food from Heaven, what use have they for the human? They have the shape of human beings but are without what is essentially human . . . and therefore "that's it, that's not" are not found in their persons. Indiscernibly small, that which attaches them to humans. Unutterably vast, the Heaven within them which they perfect in solitude . . .[45]

For Zhuangzi, the "human" is associated with bias, selfishness, self-injury through personal preferences and desires, one-sided judgments, shallow breathing, overintellectualization, and lack of spontaneity. The "heavenly" is associated with the opposite characteristics, including deep breathing, lack of self-injury through preferences and desires, and a spontaneity and dynamism that come from not allowing thinking to block the Way and from a contemplative experience of complete solitude. We return to these foundations in contemplative practice. For the moment, in terms of contemplative phenomenology, the state and trait that is being commended in these passages is one that we well recognize from the scientific literature on effortless attention and flow. It suggests precisely the kind of non-intentional subjectivity that allows true sages to abandon objectification of both self and world via third-person analysis and to manifest the un-self-conscious mode of "no-person experience." This recalls the description of the Great Person in chapter 11: "In describing and sorting out shapes and bodies remain joined with them in ultimate sameness. In ultimate sameness they have no self, and without a self, from where would they get to have anything?"[46] Ultimate sameness without self refers to this being united with the flow of experience via this un-self-conscious "no-person experience." I see it as also linked to "tacit knowledge," in which cognition occurs and activities are performed effortlessly and without intentionality.

Throughout the *Zhuangzi*, this commended cognitive trait is also associated with manifesting *De* 德 (Power; Potency). Graham defines this in early Chinese philosophy as "the capacity to respond without reflection according to the Way."[47] In the Inner Chapters, we see this emphasis most clearly in the deformed and mutilated exemplars of fearless true sages in chapter 5, people like chopped foot Wang Tai, who is "aware of the Flawless" . . . not moved by death and life and who "lets his heart go roaming in the peace which is from the Power." Another example is "Uglyface T'o," as Graham translated his name, instantaneously perceived as trustworthy enough to hand over a state because he "keeps the Power whole" inside himself.

An emphasis on the importance of cultivating a cognition based on "the Power" is one of the defining philosophical tenets of the "Primitivist" writings, one that also links it to the cognitive attunement we have seen elsewhere in the text. In chapter 8, the Power is basically defined in the phrase Graham sees as quintessentially associated with this author: *xing ming zhi qing* (性名之情), which he translates as "the essentials of our nature and destiny." I would explain this further as "the spontaneous responses of our instinctual nature in response to things that happen to us in life." In chapter 8, our essential human nature is for all the senses to respond spontaneously and harmoniously on their own without the interference of social and ethical dicta, such as those provided by Confucians: "When I call someone a fine man, it is not Goodwill and Duty that I am talking about, but simply the fineness in his powers; nor when I call someone is it the Five Tastes that I am talking about but simply a trust in the essentials of our nature and destiny."[48]

This is another way to talk about the kinds of "tacit knowledge" and "effortless activity" that apprehend the world clearly when not interfered with by fixed and rigid categories and dicta about human moral behavior. Chapter 9 talks about "The Age when Power was at its utmost," a primitive Utopia when people

> lived in sameness with the birds and animals, side by side as
>   fellow clansmen with the myriad creatures . . .
> In sameness, knowing nothing!
> Not parted from their Power
> In sameness, desiring nothing!
> Call it "simple" and "unhewn."
> In the simple and unhewn, the nature of the people is found.[49]

The "simple" (*su* 素) and the "unhewn" (*pu* 樸) are famous images from *Laozi* 19, which are metaphors for states of mind in which the Way is present. I see them as symbolizing freedom from desires and from dualistic knowledge, an un-self-conscious state of pure experience in which, for the Primitivist, our instinctive tendencies to respond spontaneously and harmoniously to whatever situation arises are allowed to operate without the encumbrance of social conventions. As we see in chapter 9: "In the time of the House of Hexu 赫胥氏: the people when at home were unaware of what they were doing and when travelling did not know where they were going, basked in the sun chewing a morsel or strolled drumming on their bellies."[50]

So, for the Primitivist, how does one create a society in which the basic un-self-conscious tendencies of human nature are allowed to develop? Be led by a exemplary person (*junzi* 君子) who practices "Doing Nothing" (*wuwei* 無為):

> Only by Doing Nothing will he find security in the essentials
> of nature and destiny . . . If then a gentleman does prove able

not to dislocate his Five Organs and stretch his eyesight and hearing, then sitting as still as a corpse he will look majestic as a dragon, from the silence of the abyss he will speak with a voice of thunder, he will have the promptings which are daemonic and the veerings which are from Heaven, will have an unforced air and *do nothing* . . ."[51]

Of course the *locus classicus* of *wuwei* in the classical Daoist tradition is the *Laozi*. It is the one classical Chinese philosophical concept that has been studied by scholars informed by cognitive science, where it is frequently linked to ideas of "effortless attention," "effortless action," and "flow."[52] In the context of the Primitivist chapters, I would take it to mean not interfering with the spontaneous functioning of cognition that arises from contact between our innate natures and the environments in which we find ourselves. In our contemplative phenomenology, this is associated with "no-person experience," un-self-consciousness, and non-intentionality. It is most definitely linked to the cognitive scientific ideas of "effortless attention" and "tacit knowledge."

These different ways of presenting the transformed trait of cognitive attunement are not just found in the Inner Chapters and the Primitivist writings; they abound throughout the rest of the text. For example, in chapter 12, we find the exemplar of the gardener who is a "man in whom Power is whole . . . Someone who by illumination enters into simplicity, by *Doing Nothing* reverts to the unhewn, who identifies himself with his nature and protects his daemon . . ."[53]

In chapter 14, we find Lao Dan teaching Confucius, a common trope in the "Outer Chapters":[54]

The Utmost Persons of old borrowed right of way through the benevolent and lodged for a night in the dutiful to roam in the emptiness where one rambles without a destination, eat in the field of the casual and simple, stand in the orchards where one can keep all the fruit. To ramble without a destination is Doing Nothing, to be casual and simple is to be easily nurtured, to keep all the fruit is to let nothing out from oneself. Of old they called this the roaming in which one plucks out only the genuine.[55]

This passage brings together several of our metaphors for cognitive attunement and adds to them the concept of "the genuine" (*zhen* 真),

another symbol for this state of un-self-conscious no-person experience that is influential throughout the classical and later Daoist traditions.[56]

Commending this state is a common theme in the dialogues between Confucius and Lao Dan that Graham has collected. In chapter 21, we see the Daoist sage, who, after his bath, was ". . . so still he seemed other than human . . . as motionless as withered wood, as though he had left everything behind and parted from man to take a stand in the Unique . . ." He manifests the Power, which, in the perfected or "Utmost" Persons (*zhi ren* 至人), cannot be trained through even the most "far-reaching words." It is simply there: ". . . It is like heaven being high of itself, earth being solid of itself, the sun and moon shining of themselves . . ."[57]

Along with some of the other passages we have presented to this point, this suggests the link between a state of complete stillness and tranquility and the development of the trait of transformed cognition of which we have seen many exemplars and symbols. This becomes clear when we examine two important and related passages from the authorial voice Graham labels as "Syncretist":

> Chapter 13: "Emptiness and stillness, calm and indifference, quiescence, Doing Nothing, are the even level of heaven and earth, the utmost reach of the Way and the Power; therefore, emperor, king, or sage finds rest in them . . . Emptiness and stillness, calm and indifference, quiescence, Doing Nothing, are at the root of the myriad things . . . To have these as your resources in high estate is the Power which is in emperor, king, Son of Heaven; to have these as your resources in low estate is the Way of the obscure sage, the untitled king . . . In stillness a sage, in motion a king, you do nothing yet are exalted, you are simple and unpolished yet no one in the empire is able to rival your glory.[58]

Emptiness, stillness, calm and indifference, and quiescence are states that result from the kinds of concentrative practices we see in contemplative phenomenology. Such practices—often linked to focusing the attention on the breath or a bodily location, or some other object—gradually reduce the occurrences of random thoughts, feelings, and perceptions that roll through the consciousness of most people from moment to moment, resulting in a state of one-pointed concentration. Many of these are tied up in third-person conceptualizations of first-person and second-person experiences, creating mental structures that reinforce fixed notions of self-identity, desires, preferences, and beliefs. Concentrative practices take the focus of consciousness off these third-person conceptualizations and gradually reduce their occurrence. This *Zhuangzi* passage argues that the states of emptiness that result from these practices enable one to "Do Nothing": that is, to allow cognition to function without effort, for sages and rulers to develop the "simple and unhewn" (*su pu* 素樸) Power that enables them to act in the world through "tacit knowledge" in complete spontaneity and harmony. This result echoes those that scientists include under the category of "receptive" meditation. These ideas from chapter 13 are echoed, almost verbatim, in the following passage from chapter 15:

> Hence it is said that calm and indifference, quiescence, emptiness, and nothingness, Doing Nothing, they are the even level of heaven and earth, the substance of the Way and the Power; therefore sages find rest in them. At rest they are even and unstrained; being even and unstrained they are calm and indifferent . . . Hence it is said that sages . . .
>
> . . . Only when stirred will they respond.
> Only when pressed will they move,
> Only when it is inevitable will they rise up
> Rejecting knowledge and precedent
> They take their course from the patterns of the heavens
> (*tian li* 天理).[59]

Here the states of calmness and emptiness leading to Doing Nothing allow sages to respond spontaneously and without deliberation or intentionality. They are able to do this because they do not interfere in the effortless automatic responses that emerge because they do not interfere with the underlying "patterns of the heavens." These are the various natural guidelines that organize the activities of the myriad things enabling them to stay true on the courses laid down by their distinctive natures in response to the circumstances in which they find themselves.[60] While there is a great deal of evidence for these illumined cognitive states and traits, what about the practices that contemplative phenomenology posits create them? While there are fewer passages that discuss these practices, they are present in some of the most renowned narratives in the inner chapters.

Perhaps the most famous of them is the one in which Confucius instructs his favorite student, Yan Hui, on the best preparation for addressing a local tyrant:

> Unify your attention
> Rather than listening with your ears, listen with your mind
> Rather than listening with your mind, listen with your breathing (*qi* 氣)
> Listening stops at the ears; the mind stops at what it can objectify
> As for your breathing, it becomes empty and waits to respond to things.
> The Way gathers in emptiness.
> Emptiness is attained through the fasting of the mind (*xin zhai* 心齋)[61]

This closely resembles concentrative meditation, with its attention focused first on sounds, then on mental objects, and finally on the breath. This leads to the emptying out of the usual contents of consciousness, as one gradually "fasts" or eliminates them. The other passage that refers to contemplative practice is this equally famous one in chapter 6 in which Yan Hui gives the following advice on "sitting in forgetfulness" (*zuo wang* 坐忘) to his teacher, Confucius:

> I let organs and members drop away (*duo zhi ti* 墮支 體),
> dismiss eyesight and hearing (*chu zong ming* 出聰明),
> part from the body and expel knowledge (*li xing qu zhi* 離形屈知),
> merge with the Great Pervader (*tong yu datong* 同於大通).[62]

To "let organs and members drop away" means to gradually lose visceral awareness of the emotions and desires, which, for the early Daoists, have "physiological" bases in the various organs or orbs of *qi* circulation in the body/mind complex (*wuzang* 五臟).[63] To "dismiss eyesight and hearing" means to cut off awareness of sense perception. To "part from the body and expel knowledge" means to lose bodily awareness and banish all thoughts from consciousness. To "merge with the Great Pervader" is to become united with the Dao.

Shorter references to such practices are sprinkled throughout the text. In chapter 2, "heart like withered wood; mind like dead ashes" refers to the deep stillness of the mind that comes about from a one-pointed attentional focus that comes from concentration meditation. These two metaphors occur seven more times in the text, particularly in chapters 19–24.[64] In chapter 19, the cicada catcher becomes completely still and totally focused: ". . . it is only the wings of the cicada of which I am aware. I don't let my gaze wander or waver, I would not take all the myriad things in exchange for the wings of a cicada . . ."[65] Confucius characterizes this as "using the will in an undivided fashion and concentrating the spirit."

The mind as a mirror is another important cognitive trait that is praised in the text. In chapter 5, Wang Tai, the sage who "regards losing his own foot as he would shaking off mud . . . and who uses his mind to discover the unchanging mind beyond it," is someone with such a mind. "None of us finds his mirror in flowing water, we find it in still water. Only the still can still whatever is stilled." "If your mirror is bright dust will not settle, if the dust settles it's that your mirror isn't bright . . ."[66] In chapter 7, we read about the Utmost Persons, who "use their minds like a mirror: they do not escort things as they go or welcome them as they come, they respond and do not store (*ying er buzang* 應而不臧).[67] In the very beginning of the Syncretist chapter 13, we find a long passage commending the still mind of the sage that ". . . is the reflector of heaven and earth and the mirror of the myriad things."[68] Finally, chapter 33 contains the advice of the sage Guanyin:

> Within yourself, no fixed positions;
> Things as they take shape disclose themselves.
> Moving, be like water.
> Still be like a mirror.
> Respond like an echo . . .[69]

So the consciousness that is emptied and stilled through concentrative meditation can mirror things with complete clarity, a symbol for the effortless, spontaneous and un-self-conscious functioning of cognitive attunement. This is an expression of "no-person experience."

The dialogue between the Yellow Emperor and the Daoist sage Guang Chengzi 廣成子 in chapter 11 contains fairly specific instructions on the concentrative dimension of contemplative practice:

> . . . look at nothing, listen to nothing
> cling to the spirit and be still,
> and the body will align itself,
> always be still, always be pure,
> Do not strain your body
> Do not allow your vital essence to waver,
> And then it will be possible to live on and on.
> When the eye has nothing it sees,
> The ear has nothing it hears,
> And the mind has nothing it knows,
> Your spirit will abide in the body
> And then the body will live on and on.
> Be watchful over what lies within you
> Shut it off from being externalized
> Excessive knowledge is ruinous . . .[70]

In commending the removal of all thought and perception through the practice of developing stillness through focused internal attention, this passage touches on contemplative practices that the early practitioners of the Way regarded as longevity engendering. The goal, while seemingly specific to the Daoist tradition, has echoes in the stress reduction research of the past three decades.[71]

Finally, most of chapter 23 is devoted to an extended search for the most effective contemplative practices in which two characters, Geng Sangchu 庚桑楚 and Laozi, instruct Nanrongchu 南榮趎 on methods of cultivating emptiness and stillness that are not at all dissimilar to those commended by Guang Chengzi.

> Rid yourself of the perversities of the will (e.g., honor and fame)
> Eradicate the absurdities of the mind (e.g., false gestures and phony attitudes)
> Relinquish the attachments of Power (e.g., preferences and feelings)
> Break through the blockages of the Way . . .
> And you will be aligned, still, lucid, empty and you will take no action yet leave nothing undone."[72]

Cognitive Attunement in the "Qi wu lun"

Two of the most evocative statements about the cognitive attunement that derives from the contemplative practice of emptying and stilling the activity of consciousness in the *Zhuangzi* come from two diverse contexts, yet they nicely symbolize the states and traits so clearly spelled out in the "Qi wu lun" (Essay on seeing things as equal). In the teaching of Lao Dan to Confucius in chapter 22, we find the following statement made about the sage who closely guards "that which no increase increases and no reduction reduces":

> The Sage neither misses the occasion when it is present, nor clings to it when it is past. He responds to it by attuning himself, that's the Power; he responds to it by matching with it, that's the Way. From this course the emperors arose and kings began . . .[73]

This is the epitome of the flowing consciousness that is advocated throughout the text; it is literally cognitive attunement.

This attunement is well captured in the central metaphor of the results of the attentional training practice of "the fasting of the mind." After his pupil demonstrates to him that, indeed, he has attained a complete clearing out of his consciousness and concomitant opening it up to the Way, Confucius says: "It is easy to stop walking; but much more difficult to walk without touching the ground (*wu xing di* 無行地)."[74] "To walk without touching the ground" is Zhuangzi's metaphor for living in the world without the support of a fixed and attached self-identity. This is living in cognitive attunement to the impulses of the Way as one engages in daily living. This process is detailed in the "Qi wu lun."

This most detailed chapter in the attunement of cognition questions subjective bias in the categories of knowledge human beings create:

> For there to be "That's it" (*shi* 是) and "That's not" (*fei* 非) before they are formed in the mind would be to "go to Yue 越 today and have arrived yesterday." This would be crediting with existence what has no existence; and if you do that, even the Divine Yu 大禹 could not understand you; how can you expect to be understood by me?[75]

Categories of knowledge are true relative to the limited perspectives that create them: "What is it is also other; what is other is also it: There someone says "This is 'it' (i.e., 'true'), 'that's not (i.e., false)'" from one point of view; here we say "'That's it;' this is not,'" from another point of view. Are there really it and other? Or really no it and other?"[76] Here the ultimate veridicality of third-person experience is seen to be arbitrary and relative to the viewpoint of the observer. However, there is a perspective from which all these relatively true and false viewpoints can be "seen as equal":

> Where neither It nor Other finds its opposite is called the axis of the Way. Once the axis is found at the center of the circle, there is no limit to responding with either, on the one hand no limit to what is It, and, on the other, no limit to what is Not. Therefore I say: "The best means is Illumination (ming 明)."[77]

By direct experience of embodiment of the Way, it is possible to break free of relativistic truths and experience a mode of cognition that can, without hesitation or limit, respond to whatever realities are present in any situation. Zhuangzi conceives of this mode of experience as an illumined cognition based in a consciousness centered in the Way. Such a consciousness is utterly without bias and able to fluidly and spontaneously respond to all the viewpoints and limited visions of reality that it encounters. This "illumined" mode of cognition is so freed from bias that it has no subjective preferences: "No thing is not Other; no thing is not It. If you treat yourself as Other, they do not appear . . . This is why sages . . . open things to the lucid light of Nature; theirs too is a 'That's it which goes by circumstance' (yinshi 因是)."[78]

To rephrase: judgments of true and false, it and other, are third-person perspectives based in individual biases. They are not in any way "objective." Throughout this chapter, Zhuangzi sets up the contrast that only Graham among the myriads of translators really gets, that between a "That's it which deems" (weishi 為是) and a "That's it which goes by circumstance."[79] The former is a "fixed cognition"; the latter is a "flowing cognition." To "shi (是 deem) things" is essentially the activity of the third-person objectification of the internal and external worlds involved in rational thought. When we use "fixed cognition" to "deem," we are locked into rigid self-other, true-false distinctions—and attendant emotions—that cause all the arguments among the different philosophers of the day and cause a great deal of confusion for most everyone.

When we use "flowing cognition" to "adapt," we can function without the interference of attachment to a self-identity, thus yielding a freedom from adhering to fixed and rigid positions that enables us to alter in the moment as things alter. As the previous quote from chapter 22 says: "The Sage neither misses the occasion when it is present, nor clings to it when it is past. He responds to it by attuning himself." In terms of our contemplative phenomenology, it is as if the activity of first-person subjective consciousness, because it has previously apprehended the non-dual Way, is able to manifest its un-self-conscious, non-self-referential aspect as "no-person experience" so it can pursue a completely unbiased third-person analysis that is free of attachment to any one particular position. This creates an illumined cognition from which all other perspectives are seen as equally valid or invalid: you have no more attachment to your own personal preferences and separate point of view than to anyone else's. This is symbolized by the distinctive phrase "to treat yourself as 'other,'" as in the following:

> No thing is not 'other;' no thing is not 'it.' If you treat yourself as 'other,' they do not appear . . . This is why sages . . . open things to the lucid light of Heaven; theirs too is a 'That's it' which goes by circumstance (i.e. a Flowing cognition) . . .[80]

Keeping an unbiased Way-centered focus amid a constantly changing world attunes subjectivity to the deeper underlying power of the Way:

> Therefore when the 'That's it which deems' (fixed cognition) differentiates a stalk from a pillar, a leper from the beauty Xi Shi 西施 . . . the Way pervades and unifies them (*dao tong wei yi* 道通為)—(and sees them as equal) . . . Only those who see right through things realize how to pervade and unify . . . the 'That's it which deems' they do not use, but lodge their attention in the ordinary (flow of experience) . . .

> To lodge in the ordinary flow of experience is to manifest it;
> when you manifest it you can pervade things;
> when you pervade things you attain it
> and once you attain it you are just about there;

Then the 'That's it which goes by circumstance' (flowing cognition) comes to an end, and when it does,

> That of which you do not know what is 'so' of it you call the Way.[81]

Epistemologically, the Way is realized through a "pure experience." We cannot know it as an object via third-person experience in which we separate from it (and know it as "so"); we can only know it through "no-person experience" in which the objectifying self collapses. For Zhuangzi, to return to this pure experience of the Way from time to time attunes subjectivity so that it can pervade and unify different perspectives, enabling a spontaneous cognition that is completely unbiased and purely spontaneous. We become directly connected to the situation in which we are embedded via the Way, which pervades all underlying Patterns (*li* 理) present in this situation. To do this is later in this text called "Embodying the Way" (*ti Dao* 體道).[82]

In terms of contemplative phenomenology, "embodying the Way" implies a non-self-referential, un-self-conscious "no-person" experience in the present moment free from self-objectification; it is experience that is immediate, unbiased, spontaneous, and intuitive. So why does this mode of experience lead to a cognitive attunement and not to chaos? In the *Zhuangzi* it is because embodying the Way connects you with a deep unitive power or source that underlies you and your environment. Throughout the text there are many metaphors for this source: "the Ancestor" (*zong* 宗);[83] "the Unique" (*du* 獨);[84] "the maker of things" (*zaowuzhe* 造物者);[85] "the Great Pervader" (*datong* 大通);[86] "the Flawless" (*wujia* 無假).[87] Currently the phenomenologists and cognitive scientists we have studied do not make this seemingly metaphysical claim.

One thing about which most of our sources agree is that this cognitive attunement is quite often the source of intuition and creativity, as many passages in chapters 3 and 19 of the *Zhuangzi* detail. Cook Ding 庖丁 carving an ox, the cicada catcher reeling in insects, the skilled swimmer over the Spinebridge Falls, and the following passage about a bellstand carver are all examples:

> Woodcarver Qing 梓慶 chipped wood to make a bellstand. When it was finished viewers were amazed . . . The Marquis of Lu 魯侯 asked him his secret.

> "Your servant is a mere artisan, what secret could he have? However there is one point. When I am going to make a bellstand I take care never to waste my energies, and I make sure to fast in order to still my mind. After three days of this I do not care to keep in mind congratulations and reward . . . after

five days I do not care to keep in mind your blame or praise, my skill or clumsiness. After fasting seven days, I am so intent that I forget that I have a body and four limbs. During this time my lord's court does not exist for me . . . the only thing I do is go into the forest and observe the nature of the wood as Nature makes it grow . . . only then do I have a complete vision of the bellstand and put my hand to it. Otherwise I give the whole thing up . . ."[88]

This evocative passage reflects the techniques and results of the cognitive attunement we find throughout the text. Here there is an apophatic practice of "fasting" similar to the "fasting of the mind" in chapter 4. This is followed by a complete loss of self-consciousness and total focusing on the task of going into the forest to find the tree linked to his "vision of the bellstand." Then he can bring it home and carve it up.

As contemplative phenomenologists and cognitive scientists gradually come to include sources that are not European or Eurocentric, they will be able to develop increasingly sophisticated theories and hypotheses about the nature of human experience. And as scholars of traditional Asian thought come to see the value of phenomenological and scientific models of human experience, they will begin to recognize certain distinctive modes of experience reflected in traditional texts such as the *Zhuangzi*. Being able to identify the distinctive goal of cognitive attunement that is advocated in the *Zhuangzi* has helped us see that despite the various authorial viewpoints found in this work, that there is a compelling continuity of interest and insight that motivated the people who authored and compiled it.

Angus Graham was convinced from his own experience that contemplative states are part of our potential as human beings. He was drawn not only to direct experience of contemplative states but also to the challenge of working out their philosophical significance. This is without a doubt what he found so fascinating about the *Zhuangzi*. He would have been pleased to know that the spontaneous flowing cognition that he recognized as a central theme in the text is now being studied and researched by philosophers and scientists so that many more people can access the significant benefits he saw in such experiences. It is, indeed, "human capacity for awareness raised to its highest pitch."

Chapter 13

Against Cognitive Imperialism

A Call for a Non-Ethnocentric Approach to Cognitive Science and Religious Studies

Unreflective Ethnocentrism and Cognitive Imperialism

In a widely circulated cover article in the *New York Times Sunday Magazine* of March 4, 2007, titled "Darwin's God," the author, Robin Marantz Henig, asked the apparently scientific question:

> In the world of evolutionary biology, the question is not whether God exists but why we believe in him. Is belief a helpful adaptation or an evolutionary accident?

It is implied in the question, and it becomes apparent in the article, that Henig and her sources (anthropologist Scot Atran and others) assume that all human beings throughout time and across cultures have believed in God. Indeed, she writes:

> According to anthropologists, religions that share certain supernatural features—belief in a noncorporeal God or gods, belief in the afterlife, belief in the ability of prayer or ritual

I wish to thank the following friends and colleagues for their invaluable critiques of earlier versions of this manuscript: Henry Rosemont Jr., Matthew Duperon, B. Alan Wallace, and Mark Cladis. None is, of course, responsible for any errors of omission and commission that remain in the work.

to change the course of human events—are found in virtually every culture on earth.[1]

She further asserts:

> These scholars [scientists studying the evolution of religion] tend to agree on one point: that religious belief is an outgrowth of brain architecture that evolved during early human history. What they disagree about is why a tendency to believe evolved, whether it was because belief itself was adaptive, or because it was just an evolutionary byproduct, a mere consequence of some other adaptation in the evolution of the human brain.

"In other words," she writes, in an appropriately condescending manner as befits her own (and many others') belief system:

> Which is the better biological explanation for a belief in God—evolutionary adaptation or neurological accident?"[2]

To answer this question, I would pose another: Which is the better explanation for a modern scientist's entirely unsubstantiated assumption that all human beings believe in God—neurological accident, or deeply ingrained and unreflective ethnocentrism? In assuming that Judeo-Christo-Islamic (Abrahamic) beliefs are not just a product of our own Western civilizations but in some form are universal for all Homo sapiens, Henig and her scientific sources are falling into the same trap that has bedeviled Western assumptions about religion since, for example, the Jesuit missionaries landed in China in 1574—a trap that is well typified by the comments of one of the fathers of the field of the academic study of religion (which developed out of liberal Protestant theology). Writing in 1951, Joachim Wach baldly stated:

> There can be no "godless" religion, and only a misunderstanding can make Buddhism and Confucianism into such. Buddhism and Jainism may have started as criticisms of the traditional or of any positive characterization of Ultimate Reality, but they soon developed into genuine religions.[3]

Wach was a pioneer in the history of religions and a founding member of the Department of Religious Studies at Brown University. He strove mightily to free the academic study of religion from Christian theological influences. Yet in this quotation and throughout his book *The Comparative Study of Religion*, he makes an essentially theological assumption: that "genuine religions" must see God as the Ultimate Reality.

This kind of unreflective ethnocentrism is understandable—although not at all justifiable—in someone thinking and writing almost seven decades ago. That it still persists in subtle forms among scholars of religion and in grosser forms among the scientists whose work is reviewed in the *New York Times Sunday Magazine* clearly indicates how, for modern Westerners, our religious upbringing—the ways in which we have been brought up to understand religions, whether we embrace them or reject them—is still deeply entrenched within our own everyday perspectives. Clearly, the academic study of religion has failed to make much of a dent in our cultural assumptions on the topic, and I would attribute that failure to the field's inability to free itself from these very culturally defined categories of religion—in other words, to our own "unreflective ethnocentrism," and to our obsession with arguing with one another from within it.

Popular and influential studies of religion by social scientists are unfortunately confined within these very limited understandings of religion as well. The anthropologist of religion Pascal Boyer is characteristic of these approaches, and his understanding of religion is quite compatible with that of Scott Atran. Boyer, who purports to "explain religion" using the lens of cognitive science, argues that *all* religions contain "supernatural notions"[4]—including notions of

> a variety of artifacts, animals, persons, plants: concepts of floating islands of mountains that digest food. . . . These are found in folktales and correspond to a small catalogue of templates for supernatural concepts. We also find that a particular subset of these concepts is associated with more serious commitment, strong emotions, important rituals, and/or moral understandings. An association between a supernatural concept and one or several of these social effects is our main intuitive criterion for what is religious.[5]

Here and elsewhere in his writings, Boyer assumes that "supernatural concepts" are one of the essential defining characteristics of religion and that these are caused directly by specific cognitive templates. They include anthropomorphic ideas about God or gods, including intentional agency—and, further, he goes so far as to assert, they are never based on actual experience. He writes:

> It is also striking that the details of such representations [of supernatural agents' actions in the world] are generally derived not from what one has experienced but rather of what others have said. People take their information about the features of . . . gods, to an overwhelming extent, from socially trans-mitted information, not direct experience.[6]

Arguing from observations of relatively primitive cultures, Boyer extends them to all religions and includes in his purview all Christian beliefs about the nature of God, which he considers to be the supernatural agent par excellence.[7] He never once stops to consider that there are religious traditions that put absolutely no stock in anything supernatural. Nor does he seem to know that some traditions derive their concepts and understanding of the functioning of consciousness completely empir-ically, grounded in experience—experience that is direct and that can be proven again and again by contemplatives and "contemplative scientists" who follow the same procedures of working in the common laboratory of their own consciousnesses.

The entire concept of "supernatural beings" and "supernatural agency" is drawn from worldviews that seek causes for natural events in forces or powers that cannot be perceived within the natural world. The classical Christian notions of an anthropomorphic God, the creator separated from creation by an unbridgeable gulf, certainly fit this model, as Boyer points out. However, in his unreflective ethnocentrism, Boyer demonstrates that he is completely unaware that in some of the major contemplative traditions of the non-Western world, such as foundational Daoism and Confucianism in China and Theravada Buddhism in South Asia, supernatural powers or forces are either absent or play a relatively insignificant role.[8] The Daoist Dao (Way) is very much a force inherent in the universe; it is certainly not supernatural. The Theravada concept of no-self (*anatta*) is not even a force: it is a mode of cognition. It can be argued that the foundational Confucian tradition, too, contains no supernatural powers: its concept of *tian* 天 (usually translated as "heaven") is, like the Daoist Dao, clearly subject to natural laws.[9] As Henry Rose-mont Jr. has unequivocally stated, these three traditions simply do not presume the existence of a transcendent, supernatural realm:

No such metaphysical claims invest Buddhist, Confucian or Daoist texts as I read them, and while these latter religions, and all others, have supernatural entities described in their oral or written canons, these entities remain altogether linked to the world.[10]

Clearly, Boyer, Atran, and anthropologists and cognitive scientists who have proposed reductive attempts to explain religion by reference to evolutionary processes are working with models of religion heavily influenced by their own personal cultural experiences. They demonstrate no awareness that the Asian contemplative traditions pose an exception to their universal assumptions about religion. Thus their unreflective ethnocentrism has led them to restrict their sources to religions that fit into the accepted cognitive models of their own European religious traditions. Their deep commitment to these cognitive models is troubling at best and leads to bad science at worst. This is the first of the issues I wish to address in this discussion.

There is a second, related issue that is just as deeply entrenched and unreflective. It is the assumption that our European religious conceptions—together with our philosophical and now scientific conceptions—of human experience contain the only possible veridical models. Thus any tradition that posits veridical cognition that does not fall within these models is ipso facto false and delusional. There are a number of key beliefs associated with this assumption. One is that human experience cannot possibly occur that is not totally conditioned by preexisting cognitive categories. This position is forcefully stated by Steven Katz in his influential essay "Language, Epistemology, and Mysticism":

> Let me state the single epistemological assumption that has exercised my thinking and which has forced me to undertake the present investigation: There are *no pure (i.e., unmediated) experiences*. Neither mystical experience nor more ordinary forms of experience give any indication, or any grounds for believing, that they are unmediated. . . . This epistemological fact seems to me to be true, *because of the sorts of beings we are*.[11]

Yet mystical traditions the world over argue that it is only when these mediating cognitive categories are stripped away that genuine intuitive knowledge and clear cognition can begin to develop, yielding experience that is truly noetic, as William James put it.[12] Katz, of course, never attempts to explain why, if all mystical experiences in their entirety are culturally mediated, mystics the world over concur in asserting that these experiences are ineffable. Katz's arrogant position thus rests on the assumption that he, as a modern European child of the Enlightenment, understands more about what the world's great mystics have experienced than those mystics themselves. This is a form of the ethnocentric hubris that is characteristic of the European imperialists who once dominated the world in the name of their cultural superiority. Katz's view is thus one example of an epistemologically blinkered attitude that I would like to call "cognitive imperialism."

The ultimate implication of this attitude for the study of religion and human cognitive possibilities is far reaching: namely, that mystical experience cannot be veridical. Nor, for that matter, can any subjective experience, which, after all, can only be a product of the preexisting categories. Thus, in this view, our subjective experience can tell us nothing new and nothing true about the world because we can only cognize the world through the categories imprinted within us by our historical and cultural context. Subjective experience, in this view, is relative and individualistic and has no claims to truth that anyone else must take seriously. Religious experience only tells us what our religion already knows, so there is absolutely no point in trying to understand or assess it, because it yields no genuine "objective" knowledge about the world. In departments of religious studies throughout North America, this has led to a profound lack of interest in religious experience—for William James, the very essence of religion—and to a shift in scholarship in the field not just to historical research but to historicism, the approach to critical study that asserts that a text can only be understood as a product of the social, historical and political forces of its time.

Historicist Reductionism:
The Reigning Paradigm in the Study of Religion

Unreflective ethnocentrism, and its concomitant cognitive imperialism, then, not only reach deeply into the fields of anthropology and the cognitive sciences, but also have become prominent features of the academic study of religion in North America. As we approach the second decade of the twenty-first century, the field of religious studies has gradually moved away from its origins in Christian theology and has gone through a number of developmental phases. During the first, the field separated its mission from that of the chaplaincy, and during the second, it introduced what one scholar has called the "historical-scientific-philosophical study of religions committed to an underlying ideal of detached objectivity and value-neutral inquiry."[13] To a considerable extent, historical and social scientific studies have gradually come to dominate research and teaching in North American religious studies departments. For example, the recent publications of one US university's department of religious studies include the following topics: "Israelite Interment Ideology"; "Women's Religions among Pagans"; "Olfactory Imagination in Ancient Christianity"; "Letter Writing in Greco-Roman Antiquity"; and "Jewish Piety in Antiquity."

Lest this one example seem idiosyncratic, let us examine the list of monographs published during the last decade by the American Academy of Religion, the professional association for the field. Therein titles such as the following predominate: "Crossing the Ethnic Divide: The Multiethnic Church on a Mission"; "Daoist Monastic Manual: A Translation of the *Fengdao Kejie*"; "History of the Buddha's Relic Shrine"; "Making Magic: Religion, Magic and Science in the Modern World"; and "Moses in America: The Cultural Uses of Biblical Narrative." Such historical and sociological studies dominate the AAR's list of publications, together with such theological studies in the Abrahamic traditions as these: "Intersecting Pathways: Modern Jewish Theologians in Conversation with Christianity"; "Opting for the Margins: Postmodernity and Liberation in Christian Theology"; and "Feminist Theology and Christian Realism."

In the academic journals and other publications that concentrate exclusively on the religious traditions of Asia, we find a similar emphasis on historical and social scientific studies—although, of course, publications on theology are absent. For example, among the articles published in the 2005 and 2004 issues of the *Journal of Chinese Religions*, we find the following topics: "A Cultural History of Muslims in Late Imperial China"; "Prehistoric Images of Women from the North China Region: the Origins of Chinese Goddess Worship?"; and "Fame and Fortune: Popular Religion and Moral Capital in Szechuan." Among the books reviewed were these: *Pilgrimages to Mount Tai in Late Imperial China*; *The Confucian Transformation of Popular Culture*; and *Religion in Modern Taiwan: Tradition and Innovation in a Changing Society*. Only rarely are there reviews of books on philosophy. Two such books are *Buddhist Phenomenology: A*

Philosophical Investigation of Yogacara Buddhism and the Ch'eng Wei-shih Lun and *After Confucius: Studies in Early Chinese Philosophy.*

I am not arguing here that historical and social scientific studies of the various religious traditions are not valuable. Far from it: they are extremely valuable in contextualizing religious experience and helping us clarify differences between our own modern perspectives and those of the authors of ancient religious texts. In my own scholarship, I have often done very detailed historical and text-historical studies of foundational Daoist religious and philosophical works.[14] However, that such scholarship dominates the field provokes a deeper question: Why this almost total retreat from serious consideration of religious experience? Why has the role of subjective experience in religion been totally abandoned as a subject of academic study?

A partial explanation can be found in the historical development of the field of religious studies. The field emerged from liberal Protestant theology in the period immediately before and after World War II, and so in the early stages, the concerns of Christian theology predominated. The issues that were studied included the existence and nature of God, the balance between faith and reason, religious experience as source of information about the nature of God, miracles, and the importance of the historicity of Jesus in particular and of New Testament narratives in general. As the field gradually moved away from explicitly Christian theological concerns and toward an attempt to consider other religious traditions of the world on an equal footing, the field nonetheless continued to think about religion in the terms and categories of Christian theology. For example, the following conceptual categories still dominate approaches in the field: soteriology (how people are saved—note that this implies a Power that does the saving); metaphysics (a field of study that implies the existence of nonphysical, world-transcending supernatural power); ontology (which implicitly posits an ultimate Being in the world); and cosmogony (which implies that the universe had a unique and discrete beginning). Yet all of these concerns betray an Abrahamic—and, in particular, a Christian—worldview that was presumed to be universal. By contrast, for example, in Chinese cosmogony, to quote the famous scholar of Chinese science Joseph Needham: "The world had always existed and always would and the point was to figure out not where it came from but how to live within it."[15]

To a great extent, the strong emphasis on historical and social-scientific models that now dominates the field of religious studies represents a forceful attempt to move the field away from Christian concerns and values and to develop a more neutral perspective from which to study all religions (although the Christian obsession with historicity persists, especially with regard to Jesus).[16] Nonetheless, it is apparent that this attempt at value-neutrality has not been entirely successful, as I have attempted to explain. Despite this, popular critics of the field such as Russell McCutcheon have completely missed this point: they mistake historicism and reductionism for "critical method," entirely ignoring the unreflective ethnocentrism that undergirds these methodologies. McCutcheon focuses on dividing scholars in the field into two camps: "critics" (who have this presumed position of neutrality) and "caretakers" (essentially theologians in disguise who seek to prove the truths of religion in the guise of value neutrality).[17] The only way to be critical, and hence "good," for McCutcheon is to treat religion and religious phenomena as objects that are to be analyzed according to "naturalistic" historical and social contexts and are thus devoid of epistemic value. For him, any *subjective* involvement in the actual practices and experiences of religion—even if it is explicitly for the purposes of better understanding the religious tradition—cannot escape active or tacit *faith* in the truths that the religious tradition espouses. Thus McCutcheon does not escape the cognitive imperialist assumptions of Atran and Boyer; his concept of religion is totally derived from Abrahamic traditions: it's all about faith, belief, God, and the supernatural. This ignorance of the contemplative traditions of the non-Western world demonstrates the kind of continued shocking failure of so many scholars of religion—who put such a high value on contextualizing the religions they study—to contextualize themselves.

This failure at self-contextualization is particularly ironic for those who consider themselves critical scholars of religion, because much of their historical and social-scientific research is dominated by historicist agendas that assert that all aspects of religion—particularly the epistemic insights that derive from their practices—are totally determined by their historical and social context. According to this way of thought, religious experience must never, without exception, be studied from the insider, first-person perspective. That perspective is denied to scholars because, in this view, our only viable choice is to study religion from the outside in. Only its external qualities are available to us; only these outer aspects of religion are potentially veridical.

There is a series of related reasons for this historicist reductionism. There is space here only to mention them. Historicist reductionism is based on certain epistemological assumptions that derive from European thought, as it has descended from its two most influential figures, Descartes and Kant. From these two thinkers, an emphasis on the importance of rational thought and on the deep insinuation of categories of thought into every conceivable human experience has served as the intellectual support for the development of historicist and social-scientific approaches to the study of religion. In effect, these approaches constitute a set of "external studies" that only examine the "objectively observable" aspects of religions, such as their institutions, the interaction of their institutions with society, their internal power relations, and so on. The effect is to exclude religious experience and human subjectivity from serious critical examination because they are internal. Yet it is precisely these internal experiences that for William James were the very heart of religion and that should still be the very heart of any serious approach to studying both religion and human cognition:

> In one sense at least the personal religion will prove itself more fundamental than either theology or ecclesiasticism. Churches, when once established, live at second-hand upon tradition; but the founders of every church owed their power originally to the fact of their direct personal communion with the divine. Not only the superhuman founders, the Christ, the Buddha, Mahomet, but all originators of Christian sects have been in this case;—so personal religion should still seem the primordial thing, even to those who continued to esteem it incomplete.[18]

Thus for James the subjective religious experience of human beings (what he calls in the quotation above "personal religion") is the very essence of religion, yet it is seriously ignored in the modern academy. All this has far-reaching implications. By completely abandoning the subjectivity of religion as a serious topic of rational inquiry, we have abandoned the field entirely to religious practitioners, who may indeed place dogmatic faith in the truths of their religion as the primary article of practice. By turning our backs on the systematic exploration of religious subjectivity from the inside out, so to speak, we have also cut ourselves off from a valuable approach to the many problems of human existence. We have ignored a valuable source of empirical knowledge that has been well developed in the contemplative traditions of Asia, and we deny ourselves a potentially valuable method for studying these traditions.

I would argue that the very reason we have become so devoted to historicist approaches to religion is that we are still dominated by the cognitive imperialist bias. The limited view of human cognition that it entails developed from the struggles of the European Enlightenment and the split that arose therein between science and religion. Alan Wallace argues that this perspective had led to what he calls a kind of "metaphysical realism" that results in an "objectivist" view of the world whose principles are as follows:

1. The real world consists of mind-independent objects;

2. There is exactly one true and complete description of the way the world is;

3. Truth involves some sort of correspondence between an existing world and our description of it;[19]

4. That it is not only possible but desirable for scientists and scholars to describe the world from the "God's-eye" viewpoint of a completely detached, objective, and value-neutral observer.[20]

As Wallace has cogently argued, this is the foundation of the scientific materialism that so dominates our modern understandings of the world and ourselves. What is missing is precisely that subjectivity which is the basis of all our experience of ourselves and the world. On the scientific level, human subjectivity is the source for all the conceptual models we develop to explain the underlying structures of the world in the physical sciences and the underlying structures of consciousness in the cognitive sciences. All scientific experimentation used to establish these underlying "truths" is also a product of human subjectivity. Thus, despite all the principles of experimental science that attempt to establish objective standards for research, they all, in the last analysis, are derived by human beings, and therefore they are grounded in human subjectivity. Because of our headlong quest for scientific certainty in an objectivist-materialist world, we have in general ignored this important foundation, and this is true not only for scientists but for scholars of religion as well.

Ruling out the systematic exploration of human subjectivity on the grounds that it is not a veridical epistemological source has given both scientific researchers and religion scholars a considerable amount of control over their subject matter and a rationale for their approach, yet at the same time it severely restricts it. If human cognition can be effectively reduced to the product of preexisting historical, social, and political forces, then it can be valuable to study only as a product of these forces, and it provides no new insights in its own right. Yet the very history of human inventiveness flies in the face of this notion, for if people only experience what their culture imprints on them, how can anything new arise? Clearly something else must be going on. We cannot understand this something else without fully appreciating the importance of subjectivity.

Furthermore, by failing to explore human subjectivity, scholars of religion and cognitive scientists remain blind to the very personal, subjective, ethnocentric, and cognitive imperialistic biases of their own approaches. Failing to contextualize their own methodological positions, they are very much reminiscent of those whom Nagarjuna criticizes for failing to apply emptiness to their own arguments: "Emptiness wrongly grasped utterly destroys the dumb-witted, like a snake picked up by the wrong end or a magical spell incanted backwards."[21]

The Intersubjective Universe

The objectivist model of the universe that underlies the unreflective ethnocentrism and cognitive imperialism pervading the fields of cognitive science and religious studies is not without challenge, if we would only expand our vision to include non-Western sources. Alan Wallace, Francisco Varela, and Evan Thompson have explored Buddhist visions of the universe and how these can inform the development of new models in understanding how the subjective and objective perspectives can mutually inform one another in order to give a more accurate and more scientific vision of the world, and I return to these a bit later. But first I wish to examine a cosmology of considerable antiquity that poses a serious challenge to European objectivism: the Chinese model proffered by the classical Daoist thinker Zhuangzi 莊子.

The Vision from Classical China

Zhuangzi, one of the foundational thinkers of the Daoist tradition, lived, taught, and wrote around the year 300 BCE. If the arguably more famous

Laozi 老子 analyzes the Way—the force that interfuses all phenomena yet cannot be fully known as an object—from the position of a neutral observer, Zhuangzi does so from a position that is clearly enmeshed within the subjective.[22] Arguing that any "objectivist" position contradicts itself, Zhuangzi criticizes the philosophical schools of his day for affirming their own limited truths as if they were universal:

> For there to be [objective standards of] true and false before they have formed in the human mind would be [as ridiculous as the Sophistic saying] "I go to [the state of] Yue 越 today but I arrived yesterday." This would be crediting with existence what has no existence; and if you do that, even the mythological sage Yu 禹 could not understand you, and how can you expect to be understood by me?[23]

The true nature of phenomena cannot be known from an independent, value-neutral position because there is no one perspective from which all agree on that truth. As Zhuangzi says,

> If being so is inherent in a thing, if being acceptable [in debate] is inherent in a thing, then from no perspective would it not be so, from no perspective would it not be acceptable.[24]

The reason for this is that our knowledge of that thing is always subjective and relational:

> Without an other there is no self; without self there is no choosing one thing over another.[25]

The problem for Zhuangzi is that we fail to recognize that all attempts to assert objective truths from a fixed standpoint are contingent and nonabsolute:

> Saying is not just blowing breath; saying says something: the only trouble is that what it says is never fixated. Do we really say something? Or have we never said anything? If you think saying is different from the chirping of fledglings, is there proof of the distinction? Or isn't there any proof? By what is the Way hidden that there should be a genuine or a false?

> By what is saying darkened, that sometimes we say that "this
> is true" and "that is false"? Wherever we walk, how can the
> Way be absent? Whatever the standpoint, how can a saying
> be labeled as false? The Way is hidden by the formation of
> the lesser, saying is darkened by its foliage and flower. And so
> we have statements that "this is true" and "that is false" each
> made by [the rival schools] of the Confucians and Mohists,
> by which what is true for one of them for the other is false,
> and what is false for one of them for the other is true. If you
> wish to affirm what they deny and deny what they affirm, the
> best means is Illumination.[26]

Zhuangzi suggests here that there is a way to cognize the world from a
perspective that is free of the limitations of the relativity of subjective
truths:

> What is It is also Other; what is Other is also It: There
> someone says "This is true, that's false" from one point of
> view; here we say "This is true, that's false" from another
> point of view. Are there really It and Other? Or really no It
> and Other? Where neither It nor Other finds its opposite is
> called the Axis of the Way. Once the axis is found at the
> center of the circle, there is no limit to responding with
> either, on the one hand, no limit to what is It and, on the
> other, no limit to what is not. Therefore I say: "The best
> means is Illumination."[27]

Once again Zhuangzi suggests another mode of cognizing the world
using what he calls "illumination," the perspective that is identical to
the perspective of the Way, a position that transforms the common rigid
cognition from a fixed, self-affirming objectivist perspective to one that
is able to shift with the constantly changing circumstances:

> Therefore when fixated cognition picks out a stalk from a
> pillar, a hag from beautiful Xishi 西施, things however peculiar
> and incongruous, the Way pervades and unifies them. As they
> divide they develop, as they develop they dissolve. All things
> whether developing or dissolving revert to being pervaded and

unified. Only those who penetrate this know how to pervade and unify things. They do not use fixated cognition, but find temporary lodging places in [the transformations of] daily life. It is in daily life that they make use of this perspective. It is in making use of this perspective that they pervade things. It is in pervading things that they attain it. And when they attain it, they are almost there. Their flowing cognition comes to an end. It ends, and when it does, that of which we do not know what is so of it, we call the Way.[28]

For Zhuangzi, the Way is directly apprehended and affirmed in the experience of dropping away all dualistic categories such as "so" and "not so," "It" and "Other." This affirmation is the basis of being able to cognize the world as it is, a complex interrelated series of constantly changing subject-object perspectives, a complex world *not* of independent objects (including oneself) that move around in empty space, but a complex world of interdependent, multi-relational, and completely mutable subjectivities. It is hence *intersubjective* in a profound way.

How can we reach this intersubjective perspective? Through the careful, subjective deconstruction of our fixated ideas of the self, accomplished through the apophatic practices of what I have called "inner cultivation."[29] For Zhuangzi, this includes such consciousness-altering practices as "sitting and forgetting," (described in the sixth chapter of the *Zhuangzi*); the "fasting of the mind," (described in chapter 4); "putting the things we live on outside ourselves" (chapter 6); "treating our self as other" (chapter 2); and pervading and unifying (chapter 2).[30] These are elements of a contemplative practice that first involves an emptying out of the usual contents of consciousness—thoughts, feelings, perceptions—until a condition of "embodying" or being merged with the Way is realized. This is its "introvertive" mode done while sitting completely still. There is then a second resulting "extrovertive" mode, which is realized when the practitioner returns to activity in the dualistic world of subjects and objects, all the while understanding its fundamental intersubjectivity and retaining an awareness of how the Way pervades this world and one's own subjective experience. This is called many things in the *Zhuangzi*, including "letting both alternatives proceed," "finding things their point of rest on the Potter's wheel of Heaven," "flowing cognition (*yinshi* 因 是)," and, as in our passages above, "using illumination."

New Developments in Cognitive Science

There is a newly emerging movement in cognitive science that has broken free of Western epistemological biases and asserts that human experience is fundamentally both embodied and intersubjective. Pioneered by the late cognitive neuroscientist Francisco Varela and his colleagues Eleanor Rosch and Evan Thompson, this approach describes an "enactive" approach to cognition, asserting that human cognition is fundamentally grounded in the subjective experience of our minds within a physical body and is hence both simultaneously subjective and objective. As Thompson states:

> We propose as a name the term enactive to emphasize the growing conviction that cognition is not the representation of a pre-given world by a pre-given mind but is rather the enactment of a world and a mind on the basis of a history of the variety of actions that a being in the world performs.[31]

Developed to counter the deliberate omission of lived subjective experience in theories of human cognition, this perspective draws upon the hermeneutic philosophies of Heidegger and Gadamer, who argue that cognition is embodied, in the sense that it depends on being in a world inseparable from our experience of our bodies, our language, and our social history. As Varela and his colleagues state:

> If we are forced to admit that cognition cannot be properly understood without common sense, and that common sense is none other than our bodily and social history, then the inevitable conclusion is that knower and known, mind and world, stand in relation to each other through mutual specification or dependent co-origination. If this critique is valid, then scientific progress in understanding cognition will not be forthcoming unless we start from a different basis from the idea of a pre-given world that exists "out there" and is internally recovered in a representation [in here].[32]

In other words, human cognition is not at all a subjective representation of an objective world; it is, rather, the constantly shifting enactment of a myriad of worlds of experience that are context-interactive (simultaneously subjective and objective). Citing phenomenologists Merleau-Ponty and Husserl, Thompson further argues that our very self-identity has no meaning without "Otherness" being implicated in the very structure of our consciousness:

> "I" and "other" are not simply co-relative and interchangeable, like the spatial perspectives of "here" and "there." . . . "I-ness" is already internally constituted by "otherness." Experience is intrinsically intersubjective in the sense that alterity and openness to the other are a priori characteristics of the formal structure of experience.[33]

Wallace too supports this fundamental intersubjectivity as a primary insight into human experience developed by the tradition of Indo-Tibetan Buddhism:

> The theme of intersubjectivity lies at the very core of the Indo-Tibetan Buddhist way of viewing the world. . . . According to this worldview, each person does exist as an individual, but the self . . . does not exist as an independent ego that is somehow in control of the body and mind. Rather the individual is understood as a matrix of dependently related events, all of them in a state of flux. . . . (1) The self arises in dependence on prior contributing causes and conditions. . . . In this way our existence is invariably intersubjective, for we exist in a causal nexus in which we are constantly influenced by, and exert influence upon, the world around us. . . . (2) The individual self does not exist independently of the body and mind, but rather exists in reliance upon a myriad of physical and mental processes that are constantly changing. (3) The misperception of a fixed self arises from ignorance of these insights and through conceptual imputation.[34]

For precisely these reasons, we cannot ignore human subjectivity by the intellectual trick of pretending that it doesn't exist or isn't relevant, as we find in the cognitive imperialist perspective. If we do this, we are living in what Zen master Jōshū Sasaki has called a "two-dimensional" world, one in which I appear to stand apart from a preexisting objective world affirming truths from my position of a fixed self, as if it were the only one possible. This seems to also have been well understood by Zhuangzi:

> Is this [theory] acceptable? Yes it is. Is that [theory] unacceptable? Yes it is. A Way develops as we walk it; things become so by being called so. Why are they so? They are so from where they are so. Why are they not so? They are not so from where they are not so. . . . Therefore when someone with a fixated mode of cognition differentiates between a stalk and a pillar, a hag from a beauty, things however peculiar or incongruous, the Way pervades and unifies them.[35]

In other words, from the ecstatic and illumined vision of Zhuangzi, none of the perspectives in the enacted world are anything more than relatively true to their own standpoints. One who is confined within such a standpoint has no way to see this. Only the sage who "sees right through," and whose embodiment of the Way has transformed her cognition from fixated to flowing, is able to know this and to respond without prejudice and attachment to any situation. The ability to do this is based upon the experience of embodying or merging with the Way, an experience in which the dualities of subject and object, and subject and subject, fall away. As we saw above, Zhuangzi asserts that when "flowing cognition comes to an end. . . . that of which we do not know what is so of it, we call the Way."[36]

Varela and Thompson rely on Mādhyamika philosophy instead of Daoism to deal with the nonreliance on either objectivity or subjectivity, and they speak of the realization of the fundamental groundlessness of human experience and its concomitant awareness of empathy and compassion.[37] Working within the Dzogchen tradition of Tibetan Buddhism, Wallace's position is closer to that of Zhuangzi. He speaks of the training of consciousness through śamathā (meditative quiescence) so that

> Discursive thoughts become dormant and all appearances of oneself, others, one's body and one's environment vanish as one attains experiential access to the relative ground-state of consciousness known as "substrate consciousness" (ālaya vijñāna) . . . a state of radiant clear consciousness that is the basis for the emergence of all appearances to an individual's

mind stream. All phenomena appearing to sensory and mental perception are imbued with the innate luminosity of this substrate consciousness.[38]

Each of these writers posits somewhat different sources for the intersubjective world: the Way, groundlessness and substrate consciousness. What is clear is that none of these is possible to conceive of, much less experience, if we remain trapped within the cognitive imperialist position. What is also clear is that the systematic training of consciousness through contemplative disciplines is a prerequisite for truly understanding and experiencing the role of the subjective in this intersubjective world. What Evan Thompson says about cognitive science is equally true of the study of contemplative experience in the major wisdom traditions of the world:

> I believe that a mature science of mind would have to include disciplined first-person methods of investigating subjective experience in active partnership with the third-person bio-behavioral science. "First-person methods" are practices that increase an individual's sensitivity to his or her own experience through the systematic training of attention and self-regulation of emotion. This ability to attend reflexively to experience itself—to attend not simply to what one experiences (the object) but to how one experiences it (the act)—seems to be a uniquely human ability and mode of experience we do not share with other animals. First-person methods for cultivating this ability are found primarily in the contemplative wisdom traditions of human experience, especially Buddhism. Throughout history religion has provided the main home for contemplative experience and its theoretical articulation in philosophy and psychology. . . . Thus [religion is] a repository of first-person methods that can play an active and creative role in scientific investigation itself.[39]

For Thompson and Wallace, this systematic training of the mind to investigate itself has been developed in the pan-Buddhist practices of *śamathā* and *vipaśyanā*, stopping and seeing, mental concentration and focused insight. I have argued that similar practices are present in foundational

Daoism. Both Thompson and Wallace imply that these practices can be taken out of an exclusively monastic setting and used to develop what the latter calls a genuine "Contemplative Science." I would assert that we can do this as well in the sphere of religion.

A truly non-ethnocentric study of the contemplative experiences found in the world's religions would entail a number of things. The first is that we remain open-minded to them and do not a priori commit ourselves to the historicist reductionism that assumes that these experiences are epistemologically invalid. The second entails an admission of the fact that despite pretending to be objective and value neutral, scholars of religion and human cognition have their own subjective biases that are deeply enmeshed in their cultural presuppositions about the nature of religion and in their own personal experience of it. This has everything to do with how we pursue the study of religion, the kinds of issues we select, and the arguments we attempt to prove.

It would be fascinating to hear from Boyer, Katz, and McCutcheon just what their own actual *experience* of religion has been. I would suspect it is totally Eurocentric. Rather than pretend their intellectual positions are objective, these scholars owe their audiences a full and complete explanation of their own subjective influences. (In the interests of full disclosure, I myself was raised with both Reformed Jewish and Christian Scientist influences; embraced Freud, Camus, and Sartre before college; began studying Confucianism, Daoism, and Buddhism at university; and have since done serious practice in a number of Asian contemplative traditions: Hindu, Daoist, and Buddhist, particularly in the tradition of Japanese Rinzai Zen.)

In addition to openly discussing the subjective factors that have influenced our attitudes toward the study of contemplative practices in religion, I would also recommend the pursuit of an approach that is, as Thompson suggests, both third-person and first-person. The historical and social-scientific study of religion constitutes the former, and systematic training in a contemplative tradition constitutes the latter. In effect, what I am calling for is nothing other than what former Berkeley professor Frits Staal called for more than three decades ago in his pioneering, but now unjustly overlooked, work *Exploring Mysticism*:

> If mysticism is to be studied seriously, it should not merely be studied indirectly and from without, but also directly and from within. Mysticism can at least in part be regarded as

something affecting the human mind, and it is therefore quite unreasonable to expect that it could be fruitfully studied by confining oneself to literature about or contributed by mystics, or to the behavior and physiological characteristics of mystics and their bodies. No one would willingly impose upon himself such artificial constraints when exploring other phenomena affecting or pertaining to the mind; he would not study perception only by analyzing reports of those who describe what they perceive, or by looking at what happens to people and their bodies when they are engaged in perceiving. What one would do when studying perception, in addition, if not first of all, is to observe and analyze one's own perceptions.[40]

It is my contention that contemplative experiences, all sorts of religious experiences, and human cognition itself can most productively and accurately be studied only by this dual approach. Whether or not departments of the comparative study of religions in North American universities can sufficiently free themselves from the pernicious influences of unreflective ethnocentrism and cognitive imperialism to allow this kind of dual approach to be established remains to be seen. I, for one, remain very pessimistic about the open-mindedness of the entire field.

So what are we to do if we are interested in training contemplative scientists and religion scholars in the basic methods of contemplation? Can this training only be accomplished in a monastic setting? Or is there a way to bring it into the academy to enrich not just research but also pedagogy?

The Field of Contemplative Studies

A new field of academic endeavor devoted to the critical study of contemplative states of experience is developing in North America. It focuses on the many ways human beings have found, across cultures and across time, to concentrate, broaden, and deepen conscious awareness. Contemplative studies is the rubric under which this research and teaching can be organized. In the field of contemplative studies, we attempt to:

1. Identify the varieties of contemplative experiences of which human beings are capable;

2. Find meaningful scientific explanations for them;

3. Cultivate first-person knowledge of them;

4. Critically assess their nature and significance.

That is, we study the underlying philosophy, psychology, and phenomenology of human contemplative experience through a combination of traditional third-person approaches and more innovative, critical first-person approaches. In other words, we study contemplative experiences from the following perspectives:

1. Science, particularly psychology, neuroscience, cognitive science, and clinical medicine;

2. The humanities, exploring the contemplative dimensions of literature, philosophy, and religion;

3. The creative arts, focusing on the study of the role of contemplation in both the creation and the appreciation of the visual and fine arts, creative writing, and in the various performing arts of dance, drama, and music.

Central to this approach is the understanding that contemplative experiences are not confined exclusively to religion. While various methods to attain contemplative states of consciousness can most certainly be found in religious practices, such states can also be found in a wide variety of nonreligious practices, such as making or listening to music, dancing, acting, writing poetry or prose, painting, sculpting, and even the intent observation of the natural world. Following the pioneering research on the state of optimal experience called "flow" by Mihalyi Csíkszentmihályi and his colleagues,[41] contemplative studies seeks to discover the complete range of experiences of attention, focus, tranquility, and insight and to demonstrate that even the most profound of these experiences—those deliberately cultivated in the world's great contemplative traditions—are not of a fundamentally different kind than the most shallow. All occur on a continuous spectrum of experience that can be rationally identified, scientifically researched, and subjectively experienced.

With regard to science, as the first major area of contemplative studies, there is now more than four decades' worth of scientific research into the nature of meditation and its cognitive impact. We can break down this research into four areas:

1. Clinical Applications: Meditation has been applied clinically most often by using Mindfulness-Based Stress Reduction (MBSR) and has been studied by Jon Kabat-Zinn, Zindel Segal, and Ruth Baer, among others. There are also the medical applications of Transcendental Meditation and the variant of it studied by Herbert Benson, as well as the application of yoga, qigong, and taiji.[42]

2. Cognitive Activity: This research, for example, by Amishi Jha and Stephen Kosslyn, explores how meditation influences cognitive functioning in both advanced and beginning meditators.[43]

3. Neurological Measurements: EEG and MRI research on both advanced and beginning meditators has been carried out by Richard Davidson, Jonathan Cohen, and Clifford Sauron.[44]

4. Positive Psychology, the scientific study of the strengths and virtues that enable individuals and communities to thrive, has developed in the past decade under the guidance of such researchers as Martin Seligman, Mihalyi Csíkszentmihályi, and Jonathan Haidt).[45]

All these areas of study, taken together, might well be considered contemplative science, and Alan Wallace has detailed how we might best approach such a discipline.[46] However, a full discussion of how third-person and first-person perspectives are blended in this category is well beyond what I can present here. I hope it will suffice to say that the best of these researchers do intimately combine these perspectives.

In the humanities, the second major area of contemplative studies, the focus has largely been on the study of the role of contemplation in philosophy (particularly phenomenology and philosophy of mind) in literature and in the comparative study of religion. Critical first-person methods are just beginning to be developed in the study of religion, and they are quite controversial. In this category, I would include the course I have regularly taught at Brown University for eight years now. Titled "The Theory and Practice of Buddhist Meditation," it includes both a regular weekly seminar of three hours and three one-hour "lab" sessions each week in which students try out meditation techniques that are directly related to the text we are reading in the seminars.[47]

The third major area of contemplative studies is the creative arts. Here we explore the production of contemplative states of consciousness via the actual creation of art. For example, at our program in contemplative studies at Brown, we offer several classes in which students write their own poetry in class using cues and key words from their professor. We also teach a course on how the hearing of music affects the mind.

From the perspective of an educator, what is the point of all this?

1. In general, it is to begin to give students a solid understanding—both third-person and first-person—of the range of the contemplative experiences that they may encounter in their lives: what these experiences are, how to understand them when they spontaneously occur, and how to deliberately cultivate them.

2. In particular, it is to give students practical training in a range of techniques to attain calmness, tranquility, and attentional stability.

3. The attainment of states of calmness, tranquility and attentional stability, and focus are important tools to use in:

    a. Self-exploration and self-understanding. (If the purpose of a university education is "to know thyself," there is no better means to do so than through contemplative training.)

    b. Developing a sound grasp of the nature of consciousness as a basis for further philosophical and scientific studies.

    c. First-person approaches to the study of religion. Again, religious experience is essential to the study of religion, and it is my hope that we will someday create a generation of scholars who combine historical studies of religion with firsthand experience.

William James well understood the importance of this type of training:

The faculty of voluntarily bringing back a wandering attention, over and over again, is the very root of judgment, character and will. . . . An education which should improve this faculty would be the education par excellence. But it is easier to define this ideal than to give practical directions for bringing it about.[48]

We are finally reaching the point where James's pessimism about the existence of methods for training the attention can give way to a new optimism about incorporating these methods as essential tools of higher education. I firmly believe that to do so will significantly broaden our perspectives on the nature and structure of human experience, breaking us out of the objectivism and scientific materialism that have dominated the academy for far too long. If we can accomplish this, we will finally project ourselves past a world of knowledge dominated by unreflective ethnocentrism and cognitive imperialism and into a fuller appreciation of a world in which subjective and objective fields of experience, in all their varieties, are on an equal footing.

Afterword

The "Contemplative Hermeneutic" and the Problem of *Zhuangzi*'s Inner Chapters

I would like to end this collection with a few words about the vast temporal-spatial jigsaw puzzle of the early history and philosophy of the tradition of practice and theory that came to be called "Daoism." I stand in awe of the challenge of filling in the missing pieces of this puzzle, most of which we may never know. At the same time I want to also recognize that we must approach this difficult task with as many of the tools from the toolkit of the cultural historian as we can.

The first of these is surely archaeology. Because of the archaeological discoveries of the past half century we are starting to locate and circumscribe (in the apt phrase of the title of chapter 11 of the *Zhuangzi* "Zai you" 在宥) more of these missing pieces. The manuscripts excavated from tombs that can reliably be dated from the fourth to the second centuries BCE have filled in some of these missing pieces but also extended the boundaries of the puzzle to previously unknown locations. Texts like the *Taiyi sheng shui* 太一生水 (Grand Unity Generates Water) from Guodian (ca. 310 BCE), the *Shiwen* 十問 (Ten Questions) from Mawangdui and the *Wuxing* 五行 (Five Conducts) from both tombs have enriched our understanding of the philosophical tradition via works previously unknown. These works and others like them as well as the parallel passages to extant works from the received tradition like the *Laozi* 老子 also found in both these sites have increased the challenges to certain cherished historical beliefs that have been transmitted for millennia in China.

The second of these tools is historical criticism. The post-modernist intellectual revolution has led to the serious questioning of many of the accepted historical shibboleths that have dominated Chinese historiography for centuries. I have identified a number of these in the introduction to this book as they pertain to the study of classical Daoism. I have also mentioned the importance of the challenges to the classification of the Six "Schools" of Chinese philosophy raised by Sarah Queen and by Michael Nylan and Mark Csíkszentmíhalyi that have helped us to think more critically about such traditional systems of organization.[1]

The third of these tools is textual criticism in its varied forms including textual analysis, philology, and bibliography. It is to this tool that I would like to turn my attention, especially as it pertains to the study of one of the foundational works of the classical Daoist tradition, and one to which I have devoted a significant amount of writing over the course of my academic career, as reflected in this collection. This is, of course, the Zhuangzi.

While this collection of published articles contains its fair share of textual criticism, there is a fourth tool with which I have combined it: something I would like to call a "contemplative hermeneutic." What this means is that in examining the creation and transmission of the textual record of the pre-Han and early Han traditions it is important that we always bear in mind that these texts emerge from specific social contexts that involved not just philosophy but also practices. This is particularly relevant in two recent and excellent articles on the text of the Zhuangzi by Esther Klein, and Stefan Peter Bumbacher.[2] The work of these two scholars seriously calls into question much of what we have come to believe about the nature of this collection. Their conclusions have done much to influence the scholarly consideration of this important question and as I conclude this collection I feel it is important to place their insightful textual critical work into this somewhat broader context.

As I have argued throughout the chapters of this collection, the surviving texts of the tradition later called "Daojia" 道家 (the family or lineage of the Way) by Sima Tan 司馬談 show a significant pattern of shared ideas in the categories of cosmology, self-cultivation, and political thought. These ideas constitute a kind of philosophical "fingerprint" with a unique and readily identifiable set of distinctive meanings and relationships with one another. While it is unlikely that these fingerprints indicate the existence of anything as organized as what would be called a "philosophical school" in the style of Greek Sophists or Epicureans, the commonalities in thought and practice presented in the pages of this book indicate that the people who created and transmitted these texts

shared a worldview in which the contemplative practices of inner cultivation were central. Whether it be the apophatic meditative practices of
emptying out the normal contents of consciousness called "cleaning out
the lodging place of the spirit," "wiping clear the profound mirror," "the
fasting of the mind or "sitting and forgetting," all practices that focus the
attention and lead to the flowing cognition of "cognitive attunement,"
the evidence for contemplative practices in our textual sources can no
longer be doubted. Or, at least, it is now incumbent on those who doubt
this to argue how to interpret these sources in a different way.

It is important to remember that the transmission of texts and of
practices does not occur in a vacuum; it is the result of the life activity
of the people who created them and the social organizations of those
people who transmitted them. The creation, preservation, and transmission of texts during the Warring States and early Han were not easy due
to the immense challenges of life in those several centuries before the
Han unification. This included the scarcity of writing materials and of
literate people to use them. Textual creation and transmission also had
to be fairly localized at least at first, because of the many state borders
and relentless warfare that took place within and between them during
this period. Because of this, most of the traditions for which we have
evidence must have begun locally within certain states. Further, they
very likely began with the direct teaching of distinctive practices to
students that included texts related to practices and the insights derived
from them that began with oral transmission.[3] Thus when written texts
emerge, two of the most common literary genres are rhymed tetra syllabic
verse—what I have called "early Daoist wisdom poetry"—and didactic
narratives, both of which are easier to remember than logically argued
essays.[4] Because of this, Sima Tan must have known at least representative texts and the practices they transmitted when he put together his
classification of the "Six Traditions." Even though this scheme may have
had bibliographical value it is unlikely that he created these categories
completely out of his imagination. Much more likely is that he was creating these categories based on his understanding of the transmission of
distinctive patterns of thought and practice via master-student lineages.

The point I would like to make here is that we have not yet sufficiently taken into account the implications of the distinctive practices
that Sima Tan associates with each of his "traditions" for the creation
and transmission of the texts that have survived from the Warring States
period. We have seen that for each of the traditions he identified, he

lists a specific practice (*shu* 術): ritual performance for the Rujia (the tradition of scholarship, popularly called the "Confucians"); bureaucratic management for the Fajia (the tradition of legal organization, popularly called the "Legalists"), apophatic inner cultivation and its application for the Daojia (the tradition of the Way, popularly called "Daoists"), and so on.[5] The very creation and transmission of texts that are grounded in the mastery of a foundational practice requires a social context in which organizations of people are involved, even if these organizations are as minimal as the basic structure of the teacher-student relationship. Volker Scheid, in his groundbreaking history of a 400 year old tradition of classical Chinese medicine aptly states:

> . . . a practice relies on the transmission of skills and exper-
> tise between masters and novices. As novices develop into
> masters themselves, they change who they are but also earn
> a say in defining the goods that the practice embodies and
> seeks to realize. To accomplish these tasks human beings need
> narratives: stories about who they are, what they do, and why
> they do it. Traditions provide these narratives. They allow
> people to discover problems and methods for their solution,
> frame questions and possible answers, and develop institutions
> that facilitate cooperative action. But because people occupy
> changing positions vis-à-vis these narratives, traditions are
> also always open to change. . . .[6]

Hence it is not surprising that the tradition of Inner Cultivation practice and thought that Sima Tan called "Daoism" is neither fabricated for bibliographical reasons nor homogenous. It was created and transmitted via a variety of different literary forms (narratives, rhymed verse, didactic prose, argumentative essays) and interpreted in different ways by each of the groups of authors who composed its surviving texts: those I have heuristically placed into the categories of "Individualist," "Primitivist," and "Syncretist," following the lead of A. C. Graham. However, while Graham limited these categories to sections of the *Zhuangzi*, my analysis is actually closer to that of Liu Xiaogan, who places the various sections of the book he identifies into broader historical categories that relate to other extant texts, as I have done.[7]

One of the cherished assumptions of classical Chinese literature to which Graham and Liu, and most other scholars all subscribe, is that the core of the *Zhuangzi* is the "Inner Chapters," and it is very likely written by the historical figure of Zhuang Zhou. I think the patchwork nature of most of the chapters and the variety of literary styles within them makes this a questionable hypothesis but I really don't think this is the key relevant issue. These Inner Chapters need not have been written by a single hand to constitute the core of the text. Rather, their most important quality is that they represent a consistent position with regard to certain key philosophical ideas and the contemplative practices that underlie them: the cosmology of the Way, the relativity of exclusively dualistic intellectual positions, the acceptance of change and death as a natural transformation, apophatic meditation practice, the importance of developing consummate skills in living that manifest a direct grounding in the Way and, most importantly, the emphasis on "flowing cognition" and "cognitive attunement" as essential to those consummate skills. This then links these Inner Chapters to practices and ideas also found in other early texts, as I have argued in the pages of the present volume: the four "Techniques of the Mind" (*xinshu* 心術) texts from the *Guanzi* 管子, the *Laozi*, the *Huang-Lao bo shu* 黃老帛書, and four chapters of the *Lüshi chun qiu* 呂氏春秋 (3, 5, 17, and 25). All these texts unarguably precede the Han dynasty and contain evidence for the tradition of practice and thought I have called Inner Cultivation to which the above 13 chapters in the present volume, I think, amply attest. This is not a monolithic tradition: as Scheid so aptly states. Traditions of practice change over time and we should not expect nor insist on total consistency. What we should look for, instead, is whether or not there is sufficient evidence of the sharing of practices—contemplative practices in this case—and a sufficient evidence of a common vocabulary for contextualizing these practices and understanding their results, even if the precise meaning of this vocabulary changes as the tradition evolves. So whether or not the historical Zhuangzi authored the Inner Chapters of his eponymous text is much less important than the shared understanding of apophatic inner cultivation practice that its author or authors shared with this larger pre-Han practice tradition. The recent challenges to the single authorship theory and the primacy of the Inner Chapters by Klein and Bumbacher that are otherwise quite astute have unfortunately not taken this perspective into account.

Both authors argue that there is a lack of evidence that the Inner Chapters or, indeed, the entire *Zhuangzi* (contra Liu and many others) existed as a text before the Western Han. They not only agree with most scholars that the traditional single author theory for the whole text is not viable, but also maintain that this is true of the authorship of the Inner Chapters, long thought to be the foundational core of the text. They further aver that there is no evidence that the Inner Chapters should even be regarded as that foundational core. Their arguments are essentially textual and bibliographical: because there are no citations of the Inner Chapters before the Han, no references to even their titles, and no excavated textual testimony to them, that the these seven chapters cannot be the core of the work. Both also express the opinion that Guo Xiang 郭象 (252–312 CE) completed such an extensive revision of the text when he redacted it to the 33-chapter received text from an original recension of 52 chapters that it is extremely difficult to know exactly what was in this larger, complete version and even how it was organized. This includes whether or not the received Inner Chapters were in the location in which we now find them.

Bumbacher further contends that this 52-chapter recension was likely not even the original version of the *Zhuangzi*, and that it was created out of a disordered collection of materials by the famed Han bibliographer, Liu Xiang 劉向 (77–6 BCE).[8] He is carefully trying to reconstruct both the pre-Guo Xiang and even pre-Liu Xiang version of the *Zhuangzi* and has developed a very sophisticated system of textual analysis in order to attempt this. This is an admirable project as is Klein's brilliant historicist challenge to the authority of the Inner Chapters as representing the original thought of the entire text.

I find much to agree with in their research. It is not difficult to agree that the Inner Chapters could have been either a collection of teachings of an original thinker redacted unevenly by disciples or the writings of several different thinkers who shared a common set of insights into the nature of mind and cosmos. Furthermore, it is true that we do not know the extent to which Guo Xiang expurgated the original *Zhuangzi*. However, we do know that there were seven chapters in three of the six redactions listed by Lu Deming 陸德明 (c. 606) in his *Jingdian shiwen* 經典釋文 and these seven chapters were in a section called "the inner chapters"(*neipian* 內篇) just as they are in the received text.[9] There seems little reason to doubt they were all based on the original complete 52-chapter recension. That's an important piece of evidence to which neither gives sufficient weight.

Of course one cannot know the influence that Liu Xiang had on most of the recensions of philosophical works in the Han Imperial Library that he collated as part of a major project of cleaning up the disordered collection of manuscripts it had become. However, I would ask how is Bumbacher's contention that he created his own organization for the new recensions he established any more likely than the contention that he attempted to remain true to the compositional structures of his sources? Certainly this was the case for the *Huainanzi*, which must have passed through his editorial hands.[10] Finally, since we do know that there are roughly 270 parallel passages between the *received Zhuangzi* and the *Huainanzi*, including materials from the Inner Chapters, this constitutes substantial evidence for the presence of an early recension in the court of Liu An, as I have argued in chapter 2 of the present volume.[11] Klein concurs with this. Bumbacher does not, but perhaps it is because he incorrectly asserts that I have argued that the *Huainanzi* versions of these *Zhuangzi* passages were the source for the 52 chapter recension.[12] Actually, I have contended in chapter 2 just the opposite: that the *Huainanzi* authors drew on inchoate *Zhuangzi* textual materials that had already been transmitted to them and created the 52 chapter recension of the text from these materials, not vice versa. Given their familiarity with so many passages that are now in the received *Zhuangzi* and the fact that despite this familiarity only once do they ever cite it as a source—in stark contrast to the way in which they treat their formal citations of other works like the *Laozi*—it is likely that the complete recension of the *Zhuangzi* was compiled at Huainan after the completion of the *Huainanzi* in 139 BCE. Therefore the *Huainanzi* passages that parallel the *Zhuangzi* are the closest versions we have of what Bumbacher is attempting to reconstruct: a pre-Liu Xiang recension. They cannot be ignored.

The arguments Klein and Bumbacher make against the Inner Chapters being the oldest stratum of the text also rely on citations of chapter titles of the received recension of the *Zhuangzi* that do not include chapters 1–7. Klein cites the important fact that the *Shiji* biography of the historical Zhuangzi mentions the titles for received chapter 10, "Rifling Coffers" (Qu qie 胠篋), chapter 29, "Robber Zhi" (Dao Zhi 盜跖), chapter 31, "The Old Fisherman" (Yu fu 漁父), and (as Klein perceptively points out) chapter 23 "Gengsang Chu 庚桑楚 of Weileixu 畏累虛.[13] Both scholars present details of the textual fragments now in the received *Zhuangzi* from early Western Han tombs at Zhangjia shan 張家山 (circa 170 BCE) and Fuyang 阜陽 (circa 165 BCE) that parallel passages now included in a number of chapters: an almost complete version of "Robber Zhi" (unfortunately only fragments of which have published to this point) in the former and three more chapters in the latter: 25 "Sunnyside" (Zeyang 則陽), 26, "External Things" (Waiwu 外物), and 28, "Abdicating the Throne" (Rang wang 讓王).[14] These are all from the section of the text now called "Miscellaneous Chapters" (*zapian* 雜篇), generally thought to be the final section of the book. They argue that if the Inner Chapters was the core and hence oldest stratum of the *Zhuangzi*, then why would virtually the only evidence to them before the *Huainanzi* be from the sections supposedly compiled last?

Let us set aside for the moment the fact that the excavated fragments do not explicitly say they are from the *Zhuangzi* and assume that these fragments from both tombs and the chapter titles listed by them are from an early version of the *Zhuangzi*. Following the line of argument I took in chapter 2, let's say that this version was likely not complete. Let's call it the "proto-*Zhuangzi*." Of course this could testify to the absence of the Inner Chapters in that partial version, which is what Klein and Bumbacher assume. However, another viable interpretation of this data could simply be that these particular chapters were included in this "proto-*Zhuangzi*" but were simply not physically placed at the beginning of this text. Or that they were, but the tomb occupants were not as interested in the Inner Chapters. As almost all of these references are from what many think is the final stratum of the *Zhuangzi*, this last stratum could simply have come first in the "proto-*Zhuangzi*" the tomb occupants possessed. We see an example of this kind of altered textual composition in the Mawangdui *Laozi* manuscripts, in which the second half of the text, chapters 38–81, precede the first half, chapters 1–37 in all directly transmitted recensions. This kind of compositional fluidity may have been more the rule than the exception, as Sarah Allan has insightfully noted.[15] She argues that the rolled up bamboo strips that transmitted the early recensions of many philosophical classics from the pre-Han era could not contain large texts because of the physical limitations of this textual medium.[16] As a result, the received recensions transmitted to the present may very well have been constructed in the Western Han when silk scrolls dramatically increased as the medium of textual creation and transmission. These scrolls allowed longer texts to be constructed from the shorter ones. The archaeological evidence from excavated manuscripts lends support to the hypothesis in chapter 2 of the present volume that the complete 52-chapter recension of the *Zhuangzi* was created at Huainan.

Another interpretation of this historical data derives from the hypothesis in chapter 6 of the present volume that there was a copy of an early recension, the "proto-*Zhuangzi*" at the Qin court where the *Lüshi chunqiu* was being written and compiled circa 250–240 BCE. It is here, I argued, that the author whom Graham identifies at the "Primitivist," engaging in arguments with "Confucians," Mohists," and particularly "Yangists," became the first thinker in the Inner Cultivation "traditions of the Way" to present a theory of the innate natures of humans and animals (*xing* 性). Contained in the "Outer Chapters" (*Waipian* 外篇), chapters 8, "Webbed Toes" (Pianmu 駢拇), 9 "Horses Hooves" (Mati 馬蹄), 10 "Rifling Coffers," and the first part of 11, "Locating and Circumscribing," this theory would have perhaps been of considerable interest to literati for whom, at that time, issues of human nature were most pressing, given their direct relationship to the very pressing concern of which form of governing philosophy would be most effective in a united empire. These chapters are also famous, as are chapter 29, "Robber Zhi" and, to a lesser extent, chapter 31, "The Old Fisherman," for satirical and biting criticisms of Confucians and Mohists, particularly the figure of Confucius himself. These criticisms could possibly have been appealing to the tomb occupants, but even more so to Sima Qian who, as someone trained in the Daoist traditions of "Huang-Lao," would have been irritated to see the ascendency of Confucian ideas and bureaucrats during the latter part of the reign of Emperor Wu.

Furthermore, the fact that Sima Qian lists chapter 23 as belonging to the version of the text attributed to Zhuangzi that he reports in the *Historical Records juan* 63 is important and deserves further exploration. Most of this chapter, "Gengsang Chu," consists of a narrative that begins with this protagonist, an adept who has received only a partial understanding of the Way of his teacher, Lao Dan (by then the accepted author of the *Laozi*) teaching a student named Nanrong Chu 南榮趎. He advises him in words that could have come from foundational Inner Cultivation texts like "Inward Training:"

全汝形
抱汝生
无使思慮營營. (23/65/14–16)

Keep your body intact
Preserve your vitality
Do not be agitated by anxieties.

Unclear about what this means, Nanrong then journeys to see the old master, himself, Laozi. The instructions on inner cultivation practice then given to him by the Old Master as "The basic rules for guarding vitality" (*weisheng zhi jing* 衛生之經) include many important elements that can be clearly linked to the text of the *Laozi* 55 (to be like a child, preserving potency despite crying all day without getting hoarse) and almost verbatim to the text of "Inward Training":

能抱一乎?
能勿失乎?
能无卜筮
知吉凶乎?
能止乎?
能已乎?
能舍諸人
而求諸己乎?

(In concentrating your vital energy)
Can you embrace and unite with it?
Can you not lose it?
Can you not resort to divining by shell or stalk
And still know fortune and misfortune?
Can you stop (thoughts)?
Can you cease?
Can you not search for it in others
But, instead, find it in yourself?[17]

In addition to these strong textual parallels to these two Inner Cultivation texts, there are at least nine clear parallels to the Inner Chapters, five of which come from the most important of them, chapter 2, the "Essay on Seeing Things as Equal" (Qi wu lun 齊物論), about which I have written extensively in the present volume. In the first of these, Laozi here continues advising Nanrong to have a childlike mind

ZZ 23/65/24[18]: . . . 能兒子乎? 兒子動不知所為, 行不知所之 . . .

Can you be like a child? A child when moving doesn't have a purpose to what it is doing; when walking doesn't have a destination where it is going.

This parallels phrasing and the context of purposeless activity in this passage from the Primitivist Outer Chapter 9:

ZZ 9/24/10: 夫赫胥氏之時, 民居不知所為, 行不知所之 . . .

In the age of the clan of the Hexu, when at home the people did not have a purpose to what they their doing. When on the road, did not have a destination where they were going . . .

Laozi continues with the following unlikely but deliberately chosen description of a child:

身槁木之枝而心若死灰 . . .

Its body is like a branch of withered wood; its mind is like dead ashes

This famous description of meditative trance is found at the beginning of Inner Chapter 2, in which the adept Nanguo Ziqi 南郭子綦 is just emerging from a deep state of meditative concentration "in which his self had lost its other" (*sang qi ou* 喪其耦) and is asked

ZZ 2/3/14–15: 何居乎? 形固可使如槁木, 而心固可使如死灰乎?

Where were you? Can you really make your body like withered wood and your mind like dead ashes?

The directionality of borrowing between parallel passages is notoriously complex. Nonetheless, in this instance there is strong evidence for a direction. This narrative in *Zhuangzi* 23 already borrows from two Inner Cultivation sources that are clearly chronologically earlier, the *Laozi* and "Inward Training." This narrative continues immediately to these two other textual parallels with *Zhuangzi* 10 and 2. This strongly suggests these two sources were also earlier; in this case earlier parts of an established textual tradition.

There is additional evidence that the author of *Zhuangzi* 23 continued to borrow extensively from the Inner Chapters perhaps in an effort to synthesize received inner cultivation practices. There are five other significant examples, the first of which is this:

ZZ 23/66/3–4: 知止乎其所不能知, 至矣; 若有不即是者, 天鈞敗之。

When knowing stops at what it is not able to understand, this is perfection. Those who cannot attain this will be worn down by the whetstone of the heavens. . . .

The first two sentences echo phrases in two separate sections of *Zhuangzi* 2:

ZZ 2/6/2: 故知止其所不知, 至矣 . . . 若有能知, 此之謂天府

Thus when knowing stops at what it does not understand, this is perfection. If you are able to understand this this is called the storehouse of the heavens . . .

ZZ 2/5/5: 是以聖人和之以是非而休乎天鈞.

Therefore the sage harmonizes them with his affirming and denying and rests them on the whetstone of the heavens . . .

The narrative in chapter 23 continues:

ZZ 23/66/4: 備物以將形, 藏不虞以生心 . . . 若是而萬惡至者 . . . 不足以滑成, 不可內於靈臺 . . .

Provide sustenance for your body; remain unperturbed to nurture your mind. . . . If you do this and difficulties still arrive . . . They will not be enough to disturb your development and the effect of this will not be felt in your Numinous Terrace.

This clearly parallels a different passage from the Inner Chapters:

ZZ 5/15/5 故不足以滑和, 不可入於靈府。

Thus it is not enough to disturb your harmony and cannot enter into your Numinous Storehouse . . .

This is exactly the kind of "cut and paste" borrowing that we see in the many passages of the received text of the *Wenzi* that are almost exclusively taken from the *Huainanzi* and the *Laozi*.[19] It is a clear determinant of the directionality of textual borrowing.

This next passage in chapter 23 weaves together two disparate stories from different passages in the Inner Chapters to form one complete narrative:

ZZ 23/66/23–25: 古之人, 其知有所至矣。惡乎至? 有以為未始有物者, 至矣, 盡矣, 弗可以加矣。其次以為有物矣, 將以生為喪也, 以死為反也, 是以分已。其次曰始无有, 既而有生, 生俄而死; 以无有為首, 以生為體, 以死為尻; 孰知有无死生之一守者, 吾與之為友。

The people of ancient times, their knowledge contained perfection within it. There were those who thought that there has not yet begun to be things. Perfect! Exhaustive! I can add nothing to it. The next thought that there were things and they took living to be sorrow and dying to be a return. They therefore made this distinction. The next said that in the beginning when there was nothing, then there was living, and once there was living, suddenly there was dying. To take nothingness as your head, to take living as your body; to take dying as your rump: Anyone who knows how to unify something and nothing, living and dying: I will make them my friend . . .

This is a pastiche of the following two passages:

ZZ 2/5/8 古之人, 其知有所至矣。惡乎至? 有以為未始有物者, 至矣, 盡矣, 不可以加矣。其次以為有物矣, 而未始有封也。其次以為有封焉, 而未始有是非也

The people of ancient times, their knowledge contained perfection within it. In what way was it perfect? There were those who thought there had not yet begun to be things. Perfect! Exhaustive! I can add nothing to it. The next thought there were things but there had not yet begun to have borders around them. The next thought there were borders but there had not yet begun to be affirmation and negation . . .[20]

And

ZZ: 6/17/22: 子祀、子輿、子犁、子來四人相與語曰：「孰能以无為首，以生為脊，以死為尻，孰知死生存亡之一體者，吾與之友矣。」四人相視而笑，莫逆於心，遂相與為友。

Four masters Si, Yü, Li, and Lai were talking to one another and said: "Anyone who knows how to take nothingness as your head, to take living as your spine, take dying as your rump and understand how to unify living and dying, persisting and disappearing into a single body, I will make them my friends." The four mean looked at one another and smiled; there was no reluctance in their minds and so they befriend one another . . .[21]

There are a number of other textual parallels between chapter 23 and several of the Inner Chapters:

—23/66/14   parallels 2/4/24+2/5/1
—23/67/7–8 parallels 5/15/15

Furthermore, chapter 23 contains well-known images from the Inner Chapters:

—23/67/21   Choptoes (wuzhe 兀者[22]) found in 5/13/6, 23;
          and 5/14/7
—23/67/4   Cicada (tiao 蜩) found in 1/1/15
—23/67/5   Turtle dove (xue jiu 學鳩) found in 1/1/15
—23/66/11   Moye sword (moye 鏌鋣) found in 6/18/6

Thus, the very significant evidence from the nine parallel passages and four common images that chapter 23 shares with the Inner Chapters supports the idea that its authors drew on most of the Inner Chapters as well as two earlier Inner Cultivation textual sources to construct its constituent narratives and short essays. I have not have had the time or space here to complete as thorough an investigation of these textual materials as is needed and I hope that further research will follow on this foundation. Nonetheless I hope the data I have presented here are sufficient to show that the Inner Chapter sources had to have been chronologically earlier and already in existence when chapter 23 was created. When seen in light of the evidence provided throughout the many chapters of the present volume, chapter 23 of the *Zhuangzi* appears to be an attempt at creating a short compendium of teachings about contemplative practice and its results. Given the testimony to the existence of this chapter that Klein cites, that it existed when Sima Qian wrote the biography of the historical Zhuangzi circa 130 BCE, this suggests that we need further and more extensive research before we can accept the conclusions of Klein and Bumbacher that there is no testimony to the Inner Chapters constituting the original core around which the *Zhuangzi* collection was formed.

There is as yet no compelling reason to doubt that the text of the original 52 chapter recension of the *Zhuangzi* was compiled at the court of Liu An from a "proto-*Zhuangzi*"—textual materials already in existence that had been transmitted there. Despite the lack of concrete textual testimony to the Inner Chapters before they appear in the pages of the *Huainanzi*, the internal evidence to the extensive textual borrowing in chapter 23 supports the idea that the Inner Chapters were chronologically earlier than this chapter and were very likely a part of the "proto-*Zhuangzi*."

Furthermore, as I argued in chapter 6 above, the received chapters 8–11.5 were created as part of the debates that occurred at the Qin court of Lü Buwei in the decade leading up to the creation of the *Lüshi chunqiu*. I argue further there that chapters 28 and perhaps 29–31 are Primitivist materials that were also already present in the "proto-*Zhuangzi*" that was present there as well. These chapters are well attested prior to the gathering of the Huainan circle circa 150 BCE. From the perspective of what I am calling a "contemplative hermeneutic," all of these chapters depend on the transmission not just of textual materials but of apophatic inner cultivation practice. Furthermore, the evidence about the chronological priority of the Inner Chapters to the materials in chapter 23 further questions the conclusion that these seven chapters were not the original core of the collection. This does not, by any means, as I have written in chapter 6 above, prove that there was a complete original recension of the text already being transmitted by the middle of the third century BCE, as Liu Xiaogan has contended.

It simply means that there was a lineage of teachers and students, all of whom shared a common set of apophatic meditation practices, who created and transmitted the textual materials that were redacted into the 52 chapter text of the *Zhuangzi* at Huainan circa 130 BCE.

Texts do not occur in a vacuum. They are the products of human beings who form social organizations, often traditions of teachers and students. Often, these traditions do not just derive their authority from textual sources, they derive their authority from the transmission and mastery of specific practices that lead to the insights embodied in these texts. The very fact that today we have transmitted versions of any of these pre-Han texts implies the existence of generations of authors and transmitters, copyists and bibliographers, redactors and librarians. Despite the very compelling textual scholarship of Queen, Nylan and Csikszent-mihalyi, Klein, and Bumbacher, we cannot dispense with the idea that these texts were products of traditions of teachers and students who created and transmitted them and the practices that were foundational to them. Thus it is important to add a "contemplative hermeneutic" to the other tools of the cultural historian as we continue the "long game" of putting together the many pieces of the vast jigsaw puzzle of the history of the various early traditions of Chinese philosophy and religion. It is my hope that this collection will make a small contribution towards this worthy goal.

Notes

Introduction

1. There has been considerable scholarly controversy about the definition of the term "Daoism." Rather than delve into this in detail, I accept the recent clear definition of Louis Komjathy: "Daoism is a religious tradition in which the Dao, translatable as "the Way" and "a way," is the sacred and ultimate concern. "Daoism" is shorthand for Daoist adherents, communities, and their religious expressions." I further accept his definition of the "classical period" of Daoism as extending from the Warring States through the end of the Eastern Han dynasty (480 BCE–9 CE). See *The Daoist Tradition: An Introduction* (London and New York: Bloomsbury, 2013), 3–4 and 18–19, respectively.

2. Louis Komjathy, *Introducing Contemplative Studies* (London: Wiley, 2017); Harold D. Roth, "A Pedagogy for the New Field of Contemplative Studies," in Olen Gunnlaugson and Heeson Bai, eds., *Contemplative Approaches to Learning and Inquiry across Disciplines* (Albany, NY: State University of New York Press, 2014), 97–118; Frances Grace and Judith Simmer-Brown, eds., *Meditation and the Classroom: Contemplative Pedagogy for Religious Studies* (Albany, NY: State University of New York Press, 2011).

3. For a sustained argument about this, see Harold D. Roth, "Against Cognitive Imperialism," *Religion East and West* 8 (2008): 1–23. Also see chapter 12 of the present volume.

4. Arthur Waley, *The Way and Its Power*, 1st ed (London, 193, reprint, New York: Grove Press, 1958). Waley wrote perceptively in his introduction and in Appendix III about what I would now call "contemplative techniques" and what he called "Quietism" and "yoga." He linked quietism and "Taoism" on 43–58 and in his Appendix on "Taoist Yoga" on 114–20, and he even made links with the "Techniques of the Mind" text from the *Guanzi*, but he did not pursue these ideas further, and they were generally disregarded by later scholars. I thank my old friend and colleague Russell Kirkland for this reminder.

5. H. G. Creel, *What Is Taoism and Other Studies in Chinese Cultural History* (Chicago: University of Chicago Press, 1970), 1–24, esp. 7–11.

6. *The Book of Lieh-tzu*, trans. A. C. Graham, Morningside Edition (Columbia University Press, 1990), xi.

7. Marcel Granet, *La Pensee Chinoise* (Paris, 1934); Henri Maspero, *Taoism and Chinese Religion*, trans. Frank Kierman (Amherst: University of Massachusetts Press, 1981); Maxime Kaltenmark, *Lao Tzu and Daoism*, trans. Roger Greaves (Stanford: Stanford University Press, 1969); Anna K. Seidel and Michel Strickmann, "Taoism," *Encyclopedia Brittanica*, 1975; Kristofer Schipper, *The Taoist Body* (Berkeley: University of California Press, 1994); Isabelle Robinet, *Taoism: Growth of a Religion*, trans. Phyllis Brooks (Stanford: Stanford University Press, 1997).

8. Nathan Sivin, "On the Word 'Taoist' as a Source of Perplexity," *History of Religions* 17, no. 3/4 (1978): 303–30; Michel Strickman, "On the Alchemy of T'ao Hung-ching," in *Facets of Taoism*, ed. Holmes Welch and Anna Seidel (New Haven: Yale University Press, 1979), 123–92.

9. This is because the two major divisions of the text in the received recensions, the so-called "*Daojing*" ("Canon of the Way") and "*Dejing*" ("Canon of Inner Power"), are preserved in the Mawangdui recension. For translations, see Robert Henricks, *Lao-Tzu Te-Tao Ching* (New York: Ballantine Books, 1989) and Victor Mair, *Tao Te Ching: The Classic Book of Integrity and the Way* (New York: Bantam, 1990).

10. Robin Yates, *Five Lost Classics* (New York: Random House, 1997); Edmund Ryden, *The Yellow Emperor's Four Canons, A Literary Study And Edition of the Text From Mawangdui* (Taipei: Institute Ricci, 1997). The seven Mawangdui medical texts are translated in a scholarly tour de force in Donald Harper, *Early Chinese Medical Literature: The Mawangdui Medical Manuscripts* (London and New York: Keegan Paul International, 1998).

11. Sarah A. Queen, "Inventories of the Past: Rethinking the "School" Affiliation of the *Huainanzi*. *Asia Major*, Third Series (14.1): 2001; Mark Csíkszentmihályi and Michael Nylan, "Constructing Lineages and Inventing Traditions Through Exemplary Figures in Early China," *T'oung Pao* LXXXIX, 2003. The entire notion that early Chinese teacher-student traditions can be conceived of as distinctive "schools of thought" bears the imprint of European categories that will be challenged by the research that I present in this book.

12. D. C. Lau et al., eds., *Zhuangzi suizi suoyin* (ZZSY). Ancient Chinese Text Concordance Series, Chinese University of Hong Kong (Hong Kong: Commercial Press, 2000), chapter 15, 43, lines 19–20. Translation in Graham *Chuang-tzu*, 265; and D. C. Lau et al., eds., *Huainanzi suizi soyin* (ZZSY). Ancient Chinese Text Concordance Series, Chinese University of Hong Kong (Hong Kong: Commercial Press, 1992), chapter 7, 58, lines 3–4. Translation by Harold D. Roth in John S. Major, Sarah A. Queen, Andrew S. Meyer, and Harold D. Roth (Translators, Editors, Annotators), *The Huainanzi: A Guide to the Theory*

and Practice of Government in Early Han China (New York: Columbia University Press, 2010), 250–51.

13. See, for example, the succinct summary in Komjathy, *The Daoist Tradition*, 23.

14. Michael LaFargue, *Tao and Method: A Reasoned Approach to the Tao Te Ching* (Albany: State University of New York Press, 1993).

15. John S. Major, Sarah A. Queen, Andrew S. Meyer, and Harold D. Roth (Translators, Editors, Annotators), *The Huainanzi: A Guide to the Theory and Practice of Government in Early Han China* (New York: Columbia University Press, 2010).

16. Interesting steps in this direction can be found in a number of sources. See, for example, Livia Kohn, *Early Chinese Mysticism: Philosophy and Soteriology in the Taoist Tradition* (Princeton, 1991) and *Sitting in Oblivion: The Heart of Daoist Meditation* (Three Pines, 2010); Fabrizio Pregadio, *The Way of the Golden Elixir: An Introduction to Daoist Alchemy* (Golder Elixir Press, 3rd ed., 2019); Mark Csikszentmihalyi, "Traditional Taxonomies and Revealed Texts in the Han," in *Daoist Identity*, ed. Livia Kohn and Harold D. Roth (Honolulu: University of Hawai'i Press, 2002), 81–101; Ronnie Littlejohn, *Daoism: An Introduction* (London and New York: I.B. Taurus, 2009); Stephen Eskildsen, *Daoism, Meditation, and the Wonders of Serenity* (Albany, NY: State University of New York Press, 2015); and Louis Komjathy, *The Daoist Tradition: An Introduction* (London: Bloomsbury, 2013); and *The Way of Complete Perfection: A Quanzhen Daoist Anthology* (Albany, NY: State University of New York Press, 2013).

Chapter 1

1. Yan Guocai 燕國材, *Xian Qin xinli sixiang yanjiu* 先秦心理思想研究 (Changsha: Hunan renmin chubanshe, 1980), 1.

2. Throughout this study I have translated the Chinese term *xin* as "mind" rather than "heart" or some combination of the two. To translate *xin* as "heart," while apparently quite literal, fails to convey adequately the broad range the term has in ancient Chinese. To the modern Western reader, "heart" is associated almost exclusively with the affective; to the ancient Chinese, *xin* included the affective, the cognitive, and the intuitive, all of which are properties of what we call "mind."

There are some who may object that the locating of this full range of psychological activities in the physical organ of the heart represents a significant assumption that should not be overlooked, especially in sources concerned with the physiological basis of such activities. In principle I agree, but recent research into ancient Chinese medical and philosophical literature indicates that the understanding of *xin* in these sources goes well beyond that of a physical organ. Manfred Porkert has convincingly demonstrated that the *wuzang*, far from simply being physical organs, were conceived of as spheres, or "orbs," of vital energy (*qi*). See his *The Theoretical Foundations of Chinese Medicine* (Cambridge: MIT Press, 1974). While the philosophical literature examined in the present study is earlier and less technical than Porkert's sources, this information from the medical texts is nonetheless instructive. It demonstrates a concept of physicality radically different from that of the modern West, a concept that gives primacy to systems of vital energy rather than to unique physical constituents. This indicates that in the technical literature, *xin* 心 was understood more as a physicalist metaphor than as a physical organ, and that we need not translate it as "heart" in order to be faithful to the implications of the original, which are, after all, more abstract than our own notions of the physical. Therefore, I translate *xin* as "mind" and ask the reader to conceive of it as a sphere of vital energy that passes through and includes the physical organ of the heart and is the source of feelings, desires, thoughts, and intuitions.

3. Yan, 4. Yan includes these aspects both under "psychology" and "psychological thought."

4. Herbert Fingarette, *Confucius: The Secular as Sacred* (New York: Harper and Row, 1972), 37ff.

5. Benjamin I. Schwartz, *The World of Thought in Ancient China* (Cambridge: Harvard University Press, 1985), 74–75.

6. A. C. Graham has identified five essays in the *Lüshi chunqiu* as containing the ideas of Yang Zhu and his followers: "Bensheng," "Chongji," "Guisheng," "Qingyu," and "Shenwei." See A. C. Graham, "The Background of the Mencian Theory of Human Nature," *CHHP* 6, no. 1/2 (1967): 217, 220, 227ff. Guan Feng and Graham identify four chapters of the *Zhuangzi*, 28–31 (Guan questions chapter 30), as products of the school of Yang Zhu. None of these works is datable to the time of Yang Zhu, but there is no reason to doubt they contain his basic ideas. See Guan Feng 關鋒, *Zhuangzi zhexue taolun ji* 莊子哲學討論集 (Peking: Zhonghua Publishing Co., 1962), 61–98, and Graham, "How Much of *Chuang Tzu* Did Chuang Tzu Write?," reprinted in *Studies in Chinese Philosophy and Philosophical Literature* (Singapore: National University of Singapore, Institute of East Asian Philosophies, 1986), 283–321.

7. Graham, includes chapters 15, 33, and parts of chapters 11–14 in this final stratum (specifically, 11/66–74, 12/1–6, 13/1–45, 14/1–5, locations from Harvard-Yenching Concordance). See his "How Much of *Chuang Tzu*," 313–21.

8. *Zhuangzi yinde* 莊子引得, Harvard-Yenching Institute Sinological Series Supplement no. 20 (Peking: Yenching University Press, 1947) [hereafter *HYC*] 9/4/27–8.

9. *HYC* 9/4/26ff.

10. *HYC* 19/6/92ff. I use the term "self-cultivation" to refer to various mental and physical techniques of self-discipline aimed at realizing one's innate potential.

11. I adopt Willard Peterson's translation of *shen* as "numen." See his "Making Connections: 'Commentary on the Attached Verbalizations' of the Book of Change," *HJAS* 42, no. 1 (1982): 67–122. This translation is better than others that have been proposed, but it fails to catch the association of *shen* with human psychology and what might be called "meta-psychology," that is, the experiences of self-transcendence discussed in early Daoist sources. I also use "vital energy" to translate *qi*, because it best captures its crucial link to life and vitality and because I agree with Manfred Porkert that "Within the framework of Chinese thought no notion may attain to such a degree of abstraction from empirical data as to correspond perfectly to one of our modern universal concepts. Nevertheless the term *ch 'i* comes as close as possible to constituting a generic designation equivalent to our word 'energy' " (Porkert, 167). Finally, the translation of *jing* as "vital essence" derives from contexts that are examined below.

12. These include such apparently varied practices as breath-control meditation, gymnastics (*daoyin* 導引), fasting, swallowing saliva, eating certain herbs, and sexual practices euphemistically termed "bedroom arts" (*fangshu* 房術). For two most thorough discussions of these techniques, see Henri Maspero, "Les Procedes de 'Nourrir le principe Vital' dans la Réligion Taoiste Ancien," *JA* 229 (April–June 1937): 177–252 (July–September 1937): 353–430, translated by Frank Kierman in *Taoism and Chinese Religion* (Amherst: University of Massachusetts Press, 1981), 443–554; and Joseph Needham, *Science and Civilisation in China*, 6 vols. (Cambridge: Cambridge University Press, 1983), 5:5.

13. Maspero, 413–26.

14. H. G. Creel, "What Is Taoism?," in *What Is Taoism And Other Studies in Chinese Cultural History* (Chicago: University of Chicago Press, 1970), 1–24, esp. 7–11; Fung Yu-lan, *A Short History of Chinese Philosophy* (New York: Mac-Millan, 1948), 3, 211–12.

15. Sakai Tadao 酒井忠夫, and Fukui Fumimasu 福井文雅, "Dōkyō to wa nani ka?" 道教とは何か, in Fukui Kōjun 福井康順, Yamazaki Hiroshi 山崎宏, Kimura Eiichi 木村英一, and Sakai Tadao, eds., *Dōkyō* 道教, 3 vols. (Heigawa, 1983), 1:10–17; Yamada Toshiaki 山田利明, "Shinsendo" 神仙道, in *Dōkyō*, 1:347–61; Chou Shaoxian 周紹賢 *Daojia yu shenxian* 道家與神仙 (Taipei: Zhonghua shuju, 1974), 72/f., and 185; Zhongguo Daojiao xiehui yanjiushi 中國道教協会研究室, "Zhongguo Daojiao shi tigang" 中國道教史提綱, *Zhongguo zhexue shi yanjiu* 1 (1983): 41–50. For a translation, see Man Kam Leung and Julian Pas, "An Outline of Taoist History," *Journal of Chinese Religions* 15 (Fall 1987): 61–79.

16. H. G. Creel first set forth this distinction in his article "On Two Aspects in Early Taoism," now included in *What Is Taoism?*, 37–47.

17. The term "Lao-Zhuang" seems to have first been used during the Wei and Chin Dynasties in the writings of, and about, the so-called "Neo-Daoists," Wang Bi, He Yan, Ji Kang, Xiang Xiu, Guo Xiang, and others. See He Qimin 何啓民;, *Wei Jin sixiang yu tanfeng* 魏晉思想與談風 (Taipei: Zhongguo xueshu zhuzuo jiangzhu yinyuan hui, 1967), 103–15.

I believe that the sole occurrence of the term before this time, in the *Huainanzi* (SBCK edition, 21.3a12), is an emendation made to conform to this Neo-Daoist outlook. In summarizing the twelfth essay, *Daoying*, which is devoted to illustrating ideas from *Laozi* with stories drawn from a wide variety of works, the text says that this essay "examines evidence for the techniques of Lao-Zhuang." However, whereas the *Laozi* is directly quoted forty-seven times in *Huainanzi* 12, the *Zhuangzi* is quoted once only. Therefore, I conclude that the text originally read "the techniques of Laozi," and was changed by a post–Wei-Jin redactor.

18. The references to Huang-Lao teachings and masters scattered throughout the *Shiji* and *Hanshu* are summarized in K. C. Hsiao, *A History of Chinese Political Thought*, trans. F. W. Mote (Princeton: Princeton University Press, 1979), 1:552–56.

19. *Shi ji* (Peking: Zhonghua shuju, 1959), 130.3288. This is based on the Jinling shuju 金陵書局 edition, which contains the three major commentaries, and was published during the Tongzhi reign period.

In this passage and throughout this chapter, I translate *jingshen* as "numinous essence." The terms *jing* and *shen* probably initially stood in a coordinative relationship (meaning "vital essence" and "numen"), but increasingly in Han texts, as the Naturalist philosophy of the five phases of vital energy became influential, a subordinative relationship developed. It persists today in the modern Chinese *jingshen* ("spirit," or "elan") and the Japanese *seishin* ("psyche"). At this early Han stage, it literally means "numen-as-vital essence," which I have shortened to "numinous essence." For the rationale for this translation, see the section on *jingshen* in the *Huainanzi* below. For a more detailed explanation, see my "The Early Taoist Concept of *Shen*: A Ghost in the Machine?," in *Sagehood and Systematizing Thought in the Late Warring States and Early Han*, ed. Kidder Smith (Brunswick: Asian Studies Program, Bowdoin College, 1990), 11–32.

20. Sima Qian says that his father studied Daoist treatises with a man named Master Huang 黃子. The fifth-century commentator Xu Guang 徐廣 identifies him as Huang Sheng 黃生 and says that he was fond of Huang-Lao techniques. *Shi ji*, 130.3288.

21. Ibid., 130.3292.

22. Hsiao sees Huang-Lao doctrines at the core of the *Huainanzi* and further sees the text as the "principal representative of Taoism during the Han" (572–77). I would differ with him, however, in that I suspect that Huang-Lao thought is syncretic from its inception, presumably during the third century BC, as the *Shi ji* says.

23. One of the first scholars to suggest this is Wei Yuan 魏源 (1794–1856). See the prefatory essay, "Lun *Laozi*" 論老子, to his *Laozi benyi* 老子本義. A final note to the colophon is dated 1842 (*Guoxue jiben congshu* ed. Taipei: Commercial Press, 1968), 54: 1–6. I am indebted to Benjamin Elman of University of California at Los Angeles for calling my attention to this work. For more

recent arguments, see Zhang Shunhui 張舜徽 *Zhoujin Daolun fawei* 周秦道論發微 (Peking: Zhonghua shuju, 1982), 78ff.

24. For this influential identification, see Tang Lan 唐蘭, "Mawangdui chutu *Laozi* yi ben juan qian guyishu de yanjiu qianlun qi yu Hanchu rufa douzheng de guanxi" 馬王堆出土老子乙本卷前古佚書的研究兼論其與漢初儒法鬥爭的關係, *Kaogu xue bao* 1 (1975): 7–38. Among the other early studies of the philosophy of these texts, two are quite illuminating: Uchiyama Toshihiko 內山俊彥 "Maōtai bosho *Keihō, Judaikyō, Shō, Dōgen* shō kō" 馬王堆帛書經, 十大經, 稱, 道原小考, *Tohōgaku* 56 (1978): 1–16, and Tu Wei ming, "The Silk Manuscripts of Ma-wang-tui," *JAS* 39, no. 1 (1979): 95–110.

25. See my essay "Who Compiled the *Chuang Tzu*?," in Chinese Texts and Philosophical Contexts: Essays Dedicated to Angus C. Graham, ed. Henry Rosemont Jr. (LaSalle, IL: Open Court Press, 1991), 79–128 (chapter 2 in the present volume). For the relationship between the *Guanzi* and *Huai-nan Tzu* material and the Yellow Emperor texts, see, among others, Uchiyama, and Long Hui 龍晦, "Mawangdui chutu *Laozi* yi ben qian guyishu tanyuan" 馬王堆出土老子乙本前古佚書探原, *Kaogu xuebao* 2 (1975): 23–32. Long has found similar rhyme patterns as well as textual parallels among these sources.

26. Allyn Rickett summarizes scholarly opinion on the origins of the *Guanzi*, saying that the "proto-*Guanzi*," the core around which the present text took shape in about 250 BC, was written at the Jixia Academy. Additional materials continued to be added until about 26 BC, when the text was edited by Liu Xiang. See his *Guanzi: Political, Economic, and Philosophical Essays from Early China* (Princeton: Princeton University Press, 1985), 15.

27. Hsiao, 320–22. Hsiao also states, "although the *Kuan Tzu* advocates a government of laws, neither in point of view nor in substance is it closely analogous to the works of Shen Pu-hai, Kung-sun Yang (Lord Shang), Han Fei Tzu, and Li Ssu" (321).

Rickett discusses the opinions of Hsiao and others on the nature of the text. While he disagrees with some aspects, he agrees that "there is a basic point of view pervading most of the text that clearly sets it apart from the works of the major Legalist and Confucian writers except perhaps Xunzi" (*Guanzi*, 15–17).

28. Rickett, *Guanzi*, 23.

29. A fourth text, *Bai xin* 白心 ("The Purified Mind"), is usually considered together with these, but I see no compelling reason for this, particularly in light of the virtual absence in this work of the self-cultivation theories and techniques that are so prevalent in the other three texts.

30. Guo Moruo 郭沫若, "Song Xing Yin Wen yizhu kao" 宋鈃尹文遺著考, in *Qing tong shidai* 青銅時代 (Shanghai: Kexue chubanshe, 1951), 255–81. Liu Jie's ideas are known to me through Rickett and Machida. Recent opinions from the PRC can be found in Guan Feng, 71, and Yan Kuo-ts'ai, 88ff.

31. Machida Saburo 町田三郎, "Kanshi shihen ni tsuite" 管子四扁につい
て, *Bunka* 文化 25.1 (1961): 75–102.

32. For Rickett's earlier views, see his *Kuan-tzu, A Repository of Early
Chinese Thought* (Hong Kong: Hong Kong University Press, 1965), 155–88. His
later ideas are in *Guanzi*, 22–23.

33. A. C. Graham, *Disputers of the Tao* (LaSalle, IL: Open Court Press,
1989), 100.

34. Rickett, *Kuan Tzu*, 156–58.

35. Kuo, 251–55.

36. Graham, *Disputers*, 100.

37. I have determined the critical text for the nineteen passages from
the *Guanzi* translated here by consulting two principal sources. The first is the
SBCK edition, which serves as my base-text (Shanghai: Commercial Press, 1920).
The second is the superb collection of variant readings from other editions and
textual emendations by Qing, Republican, and modern scholars assembled in
the following work: Xu Weiyu 許維遹, Wen Yiduo 聞一多, and Guo Moruo,
Guanzi jijiao 管子集校 (Peking: Zhonghua shuju, 1955). The *SBCK* reprint is
of the Zhang Ying 張瑛 traced facsimile (1878) of the oldest extant complete
edition, the Southern Song edition of Yang Zhen 楊忱, an exemplar of which
is today in the Peking National Library. Because it contains only the cyclical
date and no indication of reign period, estimates of its date of printing range
from 1164 to 1284 (Rickett, *Guanzi* 31–40). From my own brief investigation,
I would judge that this Southern Sung edition and the Ming edition of Liu Ji
劉績 (*jinshi* 1488) are the ancestors of most extant editions. The reasons why
I disagree with Guo's and Rickett's insistence that Liu Ji is a Liao Dynasty figure are detailed in my *Textual History of the Huai-nan Tzu* (Ann Arbor: AAS
Monograph Series, 1992), chapter 7. All citations of the *Guanzi* are to the *SBCK*
edition. The emendations I have adopted are indicated in my footnotes, and
most of these emendations are taken from the *Guanzi jijiao* (hereafter, GZJJ).

38. The term *zheng xing* 正形, which could be translated as "correcting
the body," has a specific meaning in the texts concerned with inner cultivation.
Because the human organism is imbued with vital energy, I take *zheng xing* to
refer to aligning or harmonizing the flow of vital energy within the physical
form (a more literal rendering of *xing*). Likewise, the term *zheng xin* 正心,
translated below in a passage found at 16.2b9, means to align the flow of vital
energy within the mind.

The notion of aligning the five systems of *qi* within the human microcosm
clearly parallels the notion of aligning the human realm in toto with the realm
of nature that Schwartz argues is the ultimate result of the philosophy and
technology of the Yin-yang/Five Phase cosmologists (Schwartz, 350–69). The
common element here is that through intentional activity, human beings can put
themselves in harmony with the inherent natural guidelines (*li*) of the cosmos.

39. For an alternate translation of this and the other passages from these three chapters of the *Guanzi*, see Rickett, *Kuan Tzu*, 158–79.

40. Reading 卒 as 萃, following the Tokugawa scholar Igai Hikohiro 猪飼彥, and 己 as 屺, following Guo Moruo (*GZJJ*, 781–87).

41. Reading 音 as 意, a variant in the late Ming edition of Chang Pang 張榜—suggested by Wang Niansun 王念孫. See *GZJJ*, 782. I have translated *yi* as "awareness" rather than the more common "ideas" and "will," which do not fit the context. The vital essence is not something that can be summoned by one's thoughts or the will, because it resists conscious attempts to control it. It is likely that in other psychological contexts in early Chinese thought, *yi* is best translated as "awareness," because to my knowledge no other term is translated to deal with this basic human experience. *Yi* is later combined with *shi* 識 in both Buddhist and contemporary psychological contexts to translate "consciousness," and it is actually first used in this way by Wang Chong in the *Lun heng* 論衡. See *Zhongwen dazidian* (Taipei: Lianhe chuban fuwu zhongxin congjing shou, 1962–68), entry no. 11107.104.

42. Reading 果 as 畢, after Wang Niansun (*GZJJ*, 782).

43. Here 禺 is a phonetic loan for 愚.

44. 得 is absent from the *SBCK* edition, but present in Liu Ji and in other major editions. *Zhuangzi*, HYC 62/23/34–5 contains these live lines in a dialogue in which Nan Rongzhu asks Laozi about the canon on defending one's nature (*wei sheng* [*xing*] *zhi jing* 衛生(性)之經).

45. I have eliminated 有 and 自 as extraneous characters, the former after Ding Shihan 丁士涵 (fl. nineteenth century), the latter after Guo Moruo (*GZJJ*, 787).

46. Reading 精 as 靜, after *GZJJ*, 44.

47. Reading 至 as 自, after Wang Niansun (*GZJJ*, 787).

48. Reading 澤 as 釋, after several scholars beginning with Liu Chi (*GZJJ*, 789–90).

49. The presence of metaphors for "physical cultivation theory" in "Neiye" has been noted by Donald Harper in "The Sexual Arts of Ancient China as Described in a Manuscript of the Second Century B.C.," *HJAS* 47, no. 2 (1987): 543–4. Harper further contends: "It is probable that both the *Laozi* and "Neiye" were recited as canons of physical cultivation theory; and that there existed an ancillary literature, either written or oral, to explain the program of cultivation allusively described in the main canon" (561).

50. Reading 精 as 情, after several scholars beginning with Yasui Ko 安井衡 (1799–1876). See *GZJJ*, 792.

51. Reading 論治 as 淪洽, after *GZJJ*, 792.

52. For an excellent study of the history and development of this meditative practice in Daoism, see Livia Kohn, "Guarding the One: Concentrative Meditation in Taoism," in *Taoist Meditation and Longevity Techniques*, ed. Livia

Kohn (Ann Arbor: Center for Chinese Studies, University of Michigan, 1989), 125–58. The role of "guarding the One" in early Chan Buddhism is analyzed in John R. McRae, *The Northern School and the Formation of Early Ch'an Buddhism* (Honolulu: University of Hawai'i Press, 1986), 136–44.

53. Many scholars conclude that 古日 has erroneously entered the text and should be excised (*GZJJ*, 633).

54. I have added this sentence from the commentarial section of "Xinshu shang" after He Ruzhang 何如璋 (fl. 1886) and Guo Moruo (*GZJJ*, 634).

55. Reading 無 as 而, after Wang Niansun (*GZJJ*, 635).

56. Reading 踈之 as 疏有, after Ding Shihan. Here ft means fen 分, according to Ting (*GZJJ*, 636).

57. Reading 未 as 大, after Ding Shihan and Guo (*GZJJ*, 636).

58. I read 因 as 出, based on parallelism.

59. Roger Ames, *The Art of Rulership* (Honolulu: University of Hawai'i Press, 1983), 57–58, 146–48.

60. Reading 乃 as 不, the variant in the Zhu Dongguang 朱東光 edition of 1579.

61. I read both instances of 虛 as similar-form corruptions for 處. The subject of the passage is the Dao. It makes no sense to talk about emptying out the Dao; the Dao is already empty. Rather, the passage speaks of the need to rest in the Dao.

62. Reading 世 as 聖, after Zhang Wenhu 張文虎 (1808–85). See *GZJJ*, 641.

63. The term *du*, which I translate as "complete solitude," implies that the self is totally devoid of all its "companions"—in other words, of all objects—just as Nanguo Ziqi is in the famous passage from the *Zhuangzi* (*HYC* 3/2/1). The technical terms for religious and mystical experience in early Daoism have not yet been adequately studied, and an analysis of all relevant occurrences of the word *du* is well outside the limits of the present study. Nonetheless, it is instructive to examine the use of this term in the *Zhuangzi* passage mentioned above, of which the author of "Xinshu shang" may very well have been aware. In this passage (*HYC* 17/6/36–40), the "Crookbacked Woman" explains how she taught Bu Liangyi: "Only after nine days was he able to put life outside him. Only after he had already put life outside him was he able to be thoroughly infused with the Light of Dawn. Only after he was thoroughly infused with the Light of Dawn was he able to see complete solitude. Only after he saw complete solitude was he able to have no past and no present. Only after he had no past and no present was he able to enter No-life and No-death. That which destroys life does not die; that which generates life does not live." This passage describes progressive stages of meditative trance ultimately leading to a total transcendence of self-identity in the experience of merging with the Dao, herein described as the ground of the cosmos that is beyond life and death. One must turn to the Buddhist tradition for comparative material on levels of inner absorption, delineated in certain texts of the Pali Canon as the nine

jhanas. For an analysis, see Winston King, *Theravada Buddhist Meditation* (State College, PA: Pennsylvania State University Press, 1982).

64. Passages in "Xinshu shang" that present a cosmology of the Dao are found at 13.1a10 and 2b5; 13.1b2 and 3a2; 13.1b6 and 3b1.

65. Reading 反 as 身, after Kuo (GZJJ, 641).

66. Reading 行者正之 義 as 正者行之義, after Kuo (GZJJ, 652).

67. I read 美 as a similar-form corruption for 義 (a phonetic loan for 義), based on the previous sentences.

68. Reading 慕 as 纂, after Yü Yüeh (GZJJ, 653).

69. Examples of this kind of connecting passage in "Xinshu shang" can be found at 13.5b3, 5b7, 6a4, and 6a9.

70. "To infer from the *Lü-shih Ch'un-ch'iu* and the *Huai-nan Tzu*, however, it appears that all works were relegated to the Eclectic category that present thought and learning not purely of one tradition, or that as literature does not qualify as *belles lettres*, thereby being eligible for listing neither under the various philosophic school divisions, nor under these for 'poetry and rhymed prose' and the like" (Hsiao, 551).

While I completely agree with Hsiao that the *Huainanzi* takes Huang-Lao doctrines as its ultimate reference point, I see the eclectic tendency it represents to be simultaneously drawing on many schools yet adhering to the basic tenets of one school—namely that of Huang-Lao. I do not see the *Huainanzi*'s eclecticism as the product of factionalism within one tradition, as Hsiao's argument implies.

71. For Needham's use of the term, see *Science and Civilisation in China* (Cambridge: Cambridge University Press, 1956), vol. 2, esp. 232–78, which is one of the most thorough studies of Naturalist thought yet undertaken in the West. Another is A. C. Graham's historical-structuralist analysis, *Yin-Yang and the Nature of Correlative Thinking* (Singapore: Institute of East Asian Philosophies, 1986), a shortened and revised version of which is found in *Disputers of the Tao*, 315–70.

72. The influence of Naturalist thought in the *Huainanzi* is superbly discussed in John Major, "Topography and Cosmology in Early Han Thought" (PhD diss., Harvard University, 1973).

73. The details of the creation of the *Huainanzi* are found in Roth, *Textual History*, chapter 1. The most detailed biography of Liu An in English is Benjamin Wallacker's "Liu An-Second King of Huai-nan," *JAOS* 92 (1972): 36–51.

74. Between 1799 and 1911, nine scholars compiled reconstituted redactions of the "Central Book" (*zhongpian* 中篇) of Huainan. Most are titled *Huainan wanbi shu* 淮南萬畢術; the title the work was known by from the time of Ge Hong (ca. 300 AD). Sun Fengyi 孫馮翼 (1799) was the first Qing scholar to compile the fragments from various sources in the indirect tradition, and his work, along with those of Mao Panlin 茆泮林 (1823–25), Huang Shen 黄奭 (1850), and Ye Dehui 葉德輝 (1891), are the most widely circulated of these.

75. Rickett, *Guanzi*, 22–23.

76. The similarity between the title of this essay and the title of the "Yellow Emperor" text from Mawangdui, *Dao Yuan* 道原, is probably not accidental and warrants further study. The former could possibly be a conscious attempt to elaborate on the latter, thus indicating that both are part of the same lineage.

77. The critical texts for the twenty-eight passages from the *Huainanzi* translated in this chapter have been determined in the following manner. The base text is the *SBCK* photolithographic reproduction of Liu Lufen's 劉履芬 1872 traced facsimile (Shanghai: Commercial Press, 1920). Liu's facsimile was copied from another facsimile that was traced in 1824 by Chen Huan 陳奐 from the original exemplar of the Northern Sung edition (ca. 1050), which was in the library of the famous Qing bibliophile Huang Peilie 黃丕烈 (1763–1825). This has been collated with the four other ancestral redactions of the eighty-seven extant complete editions of the text, identified in my book *The Textual History of the Huai-nan Tzu*, Pt. 2. These are the *Daozang* (1445), the Liu Ji (1501), the Zhu Dongguang (1579) and the Mao Yigui 茅一桂 (1580). For emendations I have consulted the major nineteenth- and twentieth-century textual critics: Wang Niansun, Gu Guangqii 顧廣圻, Wang Shumin 王叔岷, Yu Dacheng 于大成, and Zheng Liangshu 鄭良樹. Their works are cited below when used for specific emendations. For convenience, a reference to the *SBCK* edition is given for each passage. For a summary of these editions and their use in constructing a modern critical text, see H. D. Roth, "Filiation Analysis and the Textual Criticism of the *Huai-nan Tzu*," *Transactions of the Conference of Orientalists in Japan* 27 (December 1982): 60–81.

78. Reading 任 as 在, as in all the other ancestral redactions. Excising 我, after Wang Niansun, *Dushu zazhi* 讀書雜志 (1832; reprint, Taipei: Hungshi chubanshe, 1976), *juan* 9, section 1, 23a (hereafter: 9/1/23a). The section numbers correspond to the chapter numbers of the *Huainanzi*.

79. Reading 失 as 矣, as in all the other ancestral redactions.

80. Zhan He 詹何 is the late Warring States teacher who appears in stories in *Hanfeizi*, *juan* 20 and *Liezi*, *juan* 5. If we are to believe Qian Mu, he is also the Zhanzi 詹子 in *Zhuangzi*, chapter 28. See Qian Mu 錢穆 *Xian Qin zhuzi xinian* 先秦諸子繫年, 2nd ed. (Hong Kong: Hong Kong University Press, 1956), 448. According to Qian, Zhan He lived from 350 to 270 BC, might have been the Heshang zhangren 河上丈人, mentioned in the *Shi ji* as the first Huang-Lao master, and might have been the author of the *Daode jing*. For Qian's arguments, see ibid., 223–26.

81. Reading 忘 as 妄, the variant in all the other ancestral redactions.

82. The character 用 is extraneous. Wang Niansun, 9/14/4a–b.

83. Most of this passage (beginning after the passage quoting Zhan He, 14.2a5–10) occurs almost verbatim but with a slightly different arrangement in the *Hanshi waizhuan* 韓詩外傳, *zhuan* 2, entry 34 (*SBCK suoben* 縮本, 19). This work is a commentary by Han Ying 韓嬰 on one recension of the *Book of Odes*.

Han Ying was a scholar from Yan, and a contemporary of Liu An, and once debated Dong Zhongshu in front of Emperor Wu. This work was transmitted to a man from Huainan called Ben Sheng 賁生, and hence may have been present at Liu An's court, where it could have served as the basis for the *Huainanzi* passage. However, it is also possible that both works drew on a now lost source, possibly the lost writings of Zhan He. For a similar discussion of "techniques for nourishing the mind," see ibid., *juan* 2, entry 31. See also James Hightower, *Han Shih Wai Chuan*, Harvard-Yenching Institute Monograph Series, vol. 11 (Cambridge: Harvard University Press, 1952), esp. 73, 71.

84. The *Huainanzi*'s analysis of *xing* is for the most part found in essays 1, 2, 7, 11, 14, and 20. Where these essays appear to differ regarding the theory of *xing*, they are in fact addressing different aspects of *xing*. Even the apparently anomalous advocacy of a Confucian-Naturalist theory of *xing* (20.3b8)—which occurs in the context of a critique of Legalist theories of governing for failing to follow or adapt (yin) to human nature—eventually recommends nourishing the numen as the foundation of nourishing this nature (20.8bl 1). It may represent an attempt to argue that Confucian theories of *xing* are not necessarily inconsistent with Daoist theories.

85. A. C. Graham, *Later Mohist Logic, Ethics, and Science* (Hong Kong: Chinese University Press, 1978), 16.

86. The brief discussion of human nature in the Primitivist chapters of the *Zhuangzi* (8–10, 11/66–74) is the first known Daoist consideration of this term. It is undertaken to support the Primitivist critique of civilization and advocacy of a minimalistic government, and it is best characterized by one phrase: "In the pure and unhewn the nature of the people is found" (HYC 23/9/10–11). The theory of human nature in the *Huainanzi* is much more thorough and sophisticated.

87. Guang Chengzi 廣成子 was the *fang shi* who taught techniques of longevity to the Yellow Emperor in the *Zhuangzi* (27/11/28–44). For his biography, see Ge Hong, *Shenxian zhuan* 神仙傳 (Baibu congshu jicheng edition, Taipei: Yiwen yinshuguan, 1966), ser. 13, 70: 1.1a.

88. Deleting 真, after Yü Yüe. The idea that human nature is completely clear and serene suggests what Lee Yearley has called the "discovery model" of human nature. As he defines it, ". . . human nature exists as a permanent set of dispositions that are obscured but that can be contacted or discovered. People do not cultivate inchoate capacities. Rather, they discover a hidden ontological reality that defines them . . ." (Lee Yearley, *Mencius and Aquinas: Theories of Virtue and Conceptions of Courage* [Albany: State University of New York Press, 1990], 59–60). He contrasts this with a "development model" through which people cultivate innate potentials over time.

89. Emending 以有 to 有以 after Zheng Liangshu, *Huainanzi jiaoli* 淮南子斠理 (Taipei: Jiaxin Cement Company, 1968), 179. This is the reading in the Liu Ji Redaction.

90. Reading 性 as 靜, after Cheng, 34, and the *Wenzi Jiushou pian* 九守篇.

91. Reading 生 as 性, as often occurs in pre-Han and early Han texts, which frequently leave off radicals.

92. Emending 勝, to 任, after Wang Niansun, 9/14/8a. To say the vital energy is aligned means that it is flowing freely along the various pathways associated with the five orbs.

93. Emending 從事於 to 存, after Wang Niansun, 9/14/10a.

94. *Tong* is a difficult term to translate. It literally means to circulate where there is no obstruction. In the phrase *tong li*, I have translated it as "flow freely with the natural guidelines," as in the passage translated earlier at 8.4b5. Here, however, *tong* is associated with a profound mental stillness and therefore cannot be so translated. Rather, *tong* here seems to be referring to penetrating this stillness. But "penetrate," which implies movement through an obstacle, is a better translation for ta 達. It emphasizes process, whereas *tong* emphasizes the result of a process. For these reasons, I have translated *tong* as "absorbed." I understand the passage to be discussing a state of meditative concentration similar to the Buddhist *jhanas*, which are sometimes translated as "states of absorption."

95. Emending 散 to 穀, after Wang Yinzhi 王引之 in Wang Niansun, 9/1/20a.

96. To translate *wuzang*, I use "five orbs," which was first proposed by Manfred Porkert in *Theoretical Foundations of Chinese Medicine*. Each "orb" is a distinct and complex pathway of vital energy within the body and is given its unique characteristics by the particular organ that is the physical manifestation of that pathway.

97. Inserting 終 after 則. See Wang Niansun, 9/8/9a.

98. *Yijing benyi* 易經本義 (n.p.: Saoye shan fang, 1930), 3.36. For a penetrating analysis of the Xici, see Willard Peterson, "Making Connections."

99. The phrase *yang xing*, "nourishing the nature," was first advanced in the fourth century BC by Yang Zhu. Yang Zhu and his later followers believed that one's nature consisted of the numen, senses, physical body, and one's allotted life span. For details, see A. C. Graham, "The Background of the Mencian Theory of Human Nature." The *Huainanzi*'s theory of human nature is decisively different from this in that it envisions an important transcendent dimension.

100. Deleting 真, after Yü Yüe.

101. Reading 越 as 株, after Gu Guangji. Gu's emendations are taken from a reprint of the Xu Zaiheng 許在衡 1898 facsimile of Gu's hand-collated exemplar of the Zhuang Kuiji 莊逵吉 edition of 1788, published in the series *Zhongguo zixue mingzhu jicheng* 中國子學名著集成 (Taipei: Zhongguo zixue mingzhu jicheng bianxiu wei yuan hui, 1977), 85:50. By "hand-collated exemplars," I mean a copy of an edition of a text onto which collation notes and emendations have been written. This particular hand-collated exemplar is of particular value for the textual criticism of the *Huainanzi*, because in it Gu recorded all variants between the original exemplar of the Northern Sung edition and the Zhuang

Kuiji edition. The photofacsimile of the Northern Sung edition published in the *SBCK* is based on a facsimile of a facsimile of this exemplar and contains many copyists' errors not in the original exemplar, which is now unavailable. For details, see Roth, *Textual History*, chapter 5.

102. Adding 非 before 去, after Zheng Liangshu, 19, and several editions including Chuang Kuiji's.

103. Emending 淵 to 神, after Wang Niansun, 9/2/12b.

104. The *Wen xuan* 文選 commentary, *Jiang fu* 江賦 section, cites the Xu Shen 許慎 recension of the *Huainanzi* for a parallel passage in chapter 16. In this, instead of *liu mo* 流沫 "flowing foam," which makes little sense, we find *liu fan* 流緐, "surging floodwaters." Wang Niansun 9/2/13a cites a parallel passage in the *Jiu shou* chapter of *Wenzi* in which we find *liu lao* 流潦, which also means "surging floodwaters." The meaning of *fan*, "heavy flooding" (according to Xu Shen), and *lao*, "flooding" are very close. Probably in the Xu Shen recension of the *Huainanzi* the character was *fan* and in the Gao You recension the reading was *lao*. I have chosen the Xu reading. For details of these two recensions and the history of their merging, see Roth, *Textual History*, chapter 4.

105. Porkert, 195–96.

106. Reading 面 as 血, due to a copyist's error in the Northern Sung edition not present in the other ancestral redactions.

107. Omitting 之 after 行, as in the Liu Ji Redaction.

108. Adding 也 following 見, after Zheng, 108.

109. Wang Qiao 王喬, more often known as Wangzi Qiao 王子喬, and Chi Songzi 赤松子, are renowned in later Daoist literature as immortals who practiced the gymnastic exercises (*daoyin*) aimed at guiding the vital energy throughout one's being. For their biographies, see [Liu Xiang?], *Liexian zhuan* 列仙傳 (Baibu congshu jicheng, ed., Taipei: Yiwen yinshuguan, 1967), ser. 65, 18:l.12a and I. la, respectively. For a translation, see Max Kaltenmark, *Le Lie-Sien Tchouan* (Peking: Centre d'etudes sinologiques de Pekin, 1953), 109 and 35. They are also mentioned in the *Yuan you* 遠遊 poem in the *Chu ci*. See David Hawkes, *The Songs of the South* (Harmondsworth, UK: Penguin Books, 1985), 194–95, 199–200. The ideas on self-cultivation attributed to them were probably transmitted and made known to the *Huainanzi* authors by the *fangshi*. Paintings of these gymnastic exercises were found in a silk document at Mawangdui tomb number 3, and are included in an anonymous monograph, *Daoyintu dunwen ji* 導引圖論文集 (Peking: Wenwu chubanshe, 1979).

Chapter 2

1. Lu Deming's (陸德明) *Zhuangzi shiwen* (莊子釋文) quotes an otherwise unidentified scholar named Tang 唐 who questioned the inconsistencies in

chapter 28. All material from Lu is taken from his work included in Guo Qing Fan's 郭慶藩 *Jiaozheng Zhuangzi jishi* 校正莊子集釋. Taipei, 1974. This reference is at p. 989.

2. Wang Shumin 王叔岷, *Zhuangzi jiaoshi*. Shanghai, 1947, Preface.

3. Luo Miandao, *Nanhua zhenjing xun ben* 南華真經循本. Daozang edition, vols. 498–502.

4. For example, H. G. Creel, "What Is Taoism?," in *What Is Taoism and Other Studies in Chinese Cultural History* (Chicago, 1970); and Huang Gongwei 黃公偉, *Daojia zhexue xitong tanwei* 道家哲學系統探微 (Taipei, 1981). Huang's book is a comprehensive study of Taoist thought, including *Guanzi*, and is an invaluable source for the later commentarial tradition of *Zhuangzi*. However, he still attempts to present the *Zhuangzi* as if the book contained the ideas of basically one man.

5. A. C. Graham, "How Much of *Chuang Tzu* Did Chuang Tzu Write?," in *Studies in Chinese Philosophy and Philosophical Literature* (Singapore, 1986), 283–321. Guan Feng 關鋒 "*Zhuangzi* wai za pian chutan," in *Zhuangzi zhexue taolun ji* 莊子哲學討論集 (Peking, 1962), 61–98.

6. Ban Gu's *Hanshu Yiwen zhi*, Hualian edition, Taipei, n.d., 38, mentions Song Xing as a Huang-Lao scholar. Yan Shigu's 顏師古 commentary on p. 33 quotes Liu Xiang that both Song Xing and Yin Wen were at Jixia. Guo Moruo *Shi pipan shu* 十批判書 (Peking, 1962), 154, lists them as Huang-Lao thinkers from Jixia who formed one lineage of early Daoist philosophy. He further maintains that because Xunzi 荀子 did not understand the full range of Song Xing's ideas, he thought he was a Mohist (162–63). Both men are criticized in the "Below in the Empire" chapter of *Zhuangzi* (*Zhuangzi yinde*, Harvard-Yenching Institute Sinological Series #33, 33/33–41). All references to the text are from the edition in this work. See A. C. Graham, *Disputers of the Tao* (LaSalle, IL: Open Court, 1989), 95–100, for a detailed treatment of Song Xing.

7. "Mending Nature" seems very close to the Primitivist perspective. It advocates a primal Utopia, and contains the only discussion of human nature outside the Primitivist documents. The principal reason it has not been classified as Primitivist is its advocacy of the Confucian moral virtues the Primitivist despises. This advocacy is contained in only two brief lines of text in which definitions of Benevolence, Rightness, Loyalty, Ritual, and Music are linked to the Way and the Power (16/2–4). I would suggest the possibility that these lines are interpolations added by the Syncretist compiler to an essay in the Primitivist mode written by a different author (because the style is so different). A. C. Graham, *Chuang Tzu: Textual Notes to a Partial Translation* (London, 1982), 45, cites Ma Xulun on possible textual corruption here. The text makes sense without the forty-five characters beginning with 夫德 and ending with 禮也.

8. Zhuang Xing 莊幸 was a late Warring States minister from Chu whose ideas are contained in a text titled *Xing chen lun* 幸臣論. *Zhongwen dazidian* 31795.36.

9. Harold D. Roth, "Psychology and Self-Cultivation in Early Taoistic Thought," *Harvard Journal of Asiatic Studies* 51.2, December 1991 (chapter 1 in the present volume).

10. The references to Huang-Lao teachings and masters scattered throughout the *Shiji* and *Hanshu* are summarized in K. C. Hsiao, *A History of Chinese Political Thought*, vol. 1, trans. F. W. Mote (Princeton, 1979), 552–56. See also Benjamin Schwartz, *The World of Thought in Ancient China* (Cambridge, 1985), 237–54, for an excellent survey of Huang-Lao thought.

11. *Shiji*, ch. 74. Zhonghua edition (Peking, 1959), 2347, lists Shen Dao 慎道 and Tian Pian 田駢 among the Huang-Lao thinkers at Jixia. Both are criticized at *Zhuangzi* 33/41–54. *Shiji*, ch. 80, 2436, gives a lineage of Huang-Lao masters, none of whom are the Huang-Lao scholars otherwise identified at Jixia. There is as yet no scholarly consensus on the existence of any writings of any of these thinkers. Also *Shiji*, ch. 63, says that the thought of Hanfeizi and Shen Buhai were based in part on Huang-Lao. The relationship of pre-Han to Han Huang-Lao, and that (if any) of Huang Lao to Legalism, awaits further clarification, especially in light of the Huang-ti manuscripts discovered at Mawangdui. However, at this point I agree with Schwartz, op. cit., 237, that Huang-Lao is much broader in scope than the fusion of Daoism and Legalism that many scholars now take it to be.

12. The term "Lao-Zhuang" seems to have first been used during the Wei and Jin Dynasties in the writings of, and about, the Profound Learning scholars such as Wang Bi, He Yan, Ji Kang, and Guo Xiang. For details on this group, see He Qimin 何啓民 *Weijin sixiang yu tanfeng* 魏晉思想與談風 (Taipei, 1967), 103–15. See also Roth, op. cit., note 14 (chapter 1 in the present volume).

13. The most complete discussion of Religious Taoist techniques of self-cultivation are found in two sources: Henri Maspero, "Les Procédés de Nourrir Le Principe Vitale Dans La Religion Taoïste Ancienne," *Journal Asiatique* 4–6 (1937): 177–252; 7–9, 353–430; translated by Frank Kierman in *Taoism and Chinese Religion* (Amherst, 1981), 443–554; and Joseph Needham, *Science and Civilization in Ancient China*, vol. 5, part 5 (Cambridge, 1983).

These techniques involve the generation and manipulation of the Vital Energy (*qi*), the Vital Essence (*jing*), and the Numen (*shen*). These ideas are first developed in the three *Guanzi* essays and the *Huainanzi*. For details see Roth, op. cit.

14. Guan, op. cit., 61.

15. Graham, "How Much," op. cit., 317.

16. Ibid., 316.

17. A. C. Graham, *Chuang Tzu: The Inner Chapters* (London, 1981), 257.

18. Schwartz, op. cit., 248.

19. *Huainanzi*, *Sibu congkan* edition: 2/3b, 7b; 11/12b; 12/2a; 14/4b, 7a. All citations from this text and the *Guanzi* are from the *SBCK*.

20. See the observations of Schwartz, op. cit., 250ff.

21. Sima Qian 司馬遷 says that his father studied Daoist treatises with a man named Master Huang 黃子. The commentator Xu Guang identifies him as Huang Sheng 黃生, a Huang-Lao master. *Shiji*, ch. 130, 3288.

22. Ibid., 3289. For the rationale for translating *jing shen* as "Numinous Essence" (a shortened form of "Numen as Vital Essence") see Roth, op. cit., note 19, and section on *jing shen*.

23. Translated by Benjamin Wallacker in *Behavior, Culture, and Cosmos* (New Haven, 1962).

24. *Shiji*, ch. 130, 3289.

25. Ibid., 3292.

26. Guo Moruo 郭沫若, "Song Xing Yin Wen yizhu kao" 宋鈃尹文遺著考, in *Qingtong shidai* 清銅時代 (Shanghai, 1951, reprinted, Peking, 1957), 245–71.

27. Guan, op. cit., 70–80.

28. See Guo "Song Xing," op. cit., and Allyn Rickett, *Kuan Tzu: A Repository of Early Chinese Thought* (Hong Kong, 1965), 155–58. Graham, *Disputers of the Tao*, op. cit., 100, speaks of the *Neiye* as a fourth-century BCE work. A fourth text, *Baixin* 白心 "The Purified Mind," is usually considered with these other three, but because of the virtual absence of any theories of self-cultivation in this work I see no compelling reason to do so.

29. Roth, op. cit. (chapter 1 in the present volume).

30. Graham, "How Much," op. cit., 316–17.

31. Graham, *Disputers of the Tao*, op. cit., 100.

32. *De* is absent from the *SBCK* edition but present in the Liu Ji edition.

33. See note 22.

34. Maspero (Kierman), op. cit., 36, 282, 365, 368, 409, 419.

35. Rickett, op. cit., 156.

36. Textual notes: *Line 1*: I read 反 as 身, after Guo Moruo, *Guanzi jijiao*. Peking, 1955, 652; *Line 3*: Reversing the order of 行 and 正, and reading 美 as 儀, after Kuo, 652; *Line 4*: Reading 美 as 儀 a similar-form corruption, based on context.

37. Hsiao (Mote), op. cit., 570–73.

38. Roth, op. cit. (chapter 1 in the present volume).

39. Roger T. Ames, *The Art of Rulership* (Hawaii, 1983).

40. For an excellent analysis of Naturalist philosophy in the *Huainanzi*, see John Major, *Topography and Cosmology in Early Han Thought*. Unpublished doctoral dissertation, Harvard University, 1973.

41. See the analysis of the *Jing shen* essay of the *Huainanzi* in Roth, op. cit.

42. Harold D. Roth, "The Concept of Human Nature in the *Huai-nan Tzu*," *Journal of Chinese Philosophy* 12 (1985): 1–22.

43. For a tabulation of the occurrences of textual borrowings in the *Huainanzi*, see Charles LeBlanc, *The Idea of Resonance in Early Han Thought*

(Hong Kong, 1985), 83. For an analysis of the use of *Zhuangzi* material in the *Huainanzi*, see Wang Shumin, "*Huainanzi yu Zhuangzi*," in Chen Xinxiong 陳新雄 and Yu Dacheng 于大成, *Huainanzi lunwen ji* (Taipei, 1976), 27–39.

44. *Huainanzi*, 12/15b8–9.

45. For example, see the Naturalist cosmogonic interpretation in *Huainanzi* 2/1a of the famous infinite regress in *Zhuangzi* 2/49–52.

46. Guan, op. cit., 71–73; Graham, "How Much," op. cit., 318–19.

47. Graham, loc. cit., and *Chuang Tzu*, 257.

48. Graham, *Chuang Tzu*, 265.

49. Ibid., 268.

49. Ibid., 268.

50. Ibid., 271.

51. Ibid., 269.

52. Ibid., 259.

53. Ibid., 265.

54. Loc. cit.

55. While Sima Tan does not actually use the term *li*, I interpret the sentence translated above in section IIA to refer to the discovery of the natural guidelines that govern the activity of all phenomena: "(The Daoist school) is therefore able to explore the genuine basis of things" 故能究物之情.

56. Graham, *Chuang Tzu*, op. cit., 274.

57. Ames, op. cit., especially chapters 5 and 6.

58. Graham, *Chuang Tzu*, op. cit., 261.

59. Ibid., 261–62.

60. Textual notes: *Line 1*: I read 無 as 而 after Wang Niansun (Guo, *Guanzi*, op. cit., 635); *Line 3*: I read 之 as 有, after Ding Shihan (Kuo, 636); *Line 4*: I read 未 as 大, after Ding and Kuo (Kuo, 636).

61. Ames, op. cit.

62. Ibid., 149.

63. Loc. cit.

64. Ibid., 153.

65. Graham, "How Much," op. cit., 317.

66. See Lu Deming's preface in Guo Qingfan, op. cit., 6–7.

67. Ma Xulun, *Zhuangzi yizheng* (Shanghai, 1930); Graham, "How Much," op. cit., 302.

68. Wang Shumin, *Zhuangzi jiaoshi*. Wang collected 149 fragments of the lost *Zhuangzi* material and Ma, 126.

69. Guo Qingfan found fragments of the Sima Biao commentary that are not included in Lu Deming. For example, see 386, 555, 1103, 1114.

70. Wang Shumin, "*Huainanzi yu Zhuangzi*," op. cit., 39–40.

71. *Wenxuan zhu* 文選注, SBCK edition, 26/24a; 31/29a; 60/16a.

72. See Lu Deming's preface in Guo Qingfan, op. cit., 7.

73. The Kozanji manuscript edition containing seven chapters of the *Zhuangzi* (23, 26–28, 30, 31, 33) contains the lost colophon of Guo Xiang previously only known in fragmentary form in Lu Deming. It is analyzed in Wang Shumin, "Bo Jiben Gaoshansi jiuchao zhuanzi ben *Zhuangzi* can zhuan," reprinted in *Zhuzi jiaozheng* (Taipei, 1964), 549–65.

74. Wu Zeyu 吳則虞, "*Huainanzi shulu*," *Wenshi* 文史 2, 1963, 314.

75. Graham, *Chuang Tzu*, op. cit., 181–82.

76. Ibid., 199.

76. Ibid., 199.

77. Michael Loewe, *Chinese Ideas of Life and Death* (London, 1982), 182.

78. Yü Ying-shih, "Life and Immortality in the Mind of Han China," *Harvard Journal of Asiatic Studies* 25 (1965): 105.

Chapter 3

1. Harold D. Roth, "Text and Edition in Early Chinese Philosophical Literature," *Journal of the American Oriental Society* 113, no. 2 (1993): 214–27.

2. For excellent and succinct surveys of these approaches, see Edgar V. McKnight, *What Is Form Criticism?* (Philadelphia: Fortress Press, 1969), and Norman Perrin, *What Is Redaction Criticism?* (Philadelphia: Fortress Press, 1969).

3. William Boltz, "The Religious and Philosophical Significance of the 'Hsiang erh' *Lao Tzu* in the Light of the Ma-wang-tui Silk Manuscripts," *Bulletin of the School of Oriental and African Studies* 45, no. 1 (1982): 95–117. Boltz follows redaction criticism implicitly when he discusses the textual variants in the *Xianger* 想爾 *Laozi* that appear to be emendations to fit the particular ideology of the Way of the Celestial Masters (*Tianshi Dao* 天師道) Daoist sect of the second century AD.

Victor Mair, *Tao Te Ching: The Classic Book of Integrity and the Way* (New York: Bantam, 1990), especially 119–30. Mair implicitly follows form and redaction criticism in his demonstrations of the various forms of oral composition in the *Laozi* and in arguments about later editorial activity found therein.

Michael LaFargue, *The Tao of the Tao Te Ching* (Albany: State University of New York Press, 1992) and *Tao and Method: A Reasoned Approach to the Tao Te Ching* (Albany: State University of New York Press, 1994). LaFargue works explicitly with both form and redaction criticism. I wish to thank him for sending me copies of the galleys for several parts of this latter book.

4. LaFargue, *The Tao of the Tao Te Ching*, 197.

5. Ibid.

6. Dan O. Via Jr., "Editor's Forward," in Perrin, *What Is Redaction Criticism?*, vi–vii. I have changed the original "theological" to "ideological" to generalize the author's point beyond the Christian tradition.

7. I first presented this hypothesis in "Psychology and Self-Cultivation in Early Taoistic Thought," *Harvard Journal of Asiatic Studies* 51, no. 2 (1991): 599–650. The contrary hypothesis is found in Guo Moruo 郭沫若, "Song Xing Yin Wen yizhu kao 宋銒尹文遺著考," in Guo Moruo, *Qingtong shidai* 青銅時代 (Shanghai: Xinwen, 1951), 261–65. This characterization oversimplifies Kuo's position, whose details are presented below.

8. Nathan Sivin, "On the Word 'Taoist' as a Source of Perplexity," *History of Religions* 17, no. 3/4 (1978): 303–30.

9. See Roth, "Psychology and Self-Cultivation in Early Taoistic Thought," and Harold Roth, "Who Compiled the *Chuang Tzu*?," in *Chinese Texts and Philosophical Contexts: Essays Dedicated to Angus C. Graham*, ed. Henry Rosemont Jr. (LaSalle, IL: Open Court Press, 1991), 79–128 (chapters 1 and 2 in the present volume).

10. *Shiji* 史記 (Peking: Zhonghua, 1959), 130.3288–92.

11. For an analysis of Sima Tan's understanding of what he first called "Daoism," see Roth "Psychology and Self-Cultivation in Early Taoistic Thought," 604–608 (chapter 1, pp. 24–27 in the present volume); and Roth, "Who Compiled the *Chuang Tzu*?," 86–88 (chapter 2, pp. 69–71 in the present volume).

12. Guan Feng, "*Zhuangzi* wai za pian chutan" 莊子外雜篇初談, in Zhuangzi *zhexue taolun ji* 莊子哲學討論集 (Peking: Zhonghua, 1962), 61–98; A. C. Graham, "How Much of *Chuang Tzu* Did Chuang Tzu Write?," in *Studies in Chinese Philosophy and Philosophical Literature* (reprint, Albany: State University of New York Press, 1990), 283–321.

13. Liu Xiaogan, *Zhuangzi zhexue ji qi yanbian* 莊子哲學及其演變 (Peking: Zhongguo Shehui Kexue chubanshe, 1987), 84.

14. Roth, "Psychology and Self-Cultivation in Early Taoistic Thought."

15. Roth, "Psychology and Self-Cultivation in Early Taoistic Thought," especially the conclusions on 648–50 (chapter 1, p. 61 in the present volume); and Roth, "Who Compiled the *Chuang Tzu*?," especially 86–87 and 95–114 (chapter 2, pp. 69–70 and 77–96 in the present volume).

16. Roth, "Psychology and Self-Cultivation in Early Taoistic Thought"; Roth, "Who Compiled the *Chuang Tzu*?"; and Harold D. Roth, "The Inner Cultivation Tradition of Early Taoism," in *Religions of China in Practice*, ed. Stephen F. Teiser (Princeton: Princeton University Press, 1996).

17. The *Shiji* (74.2347) mentions Huang-Lao teachers at the Jixia Academy circa 300 BC and further delineates a lineage of Huang-Lao masters (80.2436), but it is difficult to definitively establish that any authored a specific text.

18. Apparently analogous practices and their concomitant results are known, cross-culturally, in many different mystical traditions. For a recent analysis of these practices under the general category of techniques of "forgetting," see Robert K. C. Forman, "Introduction: Mysticism, Constructivism, and Forgetting," in *The Problem of Pure Consciousness*, ed. Robert K. C. Forman (New York: Oxford University Press, 1990), 3–49.

19. *Mengzi*, 2A2 (the famous passage on the "floodlike vital energy"); *Xunzi yinde* 荀子引得, Harvard-Yenching Institute Sinological Index Series no. 22 (Peking, Harvard-Yenching Institute, 949), 4/2/5–10, 15–19; *Lüshi chunqiu*, for example, "The Essential Desires" (*qing yu* 情欲), 2.6a10, 2.7a9. For an excellent analysis of the Mawangdui physical hygiene texts, see Donald Harper, "The Sexual Arts of Ancient China as Described in a Manuscript of the Second Century B.C.," *Harvard Journal of Asiatic Studies* 47, no. 2 (1987): 539–93.

20. It could be argued that analogous practices and results obtain in "mystical" traditions in many different cultures. For a discussion of early Taoist mysticism in light of the comparative study of mystical experience, see Livia Kohn, *Early Chinese Mysticism: Philosophy and Soteriology in the Taoist Tradition* (Princeton: Princeton University Press, 1992), and my review article titled "Some Issues in the Study of Early Chinese Mysticism," *China Review International* 2, no. 1 (Spring 1995, in press).

21. *Zhuangzi yinde* 40/15/5; *Huainanzi*, 7.6a10.

22. A. C. Graham, "The Origins of the Legend of Lao Tan," in *Chinese Texts and Philosophical Contexts*, 111–24; *Zhuangzi yinde*, 90/33/1. The identification of the author of the *Laozi* with the figure of Lao Dan, a ritualist senior to Confucius who, in Confucian legend, taught the rites to the master himself, is a brilliant tactic of one-upsmanship that bespeaks the existence of a school developing an identity in contradistinction to its Confucian rivals. This development is further attested by the label of "*dao shu*," which suggests that the Syncretist author of *Zhuangzi* 33 thought of himself and his group as the exclusive preservers of this comprehensive philosophy, of which the other thinkers discussed in this chapter had only one aspect. The full implications of this important chapter for the early history of Daoism have yet to be worked out. One possibility is that this self-identification was known to Sima Tan and influenced his choice of the term "*Daojia*" for this group.

23. Roth, "Psychology and Self-Cultivation in Early Taoistic Thought," 607.

24. Mair, *Tao Te Ching: The Classic Book of Integrity and the Way*, 120ff.; LaFargue, *The Tao of the Tao Te Ching*, 196–98.

25. LaFargue, *Tao and Method: A Reasoned Approach to the Tao Te Ching*, 181ff. Where I disagree with LaFargue is in his contention that the sayings in "Neiye" and the *Laozi* are exclusively "experientially evocative" and not "analytically explanatory." While they are most certainly "experientially evocative," they also contain attempts to provide analytical explanations of the noetic content of their experiences of self-transformation. That they are not always consistent speaks of their newness and experimental character, not of their lack of philosophical intent.

26. Donald Harper has discussed the development and nature of such technical literature in the late Warring States and early Han in an insightful article, "Tekhnê in Han Natural Philosophy: Evidence from Ma-wang-tui Medical Manuscripts," in *Sagehood and Systematizing Thought in Warring States and Han*

China, ed. Kidder Smith Jr. (Brunswick, ME: Bowdoin College Asian Studies Program, 1990), 33–45.

27. Allyn Rickett, *Guanzi: Political, Economic, and Philosophical Essays from Early China* (Princeton: Princeton University Press, 1985), 15.

28. A. C. Graham, *Disputers of the Tao* (LaSalle, IL: Open Court Press, 1989), 95–100.

29. Allyn Rickett, "Four Daoist Chapters of the *Kuan Tzu*: The Origins of the So-called *Si shu* Chapters," manuscript, 9–15. Similar material is also found in relevant sections from the second volume of Rickett's *Guanzi* translation kindly sent to me in manuscript form by Professor Rickett. I wish to thank him for sending me these two manuscripts, both of which were very helpful in the preparation of this article.

30. Redaction criticism suggests that the small amount of prose material is the creation of the composer of the original written text or, in at least two instances where there is a radical intellectual shift (my VI.4 and XX), the interpolations of a later editor.

31. Jeffrey Riegel, "The Four 'Tzu Ssu' Chapters of the *Li Chi*" (PhD diss., Stanford University, 1978), 143–69. In an appendix to this work, Riegel presents a critical text of "Neiye" based on the manuscript of Gustav Haloun, given to him by Denis Twitchett. This critical text is divided into eighteen stanzas, of which four are further subdivided, thus yielding a total of twenty-two. However, the twenty-two stanzas of this critical text differ somewhat from my own arrangement. n.b.: Subsequently, in my book on "Neiye," I changed this number of stanzas of verses to 26. See *Original Tao: "Inward Training" and the Foundations of Taoist Mysticism* (New York: Columbia University Press, 1999).

32. Rickett, "Four Daoist Chapters of the *Guanzi*: The Origins of the So-called *Si shu* Chapters," 29–45, divides the text into fifteen sections. Within these, he finds an additional eighteen subsections, thus totaling thirty-three distinct stanzas.

33. This is the conclusion of LaFargue, *Tao and Method: A Reasoned Approach to the Tao Te Ching*, 187.

34. For passages elucidating these themes in both the core and the explanatory sections of "Hsin-shu, shang," see, for example, *Guanzi* (*Sibu congkan* ed.), 13.1a10 and 2b5, 1b2 and 3a2, 1b7 and 3b2, and 2a3 and 4a3. All textual references to the *Guanzi* in this article are to this edition.

35. The *locus classicus* of this distinctive metaphor is in the following lines: "Neiye," 16.2b10:

> 敬除其舍,
> Reverently clean out its abode
> (神之)精自來。
> And the vital essence of the numen will come on its own.
> Compare this with "Xinshu shang." 13.1a11:

虛其欲

If you become empty of desires

神將入舍。

Then the numen will enter its abode.

掃除不絜

But if your sweeping clean is not pure,

神<乃>「不」留處。

The numen will not remain there.

See also the explanatory section on this passage at 13.2b8 and another reference to this metaphor at 13.1b8, with an explanation at 13.3b8.

36. Roth, "Who Compiled the *Chuang Tzu*?," 91–92, 96–98 (chapter 2, pp. 74–75, 79–80 in the present volume).

37. Guo Moruo, "Song Xing Yin Wen i-chu k'ao," 261–65. See also Xu Weiyu, Wen Yiduo, and Guo Moruo, *Guanzi jijiao* 官子集校 (Peking: Zhonghua shuju, 1955), 658.

38. Rickett, "Four Daoist Chapters of the *Guanzi*: The Origins of the So-called *Si shu* Chapters," 19–22.

39. I first presented this hypothesis in Roth, "Psychology and Self-Cultivation in Early Taoistic Thought," 627–28 (chapter 1, p. 43 in the present volume).

40. Bernhard Karlgren, *The Authenticity and Nature of the Tso Chuan* (Goteborg: Elanders Boktryckeri Aktrebolag), 1926.

41. 16.4al0 contains two examples of *moruo* 莫若 ("there is nothing like/ as good as"), which disrupt a pattern of four-character phrases. 16.4b6 contains five similar examples in an unrhymed passage presenting a Confucian interpretation of how to curb the emotions. Because both disrupt regular patterns and the latter introduces an ideology foreign to the rest of the text, I consider them likely interpolations. Such disruptions of patterns are characteristic signs of interpolation according to redaction criticism. For further details on 16.4b6, see n.90.

42. The sole exception, at 13.6al in "Xinshu xia," is so unusual as to suggest an emendation. For Karlgren (37–38), the virtually exclusive use of *ru* for "like" is a characteristic of the language of the *Zuozhuan*.

43. Karlgren, The *Authenticity and Nature of the Tso Chuan*, 39–40, maintains that the preposition *hu* is virtually absent from the *Zuozhuan* dialect.

44. For a summary and final resolution of the debate on the nature of *wu4* between Edward Pulleyblank and A. C. Graham, see Pulleyblank, "Some Notes on Morphology and Syntax in Classical Chinese," in *Chinese Texts and Philosophical Contexts*, 34–41. For Graham's reply, see "Reflections and Replies" in the same volume, 272–73.

45. Examples of these negatives are found at "Xinshu xia": 13.4b5,6, for *bu*; 5a3,4, for *wu²* 毋; 4bl2 for *wu²* 無. W.A.C.H. Dobson, A *Dictionary of Chinese Particles* (Toronto: University of Toronto Press, 1972), 100–101, 790–92, states

that a feature of the Han literary language is this blurring of the previously distinct differences among all negatives except wu^2 無 and *bu*. He calls this "blunted usage."

46. Karlgren, *The Authenticity and Nature of the Tso Chuan*, 40–41, notes this *yü* as a Lu characteristic, but only as a conjunction between nouns. He is silent on it as a prenominal preposition.

47. Both occurrences of *zhe* in "Xinshu shang" are at 13.1a12. Two of the occurrences of *zhe* in "Neiye" are found at 16.2a11, and the other two are at 16.3a4–5.

48. Rickett, "Four Daoist Chapters of the *Guanzi*: The Origins of the So-called *Si shu* Chapters," 16–17.

49. I have used the *Sibu congkan* edition of the *Guanzi* as the basis for these tables and for my new arrangement of "Xinshu xia" showing its "Neiye" parallels. In the Appendix to this chapter, "Xinshu xia" is complete and presented in the same order in which it occurs in all extant editions. The principal difference between them and my own arrangement is that I have divided the text into seven sections. The "Neiye" parallels to "Xinshu xia" presented in the Appendix constitute about one-third of the text of "Neiye." I often refer to sections of these two texts according to my own arrangement in the Appendix. All other references to them are to the *Sibu congkan* edition.

50. Rickett, "Four Daoist Chapters of the *Guanzi*: The Origins of the So-called *Si shu* Chapters," 20–21.

51. For details, see the Appendix to this chapter.

52. The term "redaction strategy" is my own. It is suggested by the research on redaction criticism by New Testament scholars, but I am not aware of a source that has abstracted these strategies from the concrete results of this general methodology. Much of this research is very highly focused on the New Testament Gospels and makes no attempt to establish general principles that could be applied to texts of other traditions, as I am doing here.

53. All textual references in the following section are to the Chinese texts of "Xinshu xia" and "Neiye" included in the Appendix.

54. Roth, "Who Compiled the *Chuang Tzu*?," especially 86–87, 92, 96–98 (chapter 2, pp. 69–70, 75, and 79–80 in the present volume).

55. *Zhuangzi yinde*, 91/33/14.

56. For explanations of the emendations to the Chinese texts included in the main body of the article, please see the introduction to the Appendix.

57. Roth, "Who Compiled the *Chuang Tzu*?," 108–9 (chapter 2, pp. 90–91 in the present volume).

58. H. G. Creel, "The Meaning of 性命 Hsing-ming," in *What Is Taoism? And Other Studies in Chinese Cultural History* (Chicago: University of Chicago Press, 1970), 79–91.

59. In the *Jing fa*, see, for example, the arguments in "Daofa" 道法; *Mawangdui hanmu boshu* 馬王堆漢墓帛書 vol. 1 (Peking: Wenwu chubanshe,

1980) 43.5–8. For *Zhuangzi*, see, for example, *Zhuangzi yinde* 34/13/33. For "Xinshu shang," see *Sibu congkan* edition, 13.lb12 and 3b9.

60. Roth, "Who Compiled the *Chuang Tzu*?," 95–99 (chapter 2, pp. 77–79 in the present volume).

61. Harper, "Tekhne in Han Natural Philosophy: Evidence From Ma-wang-tui Medical Manuscripts," 33–37.

62. David Keegan, "The 'Huang-ti nei-ching': The Structure of the Compilation and the Significance of the Structure" (PhD dissertation: University of California, Berkeley, 1988).

63. Keegan, "The Huang-ti nei-ching," 219–33, especially 226–28 for Cang's memorial from the *Shiji*.

64. Keegan, "The Huang-ti nei-ching,"' 231.

65. Graham, *Disputers of the Tao*, 100.

66. I consider this a gloss inserted into the text by an unknown commentator, or possibly a conjectural reconstruction of a damaged original, erroneously transmitted as part of the text. Riegel, "The Four 'Tzu Ssu' Chapters of the *Li Chi*," 158, follows Haloun in deleting this clause for disrupting the rhyme pattern. Furthermore, it represents an intrusion of Confucian concepts into a text that is, with one very suspicious exception, totally devoid of them. For the exception, see below, n. 25. Finally, the text makes perfect sense without this clause.

67. Riegel, "The Four 'Tzu Ssu' Chapters of the *Li Chi*," 158, follows Haloun in emending *zhi* 至 to *lai* 來 to preserve the rhyme (德 tək; 至 tjier; 來 ləɣ) and because of the parallel in "Xinshu xia," I.B.1. The archaic Chinese pronunciations are taken from Zhou Fagao 周法高, *Hanzi gujin yinhui* 漢字古今音彙 (Hong Kong: The Chinese University Press, 1973).

68. *Guanzi jijiao*, 787. Textual contamination from line IX.6; also *yi* 義 is absent from the Yin commentary (Wang Niansun 王念孫).

69. *Guanzi jijiao*, 651. Contamination from explanatory sections of "Xinshu shang" (Tao Hongqing 陶鴻慶).

70. *Guanzi jijiao*, 652. Similar-form corruption. Emendation from parallel use of *shen* in next line (Guo Moruo).

71. *Guanzi jijiao*, 652. Phonetic loan (Liu Ji).

72. *Guanzi jijiao*, 652. Semantic emendation (Guo Moruo).

73. *Guanzi jijiao*, 652. Similar-form corruption from the common form of *zheng* 証 (Xu and Guo).

74. *Guanzi jijiao*, 790. Similar-form corruption restored from Liu Ji and Zhu Dongguang editions (Guo Moruo). The same emendation occurs in line 14.

75. *Guanzi jijiao*, 791. Graphic inversion, emended to preserve the rhyme with *yi* 一 jiet (吉 kjiet) (Wang Niansun). Also paralleled in "Xinshu xia," III.B.3.

76. *Guanzi jijiao*, 653. Similar-form corruption in lines 1 and 3 (Guo Moruo).

77. *Guanzi jijiao*, 786. Similar-form corruption, restored based on semantic context: "This is what I mean (by 'When a regulated mind lies within')." This

is the understanding of the Yin commentary, which says, *zhi xin zhi wei* 治心之謂 (This is the meaning of a 'regulated mind') (Wang Niansun).

78. *Guanzi jijiao*, 654. Similar-form corruption; semantic restoration (Guo Moruo).

79. *Guanzi jijiao*, 654. Similar-form corruption. The bronze-inscription form of *si* 司 closely resembles the standard clerical script (*lishu* 隸書) form of *luan* 亂. *Er* 而 is a phonetic loan for *neng* 能, The characters *ren suo* 人所 are restored to their proper order through a semantic emendation (Guo Moruo).

80. *Guanzi jijiao*, 785. Textual contamination from Yin commentary. Deleting *an* 安 preserves the parallel structure of the first three sentences (Xu Weiyu).

81. Riegel, "The Four 'Tzu Ssu' Chapters of the *Li Chi*," 156; *Guanzi jijiao*, 785. Emendation to preserve rhyme: *cai* 材 (dz əɣ), *shi* 時 (dji əɣ), *mo* 謀 (mjw əɣ). Wang Niansun further supports this emendation with analogous passages from other essays in the *Guanzi* and other early works.

82. *Guanzi jijiao*, 785–86. Emendation based upon the Yin commentary that preserves the parallel structure with the previous line (Xu Weiyu).

83. *Guanzi jijiao*, 655. The two characters are homophones, with the latter reading, meaning "elastic," preferred to the former, meaning "tough, hard," based on semantic context and "Neiye" parallel (Li Zheming 李哲明).

84. *Guanzi jijiao*, 789. *Xin* 信 an archaic form of *shen* 伸 (Dai Wang 戴望).

85. *Guanzi jijiao*, 656. Similar-form corruption restored from "Neiye" parallel (Liu Ji and others). Also found in line 11.

86. *Guanzi jijiao*, 790. Similar-form corruption restored from "Xinshu xia," VI.B.4 (Liu Ji and Wang Niansun).

87. *Guanzi jijiao*, 657. Similar-form corruption restored from semantic context (reward/punishment contrast) and "*Neiye*" parallel. Also found in line 3 (Yu Yue 俞樾).

88. *Guanzi jijiao*, 790. Similar-form corruption restored to preserve rhyme: *wu* 惡 (·ak); *gu* 鼓 (kw əɣ); *mu* 母 (m əɣ) (Guo Moruo). This emendation also agrees with the variant in the parallel line from "Xinshu xia" (VI.D.2).

89. *Guanzi jijiao*, 657. Similar-form corruption restored from all other editions (Guo Moruo).

90. Riegel, "The Four 'Tzu Ssu' Chapters of the *Li Chi*," 167. Similar-form corruption ("graphic error" in Riegel's terminology). Riegel supplies no justification for this emendation, but undoubtedly the parallel line in "Xinshu xia" (VII.A.4), which contains the character *ruo* 若, should be a factor. Furthermore, *huan* 患 is not usually listed in typical arrangements of the four emotions. Another factor could be the appearance of *le* 樂 in line 8.

I am very suspicious of the originality of most or all of the remainder of this passage, lines 5–12. To begin with, lines 6–8 do not rhyme. Second, lines 6–10 contain virtually the only use of *ruo* 若 in the text (for the other, see n. 31). Third, lines 5–12 contain one of the only two instances of Confucian technical terms in the entire text. Finally, these lines are introduced by the connective conjunction, *shi gu* (therefore), often an indicator of editorial comment according to the principles of redaction criticism. I suspect, therefore, that most or all of these lines represent material added to the original text of "Neiye." The identity of this commentator remains a subject for speculation that is beyond the parameters of the present study.

91. Similar-form corruption restored from semantic context.

92. *Guanzi jijiao*, 658, 788. Guo Moruo accepts Wang Niansun's emendation of *yin* 音 to *yi* 意 (similar-form corruption). He emends *yan* 言 to *yin* 音 to preserve the rhyme with *xin: yan* 言 (ngjan); *xin*, 心 (siəm); *yin* 音 (·iəm). Semantic context is a further unstated determinant of these emendations.

93. *Guanzi jijiao*, 658, 788. Emendation preserves the rhyme between *xing* and *ming*: 形 (geng); 名 (mjieng) (Guo Moruo). This also applies to the next line (XIL.19), where Guo Moruo further states that *shi* 使 and *shi* 事 were interchangeable at this period.

94. *Guanzi jijiao*, 658. Similar-form corruption restored from the variant in the Liu, Zhu and Zhao editions (Guo Moruo).

95. *Guanzi jijiao*, 658. The first emendation: Similar-form corruption restored from the Yin commentary that accompanies the text in most extant editions. The second emendation: Similar-form corruption restored based on semantic context (Wang Niansun).

96. *Guanzi jijiao*, 789. Similar-form corruption emended to preserve the rhyme between *jie* 竭 (giat) and *da* 達 (dat) (Wang Niansun).

Chapter 4

1. This summary is based on the following articles: "Psychology and Self-Cultivation in Early Taoistic Thought," *Harvard Journal of Asiatic Studies* 5, no. 2 (1991): 599–650; "Who Compiled the Chuang Tzu?," in Henry Rosemont Jr., ed., *Chinese Texts and Philosophical Contexts: Essays Dedicated to Angus C. Graham* (LaSalle, IL: Open Court, 1991); "Redaction Criticism and the Early History of Taoism," *Early China* 19 (1994): 1–46; and "The Inner Cultivation Tradition of Early Taoism," in Donald S. Lopez Jr., ed., *Religion of China in practice* (Princeton: Princeton University Press, 1996), 123–48.

2. See, for example, the important contrast made by the Syncretist author of *Zhuangzi* 33, that between those who follow the comprehensive *Dao shu* 道術 (namely, "us") and those who follow partial and incomplete techniques (*fang shu* 方術). I have elsewhere contended that this phrase testifies to the developing self-identity of the Syncretist Taoist school of the early Han and that it also could have served as the basis for Sima Tan's identification of them as the *Daojia* 道家.

3. Fukui Fumimasa, "The History of Taoist Studies in Japan and Some Related Issues," *Acta Asiatica* 68 (1995): 12–13.

4. See, for example, Daniel Brown, "The Stages of Meditation in Cross-Cultural Perspective," and John Chirban, "Developmental Stages in Eastern Orthodox Christianity," in Ken Wilber, Jack Engler, and Daniel Brown, *Transformations of Consciousness* (Boston: Shambala, 1986), 219–84 and 285–314.

5. For an analysis of breath meditation in the *Laozi*, see my "Laozi in the Context of Early Daoist Mystical Praxis," in P. J. Ivanhoe and Mark Csikszentmihalyi, eds., *Essays on Religious and Philosophical Aspects of the Laozi* (forthcoming). It includes a brief discussion of the *Zhuangzi*'s techniques of "fasting the mind" and "sitting and forgetting." These are found in *Zhuangzi yinde* 莊子引得, Harvard-Yenching Institute Sinological Index Series, no. 20 (Peking, 1947), 4/24–34 and 6/89–93.

6. *Zhuangzi yinde*, 6/36.

7. Donald Harper first noticed this structure in the twelve-sided jade knob. See Harper, "The Sexual Arts of Ancient China as Described in a Manuscript of the Second Century B.C.," *Harvard Journal of Asiatic Studies* 47, no. 2 (1987): 563.

8. Guo Moruo 郭沫若, "Gudai wenzizhi bianzheng de fazhan" 古代文字之辨證的發展, *Kaogu* 考古 5 (1972): 9.

9. Joseph Needham, *Science and Civilization in China*, vol. 2 (Cambridge: Cambridge University Press, 1956), 242. The inscription is translated and briefly discussed on p. 143.

10. Guo Moruo, 9.

11. For an excellent discussion on the use and significance of these terms in the *boshu*, see R. P. Peerenboom, *Law and Morality in Ancient China: The Silk Manuscripts of Huang-Lao* (Albany: State University of New York Press, 1993), 64–66.

12. Robin D. S. Yates, "The Yin-Yang Texts from Yinqueshan," *Early China* 19 (1994): 95–96 and 102. Yates observes an important difference: whereas the Yin-Yang texts are extremely detailed in their rules that humans must follow in order to harmonize with the greater patterns and cycles of Heaven and Earth, the *Huang-Lao boshu* are more abstract and generalized. They thus demonstrate the meaning of Sima Tan's statement about the Daoist lineage: they follow the general guidelines of the Yin-Yang lineage (*Shiji* 史記 [Peking: Chung-hua, 1959], 130.3289).

13. Harold D. Roth, "The Yellow Emperor's Guru: A Narrative Analysis from *Chuang Tzu* 11," *Taoist Resources* 7, no. 1 (1997) (chapter 5 in the present volume).

14. *Zhuangzi yinde*, 6/6–7. My translation is adapted from A. C. Graham, *Chuang Tzu: The Inner Chapters* (London: George Allen and Unwin, 1981), 84.

15. Harper, art. cit., 550.

16. Harold D. Roth, "What Is Huang-Lao?," a paper given at the 50th Annual Meeting of the Association for Asian Studies, New Orleans, LA, April 1991; and S. A. Queen and H. D. Roth, "Daoist Syncretisms of the Late Zhou, Qin and Han," in Wm. Theodore de Bary and Irene Bloom, eds., *Sources of Chinese Tradition* (revised ed., New York: Columbia University Press, in press).

17. *Mawangdui Hanmu boshu* 馬王堆漢墓帛書 (Peking: Wenwu Press), 1980, 53, lines 12–13. Characters in parentheses are alternate readings or conjectural emendations provided by the editors; those in brackets are my own conjectural emendations based on meaning.

18. I disagree completely with the conjectural restoration of these six missing graphs supplied by the editors (54, n. 71): (也。強生威。威) from a sentence in the *Shangjun shu*: 強生威。威生惠。It introduces a completely new topic, that of "strength," into the discourse and alters the meaning of the sorites that follows. My conjectural emendation continues the subject of preservation and loss of natural guidelines or patterns (*li* 理) from the previous paragraph and provides a logical link with the sorites structure that follows. Please note that the use of italics is to emphasize the textual material most relevant to the present investigation.

19. See, for example, Tian Fengtai 田鳳台, *Lüshi chunqiu tanwei* 呂氏春秋探微 (Taipei: Student Book Company, 1986), 153.

20. See, for example the following: Hsiao Kung-chuan, *A History of Chinese Political Thought*, vol. I, trans. F. W. Mote (Princeton: Princeton University Press, 1979), 556–70. Hsiao sees it as an expression of "pre-Ch'in egocentric thought" derived from the Yangists; A. C. Graham, *Disputers of the Tao* (LaSalle, IL: Open Court, 1989), 373–74, maintains that it combines "the essential elements of Legalist statecraft . . . with Confucian and to a lesser extent Mohist moralism, all inside the frame of Yin-Yang cosmolo . . . ," but concurs with Hsiao that its "organizing doctrine . . . is not Taoist but Yangist . . ."; Wu Guang 吳光, *Huang-Lao zhexue tonglun* 黃老哲學通論 (Hangzhou: Zhejiang Peoples' Press, 1985), 170–75, argues that the entire work should be classified as Huang-Lao.

21. Tian, 341–55. This total omits the thirteen essays that are part of the structural framework of the book and were probably written by the editor(s). This includes the twelve "records" (*ji* 記) essays, each devoted to listing the proper ritual observances to be observed by the ruler for each of the twelve months of the calendar and which occur at the beginning of each of the first twelve chapters. They have their own structure. It also omits the postface (*xu yi* 序意) to the first twelve chapters that is found at the end of the twelfth chapter.

22. Andrew S. Meyer, "The Huang-Lao Chapters of the *Lüshih chunqiu*," a paper given at the 53rd Annual Meeting of the Association for Asian Studies, Boston, March, 1994. Where I would qualify his argument is that there is little evidence to suggest that "Huang-Lao" is a label these thinkers applied to themselves at this time or that this label even existed before the Han. However, this does not change in any way the definite links between these chapters and the ideology of what later came to be thought of as Huang-Lao. Until this is

clarified further, I prefer simply to say that these chapters represent another form of Daoist syncretism with clear similarities to those other forms I have identified previously.

23. *A Concordance to the Lüshi chunqiu*, ed. D. C. Lau and Chen Fong Ching (Institute of Chinese Studies Ancient Chinese Texts Concordance Series, Philosophical Works, no. 12, Hong Kong: Commercial Press, 1994), 14–15.

24. Restricting desires (*jie shi yü* 節嗜欲 and relinquishing various types of biased thought (*shi zhi mo* 釋智謀 and *qu qiao gu* 去巧故) are characteristic technical terms of Syncretist Daoism. See my "Who Compiled the *Chuang Tzu*?," 96–97. They are also present in the two *Chuang-Tzu* passages on "mind-fasting" and "sitting and forgetting" cited above.

25. Harold D. Roth, "The Early Taoist Concept of *Shen*: A Ghost in the Machine?," in Kidder Smith, ed., *Sagehood and Systematizing Thought in the Warring States and Early Han* (Bowdoin University, 1989), 11–32.

26. Roth, "Psychology and Self-Cultivation in Early Taoistic Thought," 613–20 (chapter 1, pp. 30–36 in the present volume).

27. For this understanding of *shen*, see my "The Early Taoist Concept of *Shen*," 11–22 and "The Inner Cultivation Tradition of Early Taoism," 123–48, especially 126, 131, 136, 140.

28. Ibid., 162.

29. *Guanzi, Sibu congkan* 四部叢刊 edition, 16/4a2.

30. *Harvard-Yenching Concordance* [HYC], 64/23/66–70.

31. For a specific conceptual parallel, see the *Zhuangzi* passage on the "fasting of the mind," which contains the following phrase: 唯道集虛。虛者心齋也。(HYC, 9/4/28).

32. Roth, "Who Compiled the *Chuang Tzu*?," 88–92, 95–99 (chapter 2, pp. 71–75, 77–79 in the present volume).

33. *Guanzi*, 16/2b10: 敬除其舍; (神之)精將自來。

34. *Guanzi*, 13/1a10 (Statement) and 13/2b5 (Explanation).

35. This emendation to delete 乃 and replace it with 不, the variant in the Zhue Dongguang 朱東光 edition of 1579, is from Guo Moruo 郭沫若, Xu Weiyu 許維遹, Wen Yiduo 聞一多, *Guanzi jijiao* 管子集校 (Peking: Chung-hua shu chü, 1955), 634.

36. I emend the explanation to fit the sentence from the statement that it is paraphrasing.

37. This emendation is from Guo Moruo et al., *Guanzi jijiao*, 641.

38. I have emended 宜 to 正 because of the considerable semantic evidence for this from the other passages examined here and further, because of the possibility that the initial error was caused by a similar-form corruption of the original graph.

39. *Guanzi jijiao*, 641.

40. See, for example, the only discussion of meditative stages from the "Inner Chapters" of *Zhuangzi*, where Bu Liangyi is said to directly perceive his

own solitude (*jian du* 見獨), a stage directly before he is able to "be without past and present" (*neng wu gujin* 能無古今). *Zhuangzi yinde*, 6/41.

41. For an analysis of this aspect of "Xinshu shang," see my "Psychology and Self-Cultivation in Early Taoistic Thought," 620–25.

42. *A Concordance to the Huainanzi*, ed. D. C. Lau and Chen Fong Ching (Institute of Chinese Studies Ancient Chinese Texts Concordance Series, Hong Kong: Commercial Press, 1992), 7/55/20–24.

43. *Tong* usually means to circulate or to flow through without obstruction. From this comes the associated meaning of "to understand." My translation here, "to be absorbed," is an attempt to take these meanings and apply them to an epistemology of breath meditation in which the awareness, that is, the conscious focus of the adept, is the subject of this verb. When one is fully absorbed in inner meditation, there are no longer any mental obstructions to one's awareness. It is like our experience of being fully absorbed in reading a book or seeing a motion picture. In this experience, our awareness is totally absorbed in what it is experiencing and flows freely in the constantly changing objective field of the book or film. In this passage, because consciousness has been emptied through apophatic practice, the absorption is in an empty internal field, a pure numinous or spiritual consciousness in which the unitive power of the One is directly apprehended.

44. I have omitted the jade knob inscription from the table because it is unique among these passages in apparently not discussing the phenomenology of meditative stages. This uniqueness, which undoubtedly comes from its antiquity, does not disqualify it from consideration along with the other passages; indeed, it is the prototype of the rhetorical structure exhibited by all of them. However, to include its instructions for guiding the breath in the table would be like comparing apples and oranges.

45. For a discussion of these processes, see, for example, "Psychology and Self-Cultivation in Early Taoistic Thought," 611–20. For the reference to this metaphor, see *Guanzi* 16/2b10.

46. *Zhuangzi yinde*, 6/92–93.

47. *Guanzi*, 16/2a8, 2b8, 3b1, 4a6, and 16/4a1, respectively.

48. Harold D. Roth, "Some Issues in the Study of Chinese Mysticism: A Review Essay," *China Review International* 2, no. 1 (1995): 154–73; and idem, "*Laozi* in the Context of Early Daoist Meditative Praxis."

49. See the summary tables in Brown, "The Stages of Meditation in Cross-cultural Perspective," 272–84; and Chirban, "Developmental Stages in Eastern Orthodox Christianity," 300–1.

Chapter 5

1. Stephen D. Moore, *Literary Criticism and the Gospels: The Theoretical Challenge* (New Haven: Yale University Press, 1989). I wish to thank my colleague Professor Stanley Stowers for initially recommending this work to me.

2. Moore, 180 and Michael LaFargue, *The Tao of the Tao Te Ching* (Albany: State University of New York Press, 1992), 197.

3. Moore, 183 and LaFargue, 197.

4. Composition criticism is first suggested by Norman Perrin in his *What Is Redaction Criticism* (Philadelphia: Fortress Press, 1969), 65–76.

5. Moore, 179.

6. Guan Feng, "*Zhuangzi* wai za pian chutan" 莊子外雜篇初談, in *Zhuangzi zhexue taolun ji* 莊子哲學討論集 (Peking: Zhonghua, 1962), 61–98; A. C. Graham, "How Much of *Chuang Tzu* Did Chuang Tzu Write?," in *Studies in Chinese Philosophy and Philosophical Literature* (reprint, Albany: State University of New York Press, 1990), 283–321; Liu Xiaogan, *Zhuangzi zhexue ji qi yanbian* 莊子哲學及其演變 (Peking: Chinese Social Sciences Press, 1987). Part of this work has been translated into English and published as Liu Xiaogan, *Classifying the Zhuangzi Chapters*, trans. William E. Savage, Michigan Monographs in Chinese Studies 65 (Ann Arbor: Center for Chinese Studies, University of Michigan, 1994).

7. This is a simplified summary of the complex field of narrative criticism more fully described by Moore, see especially 7–14, 25–27, 41–47, 51–63.

8. Moore, 56–58.

9. For a fascinating and learned discussion of the meaning of this title, see D. C. Lau, "On the Expression Zai You 在宥," in *Chinese Texts and Philosophical Contexts: Essays Dedicated to Angus C. Graham*, ed. Henry Rosemont Jr. (LaSalle, IL: Open Court, 1991), 5–20, and Graham's reply, 267–72. I find Graham's argument more persuasive, but because his translation is rather cumbersome, I have chosen a translation that is more concise. No matter how one chooses to translate *zai you*, it is the innate nature of human beings that must be "preserved and circumscribed" according to the author in order to prevent its being damaged and ultimately destroyed by the seductive and destructive forces of civilization.

10. Robin D. S. Yates, "The Yin-Yang Texts from Yinqueshan," *Early China* 19 (1994): 83–88.

11. For a discussion of this text, see Donald Harper, "The Sexual Arts of Ancient China as Described in a Manuscript of the Second Century B.C.E.," *Harvard Journal of Asiatic Studies* 47, no. 2 (1987): 545–55.

12. *Mawangdui hanmu boshu* (Peking: Wenwu Press, 1980): section 3 of the *Shiliu jing* is on p. 65; section 9, p. 72; section 14, 79. The Yellow Emperor and his minister Li Hei are also found in section 2, pp. 62–63, but the narrative structure is different: the Yellow Emperor is not asking for teachings from Li Hei.

13. Donald Harper translates part of this instruction in Harper, 550–52.

14. I have in mind Charles LeBlanc, "A Re-Examination of the Myth of Huang-ti," *Journal of Chinese Religions* 13/14 (Fall 1985/1986): 45–64; and John S. Major, "Will the Real Yellow Emperor Please Stand Up?," unpublished manuscript obtained from author. These comprise the basis for the following summary portrayal.

15. *Mawangdui hanmu boshu*, 61, lines 1–2. For another translation, see Robin D. S. Yates, *Lost Scrolls from Mawangdui: Early Chinese Texts on Cosmology,*

Philosophy, and Government (New York: Ballantine Books, in press), author's manuscript, 88. I took the concept of an "exemplary image" from Yates.

16. *Mawangdui hanmu boshu*, 61, line 4.

17. *Mawangdui hanmu boshu*, 62; Yates, *Lost Scrolls*, 90.

18. *Shiji* (Peking: Zhonghua, 1959), chapter 130, 3289.

19. *Zhuangzi yinde* 莊子引得, Harvard-Yenching Institute Sinological Index Series 20 (Peking, 1947), 11/28 and 16/8.

20. *Zhuangzi yinde*, 24/31.

21. *Zhuangzi yinde*, 22/4.

22. *Zhuangzi yinde*, 14/13.

23. *A Concordance to the Huainanzi*, ed. D. C. Lau and Chen Fong Ching, The Institute of Chinese Studies Ancient Chinese Texts Concordance Series (Hong Kong: The Commercial Press, 1992), 14/134/2.

24. *Dōkyo jiten*. Comp. Fukui Bunga, Yamada Toshiaki, et al. (Tokyo: Heiho Publishing Co., 1994), 147, 302.

25. Guo Qingfan 郭慶藩, *Zhuang Tzu jishi* 莊子集釋, 1st ed., 1894/5. *Jiaozheng* 校正 *Chuang Tzu chi-shih* (Taipei: World Publishing Company, 1974), 379.

26. Harper, "Sexual Arts," 550–53.

27. Harper, "The Sexual Arts," 547.

28. *A Concordance to the Lüshi chunqiu*, ed. D. C. Lau and Chen Fong Ching, The Institute of Chinese Studies Ancient Chinese Texts Concordance Series, Philosophical Works 12 (Hong Kong: The Commercial Press, 1994), 17.4/102128; and *A Concordance to the Huainanzi*, 19/206/10.

29. *Dōkyo jiten*, 147.

30. The translations from this narrative and the one that follows in *Zhuangzi* 11 are largely my own, but I have consulted the following other translations: Burton Watson, *Chuang Tzu* (New York: Columbia University Press, 1968), 118–23; A. C. Graham, *Chuang Tzu: The Inner Chapters* (London: George Allen and Unwin, 1981), 177–79; Victor Mair, *Wandering on the Way: Early Taoist Tales and Parables from Chuang Tzu* (New York: Bantam Books, 1994), 94–100.

31. *Zhuangzi yinde*, 11/46.

32. One of the prevailing themes in this work is the importance of coordinating human institutions with the greater patterns of Heaven and Earth, complying with them rather than deviating from them; deviation causes great disasters to befall human beings and their environment. For an insightful analysis of this text, see R. P. Peerenboom, *Law and Morality in Ancient China: The Silk Manuscripts of Huang-Lao* (Albany: State University of New York Press, 1992).

33. *Zhuangzi yinde*, 11/51.

34. *Zhuangzi yinde*, 11/32. This turn of phrase is from Graham.

35. *Zhuangzi yinde*, 7/30.

36. For this argument, see my article "Redaction Criticism and the Early History of Taoism," *Early China* 19 (1994): 1–46.

37. The details of these practices in "Inward Training" are discussed in a number of works. Those most focused on inner cultivation are "Psychology and Self-Cultivation in Early Taoistic Thought," *Harvard Journal of Asiatic Studies* 51, no. 2 (1991): 599–650 (chapter 1 in this volume); and Harold D. Roth, "The Inner Cultivation Tradition of Early Taoism," in *Religions of China in Practice*, ed. Stephen F. Teiser (Princeton: Princeton University Press, 1996): 123–48.

38. Harold D. Roth, "Evidence for Stages of Meditation in Early Taoism," *Bulletin of the School of Oriental and African Studies* 60 (1997): 295–314 (chapter 4 in the present volume).

39. Harold D. Roth, "*Lao Tzu* in the Context of Early Taoist Mystical Praxis," in *Essays on the Religious and Philosophical Aspects of the Laozi*, ed. P. J. Ivanhoe and Mark Csikszentmihalyi (Albany: State University of New York Press, 1999), 33–58 (chapter 7 in the present volume).

40. *Zhuangzi yinde*, 11/38–39.

41. *Zhuangzi yinde*, 11/53–54.

42. *Zhuangzi yinde*, 11/40–42.

43. Another possible interpretation of the story is that rulership should be completely rejected in favor of spiritual cultivation. However, I do not think that this is the case for several reasons. First, Guang Chengzi tells his pupil that if you "attentively guard your own person, things will flourish by themselves." If the concern were only for individual cultivation, no mention would be made of other things. Second, Guang Chengzi states that his Way was practiced by the "emperors of the past" and will be by the "kings to come." This indicates an interest in rulership. On the other hand, one could see the narrative viewpoint as rejecting Naturalist theories, yet Guang Chengzi accepts the efficacy of Heaven and Earth and yin and yang in controlling the various patterns, phenomena, and events in the cosmos. Perhaps he is rejecting all the various restrictions dictated to humans in some of the Naturalist texts, implicitly suggesting that if what the Naturalists say is true about yin and yang and the seasonal alternations, then people will just do the right thing at the right time without the need for government intervention. Yet we must remember here that there is a kind of "intervention" recommended: the ruler must become united with the very source of all these patterns and things if the world is to be well ordered.

44. A. C. Graham, "How Much of *Chuang Tzu* Did Chuang Tzu Write?," in *Studies in Chinese Philosophy and Philosophical Literature* (reprint, Albany: State University of New York Press, 1990): 283–321.

45. Graham, *Chuang Tzu*, 216–11.

46. Graham, *Chuang Tzu*, 184–85.

47. Graham, *Chuang Tzu*, 150, 268, and 261–62, respectively.

48. See my "Who Compiled the *Chuang Tzu*?," in *Chinese Texts and Philosophical Contexts: Essays Dedicated to Angus C. Graham*, ed. Henry Rosemont Jr. (LaSalle, IL: Open Court, 1991), 115–18.

49. *Zhuangzi yinde*, 11/15–16; Graham, *Chuang Tzu*, 212.

50. See, for example, Peerenboom's discussion of Huang-Lao epistemology in Peerenboom, 70–73.

51. Roth, "Evidence" (chapter 4 in the present volume).

52. *Mawangdui hanmu boshu*, 65, 1.4–5.

53. I accept the editors emendation to *tian from tan* 談. *Mawangdui hanmu boshu*, 65, n. 48. Notice that when the Yellow Emperor comes to see Guang Chengzi for a second audience, he is also in this same position.

54. See, for example, *Zhuangzi yinde*, 15/19 and *Guanzi* (*Sibu congkan* edition), 16.3a2; *Chuang Tzu*, 15/11 and *Guanzi* 13.2a2 and 4a3; and *Chuang Tzu* 15/12 and *Huai-nan Tzu* 14.4b.

55. *Zhuangzi yinde*, 15/8 and 13/7.

56. *Zhuangzi yinde*, 15/16; *Shiji*, 130.3289.

57. *A Concordance to the Huainanzi*, 14/134/2.

58. Harold Roth, "Who Compiled the *Chuang Tzu*?," especially 118–23 (chapter 2, pp. 100–104 in the present volume).

Chapter 6

1. A. C. Graham, *Chuang Tzu: The Inner Chapters*. London: George Allen and Unwin, 1981. 1986 (first paperback edition). Repr. Indianapolis: Hackett Publishing Co., 2001. Please note that we have retained the earlier Wade-Giles romanizations e.g. "*Chuang Tzu*" instead of the currently accepted *pinyin romanizations* e.g. "*Zhuangzi*" if they are used in the Chapters or articles being studied or cited

2. Guan Feng, *Zhuangzi zhexue taolun ji* 莊子哲學討論集 (Beijing: Zhonghua, 1962), pp. 61–98.

3. These three types of literary criticism were developed in New Testament studies and were being propounded and debated during the 1930's and 40's while Graham was a college student. Form criticism is an analysis of the standard genres in which the oral and early written tradition is cast in the effort to interpret each in terms of its concrete historical setting. Redaction criticism is an analysis of the philosophical positions of the people who wrote and compiled texts and the application of this analysis to discover their historical circumstances. Composition criticism examines the literary techniques of the early redactors and how they assembled their inherited material to create unified works. All three criticism overlap. For details see Stephen D. Moore, *Literary Criticism and the Gospels: The Theoretical Challenge*. (New Haven: Yale University Press, 1989), 179–83 and Michael LaFargue, *The Tao of the Tao Te Ching* (Albany: State University of New York Press, 1992), 179.

4. A. C. Graham, "Two Notes on the Translation of Taoist Classics," in *A Companion to Angus C. Graham's* Chuang-tzu: The Inner Chapters. Harold

D. Roth (ed.) Society for Asian and Comparative Philosophy Monograph No. 20 (University of Hawaii Press 2003, 130–56).

5. Graham, "Two Notes," 142.

6. Textual citations from the *Zhuangzi* are taken from the edition in *Zhuangzi yinde* 莊子引得. Harvard-Yenching Institute Sinological Index Series no. 20 (Beijing, 1947). They follow the format "chapter x /line number y."

7. This reconstruction is explained most completely in A.C. Graham, "How Much of *Chuang Tzu* did Chuang Tzu Write?" In *A Companion to Angus C. Graham's Chuang-tzu: The Inner Chapters*. Harold D. Roth (ed.) Society for Asian and Comparative Philosophy Monograph No. 20. University of Hawaii Press 2003, 58–103.

8. Ma's research is published in his collection, *Yuhan shan fang ji yishu* 玉函山房輯佚書. Changsha, 1883; Tao's thorough collection of the lost Xu Shen 許慎 commentary to the *Huainanzi*, *Huainanzi Xu zhu yitong gu* was first printed in 1881. This genre of reconstituted redactions has largely been overlooked in Western scholarship and merits further examination.

9. See Wang Shu-min 王叔民, *Zhuangzi jiaoshi* 莊子校釋 (Shanghai: Commercial Press, 1947), 1383–1414.

10. Liu, like many Chinese scholars whose work he summarized, considers these chapter to be written by later followers of Chuang Tzu and he groups them together with chapters 17–22 as the products of the "Transmitter School" who continued the ideas of their founder. See Liu, *Classifying the Zhuangzi Chapters*. Michigan Monographs in Chinese Studies no. 65 (Ann Arbor: Center for Chinese Studies, University of Michigan, 1994), 83–121.

11. Harold Roth, "Who Compiled the *Zhuangzi*?" in *Chinese Texts and Philosophical Contexts: Essays Dedicated to Angus C. Graham*, ed. Henry Rosemont Jr. (LaSalle, Ill.: Open Court, 1991), pp. 115–18 (chapter 2, pp. 97–100 in the present volume).

12. Brian Hoffert, "*Chuang Tzu*: The Evolution of a Taoist Classic." Ph.D. diss. Harvard University, 2001.

13. Liu, *Classifying the Zhuangzi Chapters*, pp. 1–45. This is a partial English translation of his 1985 doctoral dissertation at Peking University, *Zhuangzi zhexue ji qi yanbian* 莊子哲學及其演變: Zhongguo shehui kexue chubanshe, 1988.

14. Wang, *Zhuangzi jiaoshi*, 1434–38.

15. Liu, *Classifying the Zhuangzi Chapters*, pp. 134–47. Liu, like Guan Feng, omits chapter 30 which he says bears no relationship to anything else in the text. However he fails to explain why it's there.

16. Liu, *Classifying the Zhuangzi Chapters*, 137.

17. Liu, *Classifying the Zhuangzi Chapters*, 121–34.

18. D.C. Lau and Chen Fong Ching (eds.), *A Concordance to the Lüshi chun qiu*. Hong Kong: The Commercial Press, 1994, pp. 379–83 and 872–81. Here I found 197 instances of post-verbal *hu* contrasted with 722 instances of post-verbal *yu*. In the *Huainanzi*, by contrast, I found 110 instances of the

former and over 1100 instances of the latter. D.C. Lau and Chen Fong Ching (eds.), A *Concordance to the Huai-nan Tzu.* Hong Kong: The Commercial Press, 1992, pp. 511–14 and 954–66.

19. Liu, *Classifying the Zhuangzi Chapters,* 89–121. Liu presents phrases or terms from each of these Mixed Chapters that are similar to or identical with phrases or terms in the "inner chapters." While these may be correct, they cannot be used to establish that the entire chapter shares the same philosophical position. Graham's work clearly establishes that these chapters do contain material related to the Inner Chapters as well as material related to all other philosophical positions found in the book.

20. Roth, "Who Compiled the *Zhuangzi?*" 79–128 (chapter 2 of the present volume).

21. Graham, "Reflections and Replies." In *Chinese Texts and Philosophical Contexts: Essays Dedicated to Angus C. Graham,* ed. Henry Rosemont Jr. (LaSalle, Ill.: Open Court, 1991), 279–83.

22. Andrew Seth Meyer, "Late Warring States Daoism and the Origins of Huang-Lao: The Evidence from the *Lüshi chun qiu.*" Unpublished manuscript. 1996.

23. For details of this practice see my *Original Tao,* chapter 4 and my article "Evidence for Stages of Meditation in Early Taoism." *Bulletin of the School of Oriental and African Studies* 60:2 (June 1997): 295–314 (chapter 4 of the present volume).

24. The Syncretist theory of the hierarchical nature of government patterned after the greater patterns of Heaven and Earth is most clearly presented in *Zhuangzi* 13/27–36, Graham, pp. 261–62.

25. John Knoblock and Jeffrey Riegel, *The Annals of Lü Buwei: A Complete Translation and Study.* (Stanford: Stanford University Press, 2000), 422. *A Concordance to the Lüshi chun qiu,* 17.4/103/19–21.

26. Liu, *Classifying the Zhuangzi Chapters,* 50–61.

27. The Robber Zhi story. Graham, *Chuang Tzu: the Inner Chapters,* 207; Knoblock and Riegel, *The Annals of Lü Buwei,* 251. *A Concordance to the Lüshi chun qiu,*11.4/55/25–56/4.

28. Graham, *Chuang Tzu: the Inner Chapters,* 174; Knoblock and Riegel, *The Annals of Lü Buwei,* 515. *A Concordance to the Lüshi chun qiu,* 20.2/129/30–130/6. The next two LSCQ references are Knoblock and Riegel, 220, *A Concordance to the Lüshi chun qiu.* 9.5/47/1 for Cook Ding; and Knoblock and Riegel, 331–32 and *A Concordance to the Lüshi chun qiu.*14.8/78/14–24.

29. *Zhuangzi yinde,* 10/6–8.

30. Qian Mu, *Xianqin zhuzi xinian* 先秦諸子繫年 1st ed. 1935. Rev.ed., 1956; repr., Beijing: Zhonghua, 1985, pp. 524–74. There is some disagreement about what this phrase "twelve generations" refers to. Chen Guying *Zhuangzi jinzhu jinyi* 莊子今注今譯 254–55, identifies Tian Chengzi as Qi Prime Minister Chen Heng 陳恆, who in 481 BCE murdered Duke Jian 簡公 and stole the state.

However to do this gives us only nine changes of rule until the fall of Qi. If we identify him instead with Tian Qi, who also murdered a Qi ruler and put a puppet on the throne, then we have an extra three changes of rule. Wang Shumin, (*Zhuangzi jiaoshi* 348–49), shows that the character *shi* 世 (generations), is an error for *dai* 代 (dynasty, change of rule). Thus the passage is talking not about entire generational changes but changes of rule. Wang however, identifies Tian Chengzi with Tian Zhuangzi 田莊子 and argues that we should date these changes of rule from the latter's death in 411 B.C.E. Part of the problem is how to count twelve of these changes. The Tian family held ministerial posts in Qi for generations before they committed regicide and established a line of puppet rulers in Qi starting in 489 B.C. They did not officially put themselves on the throne until 386 B.C.E. According to Qian Mu's historical table, we can count twelve changes of rule from 489 B.C., including, of course, the puppet dukes who were the official rulers of Qi while the Tian family really controlled the power. Wang seems to want to begin his count with the official Tian ascent to the throne but then has to go back for two more Tian family ministers in order to reach the proper count. This analogy to a powerful ministerial family controlling a weaker ruler may have been intentionally used by the Primitivist to satirize Lü Buwei's power over the young Qin king who eventually, after removing Lü from power, became the First Emperor. See below for a further discussion of this.

31. Knoblock and Riegel,11–13. While Han did not fall until 230 B.C., Zhao not until 228, and Wei not until 225, Qin annexed large amounts of territory during these campaigns and killed many soldiers and civilians, thus seriously undermining the strength of these states and making them ripe for the final conquest.

32. I have examined concordances to the following works and none contain the phrase in question: *Lun yu* 論語, *Mengzi* 孟子, *Xunzi* 荀子, *Laozi*, *Guanzi*, and *Hanfeizi* 韓非子.

33. To be specific, the phrase is found three times in chapter 8 (in lines 8, 12, and 30) and four times in the first part of chapter 11 (in lines 8, 10, 11, and 14). The other two occurrences are in chapter 14 (14/73) and chapter 24 (24/2), both passages that Graham concludes are Primitivist. See his section "Episodes related to the Primitivist"(*Chuang Tzu: the Inner Chapters*, 214–15).

34. The use in 17.5/104/6 is simply of *xing ming* but the context implies the full phrase.

35. There are six sporadic references to the term *xing* in three "school of *Zhuangzi* chapters:" 17/37, 19/11, 52, 53, 54, and 20/61). The last four are in passages that feature Confucius and seem to be borrowing the idea; the first is about the nature of all things and not human nature; 19/11. None of these even faintly suggest a unique Daoist theory.

36. This summary of Yangist ideas is primarily based on five *Lüshi chun qiu* essays: 1.2, 1.3, 2.2, 2.3, and 21.4, and also draws on material in *Zhuangzi*

28 and 30. It is taken from my article "*Zhuangzi.*" *Stanford Encyclopedia of Philosophy.* November 2001.

37. *A Concordance to the Lüshi chun qiu.* 2.3/8/20–23; the translation is my own.

38. *Zhuangzi yinde*, 8/26–31, Graham, *Chuang Tzu*, 202–3. I have modified it slightly.

39. *Zhuangzi yinde*, 16/4, Graham, *Chuang Tzu*, 171.

40. *Zhuangzi yinde*, 9/10–11, Graham, 205. The Simple and Unhewn are defined in *Laozi* 19 as being selfless and desireless.

41. *Zhuangzi yinde*, 9/16–19, Graham, 205–6.

42. Knoblock and Riegel, 12–32, cover this in greater detail.

43. Knoblock and Riegel, 67–68.

44. Knoblock and Riegel, 292–93.

45. Knoblock and Riegel, 380–81. I accept their emendation of the graphic error *yuan* 遠 to *da* 達.

46. Knoblock and Riegel, 419–21.

47. Knoblock and Riegel, 423–25. The third use of our phrase lacks the final "*zhi qing*," but I think it is implied by the context.

48. Knoblock and Riegel, 630–32.

49. Roth, "The Concept of Human Nature in the *Huai-nan Tzu. Journal of Chinese Philosophy* (1985): 1–26.

50. The concluding paragraph to this narrative in the *Lüshi chun qiu* takes a Confucian turn towards Rightness that the Primitivist would not approve, but this does not mean that the understanding of "the essentials of nature and destiny" implied here could not have been taken from the Primitivist and then applied to a Confucian argument. This suggests he was part of debates in the Lü Buwei circle but that he did not write anything that was included in the final version of the text.

51. *Zhuangzi yinde*, 10/19; Graham, *Chuang Tzu*, 208.

52. *Zhuangzi yinde*, 11/15–16; Graham, *Chuang Tzu*, 212.

53. *Zhuangzi yinde*, 2/55. For an interesting discussion of this phrase see D.C. Lau, "On the Expression Zai You 在宥" In Henry Rosemont (ed.), *Chinese Texts and Philosophical Contexts*, 5–20.

54. Andy Meyer first suggested that *Zhuangzi* 28 is a collection of Yangist stories made by the Primitivist in a paper he gave at a meeting of the Warring States Working Group in the fall of 1998. I do not have the paper but recall talking to Professor Meyer about it at that time.

55. *Zhuangzi yinde*, 27/1–10; Graham, *Chuang Tzu*, 106–7. This means taking an intellectual position and using a narrative to demonstrate its veracity. But ultimately abandoning it if the situation changes. This likely derives from the idea of "discarding fixed cognition and finding things their lodging-places in the practical" (為是不用而寓諸庸 . . .) from *Zhuangzi yinde* 2/34.

56. Like most scholars I am still not sure what to make of chapter 30, "The Discourse on Swords."

57. *Zhuangzi yinde*, 29/71–74; Graham, *Chuang Tzu,*, 240–41. The term *xing* is extremely rare outside the Primitivist chapters but it occurs thrice in "Robber Zhi:" 29/86, 89, 98.

58. *Zhuangzi yinde*, 31/31, 37, 49; Graham, *Chuang Tzu*, 251–53.

59. Liu, *Classifying the Zhuangzi Chapters*,138–39.

60. Liu, *Classifying the Zhuangzi Chapters*, 125, 128, 133. Liu's links between "Menders of Nature" and the Inner Chapters are much more persuasive than his two extremely weak links between it and the "Huang-Lao" material.

61.*Zhuangzi yinde*, 16/3–4; Graham, *Chuang Tzu*, 171.

62. Chen Guying 陳鼓應 *Zhuangzi jinzhu jinyi*. 莊子今註今譯 (Taipei: Zhonghua, 1983), 403.

63. This translation is based on Graham's but I have edited it to make it consistent with other translations of mine throughout this essay. The italicized text constitutes 37 characters; Chen would expand this to 54 by adding the sentence immediately before and the one immediately after this section but I see no reason to do this. He would also excise the passage as not the words of Zhuangzi. See Chen, *Zhuangzi jinzhu jinyi*, 403.

64. "Menders of Nature" 16/17 uses the partial phrase *xing ming*, rare outside the Primitivist essays and passages related to them.

65. For details on this theory, see Roth, "Who Compiled the *Chuang Tzu?*" (chapter 2 in the present volume).

66. Roth, *Original Tao: Inward Training and the Foundations of Taoist Mysticism*, 198–203.

Chapter 7

1. For a thorough summary of these debates about affiliation, see John S. Major, Sarah A. Queen, Andrew S. Meyer, and Harold D. Roth (Translators, Editors, Annotators), *The Huainanzi: A Guide to the Theory and Practice of Government in Early Han China* (New York: Columbia University Press, 2010), 27–32.

2. For details of text creation and writing during this period, see the classic work, Tsuen-Hsuin Tsien, *Written on Bamboo and Silk: The Beginnings of Chinese Books and Inscriptions* (Chicago: University of Chicago Press, 1962).

3. The surviving evidence for the social organization of the early Confucian tradition has been thoroughly analyzed in E. Bruce Brooks and A. Taeko Brooks, *The Original Analects* (Columbia, 2001).

4. Mark Edward Lewis, *Writing and Authority in Early China* (Albany, NY: State University of New York Press, 1999), 5.

5. Fukui Fumimasa, "The History of Taoist Studies in Japan and Some Related Issues," *Acta Asiatica* 68 (1995): 12–13.

6. *Shiji* 史記, *Bona* edition, ch. 130, 3a–6b. For a translation and analysis of Sima Tan's "On the Six Intellectual Traditions," see Sarah A. Queen and Harold D. Roth, "A Syncretist Perspective on the Six Schools," in *Sources of Chinese Tradition* (rev. edition), ed. William Theodore deBary and Irene Bloom (New York: Columbia University Press, 1999), 278–82.

7. The three major recent articles on this topic are Sarah A. Queen, "Inventories of the Past: Rethinking the "School" Affiliation of the *Huainanzi*. *Asia Major*, Third Series (14.1) 2001; Mark Csíkszentmihályi and Michael Nylan, "Constructing Lineages and Inventing Traditions Through Exemplary Figures in Early China," *T'oung Pao* LXXXIX, 2003; Kidder Smith, "Sima Tan and the Invention of Daoism, 'Legalism,' et cetera," *Journal of Asian Studies* 62, no. 1 (2003): 129–56. For an analysis of how Sima Tan's ideas about the "Daoist tradition" are derived from the pre-Han sources of "inner cultivation," see my article "Psychology and Self-Cultivation in Early Taoistic Thought," *HJAS* 51, no. 2 (1991), especially 604–6.

8. For a synthetic overview of this research, see *Original Tao: Inward Training and the Foundations of Taoist Mysticism* (New York: Columbia University Press, 1999), 173–203. The "Techniques of the Mind" is the title of two short texts in the seventy-six-text *Guanzi* compendium. Together with "Inward Training" and "The Purified Mind," they constitute a group that in modern scholarship is referred to as the four "Techniques of Mind" works. The relevant chapters of the *Lüshi chunqiu* are 3, 5, 17, and 25.

9. These categories are initially presented in Harold D. Roth, "Who Compiled the *Chuang Tzu*?," in Henry Rosemont Jr., ed., *Chinese Texts and Philosophical Contexts: Essays Dedicated to Angus C. Graham*, 78–128 (LaSalle, IL: Open Court Press, 1991) (chapter 2 in the present volume).

10. *Zhuangzi* 6/19/20–1. All *Zhuangzi* references are to D. C. Lau, ed., *Zhuangzi zhuzi suoyin* 莊子逐字索引. The Institute for Chinese Studies Chinese Text Concordance Series (Hong Kong: Commercial Press, 2000). In these ICS critical texts, emendations are given in the following format: (a) [x]: "character a is emended to character x." The translation is modified from A. C. Graham, *Chuang-tzu, the "Inner Chapters"* (London: Allen and Unwin, 1981), 92.

11. References to chapters of "Inward Training" (Neiye) are from Roth, *Original Tao*, which contains both a critical Chinese edition and facing translation. Here, Roth, 94–97.

12. See, for example, *Zhuangzi* 9/23/29; 12/29/16; 20/53/24+25; 23/65/6; 25/76/17.

13. Such phrases are widespread in early Inner Cultivation texts. See, for example *Lüshi chunqiu* 3.4/15/1; 25.3/162/20–21; *Zhuangzi* 15/41/27, and my analysis in Roth, "Evidence for Stages of Meditation in Early Taoism," *Bulletin of the School of Oriental and African Studies* 60, no. 2 (June 1997): 295–314 (chapter

4 in the present volume). *Lüshi chunqiu* references are to D. C. Lau, ed., *Lüshi chunqiu zhuzi suoyin* 呂氏春秋逐字索引, The Institute for Chinese Studies Chinese Text Concordance Series (Hong Kong: Commercial Press, 1994).

14. *Guanzi* 13.1/95/29l; *Laozi* chapter 10; *Zhuangzi* 5/13/18, 27. *Guanzi* references are to D. C. Lau, ed., *Guanzi zhuzi suoyin* 管子逐字索引, The Institute for Chinese Studies Chinese Text Concordance Series (Hong Kong: Commercial Press, 2001).

15. See, for example, Cahn and Polich, "Meditation States and Traits: EEG, ERP, and Neuroimaging Studies," *Psychological Bulletin* 132, no. 2 (2006): 180–211.

16. *Zhuangzi* 6/19/21.

17. *Zhuangzi* 2/5/1.

18. See H. D. Roth, "Psychology and Self-Cultivation in Early Taoistic Thought," *Harvard Journal of Asiatic Studies* 51, no. 2 (December 1991): 599–650 (chapter 1 in the present volume).

19. *Zhuangzi* 18/48/7, 22/60/14, 25/76/6; *Lüshi chunqiu* 25.3/162/23.

20. Paraphrased from *Zhuangzi* 9/23/27.

21. In an earlier work, I have presented evidence for a remarkable consistency across texts as early as the *Huang Lao boshu* (ca. 300 BCE) and as late as the *Huainanzi* (139 BCE) in terms used for stages of meditation. See H. D. Roth, "Evidence for Stages of Meditation in Early Taoism," *Bulletin of the School of Oriental and African Studies* 60, no. 2 (June 1997): 295–314 (chapter 4 in the present volume).

22. *Guanzi*, 13.1/96/14; *Zhuangzi* 13/34/22, and 33/98/1.

23. Totals and all subsequent references to the *Huainanzi* are taken from D. C. Lau, ed., *Huainanzi zhuzi suoyin* 淮南 子逐字索引, The Institute for Chinese Studies Chinese Text Concordance Series (Hong Kong: Commercial Press, 1992). Totals for the character "Dao" are from 345–50; for the character "*ren*" are from 764–65. This sentence quoted is from *Huainanzi* 11/93/20.

24. For this theory, see Major, Queen, Meyer, and Roth, *The Huainanzi*, 14–20. The twenty-first and final chapter, "A Overview of the Essentials" ("Yao lüe" 要略), is a summary of the rest of the book. My reflections about the structure of the *Huainanzi* chapters do not include this final summary, which has its own purpose and structure.

25. HNZSY 21/223/21ff. All references are to the edition of the *Huainanzi* in D. C. Lau, ed., *Huainanzi zhuzi suoyin* 淮南子逐字索引, The Institute for Chinese Studies Chinese Text Concordance Series (Hong Kong: Commercial Press, 1992). I largely follow this text and its emendations, which are given in the framework (character X is emended to) [character Y]. The translations are from Major, Queen, Meyer, and Roth, *The Huainanzi* (HNZ). For this passage, see 848–49.

26. Charles Leblanc, "*Huainanzi*," in Michael Loewe, ed., *Early Chinese Texts: A Bibliographical Guide* (Berkeley: Society for the Study of Early China

and The Institute of East Asian Studies, University of California at Berkeley, 1993), 189–95.

27. Martin Kern, "Language, Argument, and Southern Culture in the *Huainanzi*: A Look at the 'Yaolue,'" in *The Huainanzi and Textual Production in Early China*, ed. Sarah A. Queen and Michael Puett (Leiden: Brill, 2014), 124–50.

28. In his Harvard Workshop presentation, Meyer argues that *Huainanzi* 1 is therefore more foundational than *Huainanzi* 2, and I do not fundamentally disagree with this. However, I think that *Huainanzi* 2 is also an important part of the foundation for the rest of the text and must be considered together with *Huainanzi* 1 when detailing the basic ideas that provide the foundational philosophy that appears in most of the "Root Passages" of the entire text. Especially important from *Huainanzi* 2 is the idea of historical devolution.

29. HNZSY 1/1/3–8; HNZ, 48–49.

30. The "Techniques of the Mind" is the title of two short texts in the seventy-six-text *Guanzi* compendium. Together with "Inward Training" and "The Purified Mind," they constitute a group that in modern scholarship is referred to as the four "Techniques of Mind" works. By the time of the *Huainanzi*, this phrase was probably used as a general term for what I have called "inner cultivation" practice. For further information, see Roth, *Original Tao*, 15–30.

31. HNZSY 1/4/22–5. HNZ, 59.

32. HNZSY 1/8/14. HNZ, 71.

33. For a detailed argument on this point, see Harold D. Roth, "Nature and Self-Cultivation in *Huainanzi's* 'Original Way,'" in *Polishing the Chinese Mirror: Essays in Honor of Henry Rosemont Jr.*, ed. Marthe Chandler and Ronnie Littlejohn (New York: Global Scholarly Publications, 2007), 270–92 (chapter 10 in the present volume).

34. See Harold D. Roth, "An Appraisal of Angus Graham's Textual Scholarship on the *Chuang Tzu*," in *A Companion to Angus C. Graham's* Chuang-tzu: The Inner Chapters, ed. Harold D. Roth, Society for Asian and Comparative Philosophy Monograph No. 20. University of Hawai'i Press, 2003), 198–207 (chapter 6 in the present volume); and A. C. Graham, "How Much of *Chuang Tzu* did Chuang-tzu Write?," reprinted in Roth, *Companion*, 58–103.

35. HNZSY, 1/8/15–17. HNZ, 71.

36. *Mawangdui Hanmu boshu* 馬王堆漢墓帛書 (Peking: Wen-wu Press), 1980, 53, lines 12–13.

37. HNZSY, 1/7/9–10. HNZ, 67.

38. This line occurs in the famous "fasting of the mind" passage in ZZ 4/10/7.

39. HNZSY, 2/14/6–11. HNZ, 101.

40. HNZSY, 7/54/24–55/5, HNZ, 241.

41. *HNZSY*, 14/132/15–16. HNZ, 537. See also extensive references to "The Genuine" (*zhen ren* 真人) in *Zhuangzi*, especially in chapters 6 and 24.

42. *HNZSY*, 6/50/4–5. HNZ, 215. The Ancestor (*zong* 宗) is a metaphor for the Dao.

43. This claim is paralleled in HNZ 2 (87–88; *HNZSY*, 2/11/16) where it argues similarly: "Sages, in the use of their mind, lean on their natures and rely on their spirits. They [nature and spirit] sustain one another and [so sages] attain their ends and beginnings. Thus when they sleep they do not dream and when they awaken they are not sad."

44. *HNZSY*, 10/82/15–17; HNZ, 349. Chapter 14 (*HNZSY*, 14/138/17–18; HNZ, 559) states similarly: "When affairs arise the sage regulates them, When things appear the sage responds to them."

45. *HNZSY*, 8/61/6–7; HNZ, 267.

46. *HNZSY*, 11/93/20; HNZ, 397.

47. *HNZSY*, 12/105/3–7; HNZ, 439–40.

48. *HNZSY*, 15/142/2122; HNZ, 580.

49. *HNZSY*, 15/144/1; HNZ, 584.

50. *HNZSY* 16/154/3–8; HNZ, 625.

51. *HNZSY*, 17/168/9–12; HNZ, 665. To roam (*you*) in accord with the greater patterns of the cosmos perfectly expresses early Daoist ideal from *Zhuangzi* 1 and the later Daoist idea of adaptation with these patterns (*yin tiandi zhi li*). See Harold D. Roth, "Who Compiled the *Chuang-tzu*?," in Rosemont Jr., *Chinese Texts and Philosophical Contexts* (Open Court: 1991), 79–128, especially the table on 96–98 (in the present volume, chapter 2, Table 2.1).

52. *HNZSY*, 18/185/23–4; HNZ, 720.

53. *HNZSY*, 19/203/13–15; HNZ, 770.

54. *HNZSY*, 20/210/5–6; HNZ, 796–97.

55. As noted above, chapters 4 and 5, because they are similar to chapter 3 in their quasi-technical vocabulary and literary style, may be thought of as forming a sub-unit with chapter 3; thus the cosmogonic "Root Passage" that begins 3 may be intended to cover 4 and 5 as well. Chapter 9 is discussed below.

56. This sentence breaks the parallelism of the whole passage; we suspect that the text might have originally read "his officials receive the admonitions [of others]."

57. *HNZSY*, 9/67/3–6; HNZ, 295–96.

58. This line echoes the famous opening lines of the *Zhongyong* ("Doctrine of the Mean").

59. Like 8.3 above, which this passage closely resembles, these lines paraphrase *Laozi* 38.

60. *HNZSY*, 11/93/20–22; HNZ, 397.

61. This refers to two forms of ancient ritual practice. Straw dogs were made to carry the transgressions of the community; earthen dragons were fashioned to pray for rain.

62. *HNZSY*, 11/98/25–56 and 11/99/15–17; *HNZ*, 412, 414.

63. The *xiang* 象 *and diti* 狄鞮 were interpreters employed to facilitate interactions between the Chinese Central States and their "barbarian" neighbors. See the similar phrasing that appears in the *Lüshi chunqiu:* "[All states] that do not use the *xiang* and *di* interpreters" (*LSCQ* 17.6/105/16). Their exact functions are unknown. See Chen Qiyou 陳奇猷, *Lüshi chunqiu jiaoshi* 呂氏春秋校釋, 2 vols. (Shanghai: Xuelin chubanshe, 1984), 2:1108, 1112n.7; Zhang Shuangdi 1997, 2:1134n.8; and 20.8.

64. *HNZSY*, 11/95/24–96/1; *HNZ*, 403–4.

65. Lee Yearley, "Idea of Human Excellence," in William Schweiker, ed., *The Blackwell Companion to Religious Ethics* (Oxford: Wiley-Blackwell, 2005), 45–52.

66. *HNZSY*, 11/96/1–3; *HNZ*, 404.

67. Here I follow the semantic emendation of Qing textual critic Yuyue as listed on 96, n. 5 in *HNZSY*.

68. *HNZSY*, 11/96–7–16; *HNZ*, 405.

69. For these arguments, see Griet Vankeerberghen. *The Huainanzi and Liu An's Claim to Moral Authority*, SUNY Series in Chinese Philosophy and Culture (Albany: State University of New York Press, 2001), 2–5; Sarah A. Queen, "Inventories of the Past: Re-Thinking the 'School' Affiliation of the *Huainanzi*," *Asia Major*, Third Series, 14, no. 1 (2001): 51–72; and Judson Murray, "A Study of 'Yaolüe' 要略, 'A Summary of the Essentials': Understanding the *Huainanzi* through the Point of View of the Author of the Postface," *Early China* 29 (2004): 45–110.

70. *HNZSY*, 21/228/30–31; *HNZ*, 867.

71. Harold D. Roth, "Psychology and Self-Cultivation in Early Taoistic Thought," *Harvard Journal of Asiatic Studies* 51, no. 2: 599–650 (chapter 1 in the present volume).

72. See for example, Russell Kirkland, *Taoism: The Enduring Tradition* (Routledge, 2001), 31–65. Kirkland emphasizes the differences between these early Daoist sources, implies that they therefore could not be part of a distinct "Daoist tradition," but cannot help but use that exact phrase in quotation marks when talking about this distinctive intellectual viewpoint in the pre-Han period. For a discussion of the *Huainanzi* as an "eclectic work," see Griet Vankeerbergen, *The Huainanzi and Liu An's Claim to Moral Authority* (Albany, NY: State University of New York Press, 2001), 4–5. By "eclectic," she avers that the *Huainanzi* embraces many intellectual traditions but prefers none. My argument is that it is "syncretic" precisely because it synthesizes ideas from many traditions within a Daoist inner cultivation framework.

73. Alistair McIntyre, *After Virtue*, 221.

74. Volcker Scheid, *Currents of Tradition in Chinese Medicine*, 9.

Chapter 8

1. Wing-Tsit Chan, *A Sourcebook in Chinese Philosophy* (Princeton: Princeton University Press, 1963); Benjamin Schwartz, *The World of Thought in Ancient China* (Cambridge: Belknap Press, 1985); Walter Stace, *Mysticism and Philosophy* (London: Macmillan Press, 1960; reprint, Los Angeles: Jeremy P. Tarcher, 1987); Wayne Proudfoot, *Religious Experience* (Berkeley: University of California Press, 1985). Specific references are given as the ideas in these works are discussed below.

2. D. C. Lau, trans., *Chinese Classics: Tao Te Ching* (Hong Kong: Chinese University Press, 1982), xxv–xxvii; Chad Hansen, "Linguistic Skepticism in the *Lao Tzu*," *Philosophy East and West* 31, no. 3 (July 1981): 321–36.

3. Chan, *Sourcebook*, 137.

4. Stace, *Mysticism*, 168, 255.

5. Proudfoot, *Religious Experience*, 126–29.

6. Livia Kohn, *Early Chinese Mysticism: Philosophy and Soteriology in the Taoist Tradition* (Princeton: Princeton University Press, 1992), 34.

7. Kohn, *Early Chinese Mysticism*, 45–52. For a critical assessment of this work, see my review article "Some Issues in the Study of Chinese Mysticism: A Review Essay," *China Review International* 2, no. 1 (Spring 1995): 154–73.

8. Schwartz, *World of Thought*, 192–201.

9. Harold D. Roth, "Psychology and Self-Cultivation in Early Taoistic Thought," *Harvard Journal of Asiatic Studies* 51, no. 2 (1991): 599–650 (chapter 1 of this book); and "Who Compiled the Chuang Tzu?," in *Chinese Texts and Philosophical Contexts: Essays Dedicated to Angus C. Graham*, ed. Henry Rosemont Jr. (LaSalle, IL: Open Court, 1991), 79–128 (chapter 2 of this book).

10. Harold D. Roth, "Redaction Criticism and the Early History of Taoism," *Early China* 19 (1994): 1–46 (chapter 3 of this book).

11. See the first traditional occurrence of this term in *Zhuangzi*, 6/73. *Zhuangzi yinde* 莊子引得. Harvard-Yenching Institute Sinological Index Series no. 20 (Peking, 1947). All references to the *Zhuangzi* are from this edition. In this passage, in a dialogue between Confucius and Zigong in which the former explains to the latter how the Daoist sage Sanghu and his friends "are at the stage of being fellow men with the maker of things, and go roaming in the single breath that breathes through heaven and earth," we read that it is through the techniques of the Way that such men can forget themselves. A. C. Graham, *Chuang Tzu: The Inner Chapters* (London: Allen and Unwin, 1981), 89–90. The only other use of this term in the *Zhuangzi* is also significant. It occurs in the thirty-third and final chapter, "Below in the Empire" (*Tianxia* 天下), in which the comprehensive Way of Heaven and Earth advocated by the Syncretist author is contrasted with the "techniques of one-corner" (*fang shu* 方術) found in other, less complete teachings, such as those of Zhuang Zhou himself (*Zhuangzi* 33/1ff; Graham, *Chuang Tzu*, 274ff). These two occurrences,

separated by a century and a half and found in both the "Individualist" and "Syncretist" sections, serve as bookends to indicate an important continuity in this tradition's self-understanding and demonstrate how the "techniques of the Way" developed beyond breathing methods to include methods of political and social organization.

12. My hypothesis on the origins of Daoism is that it began as a lineage of masters and disciples who practiced and transmitted a unique form of guided breathing meditation involving this regular circulation of vital breath. Political and social concerns and naturalist techniques and philosophy represented later developments. One of the strongest pieces of evidence for this is presented in my article "Redaction Criticism and the Early History of Daoism"(see chapter 3), in which I demonstrate that "Inward Training," a collection of verses on this practice of guiding the vital breath that dates from the origins of Daoism, was deliberately summarized and restated in the much later work, "Techniques of the Mind II." This deliberate abridgment and restatement was done for the purposes of commending this practice of inner cultivation to rulers as one of the principal arcana of governing.

13. For the former, see Catherine Despeux, "Gymnastics: The Ancient Tradition," in *Taoist Meditation and Longevity Techniques*, ed. Livia Kohn, vol. 61, Michigan Monographs in Chinese Studies (Ann Arbor: University of Michigan Center for Chinese Studies, 1989), 225–62. The precise relationships between these two techniques and their practitioners is still unclear. However, by the time of *Zhuangzi* 15, which criticizes the practitioners of "gymnastic" exercises, the groups who advocated these two techniques seem to be clearly differentiated (*Zhuangzi yinde* 15/5–6).

14. I use the term "apophatic" in its more general and original sense of "(of knowledge of God) obtained by negation," *Concise Oxford Dictionary Sixth Edition* (Oxford: Oxford University Press, 1976). It has come to be associated with a particular mode of approach to the nature of God in the writings of Christian mystics, the so-called "*via negativa*," in which God is described using negative language. I consider this a subset of "apophasis," and I wish to clarify that I use the term more broadly to indicate a method of negating the self in order to facilitate an experience of the Absolute, however that is conceived. While more culturally specific than my own use, A. H. Armstrong argues for this kind of more general meaning of apophasis in *Plotinian and Christian Studies* (London: Variorum, 1979), especially in essays XXIV and XXIII. I wish to thank Janet Williams of the University of Bath for this reference.

"Inner cultivation" (*neixiu* 內修) refers to the apophatic methods of emptying the mind practiced by the various master-disciple lineages of early Daoism. Its *locus classicus* is in the "Inward Training" text of the Guanzi, which is discussed below. "Self-cultivation" (*zixiu* 自修) is a more general term that I take to refer to all methods of practical discipline aimed at improving oneself and realizing one's innate nature and potential to the fullest. Self-cultivation was practiced by Confucians and Yangists as well as Daoists. Daoist self-cultivation is what I call "inner cultivation."

15. Michael LaFargue, *The Tao of the Tao Te Ching* (Albany: State University of New York Press, 1992); *Tao and Method: A Reasoned Approach to the Tao Te Ching* (Albany: State University of New York Press, 1994). The former book is an abbreviated version of the latter. Both contain the same translation of the *Laozi*.

16. The Individualist aspect is the earliest. It advocates a cosmology of the Way and the inner cultivation practices that I adumbrate in the present chapter. Its representative extant texts are *Guanzi*'s "Inward Training" and the "Inner Chapters" of the *Zhuangzi*. The Primitivist contains the same cosmology of the Way and inner cultivation practices as the former but to these adds a political philosophy that rejects social conventions (especially Confucian and Mohist) and recommends returning to a political and social organization based on small agrarian communities. Its representative works are the *Laozi* and chapters 8–11 (1–57) and 16 of the *Zhuangzi*. The Syncretist embraces the same cosmology and inner cultivation practices as the other two aspects but in its political thought conceives of a complex, hierarchically organized society whose customs and laws are modeled on the overarching patterns of heaven and earth and that freely uses relevant techniques and ideas from other intellectual lineages. Representative texts include the "*Huang-Lao* silk manuscripts" from Mawangdui 馬王堆, chapters 12–15 and 33 of the *Zhuangzi* and the *Huainanzi*. For further details, see my "Psychology and Self-Cultivation," especially 599–608 (chapter 1, pp. 21–27 in the present volume); "Who Compiled the Chuang Tzu?," especially 80–88 and 95–113 (chapter 2, pp. 63–71 and 77–95 in the present volume). See also A. C. Graham, "How Much of Chuang Tzu Did Chuang Tzu Write?," in *Studies in Chinese Philosophy and Philosophical Literature* (Albany: State University of New York Press, 1990), 283–321; and Liu Xiaogan, *Zhuangzi zhexue ji qi yanbian* 莊子哲學及其演變 (Peking: Chinese Social Sciences Press, 1987).

17. This presentation is not intended to be comprehensive but deals principally with the theoretical role of mystical praxis and its relationship to mystical experience. I differ from Kohn by focusing more on the phenomenological and typological studies of William James and Walter Stace and "anti-constructivists" such as Donald Rothberg, which seriously entertain the possible veridicality of the epistemological claims of the mystics, rather than on the "constructivist" theories of Steven Katz, Wayne Proudfoot, et al., which reject the veridicality of such claims. For details, see my "Some Issues," 161–68.

18. William James, *The Varieties of Religious Experience* (1902; reprint, New York: Penguin Books, 1982), 380–81.

19. This fifth characteristic is implicit. James uses the transforming influence of mystical experience as a means of clarifying where they differ from religious experiences in general, but he does not include it in his list of characteristics. See 381–82, 400–1, 413–15.

20. Peter Moore, "Mystical Experience, Mystical Doctrine, Mystical Technique," in *Mysticism and Philosophical Analysis*, ed. Steven Katz (London: Oxford University Press, 1978), 101.

21. Stace, *Mysticism*, 67–87.

22. See Robert K. C. Forman, ed., *The Problem of Pure Consciousness, Mysticism and Philosophy* (New York: Oxford University Press, 1990).

23. The two modes correspond well with Stace's introvertive and extrovertive mystical experiences. Where I would differ from him is in his devaluing the latter (Stace, *Mysticism*, 132); I see no evidence of this in early Daoist sources. See "Some Issues," 160–62.

24. These concepts are discussed throughout Stace's third chapter, "The Problem of Objective Reference." Note that at the time Stace was writing, the term "Hinayana" (Lesser Vehicle) was thought to be appropriate. Today, appreciating that this term is a polemical and deprecatory label, we would likely substitute the terms "Theravada."

25. The foremost champion of the latter position is Steven Katz. See his "Language, Epistemology, and Mysticism," in Steven Katz, ed., *Mysticism and Philosophical Analysis* (Oxford: Oxford University Press, 1978), 22–74, especially 26.

26. Moore, "Mystical Experience," 113.

27. Moore, "Mystical Experience," 113.

28. Robert Forman, "Mysticism, Constructivism, and Forgetting," in Forman, *Problem*, 3–49, especially 3–9, and 30–43.

29. Donald Rothberg, "Contemporary Epistemology and the Study of Mysticism," in Forman, *Problem*, 184.

30. Rothberg, "Contemporary," 186.

31. Daniel Brown, "The Stages of Meditation in Cross-Cultural Perspective," in *Transformations of Consciousness and Contemplative Perspectives on Development*, ed. Ken Wilber, Jack Engler, and Daniel Brown (Boston: Shambala, 1986), 263–64. In his analysis of the results of this study, Brown states that he has discovered "a clear underlying structure to meditation stages, a structure highly consistent across traditions . . ." which, despite the "vastly different ways they are conceptualized," "is believed to represent natural human development available to anyone who practices" (223).

32. Rothberg, "Contemporary," 186.

33. Forman, *Problem*, 8. This is a deliberate strategy on the part of Forman, who recognizes that this extrovertive form can be a more permanent mystical state that is typically thought of as a more advanced stage in the mystical journey. He omits it, not out of disregard, but in order to limit the focus of his collection of essays.

34. Roth, "Some Issues."

35. Roth, "Some Issues," 159–61. See also n. 14, which calls for further research to clarify various types in a continuum of extrovertive mystical experience.

36. Roth, "Some Issues," 167–68.

37. Brown, "Stages of Meditation," 221–22.

38. LaFargue, *The Dao*, 61.

39. *Zhuangzi yinde*, 6/92–93.

40. In this chapter, I most often use the text of the received recension of the *Laozi* as found in the edition of D. C. Lau, *Tao Te Ching*. However, whenever I find their readings preferable, I also make use of the Mawangdui manuscript redactions as found in the edition of Robert Henricks, *Lao-Tzu Te-Tao Ching* (New York: Ballantine Books, 1989). Translations are my own unless otherwise noted. I explain the unique elements of it when I fully analyze this passage below.

41. Lau, *Tao Te Ching*, xxxvii.

42. Chan, *Sourcebook*, 144.

43. *Zhuangzi yinde*, 6/92–93; Graham, Chuang Tzu, 92. I deviate only in translating *tong* 同 as "merge" instead of "go along."

44. I follow Graham in understanding *zhiti* as the four limbs or members and the five orbs or visceral organs that are the physical manifestations of the five basic systems of vital energy in the human body. This is preferable to the alternative "drop off limbs and body" because two lines later the text refers to parting from the body (*lixing*), which would be redundant if the second interpretation were taken. For the associations of the emotions with the various internal organs or "orbs," see Manfred Porkert, *The Theoretical Foundations of Chinese Medicine* (Cambridge: MIT Press, 1974), 115–46.

45. On the imagery of the character "Dao" in *Zhuangzi*, see A. C. Graham, *Disputers of the Dao* (LaSalle, IL: Open Court Press, 1989), 188: "Chuang-tzu . . . sees man as coinciding with the Way by ceasing to draw distinctions. To be on the unformulable path is to merge into the unnameable whole, so that what we are trying to pin down by the name 'Way' is revealed as nothing less than the universe flowing from its ultimate source . . ."

46. For the link between psychological states and physiological substrates, see Roth, "Psychology and Self-Cultivation," 599–603 (chapter 1, pp. 21–23 in the present volume).

47. *Guanzi*, *Sibu congkan* edition, 16.2a5, 2b6, 3b6. All textual citations for the *Guanzi* are to this edition. For translations, see Roth, "The Inner Cultivation Tradition of Early Daoism," 131–32.

48. *Guanzi*, 16.5a4, 5a5, 1h10, and 4a2. For translations, see Roth, "Inner Cultivation," 133–34, 130, and 133.

49. *Guanzi*, 16.3b6.

50. See, for example, the other famous passage on meditation, the "fasting of the mind" dialogue, also between Confucius and Yan Hui (wherein Confucius is now the teacher): *Zhuangzi yinde*, 4/24–34: Graham, *Chuang Tzu*, 68–69.

51. Harold D. Roth, "Evidence for Stages of Meditation in Early Daoism," *Bulletin of the School of Oriental and African Studies* 60, no. 2 (1997): 295–314 (included as chapter 4 in this book). These important sources for early Daoist mystical praxis include the "HuangLao boshu," chapters 3, 5, 17, and 25 of the

Lüshi chunqiu, chapters 15 and 23 of the *Zhuangzi*, and the "Inward Training" and two "Techniques of the Mind" works from the *Guanzi*.

52. Brown, "Stages of Meditation," 230–45 and 272–76.

53. Lau, *Tao Te Ching*, 77.

54. The restriction of the senses through focusing on the breathing is discussed in Brown, "Stages of Meditation," 232–24. As a result, the meditator becomes "less sensitized to external events and more to internal events" (233).

55. Brown, "Stages of Meditation," 232–33.

56. Brown, "Stages of Meditation," 233.

57. According to the *Baopuzi* 抱朴子 (ca. 300 CE), the "lower cinnabar field" is located 2.4 inches below the navel. It is one of the major locations of the One in the human being. In the later *Huangting jing* 黃庭經, the Daoist adept makes the vital breath circulate through the lower cinnabar field, where it helps to nourish and retain the vital essence. In the Tang dynasty meditation texts of Sima Chengzhen 司馬承禎, fixing the attention on the lower cinnabar field is a technique used to control the desires and emotions. See Livia Kohn, "Guarding the One: Concentrative Meditation in Taoism," and "Taoist Insight Meditation: The Tang Practice of Neiguan," in *Taoist Meditation and Longevity Techniques*, ed. Livia Kohn, 135 and 194–95, respectively; and Henri Maspero, "An Essay on Taoism in the First Centuries A.D.," in Henri Maspero, *Daoism and Chinese Religion*, trans. Frank Kierman (Amherst: University of Massachusetts Press, 1981), 339–45.

58. *Huainanzi*, *Sibu congkan* edition, 8.8a1–3. All references to the text of the *Huainanzi* are to this edition.

59. Roth, "Who Compiled," 96 (chapter 2, Table 2.1, p. 79 in the present volume), finds this phrase in "Techniques of the Mind I," chapters 13 and 15 of the *Zhuangzi*, and chapters 1, 6, and 7 of the *Huainanzi*. I can add *Lüshi chunqiu* 3.4 to this list (see "Evidence for Stages of Meditation in Early Taoism," 302) (chapter 4, Table 4.1, pp. 170–71 in the present volume).

60. I follow Henricks, 234, in moving the first line of chapter 20 to the last line of chapter 19, where it constitutes the third of the three statements indicated above in the text of chapter 19.

61. Here I follow the Mawangdui B manuscript reading from Henricks, 219: *zhi xu ji ye; shou jing du ye* 至虛極也守靜督也.

62. *Zhuangzi yinde*, 4/28.

63. I follow Lau in emending the negative *bu* 不 ("not") to *er* 而 ("and"), based on semantic considerations. Lau, *Tao te Ching*, 23.

64. LaFargue, *The Dao*, 245.

65. For the purposes of this chapter, I have taken the concept of the One to be the functional equivalent of the Way as it is manifested within the phenomenal world. This certainly seems to be the implication of chapter 39 in which the most important phenomena (Heaven, Earth, numen, the valley, the myriad things, sage rulers) each attain their essential defining characteristics as the result of the One. Chapter 42, in which we read that the "Way generated the

One," indicates that there is some difference between them. This could simply mean that there is a certain aspect of the Way that transcends its manifestation as the solitary unifying power within the phenomenal world. For a fuller discussion of the polysemy of the concept of the One in the Daoist tradition, see Livia Kohn, "Guarding," 127–37.

66. Here I follow the Mawangdui variant *jin zhi Dao* 今之道 (not *gu zhi Dao* 古之道; Henricks, 215), because it better fits the phenomenological interpretation I have been developing in this chapter. The Way, as both the source merged with in introvertive mystical experience and the constant source of the universe from before its beginnings, is directly experienced in the present (not past, as in the received versions). Because it has existed from antiquity, if one knows it in the present, one can know it in the past and, through it, "know the ancient beginnings."

67. Lau, *Tao te Ching*, 33–34.

68. *Zhuangzi yinde*, 2/38–40.

69. The phrase *dai ying po* 戴營魄 is extremely problematic and has puzzled commentators since *Heshanggong* 河上公. The po is the "bodily soul," associated with yin, and the counterpart of the "spiritual soul" (*hun* 魂) associated with yang. The former governs the body; the latter governs the mind. They work harmoniously together during life, but separate after death, the po returning to Earth and the hun to Heaven. According to Yu Yingshi 余英時, the former concept developed first; there are a few references in the oracle bones. The concept of hun seems to have been derived from it and is intended to represent the locus of daily conscious activities, somewhat akin to our modern notion of the conscious mind, in my interpretation. Along these lines, I would suggest that we might think of the po as rather like our modern notion of the unconscious mind. That is, the mental phenomena we now associate with the conscious and unconscious minds were explained in early China by the concepts of the hun and po. Eduard Erkes follows the *Heshanggong* commentary by taking the term ying as the functional equivalent of hun; he suggests it was a variant of *ling* 靈 in Chu dialect. Thus, a literal translation of this phrase would be "to sustain the conscious and unconscious souls." I have rendered it more freely because the constant activity of these two aspects of the mind does constitute "the daily activity of the psyche." For more information, see Yu Yingshi, "O Soul, Come Back!' A Study of the Changing Conceptions of the Soul and Afterlife in Pre Buddhist China," *Harvard Journal of Asiatic Studies* 47, no. 2 (December 1987): 363–95; and Eduard Erkes, trans., *Ho-Shang-Kung's Commentary on Lao-Tse* (Ascona: Artibus Asiae, 1950), 141–42.

70. *Guanzi*, 16.2b1–3. Translated in Roth, "Inner Cultivation," 133.

71. *Guanzi*, 16.5a2–4.

72. Kohn, "Guarding," especially 154–56.

73. *Guanzi*, 16.4a2–7. Close parallels of this passage are found in "Techniques of the Mind II" from *Guanzi* (13.5a2) and in the "Gengsang Chu" chapter of *Zhuangzi* (*Zhuangzi yinde*, 23/34–35).

74. Lau, *Tao Te Ching*, 15. The mirror is one of the most important metaphors in Chinese religious thought. The mirror is often seen to symbolize the clarified mind of the sage, which reflects things exactly as they are without even an iota of personal bias. For further details, see the pioneering study by Paul Demieville, "Le miroir spirituel," *Sinologica* 1, no. 2 (1948): 112–37.

75. *Guanzi*, 16.2b9–3a1.

76. *Guanzi*, 13.1a11.

Chapter 9

1. Victor Mair, *Experimental Essays on the Chuang Tzu* (Honolulu: University of Hawai'i Press, 1983); and Paul Kjellberg and P. J. Ivanhoe, *Essays on Skepticism, Relativism, and Ethics in the Zhuangzi* (Albany: State University of New York Press, 1996). I share the same assumptions as the scholars included in these two volumes that there is one author of the "Inner Chapters," and I follow existing conventions in referring to him as Zhuangzi.

2. I am fully aware that the text of the *Zhuangzi* contains a number of distinct authorial voices, and I accept Angus Graham's identification of them in his seminal study, "How Much of *Chuang Tzu*." The present study is principally concerned with the "Inner Chapters" (ch. 1–7), which most concur are the product of a single hand, usually thought to be the man after whom the collection was named. While I am not convinced that all the passages collected in these chapters are by a single author, I do maintain that they express a sufficiently consistent vision. For convenience, and in the absence of a viable alternative, I adopt the traditional practice and identify this author as "Zhuangzi."

3. Harold D. Roth, "Redaction Criticism and the Early History of Taoism," *Early China* 19 (1994): 1–46 (chapter 3 in this book); "Evidence for Stages of Meditation in Early Taoism," *Bulletin of the School of Oriental and African Studies* 60, no. 1 (June 1997) (chapter 4 in this book); and Roth, "*Laozi* in the Context of Early Daoist Mystical Praxis," in *Religious and Philosophical Aspects of the Laozi*, ed. P. J. Ivanhoe and M. Csikszentmihalyi (Albany: State University of New York Press, 1999) (chapter 8 in this book).

4. Donald Harper has accomplished seminal work in translating the texts of this tradition: *Early Chinese Medical Literature: The Mawangdui Medical Manuscripts* (London: Royal Asiatic Society, 1998). He has also begun an important analysis of how this tradition relates to the early texts of Daoism in this book and in an article "The Bellows Analogy in *Laozi* V and Warring States Macrobiotic Hygiene," *Early China* 20 (1995): 381–92.

5. Walter Stace, *Mysticism and Philosophy* (London: Macmillan Press, 1960; reprint, Los Angeles: Jeremy P. Tarcher, Inc., 1987), 111, 131.

6. Ibid., 66.

7. Harold D. Roth, "Some Issues in the Study of Chinese Mysticism: A Review Essay," *China Review International* 2, no. 1 (1995): 154–72.

8. Stace, 9, 132.

9. Lee Yearley, "The Perfected Person in the Radical *Chuang-tzu*," in *Experimental Essays on Chuang-tzu*, ed. Victor H. Mair (Honolulu: University of Hawai'i Press, 1983), 125–48.

10. Ibid., 131.

11. Chad Hansen, "A Tao of Tao in *Chuang-tzu*," in *Experimental Essays on Chuang-tzu*, ed. Victor H. Mair (Honolulu: University of Hawai'i Press, 1983), 24–55.

12. All references to the text of the *Zhuangzi* are to the following edition: *Chuang-tzu yin te*, Harvard-Yenching Institute Sinological Index Series no. 20 (Peking, 1947).

13. See Roth, "Evidence" and Roth, "*Lao Tzu* in the Context" (chapters 4 and 8 in the present volume).

14. I deviate from Graham's translation only in translating *tong* 通 as "merge" instead of "go along," and *datong* 大通 as the "Great Pervader." References to the Chinese text are to the *Chuang tzu yin te*, Harvard-Yenching Institute Sinological Index Series no. 20 (Beijing, 1947).

15. I follow Graham in understanding *zhi ti* as the four limbs or members and the five orbs or visceral organs that are the physical manifestations of the five basic systems of vital energy in the human body. This is preferable to the alternative "drop off limbs and body" because two lines later the text refers to parting from the body (*li xing* 離形), which would be redundant if the second interpretation were taken. For the associations of the emotions with the various internal organs or "orbs," see Porkert, 1974, 115–46.

16. Hansen, in Mair, 45.

17. Lisa Raphals, "Skeptical Strategies in *Zhuangzi* and Theaetetus," in *Essays on Skepticism, Relativism, and Ethics in the Zhuangzi*, ed. Paul Kjellberg and Philip J. Ivanhoe (Albany: State University of New York Press, 1996), 26–49.

18. Ibid., 30.

19. Ibid., 30–31.

20. P. J. Ivanhoe, "Zhuangzi on Skepticism, Skill, and the Ineffable Dao," *Journal of the American Academy of Religion* 64, no. 4 (1993): 639–54.

21. Ibid., 641.

22. Ibid., 642–43, 648–49.

23. Ibid., 645.

24. Ibid., 653.

25. A. C. Graham, "*Chuang Tzu's* Essay on Seeing All Things As Equal," *History of Religions* 9 (October 1969–February 1970): 137–59.

26. Hansen, in Mair, 34.

27. The two pairs of Graham's English translations of *shi* and *fei* are from his book *Chuang Tzu: The Inner Chapters* and from the *History of Religions* article, respectively.

28. My translation departs from Graham's (CT: Inner Chapters, 53–54). The key departure is my rendering of the verbal phrase *tong weiyi* as "to pervade and unify" rather than Graham's "interchange and deem to be one." I feel this better captures the activity of the Way and of the sages who identify completely with it: the Way pervades everything and in pervading them unifies them. They are unified to the extent that each and every thing contains the Way within it; and they are unified in that, from the perspective of the Way within, each thing is seen to be equal. Because they attain this Way, sages can have the exact same perspective.

29. Raphals, in Kjellberg and Ivanhoe, 33, and 46 n.34, respectively.

30. I take the title of the waterfall from Victor Mair 1994, 182. Mair's consistent translation of such names in order to give the reader a sense of their implications in Chinese is one of the strengths of his translation.

31. The bell-carver (19/54–57) and Yan Hui (4/29–32) both practice a fasting of the mind in order to cultivate stillness and emptiness. This is another indication of the importance of inner cultivation practice in developing the *yinshi* mode of extrovertive mystical consciousness.

Chapter 10

1. "Inner cultivation" is the term I use to refer to the apophatic practices of emptying the mind in order to realize the Way that are found in all early Daoist works. For details, see Harold D. Roth, *Original Tao: Inward Training and the Foundations of Taoist Mysticism* (New York: Columbia University Press, 1999), 7–9 and passim. This activist Daoist position belongs to the Syncretist phase of the early Daoist tradition that is sometimes identified with the "Huang-Lao" intellectual position. For a good overview, see Sarah Queen and Harold D. Roth, "The Huang-Lao Silk Manuscripts," in *Sources of Chinese Tradition*, 2nd ed., ed. Irene Bloom and Wm. Th. De Bary (New York: Columbia University Press, 1999), 241–43; John S. Major, *Heaven and Earth in Early Han Thought: Chapters Three, Four, and Five of the Huainanzi* (Albany: State University of New York Press 1993), 8–14.

2. For a classical formulation, see Rudolph Otto, *The Idea of the Holy*, trans. John W. Harvey (Oxford: Oxford University Press, 1925). For the effects on the laws of nature, see Joseph Needham, *Science and Civilisation in China*, vol. 2 (Cambridge: Cambridge University Press, 1956), 533–39.

3. In his analysis of the presence of laws of nature that serve as the foundation for human natural laws in the *Huang-Lao boshu*, Randall Peeren-

boom has made a similar argument. See R. P. Peerenboom, *Law and Morality in Ancient China: The Silk Manuscripts of Huang-Lao* (Albany: State University of New York Press, 1992), 19–29.

4. D. C. Lau and Chen Fong Ching, eds., *A Concordance to the Huainanzi* (Hong Kong: Commercial Press, Institute of Chinese Studies Ancient Chinese Texts Concordance Series, 1992); and D. C. Lau and Roger T. Ames, trans., *Yuan Dao: Tracing Dao to Its Source* (New York: Ballantine: 1998).

5. Kusuyama, Haruki 楠山春樹, *Enanji* 淮南子, 3 vols. (Tokyo: Meiji shôin, 1979, 1982, 1988). Zhang Shuangdi 張雙棣, *Huainanzi jishi* 淮南 自校 釋, 2 vols. (Beijing: Beijing daxue chubanshe, 1997).

6. References to the Chinese text of the *Huainanzi* are to the edition in D. C. Lau and Chen Fong Ching, eds., *A Concordance to the Huainanzi* (Hong Kong: Commercial Press, Institute of Chinese Studies Ancient Chinese Texts Concordance Series, 1992). They follow the format: chapter/page/line. In the following translations from "Yuan Dao," block prose is continuous, parallel prose is laid out line by line from the left margin of the quotation, and true verse is indented. All translations are my own.

7. Roger Ames identifies this principle as one of the fundamental ideas in *Huainanzi* 9. See Roger Ames, *The Art of Rulership* (Honolulu: University of Hawai'i Press, 1983).

8. Peerenboom 1992, 42–45, discusses the range of meaning of *tian* in early Chinese philosophical literature and decides upon "nature" as the best translation in his sources.

9. Chen Guying 陳古應, *Huangdi sijing jinszhu jinyi* 黃帝四經今注今意 (Taipei: Commercial Press, 1995), 155–56.

10. Sarah Allan, *The Way of Water and Sprouts of Virtue* (Albany: State University of New York Press, 1998); and Sarah Allan and Crispin Williams, eds., *The Guodian Laozi: Proceedings of the International Conference, Dartmouth College, May 1998* (Berkeley: University of California, Institute for East Asian Studies, 2000).

11. The concept of realizing the deepest aspects of your own innermost being is a constant in the early Daoist "inner cultivation" tradition harkening back to its oldest extant source, the "Inward Training" (*Neiye* 內業) chapter of the *Guanzi* 管子. I have discussed this at great length (see Roth 1999, and in chapters 1–4, 7 and 9 in the present volume). Early Daoists conceived of a number of closely related aspects at the core of your innermost being including the spirit and its vital essence and ultimately the Way itself.

12. The "Techniques of the Mind" is the title of two short texts in the seventy-six-text *Guanzi* compendium. Together with "Inward Training" and "The Purified Mind," they constitute a group that in modern scholarship if referred to as the four "Techniques of Mind" works. By the time of the *Huainanzi*, this phrase was probably used as a general term for what I have called "inner cultivation" practice. For details, see Roth, 1999, 15–30.

13. For Graham, chapters 8 through the first part of 11 of the *Zhuangzi* were written by a single author whose literary style and intellectual viewpoint are unique in the work. He deemed this author the "Primitivist." See A. C. Graham, "How Much of *Chuang-tzu* did Chuang-tzu Write?," in A. C. Graham, *Studies in Chinese Philosophy and Philosophical Literature* (Albany: State University of New York Press, 1990), 283–321.

14. Michael Saso, *Taoism and the Rite of Cosmic Renewal* (Pullman: Washington State University Press, 1972), 45–51, presents a series of translations from the opening sections of *Huainanzi* 1, 3, and 7 that he argues contain many of the fundamental ideas of religious Daoism.

15. Roth in Harold D. Roth, *The Textual History of the Huai-nan Tzu* (Ann Arbor: Association for Asian Studies Monograph No. 46. 1992), 144–47, notes the existence of Northern Song taboos in the *Huainanzi* redaction in the Zhengtong 正統 *Daoist Canon* of 1445, thus indicating that it was based on an edition from this earlier recension.

Chapter 11

1. Sarah Allan, *The Way of Water and Sprouts of Virtue* (Albany: State University of New York Press, 1997).

2. An excellent example of this can be found in the writings of Cheng Yi 程頤 (1033–1107) in Wm. Theodore de Bary and Irene Bloom, *Sources of Chinese Tradition* (New York: Columbia University Press, 1999), 1: 689–91.

3. *Mengzi* 孟子 10.1 (*Wan zhang xia* 萬章下) Ancient Texts Database [CHANT], Chinese University of Hong Kong Institute of Chinese Studies Ancient Chinese Texts Concordance Series, supervising eds., D. C. Lau and Chen Fong Ching. All Chinese texts are taken from this Database, unless otherwise noted.

4. *Mencius 5B.1*. Irene Bloom, *Mencius* (New York: Columbia University Press), 111. Most English translations of Mencius, such as those of Bloom and D. C. Lau, follow a different numbering scheme than the CHANT edition.

5. Stephen Little, *Daoism and the Arts of China* (Berkeley: University of California Press, 2000), 170–71; Phillip Clart, "The Jade Emperor," in *The Encyclopedia of Daoism*, ed. Fabrizio Pregadio (Oxford: Routledge, 2008), 1:1197–98.

6. *Shuowen* definition and commentary taken from citation in *Zhongwen dacidian* 中文大辭典 (Taibei: Guanghua Publishing, 1973), 6: 455.

7. *Mengzi* 11.7 (*Gaozi xia* 告子下) (CHANT).

8. Modified from Bloom, *Mencius*, 126. Unless otherwise noted, all translations are by the author.

9. *Mengzi* 14.19 ("Jinxin xia" 盡心下) (CHANT).

10. *Xunzi* 23 ("Xing e pian" 性惡篇), para. 1 (CHANT).

11. *Guanzi, juan* 卷 18.2(九守, *pian* 55), para. 9 (CHANT). The received text of the *Guanzi* follows a distinctive arrangement in which 76 *pian* are arranged

in 24 *juan*. I have provided paragraph numbers for the CHANT editions here and elsewhere to facilitate the location of specific passages in this electronic database that contains no numbered pages.

12. *Lüshi chunqiu*, *juan* 3.3 ("Xian ji" 先己), para. 1 (CHANT).

13. *Cou li* (腠 理) are the lines in the inner layer of connective tissue that cover muscles, ligaments, tendons, and joints. (*Grand Dictionnaire Ricci de la Langue Chinoise* [Paris: Association Ricci, 2001], entry 11436, vol. VI, 131.) Vital energy circulates through this system of veins and animates these structures and the skin above them. This is a term found in the Chinese medical traditions.

14. Translation modified from John Knoblock and Jeffrey Riegel, *The Annals of Lü Buwei* (Stanford: Stanford University Press, 2001), 102.

15. *Lüshi chunqiu*, *juan* 5.4 ("Shiyin" 適音), para. 2 (CHANT).

16. Translation is the author's. See Knoblock and Riegel, *Annals*, 143 for a different interpretation.

17. Harold D. Roth, *Original Tao: Inward Training (Nei-yeh) and the Foundations of Taoist Mysticism* (New York: Columbia University Press, 1999).

18. See Harold D. Roth, "Psychology and Self-Cultivation in Early Taoistic Thought," *Harvard Journal of Asiatic Studies* 51, no. 2 (December 1991): 599–650 and "Redaction Criticism and the Early History of Taoism," *Early China* 19 (1994): 1–46 (chapters 1 and 3 in the present volume). See also Russell Kirkland, *Daoism: The Enduring Tradition*. Routledge, 2004) and Ronnie L. Littlejohn, *Daoism: An Introduction* (London and New York: I. B. Taurus, 2009).

19. Roth, "Psychology" and "Redaction Criticism" (chapters 1 and 3 in the present volume).

20. Louis Komjathy, *The Daoist Tradition: An Introduction*, chapter 2 (London: Continuum, 2013) provides a spirited defense of this terminology.

21. These phrases are found, respectively in *Guanzi*, *juan* 13.1 ("Xinshu shang" 心術上, *pian* 36), para. 2; *Laozi*, *zhang* 章 10; *Zhuangzi*, *juan* 4 ("Renjian shi" 人間世), para. 5, and *juan* 6 ("Dazong shi" 大宗師), para. 18 (CHANT).

22. For details on these states, see Harold D. Roth, "Evidence for Stages of Meditation in Early Taoism," *Bulletin of the School of Oriental and African Studies* 60, no. 2 (June 1997): 295–314 (chapter 4 in the present volume).

23. For this latter phrase, see *Zhuangzi*, *juan* 6 ("Dazong shi" 大宗師), para. 18 (CHANT).

24. For details, see Harold D. Roth, "*Lao Tzu* in the Context of Early Taoist Mystical Praxis," in *Essays on Religious and Philosophical Aspects of the Lao Tzu*, ed. Mark Csikszentmihalyi and P. J. Ivanhoe (Albany: State University of New York Press, 1999), 59–96 (chapter 8 in the present volume).

25. Harold D. Roth, "Bimodal Mystical Experience in the Qiwulun of Zhuangzi," *Journal of Chinese Religions* 28 (2000): 1–20 (chapter 9 in the present volume). "Flowing cognition" is my interpretation of Graham's very literal translation of *yinshi* 因是 as "the That's It that goes by circumstance." As explained

in this chapter, this refers to cognizing a situation from attachment to any one fixed way of seeing it.

26. *Laozi*, *zhang* 65 (CHANT).

27. *Laozi zhuzi suoyin* 老子遂 字索引 Chinese University of Hong Kong Institute of Chinese Studies Ancient Chinese Texts Concordance Series number 24. Supervising eds., D. C. Lau and Chen Fong Ching (Chinese University Press, 1996), chapter 65, line 20, p. 140. The CHANT Database does not include the commentaries of Wang Bi 王弼 and Heshang Gong.

28. *Zhuangzi*, *juan* 3 ("Yangsheng zhu" 養生主), para. 3 (CHANT).

29. *Zhuangzi*, *juan* 15 ("Keyi" 刻意), para. 2 (CHANT).

30. For this dating, see Roth, *Original Tao*, 23–27.

31. *Guanzi*, *juan* 16.1 (*pian* 49, "Neiye"), para. 3 (CHANT).

32. Roth, *Original Tao*, 54. Verse numbers are taken from this source.

33. *Guanzi*, *juan* 16.1 (*pian* 49, "Neiye"), para. 18 (CHANT).

34. See note 13.

35. Roth, *Original Tao*, 96.

36. *Guanzi*, *juan* 16.1 (*pian* 49, "Neiye"), para. 5 (CHANT).

37. Roth, *Original Tao*, 62. The "patterns of the One" are the various natural guidelines through which the Way penetrates the universe. They serve to structure the natural development of all phenomena and form a normative substructure for their interactions with one another.

38. For tentative dating, see Roth, *Original Tao*, 23–37. Textual emendations are all taken from Xu Weiyu 許維遹, Wen Yiduo 文一多, and Guo Moruo 郭沫若, *Guanzi jijiao* 管子集校 (Beijing: Zhonghua, 1955), 633–49.

39. *Guanzi*, *juan* 13.1 (*pian* 36, "Xinshu shang"), para. 1 (CHANT).

40. The division of "Xinshu shang" into verses is my own; the later commentary to each verse occurs within the undivided original text, but is obvious with careful analysis. These translations are from my unpublished manuscript translation of all four "Techniques of the Mind" chapters from the *Guanzi*: "The Resonant Way: Daoist Texts from the *Guanzi*."

41. Deleting *guyue* 故曰 (therefore it says) at the start of the sentence, following many scholars.

42. Moving this sentence here from a position in the comment section (just before the final line) to which it was erroneously displaced, following Guo Moruo, *Guanzi jijiao*.

43. *Guanzi*, *juan* 13.1 (*pian* 36, "Xinshu, shang"), para. 12 (CHANT).

44. *Guanzi*, *juan* 13.1 (*pian* 36, "Xinshu, shang"), para. 5 (CHANT).

45. Emending *zhi* 執 (grasp) to *shi* 势 (condition), the reading in other major editions (Guo Moruo, *Guanzi jijiao*).

46. *Huainanzi*, *juan* 21 ("Yao lüe" 要略), para. 21 (CHANT).

47. John S. Major, Sarah Queen, Andrew S. Meyer, and Harold D. Roth. *The Huainanzi: A Guide to the Theory and Practice of Government in Early Han*

China, by Liu An, King of Huainan (New York: Columbia University Press, 2010), 860.

48. *Huainanzi, juan* 1 ("Yuan Dao xun" 原道訓), para. 5 (CHANT). The suffix *xun* 訓 ("explicated") is added in the CHANT edition to the first 20 chapters titles. It is superfluous for chapter 21, which is a summary of the previous twenty chapters. However, if one is to be precise, this suffix was originally only found in the editions of the Gao Yu recension, and it should not be added to the chapters titles for the extant recension, which is a conflation of thirteen chapters from the Gao recension and eight from the recension of latter Han grammarian, Xu Shen. For details, see Harold D. Roth, *The Textual History of the Huai-nan Tzu*. Ann Arbor: Association for Asian Studies, 1992, 43, 79–112.

49. Major, et al., *The Huainanzi*, 53.

50. *Huainanzi, juan* 14 ("Quanyan xun" 詮言訓), para. 8 (CHANT).

51. Major et al., *Huainanzi*, 539–40.

52. *Huainanzi, juan* 11 ("Qi su xun" 齊俗訓), para. 13 (CHANT).

53. Major et al., *The Huainanzi*, 405–6.

54. *Huainanzi, juan* 11 ("Qi su xun"), para. 16 (CHANT).

55. Major et al., *The Huainanzi*, 408.

56. *Huainanzi, juan* 14 ("Quanyan xun"), para. 18 (CHANT).

57. Major et al., *The Huainanzi*, 547 (modified).

58. *Huainanzi, juan* 1 ("Yuan Dao xun"), para. 7–8 (CHANT).

59. Major et al., *The Huainanzi*, 55.

60. *Huainanzi, juan* 9 ("Zhu shu xun" 主術訓), para. 14 (CHANT).

61. Major et al., *The Huainanzi*, 304.

62. *Huainanzi, juan* 11 ("Qi su xun"), para. 24 (CHANT).

63. Major et al., *The Huainanzi*, 417.

64. *Huainanzi, juan* 14 ("Quanyan xun"), para. 20 (CHANT).

65. Major et al., *The Huainanzi*, 548–49.

66. For a fuller argument about this "normative natural order," see Harold D. Roth, "Nature and Self-Cultivation in *Huainanzi's* 'Original Way,' " in *Polishing the Chinese Mirror: Essays in Honor of Henry Rosemont Jr.*, ed. Marthe Chandler and Ronnie Littlejohn (New York: Global Scholarly Publications, 2010), 270–92 (chapter 10 in the present volume).

67. *Huainanzi, juan* 1 ("Yuan Dao xun"), para. 26 (CHANT).

68. Major et al., *The Huainanzi*, 71.

Chapter 12

1. A. C. Graham, "Mysticism and the Question of Private Access," in *Reason within Unreason: Essays on the Outskirts of Rationality*, ed. David Lynn Hall (LaSalle, IL: Open Court Press, 1992), 281–82.

2. The series of four radio programs for *Ideas* was broadcast on the CBC in February 1982 when I was in Sendai, Japan. I still use copies of them today in my teaching.

3. Harold D. Roth, "Contemplative Studies: Prospects for a New Field," *Teachers College Record* 108:9 (2006) (Columbia University), 1787–1815; "Against Cognitive Imperialism," *Religion East and West* 8 (2008): 1–23 (chapter 13 in the present volume); "A Pedagogy for the New Field of Contemplative Studies," in *Contemplative Approaches to Learning and Inquiry Across Disciplines*, ed. Olen Gunnlaugson and Heeson Bai (Albany: State University of New York Press, 2014), 97–118.

4. A. C. Graham, "Mysticism and the Question of Private Access," in *Reason within Unreason*, 265–82.

5. Graham, "Mysticism," 265.

6. Graham, "Mysticism," 277.

7. I have borrowed this idea of "attunement" from Jung Lee, *The Ethical Foundations of Early Daoism* (London: Palgrave-Macmillan, 2014). Lee speaks of "ethical attunement" as a result of practices advocated in the *Zhuangzi*.

8. Roth, "A Pedagogy for the New Field of Contemplative Studies," 98–99.

9. The former have been studied extensively as examples of the "optimal experience" he calls "flow" by psychologist Mihalyi Csíkszentmihályi. See *Flow: Towards a Psychology of Optimal Experience* (New York: Harper and Row, 1990). The latter have been studied during the past century under the general category of "mysticism or "mystical experience." For a superb overview article, see Jerome I. Gellman, "Mysticism and Religious Experience," in *The Oxford Handbook of the Philosophy of Religion*, ed. William Wainwright (Oxford: Oxford University Press, 2005), 138–52.

10. See, for example, the collection of scientific research in Brian Bruya, ed., *Effortless Attention: A New Perspective in the Cognitive Science of Attention and Action* (Cambridge: MIT Press, 2010). See also two books by Edward Slingerland: *Effortless Action: Wu-wei As Conceptual Metaphor and Spiritual Ideal in Early China* (Oxford: Oxford University Press, 2007) and *Trying Not to Try: The Art and Science of Spontaneity* (Crown, 2014).

11. Francisco J. Varela and Jonathan Shear, "First-Person Methodologies: What, Why, How?," in *The View from Within: First-Person Approaches to the Study of Consciousness*. Published as a special issue of the *Journal of Consciousness Studies* 6, no. 2–3 (1999) (Bowling Green, OH: Imprint Academic), 1.

12. Francisco Varela, Evan Thompson and Eleanor Rosch, *The Embodied Mind* (Cambridge, MA: MIT Press: 1991).

13. Evan Thompson, "Empathy and Consciousness," in *Between Ourselves: Second-Person Issues in the Study of Consciousness*, ed. Evan Thompson. Published as a special issue of the *Journal of Consciousness Studies* 8, no. 5–7 (2001) (Bowling Green, OH: Imprint Academic), 1.

14. Dan Zahavi, "Beyond Empathy: Phenomenological Approaches to Intersubjectivity," in *Between Ourselves*, ed. Evan Thompson, 166.

15. Evan Thompson, "Empathy and Consciousness," 1.

16. For an excellent recent summary of a plethora of this research, see Richard Davidson, *The Emotional Life of the Brain* (New York and London: Plume, 2012).

17. William James, *Essays in Radical Empiricism and a Pluralistic Universe* (New York: Peter Smith, 1967; first edition 1929), 74.

18. Yoko Arisaka, "The Ontological Co-Emergence of 'Self and Other' in Japanese Philosophy," in *Between Ourselves*, 202.

19. Arisaka, 202.

20. Arisaka, 203.

21. Nishida, Kitarō, *An Inquiry into the Good* (*Zen no kenkyu* 善の研究), trans. Christopher Ives and Masao Abe (New Haven: Yale University Press, 1990). Author's preface, xxx

22. The ultimate ground of consciousness and the world in the foundational Yogācāra work, *The Laṅkāvatāra Sutra*, is "mind only" or the ultimate Storehouse Consciousness (*Pāramālaya vijñāna*). For an excellent summary of this complex work, see Mark A. Ehman, "The Laṅkāvatāra Sutra," in *Buddhism: A Modern Perspective*, ed. Charles S. Prebish (University Park: Pennsylvania State University Press, 1975), 112–17.

23. The "brain sciences" include psychology, cognitive science, and neuroscience, and various overlapping fields of research such as "cognitive neuroscience."

24. Aaron Seitz and Takeo Watanabe, "The Phenomenon of Task-Irrelevant Perceptual Learning," *Vision Research* 49, no. 21 (October 2009): 2604–10.

25. Aaron Seitz, "Task Irrelevant Perceptual Learning," in *Encyclopedia of the Sciences of Learning*, ed. Norman M. Seel (New York: Springer, 2012); 3270–72.

26. Paul Hager, "Tacit Knowledge," in *Encyclopedia of the Sciences of Learning*, ed. Norman M. Seel (New York: Springer, 2012): 3259–61.

27. Brian Bruya, "Introduction: Towards a Theory of Attention That Includes Effortless Attention and Action," in *Effortless Attention: A New Perspective in the Cognitive Science of Attention and Action*, ed. Brian Bruya (Cambridge, MA: MIT Press, 2010), 1.

28. Rael B. Cahn and John Polich, "Meditation States and Traits: EEG, ERP and Neuroimaging Studies," *Psychological Bulletin* 132, no. 2 (2006): 180–211. The information about neuroscientific studies of meditation presented here is taken from this excellent overview article.

29. Cahn and Polich, 181.

30. Cahn and Polich, 181. I have replaced their category of "mindfulness" with that of "receptive meditation," as in the following source: James Austin, "The Thalamic Gateway: How Meditative Training of Attention Evolves toward Selfless Transformations of Consciousness," in Bruya, ed., *Effortless Attention*,

375–77. "Mindfulness" is a technique and result that can be used for either concentrative or receptive meditation.

31. Austin, 377.

32. Britta K. Hölzel, Sara Lazar, Tim Gard, Zev Schuman-Olivier, David R. Vago, and Ulrich Ott, "How Does Mindfulness Meditation Work? Proposing Mechanisms of Action From a Conceptual and Neural Perspective," *Perspectives on Psychological Science* 6, no. 6 (2011): 537–59.

33. Francisco Varela, "Neurophenomenology: A Methodological Remedy for the Hard Problem," *Journal of Consciousness Studies* 3, no. 4 (1996): 330–50.

34. Angus C. Graham, "How much of *Chuang Tzu* did Chuang Tzu Write?," in A. C. Graham, *Studies in Chinese Philosophy and Philosophical Literature* (Albany: State University of New York Press, 1990). Harold D. Roth, "An Appraisal of Angus Graham's Textual Scholarship on the *Chuang Tzu*," in *A Companion to Angus C. Graham's Chuang Tzu: The Inner Chapters*, ed. Harold D. Roth (Honolulu: University of Hawai'i Press, 2003). The Society for Asian and Comparative Philosophy Monograph 20, 181–220 (chapter 6 in the present volume).

35. Three recent works address many issues surrounding the text and composition of the *Zhuangzi*. Most relevant for our concerns is the issue of whether or not the first seven "Inner Chapters" of the *Zhuangzi* contain the original core around which the text formed and whether or not they can be attributed to the historical figure of Zhuang Zhou, as maintained by Graham and myself. Liu Xiaogan's 劉笑敢 newest work on this topic examines a wide range of opinions and concludes that the inner chapters should be taken as the core of the text and represent the work of the historical figure; and that the outer and miscellaneous chapters can be roughly attributed to the followers of Zhuang Zhou. See Liu Xiaogan, "Textual Issues in the *Zhuangzi*," in *Dao Companion to Daoist Philosophy*, ed. Xiaogan Liu (Dordrecht: Springer, 2015), 129–57.

David McCraw, in *Stratifying Zhuangzi: Rhyme and Other Quantitative Evidence*, Language and Linguistics Monograph Series, vol. 41 (Taipei: Institute of Linguistics, Academia Sinica, 2010), uses his own system of rhyming patterns in the *Zhuangzi* to argue that the presence of many "non-canonical cross-rhymes" in the Inner Chapters proves that they could not have been written by a single author. Reviewers have commented on the confusing presentation of his methodology and results, calling this "opaque to the point of incomprehensibility" (Richard Lynn, *Journal of Chinese Studies* no. 54 [January 2012]: 335–59). Linguist David Branner (*Journal of the American Oriental Society* 130, no. 4 [2010]: 653–54), further questions both McCraw's methodology and conclusions: "In the case of the *Zhuāngzǐ*, the fact that there are a great many noncanonical "cross-rhymes" could indeed point to multiple authorship, with each hand characterized by a different cross-rhyming pattern. Could it also point to a single author writing in a style that allows for non-canonical rhyming, or even simply trying to sound non-canonical?" He concludes: "In short, this book should not have been published in its present form. It deals with an important question but is confusing and awkwardly composed. . . . its rambling and hesitant presentation makes me wonder about the soundness of its findings."

In "Were There Inner Chapters in the Warring States?: A New Examination of Evidence About the *Zhuangzi*," *T'oung Pao* 96 (2011): 299–369, Esther Klein has put forth a well-researched and well-argued analysis of the composition of the *Zhuangzi*. In it, she theorizes that while there must have been a pre-Han version of the text that contained most of the materials that are in the work today, the compilation of the original fifty-two-chapter recension, later excised to thirty-three by Guoxiang, is likely a Western Han event, possibly—as I hypothesized in the original *festschrift* for Angus Graham—at the Huainan court of Liu An. (See Harold D. Roth, "Who Compiled the *Chuang Tzu?*," in *Chinese Texts and Contexts: Essays in Honor of Angus C. Graham*, ed. Henry Rosemont Jr. [Lasalle, IL: Open Court Press, 1991], 79–128 [chapter 2 of the present volume].) She contends further, contrary to accepted opinion, that the Inner Chapters are likely to have been the *last* section of the text compiled, put together because of—or to form—a coherent philosophy. She concludes that the time has come to stop thinking of there being one author of the Inner Chapters and most certainly to stop thinking of this author as the reputed historical personage of Zhuang Zhou.

While there is something to commend in each of these sources, all fail to seriously consider the experiential dimension to which many passages in the text attest. (To be more precise, McCraw summarily dispenses with this in a comment on 48–49.) If, as I am arguing, a contemplative practice and its results are attested throughout the text, the reliance on a historical tradition in which this practice was handed down from teacher to students is a necessity. Then as now, it is clear that one cannot derive an effective contemplative practice from reading about it in a book. As I have argued in the first Graham *festschrift*, there is reason to theorize that this tradition continued into the Han and was present at the Huainan court. While it is not possible here to fully assess the impact this argument has on the evidence for the compilation of the text, it *is* possible to take something from each of their works: 1. With Liu, I think that the material now in the Inner Chapters was part of the original stratum of the book; 2. With McCraw, I think that it is possible that not all the Inner Chapters were written by one person; I do think that there is a consistency in literary styles and in philosophy that makes these chapters the core of the text; 3. With Klein, I think that the work was likely compiled at the court of Liu An from materials that existed in the late Warring States.

36. Roth, "Who Compiled the *Chuang Tzu?*"

37. I am using "cognitive" to encompass the entire range of responses of consciousness to its environment, including intellectual, emotional, intuitive, aesthetic, and even "spiritual." All these aspects of consciousness contribute to the total apprehension or cognition of the whole from moment to moment

throughout the full range of third-, second-, first-, and no-person experience. This full range is included in classical Daoist ideas about the activity of consciousness or of the "heart" or "mind."

38. Graham, *Chuang Tzu: The Inner Chapters* (London: Allen and Unwin, 1981), 43–44. All references to the text are from the edition in D. C. Lau et al., eds., *Zhuangzi suizi suoyin* (ZZSY). Ancient Chinese Text Concordance Series, Chinese University of Hong Kong, Philosophical works no. 43 (Hong Kong: Commercial Press, 2000), 1/1/15–21 (chapter 1/page 1/ lines 15–21.).

39. Graham, *CT*, 45 (modified). ZZSY 1/2/2–3.

40. Graham, *CT*, 95. ZZSY 7/20/16.

41. Graham, *CT*, 150. ZZSY 11/28/31–32.

42. Graham, *CT*, 131–32; ZZSY 12/31/19.

43. Graham *CT*, 69. ZZSY 4/10/5–6.

44. Graham, *CT*, 84–85 (modified). ZZSY 6/15/29–16/9.

45. Graham, *CT*, 82. ZZSY 5/15/20–25. I have emended Graham's translation to be gender neutral whenever possible.

46. Graham, *CT*, 150. ZZSY 11/28/31–32.

47. Graham, *CT*, 81.

48. Graham, *CT*, 202–03. ZZSY 8/23/9–10.

49. Graham, *CT*, 205. ZZSY 9/24/1.

50. Graham, *CT*, 205. ZZSY 9/24/10.

51. Graham, *CT*, 212. ZZSY 11/26/25–27.

52. See, for example, Brian Bruya, "The Rehabilitation of Spontaneity: A New Approach in the Philosophy of Action," *Philosophy East and West* 50, no. 2. And Edward Slingerland, "Towards an Empirically Responsible Ethics: Cognitive Science, Virtue Ethics, and Effortless Attention in Early Chinese Thought," in Bruya, *Effortless Attention*, 248–86.

53. Graham, *CT*, 186–87. ZZSY 12/32/22–24.

54. So common, in fact, that Graham has put together a section of these passages, seven in all. They come from chapters 12–14 and 21–22. Graham, *CT*, 126–34.

55. Graham, *CT*, 129–30. ZZSY 14/39/27–28.

56. See, for example, the second chapter of the *Huainanzi* titled "Activating the Genuine," in *The Huainanzi: A Guide to the Theory and Practice of Government in Early Han China*, translated, annotated, and introduced by John S. Major, Sarah Queen, Andrew S. Meyer, and Harold D. Roth (New York: Columbia University Press, 2010).

57. Graham, *CT*, 130–31. ZZSY 21/57/20–25.

58. Graham, *CT*, 259–60. ZZSY, 13/34/16–22.

59. Graham, *CT*, 65. ZZSY, 15/41/24–28.

60. For an analysis of this important concept of *Li* (patterns), see Harold D. Roth, "The Classical Daoist Concept of Li and Early Chinese Cosmology," in *Studies in Honor of Li Xueqin*, ed. Wen Xing, Early China 35–36 (Berkeley:

The Society for the Study of Early China, 2012–2013), 157–84 (chapter 11 in the present volume).

61. Graham, *CT*, 68–69. ZZSY 4/10/1–4 (modified).

62. Graham, *CT*, 92. ZZSY 6/19/17–22.

63. For details, see Manfred Porkert, *The Theoretical Foundations of Chinese Medicine* (Cambridge, MA: MIT Press, 1974), 108–52.

64. ZZSY: 2/3/15; 19/50/14; 20/55/12; 21/57/21; 22/61/1; 23/65/23; 24/70/19.

65. Graham, *CT*, 138. ZZSY 19/50/12–16.

66. Graham, *CT*, 77. ZZSY 5/13/18–21.

67. Graham, *CT*, ZZSY, 7/21/21 (modified).

68. Graham, *CT* 359–60. ZZSY, 13/34/1–24.

69. Graham, *CT*, 281. ZZSY 33/99/29–30.

70. Graham, *CT*, 178. ZZSY 11/27/23–28.

71. Concentrative meditation is one of the techniques included in the toolbox of the practice of "Mindfulness Based Stress Reduction." See Jon Kabat-Zinn, *Full Catastrophe Living* (New York: Delta, 1990).

72. ZZSY 23/67/8–11. For an alternate translation, see Victor Mair, *Wandering on the Way* (New York: Bantam, 1994), 234.

73. Graham, *CT* 132–33. ZZSY, 22/61/16, 21–23.

74. Graham, *CT*, 69. ZZSY 4/10/5.

75. Graham, *CT*, 51 (modified). ZZSY 2/4/9–10.

76. Graham, *CT*, 53. ZZSY 2/4/18–19.

77. Graham, *CT*, 53. ZZSY 2/4/19–20.

78. Graham, *CT*, 52. ZZSY 2/4/16.

79. He first cracked this in the following article: A. C. Graham, "*Chuang Tzu's* Essay on Seeing All Things as Equal," *History of Religions* 9 (October 1969–February 1970).

80. Graham, *CT*, 52. ZZSY 2/4/16.

81. Graham, *CT*, 53–54. ZZSY 2/4/26–5/3.

82. ZZSY 22/62/14–15.

83. ZZSY 5/13/13; 7/21/15; 13/34/22; 22/61/20; 33/97/15.

84. ZZSY 6/17/14; 7/21/19; 11/27, 28; 20/54/3; 33/99/27.

85. ZZSY 6/17/25,27; 6/18/19; 7/20/14; 19/50/1,3; 32/95/19; 33/100/10.

86. ZZSY 6/19/21; 17/46/27.

87. Graham, *CT*, 76–77. ZZSY 5/13/11–15.

88. Graham, *CT*, 135. ZZSY 19/52/4–8.

Chapter 13

1. Robin Marantz Henig, "Darwin's God," *New York Times Sunday Magazine*, March 4, 2007, 39.

2. Ibid.

3. Joachim Wach, *The Comparative Study of Religions* (New York and London: Columbia University Press, 1958, paperback edition, 1961), 37.

4. Boyer's use of the term *supernatural notions* can only be described as deriving from common parlance. Neither in this article nor in his larger study, *Religion Explained*, does he attempt to provide a clear definition of this term. Of course, to a great extent it depends on how one defines what it means to be "natural." This has varied considerably in European religious and scientific thought, to say nothing of non-European philosophies. For the purposes of this study, we also use *supernatural* as Boyer seems to: to refer to experiences, events, forces, or beings that operate beyond what a society defines as "natural," that is, subject to the laws of nature. For the history of how such concepts led to the rise of scientific materialism in Europe, see B. Alan Wallace, *The Taboo of Subjectivity* (Oxford and New York: Oxford University Press, 2000), 41–56. For a study of these concepts in Christian theology, see Paul Draper, "God, Science, and Naturalism," in William Wainwright, ed., *The Oxford Handbook of Philosophy of Religion* (Oxford and New York: Oxford University Press, 2005), 272–303.

5. Pascal Boyer, "Gods and the Mental Instincts that Create Them," in James Proctor, ed., *Science, Religion, and the Human Experience* (Oxford and New York: Oxford University Press, 2005), 240.

6. Ibid., 244.

7. Ibid., 247.

8. There are, of course, important contemplative traditions in Christianity that Boyer ignores; whether or not they hold supernatural beliefs is a contentious issue beyond the scope of this chapter.

9. Over the years there has been a lively debate on whether or not this key Confucian concept can be understood within the confines of Abrahamic notions of natural/supernatural or transcendent/immanent. This debate is resumed in the pages of the superb *festschrift, Polishing the Chinese Mirror: Essays in Honor of Henry Rosemont Jr.*, ed. Ronnie Littlejohn and Marthe Chandler (New York: Global Scholarly Publications, 2008). See, in particular, Littlejohn's "Did Kongzi Teach Us How to Become Gods?," 188–211 and Rosemont's response, 382–88.

10. Henry Rosemont Jr., *Rationality and Religious Experience: The Continuing Relevance of the World's Spiritual Traditions* (LaSalle, IL: Open Court Press, 2001), 43.

11. Steven Katz, "Language, Epistemology, and Mysticism," in Steven Katz, ed., *Mysticism and Philosophical Analysis* (Oxford and New York: Oxford University Press, 1979), 26. The emphases are mine.

12. For James's classic identification of the basic phenomenological elements of mystical experience, see his *The Varieties of Religious Experience* (1902; reprint, New York: Penguin Books, 1982), 380–81. This apophatic process of deepening insight through removing the basic categories of everyday cognition is perhaps best seen in the early Daoist tradition, where the progressive emptying

out of the contents of consciousness results first in a state alternately described as being completely empty, attaining the One, or merging with the Dao. This is then followed by the arising of a attachment-free cognition that spontaneously perceives, knows, and acts in complete harmony with the greater forces of the cosmos. For details on these processes, see two articles of mine: "Evidence for Stages of Meditation in Early Taoism," *Bulletin of the School of Oriental and African Studies* 60, no. 2 (June 1997): 295–314, and "Bimodal Mystical Experience in the 'Qiwulun' of *Chuang Tzu*," *Journal of Chinese Religions* 28 (2000): 1–20.

13. Sumner B. Twiss, "Shaping the Curriculum: The Emergence of Religious Studies," in Mark Hadley and Mark Unno, eds., *Counterpoints: Issues in Teaching Religious Studies* (Providence, RI: Department of Religious Studies, Brown University, 1995), 33. Although written as a study of a particular department, it is a case study for the entire field.

14. See, for example, Harold D. Roth, *The Textual History of the Huai-nan Tzu* (Ann Arbor: Association for Asian Studies, 1992).

15. This quote is taken from an interview I did in 1981 with Needham that was incorporated into the radio program "Divination and Cosmology in Ancient China," on *Ideas* (Canadian Broadcasting Corporation, February 9, 16, 23 and March 2, 1982). This particular broadcast was the first, on February 9.

16. The search for the historical Jesus is a topic that has roiled Christian theology for more than four centuries; however, no era has been so engaged in this topic as that of the past half-century, when the theological quest to establish the historicity of Jesus as an example of the working of the Divine in the world has been challenged by the critical techniques of historical scholars who have attempted to differentiate reliable data from myth and pious elaboration. Representative writings in this massive corpus include Albert Schweitzer, *The Quest for the Historical Jesus* (1909; reprint, New York: Dover, 2005); Norman Perrin, *Rediscovering the Teaching of Jesus* (New York: Harper and Row, 1967); John Dominic Crossan, *The Historical Jesus: The Life of a Mediterranean Jewish Peasant* (New York: Harper and Row, 1993); E. P. Sanders, *The Historical Figure of Jesus* (London and New York: Penguin Books, 1993); Robert Funk et al., *The Five Gospels: The Search for the Authentic Words of Jesus* (San Francisco: Harper San Francisco, 1993).

17. Russell McCutcheon, *Critics Not Caretakers: Redescribing the Public Study of Religion* (Albany: State University of New York Press, 2001) is probably the most direct statement of this thesis; his *Manufacturing Religion* (Oxford and New York: Oxford University Press, 2003) argues this critique in terms of the presumed clash between "insider" and "outsider" perspectives in the study of religion. His critique of the study of religion as a special sui generis phenomenon in the latter volume is not without merit, but he doesn't go far enough to break away from the European cultural presuppositions that support objectivist historicism and social-scientific reductionism to attain a truly unbiased perspective.

18. James, *Varieties*, 42.

19. B. Alan Wallace, "The Intersubjective Worlds of Science and Religion," in Proctor, *Science, Religion, and the Human Experience*, 309.

20. B. Alan Wallace, *The Taboo of Subjectivity* (Oxford and New York: Oxford University Press, 2000), 41–56.

21. *Mulāmadhyamika kārikās* 24.11.

22. I use the names Laozi and Zhuangzi as conventions to refer to the philosophical arguments made within those works; I do not intend to imply that there was a real historical person named Laozi who authored this work (there was not). The historical Zhuangzi, or Zhuang Zhou 莊周, was author of perhaps chapters 1 to 7 (the "Inner Chapters") of the *Zhuangzi* text. For the former, see A. C. Graham, "The Origins of the Legend of Lao Tan," in Livia Kohn and Michael LaFargue, *Lao-Tzu and the Tao-te-Ching* (Albany: State University of New York Press, 1998), 23–40. For the latter, see Graham, "How Much of *Chuang Tzu* did Chuang Tzu Write?," in Harold Roth, ed., *A Companion to Angus C. Graham's Chuang Tzu: The Inner Chapters* (Honolulu: University of Hawai'i Press, 2003), 58–103; and Harold Roth, "Who Compiled the Chuang Tzu?," in Henry Rosemont Jr., ed., *Chinese Texts and Philosophical Contexts: Essays in Honor of Angus C. Graham* (LaSalle, IL: Open Court Press, 1991), 79–128 (chapter 2 in the present volume).

23. Angus C. Graham, *Chuang-tzu: The Seven "Inner Chapters" and Other Writings from the Book Chuang-tzu* (London: Allen and Unwin, 1981), 51 (modified).

24. Ibid., 53 (modified).

25. Ibid., 51 (modified).

26. Ibid., 52 (modified).

27. Ibid., 53. My translation departs from Graham's in rendering *shi* 是 and *fei* 非 as "true" and "false" rather than Graham's insightful but idiosyncratic translations of "that's it" and "that's not."

28. My translation departs from Graham's on 53–54. The key departure is my rendering of the verbal phrase *tong wei yi* 通為一 as "to pervade and unify" rather than Graham's "interchange and deem to be one." I feel this better captures the activity of the Way and of the sages who identify completely with it: the Way pervades everything and in pervading them unifies them. They are unified to the extent that each and every thing contains the Way within it; and they are unified in that, from the perspective of the Way within, each thing is seen to be equal. Because they attain this Way, sages can have the exact same perspective. I have also provided a different and I hope clearer translation of two important compounds, *weishi* 為是 and *yinshi*. Graham's extremely precise translations of these terms as "the That's It which Deems" and "the That's It which goes by circumstance" are insightful but overly technical for the educated reader. I have chosen to translate these compounds in a way that incorporates my interpretation of their meaning as "fixated cognition" and "flowing cognition."

29. Harold D. Roth, *Original Tao: Inward Training (Nei-yeh) and the Foundations of Taoist Mysticism* (New York: Columbia University Press, 1999).

30. For information on Zhuangzi's inner cultivation practices, see Roth, *Original Tao*, 153–61. For a study devoted to this subject, see "Bimodal Mystical Experience in the Qiwulun of Chuang Tzu," *Journal of Chinese Religions* 28 (2000): 1–20 (chapter 9 in the present volume).

31. Francisco Varela, Eleanor Rosch, and Evan Thompson, *The Embodied Mind* (Cambridge, MA: MIT Press, 1991), 9.

32. Varela et al., *Embodied Mind*, 150.

33. Evan Thompson, "Empathy and Human Experience," in Proctor, *Science, Religion and the Human Experience*, 273.

34. B. Alan Wallace, "Intersubjectivity in Indo-Tibetan Buddhism," *Journal of Consciousness Studies* 8: 5–7 (2001): 209–10.

35. Graham, *Chuang-tzu*, 53 (modified).

36. Ibid., 54 (modified).

37. Varela et al., *Embodied Mind*, 217–54.

38. B. Alan Wallace, *Contemplative Science: Where Buddhism and Neuroscience Converge* (New York: Columbia University Press, 2006), 15–16.

39. Thompson, "Empathy and Human Experience," in Proctor, *Science, Religion and the Human Experience*, 261–62.

40. Frits Staal, *Exploring Mysticism* (Berkeley and Los Angeles: University of California Press, 1975), 123–24.

41. Mihalyi Csíkszentmihályi, *Flow: The Psychology of Optimal Experience* (New York: Harper and Row, 1990).

42. The pioneering works in these areas are Jon Kabat-Zinn, *Full Catastrophe Living* (New York: Delta, 1990) and Herbert Benson, *The Relaxation Response* (New York: Harper, 1975). See also Ruth A. Baer, "Mindfulness Training as a Clinical Intervention: A Conceptual Review," *Clinical Psychology: Science and Practice* 10, no. 2 (Summer 2003), 125–43; and Scott Bishop et al., "Mindfulness: A Proposed Operational Definition," *Clinical Psychology: Science and Practice* 11, no. 3 (Fall 2004): 230–41.

43. Jha's Lab at the University of Pennsylvania is doing cutting-edge research on the cognitive impact of contemplative practices. See, for example, her article A. P. Jha, J. Krompinger, and M. J. Baime, "Mindfulness Training Modifies Subsystems of Attention," *Cognitive, Affective, & Behavioral Neuroscience* 7 (2007): 109–19.

44. The basic scientific research in these areas is voluminous. I refer the reader to the excellent summary article of research through the year 2000: Jensine Andresen, "Meditation Meets Behavioural Medicine," *Journal of Consciousness Studies* 7:11–12 (2000), reprinted in Jensine Andresen and Robert K. C. Forman, eds., *Cognitive Models and Spiritual Maps* (Charlottesville, VA: Imprint Academic, 2000), 17–73. Another more recent summary of research that focuses on Tibetan Buddhist Meditation is Antoine Lutz, John D. Dunne, and

Richard J. Davidson, "Meditation and Neuroscience: An Introduction," in Philip Zelazo, Morris Moscovitch, and Evan Thompson, eds., *The Cambridge Handbook of Consciousness* (Cambridge: Cambridge University Press, 2007), 499–555. There are two works by James Austin that present the neuroscience of Japanese Zen Buddhist contemplative experience: *Zen and the Brain* (Cambridge, MA: MIT Press, 1998) and *Zen-Brain Reflections* (Cambridge, MA: MIT Press, 2006).

45. Two leading works in this very new area are Martin Seligman, *Authentic Happiness* (New York: The Free Press, 2004) and Jonathan Haidt, *The Happiness Hypothesis: Finding Modern Truth in Ancient Wisdom* (New York: Basic Books, 2006).

46. Wallace, *Contemplative Science*.

47. For a discussion of the pedagogical theory surrounding this, see my article "Contemplative Studies: Prospects for a New Field," *Columbia Teacher's College Record Special Issue on Contemplative Education*, vol. 108, no. 9 (September 2006): 1787–1816.

48. William James, *The Principles of Psychology* (New York: Henry Holt, 1890), vol. 1, 424.

Afterword

1. Sarah A. Queen, "Inventories of the Past: Rethinking the "School" Affiliation of the *Huainanzi. Asia Major*, Third Series (14.1) 2001; Mark Csíkszentmihályi and Michael Nylan, "Constructing Lineages and Inventing Traditions Through Exemplary Figures in Early China," *T'oung Pao* LXXXIX, 2003.

2. Esther Klein, "Were There Inner Chapters in the Warring States?: A New Examination of Evidence About the *Zhuangzi*," *T'oung Pao* 96 (2011): 299–369; For a critique see Liu Xiaogan, "Textual Issues in the *Zhuangzi*," in *Dao Companion to Daoist Philosophy*, ed. Xiaogan Liu (Dordrecht: Springer, 2015), 129–57; Stephan Peter Bumbacher, "Reconstructing the *Zhuangzi*: Preliminary Considerations." *Asia* (2016) (70:3) 611–74.

3. For more detailed arguments see above chapters 1, 2, and 7. See also, Mark Edward Lewis, *Writing and Authority in Early China* (Albany: State University of New York Press, 1999), 5 ff. See also Harold D. Roth, *Original Tao: Inward Training and the Foundations of Taoist Mysticism* (New York: Columbia University Press, 1999), 173–203.

4. See Roth, *Original Tao*, 190–93. Dirk Meyer, *Philosophy on Bamboo: Text and Production of Meaning in Early China* (Leiden: Brill 2012) has made a perceptive distinction between two types of early Chinese texts. "Context-dependent" texts rely on "outside information for getting their concerns across, such as oral instructions from a teacher. "Argument-dependent" texts are self-contained and rely on logical argumentation and internally consistent terminology to convey meaning. See, in particular, 227–29. I would disagree with Meyer, however, in his contention that the former group depend on such specific situational con-

textualization that they become impossible to fully understand once they have been transmitted out of their initial setting or location. At least in the Inner Cultivation tradition, it is possible by inference from contemplative hermeneutic, to reconstruct some of that original setting and hence some of the original meaning. Finally, of course, actual philosophical works are sometimes cross-overs between these two categories and thus provide interesting possible combination.

5. *Shiji* 史記, *Bona* edition, ch. 130, 3a–6b. For a translation and analysis of Sima Tan's "On the Six Intellectual Traditions," see Sarah A. Queen and Harold D. Roth, "A Syncretist Perspective on the Six Schools," in *Sources of Chinese Tradition* (rev. edition), ed. William Theodore deBary and Irene Bloom (New York: Columbia University Press, 1999), 278–82.

6. Volcker Scheid, *Currents of Tradition in Chinese Medicine: 1626–2006* (Seattle: Eastland Press, 2007), 9.

7. For his most recent thinking on this topic see See Liu Xiaogan, 劉笑敢 "Textual Issues in the *Zhuangzi*," in *Dao Companion to Daoist Philosophy*, ed. Xiaogan Liu (Dordrecht: Springer, 2015), 129–57.

8. Bumbacher, 643–50.

9. Klein, 302.

10. Harold D. Roth, *The Textual History of the Huai-nan Tzu*. Association for Asian Studies Monograph #20 (Ann Arbor: The Association for Asian Studies, 1992), 55–58. Despite the evidence that Liu Xiang established the received recension of the *Huainanzi*, there is absolutely no evidence—either internal to the text or external to it—that he altered the structure or contents of the original work.

11. Wang Shumin 王叔民. "*Huainanzi yu Zhuangzi* 淮南子與莊子." In Wang Shumin, *Zhuzi jiaozheng* 諸子斠證 (Taibei: World Publishing, 1964), 573–86. For a tabulation of the numbers of these *Zhuangzi* parallels in the *Huainanzi*, see Charles LeBlanc, *Huainanzi: Philosophical Synthesis in Early Han thought: The Idea of Resonance (Gan-ying* 感應 *with a Translation and Analysis of Chapter Six* (Hong: Kong: Hong Kong University Press, 1985), 83.

12. Bumbacher, 636–39. He uses four examples of passages in which the received *Zhuangzi* and the *Lüshi chun qiu* agree against *Huainanzi* parallels that are in all these cases shorter. However he assumes incorrectly I think that the *Huainanzi* version of the *Zhuangzi* text was already fixed at the time the *Huainanzi* was created and there is every reason to believe it was not. Further, he assumes that the *Huainanzi* is always attempting to be faithful to its source in what I am herein calling the "proto-*Zhuangzi*" materials it received and there is no reason to assume that either.

13. Klein, 318–19, n.53.

14. Klein, 349–51; Bumbacher, 631.

15. Sarah Allan, *Buried Ideas: Legends of Abdication and Ideal Government in Early Chinese Bamboo-Slip Manuscripts* (Albany: State University of New York Press, 2015), 27–37.

16. Bamboo strips or "slips" (Allan) were held together with leather or silk chords passed through holes in the tops and bottoms of the strips. They were then were rolled up like a much more flexible version of snow fence. These rolled up scrolls of bamboo strips (*pian* 篇) took up much more space then silk scrolls (*juan* 卷) and could thus hold fewer texts. Allan, 27–30.

17. Harold D. Roth, *Original Tao: Inward Training (Nei-yeh) and the Foundations of Taoist Mysticism*, (New York: Columbia University Press, 1999), 82–83. Verse XIX, lines. 3–8.

18. All references to the text are from the edition in D. C. Lau et al., eds., *Zhuangzi suizi suoyin* (ZZSY). Ancient Chinese Text Concordance Series, Chinese University of Hong Kong, Philosophical works no. 43 (Hong Kong: Commercial Press, 2000), 23/65/24 (chapter 23/page 65/ line 24.). The translations are my own unless otherwise indicated.

19. Charles Le Blanc, *Le Wenzi À La Lumière de L'Histoire et de L'Archéologie* (Montreal: Les Presses de L'Université de Montréal, 2000). See, in particular, ix–xiii, 1–10, and 43–45.

20. A. C. Graham, *Chuang Tzu: The Inner Chapters* (London: Allen and Unwin, 1981), 54.

21. Graham, *Chuang Tzu*, 87–88.

22. Here I follow the variant 兀 *wu* "footless" instead of 介 *jie* "armored" from the third century CE redaction of Cui Zhuan 崔 譔 cited in Lu Deming's *Jingdian shiwen* 經典釋文 (circa 606) in Wang Shumin 王叔民, *Zhuangzi jiaoquan* 莊子校詮. 2nd ed. (Taibei: Commercial Press, 1994), 913–14.

Appendix 1

The Chapters of the *Zhuangzi*

Chapter Number and Title	Roth Title Translation	Graham Title Translation
INNER CHAPTERS		
1. Xiaoyao yu 逍遙遊	Free+Easy Wandering	Going rambling without a destination
2. Qi wu lun 齊物論	Essay on Equalizing All Things	The sorting which evens things out
3. Yang sheng zhu 養生主	Mastery in Nurturing Vitality	What matters in the nurture of life
4. Ren jian shi 人間世	Within the Human World	Worldly business among men
5. De chong fu 德充符	Symbols of Perfected Inner Power	The signs of fullness of Power
6. Da zongshi 大宗師	The Great Ancestral Teacher	The teacher who is the ult. ancestor
7. Ying di wang 應帝王	Responding to Emperors+Kings	Responding to the Emperors+Kings
OUTER CHAPTERS		
8. Pianmu 駢拇	Webbed Toes	Webbed toes
9. Mati 馬蹄	Horses' Hooves	Horses' hooves
10. Qu qie 胠篋	Raiding Coffers	Rifling trunks
11. Zai you 在宥	To Preserve and Circumscribe	Keep it in place and within bounds

continued on next page

Chapter Number and Title	Roth Title Translation	Graham Title Translation
OUTER CHAPTERS *(Continued)*		
12. Tian Di 天地	The Heavens and the Earth	Heaven and Earth
13. Tian dao 天道	The Way of the Heavens	The Way of Heaven
14. Tian yun 天運	The Circuits of the Heavens	The circuits of Heaven
15. Keyi 刻意	Ingrained Opinions	Finicky notions
16. Shan xing 繕性	Mending Nature	Menders of nature
17. Qiushui 秋水	Autumn Floods	Autumn floods
18. Zhile 至樂	Ultimate Joy	
19. Da sheng 達生	Understanding Life	Fathoming nature
20. Shan mu 山木	The Mountain Tree	
21. Tian Zifang 田子方	Tian Zifang	
22. Zhi beiyou 知北遊	Knowledge Wanders North	Knowledge roams north
MIXED CHAPTERS		
23. Geng Sangchu 庚桑楚	Geng Sangchu	
24. Xu Wugui 徐無鬼	Xu Wugui	
25. Ze yang 則陽	Zeyang	
26. Waiwu 外物	External Things	
27. Yuyan 寓言	Goblet Words	
28. Rang wang 讓王	Abdicating Kingship	Yielding the throne
29. Daozhi 盜跖	Robber Zhi	Robber Chih
30. Shuo jian 說劍	Discoursing on Swords	The discourse on swords
31. Yufu 漁父	The Old Fisherman	The old fisherman
32. Lie Yukou 列禦寇	Lie Yukou	
33. Tianxia 天下	All Under the Heavens	Below in the empire

Appendix 2

The Chapters of the *Huainanzi* 淮南子

Chapter 1: *Yuan dao* 原道 Originating in the Way
Chapter 2: *Chu zhen* 俶真 Activating the Genuine
Chapter 3: *Tianwen* 天文 The Celestial Patterns
Chapter 4: *Dixing* 地形 The Terrestrial Forms
Chapter 5: *Shice* 時側 The Seasonal Rules
Chapter 6: *Lan ming* 覽冥 Surveying Obscurities
Chapter 7: *Jingshen* 精神 The Quintessential Spirit
Chapter 8: *Benjing* 本經 The Basic Warp
Chapter 9: *Zhushu* 主術 The Ruler's Techniques
Chapter 10: *Miaocheng* 繆稱 Profound Precepts
Chapter 11: *Qi su* 齊俗 Equalizing Customs
Chapter 12: *Daoying* 道應 The Responses of the Way
Chapter 13: *Fanlun* 氾論 Boundless Discourses
Chapter 14: *Quanyan* 詮言 Explanatory Sayings
Chapter 15: *Binglue* 兵略 An Overview of the Military
Chapter 16: *Shuishan* 說山 A Mountain of Persuasions
Chapter 17: *Shuilin* 說林 A Forest of Persuasions
Chapter 18: *Renjian* 人間 The Human World
Chapter 19: *Xiuwu* 修務 Cultivating Effort
Chapter 20: *Taizu* 太族 The Exalted Lineage
Chapter 21: *Yaolüe* 要略 An Overview of the Essentials

Index